Power in Eden

Power in Eden

The Emergence of Gender Hierarchies in the Ancient world

Bruce Lerro

TRAFFORD BOOKS

Note for Librarians: a cataloguing record for this book that includes Dewey Decimal
Classification and US Library of Congress numbers is available from the Library and
Archives of Canada. The complete cataloguing record can be obtained from their online
database at:
www.collectionscanada.ca/amicus/index-e.html
ISBN 1-4120-2141-3
Printed in Victoria, BC, Canada

TRAFFORD

Offices in Canada, USA, Ireland, UK and Spain
This book was published *on-demand* in cooperation with Trafford Publishing. On-demand
publishing is a unique process and service of making a book available for retail sale to the
public taking advantage of on-demand manufacturing and Internet marketing. On-demand
publishing includes promotions, retail sales, manufacturing, order fulfilment, accounting and
collecting royalties on behalf of the author.
Book sales for North America and international:
Trafford Publishing, 6E–2333 Government St.,
Victoria, BC v8t 4p4 CANADA
phone 250 383 6864 (toll-free 1 888 232 4444)
fax 250 383 6804; email to orders@trafford.com
Book sales in Europe:
Trafford Publishing (UK) Ltd., Enterprise House, Wistaston Road Business Centre,
Wistaston Road, Crewe, Cheshire CW2 7RP UNITED KINGDOM
phone 01270 251 396 (local rate 0845 230 9601)
facsimile 01270 254 983; orders.uk@trafford.com
Order online at:
www.trafford.com/robots/03-2690.html

10 9 8 7 6 5 4 3 2

Contents

Figures

Preface

When I first became fascinated with the ancient world fifteen years ago, I had two major questions. One had to do with the difference between magic and religion and how this was grounded in in economic and political changes in the ancient world. The second had to do with the roots of exploitation. Marx and Engels had argued that tribal societies were practicing egalitarian "primitive communism." But they were vague about when this began to change. Since gender stratification seemed to be the oldest form of inequality I wanted to understand how men came to have power over women.

Usually in these matters one question leads to many qualified answers, which lead to deeper, more refined questions, which lead to sharper answers. After twelve years of writing, speaking, thinking, and testing my manuscript on students I had answers to my first question and a lot more new questions I hadn't bargained for. The results were published in my first book, *From Earth Spirits to Sky Gods.* As I was writing on the subject of magic and religion, of course gender issues were mixed in along he way. Did magic support women or men more? What about religion? Was there anything about religion that supported or discouraged gender stratification that was different from magic? At first I thought I could address my original question about sacred traditions and the origins of gender hierarchies in a single volume, but the more I wrote the more I wished to treat the origins of gender inequalities as a separate question. After five more years of work I have some answers that I am satisfied with. Whether I answer *your* questions, of course, is a different matter.

I wish to thank Nancy Brumback for giving me a forum in her classes in which to present my findings. Thanks to my students for always clamoring for more about this subject whenever I raised it in other courses. Salutations go to Robin Oldham and Jean Santullo for blazing a trail through the first draft of the manuscript with good cheer, despite probably wishing to strangle me, if not worse. Thanks to Richard Heinberg who not only brought a public voice into my work through his editing, but was able to pose great content questions for which I was most grateful. Thanks to Russell Kilday-Hicks for doing the indexing amidst his busy schedule. Thanks to Amy Altschul for a scrupulous job of proofreading and to my wonderful artist friend Ricardo Valbuena for working on the cover. Hats off to Laura Pringle and Brian Slater of Trafford Press for answering my questions in such a cheerful and down-to-earth manner. Thanks lastly to my wonderful partner, Barbara MacLean, who by her intelligence, perseverance, sensitivity, warmth, practicality, and humor shows what women are capable of if given half a chance.

What I am most proud of in this book is the depth of the work of the scholars I have drawn from. Marvin Harris, V.G. Childe, Leslie White, Marshall Sahlins, Elman Service, and Peggy Reeves-Sanday provided me with a grounding in materialist anthropology. In macro-sociology Gerhard Lenski, Steve Sanderson, Janet Chafetz, and Rae Lesser Blumberg provided an overall direction to the movement of the early societies. Thanks to Tikva Frymer-Kensky Lucy Goodson, Christine Morris, Lotte Motz, Cynthia Eller, and Phillp Davis for having the nerve to challenge Goddess fundamentalism in a respectful manner. In evolutionary psychology thanks to Dave Buss, Steven Gaulin, and Donald Mc Burney; in the analysis of warfare in tribal societies thanks to Lauwrence Keeley and Raymond Kelly. I was aided immensely by the work of Robert Drews and J.P. Mallory when it came to understanding warfare and invasions in the Bronze and Iron Ages. Thanks to Victor Clube, Bill Napier, Duncan Steel, Mike Baillie, and Benny Peiser for courageously arguing that astronomical events do have something to do with natural disasters. Thanks to Mark Edmund Lewis, Ram Sharn Sharma, and Uma Chakrayarti for expanding my understanding of the place of China and India in the Axial iron Age. In the field of environmental psychology hats off to Yi-Fu Tuan, David Sack, and Lyn Lofland for their insights into how places and spaces affect social psychology.

In the field of technology the work of Marshall McLuhan, Harold Innis, Eric Havelock, Walter Ong, Jack Goody, and Robert Logan has been pivotal in my understanding of how writing affects sense ratios on the one hand, and cognition on the other. Thanks to the work of Denise Schmandt-Besserant for tracing the emergence of writing to economics.

I would also like to acknowledge my debt to the socio-historical school of psychology—Lev Vygotsky, Alexander Luria and A. N. Leontiev—who insisted in rooting psychology in social evolution and world history. Finally, thanks to the great social psychologist George Herbert Mead for his insistence that even the most seemingly private dimension of psychology is rooted in society. Having these scholars at my back gives me a substantial tailwind. Whether, in synthesizing their work, I fly or crash is for you and others to decide.

Introduction

Why do men monopolize most technological, political, and economic power in complex societies? Have the inequalities in power between men and women always existed, or did gender stratification have an origin in time? To what extent is it hardwired into our biology? How much of it is built from socio-ecological forces? Do men and women treat each other any differently under social stress? What happens to gender relations during natural disasters, famines or plagues? If gender stratification had an origin in time, did it appear all at once, or did it arise subtly and gradually over thousands of years? Were there once matriarchal societies as claimed by some feminist spiritualists? Does reverence for goddesses go all the way back to the Paleolithic Age? Is there a necessary and direct connection between the presence of goddesses in society's pantheon and the reverential status of women in that society? Were ancient tribal societies peace-loving before being invaded? When gender hierarchies emerged, were there discernible stages, was it random, or is the origin of gender inequalities too complex to sort out? How much were women responsible for their fall into subordination? Were they simply victims of circumstances or do they bear some responsibility? If so, how much? Bronze Age agricultural states were the most oppressive societies to women in history, yet we are hard-pressed to find instances of mobilization and revolution; why was there no feminist movement in the ancient world?

In what follows I will attempt to answer these important questions and many others with a reconstruction (based on the best existing evidence and research) of the multidimensional events and processes that led to the emergence of institutionalized male dominance beginning in the late Neolithic Age and ending in the Axial Iron Age in 500 BCE. I will show how socio-ecological transformations across a period from 6000 BCE to 500 BCE and across five social formations (hunting-gathering bands, simple and complex horticultural villages, agricultural states, and commercial states) were responsible for the dominance of a few men over most women and most other men.

My principal claims are that ecological and demographic forces such as periodic population pressure and resource depletion created great social stresses to which men and women reacted differently. These forces also catalyzed new social processes in the Bronze Age, including the rise of political centralization, economic stratification, the invention of the plow, and hieroglyphics. The new gender hierarchies were deepened by the emergence of coined money, the alphabet, and iron tools, all of which consolidated male dominance. These material forces were sustained and legitimized by the sacred movement from animism to polytheism to monotheism. Lastly, these socio-ecological dynamics led to changes in the ways people thought and perceived their world; these psychological changes were epitomized in the appearance of the individualist self and a new form of reasoning, which I call "hyperabstract" cognition.

The existing literature on the subject of male dominance falls into at least four categories.

The first consists of the writings of Goddess advocates (whom I'll also refer to as Neo-pagans and feminist spiritualists) who claim that history has been misrepresented and fails to acknowledge that pre-Christian sacred beliefs were more pro-woman and that women's status in pre-state societies was equal to or higher than that of men. This group tends to ignore the work of most anthropologists and archeologists, regarding the latter as members of a patriarchal conspiracy.

The next group consists of anthropologists and archeologists who for the most part dismiss the claims of Goddess theorists—but rarely answer them directly. Hence the layperson does not become acquainted with the full range of evidence or the arguments surrounding it. By default, goddess advocates control the trade publications. At the same time, because anthropologists and archeologists are specialists, they often don't take an interdisciplinary approach. While they are usually aware of macrosociology (the study of large-scale social change), political science, and economics, they often have less grasp of how comparative psychology and religion might contribute to an understanding of the origins of female subordination.

Standing opposed to both spiritually-oriented goddess advocates and socially-oriented anthropologists and archeologists are the sociobiologists and evolutionary psychologists, who explain gender hierarchies from sexual and natural selection deep in our evolutionary background, before human societies formed. They argue that while not all aspects of gender relations can be explained by biology, the most important usually can be. For them, social dynamics cannot produce anything new that could override biology.

Finally, there are macrosociologists and liberal or socialist advocates, who explain power differentials between genders in terms of politics, economics, and to a lesser extent, ecology and demography. While I am most sympathetic to this group, they often tend to explain gender differences as resulting from capitalism and to ignore the presence of gender hierarchies long before the emergence of capitalism. Secondly they tend to be "biophobic"—that is, they immediately reject any biological explanation for political reasons as being inherently reactionary. At least some might be called "social constructivists."

My work draws primarily on—and synthesizes—the arguments of anthropologists, archeologists, and macro-sociologists, while

granting some ground to evolutionary psychologists. While I am sympathetic to the uses of Goddess spirituality for women *today,* I disagree with almost everything the Goddess advocates say about ancient history.

This book is grounded in existing scholarship and it is inclusive of many fields. Moreover, it fills what I perceive as a large gap in the existing literature:

- Most books on the subject try to explain differences in power between genders from either a biological or a social standpoint. While I clearly favor emphasizing social explanations, I include a discussion of the discipline of evolutionary psychology. More importantly, I specify which gender differences have a biological basis and which have a social basis, and discuss how these interact.
- Most books on the subject discuss Goddess spirituality movement claims for an ancient matriarchy, but these books are either naively praiseworthy (the works of true believers) or flippantly dismissive. While am I highly critical of the Goddess movement's attempt to revise world history, I try to bridge the gap between academics and advocates: I try to give matriarchalists a fair hearing.
- My work is interdisciplinary; I draw from the fields of anthropology and macro-sociology, archeology, geography, astronomy, political sociology, comparative religion, socio-historical psychology, and evolutionary psychology.

I have not done original research that brings new facts to light. What I *have* done is to bring together existing materials produced by first-rate scholars in many fields, and put these materials together in new ways.

Existing theories of the origin of gender hierarchies tend to be either materialist or idealist. The theories of anthropologists, archeologists and macrosociologists that explain changes in society from a combination of tangible factors such as population pressure, resource depletion, technological changes, or political and economic dynamics are materialist; those that derive their explanations from the realm of values, morals, and sacred beliefs are idealist. Materialist theories typically do not have a well-developed explanation of how *sacred meaning making systems tend to legitimize* gender hierarchies. On the other hand, idealist theories tend to ignore material factors and world history. Chapter 3, on Goddess ideology, criticizes idealist attempts to explain the technological, economic, and political transformations that occurred in ancient times on the basis of shifts in sacred beliefs. However, chapters 12 and 13, on the movement from earth-spirit magic to sky-god religion, are designed to fill the gap left by materialist authors.

Materialist theories typically do not provide a sufficient explanation for how society gets internalized inside people's minds and hearts—that is, into their psychology. Materialist theories tend to see people as victims of circumstances. Without a psychological theory we cannot begin to understand how and to what degree women colluded with material forces that imposed subjugation.

In chapters on collectivist versus individualist selves (16), concrete thinking vs. hyperabstraction (15) and proximate vs. long-distant sense-ratios (14), I show how a psychology of subordination is built out of the demographic, ecological, technological, economic, and political structures that materialist theories have identified. I apply Vygotsky's socio-historic theory of learning to show how society gets inside of people and

how society gets reproduced when people go to work.

Previous authors have argued that the biophysical setting affects gender relations. But in chapters 10 and 11, on natural disasters in the Bronze Age, I argue that radical climatic downturns resulting from Earth's passage through the debris of a comet or asteroid created stress between men and women that went beyond that engendered by the normal inability of societies to address ecological and demographic constraints.

To my knowledge, no previous theorist has addressed the question of why there was no women's movement in the ancient world. Chafetz, in *Gender Equity* (1988), goes into detail about the conditions under which women's movements emerged. But her application begins after the Axial Iron Age. In my chapter on dissent, mobilization, and revolution (17) I try to answer the question, Why was there no women's movement in this specific time period? I do this by applying contemporary theories of social movements (including that of Chafetz) and comparing current conditions to those in the ancient world.

I have developed a five-phase stage theory of female subordination that goes through four cycles. Each cycle corresponds to a historical period, beginning with the late Neolithic Age and ending with the Axial Iron Age. During this period of time there were many instances when technological change led changes in the economy and political system. Other times the political and economic system changed faster than the sacred beliefs and the psychology of people. This way of looking at social change can explain why there is no necessary correlation between the presence of goddesses (belief systems) and the economic status of women.

This work is divided into six parts, which are organized around my stage theory and the cycles of female subordination. Part I sets up the justification and orientation for the book.

Chapter 1 explains what the study of history has to do with gender relations today. In it, I argue against the notion that history is made by extraordinary individuals, or that the most important events in history consist of official political events such as wars, congresses, and treaties. I claim that everyone is always producing history and that everyone is responsible for what becomes of world history. I follow Marvin Harris and other materialists in claiming that so far social evolution is the conflicted story of class and gender struggles, which are driven by population pressure and resource depletion.

Chapters 2 and 4 are orientation chapters, one based on the description of social evolution and the other on theories of the emergence of gender hierarchies. Chapter 2 provides an overview of the political, economic, and technological transformations in ways of life of people, from hunter-gatherers in the Paleolithic Age to commercial farmers in the Axial Iron Age. This chapter also contains a brief description of the changes in mating and childrearing practices that occurred during this period.

Chapter 4 focuses on three kinds of socio-ecological theories of gender inequalities. These include Marxist theories, which are basically economic and political, including the work of Engels, Sacks, and Vogel. Next I cover the ecological theory of Reeves-Sanday. Finally I present the work of Janet Saltzman Chafetz. Since hers is the most complete theory, I address it in more depth. In the last section I present an outline of how to build from her theory and fill some gaps in it.

With the justification for studying history, an orientation to the anatomy and dynamics of ancient societies, and a survey of various socio-ecological theories of female subordination in place, I turn to Goddess spirituality. In Chapter 3 I address Neo-pagan attempts to link changes in the status of women to the presence or absences of goddesses in the ancient world. In the first section I describe the overall claims and

the underlying values that inform Goddess spirituality. Then I raise a series of questions which Goddess ideology claims to answer. The discussion of these questions throughout the chapter will help the reader to decide whether matriarchies are likely ever to have existed.

In Part II I describe the origin and consolidation of male dominance. Chapter 5 begins by analyzing two theories of the origins of inequality between groups within any given society. The next section presents Peggy Reeves-Sanday's theory for the origins of *gender* hierarchies in tribal societies, based on social stress grounded in ecological and demographic crisis. In the last section I attempt to synthesize the origins of rank and caste stratification theory with Reeves-Sanday's theory of gender stratification.

In chapter 6, I revisit the history of social evolution presented in chapter 2, but this time only from the perspective of the evolving status of women. It is in this chapter that I introduce the five stages of female subordination. They include enmeshment, coercion, legitimization, internalization and collusion. I present an overview of how these stages have unfolded through four cycles—one cycle for complex horticultural societies, two cycles for the Bronze Age agricultural states, and one cycle for Iron Age commercial farming societies. Different cycles emphasize different steps of the stages and de-emphasize others. With this outline in place the rest of the book will follow the stages, with each part devoted to a stage.

Part III shows how the forces of biological constraint, political coercion, and natural disasters operated in producing gender hierarchies. Chapters 7 and 10 address non-social constraints. Chapter 7 addresses biological differences between men and women and chapters 10 and 11 discuss possible geophysical, climatic, and astronomical impacts on gender relations. Chapters 8 and 9 discuss the impacts of war and migration in the ancient world on the emergence of male dominance.

I begin chapter 7 by presenting an overview of differences in the work that men and women do regardless of the type of society they live in. Next I present an theory of human nature derived from evolutionary psychology, which challenges the belief that biological hardwiring is unchanging, that it overrides learning and culture, and that it is inherently politically conservative. I describe how sexual selection explains some differences between men and women, but by no means all of them or even the most important ones. In sections on gender differences in aggression, power, and conflict I argue against the idea that institutionalized male dominance was a conspiracy. I close the chapter by listing seven of my own reservations about evolutionary psychology.

Chapter 10 deals with a subject that many readers might initially find tangential—evidence of the impact of comet debris in the beginning middle and end of the Bronze Age. However, as I attempt to show, these astronomically-based natural disasters powerfully affected all human societies, and altered gender relations in at least some societies. The first section of this chapter differentiates neo-catastrophism from the old religious catastrophism and argues that it is no longer controversial to assert that most, if not all planets have been bombarded by comets, asteroids, or both. At the same time, it is generally accepted that during the Bronze Age natural disasters periodically disrupted the civilizations of Egypt, Mesopotamian, China, India, and Greece. The only remaining controversy is over whether these disasters were purely geological or were caused by astronomical impacts. I also discuss how these natural disasters could have triggered climate change and famine.

Chapter 11 makes explicit how these natural disasters affected gender dynamics. In the first section I examine men's and women's responses to natural disasters in today's world. I then proceed to compare natural disasters today to what we know about those that occurred in the ancient world. In the third section I come back

to the present and assess how men and women differ in how they deal with stress. Then I comb through research on how men and women differ in response to the stress caused specifically by natural disasters. Finally I synthesize the work in the first four sections by building a scenario of how men and women might have treated each other during natural disasters in the Bronze Age, and draw out the implications for institutionalized male dominance.

Chapters 8 and 9 discuss the impact of primitive and civilized warfare on gender relations. Chapter 8 challenges romantic notions of tribal societies as being peaceful, and warfare as being solely caused by the rise of stratification and the state. As archaeologist Lawrence Keeley has shown, while the absolute number of casualties was lower in tribal societies, homicide rates were actually higher than in state societies. Keeley shows that warfare in the form of ambushes was constant. Since men primarily did the fighting, this state of affairs was no boon for gender equality. There have indeed been warless societies, and I identify the conditions under which they arose and what this meant for gender relations.

In chapter 9 I discuss how the technological changes introduced in the Bronze Age by chariot warfare and in the Iron Age by cavalry and infantry affected the relations between societies. Some of these technologies were more democratically accessible, making it possible for pastoral people to disrupt and conquer more complex societies. This last point is important to the discussion of gender hierarchies because, as Nisbett has shown, herding societies have possibly the most "machismo" ideology of any.

No society can control its castes, classes, or genders by coercion alone. It must justify its rule through legitimizing institutions and their ideologies. Part IV contains three chapters that discuss how male dominance is explained and justified—that is, legitimized.

After explaining some of the differences between primitive magic, secondary magic, and religion, I argue that goddess reverence arose during secondary magical times at a point when women were clearly subordinate to men, and that belief in goddesses justified their subordination. As Frymer-Kensky shows, the movement from the middle to the late Bronze Age was a downturn for belief in goddesses, that they went not from being revered to being subordinate, but from being subordinate to being marginalized. I conclude that secondary magic both supported and contradicted women's social status in the Bronze Age, depending on the social caste of the women. It is too simplistic to say that polytheism supported women and the rise of monotheism was their downfall.

Chapter 13 shows that while the rise of sky-god religion legitimized the subordination of women, in some respects—at least among the Hebrews—aspects of monotheism challenged the legitimacy of polytheistic secondary magic. Frymer-Kensky argues that the rise of Archaic religion among the Hebrews conferred some improvements in women's material status. Both the religious and secular philosophies of China, Greece, and India continued to legitimize women's subordination.

Chapter 14, a study of environmental psychology, both closes our discussion of the second, legitimization phase of the subordination of women, and anticipates the third, internalization phase. I set up the discussion of gender hierarchies by first showing that all societies organize their physical environment into "places" and "spaces." These correspond to the security-seeking and adventure-seeking tendencies in human beings, which tend to get projected onto the physical environment. In addition, people do not use the senses equally. Some senses become more specialized based on the ecological setting inhabited and the tools that people find at their disposal. Following McLuhan and the communication theorists, I claim that technology is "extra-somatic sensitivity." This means whichever senses a tool

demands for its use gradually become more refined, while those senses that are not used with tools weaken. As we will see, men and women used spaces and places differently, and also developed their senses to differing degrees. The masculine priority of spaces over places and the prioritizing of the sense of sight among upper middle class men legitimized male dominance, while the use of the proximate senses among women contributed to women's internalization of gender hierarchies.

In Part V, I discuss two psychological phenomena that arose during the Bronze and Iron Ages from which women were excluded—hyperabstract reasoning and the individualist self. Both contributed to women's subordination.

Chapter 15 discusses Vygotsky's sociogenic theory of the origins of new, higher psychological functions. Vygotsky argues that, as people cooperate in learning how to use new tools, they stretch beyond their given level of functioning. It is only later that they internalize these skills. In the case of Bronze Age societies, the division of labor between mental and manual workers gave mental workers a chance to use two new tools that developed their ability to think more abstractly—writing and money. These tools were used in the service of political centralization and empire-building. Since they were principally in the hands of men, women did not have much of a chance to learn to think in a hyperabstract way. This negatively affected their capacity to challenge the existing order and to build a coherent ideology of opposition.

Chapter 16 begins with a description of the building blocks all individuals in society must learn in order to become fully socialized (as discussed in the work of George Herbert Mead). While theories of individualist and collectivist selves are very popular in cross-cultural psychology, no one to my knowledge has previously suggested how Mead's building blocks of socialization might be incorporated in the production of individualist and collectivist selves. This is what I set out to do.

Following cross-cultural psychologists, I argue that tribal societies have horizontal collectivist identities while people in agricultural civilizations have vertical collectivist identities. Horizontal collectivism refers to the egalitarian political status of these groups, whereas vertical collectivism refers to the stratified status of collectivists in these societies.

While I agree that individualism intensifies with the rise of capitalism, I argue that it has its origins in the Axial Iron Age, with the great sages, prophets, and philosophers. While both men and women were collectivists prior to the Axial Iron Age, a few middle- and upper-middle-class men developed individualist selves. This added to women's internalization of subordination, because the values of collectivism—putting the kin group before themselves, learning how to take rather than make roles, having an external locus of control—worked against challenging the existing order, organizing other women, and taking personal responsibility for the results.

Part VI contains a single chapter (chapter 17), which completes my discussion of the cycle of subordination. I open the chapter with a rapid survey of all of the events in the ancient world that led to women's subordination (this is a review of chapters 5 through 16). I then re-present the four cycles of subordination and the five stages of each cycle and link them to events in the ancient world. Then in section two I rework Janet Saltzman-Chafetz's theory to include the events described in chapters 5 through 15. In the next section I draw on research on social movements to identify eleven conditions under which movements are likely to arise. Then I compare these conditions to the circumstances of the ancient world. I find that virtually none of the conditions that allow social movements arise then existed. The implication is that the conditions for women to

overcome subordination are much better today than they were in the ancient world.

Figure A at the end of this section gives a visual overview of the journey.

Several qualifications may help the reader be clear about what am I *not* arguing for.

(1) A convolute vs. an evolute theory of social evolution. I am not implying that once qualitative changes in human societies—such as the change from hunting-gathering to horticulture, or the change from rank to stratified relations—are introduced in one society, all other societies suddenly follow suit. Such a theory would be "convolute," which means that each stage in the process of social evolution swallows up all previous stages. Instead I am suggesting an "evolute" theory of social evolution in which existing means of subsistence and political institutions either continue untouched alongside new forms or enter into a hybrid combination of old and new as a result of trading, coercion, or imitation.

Furthermore, the same distinction applies within societies. The fact that a novel institution, idea, or tool has been adopted by a society does not mean that it will be used by all social classes. For instance, when the universalistic religions were introduced in the first millennium, they first affected the middle and upper classes. Peasants continued to practice primitive magic while artisans and merchants probably practiced a hybrid of both. (See chapters 11 and 12 for details.)

(2) Some theories about the truth of what occurred are better than others, but no contention will be absolutely certain because evidence is piecemeal and uneven. Archeology can give us reliable information about the technological base of a society and the extent to which it was egalitarian or stratified. However, we can know much less about a people's sacred practices or their psychology unless they left written records. This means that we will know much less about the sacred beliefs and psychology of tribal societies who lived in the Stones Ages than people living in state societies in the

Bronze and Iron Ages. In both cases we must combine archeology with an anthropology of modern tribal and state societies and infer backward. While this is dangerous business, many scholars have done just this. The best we can do is to aspire to a reconstruction that falls between plausible and probable.

The absence of a theory that is *certain* does not justify arguing that all theories are of equal weight and are interchangeable. Some theories, while possible, are far-fetched and wind up causing more new problems than they purport to solve. Thus if someone argues that the Egyptian pyramids were built by people from outer space, this theory undermines many archeological and anthropological facts that are integrated and fit together well. In order to accommodate the new theory these established facts will have to be reintegrated, not simply undermined and left hanging. The point is to explain the most new information with the simplest theory, which causes the least problems for what has already been established. In addition, the inability to prove that something *didn't* happen is not evidence that it *did* happen. For example, we cannot prove that aliens have not landed on Earth at some point in its history. However, the burden of proof is on those who make the claim, not on those who oppose it.

(3) Descriptions of phenomena from the point of view of outsiders must be distinguished from the point of view of the participants. Marvin Harris makes a distinction between "etic" and "emic" interpretations. Etic interpretations are interpretations of people's actions and beliefs using the categories of the observer. Emic interpretations are inferences about another's society's practices or beliefs using the categories of the participants. Both are necessary. Each has its strengths and weaknesses.

Power in Eden looks backward in time to challenge the conventional views of the way history has been presented, and from this draws new meaning for our present and future. My work aims to show that world history has a

great deal to teach us not only about the possible origins of gender hierarchies, but also about how they are reproduced over time. The experiences of hunter-gatherers, horticulturalists, and people in the great early civilizations of the Sumerians, Egyptians, and Greeks are object lessons that can tell us about the conditions under which hierarchies emerge. This is information that is vitally relevant today.

*   *   *

Before beginning our journey I would call the reader's attention to two introductory figures that will give us a visual map of our journey. We will revisit Figures A and B throughout this text.

Figure A displays the five major forces that impacted the emergence of gender hierarchies: biological, psychological, social, ecological-demographic, and geological-astronomical.

Each of these forces is given a shape, which is indicated in the chart. Lastly, I have coded the type of influence each has had on women. These include a pervasive impact, a periodic impact, and an emergent impact. As we proceed throughout the book, we will identify these five forces with particular historical events.

Figure B provides an overview of five stages of female subordination, including enmeshment, coercion, legitimization, internalization, and collusion. These terms will be defined in chapter 6. Notice that different parts of the stages are in bold as we move from the upper to the lower part of the page. These five stages go through four major cycles from the late Neolithic Age to the Axial Iron Age. To the right of the cycles is a description of the society in terms of its material culture, its sacred beliefs, and its psychology. Some of the elements of the stages are in bold in some cycles and not in others, because as societies change, the means of subordination change.

What is the difference between the two figures? Figure A simply gives us an overview of different forces. It does not tell us how they impact women. Secondly, as we will see, these forces do not interact in a coherent direction. Thirdly, Figure A includes a wider range of impacts, including population-ecological dynamics as well as geology-astronomy and biology. Figure B presents a more specified description of a social-psychological-social process of how subordination emerges and is sustained. It is directional, in that the events in the ancient world can be meaningfully organized into the five stages. Figure B is also more historically specific as the four cycles of subordination actually present us with specific social structures and world changes. Both of these Figures will be useful to us in different ways.

Figure A Overview of the Forces Impacting the Emergence of Institutionalized Male Dominance

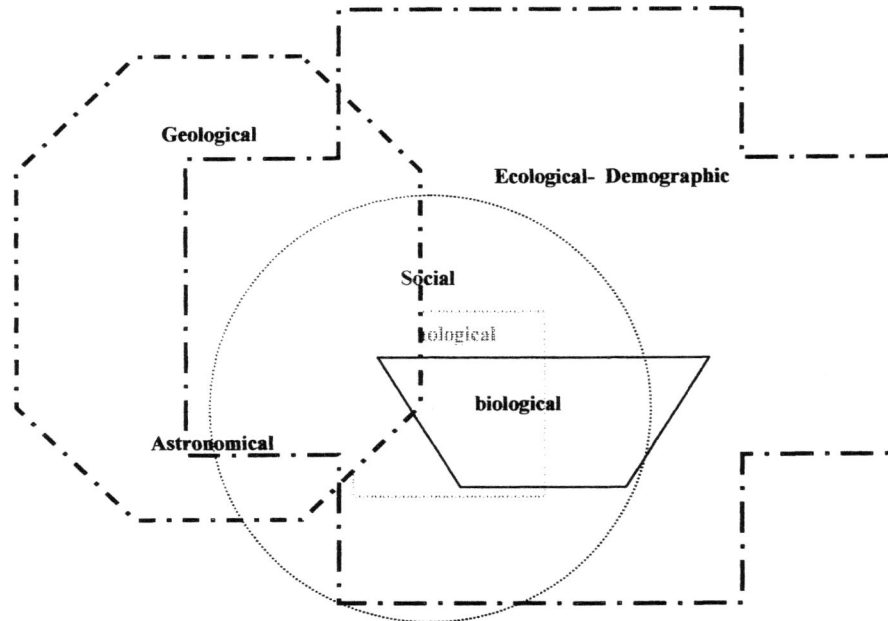

Geological

Ecological- Demographic

Social

ological

biological

Astronomical

FORCES OF IMPACT

Biological = inverted trapezoid
Psychological = square
Social = circle
Ecological-demographic = cross
Geological-astronomical = octagon

TYPES OF INFLUENCE ON WOMEN

Pervasive impact = hard line
Periodic impact = dash dots
Emergent impact = dots

COMMENTARY:
Note how these shapes overlap each other. This means that most of these dimensions interact with each other while maintaining some independence. For example the biological realm of genes, hormones and anatomy is influenced by all other realms. The same is true for psychology. When we go into larger systems we see more independence. For instance in the social world much of it lies behind the realm of biology and psychology but is impacted by ecological-demographic, geological and astronomical realms. Finally the ecological-demographic and geological-astronomical have some impact on society but they are also independent from society, psychology and biology.

Figure B Five Stages and Four Cycles of the Emergence of Gender Hierarchies

Phases of Subordination

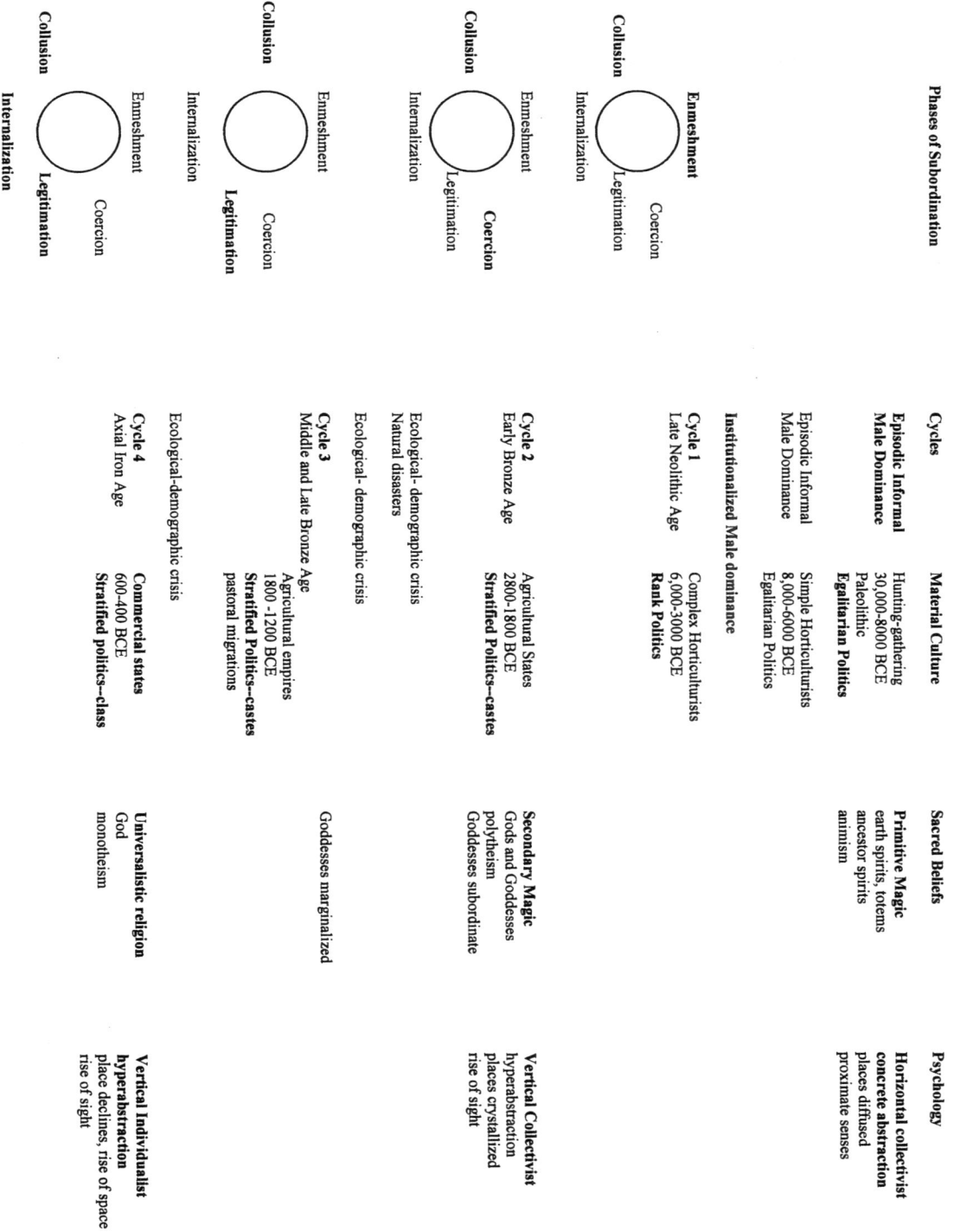

Enmeshment · Collusion · Coercion · Internalization · Legitimation

Cycles	Material Culture	Sacred Beliefs	Psychology
Episodic Informal Male Dominance	**Hunting-gathering** 30,000-8000 BCE Paleolithic **Egalitarian Politics**	**Primitive Magic** earth spirits, totems ancestor spirits animism	**Horizontal collectivist** **concrete abstraction** places diffused proximate senses
Episodic Informal Male Dominance	Simple Horticulturists 8,000-6000 BCE Egalitarian Politics		
Institutionalized Male dominance			
Cycle 1 Late Neolithic Age	Complex Horticulturists 6,000-3000 BCE **Rank Politics**		
Cycle 2 Early Bronze Age	Agricultural States 2800-1800 BCE **Stratified Politics—castes**	**Secondary Magic** Gods and Goddesses polytheism Goddesses subordinate	**Vertical Collectivist** hyperabstraction places crystallized rise of sight
Ecological-demographic crisis Natural disasters			
Ecological-demographic crisis			
Cycle 3 Middle and Late Bronze Age	Agricultural empires 1800-1200 BCE **Stratified Politics—castes** pastoral migrations	Goddesses marginalized	
Ecological-demographic crisis			
Cycle 4 Axial Iron Age	**Commercial states** 600-400 BCE **Stratified politics—class**	**Universalistic religion** God monotheism	**Vertical Individualist** **hyperabstraction** place declines, rise of space rise of sight

Part I

Justification and Orientation

Chapter 1

History-Shaping:
Why the Past Matters

1. Why study history?

Why read a book about the past? After all, isn't history about past institutions, past wars, dead people? This could only interest academics. What does the past have to do with the present and future?

Perhaps it seems reasonable that the study of wars, dates, and the lives of famous men might be irrelevant not because the past itself is irrelevant, but because our view of the past is partial and skewed. Until recently, history books described only the actions of extraordinary people—kings, generals, heads of state, or scientific or artistic geniuses. This kind of history leaves the mundane life of the average person almost completely out of the picture. The contribution of the majority of people to the shaping of societies constitutes a history that is still in the process of being written. The history of class, ethnic, and gender struggles has surfaced in academia relatively recently and, though incomplete and still largely unknown to the general public, is now unavoidable in serious discussions about the past. While the "people's historians" offer an alternative view, it is not a monolithic one; they contest among themselves which events should be chosen for description and how those events should be interpreted.

These developments represent an important step forward. However, despite them, most people still fail to see the relevance of history to the present and the future. History is what has already happened; it is the imperfect record of an objective past that has occurred, has impacted us for better or worse, and vanished, giving us no further opportunity to modify it. Yet, at the same time, the hot molten lava of past struggles becomes crystallized in the institutions of the present; in this sense the past is solidified in the present. Also,

past struggles can be reinterpreted and reorganized, for better or worse, in terms of our present and future. All groups, both in power and struggling for power, reinterpret history in the service of their own cause. If that were not so, there would not be so many different interpretations of the same historical events. History is political; it has never been the impartial study of objective events for its own sake.

The study of history can be subversive because it can expose the relativity of our most cherished institutions—private property, wage labor, institutionalized leadership, the virtue of acquisitiveness, individualism, and the worship of male deities. History can open up our imaginations by enabling us to learn from the beliefs and practices of early societies and, on the basis of what we have learned, to reorganize our future. This subversive approach to history centers on a study of past problems, and how the previous societies attempted to solve problems—as well as on the unintended consequences that resulted from chosen solutions.

Conversely, not knowing about the past leaves us vulnerable to the belief that the current order of things is more or less the way it has always been, and by implication, the way it will always be. It means our social problems, social solutions, and the consequences that follow have no link to the past.

Here, in summary, are the reasons for studying history:

- It is about the average person;
- It is about the present *and* future;
- It is malleable and open to change;
- It exposes the relativity of our present institutions;

- It can help us to reorganize our present and future;
- It reduces the chances of repeating past mistakes.

2. The dimensions of society

Describing historical events without referring to the types of society they occur in is like a drawing of the human figure in motion with no understanding of how the skeleton or the muscles of the body interact to create certain possibilities and constraints to movement. History can only occur through the construction of relatively stable socio-cultural systems. A natural catastrophe in a hunting-and-gathering society will not have the same impact as it will in an industrial capitalist society. It is impossible to make sense of ecological crises, inventions, and famines without a prior understanding of the type of social structure they are impacting. World history occurs in concrete social systems—hunting and gathering societies, simple and complex horticultural villages, nomadic herding societies, and agricultural states.

As we will see in the next chapter, there are qualitative differences between bands, tribes, chiefdoms and state societies. Yet all societies have to adapt to their ecological settings and develop systems for producing and reproducing their existence across generations.

Anthropologist Marvin Harris (1977, 1979, 1988) has divided all social systems into three subsystems—the social infrastructure, structure, and superstructure. It is these subsystems that enable human beings to reproduce their existence. (See Figure 1.1 for an overview.)

Activities in the social *infrastructure* involve the most immediate necessities in food production—whether people will hunt, gather, fish or plant. Whether people find themselves in steppes, deserts, jungles or plains affects the kind of society they will build. The kind of soils, plants, and animals that are available, as well as the climate and topography affect how work and leisure patterns play out and constrain the way of life that is possible. Once all of this is established, people have to discover the process of how they can work most efficiently, so as to gain the most yield with the least amount of effort. In order to do this an elementary division of labor is established which includes designing tools, devising ways of harnessing energy, and determining the length of the workday.

In Harris's system, the social infrastructure involves not only the production and distribution of goods, but the reproduction of the next generation. This entails regulating the size of the population through birth control methods and sexual and marital practices. Child-rearing practices and the various factors that determine mortality rates also figure into the infrastructure, which as a whole determines both the production and reproduction of society.

Producing goods however, is only the beginning. There must be methods of determining who gets what, when, where and how. Thus a primary aspect of the second dimension of a society—its *structure*—is its economy, or system for exchanging goods and services once they are produced. Further, the economy involves decisions about how much gets produced. In societies with rank and stratified social relations (which we will discuss in the next chapter), the asymmetrical ratio of distribution is justified by status, prestige, and the ownership or non-ownership of property.

The second major department within the social structure is a society's politics. Politics in its original sense means the "policy" governing society in two senses: projecting the future direction of the society, and maintaining and regulating the existing social institutions—that is, sustaining order. The establishment of social policy is rarely a smooth process. Especially in rank and stratified societies, different subgroups within society cooperate, compete, and struggle for political power. The political and the economic systems are interrelated, and both concern the public world. However, all societies have a more private "domestic" economy in which families, extended families, and kin groups exchange goods and services. While the public and domestic political economies interact, the public political economy has more power to determine the domestic economy than the reverse.

As the saying goes, "man does not live by bread alone." People in all societies seek meaning about what they are doing. Meaning-making systems include science, art, law, and sacred systems—which, according to Harris, more often than not

Figure 1.1 Dimensions of Society

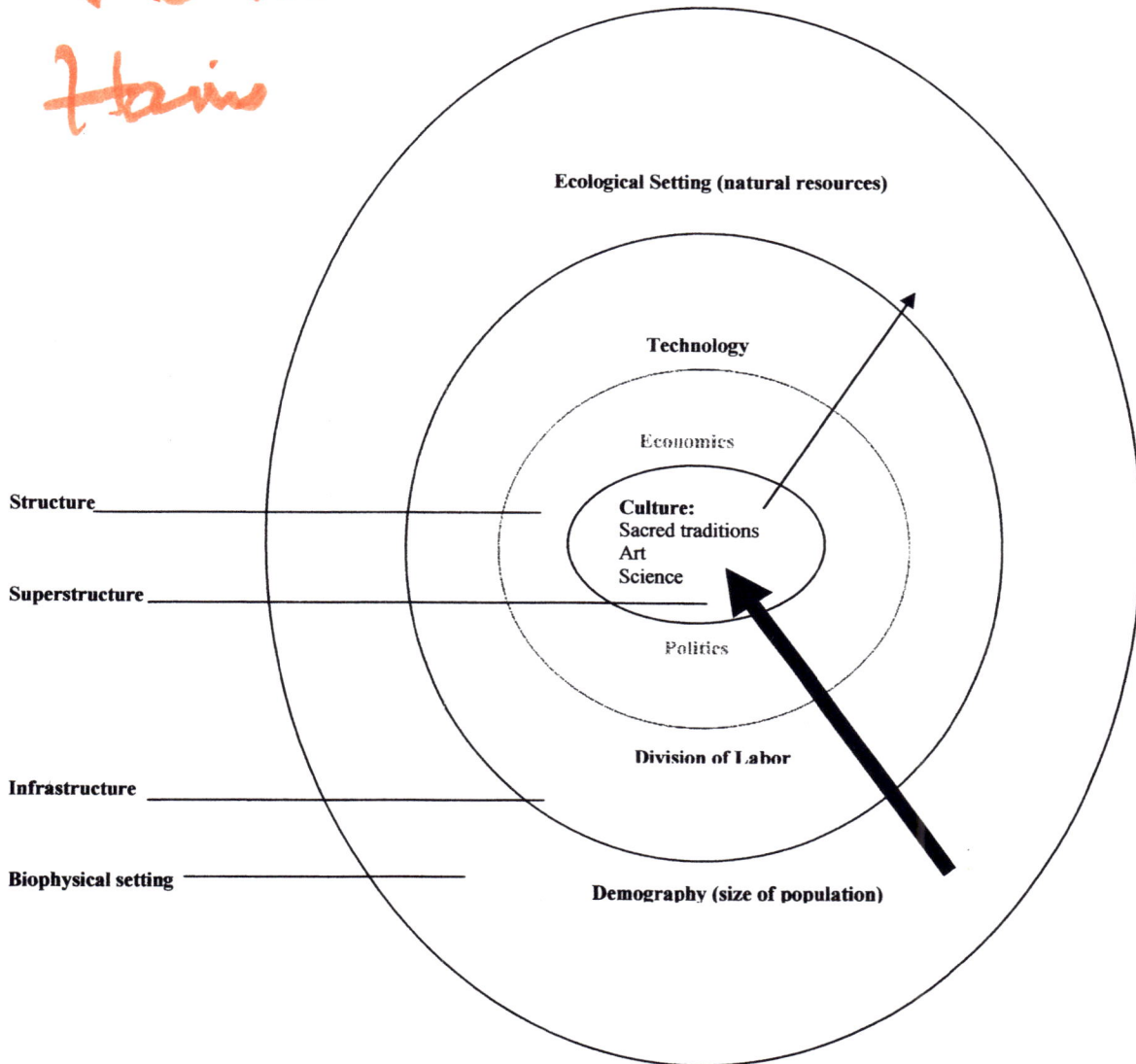

Ecological Setting (natural resources)

Technology

Economics

Culture:
Sacred traditions
Art
Science

Politics

Division of Labor

Demography (size of population)

Structure

Superstructure

Infrastructure

Biophysical setting

Materialist theory of social change:
Population pressure and resource depletion creates a crisis
that instigates technological innovation and /or
political and economic reorganization. There is a generational
lag that occurs before culture changes to express changes
originating from the outer levels. Mostly cultural expressions
legitimize what has already gone on in the biophysical,
infrastructural and structural dimensions of society.

The arrows are meant to indicate that while all dimensions
mutually impact each other, they are not equal.
The larger arrow indicates the more powerful direction
goes from biophysical setting to infrastructure to
structure to superstructure.

serve to justify in people's minds what they are already practicing in their work. These meaning-making systems can also inspire people to look beyond the mundane necessities of working, eating, and breeding. This dimension is called the society's *superstructure*, and is often simply referred to as its "culture."

For purposes of this book, the most important part of Harris' description is his claim about how these three subsystems interact over time. When most of us are taught about world history we are presented with a picture that presupposes that social change proceeds from the top down, moving from the social superstructure and descending to the structure and infrastructure. This is an "idealist" presentation of history, in that it assumes the social world changes because of extraordinary ideas, knowledge systems, or morals.

Harris argues that this is incorrect. Social evolution is rarely determined by people's values and ideas—whether they be sacred or scientific. In fact, in nearly every instance social change begins with a crisis of population pressure and resource depletion. If the crisis is bad enough and the society doesn't become fragmented (people abandoning it or joining other societies), people will by trial and error develop new technologies and economic-political systems that temporarily relieve the crisis. The superstructure is usually the most conservative dimension of society and the last to change. In Harris's model, the social infrastructure and structure are like the arms of a galaxy whirling very quickly. The superstructure is like the galactic core, whose rate of movement is slower. Harris backs up his claim with evidence that hunting-and-gathering, horticultural, and agricultural societies all change from the bottom up. Following Harris, my position in this book is "materialist," in that I am convinced that tangible, biophysical, and technological-economic processes determine beliefs, knowledge systems, and values far more often than the reverse.

This linear description of the movement from infrastructure to structure to superstructure does not mean that the superstructure is powerless and doesn't have any influence. It just means its influence is comparatively weak. In reality, all three dimensions are interpenetrating. But the dynamics are not equally weighted. Lastly this description is not meant to suggest that in practice people in societies first build the infrastructure, then the structure, and finally the superstructure. All three subsystems are built co-extensively in time. But as they are building all three subsystems, each subsystem is not affecting people's material life equally. The infrastructure and structure of society are impacting and determining people's lives more forcefully.

3. How humans shape society: cooperation, externalization, objectification, and internalization

Like all other animals, we humans have to earn a living in the environment in order to meet our needs. Each species has a specific activity, a "species activity," unique to itself by which adaptation is accomplished (for example, building dams is the species activity of beavers). All animals work—i.e., they expend energy in a focused way over time in order to survive and reproduce. But the overwhelming majority of animals do not deliberately cooperate with other members of their own species, except in caring for their young. They complete all processes of work essentially alone. The simple biological strategy of most other animals is to graze, forage, or chase down prey in solitude.

Considered in isolation, without society or culture, and relying only on physical prowess, a human being is a mediocre competitor to other large-bodied mammals. Other animals can run faster, jump higher, and have greater sensory acuity. It is our social strategies that have made us the dominant large-bodied species on the planet, and these social strategies entail cooperation. It is our ability to cooperate with other human beings that gives us the edge over the rest of the animal kingdom. We cooperate by (a) pooling our resources, (b) creating a division of labor, and (c) working to a common end. Cooperation creates a social whole that is more than the sum of its parts.

Human societies emerged as an adaptive strategy of *Homo sapiens* to compensate for our physiological mediocrity. But society does far more than help us to survive and reproduce. Society is responsible for completing our humanization and expanding it over the course of history.

Cooperation changes human species-activity from work to labor. In laboring, we accept roles. Members of a hunting band agree beforehand that some will join together to frighten the game, while others will wait in ambush. Later, if they have been successful, they will share the kill with other members of the band who have stayed behind at the campsite. After all have finished consuming the edible parts of their prey, those members who did not participate in the hunt are expected to engage in other roles, such as sewing the carcass and tanning the leather of the animal.

None of these roles, other than that of waiting in ambush, directly leads to biological satisfaction. In fact, the strategy of frightening the game, taken by itself, would be maladaptive: it would probably diminish the chances of a successful outcome. But as a socio-cultural strategy, frightening the game is effective because others have agreed to be waiting for the game when it falls into their trap. This cooperative strategy, and others like it, are so effective that they have enabled our species to dominate the globe.

Over time, our species has built a network of social institutions around the Earth that changes, and is changed by, our biophysical environment. Society becomes akin to what Teilhard de Chardin termed a "noosphere"—a "super-organic" planetary feedback system, a "socio-sphere" nested within the biosphere. It is within this socio-sphere that history takes shape. The dynamics taking place among other animals within the biosphere over time could be called "evolution." "History" is a unique kind of evolutionary activity that goes with the building of a socio-culture. Without a socio-culture there would be no history. With the few exceptions of those other animals that have some socio-culture, the human species is the only species on earth that produces history. History consists of socio-cultural systems changing over time.

Summing up:

Non-human animals	Human beings
work	labor
little or no cooperation	cooperation: social roles
biological evolution	socio-cultural evolution
evolution without history	evolution with history

The heart of cooperation is the creation of division of labor, or role-making. When groups divide up to perform complementary roles, they create an interdependency. By relying on each other, the people create synergistic results. They obtain more food per capita with less risk than could any single member working alone. There is no longer a direct relationship between biological needs and biological strategies. The ends may be biological, but the means are socio-cultural.

When a hunting-and-gathering society first begins to divide up the tasks, the people need to discuss what to do: "You go over here and frighten the game; you go here and wait in ambush; you stay back at the camp and prepare for a feast." But then, after a few practice runs, the group members no longer need to discuss who is going to do what because the roles have been internalized. Each person reciprocally typifies the process in his or her head. (Berger 1967) The internal dialogue probably goes something like, "Aha, here he or she goes again playing that role. This is my cue to play this role."

The internalization of laboring activities allows old roles to be mastered to the point where they become subconscious. Each person can now anticipate what the others will do. "There she goes again" becomes "there we go again." The socialization activity initially is consciously undertaken. But once internalized cues kick in, each person engages in roles automatically. This frees up the individual's conscious mind to deepen existing skills or learn a wider set of roles.

So the more roles we internalize, the more human we become. The more roles can be typed and then formed into social habits, which can be counted on to recur, the more the mind knows its social place in relation to what other humans are doing. In this model, history does not "begin" with writing and civilization, because this would exclude all the laboring and role-making of pre-state societies. History begins with the construction and reproduction of all human societies, starting with hunter-gatherers.

People are not, however free to build roles from scratch. Throughout our lives we are limited by the tools, institutions, and beliefs that are passed on to us from previous generations. An individual is born into a particular type of society, within a given subgroup of that society, at a particular point in history. Nothing can be done about that. And these constraints define what the person has to work with. As an adult, through one's goals and actions, one not only cooperates with others, but also competes with the goals and actions of others. That encounter is an inseparable part of social life. Furthermore, competition between people is not a democratic "free-for-all." Since the rise of stratified states 5000 years ago, most people have little or no political or economic power at their disposal to enable them to compete with the real power-holders in society. In all these ways, people are the objects of history.

At the same time, while individuals are in one sense subservient to forces which are much more powerful than themselves, the institutions and social tools of previous generations contain the raw materials necessary to overcome these constraints. Each person still has responsibility for what is made of his or her circumstances. Through learning language, and through learning to take on roles, we are training ourselves to become weavers, not simply yarn to be woven into what history becomes. As adults, the quality of what we bring to our work, the morals and beliefs we hold dear, and the way we raise our children are all aspects of being a human subject.

Individuals then, are both objects and subjects of society, both products and co-producers of society. What is more, the process of being a product and co-producer is going on all the time.

The process of being a subject and object of history has nicely been broken down by Berger (1967) to include three moments: externalization, objectification, and internalization. For example, every day a person goes to work, her labor, along with everyone else's labor, literally produces society for another day. Every morning a person wakes up, she is "pregnant" with the power of reproducing society for another day. As people express their subjectivity and creativity on the job, society is reproduced. We are each pregnant with a little part of the birthing process of society for that day. The fact that this *externalization* potential stands behind both society and history can easily be seen if there is a natural disaster or a general strike. Society comes to a halt. It can only resume its normal rhythms through the concrete cooperative action of people. As long as people withhold their laboring activity, social reproduction is temporarily halted. So on the one hand, society is a human product, and we are the producer of it.

On the other hand, both the process of creation on the job and the goods and services which result from our joint actions of role-taking produce synergetic results. The outcomes and consequences of the consumption of these goods and services by others are beyond the power of any individual to control. Our actions are *objectified* in the substance of what gets produced. However much we "externalized" ourselves by laboring, the outcome of what people actually do with the goods and services produced confronts these producers as something new, as both more than and less than we bargained for. Externalization is the process of making something. Objectification is the product made, along with other people's reaction to it.

Last, there is the stage of *internalization*. It is here that the person digests the difference between what was intended in the process of externalizing their social being and what actually happened to the product (objectification). This internalization is an evaluation of the results in the service of future cycles, beginning with externalization. This cycle repeats itself over the course of history.

Figure 1.2 Humanity as the subject-object of history.[*]

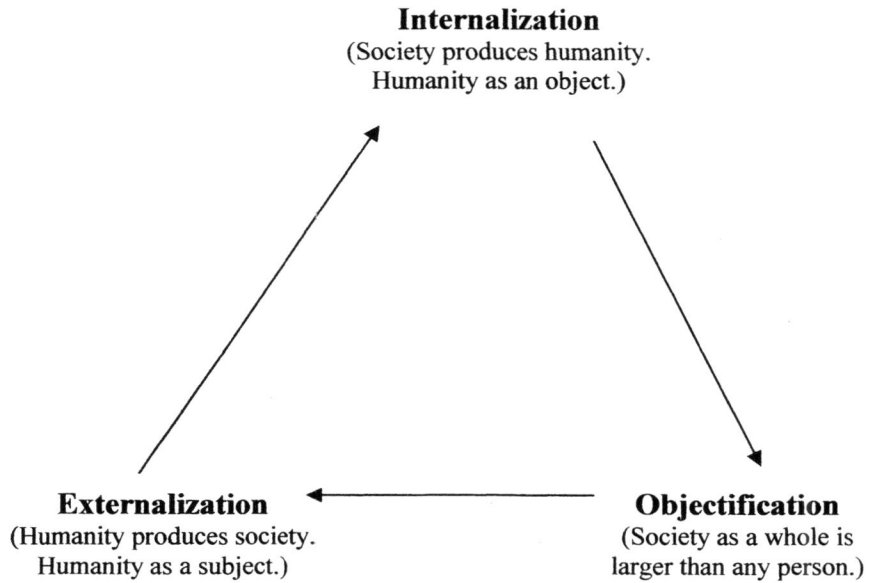

Internalization
(Society produces humanity.
Humanity as an object.)

Externalization
(Humanity produces society.
Humanity as a subject.)

Objectification
(Society as a whole is
larger than any person.)

---

[*] This cycle turns into an irreversible *spiral* of prosperity or decadence over time, and this is human history.

Let's take a concrete example. Suppose you are an actress and along with others in your theater company you've been rehearsing for a play for weeks. Every day that you go to rehearsal, you are externalizing your being as you shape the form of this social activity (putting on plays). On opening night and all the subsequent performances, your performance is objectified. It is now subject to feedback from the world—as gauged by the number of tickets sold, as well as by audience response, critical reviews, and wages. When the play is over the actors and actresses internalize the outcome. They take in and evaluate the feedback and make judgments about future plays.

When we objectify and internalize, we are a product of society. When we externalize ourselves, we are co-producers of society. History is the result of the process of externalization, objectification, and internalization of societies over time and across space around the world.

In sum, externalization is the process of laboring, objectification is the outcome of the laboring, and internalization is the evaluation of laboring, or the discrepancy between externalization (what was produced) and objectification (how it was received). All three moments both reproduce society and socialize the individual. See Figure 1.2.

All roles and work patterns are not freely constructed from scratch every day. Roles are institutionalized; and customs, habits, and coercion insure continuity from day to day. But while there may be pre-programmed roles, the enactment of the "play" can only occur through the performance of social roles by living actresses and actors. It is the average person more than the extraordinary one who, for better or worse, makes the drama real on the stage of history.

Finally, the collective activity of reproducing society through externalization, objectification, and internalization over time produces both conflict and order. On the one hand, humanity's labor reproduces continuity, integration, cohesion, consensus, and predictability from generation to generation. But at the same time, humanity's labor also produces outcomes that are novel, competitive, conflicted, and that sometimes result in crisis. In reproducing our society we reproduce traditional institutions of constraint,

while also producing possibilities for challenging those institutions.

My emphasis on the average individual as a history-shaper does not imply there is no place for extraordinary individuals who also write the scripts of history. But these scientists, artists, and politicians are essentially mental workers who couldn't have done their work if it weren't for the everyday work of farmers and "blue-collar" workers who provide the food and construct the buildings, roads, and machines that directly or indirectly make this extraordinary work possible. At the same time, not only are extraordinary individuals the beneficiaries of the work of the lower classes, but the work of privileged groups impacts the average person too. The work of Alexander Graham Bell on the telephone, for example, changed the communication patterns of the average person dramatically. Extraordinary people are also products and co-producers of the externalization, objectification, and internalization processes.

Let us review the relationship between the socio-cultural dimensions of society, world-history and laboring. In order for people to meet their needs and desires, they have to earn a living in their environment; therefore, human beings labor. The process of laboring involves a specialization of tasks and the use of tools to devise and take on roles. This laboring process—

- satisfies needs and desires
- humanizes us
- breathes life into macro and micro social processes—
  (a) building and sustaining the social infrastructure, structure, and superstructure of society
  (b) catalyzing externalization, objectification and internalization
- spreads the "sociosphere" in space, i.e., around the planet, creating order and continuity as well as novelty and conflict
- extends the "sociosphere" in time, shaping a human world-history
- creates unintended consequences in our biophysical environment.

Laboring is the activity that reproduces society and history. Laboring might be defined as the totality of collective human effort, both physical and intellectual, that is expended on the shaping and reshaping of socio-culture over time and across space.

4. Social amnesia: reification and alienation

In the last section we discussed role-making and role-taking as the basis of cooperative labor. Following Berger, I argued that role-making arises out of discussion, while role-taking occurs once the initial roles have been mastered: they are acted on subconsciously, becoming habits. The blessing and the curse of role-creating occur when the original roles that were improvised by adults of a given hunting-and-gathering society are transmitted to the next generation—i.e., institutionalized.

The blessing is that the next generation is spared the task of having to invent roles for the first time and work out the bugs. The curse is that since the members of the new generation did not themselves construct these roles, they lack the same active, exploratory relationship to them. The daughters and sons inherit the roles their parents constructed. But since they didn't participate in shaping those roles, their relationship to these roles is more passive. Over generations, it becomes more difficult to imagine that these roles are malleable. They seem harder to change, or even to imagine as being different than they are. The internalized cue of the next generation might no longer be "there we go again," but "this is how things are done."

Our roles humanize us, and at the same time they have the potential to make our minds and bodies passive. We become automatic humans—humanoids. As long as the individual is actively constructing her or his roles, the act of playing out those roles seems tenuous and changeable, almost playful. But once the roles are passed on to the next generation, they become institutionalized and ossified in the body and mind of the individual as well as in society.

The old role-making habits become simple role-taking habits. Roles become crystallized at the macro-level in historical institutions, and are experienced as being beyond the control of the individuals who currently embody them. Institutions appear to have a life of their own, and

confront the individual as external and coercive things about which nothing can be done. Still, no matter how difficult it may be to imagine, we have far more freedom to shape and change these roles collectively than we usually think, granting that some social circumstances are more difficult to change than others.

The process of conceptualizing a social institution as a "thing" divorced from cooperative labor is called *reification*. The transformation of role-playing from an experience of "here we go again" to one of "this is how things are done" is an example of reification. Suppose I am at work and someone new on the job challenges the role I am playing in order to get a particular project done. If I rigidly say, "this is how things are done," without considering that this particular situation might be unique, I am reifying the social situation. First, I am renouncing my capacity to change the role I am in. Second, I am giving up or projecting my own power to change roles by allowing myself to be enslaved to customs developed by previous workers. Third, these customs appear to me to be out of our control and have a life of their own. "Who am I to change these customs? This is the way things have always been done." Finally, the customs are not conceived of as having both good and bad qualities that are evolving. Rather, they are understood as static—as all good; or, if we happen to be rebelling against them, as all bad.

Let me define reification more robustly. Reification is a psychological process by which individuals turn social processes and products into things. Social processes and products include roles, language, and institutions. Reification is a kind of amnesia in which humans forget that we are the agents and ends of all social activities. Roles, language, and institutions are means to our ends, not ends in themselves. Reification turns means into ends. From the example above, in its full-blown form, reification can be broken down into four moments

(1) a renunciation of ourselves as the agents or subjects of our creations;
(2) a projection of our power out of ourselves onto our creations;
(3) a rigidification of our creations into a status which appears beyond our control; and

(4) a caricaturization of our creations as having either all good or all bad qualities.

While reification is a collective illusion, in another sense it is real. On one hand, it presents social reality in a false form. In fact, human collective creativity (labor) stands behind all social processes and products. Reifications are illusions about how society is actually built and sustained over time. But on the other hand, when people act as if society were actually a thing standing above individuals, it gives society a certain kind of reality because people's actions support that illusion. In other words, when people are mobilized around what we may think is an illusion, the illusion becomes real in the sense that we have to deal with all of the problems that real people add to a situation through actions based on their beliefs.

But is the tendency to reify society the only problem that stands in the way of people becoming more active as social shapers? If people didn't have all of these misunderstandings, would we be free to create any type of society and history we wished?

The difficulty with this formulation is that it makes the problem of why societies tend to resist change only a question of social-psychological misunderstandings, or some sort of cognitive error. This ignores the economic and political constraints that are real obstacles in changing society.

Another reason, as Marx and Engels pointed out over 150 years ago, is that people become "alienated"—that is, they lose control over the infrastructure, structure, and superstructure of society. With the rise of agricultural states, societies became stratified, with elites using coercive force to mobilize alienated castes to labor in all three dimensions of society while extracting a huge surplus of goods and services for themselves. Because they had the backing of a military, they could force the majority to work longer and harder against their will and despite their resistance. Besides surrendering goods and services, the alienated castes paid rent and taxes on land, and had to be available to fight wars and work on state projects.

But alienation cannot be achieved by state coercion alone. Social institutions must be built that justify and support coercive power so that the

need for armed force is not always immediately present. Legitimation is the set of superstructural institutions and processes used by those with coercive power to induce those in submissive positions to comprehend their submission as being (a) necessary (rather than questionable); (b) socially beneficial to all, including themselves (rather than exploitive); (c) as part of a cosmic order (as opposed to a social arrangement); (d) as inevitable (rather than changeable); and (e) as eternal (rather than historical). The socializing institutions in the ancient world that performed this function included both sacred authorities and the government—which were often one and the same; and these were in turn supported by the kin group and the family.

I use the term "Ideology" to mean an integrated system of political and economic ideas that emerges in stratified societies among competing castes or classes to explain and justify each's struggle for power. Ideology overlaps all meaning-making systems in the superstructure but is not identical with them. For instance, art in a given society can either support the status quo or undermine it. Sacred beliefs can justify the rulership of a king, or they can—through the efforts a cult or sect—threaten the power of the elite. Ideologies have at least six dimensions: they provide knowledge and beliefs about the past, present and future political and economic world; they appeal to emotions; they provide norms and values; they promote goals and plans; they are enacted in rituals; and they have a social base among various sectors of the population.

Ideology limits the ability of any caste or class to see the world with any absolute objectivity. Thus the way any given group sees the world cannot be completely separated from the political and economic struggles between various stratified groups.

While ideology is a body of ideas, legitimation requires material processes and institutions by which ruling-class ideology is transmitted. Certainly, the lower classes can house ideologies of resistance in their own counter-institutions, but this would not be a legitimizing process, but a "counter-legitimation."

With state coercion and legitimation in place, most alienated people retreat from public life and from technological, economic, and political decision-making processes. Most people in stratified societies are aware of having needs and desires, possessing a skill, receiving a wage, satisfying a need, raising a family, and believing in deities. In order to satisfy their needs, people are aware that they need to go to work. But most are only dimly aware that their labor has collective, macro-social consequences that go far beyond their personal and domestic agenda.

In the process of working, we also reproduce the institutions of our society, indirectly participate in the reproduction of other societies around the world, and impact our biophysical ecology. And doing this day after day, we are shaping society.

It is important to keep in mind that alienation is a political and economic process of losing control over our collective-creative species activity —labor. In contrast, reification is a psychological process that can occur in any society, including those that are egalitarian. When people are alienated they are still shaping history, but they are sleepwalking through it. Let's take an example.

Suppose I go for a cup of coffee from a vending machine on my morning break. That cup of coffee I'm drinking has the labor of thousands of people contained in it—including people on the coffee and sugar plantations, and all the workers who ship and deliver the coffee to our country. That is collective-creative activity. They are shaping world history by their labor. But how can that work be creative? Those people on the sugar and coffee plantations don't sit down with other people and coordinate their efforts. They just do what they are told. As for creativity, harvesting sugar cane is hardly creative. Furthermore, those people usually don't give a damn about the rest of the workers who are responsible for getting the coffee to the U.S., nor do they care about who is going to drink it, or the quality of the coffee itself.

What most workers care about is not getting in trouble, not losing their job, increasing their wages, and bettering their working conditions. Whatever creativity they express relates either to finding ways to goof off on the job or to picking faster (if they are paid piecemeal). Real creativity is expressed negatively in avoiding the requirements on the job; it is expressed positively when they get off work. As Marx said, the majority of human beings feel most human when they are not working and more like animals when they are working.

Of course the cooperation and creativity of workers on coffee and sugar plantations is limited in scope, given that we live in a stratified society and they are working-class and have to take orders. Other members of the society—artists, writers, musicians, and architects, for example—are able to exercise much more creativity; while still others—such as entrepreneurs and athletes—tend to be much more competitive than factory or agricultural workers are. But even if all of the people in the system as a whole were competing with each other or being creative to the same degree, the social process instituted by the human species taken *as a whole* would still have to be considered essentially cooperative and creative. The very fact that a species can harness the fertility of the soil to meet its needs is a major achievement that distinguishes us from the rest of the animal kingdom. We coordinate our efforts through occupational specialization, and the product can ultimately be transported across oceans. That's an enormous feat, and we would be shortsighted to take it for granted.

I will summarize my argument so far. People don't intentionally act to produce society, yet their actions produce it nevertheless, behind their backs as it were. All that humans intentionally do is merely to try to satisfy needs and desires. But in order to do this, they have to work at a specific job, receive a wage or a salary, and thereby satisfy their needs. However, in the process, people produce more than they realize. They inherit the tools, institutions, and belief systems of previous generations, which they inadvertently reproduce in the process of satisfying their needs. Whatever the individual's immediate personal or family needs, his or her work responsibilities demand that more goods and services be produced than are necessary for private consumption. In order for the individual members of the society to get their needs and desires satisfied, a super-personal system of production, decision-making, circulation, and distribution must be set up, maintained, and in some cases, transformed.

As people become more politically and economically alienated, they become less and less aware of macro-social processes, which become more or less unconscious and over which they have diminishing control. In spite of their alienation, and in spite of the fact that individuals and families are to a large degree "out for themselves," they nevertheless inadvertently reproduce larger systems and processes—they feed people they will never know, reproduce social institutions they have no power to control, and impact the biophysical environment in ways they do not understand. Part of their activity is conscious, but a much larger part is unconscious. I call the inability to grasp the full implications of cooperative labor, either because of reification or alienation, "social amnesia."

People are conscious of

- needs/desires
- biological reproduction (raising a family)
- choice of labor (this is not very relevant in ancient rank and stratified societies)
- playing roles as given
- wages or salaries received
- satisfaction/dissatisfaction with needs
- identification with superstructural sacred traditions,

while the following are relegated to the realm of "social amnesia":

- the fact that roles are changeable
- the reification of society
- alienation from society
- inadvertent reproduction of local social institutions (externalization, objectification, internalization)
- reproduction of international societies (through trade)
- social impact on biophysical ecology

Until now there has never been a time when human beings as a species have intentionally remade these institutions with the intention of changing history. In order for history to become a conscious process, people would have to overturn and restructure the stratification system, which would allow us collectively to take hold of that system. Then it would be possible to design our future, not just improvise it. We would become conscious history-makers, not just unconscious history-shapers.

5. A summary, and a discussion of some mysteries about gender inequalities

The process of history shaping involves three participating dimensions—the individual, society, and the biophysical environment. In the process of trying to satisfy our individual needs, we must engage in mediated social relations. In working together to satisfy needs, we use up natural resources and change the ecological niche we inhabit. As a result, socio-cultural systems accumulate wear-and-tear and undergo periodic crisis. People have to decide on new ways of engaging this environment and have to build new forms of social organization to better adapt to these biophysical changes. If successful, they produce new means by which to satisfy individual needs. Individuals then develop new needs, and this results in changed social systems and changed ecological conditions. Changes in both these larger systems in turn provide new vehicles by which old individual needs may be gratified and new needs stimulated or discovered. All of this occurs despite reification and alienation.

History-shaping can be defined as the necessary, recurrent, irreversible, and accumulating process of the collective laboring of the entire human species in the past, present, and future. Figure 1.3 summarizes the chapter by contrasting how history in this book will differ from traditional presentations. The last three contrasts in this Figure have not been discussed in this chapter, but will be covered in later chapters.

Up to this point I have discussed history-shaping as if men and women have experienced these processes identically. But they have not. While the rise of rank and stratified power relationships affected most men and all women the same, it has also entailed a gender entitlement process, which is embedded in and yet distinct from the processes discussed in this book so far. For example:

(1) Even in egalitarian hunting-and-gathering societies, under certain conditions what I will later call "informal" male dominance emerges; there is no corresponding informal female dominance;

(2) though leadership in hunting-and-gathering societies and in simple horticultural societies is

tenuous, whatever leadership emerges is virtually always by men;

(3) once privilege and vertical power emerge in rank and stratified societies, it is a few men who are privileged and wield power;

(4) in all pre-state societies—egalitarian and rank—women have always had responsibility for raising children in addition to working in public;

(5) the overwhelming majority of pre-state societies trace descent along the male rather than the female line;

(6) in pre-state societies women go to live in the male's kin-group home area more often than the male goes to live in the female's kin-group area;

(7) to the extent that pre-state societies allow nonmonogamous marriages, such marriages consist of one man marrying many women far more often than the reverse;

(8) when there are wars it is virtually guaranteed that men will fight and women will be considered the "spoils of war."

The purpose of these statements is to show that the roots of gender hierarchies go deeper into social evolution than the origins of political rank and stratification. They can be seen in rudimentary form as far back as hunting-and-gathering societies under certain conditions. Therefore, an explanation of the roots of gender hierarchies will include, but go beyond reification and alienation as explanations.

How then did it come to be that some men dominated in the areas of leadership, politics,

economics and the military and acquired privileges in tracing of lineage, residency and in child-rearing. How did it come to be that all men had some privileges over all women? Why don't we find some societies where women dominate in these areas?

Typical responses to questions about why men came to subordinate women include the argument that men are biologically stronger than women, or that women were victims of coercive social forces beyond their control. Another approach is to "blame the victim" and contend that women prefer to be in a subordinate position. I reject all of these arguments.

If we accept the belief that women are simply victims of circumstances, we deny women their role in co-producing society. Women have always been actors and agents in history. If we shelter women from their collective responsibility as social producers we also deny them the power to change these circumstances. We deny their social agency.

Before discussing this issue in more depth, let us first explore what ancient social formations were really like. Where were they located? How large were they? How did people in them make their living? How many hours did they work? What kinds of tools did they use? What rules did they have for distributing their products? Did they believe in one god, many gods or no gods? What were their mating practices? How did they raise their children? How did they handle group conflict? These are the topics of the next chapter.

Figure 1.3 Contrasting Views of History

Traditional U.S. View	Categories	View of This Book
about the past	**subject matter**	about the past, present and future
begins with writing, states, cities	**origins**	begins with socio-culture in Upper Paleolithic Age
extraordinary events: wars, inventions, congresses	**what events matter**	mundane events: working and breeding
made by extraordinary men: kings, generals, politicians	**who makes events**	primarily made by the average men and women laboring
labor has little to do with history	**place of labor**	labor is the collective activity that makes society and history possible
objectivity, impartiality already given	**place of objectivity**	objectivity-- something to be striven for and inseparable from class and gender struggles
discrete, unconnected events	**relationship between events**	a process of interconnected, evolving events
implicit or no relationship	**relationship between history and society**	types of societies are the basic unit of history
extraordinary ideas, beliefs, values (idealist)	**ultimate cause of change**	1) population pressure and resource depletion 2) technology 3) economics (materialist)
inevitably out of control of the majority	**locus of control in the past**	improvised by majority due to reification and alienation.
inevitably out of control of the majority in the future	**locus of control in the future**	potentially can be designed by the majority in the future
free will of heroic individuals	**human motivation**	improvised collective actions to keep things from getting worse individual is both a product and co-producer
progress	**meaning of history**	improvised evolution
voluntarily designed by few individuals	**agency/constraint**	structured, but not pre-determined irreversible, cumulative, with periodic crisis

Chapter 2

The Anatomy of Ancient Societies:
From Paleolithic Bands
to Axial Iron Age States

1. Egalitarian Societies

In this chapter, my purpose will be to examine briefly how the material cultures of the primary historic social systems—tribal hunting-and-gathering bands, horticultural and agricultural societies, and agricultural states—are organized, with a special emphasis on their politics.

In learning about how these past societies functioned, it is difficult to avoid making comparative judgments about our own present society. One should not undertake such comparisons too hastily. One of the major goals of this book is to cultivate a "historical imagination," which entails learning to appreciate the entirety of a social system, with all its strengths and weaknesses, given its unique place in world history.

However, since comparative judgments are inevitable, it is worth commenting at the outset on what form those judgments are likely to take. An important function of this chapter is to show that the conventional tendency to characterize the historical transitions of humanity from tribal organization to state societies as "progress" is problematic. But at the same time, it is just as simplistic to embrace a "degeneration" theory, which romanticizes tribal societies as the ideal. I will reject both of these perspectives in favor of one that I call "improvised evolution."

(A) Paleolithic Hunter-Gatherers

We begin with the Upper Paleolithic Age, beginning approximately 30,000 BCE, in which all humans lived in foraging societies. These societies averaged between 50–100 members who lived nomadically in bands of nuclear families. These families stayed with other families or separated from them based on seasonal changes and the abundance or scarcity of natural resources. They stayed together when they needed protection from the elements or had to defend themselves; they separated when smaller groups could more effectively harvest resources.

There was an elementary division of labor, with men practicing hunting and women gathering nuts, berries, roots, tubers, leaves, and small animals such as crayfish, insects, etc. As Sanderson (2001) points out, while hunting is the predominant means of subsistence in roughly two-thirds of hunting-and-gathering societies, whether hunting or gathering is primary depends on the climate. Gathering constitutes a larger part of the diet in warm or hot climates, while hunting dominates in the colder climates with less vegetation. The tools used were made of stone, wood or bone. This division of labor between hunting and gathering does not imply that it was full-time. In these simple societies, many work practices were performed by each nuclear family separately, with minimal coordination between families, and no public institutions.

The cases where women were big-game hunters were probably rare. According to Lenski (1987) there were several reasons for this, some of them biological. Hunting with bows and spears requires speed, agility, and upper-body strength, in which men excel. This difference is exaggerated in the later stages of pregnancy. Because of the physiological demands of pregnancy and lactation, women have a higher ratio of fat to muscle than men. This provides them with nutritional reserves to draw on during food shortages. With training, the average woman can develop her muscles to a level that equals or exceeds that of the average man—and some women are of course innately larger and stronger than some men to begin with. But when women's ratio of body fat drops below 15 percent, they often cease to ovulate and become infertile. Thus muscular development in women appears to conflict with their societally more essential role of child-bearing. As a likely consequence, if there ever were societies that used women extensively in hunting, they probably did not survive because of low birth rates.

While the work life of hunter-gatherers was partly specialized based on age and sex, specialization did not necessarily imply hierarchy or centralization. Having a special domain of activities for each group doesn't imply power of one group *over* another. In the case of women, the gathering they did was highly valued and they participated actively in group decision-making.

In the previous chapter I defined *power* as the social capacity to harness energy and labor in order to meet needs and desires. *Politics* is the method or means of achieving power. This can be done with or without social hierarchies. The result of this process is the determination of who gets what, when, why, and how. Politics regulates existing power in the present, maintaining order and punishing infractions, but also navigates power relations over time.

Hunter-gatherers have been characterized by Morton Fried (1967) as "egalitarian" in their power relations. This means that positions of entitlement are open, so that all those people who have the talent to occupy them can achieve them. It also means that everyone has access to basic resources and tools, helps determine social policy for the future, and regulates power in the present. If power is exercised in the context of egalitarian social relations, the result is a form of politics with "horizontal power" as its base. Horizontal power is the harnessing of energy to do work in a way in which all groups control all dimensions of society—infrastructure, structure, and superstructure.

Hunting-and-gathering societies had no permanent leadership and made most decisions by consensus. What leadership existed was "situation-specific." This means there were no institutions of office. When a situation emerged which required a special skill, someone with that skill took responsibility for leadership *in that situation*. When the situation was either resolved or dissolved, the power of the leader dissolved with it.

Perhaps it is difficult to imagine that a temporary leader wouldn't turn into a permanent one. It might seem that, after a while, people would inevitably get lazy and stop paying attention; and before they knew it, they have a tyrant on their hands. Remarkably, though, this was not the case.

We must keep in mind that, in egalitarian societies, people in positions of leadership were hardly objects of envy. They were not spared from working at mundane tasks; indeed, leaders were probably the *hardest* working members of the group. Leaders gained their reputations by their generosity. Perhaps the experience of being a leader in a hunting-and-gathering society resembled, in some ways, the experience of leaders of today's volunteer groups or non-profit organizations, who typically reap modest material rewards though they work very hard indeed.

This does not mean that every aspect of society was leveled. Some people had more influence and prestige than others, but influence and prestige did not translate to privilege or power. Influence is the capacity to get people to act by persuasion or example without invoking coercion. This capacity is based on a skill or talent that cannot automatically be passed on to a son or daughter. Prestige is the degree of honor accorded one by other people. Leadership in egalitarian societies brought prestige and influence, but it brought no surplus of material goods, no more leisure time, and no coercive power over others. The performance of the leader was subject to community discussion and evaluation. Any leader who slacked off or was abusive ceased to have influence or prestige. What compensation existed was either the intrinsic enjoyment of the work, or the admiration shown by other members of the community. Leaders continued at their tasks because there was no one else to do the work, and because the work was important.

To say that leadership was situation-specific in hunter-gatherer societies does not mean *anyone* could be a leader in any situation. After all, in every society there are people who have natural gifts or talents. It would be self-defeating for a society not to take advantage of those skills. But in hunter-gatherer societies, even people who *never* took a turn in leading *any* activity were still party to all decisions that affected themselves and their interests.

It is an oversimplification to say that all hunting-gathering societies were nomadic. Their patterns of mobility, size, and political organization were dependent on the geography of the land they inhabited and on whether available natural resources were concentrated or dispersed. Beginning in the 1980s, *optimal foraging theory* attempted to identify the conditions under which a particular food would be chosen to be exploited (using the diet-breath model), and whether and when people would move to new areas (the patch-choice model).

According to the diet-breath model, a foraging society's decision to exploit a particular food is determined by the ratio between the amount of work expended searching for and handling the food, as compared to the net energy derived from that food item. Thus the choices people make are not solely determined by nutrition; the amount of effort it takes to find the resource, and the time it takes to prepare the food after it is acquired, also figure into the equation.

The patch-choice theory identifies the conditions under which hunter-gatherers will stay in one area or leave for another. In this case, the determining factors revolve around the costs of moving—which include the type of terrain to be crossed, the distance to the next prospective camp, and the resources needed in order to make the trip.

Dyson, Hudson and Smith, in Sanderson (2001) present four possible scenarios:

(1) *High resource density, low resource predictability.* Here groups will be highly mobile, will share information about the state of resources, and territoriality will be low (because of constantly shifting territories).

(2) *High resource density, high resource predictability.* Here territoriality is prominent because the benefits of defending dense resources outweigh the costs.

(3) *Low resource density, low resource predictability.* Here groups are highly dispersed and highly mobile. Territoriality is absent because the costs of defending resources outweigh the benefits.

(4) *Low resource density high resource predictability.* Here groups tend to remain in areas of predictable resources, and any territoriality that develops is a "passive territoriality."

According to this theory, the degree to which people will become territorial is not static, but depends on the degree of concentration of available resources, and on the ease of their accessibility. High resource density and high resource predictability will tend to make people more territorial, because this situation provides the most in resources for the least amount of work. People will understandably tend to become possessive about a territory with these characteristics, because the alternatives (sharing the territory with others or moving) are less desirable; thus the energy expended in fighting to retain exclusive rights to such a territory is energy well spent. But under these conditions, members of foraging societies face an interesting problem, in that the population will tend to expand and families will begin to compete for resources. If conflict results, then the various groups involved will have to weigh the costs and benefits of staying put against the costs and benefits of moving to another location. If they stay, they face continued conflict and possible subordination by victorious groups; but they benefit by remaining well-fed and not having to move. If they withdraw from the area to avoid conflict and potential subordination, they will probably have to work harder, live under more difficult geographical conditions, and subsist on less nutritious food.

Low resource density and low resource predictability mean that people have to work harder to gain access to resources; and, because the resources are less predictable, the people often come up empty-handed. Foragers will be the least territorial here because there is little worth defending.

How could people have known what the best alternatives were? I am not arguing that this decision-making process was consciously undertaken, in the sense that calories of food energy and human effort were calculated and compared. I am suggesting that, over thousands of years of trial and error, behaviors evolved that helped hunter-gatherers survive better than their human and non-human competitors; the accumulating wisdom regarding what resources were worth pursuing, and when and under what conditions it was advisable to move, were gradually and unconsciously incorporated into cultural institutions. Only in retrospect can these choices be understood in terms of optimization of benefits over costs.

The economy of any society is the means by which goods and services get distributed. The economies of hunter-gatherers are difficult for anyone living in an industrial capitalist society to understand. As Polanyi (1957) has pointed out, pre-state economies are inseparable from social interdependencies and obligations. There is no separate "market" that is autonomous and independent of socialization, customs, and rituals.

The most important goods and services were shared in a spirit of what Sahlins (1966) called "generalized reciprocity." This meant giving among equals without explicit calculation or expectation of where or when giving would be reciprocated. Trade, where it occurred, involved only relations with strangers—people from foreign tribes. Within the society itself, any calculation of labor expended, or introduction of money to mediate relations between people, was taboo. In our society, relations between family members or close friends are still conducted using generalized reciprocity. What boggles the imagination is

that, in hunting-and-gathering societies, generalized reciprocity extended beyond intimate contacts *to the entire society*. Individuals did not independently calculate how to "get ahead" materially in relation to others. In this sense, Marx and Engels were right to label these economic relations as "primitive communism."

In generalized reciprocity, every exchange was understood within a larger context in which the prime goal was to make the world sacred. From an etic (for a definition of this word, see the Introduction) standpoint, the benefit of this would have been to promote solidarity within the group. Sometimes generalized reciprocity extends to other groups, because when strangers become friends there is less danger of attack.

Early anthropologists typically speculated that the workload in tribal hunter-gatherer societies must have been heavier than that in later agricultural state societies; and that, because more complex societies have more sophisticated technology, there must have been an increase in the amount of leisure time in complex societies for the average person. Anthropologist Marshall Sahlins (1972) challenged this assumption, finding on the basis of cross-cultural studies that, on average, typical hunter-gatherers worked only fifteen to twenty hours per week! They spent the rest of their time playing, sleeping, or visiting. It is important to note that the studies cited in Sahlins' work were done in a period of history (the last 400 years) when most hunter-gatherers were being—or had already been—*driven out of* the more lush environments by state societies, and were subsisting in marginal, often desert, environments. It is likely that, in earlier eras, when there was little or no competition for land (e.g., in African environments not subject to the last Ice Age), hunter-gatherers worked even less.

People in industrial capitalist countries commonly assume that individual private property has always existed. In fact, *individual* ownership of property was the exception before the Axial Iron Age. When Victorian anthropologists discovered that tribal societies had group property, they went on to suppose that people in such societies shared *everything*, including marriage partners. This has been shown to be inaccurate. Hunter-gatherers shared the material goods that mattered most to them, such as land, food, and tools needed by the whole group—but not marriage partners. In fact, *ownership was seen as the right to give something away.* Generosity was given a high moral value.

Yet all of this sharing and generosity did not proceed simply from a spirit of altruism. Hunter-gatherer economic relations served the self-interest of the participants. Individual survival was inseparable from group self-interest. Furthermore, people couldn't *afford* to accumulate wealth even if they wanted to, given their life-style. Possessions were limited to what could be carried. And there was no specialized military group to protect and serve those who might have had the desire to accumulate wealth.

Parents in hunter- gatherer societies did not need or have many children, at least partly because the activities of hunting and gathering don't easily lend themselves to child labor. It could be argued that child labor in food gathering might have given women more time to develop hunting skills, but other factors intervened. In order to keep the number of births down, and also because there was no safe and adequate substitute for mother's milk, women in most of these societies nursed their babies for at least two to four years. Since nursing infants need to be fed often, mothers were not able to roam as widely and quickly as big game hunting requires. They were, however, available for small game hunting. The mating practices of hunter-gatherers, according to O'Kelly (1986), were typified by serial monogamy. Divorce was common, but divorced individuals proceeded to find other partners. Polygamy was rare. Hunter-gatherers were sexually liberated as compared with people living in agricultural states. Standards of sexual behavior for women did not differ dramatically from those for men; female virginity was not a serious issue, and wife-beating was rare. Compared to women in any other societies, women in hunting-and-gathering bands had a very good life. Permissive attitudes towards sexuality were reflected also in child-rearing practices. Children were allowed

to explore their sexuality, provided they didn't do so in front of the adults. Hunters and gatherers did not have large families: on average, parents had two to four children, and raised them to be self-sufficient and independent.

According to Lenski (1987), population growth in hunting-gathering societies was virtually nonexistent. This was, in part, because of high death rates from natural causes (the average life-span—factoring in high infant mortality—was somewhere between 28 and 33 years). It was also due to the fact that women who are nursing infants are less likely to ovulate. Choice also played a role. One study revealed that infanticide was practiced in 80 of 86 hunting and gathering societies, while another study found that abortion was practiced in 13 of 15 societies studied. Some scholars estimate that between 15 and 50 percent of all live births ended in infanticide.

In sum, if freedom and equality are ideals toward which to strive, then hunter-gatherer societies embodied those ideals to a greater degree than any other societies in human memory. Whether we speak of the large amounts of leisure time, the expectation of generosity in economic exchanges, the lack of private property, the absence of accumulated wealth, the fluid nature of leadership, the consensual decision-making process, or the relative gender parity, these societies more than any other in history deserve to be thought of as egalitarian.

However, all this freedom and equality required the maintenance of low population levels, which in turn often required infanticide. Before we jump to the conclusion that hunter-gatherers had little respect for the sacredness of individual life, we must keep in mind that in primitive magic there is no individual soul or individual life after death. In fact a baby is not considered a member of the community until he or she is initiated through ritual.

(B) Neolithic Simple Horticulture Societies

During the period between 13,000 and 7,000 BCE, the supply of large game mammals around the world dwindled. In North America, giant bison, horses, oxen, elephants, camels, and antelopes were hunted to extinction; in Europe, the same fate met the woolly mammoth, woolly rhinoceros, steppe bison, and giant elk. Meanwhile, human population density was increasing, probably due to the exploitation of new habitats opened up by the retreat of ice sheets and to the temporarily abundant food supply resulting from unrestrained harvesting of large game animals in those new habitats. Increasing population, combined with a growing scarcity of resources as game animals were over-hunted, meant that the old survival strategies were proving increasingly inadequate. A new way of making a living had to be invented that would feed more people, and it had to be done in a smaller space.

During a period of about 4,000 years called the Mesolithic period, foragers switched to small game hunting and began planting temporary gardens. By 8,000 BCE, especially in the Near and Far East and Eastern Europe, societies began to practice horticulture in settled villages. Simple horticultural societies predominated on the globe from 8,000 to about 6,000 BCE.

Simple horticulturalists lived in larger groups (100-300) than did hunter-gatherers, and in more constricted areas. Because of this, people's commitments to each other grew: families bonded into kin groups, and clans formed, along with secret societies and other specialized bodies. The etic function of many of these groups is to lessen the conflicts likely to arise in large groups, where the cost of moving is less an option than in nomadic foraging societies, and to protect themselves against famine.

In hunting-and-gathering societies, the nuclear family is not obligated to share with other families, and no social institutions existed to enforce resource redistribution. What was shared was shared voluntarily. One of the sources of conflict in horticultural societies is the expectation that nuclear families produce for the kin group as well as their family. As might be imagined, nuclear families must have had mixed feelings about this. Anthropologists have often reported incidents of families *hiding* their food supply when a loafing kinsman appeared on the scene. On the surface, the

family was cordial and observed the proper etiquette, but underneath they resented having to give to a kinsman who was not pulling his weight. Thus obligations arising from bonds between kin were probably often regarded as onerous. On the other hand, when a harvest was bad and times were difficult, nuclear families were probably relieved to be members of a kin group.

Direct confrontation between people would have been a problem, and thus community members would have developed ways to avoid confrontation—just as members of extended or nuclear families find ways to avoid confronting each other today. Over the course of the year, people would get lost in the mundane squabbles of daily life. They needed periodic group activities that would provide members with an opportunity to release these tensions, to forgive and forget. Where their livelihood was at stake, they had to learn how to promote group solidarity at all costs.

Ceremonies became more elaborate in simple horticulture societies, as a means to promote solidarity and minimize family-kin conflicts. In hunting-and-gathering societies, where land was plentiful, groups were more likely to confront each other over misunderstandings because people knew that if the conflict wasn't resolved, there was not a great cost in moving. But in planting societies the costs of direct confrontation were greater because the price of moving was higher. Therefore people in planting societies had to devote more time to working out their problems. From an etic standpoint, one of the functions of a ritual is to allow people to express their hostilities and tensions through dramatization rather than through direct confrontation. Sacred rituals provided predictable, periodic opportunities to forgive and forget. These ceremonies were typically coordinated with the turning of the seasons.

At this point, it is important we distinguish between *horticulture* and *agriculture,* since these words are often used interchangeably. Horticulture is the form of planting which existed in Neolithic tribal societies. Agriculture originated in Bronze Age states. Horticulture is the cultivation of small gardens of fruits and vegetables. Agriculture involves the cultivation of grains in large, permanent fields. Horticultural societies typically use a "slash-and-burn" technique. New grounds are cleared by cutting and then burning existing vegetation, especially shrubs and small trees. Larger trees are left standing, but are killed by 'girdling'—i.e., cutting a circular strip of bark all the way around the trunk, thus stopping the flow of nutrients from the roots to the branches. When all the existing vegetation is burned to the ground, the resulting layer of ash provides mineral nutrients for the season's planting. In a few years, when the soil is exhausted, the people move to another location nearby. The abandoned plots are allowed to lay fallow for twenty to thirty years before the tribespeople return to plant again.

Compared to hunters and gatherers, horticulturalists are more settled. But compared to agriculturalists, horticulturalists are more nomadic. This is because agriculturalists can cultivate the land more efficiently than horticulturalists. The type of technology a planting society possesses dictates how settled they really are. Why is this?

Horticulturalists use digging sticks, whereas agriculturalists use plows. A digging stick cannot penetrate very deep into the ground; thus horticulturalists weren't able to access soil nutrients much below the surface. With a digging stick, it is also hard to get deep enough into the ground to root out weeds, and the presence of weeds undermines productivity. In addition, a certain portion of the land must remain untouched and be allowed to revert to wilderness so that it recovers its nutrients. When cultivated areas are exhausted, the group must move on. All of this means that horticulturists ran out of space quickly if there was any significant rise in population. In contrast, agriculture permitted people to stay in one place longer, because the plow exploits the nutrients in the soil more fully.

The evolution from hunting and gathering to horticulture had an important impact on the work activities of men and women. Women probably led the revolution from foraging to planting because planting is closer to gathering than it is to hunting. They took the lead in seeding, tending, and harvesting the plants. They learned about the healing properties of plants. Women also protected, fed, and cared for many of the small animals brought back alive, eventually leading to animal domestication. Men did the unskilled labor of clearing the brush and preparing the ground while doing occasional hunting.

This division of labor resulted in an increased segregation of men and women. Men worked in teams clearing the land, while women worked together planting. In many horticultural societies that have been studied by ethnologists, men and women do not even live together, but stay in separate houses. As people adopted horticulture in the Neolithic Age, there must have been a loss of prestige for the men, as they were forced to exchange the adventure of big game hunting for the less-skilled work of clearing land for women's planting.

The shift from hunting and gathering to horticulture also led to a shift from exchange among equals (reciprocity) to centralized exchange. Horticultural societies produced more food per capita than hunter-gatherer societies, but in important ways they were more vulnerable. Not only were horiculturalists more dependent on fellow social members, but they were more dependent on other groups for trade. Since they domesticated and planted only a narrow range of crops, and since they tended to stay in one place longer and thus could not access free-roaming game animals as well as nomadic hunter-gatherers could, horticulturalists did not enjoy as balanced a diet as their hunter-gatherer ancestors. The early gardeners were typically protein-deficient. The only way they could supplement their diets was through trade—producing more of what they could produce, and exchange it for what they couldn't. Coordination of material production thus became a necessity. The society as a whole needed a subsystem to manage the economic exchange of goods that went beyond informal exchanges between families. The society required a public economy, in addition to a domestic economy. The solution was the phenomenon of the "big man."

"Big men" played the role of hard-working, public-spirited individuals who exhorted their families and neighbors to work toward accumulating surplus food that could be given away at a big feast. During the feast, the big man ostentatiously redistributes the extra food, thus acquiring prestige and influence in the community. According to Harris (1977), regardless how the big man rationalizes his own actions, or how members of the society make sense of what he is doing, etically he is inadvertently training people to produce more than is needed for just the family and the kin-group. By training himself and others to work this way, he is "teaching" all involved how to share in a more systematic and efficient way in a public economy. The big man is not an institutional office of all simple horticulture societies; where it occurs, it is voluntarily chosen by a few individuals who compete with each other.

One psychological interpretation of bigmanship and the male secret societies which first emerge in horticultural societies is that they offered some compensation for the deterioration of men's occupational status from big game hunters to forest clearers.

Anthropologists report that the adventure of hunting big game is highly regarded and brings a great deal of prestige. When the big game began to run out, between 13,000 and 7,000 BCE, men must have begun hunting small game with women and children. Because small-game hunting is less dangerous, the experience must have been disappointing and probably involved a loss of status. At the same time, gathering maintained its status as a worthy skill. Eventually even small-game hunting became an insignificant source of food, and with the rise of horticulture men's only contribution to work was clearing the land for planting. This was neither satisfying nor prestigious. Meanwhile, women were learning about planting and harvesting, and about the medicinal properties of plants. Men must have been somewhat envious of the women during this period. As compensation, men invented secret societies that excluded women; and they stressed the importance of clans, whose function is protection. In addition, they acquired additional prestige by becoming big party throwers, displaying generosity to all.

I am not suggesting that male psychological insecurity caused the beginning of public economies and centralized redistribution, only that it might have been an initial motive. Often people's psychologically-motivated actions have political or economic repercussions; occasionally these repercussions result in changes to social systems that are preserved because they serve some function that was previously nonexistent, or of which the people were unaware. People in simple horticultural societies needed to build a public economy in order to survive. But they discovered a way to do so not through conscious economic analysis and strategic planning, but by stumbling onto it, with motives that were not economic at all.

It is tempting to assume that the emergence of big men was the beginning of male dominance and social stratification because these individuals took on some leadership functions and were able to mobilize people to do what they wanted. But, as we will see in later chapters, in order for male dominance to exist, it must have institutional backing. While I am not suggesting that the big man's motives were selfless, his goals were influence and prestige, not an increase in material wealth at the expense of others. More importantly, as an unintended consequence, he encouraged the habit of producing a surplus, since not all of what was produced for the feast was consumed. The rest was stored, available either in case of a bad harvest, as wealth for trade for other products, or as "bait" in forming alliances.

If the big man had really been accumulating power, he would have needed some institutionalized coercive force to protect that power. Simple horticultural societies had no such institution—no police or military force to protect the big man from popular protests or to enforce his will. As Sahlins (1972) argued, big men had to "make their own power" through acts of generosity, bravery, oratory skills, charisma, or managerial ability. The big man had to goad, bait, or persuade people to help him prepare for the feast. If the feast didn't go well and one of his competitors won the contest for generosity, his followers deserted him. His followers only helped him prepare for the party in the hope that he would outdo competing big men. His winning added to their own prestige.

How did those members of society not involved in the process of throwing these "parties" feel about them? They probably had mixed opinions. In times of bad harvest, people were likely glad for the leftovers collected and set aside after the feast. However, when the harvest was good, people might have thought the whole process of throwing feasts a little silly.

It is only in complex horticultural societies (which we will study in the next section) that the public economy becomes institutionalized, existing across generations. The "big man" was not an office that that could be handed down. The death of a big man often meant the end of centralized distribution of goods within and between societies. In protein-deficient horticultural societies where moving was not an easy option, this was a dangerous situation.

Let us turn from the economies of simple horticulturalists to their marriage and childrearing practices, as compared with those of hunting-and-gathering societies. According to O'Kelly (1986), in horticultural societies the spouse relationship is not as important as the relationship between brothers and sisters. In fact, kinship relations are generally built around brothers and sisters. This makes good sense in terms of promoting social stability. Planters rightly sensed that a brother or sister relationship was far less likely to "break up" than was a marriage relationship, with all its storm and stress. In addition, O'Kelly points out that the sexual attitude men have towards women changed in these societies. Women were seen by men as dangerous polluters (through menstruation), and men's attitude toward sex gained a strong element of fear that had never existed in foraging societies.

Polygamy (the practice of having more than one mate) typically exists in one of two forms: *polygyny*, in which a man has more than one wife; or *polyandry*, in which a woman has more than one husband. Anthropologists have found that, in societies where polygamy exists, it is far more likely to take the form of polygyny than polyandry. Polygamy of either form is rare in hunter-gatherer societies. However, polygyny is common in simple horticulture societies, a fact that would seem to contradict the belief held by many that women in such societies enjoyed high status. Yet there are some circumstances in which polygyny can benefit women. In simple horticultural societies, where women are involved in communal work patterns and eat and sleep together, it can make life easier economically for a group of wives to live and work together in a domestic arrangement. In terms of labor-load, a monogamous marriage may be far more demanding.

As we shall see later, however, in complex horticultural societies the meaning of polygyny changes. Here it is used for purposes of status and display by prominent men in these ranked societies. Polygyny among chiefdoms is set in a context of institutionalized male dominance in which women are supervised.

In horticultural societies, people have more children than in foraging societies because planting lends itself more easily than hunting or gathering to child labor. But as can be imagined, because people are living in close proximity, children are raised to be obedient rather than independent, due to the added social pressure to get along.

Until the 1960s, anthropologists assumed that the shift from hunting and gathering to planting was an advance for the human species. The reasons offered were that, with planting, the food supply was more stable, people didn't have to keep moving around, and there was more leisure time. Mark Cohen, in *The Food Crisis in Pre-history* (1977), argued instead that hunter-gatherers knew about planting for hundreds, perhaps thousands of years before it was implemented, but did not adopt it because it did not in fact offer as good a life.

From what we know now, hunter-gatherers did not experience the shift toward a sedentary lifestyle as a relief or an advance. There was work involved in setting up systems to minimize group conflict. As for the reliability of the food supply, it is true that big-game hunting provided a less reliable source of food than gardening. However, the gathering of fruits and nuts by women in foraging societies made up for the unpredictability of big-game hunting. Finally, planting did not increase the amount of free time for the average person. People in simple horticultural societies worked at least 25 hours a week (Lenski, 1987), a significant increase from the 15 to 20 hours reported by Sahlins (1972) for hunter-gatherers.

2. Rank Societies: Neolithic Complex Horticultural Societies

Nomadic hunter-gatherer bands and simple horticultural societies had no institutionalized leadership. Leadership was either situational or episodic (as with big men). When did centralization and political hierarchies emerge, and why?

Complex horticultural societies appeared in isolated parts of the world between 6,000 and 3,000 BCE. As noted in chapter 1, qualitative change in social systems in the ancient world came about as the result of a crisis—usually resource depletion and population pressure. However, some simple horticultural societies faced additional problems, including: (a) a dry climate; (b) land that was biophysically circumscribed (surrounded by mountains, deserts, or water); or (c) a scarcity of natural resources even prior to human activity.

Each of these problems could be allayed—at least temporarily—through increased centralization. Centralized irrigation systems were more conducive to horticultural production than were uncoordinated struggles between villages for dry, unproductive land; but the building of such systems required a central coordinator of the work force. Horticultural societies that lacked natural resources could benefit from the institutionalization of a regular trading system, as opposed to the erratic trading systems of most simple horticulture societies; but in order to have enough goods to trade, a surplus of raw materials and goods would have to be produced within the society. The question of whether centralization was imposed or voluntarily accepted is one that we will take up later. For now, it is enough to point out that centralization did provide tangible benefits.

The subsistence vulnerabilities of simple horticultural societies in crisis were too severe to allow a public economy—which had proven its usefulness—to rise or fall based on a volunteer system of bigmanship. The culturally adaptive response was to organize production more efficiently by centralizing society and creating a hierarchical division of labor. Thus the big men of some simple horticultural societies became the chiefs of the earliest complex horticultural societies.

While simple horticultural societies consist of between 100 and 500 people, usually living in a single village, complex horticultural societies vary greatly in size—perhaps one thousand to a few thousand people living in anywhere from two to six villages. The Trobriand islanders offered typical examples of the small chiefdom, while the societies of the Polynesian islands were the largest known chiefdoms, with numbers approaching 50,000 people.

Complex horticultural societies were still based in kin-groups and clans, but these were now organized hierarchically. At the bottom of the hierarchy were the commoners, who engaged in food production and specialized crafts. Over them stood district administrators, who mediated between the chief at the top of the social pyramid and the commoners at the bottom. Usually district managers served as heads of their local villages. At the apex of the system as a whole stood the chief and his kin.

With the rise of chiefdoms, egalitarian political relations ended and were replaced by *rank* relations. According to Fried (1967), rank relations positions are limited so that not all individuals with sufficient talent to occupy positions of status can achieve them. (See Figure 2.2 for a more specific contrast between egalitarian, rank, and stratified political relations). The difference between egalitarian and rank relations can be seen by contrasting the differences in power between a big man and a chief.

Sahlins (1972) argues that a big man could only *ask* people to help him produce a surplus. The chief, on the other hand, had the authority to break into the domestic economy and *demand* some production for the public economy. He could *command* extra output from groups lower in the hierarchy. Further, while a big man was not authorized to represent the group in any important function, the chief represented the group in both peace and war. The social role of the chief was to be at the head of an expanding society, and to provide an integrating function of managing irrigation systems and coordinating redistribution and trade systems.

At the same time, the chief began accumulating privileges of his own. Privilege might be defined as special access to material benefits or opportunities based on birth, office, or membership in a certain group, without the requirement of having to do something in return. In this case the chief retained a significant amount of the social surplus produced for his kin and minions before it was redistributed to the commoners. He had a larger garden-plot, and a separate storage center and residence. He was exempt from manual labor, wore prestigious décor forbidden to others, and his status was hereditary. Rank political relations entitled the chief to these benefits.

The leadership privileges of a chief differed dramatically from those of a big-man. Since the right of a chief to lead was hereditary, that meant he didn't need the big man's oratory skills and charisma. The chief was believed to have descended from the ancestor spirits, and that was more than enough to justify his privileges and authority over people. The chief did not need to work to demonstrate generosity; he had been born with admirable qualities simply because of his special relationship with the ancestors or the totem.

These privileges, however, did not add up to anything like the power that exists among the ruling castes or classes in stratified societies. For example, the chief did not own any private property. The land was seen as chiefly property that he "holds" for the ancestor spirits. The chief could regulate distribution once food or artifacts had been produced. He could also command a commoner to produce a surplus beyond what the commoner's family or kin-group needed in order to survive. But the chief could not monopolize the basic resources of life or the tools used to reproduce the life of the commoners. In rank relations, commoners maintain control over production—what gets produced, when it gets produced, and how it gets produced. However, commoners lose

control over the distribution process. The chief could not control production because there was no military to back him up. His pre-state society could not afford that kind of social specialization.

When we compare the life of the average person (a commoner) in a chiefdom, a foraging society, and an agricultural society, we see a rough progression—or retrogression. The life of a commoner in a chiefdom was probably worse than the life of an average nomadic hunter-gatherer or a commoner in a simple horticultural egalitarian society; however, it was generally better than the life of a peasant in an agricultural state.

Sexual relations, family life, and the erotic life for women in chiefdoms reveal increasing inequalities. For unmarried chiefly women, standards of sexual behavior were liberal; but once these privileged women were married, standards became sexually repressive. For commoners, standards of sexual expression were permissive, but commoner women were not protected from rape or wife-beating. The community did not come to her defense the way it would if the women were of the chief's family. We will study the life of women in chiefdoms in much more depth in chapter 6.

The childrearing practices in chiefdoms are the same as in simple horticultural societies. People raise more children than in foraging societies, but the children are probably taught to be more compliant because they are living in a ranked society.

3. Stratified Societies: Bronze Age Agricultural States

What happened to cause complex horticultural societies to evolve into states? The theory of progress embraced by early anthropologists supposed that social complexity arose from the desire to improve the technology, from hunger for material wealth, and from the longing for more leisure time. Contemporary theories of social evolution claim that none of these motivations were operative.

Figure 2.1 Simple Horticultural vs. Complex Horticultural Societies *

Simple Horticulture	Dimension	Complex Horticulture
Depletion of resources High population density	**Conditions of Emergence**	Depletion of resources High population density Limited pristine resources Arid climate Geographical circumscription
8,000 BCE	**First Time of Appearance**	6,000 BCE
Villages 100-500 people	**Size**	2-6 villages at least 1,000 people
Federation	**Social Organization**	Centralization (political hierarchy)
Egalitarian	**Political Relations**	Rank
Big-man	**Leadership**	Chief
Egalitarian redistribution	**Public economy**	Partial redistribution

Big-Man	**Conditions of Power**	**Chief**
Makes power Depends on personal qualities, which cannot be inherited: generosity, bravery, oratory skills, charisma, perseverance, managerial skills		*Comes to power: office* Passed on through heredity. May or may not have skills. Descent from ancestor spirits
Can attract, but can't compel "To be generous is to be noble."		Can compel "To be noble is to be generous."
Redistribution of wealth within society. Manager of trade.	**Functions**	Redistribution of wealth within society. Manager of institutionalized trade
Representative at intra-group ceremonies. Spontaneous festivals and feasts. Can only control own domestic economy. Doesn't have command over political economy.		Representative of group to other groups. Offers protection to the group. Can control political economy and command extra output from commoners.

*Adapted from Sanderson (1991)

According to some social evolutionists, chiefdoms became states for the same reasons simple horticultural societies evolved into complex horticultural societies: they inhabited dry climates, were geographically circumscribed, and were poor in pristine natural resources.

Complex horticultural villages had grown to encompass several thousand people. Regional population densities were in excess of twenty to thirty people per square mile. Crowding problems were worsening. The "slash-and-burn" techniques described earlier could not continue to work under these conditions. Not only was the soil eroding, but also these techniques required space: a portion of the land had to be left to revert to wilderness, and this limited the amount of land that people could use to live on. As population densities increased, this problem intensified.

Chiefdoms in crisis had to find a new strategy for food subsistence. How could a growing population reproduce its existence and not have to move? Two developments provided the solution—the plow and the domestication of cattle.

The plow and the domestication of cattle made it possible to extend farming into new zones and to intensify farming in the old ones. According to Lenski (1987), controlling weeds and maintaining the fertility of the soil were the two principal problems for all farmers. Weeds multiplied faster than horticulturalists could root them out with their hoes or digging sticks. And over time, the soil's nutrients seeped deeper into the ground, below the reach of plants and too deep to be brought back to the surface. The plow turns the soil at greater depth; it buries weeds and adds humus to the soil; it also brings to the surface those nutrients that had previously seeped below the root level. The first plows were made of wood, but some were made of copper and were dragged and guided by small teams of farmers working together. The domestication of cattle to pull the plow made farming far less labor-intensive.

As should be evident from this description, planting was not a once-and-for-all discovery, resulting from the inspiration of some heroic individual. Its discovery and development was a collective process that took thousands of years. Cohen (1977) pointed out that the enrichment of soil, the planting of seeds, the removal of competing species of plants, the irrigation of plants, the clearing of land, and the transport of species beyond their native ecological sites all constituted a groping process, not a discovery.

The continuing growth in population densities, and the increase of the amount of food surpluses available under agricultural methods, necessitated more social coordination. Though the state served to protect the interests of the ruling caste, it also provided an integrating function in further centralizing irrigation systems, systematizing trade with other societies, and coordinating relations between groups. Once grains could be domesticated (instead of being used in their wild state), they could be stored for long periods. This large stored surplus would allow the ruling group to pull larger sectors of the population away from food production and permit (or force) them to develop other specialized occupations.

Harnessed animal energy found uses other than that of farming. The casting of tin and copper into bronze not only improved the durability and flexibility of tools and weapons, but enabled the manufacture of bronze wheel rims—leading to the development of a whole new form of transport. Animals could carry the upper castes around on chariots. But chariots required roads, at least in the cities. The pace of society quickened. As time accelerated, space expanded. Ships were built for the trading of commodities over long distances. While the crises these societies had faced were more severe than those faced by chiefdoms, their increasing centralization and their technological innovations would allow them not only to resolve the crises but to develop new ways of life not directly connected to crisis management.

The first states emerged between 3000 and 2000 BCE, initially in Egypt and Mesopotamia, later in China and India. The population of these agricultural states ranged from 10,000 to 100,000 people. These societies were *stratified*. This means that status positions were exclusionary, with great differences in access to the infrastructure, structure, and superstructure of society. The ruling class wielded what I call *vertical power*—the monopolizing, by the use of coercion backed by military specialists, of the means to harness energy and labor. The ruling group could impose its will on the lower groups against their will and despite their resistance. The lowest groups had lost control of the products of their labor, most of the processes of laboring, and most of their leisure time.

Agricultural States were typically composed of eight or more castes. At the top were the king and queen and their family, followed by the priests and priestesses. Priests were originally administrators. They kept track of all transactions and interpreted the will of the goddesses and gods into written sacred myths. The society's ability to store grain gave the king and the ecclesiastical hierarchies greater powers that the chiefs in complex horticultural societies had, because grain could be hoarded much longer than fruits and vegetables. It was part of the job of the newly emerged military specialists to protect these hoards.

Below the military were the merchants and artisans. They produced for an external market as well as for the royal household. Merchants traded in the artifacts the artisans produced for foreign goods. Merchants in agricultural states had much less autonomy than those in industrial capitalist states, since trade was tightly administered by the State. Lenski (1987) argues that agricultural states were "command" economies with a state-controlled market, not free markets.

In the city, the next caste below the artisans consisted of what Marx called the "lumpen proletariat." These were people living by their wits—beggars, thieves, and prostitutes. All people living in the cities composed, according to Lenski (1984), about 10% of the total population of the state.

The lowest caste in cities within these societies were slaves. They were the property of the royal household or of the aristocratic class. In agricultural states, most of the slaves were women and children who worked in various jobs within the royal household. Women and children were worth more alive then dead, since they could provide the king with children as part of his harem, and do simple menial work.

Most female slaves wouldn't run away. Where would they have gone? Most people will not leave a miserable situation for something completely unknown which may be worse. Besides, in some ways the life of a domestic slave was better than that of some of the "free" castes, certainly than that of peasants. Male slaves presented a different problem. It is more difficult to enslave a man than a woman. To force formerly free warriors to work in fields with copper hoes would require armed soldiers to watch them. A copper hoe is not much different from a copper hatchet (the warriors' weapon).

The last caste consisted of the peasantry living in the country and producing all of the food. The life of an agricultural peasant was considerably worse than that of a commoner in a chiefdom. In stratified societies there are thousands of people to produce for and the exploitation of peasants' labor was thus severe. In addition to having to produce food for others, the peasant was heavily taxed, conscripted to fight wars, and recruited to build public works such as monuments. Why didn't the peasants run away? There was no place to go. These states arose in geographical settings where escape meant migrating into a desert or into the mountains and having to learn a new form of subsistence.

Life for the average person in an agricultural state was therefore less desirable than it was for the inhabitants of pre-state societies. In agricultural societies, the ruling class controlled at least 50 percent of the total wealth produced. This meant that most people had to live on less. The goods and services obtained through trading were appropriated by the governing class, rather than fed back into the social body as a whole. The newly-invented wheeled vehicles weren't used by the lower classes, but for the military purposes of the rulers or for public display. There was neither public education nor mass communication. Only the upper classes were literate. Political parties did not exist. Power was hereditary, or conferred by appointment. Most people suffered from a lack of variety in their diet, which translated into chronic vitamin, mineral, and protein deficiencies. In hunting-and-

**Figure 2.2 Evolution of Political Entitlements and Status
Stone and Bronze Ages***

Egalitarian	Rank	Stratification
Hunter-Gatherers/ Simple Horticultural	Simple Horticultural Complex Horticultural	Complex Horticultural Agricultural States
All positions of valued status are open to all	Status positions are limited	Status positions exclusionary
Unlimited access to basic resources	Limited access to basic resources	Extreme constriction of access to basic resources
Average person has control over production, circulation, and ownership	Average person has control over production, loses control over circulation and ownership	Average person has no control over production, circulation and ownership. Must work very long hours
Situational leaders have influence and prestige only	Chief has influence, prestige and privileges	Divine kings and priests have influence, prestige, and privileges
Horizontal power	Proto-vertical power	Vertical power
Neither coercion nor legitimacy	No coercion but legitimacy to rule	Both coercion and legitimacy

* Adapted from Fried (1967) and Sanderson (1991)

gathering societies, a more balanced diet was achieved with far less labor.

The status of women in agricultural states was worse than in any of the previous social formations. Women lost control of planting, as men worked plows harnessed to large animals. For the first time in history most women did not work in public, but rather in domestic households supporting the cottage industry of spinning, weaving, and canning. They become more economically dependent on their husbands and more isolated from other women.

Polygyny continued among the upper castes, as a means either to enhance status or seal political alliances. Birth rates were higher than in any previous type of society, as peasants reacted to their extreme poverty by producing as many sons as possible to labor in the fields. The status of women was so low that a dowry was offered to a prospective mate for purpose of taking the daughter off the hands of her family. As might be expected, child-rearing practices emphasized discipline and obedience. This socialized children to reproduce the caste system as adults. We will explore the status of women in agricultural states further in chapter 6.

I will now summarize the difference in wealth between ranked complex horticultural societies and stratified agricultural states. In the rank relations of chiefdoms, the chief had some definite privileges, but he did not have the coercive vertical power to monopolize the basic resources of life or to control the production process. In the stratified relations of agricultural states, kings and priests had the power to do both. Peasants had to work much harder, and had to produce on command.

The actual practice of the people who built agricultural states contradicts theories of progress in a number of ways. First, agriculture was a gradual collective evolution, not a sudden, individual discovery. Neither was "civilization" designed as a fully worked-out plan in the minds of the participants. People discovered what they were getting into as they were in the process of building it. Agricultural civilizations were improvised, not designed. Lastly, agricultural states emerged in spite of the resistance of most of their inhabitants. People

in pre-state societies didn't care about "growth" or "innovation" for their own sake. They were quite content to reproduce the old ways. It was only after the old ways were repeatedly proven not to work any longer that they considered other options. But the exercise of these options must have taken place amidst anxiety, skepticism, and resistance.

4. Archaic Iron Age Herding Societies

We now turn to a type of non-state society— those that subsist by animal herding—that has had a great deal of impact on world history, despite its typically modest size and minimal technological kit.

Most herders move frequently, and are thus classifiable as "nomadic." There are various stereotypes of nomads, which we must address before proceeding to discuss their way of life. According to Thomas Barfield (1993), these stereotypes run typically along the following lines:

- Herders subsist entirely on meat an milk products.
- Herders never have contact with villages or cities except to loot or burn them.
- The treatment of women is worse than in state societies.
- Herders are unreasonable because (a) they do not understand the rules of civilized societies, or (b) they do not make a distinction between the natural and the social worlds.
- Herders are reasonable but they use their reason for evil purposes.
- Herders attack other societies solely for the purpose of conquering them.
- Herders envy civilized societies and wish to assimilate into them or wish their society could be more like them.
- Herders have the freedom to do what they want and are not bound by relationships the way settled communities are.
- Being nomadic means a society is constantly moving (i.e. every day) and

the people do not know where they are going; they are meandering.

- Pastoral societies are in need of "development," as for example, learning to farm.

As we will see in this section, many of these stereotypes are either completely wrong or are highly questionable.

Barfield (1993) compares five different types of pastoral nomads around the world living in various ecological zones. The first category, comprising East African pastoralists, includes the Nuer, who domesticate cattle in the South of Sahara grasslands; the Bedouins, who herd camels in the desert zone of Arabia; and the Basseri and the Lurs, who primarily domesticate goats and sheep in the Anatolian and Iranian plateaus. In the Eurasian steppe from the Black Sea to Mongolia groups of pastoralists rode horses across flat grasslands and mountain ranges; these included the Cimmerians and Scythians in ancient times, and of course Chinggis Khan and the Mongolian empire; and still more recently the Kazak and the Kirghiz. Please scan my chart at the end of this chapter for a comparative overview.

Pastoral societies illustrate the cultural ecological theory of Marvin Harris. According to Harris, the kind of physical ecological setting—mountains, valleys, plains—determines the kind of biological resources that will be found there. These biophysical constraints determine the *infrastructure* of society—how the people in a society will make their living, including which plants and animals they will use as resources and how they will use them. The political and economic system (Harris's *structure*) will ultimately depend on the biophysical ecology and on the social ecology— i.e. whether pastoral societies are surrounded by other tribal societies or by states.

Pastoral societies rely upon domesticated animals—horses, camels, sheep, and goats. Why does a given society rely upon one animal but not others? Barfield names four criteria:

- The animal must be well adapted to regional ecological conditions. There

is a high correlation between the original zone of domestication for a species and its emergence as a key animal.
- Large numbers of the animal must be able to be supported by the environment.
- The key animal's needs must take precedence over those of other stock.
- The key animal must in some way provide benefits with regard to the nomad's social, political, or economic competition with other societies, and benefits also in regulating relations within its own society

Let us consider these four criteria in more detail. First: *The animal must be well adapted to regional ecological conditions.* Thus, according to Barfield,

> The exact composition of a herd depends on the local environmental conditions. For example the percentage of goats is higher in regions with marginal pasture because goats can browse on plants that grazing sheep would not touch. For similar reasons, the number of horses is highest where pastoralists have access either to dependable pastures or to grain or hay purchased from farmers. In arid areas, particularly along the edge of deserts, where raising horses is an expensive luxury, camels and donkeys often completely replace them. . . . Cattle are believed to fare poorly on long migrations and they require better pastures and more regular watering. (Barfield 1993, 95)

Barfield closes his point with a proverb: "If you see a cow you are near a village, if you see a goat you are near a camp, if you see a camel you are lost."

Here is a table of the primary types of herd animals and their adaptability to nomadic pastoral conditions:

Most adaptable	Less adaptable	Least adaptable
goats	sheep	cattle
camels	horses	
yaks		

Large numbers of the animal must be able to be supported by the environment. If it costs too much to maintain an animal, that animal may still be used, but not as the key animal. The key animal must be a necessary component of everyone's herd and not restricted to a minority. This criterion also provides a basis for economic democracy, because if each family has a herd, then any family can move with the economic resources (their animals) if the political climate becomes unfavorable.

The key animal's needs must take precedence over those of other stock. This affects the migration patterns and the composition of the overall herd. For example:

the yak's requirement of a high-altitude habitat means that Tibetan pastoralists can only raise specialized breeds of sheep and goats that are also adapted to the rigors of highland living. Similarly, the reason deep-desert nomads specialize exclusively in raising camels is not because they have an aversion to other animals, but because only the camel can survive with so little available water. (Barfield 1993, 11)

There are at least three categories of pastoral animals, based upon their uses:

- Production animals yield meat, milk, wool, or hides for consumption or trade; these include sheep, goats and cattle.
- Transport animals provide mobility; horses, donkeys, yaks, and camels are examples.
- Protection animals guard the other animals; the primary protection animal is the dog.

The categorization of animals into these three functions should not be too rigid, because some pastoral societies are stricter in their division of labor among animals than are others. For example, although goats are primarily used for their byproducts, the Drokba of Tibet use them as pack animals to carry salt. Camels are primarily used in Arabia as transport animals, but in the Eurasian steppes camels are used not only as baggage animals but they are milked, used for their hair, and are occasionally eaten. Horses are ridden, but mares are sometimes milked and horsemeat is widely eaten.

Despite the fact that sheep and goats do not have the status of horses on the Eurasian steppe or the yak in Tibet, they are still the economic mainstay in both areas. This is because they mature quickly and have high rates of reproduction. The minimum time it takes for a camel herd to double is nine years; for cattle it takes 6.5 years; whereas for sheep and goats it takes only three years. In addition, sheep and goats take less labor to herd and their byproducts are more readily marketable than those of camels.

Regardless of the proportion of animals, while attempting to maximize herd size several conditions must be considered:

- The household's need for meat
- The household's need for animal products
- The needs of people to sell animals in markets for grain or other products not easily available.

Barfield makes the important point that, unlike paper investments, investments in animals have to factor in the age of the animal and how likely it is to survive a bad winter season.

The key animal must in some way provide benefits in the nomad's social, political, or economic competition with other societies and in regulating relations within its own society. Among East African pastoralists, cattle help define marriages, friendships, sacred ceremonies, and conflicts. The Bedouins were for most of their history not subject to attack because sedentary societies could not pursue or even find them in the desert. The horse, together with the development of military technology, gave steppe nomads great advantages over their enemies. In the case of Southwest Asia, sheep and goats were especially adaptive since these societies were more economically dependent on the sale of their products to town, village, and city markets.

In sum, the reason a society chooses one animal over others as key is that the animal has already adapted to its environment and can reproduce in large enough numbers to allow the society to make a living in the environment and provide political benefits between societies and within its own society.

As Barfield points out, pastoralists do not wander. They know where they are going and why. For instance, if nomads inhabit a mountainous area, they

> may spend the winter in the lowlands, move to the foothills in the spring, to the high mountain pastures in the summer and return in the fall. If they attempted to stay in one place the whole year round they would soon find themselves short of pasture and subject to climatic extremes. That their animals could not easily survive: in the winter the mountains are covered with snow, while the lowlands in summer are extremely hot. . . . It is the nomads' willingness to migrate with their animals that permits them to raise a far greater number of animals than they could possibly support on the limited natural pasture in any one place. (Barfield 1993, 12)

The number of moves pastoralists make in a year depends on (a) the types of animals in their herds, (b) the quality of pasture available, (c) the severity of the climate, (d) the availability of water, (e) the distance to be traveled, (f) the difficulty of the topography, (g) the right of inclusion or exclusion to the land upon their arrival, and (h) the competition for land. How long they stay depends on the same factors.

In other words, the more favorable the pasture available, the more diverse the animal stock, the milder the climate, and the more water available, the less they will have to move—if we assume there are no other societies around. However, in such a case it is unrealistic to assume that no other societies will be around to compete, given that people in all societies want to gain the greatest resource benefits from their environment for the least amount of work. It is likely that the better the biophysical ecology the more the social ecology will be competitive. This means that groups may have to move for political rather than biophysical environmental reasons.

Conversely, the worse the pastureland, the more dependent the people are likely to be on single animals. If poor land is combined with a difficult climate and lack of water, the people will migrate frequently. They are less likely to experience socio-ecological competition because of the harsh way of life.

Having less variety of animals to choose from will make herders more dependent on other societies for the products they cannot get from their own animals. They can withdraw in order to maintain independence and make due with less accumulation of goods, but they will still be dependent on some products. This will entail longer trading distances. Under some ecological settings, as in Arabia and in the Mongolian steppe, pastoral nomads have a favorable balance of trade with sedentary societies, yet trade they must.

Summing up:

Good biophysical conditions → social ecological competition;
Difficult biophysical conditions → more socio-ecological dependence but less competition.

Both of these conditions can lead to either trading or raiding options.

In pastoral societies, internal political organization is largely determined by external conditions. Broadly speaking, the harsher the climate, the worse the pasture land, the more general the lack of water, then the more egalitarian pastoralists are likely to be. This is because they are more dependent on each other and can accumulate less. The better the climate, pastureland, and water availability, the less pastoralists have to travel. The less they travel, the more potential they have to accumulate. Whether the accumulation of goods comes from within their own societies or from trading with other societies, the more they accumulate the more conflicts can emerge over the distribution of resources. Kinship relations remain but tend to become ranked or stratified.

In addition, as said earlier, the better the biophysical ecology the more pastoral societies will have to compete for occupancy. The more competition there is, the greater the chance for wars. Wars require a reorganization of the political system from decentralization towards more centralization, resulting in either rank or stratification. In some cases, kinship relations are overridden.

If pastoral societies have consistent contact with centralized state societies, either in trade or in war, this changes their internal political organization. For example, Central Eurasian nomads formed empires that involved hundreds of thousands of people who were not organized along kinship lines. So too, Near Eastern tribes had complex economic relations with sedentary towns, which required a permanent leader to negotiate with the state. On the other hand, pastoralists of East Africa dealt only with other tribal societies, and because of this their society remained decentralized. In fact there is a correlation between the degree of hierarchy and centralization a pastoral society faces in another society and the degree of hierarchy it sets up internally. As Barfield points out,

> there is an arc of growing centralization running from East Africa to the steppes of Mongolia with four increasingly complex types of tribal organization:
> 1. Age sets and acephalous segmentary lineages in sub-Saharan Africa where tribal societies encountered few state societies.
> 2. Lineages with permanent leaders but no regular supratribal organization in North Africa and Arabia where tribal societies faced regional states with which they had symbiotic relations.
> 3. Supratribal confederations with powerful leaders who were part of a regional political network within large empires, distributed throughout the Iranian and or Anatolian Plateaus, linking tribes to states as conquerors or subjects.
> 4. Centralized tribal states ruling over vast distances on the steppes of Central Eurasia, north of China and Iran supported by predatory relationships with neighboring sedentary civilizations.

In general, all pastoral societies are patrilineal. The men work with whatever large animals exist—camels, horses, or cattle. They herd, milk, and water the animals and they are responsible for protecting them from thieves. Men dominate the world of politics both within and between societies. Women prepare food, pack and unpack the tents, and process the by-products of the animals, making yogurt, cheese, and butter. In pastoral societies in Southwest Asia, where sheep and goats are the major animals, men and women work together. However, in societies in which there is a combination of large and small animals, the women work with sheep and goats. In pastoral societies in the South Sahara grasslands, where the ecological setting lends itself to horticulture as a supplement, women take this work on. But what does this division of labor tell us about the relative status of men and women in these societies?

As we will see in chapter 5, Peggy Reeves-Sanday, in her cross-cultural study of gender and political power, found when the means of subsistence consists of large animals, men tend to dominate society to a greater degree. Rae Lesser Blumberg has argued that women's status is greatly determined by the status in which her work is held by society as a whole. Further, the extent to which women work in public is also a major contributor. This means that the maximum condition for gender equality is when (a) large animals are not a major form of subsistence, (b) the work that women do is highly valued, and (c) the work is done in public.

In East African societies the animals primarily used are cattle, which by the above criteria would tend to support higher status for men. Yet this is tempered by a number of factors. For one thing, the Nuer also herd sheep and goats, which is done in public and is women's work. In addition, this environment supports horticulture, which is also public work and is done by women. As a result, women enjoy a fairly high status in this society. Women suffer perhaps the lowest status in Arabia, where no horticulture was possible and sheep and goats were herded only on the margins of the desert. Meanwhile, men worked with camels. The situation lies somewhere between these extremes in the case of the Anatolian and Iranian plateau: on one hand sheep and goats are the main source of income, giving women valuable public work; while in the highlands, camels, donkeys, and horses carry baggage and people, yielding high status for men.

In the Eurasian steppe from the Black Sea to Mongolia the situation is more complicated. Despite the association of this area with horses and wars, sheep and goats—not horses—were the economic mainstay. These animals, as usual, were controlled by women. It is easy to assume that when societies are warlike women's status will plummets and that women will do better in times of peace. This is not necessarily the case, for in pastoral societies women can be recruited to fight:

> Women in steppe nomadic pastoral societies had more authority and autonomy than their sisters in neighboring sedentary societies or pastoral societies in other regions. . . . Although in formal terms these societies were strongly patrilineal, in many groups steppe nomadic women participated in tribal politics and sometimes even war. (Barfield 1993, 146)

O' Kelly (1986) claims that men in these societies tended to be emotionally distant, that wife beating was common, and that sexuality was restrictive for women. Virginity was important, and sexual intercourse was seen by the men as being polluting. ·

Child-rearing practices in herding societies had some similarities to those in foraging societies, as well as some similarity to those of horticulturalists. Herders were not permissive and demanded compliance, but they also encouraged independence and aggressiveness, especially in male children. This made sense, since herding is a hard way to make a living.

Pastoral nomads, whether men or women, did not envy the lives of people who planted for a living, especially people in agricultural societies. Herders saw farmers as plodding, dependent, lacking a sense of adventure, and slavish to authority. Though it is fair to say the men in pastoral societies had more "machismo" than those in other societies, this does not necessarily mean that women were required or assumed to be nurturing, dependent, and soft. Given the difficult environmental circumstances, it sometimes didn't pay for either men or women to develop "soft" qualities.

Earlier in this section it was mentioned that herding societies sometimes trade and sometimes raid. As we will see in more detail in chapter 10, there were very unusual ecological stressors in the Bronze Age in pastoralists' immediate environment that may have induced them to attack. Between 3000 and 1000 BCE, natural catastrophes weakened all societies of the Near East. Simple horticultural societies were probably the most vulnerable to herders because they were settled, couldn't move easily, and lacked any kind of specialized military to defend themselves against raids.

Simple horticultural societies could be not only raided, but permanently conquered. Both horticultural and herding societies have kin-groups. What probably occurred is that after herding groups raided horticultural societies, they reorganized the latter into a hierarchical form and put themselves at the top of the social pyramid.

Unlike the leaders of a chiefdom, the leaders of a conquering herding group would not have had the legitimate authority of chiefs who had risen from the ranks. The chief in a complex horticultural society never conquered his people in order to attain the benefits he enjoyed. In addition, the chief was seen as a blood relative of the totem or ancestor spirit. The indigenous sacred system legitimized his rule. This was not the case for pastoralist leaders. For at least the first two generations, the conquered people would not have looked to their overlords as kin. The social mixture of herders and simple horticulturists must have looked somewhat like the feudal caste system of medieval Europe, with the dominant herders offering "protection" in exchange for the labor of the conquered.

In the shifts from hunting and gathering to simple and complex horticulture to agriculture, we see a series of interlocked trends, including growth in population, increasing specialization of labor, increasing complexity of technology, growth in material wealth, and increasing economic differences between people. Herding societies' conquest of simple horticultural societies marks a break with these trends. Compared to the Bronze-Age agricultural states, herding-horticulture societies showed decreases in population, social complexity, material wealth, inequality, and advances in the harnessing of energy.

5. Stratified Societies: Axial Iron Age Maritime States

Between 1000 BCE and 400 BCE a great revolution occurred in state civilizations—a revolution best typified by developments in the Greek city-state of Athens. There, caste relations characteristic of Bronze-Age states were challenged and greater mobility emerged within the newly-formed social classes. The invention of iron tools made life a little easier for farmers because the new tools were stronger, more durable, and more efficient than stone implements. The replacement of hieroglyphics, used by Bronze-Age priesthoods, by the alphabet made it possible for more social classes to read and write. The emergence of standardized coins made a single integrated economy possible and made bartering obsolete except on the periphery of society. Finally, the appearance of the polis made political discussion (rather than appointment or claims

of revelation) the basis of decision making for the first time since the shift from egalitarian social relations. All these conditions combined to (a) speed up the pace of all exchange between people, and (b) expand the number of participants involved.

Commercial rights and sacred rites have been long-standing enemies. Before the Axial Iron Age, commercial relations within society were either forbidden or marginalized on the periphery of society. Haggling threatened the solidarity of the group and also its relations with the spirit-world, which was thought to be immanent in society. All exchange within pre-Axial Iron Age societies was mediated by the sacred rights and obligations of kin members and clans. With the rise of coined money, commercial relations slowly eroded these kin/clan relations.

When coined money first appeared it tended to democratize economic exchanges. A poor farmer could convert a small surplus of farm produce into an easily divisible medium of exchange, buying goods of any kind without having to lug all of his tradable items to a marketplace. The availability of coined money encouraged farmers to turn from subsistence agriculture to specialized farming, such as the production of olive oil for trading. Money stimulated more trading between farmers and other classes. It made it more profitable for an artisan to make cheap goods because peasants had a fluid medium of exchange with which to purchase them.

But as coined money cleared the way for the secular exchange of goods and services, it also opened space for the emergence of other secular cultural phenomena. In particular, philosophy, science, and law found a new growth medium in the secularized society. Philosophers began to toy with materialist explanations for the circumstances of their lives, while early practitioners of science aspired to a secular relationship with nature that minimized possible connections between nature and goddesses, gods, and ancestor spirits. Meanwhile, secular laws established by a Republic replaced revelations from the gods and goddesses, which had issued from the theocratic kings of Bronze-Age states.

During the Axial Iron Age, the civilizations of the Old World—including the Egyptians, the Hebrews, the Persians, the Indians, the Chinese and the Greeks—flowered and cross-pollinated. For the Western civilizations, trade was important and centralization was difficult. Both the Hebrews and Persians began in the Archaic Age as mobile herding societies, and the climate and topography of Greece made vast centralized bureaucracies difficult to establish. However, Egypt, Mesopotamia, China, and India in the East had vast river valleys in which centralized irrigation systems could be built in order to support a large, densely concentrated populace. In these societies a centralized state emerged out of necessity.

Greek society exemplifies the differences between social *castes* on one hand, and social *classes* on the other. The latter term denotes greater potential mobility within a system of stratification. A supercentralized state was usually staffed by lifetime bureaucratic castes. Athens, in contrast, had no priestly caste. Rather than a military of full-time specialists, the Greeks had a citizen militia that could be called upon at any time, along with barbarians and mercenaries. What class struggles existed were between a land-owning and slave-owning aristocracy, a middle class of farmers, and an urban merchant-artisan class. Farmers in Greece never became a dependent peasantry always having to produce for the state, because they were not dependent on an irrigation system. Greek farmers were able to participate in political discussions at the polis. They made their living from producing wine and olive oil while domesticating goats and sheep, or fishing.

Athenian democracy did not include the entire population. Only about 20 percent of the population of Athens could claim citizenship, with women, slaves, and foreigners excluded. In addition, the participation of middle-class farmers in the polis depended on their slaves doing the work while they were gone. The state did offer its poorer citizens a stipend to participate in the polis, but this could be paid only through income generated from the Greek empire. Notwithstanding these deficiencies, Athenian democracy represented the first instance in which the social classes in a state

society other than the elite could debate the issues of the day as peers, despite differences in property or wealth.

Despite the economic, technological, and political changes going on around them, the aristocracy maintained formal political and economic power. Eventually this situation led to a crisis, which occurred after 200 years of transformation, between 800 and 600 BCE. By the 6th century BCE, the middle- and lower-class farmers were on the verge of insurrection. Eventually this led to reforms by the Greek statesman, Solon.

The lives of the women in Greece were at least as bad as those of their counterparts in agricultural states. Women could not vote or own property. Unlike the priestesses in agricultural states, women in Greece could hold no public office. There was no pubic education for women except in music. The sexual double standard that had begun in rank societies continued. Most women were married by age fifteen and were expected to remain monogamous for life. In contrast, it was acceptable for men to visit prostitutes in young adulthood, then take a wife at about the age of 30, and have a concubine in old age. According to Gerta Lerner (1986), there were three identities available to women in Greece—wife, concubine, or prostitute. A more extended discussion of the life of women in Greece awaits us in chapter six.

In the first chapter I argued that men and women have been largely unconscious history shapers. At the end of the first chapter I asserted that though both men and women alienated their powers, with the rise of rank and stratification there has been a subtle process of informal male dominance that existed periodically even in egalitarian societies.

At the end of the first chapter I posed the following problems which I have now turned into questions:

1. Why was there no informal female dominance?
2. Why, when public leadership is needed even in egalitarian societies, is that leadership always taken by men?

3. Why is it that when rank and stratification emerge it is virtually always the men who have the most privilege and wield the most power?

4. Why have women always been the ones with responsibility for raising children?

5. Why is descent traced far more often along the male line?

6. Why do women go to live in the male kin's hamlet or village much more often than the male living near the his wife's residence?

7. Why, when mating practices are non-monogamous, do men marry many women far more often than women marry many men?

8. When there are wars, why is it that men will virtually always do the fighting?

If women are history shapers too, then women have to take responsibility for addressing these historical facts. In this chapter I have tried to map out the social structures of the ancient world. We have seen that, broadly speaking, the more complex societies became, the worse were the conditions faced by women. However, none of the questions above were answered. Neither have we discussed how much responsibility women have for the circumstances identified by the eight questions above. These questions will be answered in chapter 5 and throughout the rest of the book.

We now have a composite picture of society, but we have yet to discuss in detail why societies changed, and why social circumstances changed for the worse for women in particular. In the next chapter we will examine the arguments of some Neo-pagans and spiritual feminists who attempt to address the issue of the origins of male dominance. I will call these *romantic idealist* arguments. In chapter four we will address materialist explanations for gender inequalities.

Figure 2.3 Comparison of Pastoral Societies*

East Africa	Arabia	Southwest Asia	Eurasian Steppe	Northwest Tibet
Cattle	Camels	Sheep, goats	Horses	Yak
Have sheep, goats, donkeys 6 years to mature / Mixed with horticulture	Only sheep / goats at margins 9 years to mature / No horticulture	All animals but cattle 3 years to mature	Sheep, goats vital for economy	Sheep and goats vital for economy
South of Sahara grasslands	Desert zone	Anatolian and Iranian plateau	Black Sea to Mongolia	Plateau grasslands
Construct huts	Tents	Tents	Yurts	Tents
Nuer	Bedouins	Basseri, Lurs	Kazak, Caspian Sea and Aral Seas. Kirghiz-Pamir in mountain regions.	Drokba
		8500 BCE (oldest)	(4000 BCE)	
Age sets and acephalous, segmentary lineages	Permanent leaders (sheiks) but no supertribal confederation. Leadership lasts a lifetime.	Khan subordinates local leaders. Supertribal confederations within large empires.	Centralized states ruling over vast distances (faced empires of China)	Lack tribal organization. Buddhist monasteries provide organization
No political centralization Low population density, easy mobility	More independence from sedentary societies.	Less independence, surrounded by states	Somewhat dependent but favorable balance of trade	Most dependent. Farmers worked for them, constructing storage buildings, tanning hides
30% polygamous	Less polygamous			Polyandry—two brothers
Relatives pay brideprice	Relatives pay brideprice	Nuclear families pay brideprice	Women have restrictions in choice of heirs	Dowry, but women don't lose control. Women have most independence. Siblings inherit equally.
Women not allowed to own animals	Women allowed to own animals.			
Wives self-supporting— horticulture	Wives not self-supporting— arranged marriages		Women have most independence in politics and war	

* Adapted from Barfield (1993)

Chapter 3

The Place and Misplace of Goddesses: How Goddess Ideology Confuses Women's Status

1. Claims and values

In the beginning men and women lived in harmony and peace. We were once one with nature and there were few differences between us in social power or wealth. Women had a special place in early tribal societies: their motherhood was revered, they held positions of authority, and they practiced forms of magic centered on the worship of a monotheistic Goddess. Figurines of Goddesses have been discovered, proving there was once a great women's religion. Throughout the Bronze Age, hunters and pastoralists from Central Asia invaded these peaceful societies creating social hierarchies, wars, and the beginnings of male dominance. All of this was later sanctioned by the worship of otherworldly, transcendent male deities that eventually coalesced to become a monotheistic God. The Goddess was discredited and went underground, being kept alive in later years by peasant communities in the magical practice of witchcraft. Today the Goddess has resurfaced as a focus of women's spirituality.

These are the claims about history and social evolution made by many Neo-Pagan or spiritual feminists. To be sure, not all people associated with the Goddess movement believe all of these claims. However, the summary above is probably a fair one, in that each of its elements is repeated in the writings of nearly all of the movement's leaders.

How plausible are these contentions in the light of anthropology, archaeology, macrosociology, political science, world history, mythology studies, and comparative religion? Were there once matriarchies or matrifocal societies? Does reverence for

goddesses go all the way back to the Paleolithic Era? Can all or most of the figurines found by archaeologist Marija Gimbutas and others be classified as goddesses? If, in our society, a male god goes with male dominance, is it fair to infer that if we find evidence of goddesses in the ancient world this must indicate female dominance or at least the high status of women? Was motherhood revered in ancient societies? Is all magic goddess-centered? Is all witchcraft synonymous with goddess reverence? Were ancient tribal societies peace-loving before being invaded? Does the movement from polytheism to monotheism involve a battle among male gods, or between male and female gods? Figure 3.1 is a summary of these claims.

In addition to addressing these contentions about history, it is important to make explicit the underlying values of the Goddess movement. I agree with Philip Davis (1998) that the Goddess movement is part of a larger Romantic movement that began during the Renaissance, and sustained itself through the Enlightenment, the Industrial Revolution, and the 20th century. I will paint as sympathetic picture as I can of the Romantic movement's perspective on the world.

The Goddess movement is generally critical of Western-style political centralization and the globalization of the human community because Western civilization is not and never has been truly democratic. The movement's members tend to believe that all state societies, even those predating capitalism, serve the interests of the wealthy. They do not believe that real democracy can ever work when power is centralized. Furthermore, they resist attempts to universalize different groups of people into a universal humanity because this grouping in the past has, in practice, excluded many groups from the wealth they produced because of their class, race, or gender. At the same time, the movement is generally critical of the competitive values of capitalism and is suspicious of the preoccupation with material wealth, the accumulation of commodities, and high technology. Finally, the Goddess movement is critical of science as a way of knowing because, while proclaiming to be neutral, it actually serves the interests of the elite classes by providing the methodological base by which technologies of war can be built. For these reasons, the movement looks to the political organization of pre-state societies as a model for participatory democracy, pre-capitalist ways of conducting economic relations, and pre-scientific ways of knowing how the world works.

Because the Goddess movement often contrasts the values of tribal societies with those of state societies, it must also challenge the way world history has been presented. According to the Goddess movement, the dominant social order has placed a value judgment on social evolution by claiming that it constitutes "progress." This means that the more complex societies are, the more they have improved life for everyone. Because the movement challenges this assumption, it must either try to revise history as written or, in more extreme cases, claim that the struggle to discover an objective history is futile. Here the Goddess movement joins forces with the extreme relativism of the Postmodernists, who say that one version of history is as good as another, and that competing ways of knowing about the past are equally relevant. One common approach is to fuse the study of history with mythology. Much of the work of the Goddess movement vacillates between the attempt to revise views of what really happened in history, and the effort to reinterpret history based on ancient mythology. For obvious reasons, this latter strategy garners little sympathy from serious historians.

The system of industrial capitalism has had a impact not just on the economy and political structure of societies, but also on their sacred traditions, their ideas about non-human nature, and the collective psyche or mentality of the people. The Goddess movement believes that there is a direct connection between the nature of the perceived sacred sources and the manner in which people treat the natural world. The movement's members believe that an otherworldly, transcendental God, because he is out of the world, neglects this world and effectively colludes with elites who exploit and pillage the natural world. Conversely, when sacred sources are understood as immanent and worldly, nature is more likely to be treated with respect. According to spiritual feminists, the distant sky-god acts as if he were an absentee landlord. If Goddess advocates are skeptical about centralization and globalization in the political world, they take the same attitude toward the spiritual world. Rather than believing in a universal monotheistic deity, many people in the Goddess movement prefer a decentralized polytheism, though this is a bone of contention within the movement, as we shall see.

Patriarchal religions and atheistic non-believers have tended to use mechanistic metaphors to describe nature. The Goddess movement rejects the idea of nature-as-machine and believes that nature is alive, that the world is an organism. Even in patriarchal religions nature is often conceived of metaphorically as "mother"; The Goddess movement builds on this theme, viewing human beings and the rest of the animal kingdom as part of "her" body. Just as nature is not separate from sacred sources, so humanity is not separate from other creatures. Other animals are at least the equals of humans and we humans have no business trying to get away from nature or to improve her with scientific techniques. We need to merge with, or get back to, nature. There are also implications for our sense of time. One symptom of humanity's problems, according to Goddess advocates, is our linear concept of time. This has caused us great problems in understanding how change occurs. Nature, for the Goddess movement, works in cycles. For humanity to merge with nature we would need to understand society and our individual lives as following the cycles of

Figure 3. 1 Common Claims or Assumptions Made by the Goddess Movement

1) There were once matriarchies or matrifocal societies

2) All or most of the figurines discovered by archeologists are goddesses

3) Goddess reverence goes all the way back to the Paleolithic Age

4) All magic is synonymous with goddess reverence

5) All witchcraft is synonymous with goddess reverence

6) Ancient People revered a monotheistic goddess

7) Motherhood is the leading function of goddesses

8) There is a direct connection between the presences of goddesses in ancient societies and the prosperous material status of women

9) The rise of institutionalized male dominance was caused by invasions of pastoral nomads

10) Tribal societies were peace-loving before being invaded by patriarchal societies

11) The movement from polytheism to monotheism involved battles between male gods and female goddesses

Figure 3. 2 Composite Values of Ancient Goddess Supporters

SOCIAL STRUCTURES

1) **Simple, pre-state societies** are an ideal to strive for (small is beautiful).
Complex, large societies are inherently bad, because they are impersonal.

2) **Innocence** is more noble than experience when it comes to social evolution.
What comes earlier in time must be better. Tribal societies are the ideal.

3) **Material wealth, objects/commodities and technology** are likely to be **corrupting influences**.

4) **Science is alienating,** cold, unfeeling and doesn't address what is important in life.

5) **Cooperation and communalism** are better than competition as a way to organize social life.

6) Modern society perpetrates a **false unity of humanity,** ignoring gender, ethnic and class inequalities.

7) **Myth** is at least as important as history.
Historians reduce myth to illusionary or naive history. Support of a real "people's history," while retaining the value of mythic stories as a valuable sacred activity.

NATURE/SACRED

8) Spirit is **immanent** in nature and the individual rather than transcendent and separate from nature.
Nature is all there is. Behind nature there is only more, undiscovered nature.

9) There are many goddesses and gods--**polytheism**-- there is no single source which unites them all.*

10) Nature is understood as an **organism,** rather than a machine.

11) Goddesses are inseparable from female physiology: menstruation and childbirth.

12) **Neither organized religion nor atheism** provide meaningful answers to the big questions of life.

13) Other **animals are at least the equal of or superior** to human beings.

14) Human beings should **merge with nature.**
We have no business thinking or trying to improve her.

15) Generally, sacred communion is **experiential** and not mediated by secular or sacred authorities based on faith.

16) Change happens in **cycles,** rather than linearly.

PSYCHOLOGY

17) **Emotions, sensuality, intuition and the non-rational** are at least as good as reason or empiricism
as ways of knowing.

18) What is **subjective and personal** is better than impartiality and striving to be objective.

19) **Spontaneity** is more in touch with what matters in life than planning.

20) **Experimental gender roles** are better than traditional male and female roles.

21) When it comes down to it, **women** are inherently better than men.

_____

    * There is a counter-argument, which claims that there is a single goddess.

nature. Because the relationship between humanity and the rest of nature must be immanent, people do not need mediators and specialists to interpret sacred experience. We are all explorers together with no need for chaperones.

There are two kinds of nature—external and internal. Our bodies are an internal, microcosmic slice of the external macrocosm of nature. This has deep psychological implications. For the Goddess movement, rationality, analysis, planning, and striving to be objective are the psychological skills an individual uses to dualize or separate our bodies from the rest of nature. These rational skills lead to other dualisms: God vs. nature, nature vs. society, society vs. the individual, and the mind vs. the body. These separations are partly responsible for the problems of the modern world.

It is the non-rational part of the psyche—the part of the mind that synthesizes rather than divides—that is the true source of wisdom. The emotions, sensuality, intuition, and spontaneity are understood as virtuous. The Goddess movement believes that women have these skills more than men do and, generally speaking, though they would probably not claim this explicitly, most members act and talk as though women are inherently better than men.

There are at least two tension points that are worth pointing out. While the Goddess movement opposes traditional female roles and supports experimenting with being simply more human, there is a tension between those who want to develop the skills that men have traditionally been encouraged to claim, and those who want to elevate traditional female skills as inherently superior to male skills.

There is also a tension between the value of innocence in contrast to the value of experience. For the most part, the Goddess movement values experience over innocence but, in their contrast between tribal and state societies, they tend to romanticize tribal societies as innocent and uncorrupted. In the first chapter I criticized the theory of progress as a way to understand history. Taken in its extreme, New-Age form, the Goddess view of

history is a degeneration theory of social evolution. Instead of suggesting, as progress theorists do, that the further we go in history the better it gets, this theory argues that the earlier in time we go the better it gets. A summary chart of these Romantic values is contained in figure 3.2

According to Goodison and Morris (1998), the controversy between the supporters of Goddess theory and those who dismiss it is made worse because the two sides do not speak to each other. Those who support the theory are non-specialists, artists, psychotherapists, Neo-pagans, and amateur historians. They accuse academics—archeologists, ancient historians, and anthropologists—of intentionally ignoring evidence of a powerful female presence in ancient history. This supposed intentional hiding or overlooking of evidence of the Goddess is usually described as being part of a male conspiracy to hide real history. Contemporary specialists in relevant fields ignore the Goddess claims, dismissing them as too far-fetched to take seriously. They also suspect that the movement is motivated by an ideology of feminist reform that attempts to rewrite history in the service of that ideology.

2. Defining "matriarchy"

Victorian anthropologists, in attempting to understand the past, sometimes proposed the existence of tribal societies in which women were at least the equals of men. Part of the feminist movement has latched on to these claims to show the relativity of "patriarchal" institutions today.

However, before we address specific arguments, we need a working definition of the term "matriarchy." In chapter 1, following Marvin Harris, I argued that there are three dimensions of society—the infrastructure, the structure and the superstructure. Again, the *infrastructure* refers to the technology used along with the means of subsistence—hunting, gathering, farming, and the division of work patterns. The *structure* refers to economic and political systems, property rights, etc. The *superstructure* refers to a society's meaning making systems, including sacred beliefs, science, art, and law. Both the words patriarchy and matriarchy share the same suffix—*archy*, from the Greek *archos*, which means "rule by." Therefore, in simple terms patriarchy means the rule of men over women in the areas of the infrastructure, structure, and superstructure of society. To be consistent with the meaning of the suffix, matriarchy would have to be the reverse of patriarchy—i.e., the rule of women over men in these areas. Matriarchy would mean the control of technological, political, and economic power—the right to control production and distribution beyond the household. Women would have the military power to force men to go along with social policy, and they would control the myths by which the society lives. Have societies with these characteristics actually existed? Presumably, if they have, we should look for evidence among the Paleolithic hunter-gatherers, the Neolithic horticulturists, and the Bronze-Age agricultural states.

Before proceeding, it is important to refine our definitions of patriarchy and matriarchy a little further. It is highly unlikely that any sociologist (man or woman) would define *patriarchy* or *matriarchy* as referring to "all men" or "all women." In the case of rank and stratified societies, there is no question that those in power are men. However, the percentage of men with political, economic and technological power is small. The rest of the male population—the middle classes, the working class artisan and peasant men—are subordinate to them. All men have some privileges over women but, as we saw in chapter 2, privilege is not the same as power. A refined definition of *patriarchy* therefore would be, *the power and control exercised by a few men over all women and most men throughout the infrastructure, structure, and superstructure of society, with all men having some privileges over all women.* If we want to be consistent with what we know of patriarchal rank and stratified societies, then a *matriarchy* would be defined as *the power and control exercised by a few women over all men and most women throughout the infrastructure, structure, and superstructure of society, with all women having some privileges over all men.*

Virtually everyone familiar with the evidence of archaeology, anthropology, and history agrees that matriarchies have never existed. This category includes female and feminist scholars—such as Frymer-Kensky (1982), Ehrenberg (1985), Reeves-Sanday (1981), and Lerner (1986).

In over 1100 societies listed in Murdock's Ethnographic Atlas (most of which are pre-state societies), three quarters are patrilocal; that is, when women get married they must move to either the home of their husbands or to that of their husbands' paternal relatives. The reverse is the case only one-tenth of the time. Patrilineal descent is also much more common than matrilineal descent: children are regarded as members of their father's group five times more often than as members of their mother's descent group. Finally, societies in which men typically have multiple wives are a hundred times more abundant than societies in which women typically have multiple husbands. As Cynthia Eller (2000) writes:

> Ethnographic analogies to contemporary groups with lifeways similar to those of prehistoric time (hunting and gathering or horticulture, practiced in small groups) show little sex egalitarianism and no matriarchy. Indeed, these societies always discriminate in some way between women and men, usually to women's detriment. (Eller 2000, 180)

Residency, descent, and mating practices, which favor men, are part of what I will call in chapter 5 "informal male dominance." While these societal traits may not themselves be indictors of institutionalized male dominance, they are signs that there is a definite preponderance of customs leading to it. If the precursor of institutionalized male dominance were informal male dominance, then if matriarchies existed we would expect contemporary examples of informal female dominance in tribal societies. There is no evidence for this in the ethnographic record.

It is sometimes argued that the archeological remains at Catal Huyuk dating between 6500–5700 BCE indicate the presence of a matriarchy.

These remains reveal towns with houses and paved streets. These societies had metal, a form of writing, pottery, and weaving. Women and children had central places in the burial sites. But is this enough to show that women ruled over all three dimensions of society? Cynthia Eller doubts this:

> Feminist matriarchalists have suggested that the women under the large platform were the head of the household, while the man under the small platform was her brother or son. But there are other equally valid ways of interpreting the burial pattern. . . . (Eller, 2000, 100)

Eller offers the following alternative interpretations:

> (1) If these were sleeping platforms, perhaps women's platforms were larger because women were expected to share their beds with more people (say, their children). . . .
> (2) Perhaps the large fixed platforms belonged to the men, and they buried their wives and children under them to feel close to their deceased family members.
> (3) In actuality, very few skeletons recovered from Catalhoyuk were found complete and it is possible that individual skeletons were not buried in a single location, but split up and "shared out among various buildings or platforms within a building," just as some people are cremated today and have their ashes spread in several different locations. (Eller, 2000, 100)

At Catal Huyuk there is a disproportionate number of female skeletons compared to male skeletons, which some Goddess advocates say proves that perhaps men were not important enough to merit a burial. But, as Eller points out, this ignores the fact that when men fight in long-distance wars or engage in trading expeditions, they don't always come back alive.

At the same time, the burial sites now indicate a conventional division of sex roles.

Philip Davis (1998) points out: "Ian Hodder, who is now leading the renewed excavations at the site, has pointed out that women tended to be buried with ornaments and cosmetic boxes while men are accompanied by tools and weapons, suggesting a fairly standard distinction in sex roles." (Davis, 1998, 63)

In addition, the symbols of this society do not necessarily confirm the high place of women. For example, the bull images appear to have a very aggressive stance toward the images of breasts. One room is decorated by friezes of sculptures representing women's breasts surrounded by the lower jaw of a wild boar. In another room is a pair of women's breasts, each containing the head of a vulture whose beak protrudes from red-painted nipples. It seems to me that the association of a breast with the hard-pecking beak contradicts the image of a benign bosom, ever flowing and generous. The boar's jaw is biting, not feeding. There is no artwork showing men in a subordinate position to women.

I am not suggesting that the boar represents men or that this proves this society was patriarchal. I am arguing against evidence of matriarchy, not for evidence of patriarchy.

Goddess theorists also often mention the Minoan civilization of Crete as an example of a matriarchy. In artwork, women are shown as judges and doctors; they presumably held political office and were cultural leaders. The artwork is dominated by female figures; women are depicted with men having conversations in everyday contexts. There is no question that, for a state society in the ancient world, Minoan civilization must have featured a stronger presence of women than was the case with the civilizations of Mesopotamia, Egypt, or China. However, that does not mean that Crete was a matriarchy. Crete's economy was based on maritime trade, and positions of power (sea captain, merchant) were held by men. Eller (2000) argues that, while the archeological remains indicate that women had an unusual amount of freedom, they certainly had no more than women do in our culture, a culture which Goddess advocates call patriarchal.

What are the implications? If women did not once dominate in the sacred, political, and economic dimensions of society, does this mean that patriarchies have always existed?

The hidden assumption of those who ask us to choose between matriarchy and patriarchy as the mode of dominance in ancient societies is that rule over others was always the case. We are simply asked to choose whether it was women or men who were doing the ruling. But as I have shown in the previous chapter, in hunting-and-gathering and simple horticultural societies everyone was doing the ruling. This means that these societies were neither matriarchal nor patriarchal.

If matriarchy is simply defined as the reverse of patriarchy, then the notion of its prevalence in early societies is fairly easy to dismiss. However, some sectors within the pagan-feminist community have defined matriarchal societies differently, calling them "matrifocal." What they mean by this is the existence of egalitarian political and economic relations between men and women in material culture and the predominance of a Goddess or goddesses in sacred culture. This is a more complicated and interesting proposal. How might we test it?

Most anthropologists, archeologists, and macrosociologists agree that hunting-and-gathering and simple horticultural societies were politically and economically egalitarian. Here Goddess advocates are on solid ground. But Goddess advocates confuse the issue by insisting that the superstructure of these societies was characterized by reverence for goddesses. This presumed predominance of goddesses, together with a presumed reverence for motherhood, seem to be the major justifications for calling these societies "matrifocal."

3. Were all or most of the early figurines goddesses?

One problem with investigation of goddess reverence is that there were no written texts until the Bronze Age. The societies that are the focus of attention for Goddess theorists existed before the invention of writing (Paleolithic Europe, Catal Huyuk in Turkey, Old Europe in the Balkans, the megalithic culture of Malta, and pre-Celtic Britain). This means that we must rely solely on archeology.

The Goddess movement's contention that egalitarian societies of Paleolithic and early Neolithic times practiced goddess worship is usually substantiated by reference to the work of archeologist Maria Gimbutas, who has discovered female figurines as much as 30,000 years old. She found such figurines all over Old Europe, in the Near East, and in Southeast Asia. While there is no disputing the importance of the artifacts Gimbutas brought to light, her interpretations of what they mean is another matter.

Archaeology is very good at assessing the level of technology and the degree of social inequality in ancient societies, but it is not equipped to judge the meaning-making systems or the psychology of the society being studied. Inevitably, commentators tend to project the meaning-making systems of our own society back in time. As Goodison and Morris (1998) point out, archeologists have typically underestimated how difficult objectivity is to achieve:

> For much of the history of archaeology as a discipline this "objectivity" has obscured the importance of how the individual's experience as a human being living in a particular time and place might shape and filter understanding of the past. "The burial was accompanied by a mirror, therefore the skeleton was female." But the expectation that women (and women alone) look in mirrors is constructed around our society's attitudes to women's appearance. We cannot simply shift those behaviors and values onto another society in a distant past. (Goodison and Morris 1998, 9)

This problem is not unique to conventional academics. Any interpretation of archeological evidence is likely to unconsciously (or perhaps consciously) include the underlying assumptions and ideologies of those who study it. As Goodison and Morris point out, this is also true of the interpretations offered by Goddess theorists. For example, if a figurine has large breasts, that means it represents motherhood. If the figurine is naked, that means sexuality and fertility. These interpretations are just as subject to projections as those of conventional archaeologists.

One problem Gimbutas fails to shed light on is the criteria for judging whether a figurine is a goddess. After all, in tribal and agricultural state societies there are earth-spirits, totems, ancestor spirits, guardian spirits, spirit guides, and personal deities. How do we know the figurines are not any of these sacred presences? Miranda Green, writing on Gallo-Roman goddesses, discusses types of characteristics of deities such as:

> nudity
> disproportionate size
> reversal in weapon bearing hands
> non-human features such as wings
> otherworldly attendants appear (Goodison and Morris, 1998)

To think that what is important to people will simply be expressed in images is naïve. As Eller points out, some things rarely experienced are frequently imaged; some things often experienced are not imaged because they are too trivial, or unpleasant; and some things are thought too special to be imaged at all—such as the Jewish and Islamic God.

Further, how do we know these are sacred presences at all? How do we know they are not dolls, toys, lucky charms or erotic props? Philip Davis (1998) writes:

> As classical historian Mary Lefkowitz has pointed out (specifically in connection with Gimbutas's findings) we have no extant texts to tell us what the Old Europeans actually thought and felt about their artifacts; a statuette of a pregnant female could be anything from a Great Goddess ruling the powers of life to a mere votive offering to some indeterminate being or force. Brian Hayden highlighted the fact that Gimbutas freely attributed Goddess symbolism to objects and abstract designs which might easily be considered asexual

> or even phallic . . . nowhere is there even a mention of methodology, testing, statistics, chance variation, assumptions or rigor. (Davis, 1998, 69)

Davis then asks:

> Was a goddess the central deity of Catal Huyuk? There are various representations of humanoid females, in images and reliefs, ranging from girlish running figures to birthing mothers and perhaps aging crones. These might depict one goddess, several separate goddesses or no actual goddesses at all. (Davis, 1998, 63)

As Cynthia Eller points out, Gimbutas did her fieldwork long before the appearance of gender archeology. Where feminist archeologists expect variety in their findings, feminist matriarchalists expect uniformity. When Gimbutas describes material cultures, we see extensive detail and a variety of interpretations; but when she interprets spiritual culture, all roads lead to the Goddess.

> In *Civilization of the Goddess*, [Gimbutas] painstakingly describes the burial customs, pottery, technology . . . of various sites in Old Europe . . . giving detailed evidence of local and chronological variations. It is not until she turns to the topic of prehistoric religion that evidence from a wide array of cultures suddenly becomes grist for a single goddess mill. (Eller, 2000, 220)

Goodison and Morris (1998) also argue that the claims for the figurines being goddesses tend to ignore the socio-historical contexts in which those figurines were embedded. Under the influence of Carl Jung's timeless archetypal theory, Goddess advocates trade historical and cross-cultural variation for a changeless set of meanings that are attached to femaleness. Eller lists close to 20 different animals and approximately 60 symbols that are supposed to be clues to the presence of matrifocal societies.

This symbolic code leads feminist matriarchalists to speak as though there were no relevant differences between the essential focus of religion in Siberia in 27,000 BCE and that in Crete in 1500 BCE. They usually treat all of prehistoric Europe and the Near East as if these constituted a single cultural complex, viewing cultural variations as an epiphany of the multiplicity of the Goddess rather than as evidence of distinctive religious beliefs or systems of social organization. (Goodison and Morris, 1998, 118)

One might ask: What are the symbols and figurines that might indicate the *absence* of matrifocal societies?

Further, Gimbutas assumes that every figurine found was sacred in some way. Following Carl Jung's belief that the degenerate nature of modern civilization is due to the rise of secularism, Gimbutas assumes that in pre-modern societies there are no remains that were not sacred. There was no room in tribal societies for secular life. Every wavy or straight line is interpreted as symbolic of the Goddess rather than as a doodle. Every cup or dish is an indication of homage to the Goddess rather than simply as kitchenware for eating.

This was especially true for sexual imagery, as Eller points out:

Feminist matriarchialists have enthusiastically embraced the interpretive scheme that sees the walls of Paleolithic caves plastered with disembodied vulvas ... and its presence in cave art indicates that Paleolithic peoples valued birth, death, and rebirth. Yet as some observers note there is an undoubted resemblance between the vulvas in Paleolithic cave art and those that "would be right at home in any contemporary men's room." (Eller, 2000, 123)

While it is safe to say that a greater proportion of life in ancient societies life was devoted to sacred rituals than in our own, this does not mean the former had no secular life. It may be safe to assume that some of these figurines and symbols were used for activities involving sympathetic magic. Yet others could

have been commodities to be traded with other tribes. Complex horticultural societies and agricultural states did have peripheral markets. Everything made was not for sacred purposes.

Moreover, even when figurines were intended for sacred purposes, we may not easily be able to infer how they were used. Any modern pagan magician who sculpts can verify that not every piece made winds up acquiring sacred status. No matter what their intention is when they first sculpt a piece, many of the results are uninspiring and are thrown away or reshaped. This would partly account for the fact that most of the figurines in both Catal Huyuk and Crete (two of the Goddess matriarchicalists' strongholds) were found in the trash.

A central problem in interpreting what the figurines mean centers on the reasons people might have had to make them. The makers could have been motivated, for example, to invite future desired events, to bolster their egos, or to hide insecurities. These figurines could be magical projections, not of what their makers believed existed, but what they wanted to exist: a figurine of a pregnant woman could serve as a visualization device for a woman who wanted to get pregnant. Corpulent figurines could be projections of a desired state of health, rather than an objective representation of a sacred form. In agricultural societies, being overweight had (and has) high-status connotations.

Let us turn briefly to three societies that are often described as having been goddess-dominated. First, let us examine Catal Huyuk in present-day Turkey (the name is spelled differently by various authors):

The art of Catalhoyuk consists of plaster wall reliefs, wall paintings and figurines either carved in stone or modeled from clay. James Mellaart, the site's first excavator in the 1960's, interpreted the art as evidence of goddess worship. . . . In 1993 . . . excavations resumed under the direction of Ian Hodder. (Eller, 2000, 142)

Since then there have been a number of findings that have undermined Melaart's original belief:

Definitely female figurines have been recovered from houses, grain bins, and most commonly, rubbish heaps. . . . Female figurines are typically found at later levels of habitation and earlier styles of figurines, both animal and "humanoid," do not persist to the latest levels. If the female figurines are representations of the goddess, one must assume that the earlier inhabitants . . . either did not worship her, or did not make icons of her. This in itself casts some doubt on the matriarchicalist interpretation . . . since this site was in theory goddess worshipping from the beginning. (Eller, 2000, 143)

Eller concludes:

Most of the images feminist matriarchalists regard as female (plaster reliefs, bucrania, "breasts" around animal skills) are not definitely or even probably female; the images that are unequivocal representations of females do not persist over the entire life of the settlement, suggesting that any goddess worship associated with female figurines was not a stable and enduring feature of Catal Hoyuks's religion; hunting continued to be an important activity in symbol if not in practice, and was strongly linked to men; and death was a prominent theme. None fit the picture feminist matriarchalists paint for prehistory. (Eller, 2000, 147)

Referring to the Indus Valley civilization of the Bronze Age, Philip Davis writes:

The female figurines are of a distinctly crude quality, by comparison to the other artifacts, which is something we should hardly expect if they were representations of the Great Goddesses. Some archeologists have suggested they represent the devotional activities of the lower classes only, but this presumes a social hierarchy, which is supposed to be out of character for a pre-Aryan Goddess culture. On the other hand, these figurines may be good candidates for Peter Ucko's observation that most small figurines around the world are simply dolls. . . . Of the *finer* [my emphasis] artistic pieces which have been found, the majority actually have male subjects. (Davis, 1998, 73)

In Crete, while many women are represented in artistic context and everyday scenes, according to Eller no female figurines have been found in a definite ritual context. In addition, while "Females do predominate in Minoan art ... there are considerably more males depicted . . . than in Paleolithic and Neolithic European." (Eller, 2000, 153)

Finally:

"Snake goddesses" have been given a symbolic role out of proportion to their very modest number. Though this has been described as "a deity very popular in Minoan times" there are actually only two such figurines from the entire palace period in Crete. (Eller, 2000, 155)

4. Does Goddess reverence go all the way back to the Paleolithic Age?

Many Goddess theorists claim that worship of the Great Goddess can be traced all the way back to the Paleolithic Age. The findings of Lotte Motz about hunting societies in the Bering Strait do not confirm this, and her data are typical of other studies. The literature we have on hunting-and-gathering and horticultural societies that have been studied during the last 300 years reveals few if any instances of Goddess reverence.

As I have written in my book *From Earthspirits to Sky Gods*, modern hunting-and-gathering societies did not organize their sacred activities around deities, whether female or male. They were more interested in controlling forces—"mana"—rather than images, like goddesses or gods. When they envisioned sacred beings, these were typically nebulous nature spirits, not deities. In early horticultural societies, ancestral spirits and totems were the major beings, not goddesses.

Further, even if we grant that goddesses might have existed in Paleolithic societies, there is no continuity between the Paleolithic period and Mesolithic in this regard. As Philip Davis points out, nothing has been found in the Mesolithic Age:

> No burials have been found which can be dated to this era with any certainty. Art is almost equally absent, with only some rock paintings in Spain. . . . Interestingly these painting indicate a clear separation in sex roles. . . . This lack of evidence for a Mesolithic Goddess raises a serious challenge to any idea that there was continuity between the Paleolithic female carving and the goddess figures of later civilizations. Even if there were Goddess cultures in more recent times, these can hardly be projected back onto the Paleolithic remains when the intervening millennia are so completely devoid of supportive evidence. (Davis, 1998, 61)

On the contrary, there is at least as much evidence for the continuity of male sacred presences across history. Lotte Motz, in *The Faces of the Goddess*, argues:

> The images of horned beasts (bison) were drawn in large numbers onto the walls in a cave of Altamira in northern Spain. If we are permitted to spin a thread from the "Venus" figurines of Paleolithic ties to Middle Eastern sculptures and to the Great Lady of beasts and men, then we are permitted to spin a thread from the horned beasts of Altamira to the horned bulls of Catal Huyuk and to the mighty weather god [in agricultural states]. There exists, in fact, a pictorial continuity from the cloven footed horned creature of Trio Freres to the horn-helmeted Anatolian weather god, the cloven footed horned pan of Greece and even the cloven footed horned devil of modern folklore. (Motz, 1997, 32)

One possible rebuttal to the claim of absence of goddesses in modern tribal societies might be that the reports from explorers, missionaries, and anthropologists over the last 300 years have been saturated with patriarchal assumptions. This is probably true. But if modern pre-state societies were devoted to goddesses, or even if they used female figurines for sympathetic magical purposes, these facts would have been recorded. Consider the historical context in which these reports were processed: missionaries were seeking to convert "heathen" natives and explorers were bringing "progress" to "backward" peoples. Evidence for goddess reverence would only have served to justify both conversion and attempted subjugation.

Another objection might be that modern tribal societies are fundamentally different from their Stone-Age counterparts: perhaps they gradually became more male-dominated as a result of influence from agricultural and industrial states throughout the past 5000 years. If so, modern hunter-gatherer and horticultural societies would not provide an accurate insight into the nature of human life during the Paleolithic and Neolithic Ages. I certainly agree that this is partly the case. We will never know the nature of the sacred practices of the Stone Ages with certainty even by combining evidence from anthropology and archaeology. However, there is no third source of evidence available, and we would be foolish to ignore anthropological data even if it can be shown to have been tainted by observer prejudice. Without anthropology, archaeology can tell us almost nothing about ancient sacred practices; any attempt at speculative reconstruction becomes complete fantasy with no grounding.

5. Is goddess reverence synonymous with magic and witchcraft?

For most casual students of this subject, the relationship between goddess reverence, magic, and witchcraft is thoroughly confused, and some of the responsibility for this lies with the

Goddess movement. As we will see, ancient peoples who lived in early agricultural states showed reverence for goddesses (Demeter, Isis, Kali, etc.) as well as gods (Zeus, Attis, Vishnu, etc.). Further, ancient goddess rituals undoubtedly had magical elements. But do all magic and witchcraft therefore signify goddess reverence? The following three propositions may help to sort out the issues as I see them:

- Some magic is goddess reverence and some magic is not.
- Some magic involves witchcraft and some does not.
- Some witchcraft involves goddesses and some does not.

To begin with, people practiced magic in connection with other sacred presences— earth spirits, totems, and ancestor spirits—long before they envisioned the existence of goddesses. Goddesses emerged as part of a secondary magical tradition (see chapter 11) during the Bronze Age. Thus, while all sacred practices involving goddesses were magical, not all magic was (or is) goddess-centered.

As for the relationship between magic and witchcraft, all tribal societies that practice magic do so for at least two reasons—to benefit the community and individuals, and also to cause harm to other societies and to individuals within their society. The latter practices are referred to by anthropologists as "witchcraft." The notion that women practiced magic in tribal societies is not controversial. Both men and women did so. In agricultural states, "good magic" was sometimes practiced in conjunction with goddesses. This was also sometimes true of "black magic," or witchcraft. All goddess reverence was magical; sometimes it constituted witchcraft and sometimes it didn't. However, both magic and witchcraft were sometimes practiced without any involvement of goddesses.

Wilson (1988) is very specific about the conditions under which accusations of witchcraft are likely. Exchanges between families in egalitarian societies have some degree of tension. Interdependence is necessary at certain times of the year for cooperative hunting or planting or when there is an ecological-demographic crisis; but other times the bonds that unite families are tenuous. In order to show that public display of good cheer is not a complete sham, hospitality is expected.

In an egalitarian simple horticultural society the relationship between host and guest was *reciprocal*, an alternation of entertaining and display between neighbors as both hosts and guests. The need to keep reciprocity alive was justified by the way in which the exchange was conceived:

> One gives away what is in reality a part of one's nature and substance, while to receive something is to receive a part of someone's spiritual essence. *To keep this thing is dangerous* [my emphasis]. . . . [T]he thing given is not inert. It is alive and often personified. . . . [T]he benefits taken by man ought to be returned to their source, that it may be maintained as a source. (Wilson, 1988, 113)

Perhaps the most important motive for having people over to a kin group's private place was to show that they had *nothing to hide:*

> The generosity a host then displays is not only the mark of his respect for his guests but is also a revelation or exposure of his privacy to outsiders. Hospitality is that form of activity specifically contrived to display the private domain in public . . . as elementary political activity. (Wilson, 1988, 98)

When hospitality and kin groups failed to maintain social harmony, accusations of witchcraft appeared. In order to understand the social function witchcraft serves, it must be distinguished from shamanism on the one hand and ancestor worship on the other. According to Wilson, Shamanism is about a relationship between an individual and a spirit, while ancestor worship involves a relationship between the living and the dead. Witchcraft is about using sacred forces to affect relationships *between* people.

[T]he shaman or the patient . . . whose illness originates in possession, is the agent (or the victim) of a spirit. . . . But witchcraft is something that operates *between people* [my emphasis]. It may enlist the aid of supernatural entities like spirits through the agency of magic, but these spirits act not on their own but only at the bidding of the witch or magician. One who is possessed is "taken over" by another . . . but one who is bewitched is invaded by another person. (Wilson, 1988, 137)

Neither is ancestor worship a relationship between the living. Wilson argues that

it is possible to insert a category between shamanism and witchcraft as sources of powers . . . on people. Ancestral spirits or spirits of the dead are widely believed in by domesticated people. They, like the spirits of place, may act of their own accord, but usually for a reason: they have been upset or offended by a failure on the part of their descendants, the living, to respect them, to fulfill obligations towards them, and to observe taboos. To redress the upset balance an expiatory ritual is carried out; to ensure the continued exercise of ancestral spiritual power . . . propitiatory rituals are performed. Although individual members of a community are implicated directly in illnesses and misfortunes attributed to ancestral spirits . . . the state of relations between people is not involved. (Wilson, 1988, 137)

The formation of kinship relationships and structured hospitality is an attempt to forestall paranoia leading to accusations of witchcraft among people living in close quarters in egalitarian relationships. According to Wilson, it is an attempt to understand how some kin groups still do better than others in spite of political and economic egalitarianism. This is especially likely to occur during the winter season, when people are working less and are already in close quarters. They naturally get on each other's nerves and don't have an opportunity to let off steam or express to anyone their envies and suspicions.

Witchcraft accusations came when people perceived their neighbors to be in some way remiss and delinquent toward their obligations to entertain, to loan, to respect; and accusations occurred when people seemed to be taking advantage to be borrowing more than they loaned, to visit more than they were visited. Such importunity causes strain because it is hard to refuse a request for a loan. In a social community of equality . . . imbalance between people, exceptional talents and achievements appear contrary to the ideal. . . . [T]he exceptional success of individuals, even if based on natural endowment, is likely to be seen as a result of that person's access to hidden powers (Wilson, 1988, 139)

Witchcraft accusations are likely when people feel that a domestic household is putting the private realm before the welfare of society. Witchcraft, according to Wilson, is non-institutional justice.

Wilson points out that, among the Azande, all accusations of witchcraft take place between *neighbors,* not between kin, strangers, or people of different rank. Why could this be? Between kin groups and members of different rank (if we are talking about complex horticultural societies) there are *clear boundaries.* Strangers are a rare phenomenon in any tribal society. The relationships between neighbors are *vague.* They are probably the weakest link in the social network, and there is the least to lose from accusing a neighbor of witchcraft.

Wilson summarizes:

Witchcraft addresses the problems and difficulties that arise from living in a state . . . called unsocial sociability. Settlement compresses people together more intensively and for longer periods than living in a temporary open camp. Friction between people that might otherwise be defused by a simple parting may smolder

to ignition in the domestic situation. . . .
[T]he presence of a privacy barrier . . .
leads directly to an increase in suspicion,
uncertainty . . . improperly taken hints,
half glimpsed shadows, distorted
eccentricities, circumstantial evidence,
furtive glances, impolitic stares, uninvited
intrusions. . . . From these . . . accidents,
good and bad luck, coincidences and
discrepancies in talent . . . there arise
frustrations, envy, jealously, cunning,
deceit and cheating. Is failure to return
something borrowed on time innocent
negligence or calculated insult? (Wilson,
1988, 145–146)

In short, witchcraft is most prevalent in
simple horticultural societies, which have
egalitarian political relations, but there is
tension between neighbors living in large
numbers in close quarters because some groups
are more successful than are others.
   The idea that both magic and witchcraft are
necessarily related to Goddess reverence is a
product of the second half of the twentieth
century and serves the purposes of both
reactionary monotheists and Goddess theorists.
The link between goddesses, magic, and
witchcraft helps reactionaries to scapegoat their
competition; it serves the members of the
Goddess movement by standing conventional
religious prejudices on their head while
providing a simplified and unifying rallying
point. But for those who are interested in
historical reconstruction these political tactics
create significant problems.
   It is much less confusing to say that women
practiced magic in Stone Age and Bronze Age
societies, and that in the Bronze Age this
magical practice was linked with goddesses.
Magic and witchcraft are larger categories and
exist in all societies to a greater or lesser degree,
whether they have goddesses or not. Goddess
reverence is a subcategory of both magic and
witchcraft and only emerged at a certain point
in history, specifically in Bronze Age
agricultural states.

6. Was there ever a monotheistic Great Goddess?

To summarize my arguments so far, I am
claiming that

(a) There is no solid evidence for the existence
    of any matriarchal society, in the sense in
    which we have defined the word
    "matriarchy." This does not mean that
    patriarchies have always existed.
(b) All of the figurines Gimbutas discovered
    were not goddesses. This does not mean that
    none were goddesses.
(c) Goddess reverence does not go all the way
    back to the Paleolithic Age, but probably
    begins with Bronze-Age agricultural states.
(d) While all goddess reverence is magical, not
    all magic is goddess-centered; while goddess
    practices sometimes constituted witchcraft,
    all witchcraft is not goddess-centered.

The next bone of contention is whether the
female godhead was singular or plural.
Gimbutas herself changed her position on this
question over the years. As Davis (1998) notes:

In an early book which predates the
Goddess movement, *Goddesses and Gods of
Old Europe*, we find that she described Old
European religion as polytheistic. . . . In
*Language of the Goddess and The
Civilization of the Goddess*, however, we
see a significant change. Gimbutas now
espoused the Goddess myth in full blown
utopian form . . . this included a virtually
monotheistic religion of the Great
Goddess. . . . The change of view . . . arose
not from new fieldwork . . . but from a
change in her own perspective. (Davis,
1998, 70)

In summarizing the work of archeologists
and historians, Goodison and Morris (1998)
claim that goddesses in the ancient world were
always polytheistic:

The result has been a revelation. Not a
single, fundamental pattern universally

repeating itself, but of a picture of staggering diversity. Most of the contributors found strong evidence for female divinities, but not necessarily in the forms or roles conventionally assigned to them. (Goodison and Morris, 1998, 16)

Cynthia Eller agrees, claiming that there is not a single documented case of Goddess monotheism anywhere in the world.

German mythologist Lotte Motz, influenced by West Asian scholar Thorkild Jabobson and classicist Walter Burkert, examines female deities in specific locations around the world, including Northern Eurasia, Latvia, Mesopotamia, Greece, Anatolia, Mexico, and Japan. She concludes that, in these societies, there was not a single Goddess; rather, many goddesses performed many different functions:

Athena and Artemis are virginal; Aphrodite is involved in matters of erotic love; Hera brought forth some children, but functions above all as a wife and queen. Though these goddesses are concerned with various areas of women's lives and assist in childbirth or protect the young, the core and heart of their being is not in the dominion over death, birth, and fecundity. (Motz, 1997, 13)

In sum, in speaking of tribal societies from Lapland to the Bering Strait, Motz found not a single cosmic Mother Goddess, but rather a variety of groups of deities:

(1) supernatural owners of nature and beasts (hunting);
(2) sanctified elements of environment earth, sky, rivers (agriculture);
(3) ancestral and tribal spirits (family);
(4) goddesses concerned with needs of women; and
(5) a remote high god in heaven.

What we really need are some criteria for determining the differences between a monotheistic deity on one hand, and goddesses, gods, ancestor spirits, totems, and earth spirits on the other. Here is my own sketch of the kinds of considerations that might help us in making this important distinction:

(1) The degree of independence of the sacred presence from human influence. This can be seen in dramatization activities.
(2) The degree of power possessed by sacred presences to determine the course of human affairs. This can be seen in:
    (a) the degree of universalism as opposed to provincialism;
    (b) the degree of worship vs. reciprocity;
    (c) the extent to which the universe is planned or improvised.
(3) The degree of difference in the qualities of the sacred powers as compared to human powers:
    (a) the proportion of virtues to vices the sacred presence possesses, and
    (b) the extent to which creation myths are enacted sensually as opposed to abstractly.
(4) The degree of difference between the location or dimension the sacred presence inhabits as compared to that inhabited by the human community (how different is it from the earth?).
(5) The degree to which sacred powers are unique and not repeated by other sacred presences.
(6) The degree to which sacred beings are graded in importance, or controlled by other beings.
(7) The size of sacred images relative to the human form.
(8) The placement of the images within the community (at eye level, below, or above).

In order to accomplish this we would have to draw from archeology, anthropology, and history.

By these criteria, a monotheistic deity will express a maximum of independence, power, and unhuman-like qualities. Its qualities will be unrepeatable; it will be located far from the earth; and it will control lesser beings. Its imagery will be either absent, or, if present, larger-than-life. Moreover, images, where they exist, will be placed high above the community to inspire awe and invite worship.

Again using the above criteria, earth spirits, totems and ancestor spirits will be found to display maximum interdependence with humanity, share power, and possess qualities similar to humans. The qualities of the earth spirits will be repeated in other spirits or sources. Earth spirits will command no other sacred presences and will live close to humans. The images made of them will be to human scale or smaller and will be placed close to eye level. The qualities of the earth spirits and the places they inhabit will be similar to those of humans and to human-occupied places.

Goddesses and gods would occupy an intermediate position between these two extremes. Goddesses and gods are somewhat dependent on humanity but have more power. They have qualities that are human-like, but they are more powerful. Gods and goddesses are close at hand, yet live far away. These beings are hierarchically organized in families that are nevertheless less closed and rigid than the hierarchies commanded by monotheistic deities. Imagery of these beings will be larger-than-life and high off the ground.

In summary, earth spirits, ancestor spirits and totems are like brothers and sisters of a stature equal to that of humanity; goddesses and gods are like older sisters and brothers of humanity; while a monotheistic God (or Goddess) is like a father (or mother) to humanity.

According to most historians, real goddesses and gods did not appear until after the formation of the first agricultural states. But what is it about agricultural states that causes the people in these societies to envision goddesses and gods rather than nature spirits, totems, or ancestor spirits? For one thing, in order to believe in deities, people need to be more awe-struck. What social conditions might have existed to promote this effect?

One factor might have been the use of bronze. When craftsmen cast their sacred images in metal, the sacred presences became far less subject to wear-and-tear than clay, stone, or wood statues, less subject to decay, more wondrous and unearthly. Another factor was the invention of writing. Whatever mythological stories were told about these metal statues were bound to be written down. The myths would then seem more objective and unchanging because they would last longer.

The entire process of creating goddesses and gods as the result of bronze-casting and writing can be understood as a good example of reification, as defined in our first chapter. It is human beings, after all, who learned to cast metal and it is human beings who learned to write, yet these inventors and creators wound up paying homage to the very things they had made. In this case, the reification of human activity into superhuman goddesses and gods is more comprehensible if we examine the form of social organization of agricultural states.

If society is organized as a hierarchy of castes, in which the more powerful govern the less powerful, then over generations the lower castes will tend to build habits of submission. These habits will in turn make them more susceptible to subordinating themselves to gods and goddesses.

As we will see in chapter 12, devotion to goddesses and gods is a form of secondary magic, not primitive magic. In primitive magic, alienation didn't exist because the sacred presences that were constructed in tribal societies were thought to be influenced by magical practices. In secondary magic, the goddesses and gods are increasingly seen as independent of human influence. In Paul Radin's stage theory (1957), the full independence of deities from human influence comes relatively late in the evolution of spiritual history.

To sum up, in prestate societies there were neither gods nor goddesses. Gods and goddesses emerged in agricultural states; both were polytheistic.

7. Is motherhood the leading function of goddesses?

Those that are mothers are not sovereign, those that are sovereign are not mothers ... a sovereign and material goddess is not primordial. —Lotte Motz (14)

A closely related bone of contention concerns the dominant function of the female Godhead. Members of the Goddess movement claim that the "Great Goddess" was worshipped as a mother. People imagine their sacred presences performing activities they deem worthy. Thus, if ancient peoples' primary deity was a universal Mother, this implies (or assumes) that people in the ancient world revered motherhood. But how true is this?

On the whole, in hunting and gathering societies reverence for motherhood *per se* is not obvious. According to Lotte Motz (1997):

When we regard the beliefs of modern hunting and herding peoples of northern Eurasia, we note that their attitude toward the "mystery of the fertile womb" is far from reverent. In these regions, the climate of emotion is so deeply affected by a fear of women's biological functions, menstruation, pregnancy, and parturition that numerous rules and prohibitions were created to counteract the potential danger. To avoid defilement, the houses of the northern peoples are divided into men's and women's parts, the former "pure" and "sacred," the latter "polluted" and "profane." . . . (Motz, 1997, 7-8)

Most statues showed no clear evidence of pregnancy. . . . (10)

We do not find in myths of divine conception the awe and wonder inspired by the mystery of the fertile womb. . . . (18)

Since among the Nentsi, childbirth was considered "the most sinful of all diseases," young girls, men and their deities had to leave the dwelling at this time of crisis. (56)

We must also recall the fact that hunting-and-gathering societies have very few children and are more interested in restricting fertility than promoting it.

Some feminist matriarchicalists take the tradition of "couvade" (the male imitation of female reproductive processes) as an indication of male "womb envy," the implication being that men revered motherhood. According to Eller (2000), men had other things in mind:

L. R. Hiatt describes what he calls 'pseudo-procreation' rituals among Australian aboriginal men, rituals used to assert men's 'supernatural contribution' to conception and to 'rebirth' boys from men (to symbolically supersede their birth from women) as part of their initiation into manhood (Eller, 2000, 98)

Goddess advocates also think that when men make subincisions into their penises it is for the purpose of simulating menstruation. But this is not necessarily the case:

Singer and Desole make a rather persuasive case for regarding subincision as an effort to make human penises resemble those of kangaroos. . . . Australian aboriginal cultures stress erotic pleasure . . . the prolonged copulation of the kangaroo . . . would not go unnoticed. . . . Subincision greatly enlarges the width of the penis causing it to look more like a kangaroo's. (Eller, 2000, 212)

Anthropologist Sherry Ortner claims that generally women lose status when placed in reproductive roles, and gain status as virgins or after menopause.

This is not to say that childbirth has nothing to do with spirituality, only that the spirits involved are not goddess-mothers. Motz points out that:

The spirits aid in the birth of children and, sometimes, cattle; their role may include the shaping of the infant, or its soul, planting it in a woman's womb, setting the fate of the newborn, healing diseases and easing the course of menstruation. . . . They remain alien spirits and do not mingle with the gods of men. Their power to protect the women may be matched by a power to guard the privacy of women's rituals, paralleling the exclusion of women from the rituals of men. (Motz 1997, 58)

In other words, these spirits do not govern the lives of all members of society the way a goddess-mother might—only those of women. Men have their own sacred presences which help them with their lives. Motz goes on to discuss the birthing-spirits' limitations in range of influence, and whether these presences could be called goddesses:

> Since the deities described are deeply involved with childbirth and motherhood, and since they sometimes even shape the unborn child, it may be argued that they represent a variant form of the Great Sovereign Mother. The two configurations, however, spring from very different roots. The Great Mother was supposedly created in the reverence generated by the mystery of her fertile womb. The Goddesses of Birth, on the other hand, frequently are not mothers and are frequently too old to bear a child. They could not be symbols of fertile womanhood. They derive their power from their nature as tutelary forces that are inherited by the woman from her family. . . . These deities are indeed of high significance, but this significance did not arise in celebration of the creative aspect of female fruitfulness, but in the fears that denied a woman even a share in the protection granted by the gods of men. (Motz, 1997, 58)

Among the Inuit, motherhood was far from revered. Motz says that the image of biological motherhood was absent from their mythology, and motherhood has very low status.

In Latvia there is a women's goddess who has clearly attained a high position in belief. However,

> the great goddesses of Latvian tradition do not derive their significance from the awesome function of the fertile womb. Saule, the sun, rules the light of day, and Laima rules the fate of humans. In Latvian society, where fertility of fields stands in the forefront of concern, no great goddess of the earth has developed, nor was the fruitful earth assimilated to the fruitful womb. Mother Earth . . . is chiefly the resting place for the departed and girls do not go to Mother Earth to ask for children . . . the growth of corn and flax is bestowed above all by Jumis, a male force. (Motz, 1997, 83)

Turning to archeological evidence, Goddess advocates often claim that the size of some of the figurines found during the Paleolithic and Neolithic Periods indicate reverence for motherhood, but Eller contests this, arguing that many of them appear to be fat, rather than pregnant.

There is no question that when people began to plant and became sedentary, the fear of women receded and the importance of children increased. However, it seems reasonable to believe that the reverence for a Great Mother would have been translated into sculptures of women with children. But Motz points out that the number of figurines found with children is minimal:

> Peter Ucko studied and analyzed several hundred sculptures attributed to predynastic Egypt, Neolithic Crete, the Greek mainland and the Middle East; he found that only six of these show a woman with a child. (Motz, 1997, 11)

In speaking of Catal Huyuk, James Mellaart drew conclusions that are questionable, according to Lotte Motz (1997):

> [Mellaart] believes that the goddess is depicted in the process of giving birth. He points to the fact that beneath one of the reliefs . . . a bull's head and the goddess are not part of the same artifact. The goddess is represented by a relief made of plaster on the temple wall. The bull's head is a sculpture in the round, planted on the floor, shaped of plaster and painted clay. The form of the goddess is stylized and the bull's head is naturalistic. The scale of the two is incompatible. If the bull had indeed issued from a woman's womb, the head would be inverted, with eyes beneath the

mouth and not in an upright position. We may find in Mellaart's interpretation one of the indications of the great desire to find a "mother." (Motz, 1997, 230)

The Goddess movement often relies on the correlation of males and all things masculine with the sky, and females and all things feminine with the earth. When a sacred marriage occurs, the purpose is to support the growth of vegetation. This belief does not hold true for the agricultural communities of northern Eurasia. If the sky-god receives a wife, she dwells with him in heaven. They do not inhabit the earth together, helping the crops to grow.

The word "mother," when referring to female deities in these traditions, does not describe a biological function or a special relationship with children, but simply a title of respect. Again, Motz:

The goddesses of this study indeed show their derivation from one or more of the basic groups of North Eurasian belief, though naturally they acquired new attributes in their development within a complex society. The evaluation of the later forms of godhead yields the following conclusions:

(1) They are of varied origin and have not descended from a single being.

(2) They derive their significance from the phenomenon they rule or represent- the earth, sun, the tribal group-and not from their motherhood.

(3) They bear the stamp of their social and religious environment.

(4) Not a birth giver, but the birth helper is of great importance. (Motz, 1997, 2–3)

In turning to Mesopotamia, Motz draws the same conclusion:

The ancient Middle East, where growing and harvesting the fruit of a generous earth had supplanted a harsher way of life, is generally seen as the place where the Great Mother unfolds to the fullest flower of her creative sovereignty. This study has not found a substantiation of this claim. It is true that a birth and mother goddess is depicted as a craftsman and creator. This role is also held, however, by other gods. . . . [T]he action of birth-giving forms part of the process through which the first human is generated. This involvement . . . is a result of the value accorded to human activity rather than to a special respect for a fertile womb. Though the goddess enjoys a station of importance . . . there is no evidence that she ever ruled the other gods.

It has been claimed that with the advent of agriculture, the birth-giving powers of the earth were assimilated to a woman's powers of fertility, a claim not supported by Mesopotamian tradition. Here birth goddesses are related to the cattle byre or the birth hut, to the site of parturition, like the North Eurasian birth helpers, but not to the agricultural earth. No great goddess has arisen in this society of farmers, and the field is not envisaged as a fertile woman. Here, as well as in the other agricultural communities of this study, no sexual rites are directed to the plowed land, nor is it approached by women in their wish for children. Birth-helping goddesses on the other hand, who show a strong relation to the earth, were encountered . . . these belong to communities of herder and hunters. Here the earth is visualized in its ancestral form as a resting place of the departed, not as the site of growing grain. (Motz, 1997, 97)

Cynthia Eller concurs:

Though agricultural societies have an active, understandable concern for the fertility of their land and sometimes invoke goddesses . . . we have no record of a group that assigns the sole power for agricultural fertility to females or goddesses (Eller, 2000, 178)

In responding to the Goddess-movement claims that the belief in a Great Mother was predominant in the Near East, Motz says that the weather gods were more important:

> It is clear that the warlike deity of lightning and thunder has not been brought by an outside force, for he had developed in the agricultural regions. It is natural for a weather god to gain great importance among a farming population. Farmers, looking to the skies for life-restring rains, apparently did not spend much time in contemplating the "holy darkness of the womb." (Motz, 1997, 34-35)

According to Motz, the only mythological indication of a goddess specifically connected to biological motherhood in the ancient world is contained in the story of the love between Demeter and Persephone. But this is the exception rather than the rule.

Further, as Motz notes, the *Hastings Encyclopedia of Religion and Ethics* entry under "Pregnancy" tells us that "The many myths in which a woman was fecundated by an external agent, a spark of fire, or a gust of wind indicated that an external agent was needed to stimulate conception and that the woman was not creative through her own inner force." (Quoted in Motz, 1997, 205)

Motz concludes:

> We may safely state that the deities did not find their origin on one single archetypal creature and did not derive significance through the power of the womb. . . .
> Their importance was attained . . . through the ability to provide food of men; to guard and protect a locality; to aid in warfare; to assist in the birth of children. . . . (Motz 1997, 180)
> They do not evolve into universal creative beings. . . . (ibid., 182)
> The promotion of new life issues to some extent from the world of the departed, less from the transitory and perishable organ of a woman's body than from the enduring beneficial power of the dead. . . . (ibid., 182)

> [It was] not infants' longing for their mother's breast that shaped the contours of the divine, but the needs of adult men and women faced with the cruel exigencies of archaic life. . . . (ibid., 183)

8. Is there a direct correspondence between the presence of goddesses in ancient societies and the prosperous material status of women?

In Christian countries the sacred presence is a single male god. Using our definition of institutionalized male dominance, all Western societies today can be characterized as practicing institutionalized male dominance. This means all men have some privileges over all women while the highest positions of economic, political, and military power are dominated by men. Simplifying this to an equation we can say: male sacred power = male political/economic power. But is the reverse the case? If there were sacred female power would it equate to female political/economic power? Goddess advocates seem to think so.

After all, as Cynthia Eller points out, if Goddess spirituality is powerful inspiration for women today, then Goddess advocates believe the presence of goddesses must have been inspiring for women in ancient times as well.

While these premises seem reasonable at first glance, the reality is far more complicated.

Let us assume for the moment that goddesses in agricultural states had great power. Let us say that they had more power than the gods. We should therefore see this reflected in women's high material status. Yet the material status of most women in these societies was far worse than that of women in pre-state societies. There was an improvement in status for chiefly wives in complex horticultural societies, as they became priestesses in agricultural states. For the latter, rituals included interactions with goddesses. However, for most women in these Bronze Age societies, the worship of high goddesses did not translate to social privileges or power. Goddess advocates do not explain this contradiction.

Far from myths of goddesses supporting high material status for women, anthropologist

Bronislaw Malinowski (as quoted by Eller) argues that myth tends to promote the status quo:

> Its function "is to strengthen tradition and endow it with a greater value and prestige by tracing it back to a higher, better more supernatural reality of initial events." Such mythic charters are said to operate especially in areas of sociological strain, such as significant differences in status or power. (Eller, 2000, 177)

The relationship between women's material status and sacred presences is complicated by at least these possibilities:

(1) the presence of goddesses can coexist with the presence of male dominance in the material world;

(2) the presence of gods or a male god can coexist with improved status for women in the material world.

For example, as we will see in chapters 12 and 13, Frymer-Kensky argues that worship of goddesses in Mesopotamia was accompanied by low status of women. Conversely, the material status of most women improved when goddesses were marginalized with the rise of Hebrew monotheism in the Archaic Iron Age. As Eller notes: "Kinship can even be matrilineal in groups that insist that women are only passive carriers of men's seed, and patrilineal in groups that hear that men have no procreative role." (Eller 2000, 102)

Lotte Motz (1997) gives four specific examples of lack of correlation between the presence of goddess-worship and the high material status of women:

> [A] goddess of great potency can evolve in the midst of a patriarchal order, as did Inanna-Ishtar. The goddess Sedna dominates the religious emotions of the Eskimo, with whom women were of low account. The cult of Isis flourished in the midst of a patriarchal society and churches dedicated to the Virgin Mary rose in the patriarchal Middle Ages. (Motz, 1997, 17)

As we will discuss more in chapter 12, the relationship between goddesses and the status of women is not a simple reflection of one by the other. It is uneven and changes with the times. In stable times in Mesopotamia, the activities of goddesses expressed the subordination to gods that women had to men. As times changed, the relationship shifted. There are at least three phases that can be identified:

Phase one: An economic or social role performed by women (such as weaving) is also the domain of a goddess (early Bronze Age);

Phase two: The economic-social role formerly performed by women comes to be performed by men, but remains the domain of a goddess (middle Bronze Age);

Phase three: The economic-social role continues to be performed by men, and becomes the domain of a god (middle Bronze Age).

Peggy Reeves-Sanday (1981) concluded that, among the scores of societies she surveyed, there was a high correlation ratio between the female contribution to subsistence and the percentage of divinities worshipped that were female; there was no correlation between the number of female divinities and female status. The unstated implication is that women can work very hard at subsistence and still maintain low social status. Conversely, women can contribute very little to subsistence and still enjoy very high status.

It is assumed that if the figurines that Gimbutas found truly represent goddesses, this must mean that the women in these societies had high status. The more the members of a group are depicted in images, the more status they must have. In our own society, images of women dominate western media. But do such images mean that women have high status in our society—that is, do women wield substantial economic and political power? Few people would agree that they do. Yet goddess advocates expect us to make this simplistic association when it comes to the ancient world.

9. Did pastoral nomads' invasions cause the rise of institutionalized male dominance?

Goddess advocates rally around Maria Gimbutas' claim that, before the emergence of the Bronze Age civilizations, planting societies were attacked in three waves by Indo-European pastoralists in 4400 BCE, 3400 BE, and 2800 BCE. These pastoralists attacked on horseback and in horse-drawn wheeled chariots. They had patriarchal gods and, in the process of conquest, introduced patriarchal values. Thus pastoralists are responsible for having introduced patriarchal values into previously matrifocal Neolithic societies and perhaps even influenced the values of Bronze Age agricultural states.

There are a number of problems with this scenario, as we will see in more detail in chapter 9. While most linguists agree that there may have been a dispersal of peoples speaking Indo-European languages within the period Gimbutas claims, the question of whether the movement was a migration or an invasion is controversial. Under normal conditions, pastoralists do not have the military power to conquer complex horticulture societies, but this is not a problem for Gimbutas's theory if the Indo-European speakers had access to domesticated horses, wheeled vehicles, and chariots during the three waves she claims the invasions took place in.

Robert Drews (1993) and J. P. Mallory (1989) deny that all three of these inventions were available as far back as the fifth or even the third millennium. Nor were these inventions combined systematically until roughly the 17th century BCE. Further, when they became available, it wasn't Indo-Europeans who first used them.

While Gimbutas claims that the Russian steppes were the home of the invaders, and this is indeed the most likely geographic origin of the Indo-European language group, the people of that area don't appear to have been nearly as ferocious as Gimbutas claims:

Neither is there any positive evidence that the Kurgans from the Russian steppes were an exceptionally brutal, supremely patriarchal people. Their stock of weaponry, as it has been uncovered archeologically, does not dwarf that of Neolithic peoples to the south. (Eller 2000, 179)

The plausible alternatives are that Indo-European speakers existed in the time Gimbutas argues but they didn't have the technology to topple planting societies. While there is evidence for incursions from the Russian steppes, the time period is much later than the late Neolithic, as posited by Gimbutas. If Indo-Europeans did invade, it wasn't until at least 1700 BCE. Lastly, while it is probable that these pastoralists were patriarchal, patrilineal, and warlike, it is highly unrealistic to assume that the people they conquered were uniformly peace-loving matriarchicalists, as we will see in the next section.

The controversy over the dating is important. If intrusions or invasions occurred before the rise of state civilizations (which Goddess advocates usually agree are male dominated), then pastoral invasions can be used to explain the origin of patriarchal states. If the invasions occurred much later, then patriarchy cannot be claimed to have emerged as the result of an external social force. Instead, possible causes within pre-state societies would have to be seriously considered.

10. Were societies without institutionalized male dominance peaceful?

One of the central tenets of the story Goddess advocates tell is that hunting-and-gathering and early farming societies were peaceful until they were invaded by pastoral nomads beginning in the fourth millennium BCE. Archeological and anthropological evidence does not support this.

As we will see in chapter 8, according to the work of Keeley (1996) the rate of homicide in pre-state societies relative to the size of their population was higher than in state civilizations. Among most segmented societies (i.e., those with a division of labor beyond the family and a relatively closed group membership), warfare in the form of ambush and raids was almost constant and difficult to stop. There was no sparing of women and children, and captives were mutilated, tortured, eaten, and traded. While it is true there were some warless societies among unsegmented hunter-gatherers such as the Mbuti and the !Kung, these were far from the rule. In these societies the absence of war does not mean the absence of violence. Of the seven societies characterized by Raymond Kelly (2000) as warless, three are characterized as having physical violence between husband and wife. While it is overstating things to say that the absence of peace is the same as the presence of war, it is also an overstatement to say that warless societies are peaceful and non-violent.

Even in the Minoan civilization of Crete, by far the least warlike of any ancient civilization, the unfortified nature of towns does not mean there was no violence. If Minoan civilization had a military, it would likely have been a navy. The results of naval warfare would not be likely to show up archeologically.

11. Did the movement from polytheism to monotheism involve battles between gods and goddesses?

According to Goddess theorists, following the takeover of some planting societies by herding societies in the fourth to the second millennium, the goddesses that supposedly previously held sway were dethroned and replaced by male gods. However, this is by other accounts a highly simplistic formulation of the events. Earthspirits, totems, and ancestor spirits of tribal societies did not simply vanish with the coming of goddesses and gods in the Bronze Age; they continued to live on. Goddess advocates write as if goddesses were the only extant deities prior to the invasions.

Also, the movement from polytheism to monotheism does not involve a battle between gods and goddesses as much as it involves a battle between gods. As we will see in chapter 12, Yahweh fought against Canaanite male gods, not goddesses, in his battle for power.

Lotte Motz (1997) writes, in the case of the Hebrews, "The battle against the Canaanite baalim (males gods) is conducted more fiercely

than the fight against the Asheroth (female deities)." (Motz 1997, 36). More generally,

It is true that Tiamat, vanquished by Marduk and Medusa, slain by Perseus were drawn as female creatures. Usually, however, the adversary of the divinity is male, such as Hrungnir (Germanic) Ullikummi (Hittite) or Typhoeus (Greek). In his exhaustive study of tales of the "monster combat," Fontenrose notes that the fight may also be twofold, against a male as well as against a female enemy. The male however, is the main opponent. (Motz 1997, 35)

Sex and gender are not important features of the adversary. He is monstrous and nonhuman; he symbolizes the chaotic void as a constant threat to cosmic order. The battle is between humans and nature-beasts, mountain ranges, and the sea. . . . (Motz, 1997, 36)

Finally, as we will see in a later discussion of natural catastrophes (chapter 10), astronomers Victor Clube and Bill Napier argue that the myths describe sky battles between male gods, not between male gods and female goddesses. This occurs in Egypt between Horus and Seth; in Greece between Zeus and Typhon; in Syria between Ball and Yam; in Iran between Ohrimazd and Ahriman; and in Scandinavia between Thor and Odin.

12. Methodologicial shortcomings

How are we to account for the wide divergence between statements by specialists in the relevant fields, and the claims made by leaders of the Goddess movement? In the United States and Western Europe in the 20th century, the male-dominated world religions were in decline. As the women's movement gained strength in the 1960s, some of its shapers sought to build a women's spirituality movement to challenge the existing spiritual order. Usually reform or revolutionary movements need roots in the past in order to justify itself.

According to Philip Davis, the mythmaking of the Goddess movement began with the 1971 book *The First Sex*, by Elizabeth Gould Davis, whose work he summarizes as follows:

She argues that women were once the only sex—all humans were female. The y chromosome developed as a mutation of the x. . . . By the time men appeared, women had already created all the worthwhile arts of civilization . . . and remained in control for several millennia. Males were bred selectively for female enjoyment and men who failed to display proper subservience were exiled to the wilderness. Eventually, male resentment of this treatment broke out in violence. Out in the wilderness the Indo-Europeans and Hebrews developed their patriarchal systems and then proceeded to impose them by force on the rest of the world. (Davis, 42)

Biologists, anthropologists and ancient historians discounted Davis's book as soon as it appeared. . . . Both her selection of evidence and her interpretations of it were fatally distorted according to the normal standards of research. (Davis, 1998, 42-3)

Another major source for the Goddess movement was Merlin Stone's book *When God Was a Woman* (first published in 1976 under the title *The Paradise Papers*). In it, Stone claims that there is a direct relationship between worship of a goddess and high socio-political status of women. But as we have seen in this chapter and throughout various parts of this book, there is no necessary correspondence between the presence of goddesses and the prosperous status of women.

A prime resource for both Victorian anthropologists and the Goddess movement was the 1861 book *Mutterrecht* (usually translated as *Mother-Right*) by Johann Jakob Bachofen, a specialist in Roman law. According to Bachofen (whose evidence was derived from literature, not archaeology), humanity passed through three stages in social evolution:

(1) a pre-civilized state of nature, characterized by short-term alliances which men dominate through physical tyranny;

(2) a matriarchal stage ruled by women through their religious and moral qualities. This stage was characterized by the irrational and ruled by the moon. Exclusive marriage predominated; and

(3) a third stage, called patriarchy, which was ruled by Apollo and called the solar age.

According to Philip Davis, Bachofen's methods were highly questionable. His acknowledgments of scholars of his own time were sparse, and he believed that myths contain a core of historical fact and can supply information we lack from other sources. Bachofen argued that the use of imagination is interchangeable with rationality in the acquisition of knowledge.

Further, Bachofen tended to minimize differences between ancient cultures, collecting and combining evidence from different times and places into a unified whole. For example, Greek myths and literature like Sophocles's Oedipus at Colonus affected his interpretation of ancient Egyptian mythology. Feeling that rational scholarship drowned the spiritual significance of a text in technical details, he used spiritual correspondences to interpret myths.

Anthropologists and historians dismissed Bachofen's work. When anthropologists studied existing tribal societies they found no instances of a matriarchal stage. But Bachofen's failure to win over experts did not curb his influence among artists, psychologists, those studying comparative religion, and political radicals. For example, Bachofen's work affected Lewis Henry Morgan's interpretation of the Iroquois in *Ancient Society*. Engels drew much of his material for *The Origin of the Family, Private Property and the State* from Morgan, and indirectly imported some of Bachofen's ideas. Robert Briffault's three-volume treatise *The Mothers* also drew inspiration from Bachofen.

Bachofen's work also influenced the Cambridge scholar of Greek religion, Jane Harrison, whose book *Prolegomenia to the Study of Greek Religion* is another resource for the Goddess movement. In her book, Harrison claimed that pre-Olympian Greece was matriarchal until invaded by Indo-Europeans. Significantly, however, late in life Harrison changed her mind. Following a study of Frazer's work, (*The Golden Bough*), she came to realize that goddess worship and the tracing of descent along a female line are, by themselves, insufficient proof of female rulership of society. Further, in her second great work, *Themis*, she placed a male god Kronos at the head of the pre-patriarchal pantheon. Goddess theorists typically overlook these later revisions.

Frazer himself has been cited by the Goddess movement because of his contention that sacrifice was linked to fertility rites meant to renew the earth. Fertility rites were the origin of all religions. Though Frazer was a sincere collector of folklore and has a respected place in the history or religion, there are good reasons not to take his work too seriously, according to Ackerman:

> He wrote vast, assured tomes about primitive religion and mythology without ever leaving the library. He based his comprehensive theories on the often crude and ethnocentric reports of explorers, missionaries and traders. He lacked the idea of culture as the matrix . . . that gives meaning to social behavior and belief and thus has no qualms about comparing items of culture from the most disparate times and places. (Ackerman, 1)

Robert Graves, in his book *The White Goddess*, claimed that life in the ancient Mediterranean was dominated by the three aspects of the Goddess—maiden, mother, and crone—who was the original deity. Not only did women hold sway in society, but both men and women lived in harmony with the earth. The dynamics in early religion between a female goddess and a male god clearly favored the goddess. According to Graves, in ancient societies the cycles of the seasons were primarily determined by a female goddess who changes form and mates with a god in the summer. While the god dies in the fall, she lives on and the god is born again in the spring. It was the rise of patriarchy that split the singular

original Goddess into many goddesses. Like most other sources of Goddess research, as an historian Graves is not taken seriously by specialists in the field because of his methods and source material.

Finally, the psychologist Carl Jung was heavily influenced by Bachofen; and Jung—together with his follower, the mythologist Joseph Campbell—have done an enormous amount to spread and deepen the Goddess movement's psycho-spiritual interpretation of world history. Jung employed some of the same questionable techniques as Bachofen, drawing together images from different times and places—Hindu scripture, alchemical allegory, and psychotic hallucination. Jung's work, in turn, influenced the primary archaeologist of the Goddess movement, Maria Gimbutus, whose discoveries and theories we have discussed.

The Goddess movement's foray into history is understandable and would be praiseworthy if mythmaking were used only for spiritual and psychological purposes. However, when movement leaders make claims for the literal historical truth of their myths, they are obliged to follow the well-known scientific procedures for collecting and objectively assessing evidence. This they have not done.

If the Goddess theorists had entered the field of history with a full commitment to correcting some of the real imbalances of historical reporting about gender relations while playing by the rules of archeology, anthropology, and macrosociology, they might have made an important contribution to our understanding of the past. What they have done instead is to merge history and mythology, resisting scientific criticism by claiming that all challenges to their conclusions stem from patriarchal politics. The result is a great deal of naive writing which has sown confusion among those who, for whatever reasons, do not know or care what traditional scholarship has found about history.

Finally, Goodison and Morris argue that, in their attempt to reconstruct a literal past, Goddess theorists have adopted what are essentially authoritarian attitudes and fundamentalist principles:

There is an over-reliance on authority rather than primary evidence . . . A personality cult emerged around . . . Gimbutas. . . . We experience disquiet at the sense of the appropriation of feminism for themselves as if there were not many diverse feminisms, both within and outside of archaeology. . . . (Goodison and Morris, 1998, 13)

A Goddess movement writer may quote from what is written in a book, or on a museum label, and may even travel to the site where the figurine was found . . . but will delve no further. . . . She may then interpret the figurine as a "goddess" and move on to link it with other figurines from a different time and place. (Ibid., 15)

The narrative is presented in an authoritarian way in which the process of inference from artifact to interpretation is mystified . . . and few justifications are provided. (Ibid., 24)

The Goddess movement has many of its roots in Romanticism and many of its leading original figures have been men influenced by the Romantic movement—Michelet, Bachofen, Frazer, Graves, and Jung, to name just a few. These writers' works have, more often that not, been characterized by bad scholarship and a confusion of mythology with history.

In sum, methodologically what we have here is:

(1) weak evidence,
(2) disregard for disconfirming evidence,
(3) discouragement of those who would seek out disconfirming evidence,
(4) speculation based on no evidence,
(5) the assumption that because evidence for what happened in the ancient world is not certain, one interpretation is as good as another,
(6) a tendency to collapse historical scholarship into mythology, art, and literature,
(7) a tendency to reduce historical change within a society to eternal archetypes of goddesses, and

(8) a tendency to reduce all cross-cultural differences between societies to eternal archetypes of goddesses.

13. Conclusions

There are at least five positive conclusions to be drawn for the Goddess theorists and their claims with regard to history. First, they are right to point to a time in history when gender relations were politically and economically equal. Second, some of the figurines found by Gimbutas are likely to have been goddesses. Third, goddesses had many positive functions in Bronze Age societies, more than they did once the universalistic religions emerged. Fourth, the practice of magic, including goddess magic, long predated the rise of the great religions. And fifth and last, tribal societies did not engage in mass killings the way state societies did.

In most other instances, however, as we have seen, the Neo-pagan goddess theorists overstate their case or are simply wrong. First, there have never been any matriarchal societies, as we have defined "matriarchy." This does not mean that all ancient societies were patriarchal; tribal societies were neither patriarchal nor matriarchal. Second, many of the figurines discovered were probably not goddesses; some were male, some were non-gendered, and some were used as dolls, toys, or lucky charms. Third, there is no good evidence for goddess reverence going all the way back to the Paleolithic Age. It is more likely that it began in the Bronze Age.

In terms of sacred practices, while all goddess practices were magical, magical practices were not tied necessarily to goddesses. Magic was conducted with earth spirits, totems, and ancestor spirits long before goddesses came on the scene. Correspondingly, while some elements of witchcraft have existed in all ancient societies, witchcraft was practiced in Paleolithic and Neolithic societies before goddess reverence emerged.

Further, the goddesses within Bronze Age societies were polytheistic, not monotheistic. There was never a single monotheistic Great Goddess who was regarded as presiding over all of society. Further, motherhood was not the leading function of goddesses. While goddesses had many functions, motherhood was not a leading one. This is because most ancient societies did not think much of motherhood.

In addition, there was no direct relationship between reverence for goddesses and high material status for women. At the time Bronze Age civilizations appeared, goddesses already had subordinate status, and this justified the low status of women in these societies. In the Iron Age, with the rise of the great religions, the status of women improved slightly despite the marginalization of goddesses. In societies that can be characterized as egalitarian (hunter-gatherer and simple horticultural societies) there were no goddesses. Therefore so far as "matrifocal" means egalitarian relations between men and women in material culture and the predominance of goddesses in the sacred dimension, ancient societies were not matrifocal. Women's positive material and sacred status have never coexisted within the same society. When women lived material lives more or less on a par with men—in foraging and simple horticultural societies—the evidence for goddess reverence is absent. When goddesses emerged in agricultural states, women's material status had already deteriorated (with the exception of queens and priestesses who constituted an insignificant proportion of the population).

The rise of institutionalized male dominance was not caused by pastoral invasions, but rather by processes internal to pre-state societies. Tribal societies were far from peace loving. Their homicide rates and frequency of war were greater than in Bronze and Iron Age State civilizations, in which institutionalized male dominance emerged. Last, the transition/crisis from polytheism to monotheism did not involve conflict between gods and goddesses, but rather between male gods.

Figure 3.3 presents these conclusions in chart form.

When we return to the eight questions posed at the end of chapter 2, we find that Goddess theorists are not very helpful in answering them. Goddess theorists either have not studied the anthropological literature fully (reading selectively), or they believe that there was such a thing as matriarchal dominance, at least in the sacred realm, as a kind of article of faith. In the case of child rearing it is generally admitted that this was the province of women, but Goddess theorists have projected romanticized notions of motherhood back in time. As a whole, motherhood and child rearing were rarely if ever held as sacred activities in the ancient world. To the extent that male dominance in tribal societies is admitted, it is generally attributed to external sources—male-dominated herders or patriarchal colonialists attacking hunter-gatherers and simple horticulturists—rather than seen as emerging from within societies.

I call Goddess theorists "idealists" because they generally try to explain changes in material institutions—ecology, technology, the economy, and politics—from changes in spiritual beliefs, from the Goddess to the God. In the next chapter we will examine materialist theories of the origin of gender inequalities.

In denying most of the historical claims of the Goddess movement, my intention is descriptive, not proscriptive. I am arguing not for what ought to have happened in gender history, but what is likely to actually have happened. It is certainly comforting and inspiring to believe that there was a time when women were respected in all areas of cultural life. If that were the case, it would be easier to believe that women can again achieve full equality with men in all aspects of society today and in the future. Even if most of the historical claims of the Goddess movement are mistaken, we still can use the myths and rituals of pagan people to help build our future. More women have a better life today, at least in industrialized societies, than they ever did in agricultural states when goddesses first arose. The improvement in the life of most women in industrial societies is a solid basis for making a closer connection between women's material and sacred status in the future. To me, that project offers the best prospect for achieving the Goddess theorists' ultimate aims.

Figure 3.3 Critique of the Goddess Movement Model of Ancient History

Neo-pagan degeneration claims	Improvised social evolution claims	Christian progress implications (what is not being implied)
1) There were once matriarchies.	Tribal societies were neither matriarchal nor patriarchal.	Patriarchies have always existed.
2) All female figurines found are goddesses.	Some figurines were goddesses; others were gods, non-gendered dolls, toys, or lucky charms.	Figurines were erotic toys for pagan heathens.
3) Goddesses go all the way back to the Paleolithic Age.	Spirits, totems and ancestor spirits preceded all goddesses and gods (goddesses and gods are a product of stratified agricultural states).	There was a god before there were goddesses.
4) All magic is goddess-centered.	While all goddess reverence is magical, not all magic is goddess-centered (see #3).	Religion preceded magic. Magic is degenerate religion.
5) All witchcraft is goddess-centered.	While some goddess practitioners have used witchcraft, witchcraft has been used without reference to goddesses.	All goddess practitioners use witchcraft.
6) Goddess practice was monotheistic.	Goddess reverence was polytheistic. Only some male gods were monotheistic.	Monotheism was the original sacred form.
7) Motherhood was the leading function of goddesses.	Goddesses had many public functions to perform which were more important. In hunting-gathering societies, motherhood had low status.	Fatherhood was revered.
8) There is a direct correspondence between the presence of goddesses and high material status of women.	There is a connection between the perceived source of resource supply and the gender of the source, not between sacred status and social status of women. When goddesses were present, the status of women was low. When earth-spirits, totems or ancestor spirits were present, women were roughly equal to men.	Women have always had a second class identity.
9) Invasions by pastoralists caused institutionalized male dominance.	Institutionalized male dominance was caused by processes internal to pre-state societies.	Institutionalized male dominance has always existed.
10) Pre-state societies were peaceful.	All pre-state societies were violent. Most were warlike. The few warless societies were not peaceful.	Wars are caused by male aggression.
11) The movement from polytheism to monotheism was a battle between gods and goddesses.	The emergence of monotheism was played out mythologically more between male gods than between male gods and female goddesses.	Goddesses had no power in mythology.

Chapter 4

Socio-Ecological Theories of Gender Hierarchies

In this chapter we will focus on socio-ecological theories of gender inequality; we will address biological theories in chapter 7. Goddess theorists attempt to explain gender inequalities by the rise of male gods culminating in monotheism. This explanation is *idealist* because it tries to explain changes in material and social conditions (technology, politics, and economics) through reference to changes in spiritual practices (i.e., the development of patriarchal religion). Theories in this chapter seek to explain gender inequalities from a materialist perspective—pointing to population pressure, resource depletion, new technologies, economic stratification, and political centralization as the causative agents.

In his book *Social Inequality* (2001), Charles Hurst divides theories of gender inequity into four types: cultural, social-structural, ecological, and capitalist or Marxist. We described a type of cultural argument in the last chapter; in this chapter we will focus on the other three types, beginning with Marxist theories.

Hurst points out four issues that are important to keep in mind when considering any of these theories:

1. Women can be unequal or equal with men in a *variety* of dimensions including public power, prestige, type of work, education, and access to goods and services that make life more enjoyable and meaningful. We must be careful to maintain these distinctions and to not make sweeping generalizations.

2. Because of the variance between the activities and beliefs about genders cross-culturally, it is difficult to identify universal factors that aren't trite, without referring to biological universals.

3. It is impossible to shed the skin of one's own socialization and avoid projecting our own society's measures of what is good, prestigious, and desirable onto other societies.

4. Some theories rely on simple dichotomies in trying to understand gender inequality, such as nature vs. culture, natural vs. artificial, private domestic vs. public social. Matters are always more complex than this.

1. Marxist theories

Marxist theories of the origin of gender inequalities argue for the primacy of economic forces in determining gender dynamics. Capitalist theories of the origin of gender inequality (*not*, that is, theories invented by capitalists, but theories that tie the origin of inequality to the origin of capitalism) start with Engels' *Origins of the Family, Private Property and the State*. Engels begins by arguing that in primitive communist societies (hunter-gatherers) all resources were communally owned and there were no separate nuclear families to create a distinction between the domestic and the public economy. Because women were involved equally with men in producing goods and services, the work of both sexes was understood as equally valuable and all goods were produced for use value (rather than exchange value).

This situation changed with the development of privately owned resources in the forms of domesticated animals and land. Herding societies produced a greater surplus than was possible in hunting societies, allowing an emerging dominant social class to live off the surplus. This higher social class coerced the lower classes to produce for exchange (commodities) instead of merely for use. While class subordination occurred for both men and women, those at the top of the newly formed hierarchy were men, since they were primarily responsible for control over large animals. The kind of work that women did changed along with their status. Because men now had property, they became more concerned about who their children were and wanted more control over the nuclear monogamous family. Hurst summarizes Engels's views this way:

> [Women's] reproduction of children was now for producing heirs and workers for their own families rather than for producing another child for the social group. This domination of men over women in the nuclear family setting was for Engels, the first instance of class domination and struggle in history. "In the family, he is the bourgeois; the wife represents the proletariat." This class conflict is a "picture in miniature of what appears later in the society as a whole." (Hurst, 2000, 80)

There are a number of problems with Engels's theory and some of them will be summarized at the end of this section. Nevertheless, some Marxists attempt to correct and update Engels's theory while still preserving his insights. For example, Karen Sacks revised Engles's theory of female subordination to take into consideration what we have learned from anthropology over the last century. To do this she changed the meaning of two of Engels's major concepts, "social labor" and "production for exchange."

By "social labor" Sacks meant producing for society as a whole, whereas domestic labor meant producing only for one's own household. Further, production for use involves gift-giving. In egalitarian societies, gifts are exchanged of roughly equal value because everyone has access to material resources. (Chafetz [1988] gives an excellent summary of Sacks's and other Marxist theories; in the following discussion, I will be quoting primarily from her summary rather than from the original sources.)

However when the means of subsistence are privately . . . held, the recipient cannot return a gift of equal worth. Rather, the recipient is expected to return the favor with service. This gives the property owner the ability to harness the labor power of other for his own ends. This second situation Sacks called production for exchange. (Chafetz, 1988, 29)

Sacks believes that when women cease to produce for society as a whole as a result of the emergence of private property and production for exchange, women cease being social adults and become imprisoned in the domestic economy. Sacks argues that men are selected to do social labor because they are more mobile and because they can be more thoroughly exploited by the ruling class than women since men do not have to rear children: "[T]he necessary and important function of rearing future generations of exchange workers is forced upon women without compensation." (Chafetz 1988, 30)

Another Marxist, Lise Vogel, argues that the origins of gender hierarchies go deep into the socio-reproduction process. All labor involves two aspects—the production involved in making a specific product (for example, baskets, rugs, or pots). The other aspect involves the *reproduction* of the labor process itself. This includes restoring the equipment and tools used to make the rugs, baskets, and pots. Reproduction also involves reproducing the laborers themselves. This means food, clothing, and housing. In most societies prior to capitalism both reproduction processes were done within the domestic household.

The conditions of production—the making of a specific product or service—are mostly in the hands of men, and produciton takes place in the public realm outside the domestic household. In addition, conditions of public reproduction are in the hands of society as a whole or, in the case of stratified societies, it is the responsibility of the elite. Public reproduction means making sure the conditions for milling and brewing in the divine household of the agricultural state are in good working order. But the conditions for the *reproduction of labor* are domestic and in the hands of women. The reproduction of labor consists of (a) giving birth to a new generation of workers, (b) taking care of them before they enter the work force (as children) and when they are too old to work, and (c) nurturing them when they return home from the public realm while they are in the work force. For this, women are paid nothing, and, as we will see, this fact is instrumental in women's subordination.

Marxists believe that at least half of the social wealth that laborers produce is not reaped by them, but is pocketed by capitalists as profit. The labor of men in the public realm can be divided into necessary labor and surplus labor. Necessary labor is the part of the labor time expended on the reproduction of the person working, which translates as wages. Surplus labor is the remaining labor time that the capitalist pockets toward his own profit.

Necessary labor also includes the work of women at home, including giving birth and sustaining the other members of the household. This labor is unpaid.

It is in the interest of the ruling class to minimize necessary labor time, thereby increasing surplus labor time in order to reap the greatest possible profit. For Vogel, it is the unpaid labor of women at home that puts them at a disadvantage even as compared to lower-class men who are working for wages.

However, there is a contradiction between the short-term and long-term self-interests of the ruling class in relation to women. On the one hand the responsibilities involved in taking care of the family decreases the potential contributions of women to necessary labor in public because they have less time to work there. This works against the capitalist's short-term self-interest. However in the long run the capitalist needs women to stay home in order to prepare the next generation of workers.

In other words, in order to maximize profits, capitalists need women *both* in the public arena as workers *and* in the domestic household to reproduce workers. Since women cannot perform both functions optimally at the same time, there is a structural contradiction. If women devote themselves fully to working in the public realm, the lives of family members within the domestic household deteriorate and workers become less able emotionally, physically, and intellectually to keep up; thus the rate of productivity goes down. If women stay home full-time, that makes the work force less competitive, and it is easier for workers to organize and drive up wages. This cuts into the capitalists' profits. This contradiction has been uneasily resolved by paying men wages sufficient to take care of the whole family, while paying women nothing for their reproductive and child-care responsibilities.

The fact that working-class men receive a wage that is socially translatable into goods and services, whereas all of women's domestic labor is unpaid, gives men leverage in dealing with the family and makes women dependent on men. While lower-class men are subordinate to their bosses, they have some leverage with their wives, which they translate into power and privileges. It is in the capitalists' interest to support men's domination of women in the domestic sphere, because this distracts lower-class men from organizing with other men to fight for higher wages and more of the total wealth produced within the public sphere of work. For a summary of Vogel's argument see chart, "Total Social Wealth Produced."

While Marxist theories succeed in identifying the source of exploitation—that is, the division of labor into necessary and surplus labor—they fall short in the following ways:

1. Marx and Engels believed that primitive societies lived in kin groups and clans from the beginning and that nuclear families were a product of capitalism. Modern research into the earliest societies (hunter-gatherers) shows that nuclear families (domestic labor) existed *long before* any extended families or kin groups. Whatever part nuclear families play in supporting capitalism, their existence *per se* cannot be linked to capitalism. They provided other functions in pre-capitalist societies. Far from being a universal tool of oppression, nuclear families existed in egalitarian societies, in which women's political and economic status was equal to that of men.

2. The division of work into domestic and public labor is based on the assumption that the

Figure 4.1 Economic (Marxist) Theories of Gender Inequality

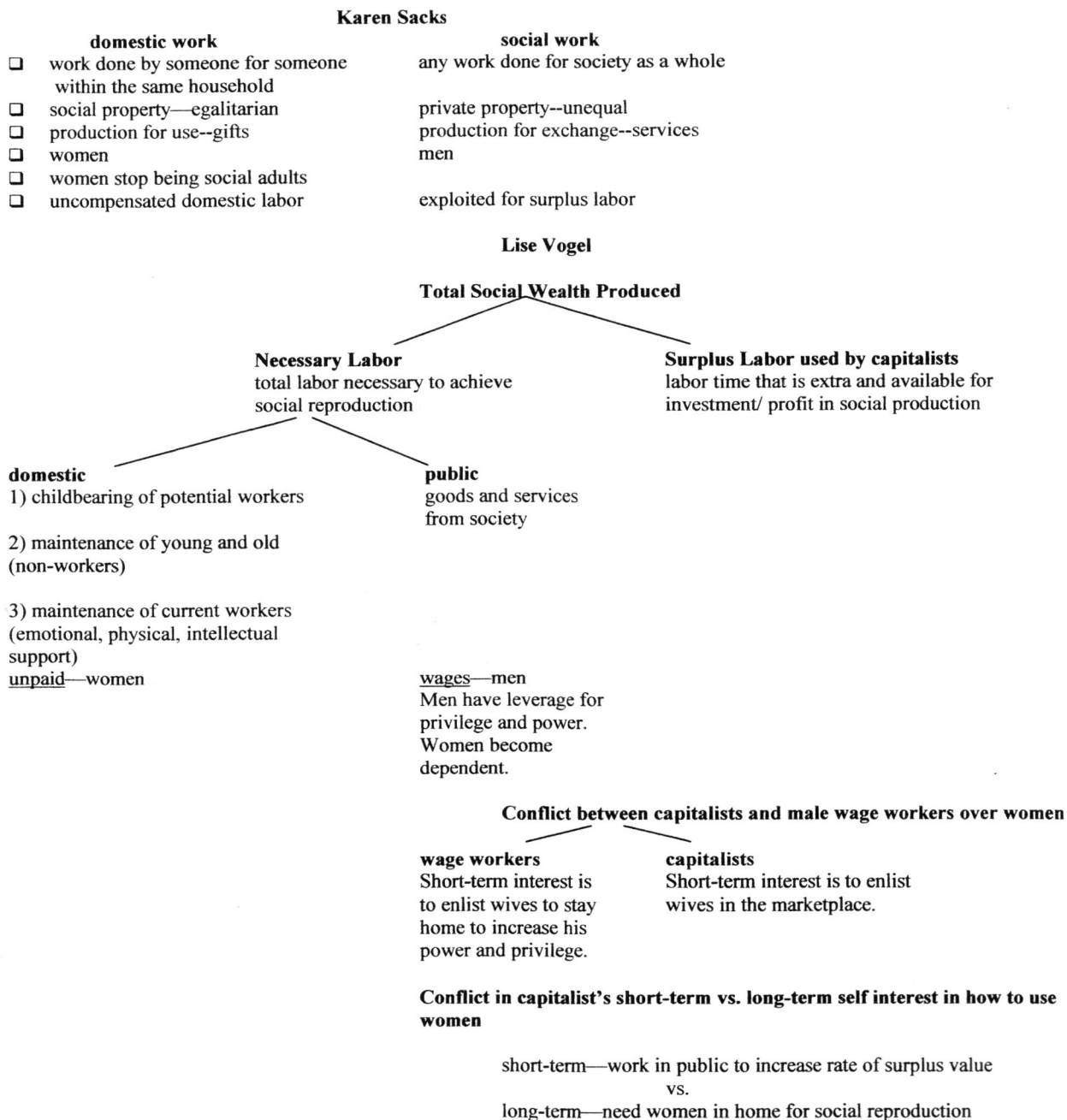

Karen Sacks

domestic work	social work
☐ work done by someone for someone within the same household	any work done for society as a whole
☐ social property—egalitarian	private property--unequal
☐ production for use--gifts	production for exchange--services
☐ women	men
☐ women stop being social adults	
☐ uncompensated domestic labor	exploited for surplus labor

Lise Vogel

Total Social Wealth Produced

Necessary Labor
total labor necessary to achieve
social reproduction

Surplus Labor used by capitalists
labor time that is extra and available for
investment/ profit in social production

domestic
1) childbearing of potential workers

2) maintenance of young and old
(non-workers)

3) maintenance of current workers
(emotional, physical, intellectual
support)
unpaid—women

public
goods and services
from society

wages—men
Men have leverage for
privilege and power.
Women become
dependent.

Conflict between capitalists and male wage workers over women

wage workers
Short-term interest is
to enlist wives to stay
home to increase his
power and privilege.

capitalists
Short-term interest is to enlist
wives in the marketplace.

Conflict in capitalist's short-term vs. long-term self interest in how to use women

short-term—work in public to increase rate of surplus value
vs.
long-term—need women in home for social reproduction

Women's unpaid domestic labor then supports:
a) the maintenance of labor force and profit for the public, political economy
b) the maintenance of male dominance within the domestic household
c) a severe spatial and temporal separation between the domestic and public economies

domestic household is essentially a *consumptive* unit in which no "social labor" is done. In fact, this is a recent development. The domestic unit in the *ancient world*, unlike the domestic unit in capitalist societies, was always a production unit and sometimes produced a surplus.

3. The division of society into a domestic and a public economy, and the association of women exclusively with the domestic economy is unique to capitalism. Since women worked in public as horticulturists and herders, they weren't nearly as dependent on men as the women in Sacks's and Vogel's scenario would have it.

4. The privileged group of chiefs in rank societies and the ruling castes in agricultural states were not nearly as systematic as capitalists in exploiting the labor of peasants. Unlike industrial capitalists, they didn't reinvest in the social infrastructure (e.g., in plants, roads, or workers) or deliberately set out to accumulate more capital. The upper castes of agricultural states engaged in Veblen's "conspicuous consumption" of exorbitant clothing, jewels, food, and drink—as well as indulging in various sexual excesses.

5. Herding societies were not the first societies in which individual private property emerged. Herders had a rotating form of group property. Engels was right to link domination by men with the act of taking care of large animals. But this occurred in complex horticultural societies as well as in herding societies.

6. Herding societies were not class societies. They were rank societies, according to Fried's typology (1967).

Marxian theories are helpful in determining the reasons for the exploitation of women in capitalist societies. The problem is that institutionalized male dominance is much older than capitalism.

2. Ecological theories

Peggy Reeves-Sanday claims that ecological and demographic pressures are the major causal determinants in the origins of male dominance. Sanday argues that, for pre-state societies that exist in lush environments and that maintain stable population densities, gender relations are more or less equal. However, when social stress arises—as a result of crowding, the scarcity of resources, or the necessity of living in a harsh environment—men and women do not deal with this stress in the same way. Men become more dominant over women under these circumstances.

A second part of her theory is that the more *segregated* work and childrearing practices become, the more men seem to dominate women. When men work at sites far away from women and are not responsible for raising their children, there is more male dominance.

A third part of her argument is that there is a relationship between the nature of basic resources and the relative power of men and women within society. When large animals are basic resources, men will be more dominant. When planting provides the basic resources, gender relations are more equal.

Sanday's research also suggests that demographics, ecology, work, and childrearing practices affect sacred beliefs. Sanday found that societies that have little social stress, have integrated work and childrearing patterns, and rely on planting for their sustenance, typically develop mythologies that are either female- or couple-oriented. Conversely, societies with great social stress, segregated work and childrearing practices, and dependence on large game have male- or couple-oriented mythology.

Sanday does little to explain the reasons for her findings. For example, why is it that under stressful conditions *women* don't become more dominant? Why do men and women deal with stress differently? Second, Reeves-Sanday does not explain why large-game hunting is correlated with increased male dominance, while planting is correlated with a minimum of male dominance. Nor does she explain why the segregation of work and childrearing leads to male dominance, while the integration of these practices does not. Why aren't women dominant when work is segregated? Finally, she tends to lump together simple and complex hunter-gatherer societies, simple and complex horticultural societies, and herding societies, and doesn't attempt to delineate precisely whether some of these tribal types might have different gender relations than others.

For example, both big-game hunting societies and herding societies deal with large animals, which presumably would be one factor supporting male dominance. Yet a simple hunting-and-gathering society is likely to have *egalitarian* political relations while a herding society has *rank* relations. Similarly, while Reeves-Sanday contends that horticulture societies will support gender equality because women do the planting, she makes no distinction between simple horticultural societies, which are egalitarian, and complex horticultural societies, which are ranked. This lack of attention to ways in which the political and economic relations of society impact gender dynamics is significant, as we shall see. We will discuss Reeves-Sanday's theory in more depth in the next chapter.

3. Structuralist theories

Rae Lesser Blumberg, the proponent of a structuralist theory of gender hierarchies, argues that the most important variables in determining gender inequality are control of the means of production and the allocation of surplus production. In the absence of this power, women will not have access to other forms of power, such as political power and knowledge bases.

More specifically, Blumberg argues not only that the means of production must be controlled but that they must be *indispensable*. Again, Chafetz's summary proves helpful:

For Blumberg, it is not women's ability to supply labor that determines their economic power—it is the demand for their labor that does so. [The demand for their labor is in turn determined by] the relative size of their contribution to total output; the short-run substitution costs at the margin of their labor (i.e. how difficult or costly it is to replace individual women workers); the extent to which they control technical expertise; the extent to which they work free from close male supervision; and the degree to which they

are able to collectively organize themselves. (Chafetz, 1988, 56)

Blumberg argues that gender stratification occurs at four levels—the household, the community, the social class (in complex societies), and the larger society as a whole. Women's power in one area is not absolute, because it can result in deterioration in a power in another area. Since men generally control the higher levels (society as a whole and the social class), more equality at the lower levels (the household and community) is less than significant. For example, a woman may convince her husband to agree with her decision to go to school to become an engineer, but if the schools she attends are male dominated and companies' hiring practices exclude women, her increased equality in the domestic household will not amount to much. On the other hand, changes for the better at class levels—women having more prestigious jobs in the work force and more economic parity with their husbands—will not necessarily lead to better relations at home. They can instead sometimes lead to spousal abuse at home at the hands of men who feel economically threatened.

Next to demand for labor, Blumberg argues that the most important factor in determining women's status is the pattern of inheritance—at least in kinship systems. The more property the woman can control, the greater her economic power. A final arena in which women's power can be sustained is in residency patterns. If a woman can continue to live among female kin after marriage, she will tend to have better economic support.

In her book *Sex and Advantage* (1984), Janet Chafetz synthesizes the work of Sanday and Blumberg and identifies 13 variables that affect the degree of gender stratification. These are gathered into three types of variables or types of causes. *Independent* variables include the systems such as the ecological setting, the demographics, and the technology used. These are the most important. *Primary* variables include the organization of work in the public and in the domestic economy. These are of secondary importance. *Secondary* variables are the ideological and stereotypical support for gender stratification. These are the least important. Chafetz's three types of variables closely correlate with the three dimensions of society described by Marvin Harris, as discussed in chapter 1.

The independent variables Chafetz includes as the most important factors in predicting the extent of gender stratification are the following:

1. Degree of environmental threat or harshness
2. Relative importance of physical strength and mobility in production
3. Population density
4. Average percent of the female life cycle devoted to childbearing and nurturance
5. Degree of separation of work and home-sites
6. Sex ratio
7. Type of technology
8. Relative societal emphasis on sustenance vs. surplus production
9. Perceived contribution to the resource base

Figures 4.2 and 4.3 represent my reworking of her findings on the *maximum* conditions for institutionalized male dominance. Figure 4.4 shows the implied conditions that *minimize* institutionalized male dominance. One of the benefits of Chafetz's work is that she distinguishes the ultimate causes from the proximate causes and points to specific feedback loops by which the variables affect each other. I will discuss more how each of the major variables interacts with other variables rather than focus on each sequentially.

To begin with, following Sanday, Chafetz claims that a physically harsh or threatening environment benefits men more than women: "The more harsh the physical environment, the greater the importance of physical strength and or mobility the productive activities will tend to be (94)." She goes on to point out how clearing new land periodically in horticultural societies or using the plow or working with large drafting animals requires great strength. A society's dependence on these activities will tend to make women more dependent on men. In addition, a difficult environment forces a society to move more often. This imposes difficulties on women who are raising children.

In addition, a harsh environment can potentially lead to wars with other societies over more fertile land. Since men almost always do the fighting, this encourages male bonding and violent ways of solving problems. Once men return from wars it is not easy to re-socialize them. The fighting of wars places higher value on boys (raising them to be warriors) and encourages female infanticide. Conversely, under conditions of ecological abundance, where a great deal of physical exertion is unnecessary to gain resources, traveling is unnecessary for the whole group and war is less of a temptation. This will work to the advantage of women.

Physical environments vary in the ease with which human beings can produce what they need to sustain life. At one extreme are deserts and the tundra where, with anything but the most sophisticated technology, it is very difficult to 'earn a living'. At the other extreme are places of moderate climate and rainfall, good soil and vegetation and extensive wildlife. . . .

In the preindustrial era, survival in a very harsh environment often depended on extensive physical mobility and strength. Pastoral societies . . . often existed in harsh environments where cultivation is difficult or impossible. Likewise, societies based heavily on hunting and fishing. . . . In areas somewhat less harsh. where cultivation is possible but difficult (because of very rocky terrain or extremely heavy vegetation) the physical labor required would be onerous compared to optimal cultivation environments. In all these cases male superiority in strength and/or mobility would tend to enhance their importance . . . sexual inequality is more extensive among Eskimos than among other hunting/gathering peoples. . . . Likewise, the desert herding societies of the Near East are among the most extreme of all societies in degree of sex stratification. (Chafetz, 1984, 83)

Figure 4.2 Chafetz's Conditions Promoting Gender Stratification

Category   **Consequences for other variables**

I Independent variables: Ecology, Demographics, Technology

1) environmental harshness/ threat
(vs. environmental abundance)
forces men to travel   use of heavier tools (more exertion)
harder on women carrying children   segregates labor between men and women
wars with other societies over scarce resources   encouragement of female infanticide: girls not as important

2) high population density
(vs. low population density)
larger number of children for women to care for   less time for women to work in public

3) high sex ratio (vs. low sex ratio)
more men than women leads to   supports environmental harshness--women as liabilities
privatization of labor and control by men   segregates labor
                                                                                             supports female infanticide

4) labor intensive technology
 (vs. capital intensive technology)
men control tools: physical strength is required   women excluded from public economy
                                                                                             loss of prestige in their labor

II Primary variables: Work and Family

5) production of economic surplus
(vs. production for subsistence)
surplus production invites trade and commodity   less prestige for women
production--men do this more

6) ownership of economic resources--land and
products of production
(as opposed to social ownership of resources)   less prestige for women
when men control this it limits women's autonomy
women work harder than men at dull, repetitive and
easily replaceable jobs

7) degree of separation of work from home-sites
(vs. integration of work at home-sites)
requires extra labor to go back and forth   women excluded from public economy
                                                                                             segregates men and women in work and childrearing

9) patrilineal descent line
(vs. matrilineal descent line)
men control how resources are passed down   in agricultural states encourages staying in a bad marriage
                                                                                             because of lack of work opportunities
                                                                                             supports male dominated religious ideology

10) patrilocal residency
(vs. matrilocal residency)
women's sexuality is more controlled   supports male-dominated religious ideology

III Secondary variable: Ideology

12) Religious support for gender inequality   supported by patrilineal descent, male ownership of
(vs. religious support for equality)   economic resources separation of home-work

13) Gender differentiation
(vs. gender integration)
stereotypes set up expectations of how genders act   supported by all variables above

Chafetz also concluded that the higher the population density, the greater the proportion of the female life cycle would be devoted to childbearing and nurturance (except in modern industrial societies, with their extensions of life expectancy, better sanitation practices, and medical technologies). Thus, in preindustrial societies with high population densities, women would have fewer options to contribute to surplus production, and would enjoy less prestige and power. Hunting and gathering societies have fewer sanitation problems than planting societies because they are not settled, but they face the same problems of low life expectancy and a lack of medical technology.

Another major variable is the gender ratio. Here a somewhat detailed explanation is required in order to convey the reasoning behind Chafetz' stance. Guttentag and Secord (1983) begin their book by stating that it is commonly believed that in all populations the number of male and female babies is almost exactly equal. However, they say that for much of human history the ratio of the numbers of adult women to men has been *unequal*.

In explaining this, they begin by naming conditions that can bring about an increase or decrease in absolute size of a population. High birth rates, low death rates, and the migration of outsiders into a society will maximally increase the size of the population. Conversely, low birth rates, high death rates, and the migration of people away to other societies will lower the size of the population. Under the latter conditions, the population will tend to be middle-aged. If a society needs a lot of children (as planting societies do), high birth rates and high death rates occurring together will tend to result in a young population. Conversely, in situations where child labor doesn't pay, low birth rates will remain low, and if modern health care is available death rates will also be low; the result will be an older population.

Regardless of the absolute size of the population, under what conditions will there be fewer women than men, or more women than men? In less warlike societies, the gender proportion will tend to remain close to 50/50. However, in societies that are more violent and are frequently at war, the proportions of men

to women vary dramatically. On one hand, many men may be killed during a war; but on the other hand, the society will place greater emphasis on having male children as replacements and female infanticide will increase. The two trends acting together rarely result in a stable population balance.

Further, Guttentag and Secord explore similarities and differences in men's and women's strategies when either gender is in short supply. When there is a *scarcity of women* are they more highly valued? Is there more courting of women? Is there more respect for motherhood? Would there be more of a commitment to a partner by a man? Are men more competitive with other men under these conditions?

These same questions can be posed in reverse. Does a *scarcity of men* result in the same treatment by women? Does a scarcity of men make them more highly revered? Do women court men more? Is there more respect for fatherhood? Are women more committed to men when men are scarce? Are women more competitive with other women when men are scare? Guttentag and Secord claim that men's and women's strategies will be different, but not for biological reasons.

Guttentag and Secord claim that the number of opposite-sex partners available to men or women has profound effects on sexual mores, marriages, divorce, and childrearing. However, scarce men and scare women differ in their strategies to deal with their situation. According to Guttentag and Secord, this is not necessarily because of biological differences between women and men, but because women—with the exception of those in hunter-gatherer and simple horticulturalist societies—lacked technological, political and economic power.

I have reconstructed the following chart (Figure 4.5) from Guttentag and Secord's work to show how men's and women's strategies differ when they are in undersupply or oversupply. The situation in which women are in oversupply or undersupply is represented in quadrants A and B; the situation in which men are in oversupply or undersupply is shown in quadrants C and D. Notice that in quadrants A and B, regardless of whether

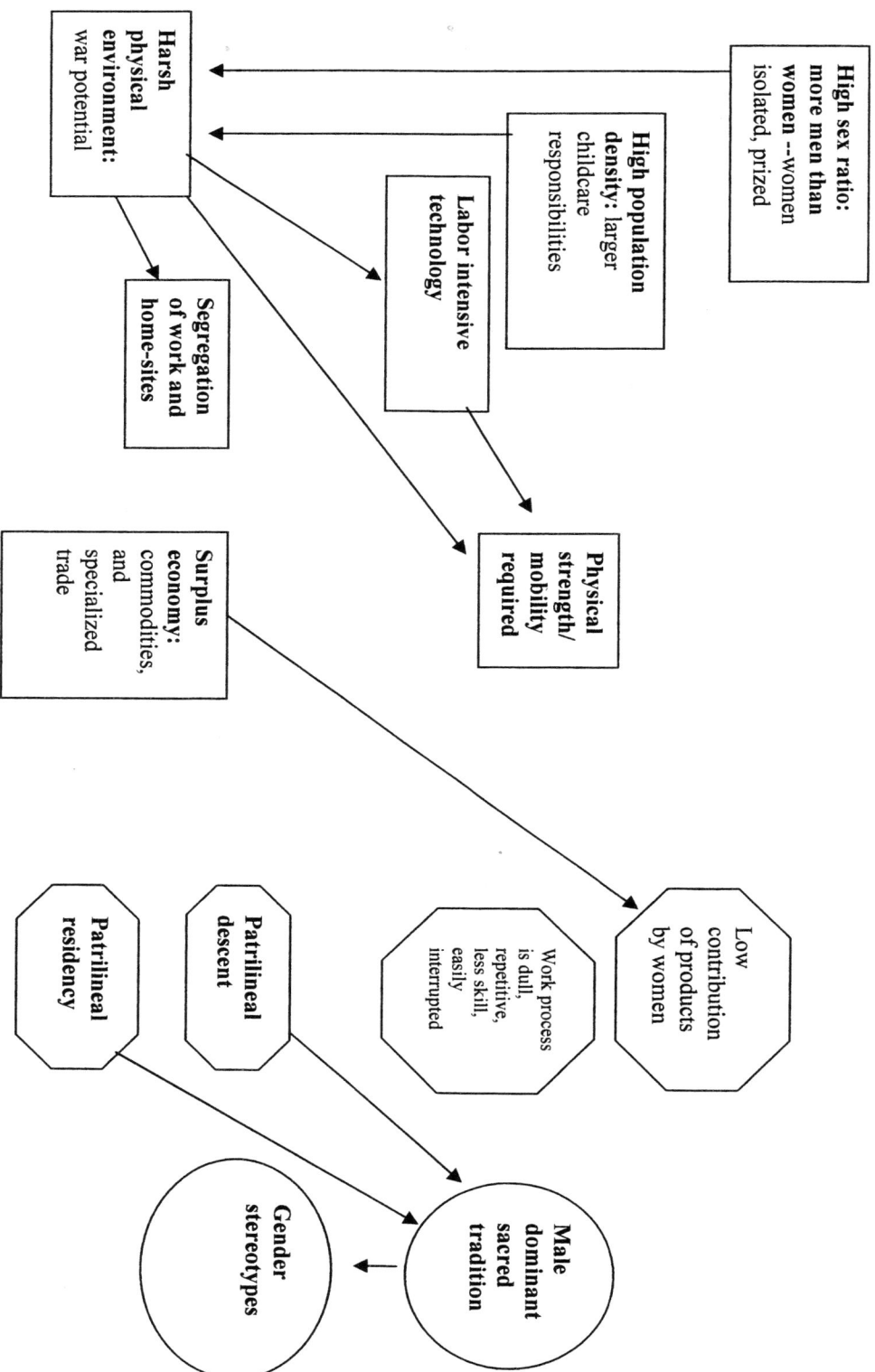

Figure 4.3 Conditions Maximizing Institutionalized Male Dominance (adapted from Chafetz, 1984)
Square is independent variable; octagon is primary variable; circle is secondary variable. Only the most powerful influences are given an arrow to keep the diagram from becoming overwhelming.

The diagram contains the following elements:

- High sex ratio: more men than women --women isolated, prized
- High population density: larger childcare responsibilities
- Harsh physical environment: war potential
- Labor intensive technology
- Segregation of work and home-sites
- Physical strength/ mobility required
- Surplus economy: commodities, and specialized trade
- Low contribution of products by women
- Work process is dull, repetitive, less skill, easily interrupted
- Patrilineal descent
- Patrilineal residency
- Male dominant sacred tradition
- Gender stereotypes

women are in undersupply or oversupply, they are not treated well. But how they are treated and what strategies they use differ.

If when *men* held dyadic power (i.e., the power accruing to either sex when it is in undersupply, thus making its members more valuable) their strategies and treatment were *the same* as those of women, quadrants C and D would result. However, the characteristics of these two quadrants are so unlike those of any known society that Guttentag and Secord have called them *imaginary* societies, and have given them special names. An undersupply of *men using women's strategies* is represented in quadrant C, which they title "Eros"; while an *oversupply of men in which women use men's strategies* is shown in quadrant D, which they call "Libertina."

Why don't women behave the same way when men are scarce as men behave when women are scarce? According to Guttentag and Secord, it is because *of differences between men and women in access to structural power*—i.e., technological, economic, and political power. In quadrants A and B, men have social structural power over women, and this affects women's strategies and treatment even when they have dyadic power, i.e., when they are scarce. In quadrants C and D women have *hypothetical* social structural power over men. The reasons the characteristics in quadrant C and D seem so unusual is that women have never had social structural power over men. Societies that corresponded to Quadrants C and D would be matriarchical.

Therefore, even when women are scarce, women do not strategize in the same way as men do, nor are they treated the same as men when men are scarce. This is because women's dyadic advantage is more than countered by men's control over social structural power. Men may treat women *differently* when women are scarce, but this situation is not necessarily better for women than one in which women are in abundance. For example, men will keep a "prized" woman home from work, preventing economic independence. Men may keep women from owning property or gaining an education. In fact, a good case can be made that under social structural conditions where there is

an oversupply of women, women have it better. This means that the loss of dyadic power that would come about if women were in oversupply might *improve* women's lives, if social structural conditions favored women.

Social structural conditions under which an oversupply of women would be countered by an improvement in women's position include: (a) if technology were capital intensive rather than labor intensive; (b) if there were opportunities to work in public; (c) if there were opportunities to become educated; and (d) if owning property were possible. At the same time, when medical technology is such that (e) contraceptives are effective so that women aren't pregnant most of the time, and (f) there are fewer pregnancy complications, an overabundance of women may work in their favor. Finally if (g) women have legal rights in the workplace in terms of equal pay and being protected from sexual harassment, and (h) the right to choose divorce, life will be better for women despite their losing dyadic power. As we will see in the last chapter, most, if not all of these conditions are unique to the industrial age, and were nowhere present in the ancient world.

In societies where men have structural power, such as in complex horticulture and agricultural states, an undersupply of women does not help women's cause. Women in agricultural states become specialists in domesticity and, among the upper classes, women are expected to cultivate their appearances, are kept as possessions, and are expected to tolerate polygyny. Since they rarely work in the public economy, their only way to be economically mobile is through marriage. Among the lower-class women, there is a greater chance for prostitution (quadrant A).

On the other hand, an undersupply of women in hunting-and-gathering and simple horticultural societies might work in women's favor, because politically and economically these societies are egalitarian. Women work in public and cannot be "kept."

Low sex ratio: more women than men women have more autonomy

Low population density: less childcare responsibilities

Abundant physical environment: less war potential

Capital intensive technology

Integration of work and home-sites

Less physical strength/ mobility required

Subsistence economy: little commodity production, little specialized trade

matrilineal residency

matrilineal descent

Work process is exciting, creative, more skill, less easily interrupted

High contribution of products by women

Egalitarian sacred tradition

Less gendered stereotypes

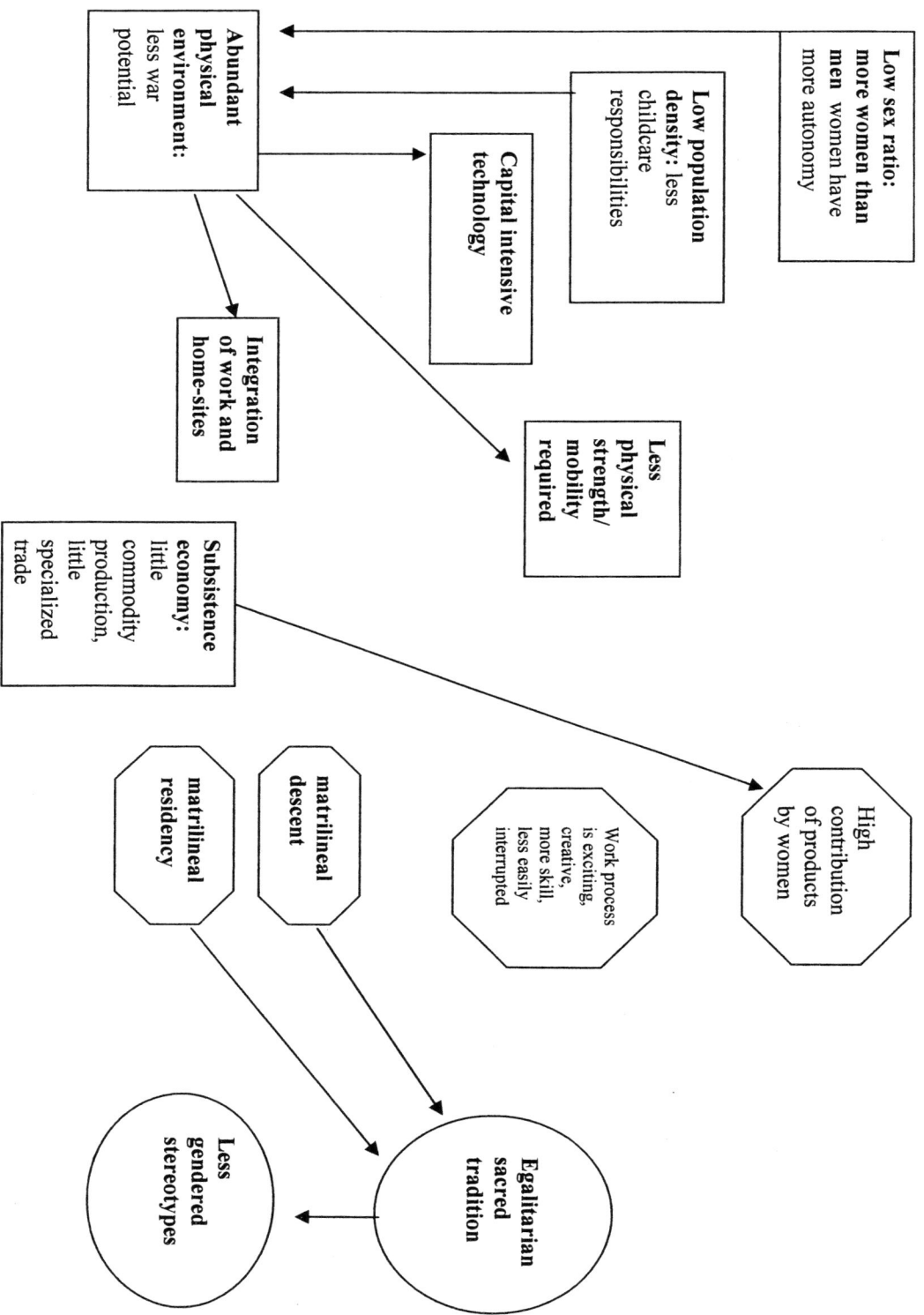

Figure 4.4 Conditions Minimizing Institutionalized Male Dominance (adapted from Chafetz, 1984)

Square is independent variable; octagon is primary variable; circle is secondary variable. Only the most powerful influences are given an arrow to keep the diagram from becoming overwhelming.

An *oversupply* of women in egalitarian societies can also work to some extent in women's favor. In fact, it is in egalitarian societies, when men are away for long periods of time in wars, that matrilineal and matrifocal social structures emerge and women assume more prestigious social roles. In such situations, there is no direct competition with men. Women are free to work in public, and sexual standards are more permissive. It is in agricultural states that an oversupply of women works against women the most, because it is in these social structures that they have the least socio-structural power.

Thus it is in conditions where men and women are politically and economically egalitarian that the condition of being in undersupply *or* oversupply can work in women's favor. In such conditions, women can move out of quadrant A or B.

However, egalitarian conditions are not enough to move women into using the strategies in quadrant C or D. As we saw in the last chapter, at no point in history have women controlled the social system and subordinated men. Therefore, in egalitarian conditions, women's strategies and treatment would fall somewhere toward the center of the quadrant diagram.

The next varible, technology, can also work for or against women. According to Chafetz, "a technology may be said to be more sophisticated than other technologies when it permits greater productivity per person, regardless of the level of human exertion required, and/or when it permits the same level of productivity with less exertion." (1984, 100) For instance, a technology that is less labor-intensive can allow more women to participate in greater numbers in the labor force. As we saw earlier, however, a technology that is very labor-intensive can actually drive women out of the labor force. A capital-intensive technology can override many other factors that might normally favor male dominance. It can overcome a harsh environment, or the need for all members of society to travel or to make war.

At this point Chafetz addresses the question of whether the real difference between men and women in physical strength and mobility (which men use to their advantage in technology) *cannot* be used as a *general* explanation for institutionalized male dominance. She cites four reasons.

First, male superiority in size and strength is relatively constant independent of time and space. Yet the degree of male dominance from society to society varies. If physical strength were a major consideration in the production of male dominance there would be no variance cross-culturally in the degree of male dominance.

Second, why single out physical strength as a major criterion in establishing gender hierarchies when no one uses it to explain other systems of stratification, such as class, caste, or slavery?

> The size/strength differences between the largest and smallest males are at least as great, if not greater than the average differences between males and females. (Chafetz, 1984, 118)

Third, though the average male is stronger than the average female, the average man does not necessarily have the power to use this additional strength against any woman in all times and places. In stratified societies, formal power is invested in the state. There is at least as much coercion between the military and non-military *men* as there is between non-military men and women.

Finally, humans are essentially a social species.

> We are impelled to live together and work collectively to extract from our environment that which we require to sustain ourselves. . . . While individuals may often be brutal, it is inconceivable that collectively males would choose to brutalize females intentionally to shape social structure to their advantage. While human nature is at least partially egocentric, in technologically simple societies self-interest is best served through cooperation and sharing. . . . Under such circumstances both the social nature of our species and enlightened self-interest

Figure 4.5 Impact of Sex Ratios in Gender Dynamics

I. Male Structural Power: Institutionalized Male Dominance

**A) high sex ratios
(undersupply of women)**

women hold dyadic power

highly valued for beauty and glamour
married women valued as wives and mothers
willing to make and keep a commitment
valued as chattel and possession
traditional roles
gain economic mobility through marriage

little career ambitions
virginity
romantic love

**B) low sex ratios
(oversupply of women)**

men hold dyadic power

devalued by society

higher divorce

feminism--political independence
difficulty with economic mobility through
marriage
stronger career ambitions
not virginity
lesbianism as an alternative

II. Female Structural Power: Institutionalized Female Dominance
(Hypothetical: Matriarchies)

**C) high sex ratios
(undersupply of men)**

men hold dyadic power

"Eros"--men acting like women

men are treated as romantic love objects
idealized in songs composed by women
physical attributes are prized
male beauty contests

men are promised financial and emotional support
women have little to do with childcare
men revere the roles of father and homemaker

wife is 2-3 years older
men are expected to remain virgins
premarital intercourse disastrous to their reputation
most degraded men are in brothels patronized by
women
men dress in a blatantly sexual way
solicit on streets: female pimps
men are better able to control their sexual impulses
than women

**D) low sex ratios
(oversupply of men)**

women hold dyadic power

"Libertina"--women acting like men
women are promiscuous
have more than one man
low regard for men
most often remain single
women are not expected to remain with men
throughout childrearing years

single parent families headed by men
men fight for economic and sexual
independence
more men are unhappy than in Eros societies

mitigate against the wholesale use of force to impose domination by one-half of the species over the other half. (Chafetz, 1984, 119)

Another important causal factor in determining gender dynamics is the extent to which a society produces for subsistence or for surplus. Producing a surplus in one area usually implies the anticipation of trade with other societies for goods and raw materials that are not to be found in the home society. Thus the society with the surplus will begin to produce commodities and trade them. Societies that produce a surplus usually develop high population densities. When this is the case, women will spend most of their time raising children and engaging in cottage industries at home. This is truer in agricultural states than in complex horticulture societies, but the impact is the same. Women have less time available to work as either artisans or as traders. Men will control these occupations.

Conversely, a subsistence economy tends to favor a closer balance in gender relations. However, if women produce a low percentage of products for a subsistence economy, they will have lower status:

. . . in societies, which produce a surplus, the extent to which the activities of each sex contribute to that surplus—exchange goods—is important. Exchange (surplus) production is typically more highly valued everywhere than sustenance production because surplus goods can be exchanged outside the family to create non-kin networks of mutual obligations. (Chafetz, 1984, 13)

Surplus production enhances the prestige and power of those engaged in production tasks.

In work life, perhaps the most important factor in determining the power balance between the genders is their relative contribution to the resource base of society. Whichever gender is perceived to contribute more will have more control over ownership, distribution, and consumption. Perception is important here, because even if one group of people objectively produces more than another, this does not mean it will be fairly compensated. For example, it could be argued that a teacher contributes more to socially necessary reproduction of culture than an athlete does, but successful athletes make salaries far larger than those of teachers. In addition to the input to the subsistence or surplus economy, another factor comes into play: the low skill level—meaning that it is easily replaceable and easily interruptible—of some women's work typically works against women's status.

We will now turn from the *independent variables* to the *primary variables* that govern women's status in societies, according to materialist theories. Chafetz claims that, within the domestic structure, there are at least three important dimensions to consider. The first is whether descent is traced though the male or the female line. The gender through which descent is traced can control whatever property and resources are passed down across generations. In simple horticultural societies, where women have relatively equal status to men, transfer of wealth is accomplished by a "bride price." In these societies, the husband must transfer wealth or labor to the bride's family upon engagement or marriage. The man's group must pay for this because a woman's labor in these societies is considered valuable. At the same time, this situation can work against women's interests, in that a woman will typically be encouraged to stay in a bad marriage because her kin group does not want to return the bride price.

In agricultural states, women's work in the domestic economy is less valued. In these conditions it is the wife's kin group who must pay her suitor's family to take her off their hands. This is called "dowry." In this case, a women's family will not encourage her to stay in a bad marriage; however, her occupational prospects outside of marriage are such that she probably would only undertake divorce as a last resort.

Residency is another primary variable. When a marrying woman must go to live with her husband's in-laws, she will tend to be more closely watched in the village and her sexuality will be more controlled. This is much less the case in hunting-and-gathering societies than in those that are horticultural, agricultural, or pastoral. When the man must go to live in the wife's village, her behavior will not tend to be controlled as much by others.

Finally, the further women have to travel from the home site, the more difficult it is for them to participate in both childrearing and public production. This leads to a segregation of labor and childrearing practices, which can easily cause misunderstandings between genders because they share a less common way of life. It can also more easily lead to stereotyping and mistrust.

With regard to secondary variables, Chafetz has little to say about ideological systems because these simply tend to support the factors already discussed. For example, the greater the degree of gender stratification the greater will be the degree of ideological support for gender inequality in sacred beliefs and morals. The higher the proportion of men to women in society (sex ratio), the more ideological support there will be for the strategies of men and women in quadrants A and B. On the other hand, the less structural inequality that exists between men and women and the more women outnumber men in the population, the more sympathetic spiritual beliefs will be toward women. Finally, the greater the sexual division of labor in the family, the greater will be the tendency to stereotype men and women. Conversely, the more the work roles in families overlap, the less is stereotyping likely.

In other words, ideology tends to legitimize what the social structure has already produced. Stereotyping seems to internalize the social structure. It is rare for ideology or stereotyping to cause the ecology, demography, technology, economy or political system to change in one direction or another.

Thus Chafetz's materialist theory of the factors impacting the origin of gender inequalities supports and underscores Harris's theory of improvised social change discussed in chapter 1.

Chafetz concludes by addressing the question of why is it that historically women have never held more social power than men. Her answer:

> . . . the degree of sex stratification is a direct function of the extent to which the organization of production permits women to contribute to the production of valued resources and to control the output of such production. The family structure also strongly affects women's status. (Chafetz, 1984, 21)

As long as women are primarily responsible for childcare, they can never equally compete with men in the public economy. This is consistent with Vogel's and Sack's theories we examined earlier. As long as childrearing is not seen as being as valuable as food gathering or the production of surplus goods, women cannot be equal, let alone superior.

> Women carry babies in their bodies and lactate, which circumscribes their physical mobility. While this can be minimized through low birthrates and bottle feeding, it cannot be eliminated and . . . such restriction due to pregnancy and nursing has been far from minimal. Most societies find it more efficient if women also do the bulk of the caretaking of children. That is, on the bases of expediency, the nurturance role is typically extended beyond the biologically based phenomenon of breast-feeding . . . it becomes more efficient to extend her domestic role to encompass other household tasks such as food preparation, and the maintenance of family possessions. (Chafetz, 1984, 22)

4. Deepening and expanding materialist theories

All materialist theories covered in this chapter try to explain the emergence of gender hierarchies by referring to either the infrastructure or the structure of society (as delineated in Harris's model).

Figure 1.1 summarizes the materialist theories discussed in this chapter. The Marxist theories of Sacks and Vogel emphasize the tension between the private, domestic economy and the public, political economy. Reeves-Sanday emphasizes the ecological-demographic crisis of overpopulation and resource depletion, which creates tension between genders. She also notes that the kinds of resources that are used and whether or not men and women work together impact the way men treat women. Blumberg emphasizes both the kind of work women do and the degree of economic control women have over it. Finally, Chafetz builds on the conclusions of Reeves-Sanday and Blumberg and adds that whether tools used are labor-intensive or capital-intensive helps determine how much power women have.

In the following chapters I hope to add the following:

1. As noted in the introduction, all materialist theories essentially ignore the power of the *superstructural* dimension to reinforce gender hierarchies. Chafetz does not discuss the superstructure in depth. Reeves-Sanday does mention that the the relative power of the genders over resources will be reflected in the culture's sacred mythology—whether it is male-, female-, or couple-dominated; however, this insight is not developed at length. My chapters 12 and 13, on the movement from magical animism to polytheism to religious monotheism, show explicitly how gender hierarchies are socially projected into sacred beliefs and mythologies. These chapters explain how changes in labor, technology, political centralization, and economic stratification are reflected in superstructural changes, causing societies to evolve from a belief in earth spirits to a belief in sky gods.

2. None of the theories discussed in this chapter has an explanation of how society gets inside of people's *psyches* and how people internalize social relations. Chafetz does mention "gender stereotypes," but only in passing.

In my chapters on self (chapter 16), cognition (chapter 15), and sense ratios (chapter 14), I show how the collective self, concrete abstraction, and the proximate senses of smell, touch, and hearing support a psychology of subordination and emerge out of the infrastructure and structure of society.

3. None of the materialist theories in this chapter discuss the impact of climate on human history. In chapter 10, I argue that there were dramatic changes in climate in the Bronze Age caused by natural disasters, and that these occurred at roughly the same time institutionalized male dominance was emerging.

4. Following the phenomenological geographers, I argue in chapter 14 that whether human ecological niches are conceived of as either "places" or a "spaces" impacts gender stratification.

5. None of the materialist theories takes on the question of the extent to which gender stratification is due to biological "hardwiring." For Marxists, discussion of biological differences is a doctrinaire taboo. For whatever reasons, Sanday, Chafetz, and Blumberg do not address the issue. In chapter 7, I discuss the strengths and weaknesses of evolutionary psychology in its emphasis on biological explanations for gender stratification.

6. There is no materialist theory to explain why women colluded with their oppression. There is no theory to explain why there was no women's movement, specifically in the ancient world. In the last chapter of this work, I draw on studies of the conditions under which social movements have arisen in the modern world and compare those conditions to the conditions in ancient society. Some of these conditions include the ability on the part of women to meet in the same time and the same place, the ability to read and write, and the presence of mass communication and mass transportation.

7. All theories in this chapter assume that the basic forces of social change proceed from the social infrastructure to the superstructure and from the superstructure into people's psyches. However, this movement is presented as if all these dimensions were changing at the same rate, as if there were no discrepancies between the rate of technological change and political change or the rate of economic change and the rate of change in sacred beliefs.

But, following Marvin Harris, we have seen that the ecological and demographic crisis occurs first, and responsive developments in the technological, economic, political, and superstructural subsystems follow. This means that there are usually contradictions across subsystems because the rates of change within the system are not the same.

In chapter 6, on the phases of female subordination, I present a five-stage process of institutionalized male dominance which encompasses four cycles, beginning with complex horticultural societies and culminating with classical Greek civilization (see Figure A at the end of the introduction). Because of the uneven rates at which the dimensions of society change, there can be periods in social evolution when women are subordinated without institutional coercion (complex horticultural societies); times when coercion exists without legitimation (early Bronze Age states), and times when legitimizing institutions exist but have not been psychologically internalized by those who are subordinated. In other words, the process of subordination is lumpy and uneven rather than smooth and symmetrical.

In summary, what I hope to add is:

1. A deepening of our understanding of the connection between the *superstructure* of societies and the material base of society.
2. A deepening of our understanding of the connection between the *psychology* of people in ancient societies and the material base of their society.
3. An introduction of a new understanding of the macrophysical impact of *climate* on society, including a discussion of catastrophic astronomical and geological events.
4. A discussion of *biological* considerations on the emergence of gender hierarchies.
5. An explanation for the uneven nature of the rate of social change through a *five-stage theory of female subordination.*
6. An exploration of the reasons for a *lack of reform or revolutionary women's movements,* specifically in the ancient world.

Part II

The Origin and Consolidation of Male Dominance

Chapter 5

Informal Male Dominance: Paleolithic and Early Neolithic Ages

1. Emergence of rank and stratification

Why did many egalitarian societies became ranked and stratified—was it merely that people are inherently greedy and it was just a matter of time before greed won out? Were ranking and stratification the inevitable results of societies becoming larger and more complex? Did inequality originate in a plot by a few conspirators?

The reasons macrosociologists have arrived at are more complex and subtle than any of these questions—taken by themselves or even together—might suggest. In chapter 1, I argued that social evolution is essentially "improvised" as a response to environmental pressures. However, we have yet to explore how the subgroups within society interact as the population grows and the resources become depleted. Will they cooperate more because of stressful conditions, or will they turn on each other? Do all subgroups typically agree on a strategy for changing their society, or are there conflicts between subgroups? What effect will the presence of subgroups with competing interests have on the determination of which strategies will win out? To what extent, if any, will coercion be involved?

In part, how the subgroups interact depends on whether the groups are egalitarian, ranked, or stratified *before* a social crisis occurs. It is easy to understand that, in societies that are already ranked and stratified, those groups that have some vertical power will have an advantage and will be able to protect their material goods and privileges during a crisis and use their power to consolidate existing inequalities. But how do *egalitarian* societies became ranked and stratified to begin with?

According to Sanderson (1991), there are two competing conflict theories of the origin of social differences between groups. One is Gerhard Lenski's *surplus* theory; the other is Sanderson's own *scarcity* theory.

Lenski claims that people strive to produce an economic surplus, and the most common way this surplus is generated is through technological advances. Once the surplus is created, it brings out the competitive side of people as they struggle over control of the surplus. The victors in the struggle then use their power to generate a greater surplus in order to increase their power, and this results in growing differences between groups. The victorious group provides integrative functions in social organization as well as exploiting other groups with its new-found power. Lenski's theory is called "surplus theory" because the generation of a surplus which results from technological advances is the original cause of social differences in entitlement and status.

Sanderson takes issue with a number of Lenski's assumptions—principally, that people seek technological innovation and welcome the change that comes with it. He also questions whether, if given a choice, people would prefer to work harder to produce a surplus rather than live on less and work less, thus having more leisure time. Lenski assumes that people are willing to produce a surplus first and struggle for its fruits later. For Lenski, egalitarian societies existed as long as they did because there was no surplus to tempt people and it is only the inability to discover new technologies that kept hunter-gatherers egalitarian. However, Sanderson argues that anthropological evidence suggests instead that culture is essentially *conservative:* People prefer to do things in traditional ways unless compelled to change; there are few incontestible examples of societies in the ancient world that have invented important new technologies and thus altered their ways of life except in response to necessity.

Sanderson's scarcity theory claims that the desire to create a social surplus is *not* shared among primitive societies. They do not automatically want to produce an excess of products because, in these societies, when people face a choice between having more and working harder or having less and having leisure, they choose the latter. Egalitarian societies are quite aware that that the production of a surplus can undermine the community. Even when they have the technology to produce a surplus they do not use it unless faced with a crisis. For example, Mark Cohen (1977) points out that hunter-gatherers knew how to plant hundreds of years before they began to rely on horticulture for the bulk of their food. Surplus creation is the end result of many other processes; it is not the ultimate generator of social inequality.

According to Sanderson, the process of change in entitlement starts not with a desire for more resources and goods, but with a crisis—population pressure and resource depletion. When a society's population increases and resources become depleted there is a struggle between groups over scarce land. The victorious group coerces political and economic reorganization for its own benefit. This restriction forces people to use the technology that had previously been suppressed in order to generate a surplus. Those now at the top of the hierarchy perform minimal coordination functions for society and mostly use the surplus to accumulate wealth and increase their leisure time. They use their position to consolidate social differences between groups, and to force the defeated groups to work harder to increase the production of social surplus.

This theory is called *scarcity* theory because it describes the emergence of hierarchy because of a lack of something—declining productivity in land, set against a rising population. In addition, Sanderson's theory assumes that people in such societies don't all agree that a surplus is needed or wanted. To the extent that a surplus is produced, it is only through the coercion on the part of the victorious group in the aftermath of a conflict with other groups.

The comparison chart Figure 5.1 summarizes some of the similarities and differences between Lenski's and Sanderson's theories.

Both Lenski and Sanderson argue that hunter-gatherers and early horticulturalists were egalitarian not because they were noble or altruistic, but because this way of life served their self-interest. They became unequal because later developments also served their self-interests.

These theories share common ground in that:

(1) the extent to which people cooperate or compete is determined by self-interest;
(2) there is a connection between lack of surplus and egalitarianism;
(3) there is a connection between the emergence of surplus and the rise of inequality;
(4) social change is generated through conflicts between groups; and
(5) groups existing at the top of the hierarchy exploit the lower groups.

But they differ over:
(1) when the technological and economic surplus takes place,
(2) when conflict between groups occurs, and
(3) the extent to which the emergent victorious groups perform integrative functions.

Lenski's theory claims that technological innovation and the prospect of generating surpluses drives social evolution. Sanderson argues that both are the product of a conflict between groups.

Lenski claims that conflicts between groups happen later, after a surplus is generated. Sanderson says that conflict between groups begins earlier over access to scarce lands.

Finally, Lenski is more sympathetic to the emergent elites than is Sanderson. Lenski claims that the victorious group discovers the exploitative possibilities of leadership after performing integrative functions for societies. Sanderson thinks the struggle over surplus and its exploitative possibilities drives the leaders to technologically, politically, and economically transform society from the beginning. Whichever group emerges victorious in a conflict will determine which strategy will prevail.

Lenski contends that a surplus comes first and that conflict between groups follows. Everyone in the society agrees that technological innovation and the creation of an economic surplus are good things, perhaps not realizing that these will entail unintended consequences. Sanderson says that conflict generates the surplus. People are not interested in technological innovation or surpluses, and will only produce them if coerced.

Thus the central issue between the two theories is this: Which comes first, the surplus or the conflict? Is the surplus produced first, voluntarily, by everyone, before the conflict emerges? Or is the conflict produced first, and the surplus follows after the victory of one of the competing groups?

For the most part, I agree with Sanderson's description of the origins of inequality, because it fits better with the reports of how modern hunter-gatherers actually live. The belief that change is better than stability, that technological innovation can be the foundation for a better way of life, and that the accumulation of a surplus of products is part of human nature are unique to industrial capitalist societies. Much of Lenski's theory is a projection of the ideology of progress back in time. Our modern attitudes toward change, technology, and the production of an economic surplus are exceptions to the rule, not the way people in most societies in history have thought.

Let us take a closer look at how egalitarian societies deal with crisis. Because a society is egalitarian, that does not mean that there is no tension among its people. When hunter-gatherers live together in bands, nuclear families are expected to share whatever game has been killed. Some of those who go out on hunting expeditions are not as skilled as other hunters, yet these individuals and their families are still given equal shares of the food; thus the nuclear families of the more skilled hunters are likely to have mixed feelings about sharing. Yet despite such tensions, during times of crisis people in such societies would still prefer to find an adaptive strategy that benefits everyone, rather than compete directly for resources and create ongoing inequalities.

During the transition between the Paleolithic and Mesolithic Ages, foragers were able to resolve the ecological crisis of running out of big game by reorganizing their means of subsistence *without creating rank relations*. Then again, at the transition between the Mesolithic and the Neolithic Ages, societies switched from hunting small game to horticulture while retaining their egalitarian relations. These crises did *not* result in the rise of inequality, but a *continuation* of egalitarian political and economic relations, with the affected societies merely adopting a different resource base.

These examples show that the emergence of inequality did not inevitably follow from a depletion of resources and a rise of population. As is still true today, crisis brings out the best and the worst in people. Periodic crises of population pressure and resource depletion intensified and dramatized whatever cooperative or competitive skills various groups already had. Crisis conditions test people, but don't cause them to behave in one single way. In egalitarian societies, it would probably have been especially easy to find an equitable strategy to resolve the ecological/demographic crisis, because all groups generally shared the same material interests.

However, a society's ability to sustain egalitarian relations when its population exceeds the available resources seems to depend on the possibility that at least some of its members can move to new territory. In all egalitarian societies in which cooperation was voluntary, if a subgroup didn't like a given social policy they could simply move, thus keeping potential conflicts from coming to a head. But when there was some pull or push to

Figure 5.1 Process of the Origin of Political Inequality

Surplus theory (Lenski)	Scarcity theory (Sanderson)

a) Assumptions

People seek change and innovation voluntarily.	People resist change unless forced.
People strive for economic surpluses.	People do not strive for economic surpluses and are suspicious of them.
People constantly strive to develop new technologies.	People do not strive to develop new technologies and suppress them until a crisis.

b) Steps in the generation of inequality

1) technological advances.	1) population pressure--suppression of technology.
2) increased economic productivity.	2) depletion of resources.
3) formation of economic surplus.	3) conflicts between groups for scarce land.
4) struggle for control over surplus. Political and economic coercion to increase surplus.	4) coercion by the victorious group to make technological, political and economic changes to generate a surplus.
5) emergence of inequality.	5) emergence of inequality.
6) leaders at first perform integrative functions later, exploitative functions.	6) leaders perform exploitative functions, integrative functions are minimal.
7) further increases in surplus production leads to increases in power of the victorious group.	7) further increases in surplus production leads to increases in power of the victorious group.

c) Commonalities
1) the extent to which people cooperate or compete is determined by self-interest.
2) there is a connection between lack of surplus and egalitarianism.
3) there is a connection between the emergence of surplus and the rise of inequality.
4) social change is generated through conflicts between groups.
5) groups existing at the top of the hierarchy exploit the lower groups.

stay together—because they were biophysically circumscribed by surrounding mountains, deserts or large bodies of water, or because they were socially circumscribed by other surrounding groups—conflicts were not so easily avoided by moving. For the people living in such societies, the creation of a hierarchy must have seemed preferable to enduring ongoing conflict. Thus, if we were to try to locate the geographic origins of inequality, we might look for times and places in prehistory when egalitarian societies located near mountains or deserts faced population pressure and resource depletion.

Until now, I have presented the emergence of inequality as being driven by a response to necessity. But will people in some situations choose rank relations in the *absence* of a crisis? Suppose there is a concentration of resources in a certain area and people gravitate to this resource in ecological circumstances that are *not* geographically circumscribed, and moving away is still a choice. Can rank relations emerge in such circumstances?

Fishing societies are typically located near a large body of water. Such a resource, if abundant, will attract many groups because much food can be obtained with little expenditure of energy. As the population expands, groups of families will vie with each other for these resources. If conflicts break out, then various groups who are part of this conflict will have to weigh the costs and benefits of staying against the costs and benefits of moving to another location.

The benefits of staying may be being well fed and not having to work hard, but these will be weighed against having to take orders from a ranked group that has successfully emerged on top as a result of the subgroup conflict. The benefits of leaving will be not having to take orders or to defer to other groups; but the cost is withdrawal to an area where resources aren't as abundant and where the group will have to work harder for what it has. Thus another possible condition for creating unequal political relations is the concentration of abundant resources in one place. Under these conditions,

societies don't create inequalities out of ecological or economic necessity, but because they are choosing less work, more resources, and mild forms of submission against harder work, less abundant resources, and maintaining political autonomy.

The case of egalitarian simple horticultural societies is somewhat different. In these societies, kin groups form outside the nuclear family and it is expected that food will be shared with kin members regardless of their contribution. The tensions within simple horticultural societies would tend to be greater, because gardening engenders a less mobile lifestyle than does foraging.

As we saw in chapter 2, when simple horticulture societies not only face population pressure and resource depletion but live in arid climates with little variety in pristine resources and are surrounded by biophysical and social constraints, groups begin to compete for scarce land. Rank relations became more tempting for a variety of reasons. Often, an irrigation system is needed because of the dry climate, and a centralized system of authority can be more efficient in managing such a system. Also, if the society lacks access to pristine natural resources, it is likely to depend on trade with other societies in order to obtain essential goods; centralization can help systematize trade. Finally, in order to have goods to trade, the society must intensify the production of whatever it is they have; and centralization can facilitate the production of a surplus. It is in these conditions of scarcity where Sanderson's theory seems to work.

A fourth reason for the emergence of rank from egalitarian societies is that property relations in horticulture societies are different from those in hunting-and-gathering societies. In the latter, the land is owned by everyone. As people settle into villages and begin gardening, kin groups tend to claim rights over sections of the land. This "ownership" does not entitle the claimants to exclude other groups from access to the land, but it does give them some proprietary benefits. When such societies face a crisis, it tends to be experienced more severely than in hunting-and-gathering societies because of the three conditions described in the

Figure 5.2 Comparison of Chiefdoms and States*

Commonalties in how they arise
> Population pressure
> Resource depletion
> Limited pristine resources
> Geographical circumscription
> Proximity to a large body of water

Commonalties in structure
> Need for irrigation systems
> Centralization
> Differential access to wealth
> Institutionalization of male dominance

How the State Differs from Chiefdoms: Biophysical and Infrastructure Dimension
> Deeper population pressure (over-crowded villages)
> More intensive cultivation of land (agriculture, not horticulture)
> Use of iron rather than stone tools (more durable, flexible)
> Use of plow, rather than hoes or digging sticks
> Greater food production
> Longer term food storage
> Greater specialization of labor and centralization
> Longer working hours for most castes
> Deterioration of diet

How the State Differs from Chiefdoms: Structure (Economics and Politics) Dimension
> Stratified rather than rank political relations
> Emergence of a military class
> Greater material wealth
> Taxation
> Conscription for wars, monumental architecture

---

* adapted from Lerro (2000) pg.55

preceding paragraph. Perhaps because of this, it is more difficult for the kin groups to cooperate rather than compete over the land. The kin group that is victorious appropriates the land of the other kin groups and attempts to centralize production, reorganize the economy, and force people to work harder—primarily to maximize and consolidate its power, and secondarily to resolve the ecological and demographic crisis. As we saw in chapter 2, big men become chiefs.

This process must have taken a more violent form when chiefdoms faced an ecological/demographic crisis in their movement from rank to stratification. There would have been the same conflict over scarce land, but this time the subgroups would not have been competing on an equal footing. In these conditions, it is not likely that a *single* strategy would have been found to be the ecological/demographic crisis, because these groups would now have had different material interests, since they were already ranked.

Some chiefly kin groups used the power they acquired to economically and politically reorganize complex horticultural villages into states. They forced people to work harder and put to use any technology that had been suppressed previously, creating even greater surplus. The chiefly kin group became the divine King and Queen of the agricultural state. The district managers of the villages in complex horticulture societies became the warriors. The shaman of tribal societies became the priest or priestess of the agricultural state. Artisans of chiefdoms lost their autonomy and became part of the divine household, working exclusively for it. Commoners of complex horticulture societies became the peasants of agricultural states.

Figure 5.2 provides a summary of the differences between chiefdoms and states.

2. Incipient gender hierarchies: informal male dominance

In the first chapter, I argued that people in all societies have to work to produce and reproduce their existence. They have to exert power—i.e., harness energy in order to do work. Further, societies build social systems—composed of infrastructure, structure, and superstructure—in order to harness that energy. Over time, many societies develop forms of entitlement and status that allow some people to work less, consume more, and decide social policy.

In chapter 2, I also discussed three broad categories of entitlement—egalitarian, rank, and stratified social relations. Further, I defined three levels of status—influence, prestige/privilege, and power. Egalitarian societies—hunting and simple horticultural societies—have horizontal power and allow for influence and prestige but not privileges. Rank and stratified societies not only have influence and prestige, but certain groups have privileges and wield vertical power.

In a more visual form:

> egalitarian societies—
> > influence and prestige
> > no privileges
> > horizontal power
>
> rank and stratified societies—
> > influence and prestige
> > privileges
> > vertical power

In the first section of this chapter I presented a model that describes the process of how these shifts in status might have occurred. However, this description is limited to the relationship between groups consisting of both men and women. It says nothing about the differences *between* men and women within and between groups. In egalitarian societies, were men and women equally using influence? Did they have the same prestige? And did they have equal access to horizontal power? In other words, is the origin of *gender* hierarchies *coextensive* with the emergence of rank and stratification in societies as wholes? Does it precede, or follow from, these other forms of hierarchy? If the formation of gender hierarchies preceded or followed the origin of rank and stratification, what did the process look like? Was it similar to or different from the seven-stage process outlined in Sanderson's model?

In chapter 3, I defined institutionalized male dominance as the power and control by a few men over all women and most men throughout the infrastructure, structure, and superstructure of society, with all men having some privileges over all women. This occurs in rank and stratified societies. More specifically, this means that some men determine technological, political, and economic power—the right to control production and distribution beyond the household, and all the decision-making processes that go with it. Men also have the military power that can force women to go along with this, and men also control the myths that people live by. This does not mean male dominance was *absolute,* however.

It would be naive to associate all political power with *public* power. Earlier, in a discussion of the political structure of hunting-and-gathering societies, I noted that not everyone has to be a formal "leader" in order to exert political power. If decisions are based primarily on *consensus,* people not in formal public decision-making roles, such as women, can still exert a great deal of political power. The Ashanti, the Iroquois, and the Dahomean women all had the right to veto male actions. Among the Cheyenne, women possessed considerable influence, being great persuaders and cajolers. Cheyenne tradition credits a woman with the founding of the Council of the Forty-Four, the oldest of their formal institutions. According to one long-time observer, the women were the *real* final authority in the camp.

Even in stratified societies, such as agricultural states, women in upper classes still influenced the decision-making processes behind the scenes and possessed great prestige, even if they did not wield social power publicly. Of course, prestige and behind-the-scenes influence were not equivalent to the power to publicly formulate social policy; however, they did prevent male power from being all-encompassing.

Gender hierarchies were coextensive with *political* hierarchies between groups—that is, rank and stratification—once political hierarchies had emerged. But if institutionalized male dominance did not emerge until the appearance of rank and stratified societies, does that imply that men and women in egalitarian societies were equal *in all respects*? Were they equal in influence and prestige? Were there seeds of institutionalized male dominance in societies that did not exhibit political rank and stratification?

To this question we must answer with an unqualified *yes.* There is abundant anthropological evidence to attest that men in egalitarian societies typically dominated public leadership, were allowed multiple marriage partners, had priority in tracing descent and residency patterns, and never had full responsibility for raising children.

It is true that not all egalitarian societies allow men all these "perks." Thus it is important to examine what conditions in egalitarian soceities seem to correlated with more, or less, informal male dominance. I will use Peggy Reeves-Sanday's ecological theory described in chapter 4 to explore this issue.

Reeves-Sanday (1981) conducted a cross-cultural study of 150 pre-state societies and found that there is a correlation between male power over women, the use of large animals as a resource base, food scarcity, crowding, invasions, or forced migrations. Conversely, there is a correlation between gender equity and the use of plants as the main resource base, sufficiency of food, the ability of people to stay in any given area as long as they want, and the presence of plenty of room in which they can spread out. Briefly: There is a definite correlation between *social scarcity and stress* with *male dominance,* and *abundance and lack of stress* with *gender equality.*

Reeves-Sanday notes that, among the Hadza of East Africa, the opposition between the sexes is more pronounced during the dry season, when camps swell and large animals congregate near a few available bodies of water. During the wet season, however, food becomes more abundant and evenly dispersed. Under these conditions, the sexes live relatively harmoniously in small, widely scattered camps subsisting on roots and small game.

Reeves-Sanday also argues that male dominance is likely to occur less frequently or with less intensity when tribal societies have *integrated* work and child-rearing patterns. Conversely, when work patterns and child-rearing are segregated, patterns of male dominance will tend to be exacerbated. For example, in big-game hunting societies, men tend to go off by themselves; whereas in small-game hunting, the whole family cooperates in the hunt. When only men go off to hunt, the women are left to rear the children alone. But if the men hunt small game, they are likely to be around to help raise the children. It makes sense that men who help with childrearing would be likely to be more patient and to learn to deal with stress more constructively, since the future of the family depends on it.

Furthermore, these shifts in material culture are reflected in mythology. Thirty-eight out of forty-three societies that rely on large-game hunting possess either couple- or male-origin sacred mythologies. On the other hand, 72% of those cultures which relied on small game had prominent female-origin myths.

Male distancing in society (being away at work and not being available for child rearing) also appears to have its reflection in mythology. Male creation myths present the beginning of the world as miraculous, coming from a distant sky or other lands. Also, there is a distance between the male deity and his creation. Creation occurs when the god crafts the first man or animals out of clay. Creation myths that emphasize the role of a female deity rely on biological metaphors. Stories are typically about creation through sexual union, and the deities are closer to the Earth. Reeves-Sanday argues that people weave their fantasies about the mythological origins of power from their perception of the forces most responsible for their necessities of life. Power is attributed to whichever sex is thought to embody the forces people depend on to meet their needs.

There are, then, *degrees* of male dominance. Even in egalitarian societies in which there isn't any privilege or vertical power, there is still influence and prestige. A kind of informal, non-institutionalized male dominance emerges in egalitarian societies when the influence and prestige of some men is enhanced under stressful circumstances, and when work and childrearing practices are segregated.

Informal male dominance (Reeves-Sanday calls it "mythological male dominance") occurs, according to her, when men use their influence and prestige, behave aggressively towards women, act bossy, and strut around, believing they are superior. However, they lack the institutionalized power to consolidate these attitudes and convert them into a systematic exploitation of women as a way of life. Also, in informal male dominance women actively combat these attitudes, humor the men, and typically do not believe that they are really inferior. Informal male dominance not only lacks in an institutional base, but fluctuates even within a given society at different times of the year.

To summarize Reeves-Sanday's work:

Informal male dominance

large animals as a resource
food scarcity, crowding, migration
segregated work patterns
segregated child-rearing
male or couple creation myths

Minimal or no male dominance

plants as a resource
food abundance, no crowding, settled
integrated work patterns
integrated child-rearing
female or couple creation myths

It seems reasonable to assume (though Reeves-Sanday herself does not make this argument) that, within the general phenomenon of informal male dominance, there are gradations, depending on how many of the conditions above are present or absent.

I will call "extreme informal male dominance" a gender dynamic in which all five conditions above are operating. This would occur when an egalitarian tribal society used large animals as a resource, experienced ecological and demographic stress, had segregated work and child-rearing practices, and had an exclusively male mythology. "Mild informal male dominance" occurs when there are stressful conditions (population pressure and resource depletion) but the work and childrearing practices are integrated. Mild informal male dominance might also occur when the work patterns are segregated, but people are living under bountiful conditions.

Let us see how these degrees of informal male dominance translate into types of societies within the social evolutionary scheme we have already developed (please see Figure 5.3 for an overview).

On the whole, institutionalized male dominance is absent in foraging societies, because there is no public economy for men to control, and there are no centralized systems of coercion that could back up that control. But *extreme informal male dominance* would have been likely to have emerged in big-game hunting societies under stressful circumstances. About 11,000 BCE, when foraging societies were running out of big game, just such circumstances probably existed. Extreme informal male dominance would also likely have emerged in some horticulture societies, just prior to the rise of chiefdoms, about 6000 BCE, where ecological and demographic stress combined with the division of labor—women planting and men clearing the land, with women being solely responsible for childrearing—to undermine egalitarian traditions.

Mild informal male dominance would occur in small-game hunting-and-gathering societies under stressful conditions. This is because, while the working conditions and childrearing practices are typically integrated (favoring women), stressful ecological or population problems would benefit men. Another social circumstance fostering mild informal male dominance would be big-game hunting societies under bountiful conditions. The segregated work-patterns favor men, but the bountiful conditions are good for women. Under these conditions, mythological creation symbolism is likely to be couple- or male-centered. A third situation when mild informal male dominance might occur is in simple horticulture societies under bountiful conditions. Here the abundance of resources and the lack of crowding tempers the segregation of labor and childrearing practices.

This period of time historically, when mild or extreme informal male dominance would have begun, would likely have been between 10,000 and 5000 BCE. This then raises interesting questions about the psychological states of "big men" who lived in simple horticultural societies in a time in which male dominance was very low. It would seem that the presence of segregated work and childrearing practices in horticultural societies would have supported informal male dominance by the big man, but under bountiful conditions this power would be mild.

The relationship of big-men to male dominance centers on the question of whether simple horticultural societies are under stress. Simple horticultural societies were predominant in the Old World between 8000 to 6000 BCE. During this period, when there was low population density and abundant resources, male dominance was mild. In fact, it makes sense that part of the *psychological* motivation to become big men was probably to acquire an influence and prestige they had *lost* since big-game hunting ceased to be an option.

Figure 5.3 The Seeds of Male Dominance in Egalitarian Societies

	Stressful	Non-Stressful
Ecological/ Demographic Pressures		
	food scarcity (resource depletion)	food abundance
	crowding (population pressure)	non-crowding
	forced migrations	voluntary migrations or sedentary
	large game animals	plants
Division of Labor:	segregated	integrated
Childrearing Practices:	segregated	integrated
Sacred Practices:	male creation mythology	female or couple creation mythology
Gender Relations:	informal or "mythological" male dominance	minimum male dominance

Types of informal Male dominance:	extreme informal male dominance male	mild informal dominance	
Anthropological/ Archeological examples:	big game hunter-gatherers under stressful conditions 12,000 BCE	big game hunters-gatherers under bountiful conditions 30,000-12,000 BCE	
		small game hunter-gatherers under stress 9,000 BCE	small game hunter gatherers under bountiful conditions 11,000 BCE
	simple horticultural societies under stress 6,000-5,000 BCE	simple horticultural societies under bountiful conditions 8,000-5,000 BCE	

Adapted from Peggy Reeves Sanday (1981) <u>Female Power and Male Dominance</u>

However, under *crisis* conditions, the prestige of a big man in a simple horticultural society would probably have turned into extreme informal male dominance. After all, even if unintentionally, the big man contributed to the building of a public (as opposed to a domestic) economy. This meant that when a *crisis* occurred in these societies, the big man would have been in an economic position to exploit his social position. In contrast, women were made more vulnerable by crisis. Eventually, big men would have been able to use their experience in the public redistribution practices to become chiefs and consolidate their power in the newly-formed ranked societies. It is in simple chiefdoms that institutionalized male dominance appears in a tenuous form.

To say that the initial motives for some men to vie for "bigmanship" were psychological does not mean that the results of the big man's actions were completely under his control. While some men may have initially become big men to overcome the insecurity that goes with a loss of occupational prestige, in a time of social crisis the position of a big-man as a centralizing agent becomes crucial in sustaining the public economy. While his motive may initially have been psychological, under stressful conditions any big man would have had to remain in his position for social reasons regardless of his initial psychological motives. Once the crisis was over, these men may have realized that they held a modest amount of power, and then began to consolidate their power over women and other men.

Just as it was a natural transition in work specialization for women to move from gathering to planting, so too would it have been a logical extension of roles for some men to move from *temporary* managers of the distribution system as "big-men" to *permanent* managers as chiefs. As we have seen, men had been the primary traders and formal decision makers even as far back as the hunting-gathering era.

But where in the evolutionary spectrum would we be most likely to find an *absence* of informal male dominance? There are two possible types of societies where conditions would foster maximum gender equality: (1) simple horticultural societies with plants as a primary resource, food abundance, no crowding, and settled conditions (though here two other conditions maximizing female equality would not have been present, because in simple horticulture societies work and childrearing practices are segregated); and (2) small-game foraging societies during the Mesolithic Period existing under bountiful conditions (these would feature integrated work and childrearing practices). However, the fact that small-game hunting rather than planting was the means of subsistence in this case worked against women, according to Reeves-Sanday's model.

In conclusion, *there were no societies I know of in which all five of Reeves-Sanday's conditions that support an absolute minimum of male dominance existed.* More importantly, *there were no societies in which informal female dominance existed.*

3. Integration of rank, stratification, and informal and institutionalized male dominance

The following is a temporal integration of the origins of *political and economic hierarchies* (rank and stratification) that we studied in section one of this chapter, combined with the origins of *gender* inequalities from section two of this chapter:

hunting and gathering; simple horticulture societies (Paleolithic, early Neolithic)
egalitiarian political-economic relations
minimum male dominance
mild or extreme informal male dominance
complex horticulture societies and herding societies (middle and late Neolithic)
rank political-economic relations
beginning of institutionalized male dominance
agricultural states, and commercial states (Bronze and Iron Ages)
stratified political-economic relations
consolidation of institutional male dominance

Let us look more closely at the relationship between the origins of political-economic inequality and the origins of gender inequality. I will compare the conditions under which egalitarian societies either *remain* egalitarian or become ranked against Reeves-Sanday's conditions under which incipient forms of male dominance appear (Figure 5.3). An overview is provided in Figure 5.4.

In the left hand column of Figure 5.4 are all of the conditions that are likely to lead to the emergence of rank societies. The left-hand column is further divided into egalitarian *hunting-and-gathering* and egalitarian *simple horticulture* societies. On the upper right hand side are the conditions under which formal male dominance is likely to emerge from informal male dominance. Notice that on the right-hand side of Figure 5.4 I have grouped hunter-gatherers and simple horticulturists together. I have found that by doing so, the contrast between the two columns is clearer. The easiest way to understand this figure is to first read each column vertically and then compare them to each other.

In reviewing the left side of figure 5.4, an important difference becomes apparent between hunter-gatherers who are foragers and simple horticulturists, in that it is easier for the former to remain egalitarian. This is because the more settled way of life makes moving in the face of conflict much more difficult. Second, a settled way of life lends itself more to the accumulation of goods. Third, clan and group property lend themselves more to group competition, whereas among hunter-gatherers there is no group property. Since most hunter-gatherers are mobile rather than sedentary, none of these additional conditions apply. Since the right side of Figure 5.4 has already been discussed (in section 2), I will move on to the comparison of the left- and right-hand columns.

Reading from left to right, social circumscription—that is, living on an island or near mountains where withdrawal is difficult or impossible—promotes *both* political and gender inequality. But whereas abundant concentrated natural resources work against political egalitarianism, it is scarcity of resources that works *against* women. Whereas the segregation of work and child rearing practices works against women, integration of work and child rearing does not necessarily lead to political inequality. Among big-game-hunting societies, egalitarian relations can be sustained, but in complex horticultural societies rank relations tend to appear. While Reeves-Sanday found that the use of large animals as a primary resource works against women, it does not necessarily lead to the emergence of rank societies. Again, big-game hunters handle large game, yet they are egalitarian. Yet large animals are present in herding societies, complex horticultural societies, and agricultural states, and these societies are either ranked or stratified.

While more *permanent settlements* are likely to lead to rank relations, there is no clear implication for gender relations. A settled way of life in simple horticulture societies promotes minimum male dominance. However, a settled way of life also correlates with rank relations in complex horticultural societies and stratfied relations in agricultural states.

The production of surpluses undermines egalitarian social relations in general and equitable gender relations as well. As Chafetz pointed out (see chapter 4), men tend to monopolize the social positions that administrate commodities and trade. These positions have high status, while women's work typically has lower prestige. In addition, because men are working in the fields to produce the surplus, they are in a better position to benefit from the surplus when rank relations emerge.

While the presence of clan and group property within a society might make rank relations more likely, Reeves-Sanday found no relationship between group property and informal male dominance. Whereas ecological and demographic crises can be managed by egalitarian societies so that they can remain egalitarian (hunting societies shifting from reliance on large game to small game; and foraging societies shifting to reliance on simple horticulture) such crises tend to foster the emergence of informal male dominance.

Whereas harsh environments, difficult climates, and lack of natural resources work against both political and gender equality, the effects of male sacred presences are not so clear. Ranked societies usually worship male ancestor spirits, but egalitarian societies also celebrate male earth spirits in myths and rituals. Thus the presence of male spirits may or may not predict political inequality. However, according to Reeves-Sanday, the presence of male dominance in creation myths usually goes with informal male dominance.

From the above we can draw three conclusions:

1. Gender inequalities between men and women *precede* political and economic inequalities between members of a society as a whole.
2. There are many more conditions that promote gender inequality than political inequality.
3. The conditions that lead to gender inequalities are more times than not *different* from the conditions that promote political and economic inequality.

Now let us turn to the conditions under which equality is maintained. When we compare each side with the other, we can see that there are some conditions that support the maintenance of both political and gender equality. They are:

1. When natural resources are abundant but dispersed;
2. When work and child-rearing practices are integrated; and

3. When the society relies on small-game hunting for its subsistence.

Small-game hunting promotes a continuation of both egalitarian relations and minimal male dominance, but for different reasons. Small-game hunting societies support the continuation of egalitarian political relations because their foraging ways discourage and accumulation of wealth. Small-game hunting supports a minimum of male dominance because there are no large animals as resources requiring intensive male work and because it promotes integrated work and child rearing practices.

How well does Reeves-Sanday's theory address the eight questions posed at the end of chapter 2? Reeves-Sanday gives us the *conditions* under which informal male dominance might emerge (harsh environments, crowding, migration, etc.). But her description of what I am calling informal male dominance at the beginning of the second section, is essentially a *social-psychological* definition. The mere fact that men behave aggressively, strut around, and believe as if they are superior does not tell us how such behavior may have translated into *concrete entitlements*—which is the point of my questions. She does not refer to Murdock's cross-cultural study, which considers the monopolization by men of public institutions such as political leadership, trading, and warring, along with descent, residency, and child-rearing entitlements *even in egalitarian societies.* She omits reference to the specific entitlements that go with informal male dominance. Adding Murdock's research would give us a more concrete definition of informal male dominance.

Also, she does not explain why there is no informal *female* dominance. *Explaining the emergence of informal male dominance is not the same as explaining the absence of female dominance.*

For example, we have already seen that there were conditions for at least some cultures during the Mesolithic and early Neolithic period that, according to Reeves-Sanday, should have been optimal for women: abundant resources, settled environments, no crowding, women either controlling the resources (planting) or sharing them with men (small-game hunting), integrated labor (the entire family hunting small game), and integrated child rearing. Why didn't these conditions lead to informal female dominance?

If gender differences in influence, prestige, privilege and power had only *socio-ecological* origins, then we should find a spectrum of societies ranging from those exhibiting extreme informal male dominance to those exhibiting extreme informal female dominance. We should find societies in which the segregation of labor and child-rearing practices supported women, where the reliance on large-animal resources conferred female power, and where food scarcity ecological/demographic crisis and the need to migrate resulted in extreme informal female dominance.

The emergence of informal male dominance can be explained socio-ecologically; the absence of informal female dominance cannot. Socio-ecology has taken us as far as it can. For answers to the question of why there is no corresponding informal female dominance we must turn to evolutionary psychology. This will be the subject of chapter 7. In the next chapter, however, we will address the emergence of institutional male dominance, its stages and cycles.

Figure 5.4 Comparison of the Origins of Political vs. Gender Inequality

RANK AND STRATIFICATION (Political Inequality)	INFORMAL MALE DOMINANCE (Gender Inequality)

How Inequality Arises
Similarities and Differences

Egalitarian Hunter-gatherers	Combined Hunter-gatherers/ Horticulturists
Biophysical or social circumscription works against egalitarianism.	Biophysical or social circumscription works against women.
Abundant, concentrated natural resources, invites large groups of people and works against egalitarianism.	Scarcity of resources works against women.
Segregation or integration of work and child rearing may or may not work for egalitarian politics.	Segregation of work and childrearing works against women.
Presence of large animals may or may not work for egalitarian politics.	Presence of large animals gives men control over resources.
Egalitarian Simple Horticulturists	
More permanent settlements discourage migration and undermines withdrawal as a strategy for conflicts.	More permanent settlements may or may not work against women.
More surplus creates competition and works against egalitarianism.	More surplus works against women. Men monopolize commodity production, trade. This work has higher prestige.
Clan and kin property works against egalitarianism.	No corresponding category.
Ecological and demographic crisis may or may not work against egalitarian politics.	Ecological and demographic crisis causes stress that works against women.
Harsh environments, difficult climates, and lack of pristine natural resources are irrelevant to egalitarianism.	Harsh environments, difficult climates and lack of pristine natural resources usually work against women.
Male sacred presences may or may not work against egalitarian politics.	Male sacred presences usually work against women.

How Equality is Maintained
Similarities and Differences

EGALITARIAN MAINTENANCE (Political equality)	MINIMUM MALE DOMINANCE (Gender equality)
When migration is possible.	When migration is unnecessary.
When natural resources are abundant but scattered.	When natural resources are abundant but scattered.
Integrated work and child rearing practices.	Integrated work and child rearing practices.
Small game hunting.	Small game hunting.
Horticulture may or may not maintain egalitarianism.	Horticulture may or may not support a minimum of male dominance.
Big game hunting may or may not support egalitarianism.	Big game hunting does not support a minimum of male dominance.

Chapter 6

Cycles and Stages of Female Subordination: Late Neolithic, Bronze and Iron Ages

1. Overview of the Stages and Cycles of Female Subordination

In this chapter I will begin by presenting a five-stage theory of female subordination. Then I will show how these five stages themselves changed as they passed through four cycles beginning in the late Neolithic Age and culminating with the Axial Iron Age. Specific events leading to institutionalized male dominance will be grouped into these stages and cycles. Figure 6.1 is a definitional overview of the five stages, and Figure 6.2 is an overview of the relationship between the five stages and the four cycles. This chapter is a pivotal one, whose purpose is both to deepen our understanding of the events discussed in chapter 2 and to lay a groundwork for the chapters in the second half of the book.

We must keep in mind that the institutionalization of male dominance does not result in every man in society having infrastructural, structural, and superstructural power over all women. Agricultural states were stratified societies in which a tiny section of male elites had institutional power not only over all women, but also over most men. When some feminist theories of male domination reduce the origins of male dominance to a kind of plot of all men to subordinate all women, they ignore the fact that the institutionalization of male dominance represented an overall deterioration in the living standards of most men as well as most women. The majority of men lost political and economic power over their lives but acquired some *privileges* over women. But privileges by themselves are not the same as public, political, and economic *power* over women.

I will begin by describing Figure 6.1. The first point to notice is that informal male dominance is not included in the any of the five stages. This is because it was unsystematic and tenuous. At the same time, I have tried to give a more robust definition of informal male dominance by citing macrosociological research without violating Reeves-Sanday's original definition. Notice that informal male dominance includes influence and prestige, but not privilege and power over women. Examples of influence and prestige include polygyny, the tracing descent along the male line, and residency after marriage with male kin. Some may feel that these constitute privilege rather than influence or prestige. I do not categorize them as privileges because informal male dominance is not institutionalized over generations and can change within a generation.

Let us turn to the stages by which male dominance becomes institutionalized. The first point to notice is that the process occurred over the course of 5000 years and it happened gradually. Female subordination cannot be attributed to discrete events that happened suddenly. Second, institutionalized male dominance changed as it passed through the four cycles shown in Figure 6.2. Institutionalized male dominance was not a "thing" that, once it emerged, remained forever the same.

The phase of *enmeshment* is specific to social conditions that (a) were previously egalitarian and later assumed modest forms of inequality, but not so much inequality as to require an external police force for its maintenance; (b) had cross-cutting rather than overlapping cleavages between groups; and (c) were characterized by the presence of a subordinate group that was only partly aware of its subordinate situation. (A cross-cutting cleavage exists when the distinctions of power and privilege between groups is not overlapping in all social domains. The subordinate group has situational privileges and power over the dominant group based on age, gender, ethnicity, language, or sacred tradition.)

Coercion occurs in all societies. Even in egalitarian societies a group can threaten to injure, exclude, or kill an obnoxious or uncooperative member. But this is informal rather than formal coercion because (a) the composition of the group is open and shifts, (b) the coercing group changes depending on the situation, and (c) the coercing group is subject to competition with other groups within that society, all of which have power to resist. Formal coercion requires institutional offices that remain intact regardless of which individuals occupy them and that remain in place over generations regardless of local situations; it also requires the monopolization by the state of the means of violence. With state coercion, differences between groups acquire overlapping cleavages, meaning that members of the subordinated group all speak the same language, practice the same spiritual tradition, are of the same ethnicity, and are engaged in the same occupation, with no privileges or power in any situation.

The third stage is *legitimation*. As we saw in chapter 1, legitimation is the activity of superstructural institutions that are monopolized by dominant groups in order to convince subordinate groups that their submission is necessary, beneficial to all, part of a cosmic order, inevitable, and eternal. These institutions usually require many years to be built and consolidated. From legitimizing institutions an ideology of dominance is built.

The fourth stage is *internalization*, whereby a subordinate group "digests" the legitimation processes and imports it into its own world view, thereby creating a mentality of submission, complete with self-doubt, timidity, and self-destructiveness, along with the typical

strategies for getting by, including deception, manipulation, betrayal, seduction, etc.

Collusion, the last stage, is the material labor subordinated groups perform over time which continues their subordination by reproducing from generation to generation the institutions responsible for their subordination. Collusion refers, for example, to the work performed by women to support military institutions that wield the coercive power, and educational institutions that wield legitimizing power, by which they themselves are oppressed

This five-stage cycle is not inevitable. During the course of history many people have rebelled against coercive institutions. They resist attempts by the established order at coercion. They resist the monopolization of tools and natural resources. They contest decisions—and often the very decision-making process—regarding what should be produced and how it should be distributed. They challenge the dominant order's control over the quality and quantity of work done. In opposing this technological, economic, and political exclusion, they may employ strikes, street fighting, or non-cooperative resistance.

Resistance movements counter legitimizing social institutions with counter-institutions that support dissent in an ongoing way. This means building alternative schools for education, either openly or secretly. It means creating some means of communicating events from the movement's own perspective through newspapers, journals, etc. It means developing a "counter-ideology" which explains to the movement's members how the world works and what alternative futures might be possible. It means developing sacred mythologies, beliefs, and rituals into which rebellion and exploration are woven. Finally, resistance movements create child-rearing practices that encourage curiosity, exploration, and the questioning of authority. They develop a language of protest for current members and pass this language of protest on to members' children.

All of these activities are internalized in a mentality of resistance that rationalizes and justifies the movement's way of life. That mentality encourages an identification with people beyond family and kin group; it encourages the ability to remain calm in problematic situations and to create and sustain roles that are novel, challenging, and discomforting. It discourages the reification of any person, object, or situation. Such a mentality must be able to weather attempts to discredit it.

In general, the building of counter-social institutions requires resistance to collusion on the job, because it is in the workplace where the dominant social institutions are reproduced. Rather than colluding through their labor to reproduce the existing order, members of resistance movements build parties and unions so they will have a presence and visibility within the system.

Finally, resistance movements develop monitoring systems for critiquing the relationship between their ideology and their practice. They engage in what Marx and Engels called "practical-critical activity." Practical-critical activity is the ongoing, collective activity which people organize to minimize their alienation and maximize the transformation of their alternative vision into a reality. Practical-critical activity among resistance movements entails allowing theory or ideology to change based on people's experience in practice, and allowing practice to be informed by improved theory.

Let us look more closely at how the five stages of submission change as they pass through the four cycles, using Figure 6.2 as a guide. In cycle one of subordination under chiefdoms, enmeshment is not accompanied by any other supporting processes prior to the collusion stage. This does not mean that all elements of coercion, legitimation, or internalization are absent. It simply means that they are weakly developed. Women who collude in complex horticulture societies are neither cowed nor convinced of their subordination. For them, enmeshment is worse than informal male dominance, but not as bad as the situation in cycle two.

The movement to the second cycle in agricultural states was driven (as are all the shifts from one cycle to the next) by a demographic and ecological crisis. The most important feature of this second cycle is that power differences between groups are enforced by a specialized military. The ruling elite of men monopolized the technology and the political economy. Women's power was systematically suppressed. This stage was experienced differently by higher-caste and lower-caste women, as we will see later in this chapter. The point to note is that the power to make women submit was rawly coercive, and not backed by any strongly developed legitimizing institution, or by conviction on the part of women that such coercion was acceptable (internalization). Collusion continued as it did throughout all cycles. Chapters 8, 9, and 10 will discuss the evolution of violence and coercion in more depth.

The third cycle of subordination occurred in the Middle and Late Bronze Ages when social institutions were built which enculturated women to accept their subordination as "natural," so as to discourage any resistance. Child-rearing practices, education, and sacred beliefs were reorganized to favor men—all aspects of the legitimation processes. Changes to sacred traditions were especially important in this regard. Mythology tells the stories of exploits of great beings and how they dealt with the fundamental problems of life. Usually, these beings are given genders. Thus, if the mythology is such that goddesses do nothing extraordinary while gods are responsible for everything noteworthy, then it is easier to justify the rule of a few men over most men and all women in this world. Once the legitimation process is in place, it is less necessary to use force to stay in power. Chapters 11 and 12 supply more detail about how sacred traditions worked to oppress women.

The fourth cycle of subordination must have occurred between the late Bronze Age and the Axial Iron Age. Over generations, women imported legitimation processes (including the reorganized mythology) into their individual world views. Women did not suddenly become passive, internalizing the social relations of subordination overnight. They must have been socialized both materially and "spiritually" over generations. Their psychological resistance had to be destroyed and then reorganized so that a recent and relative reorganization of social

Figure 6.1 Overview of All Forms of Male Dominance

Informal male dominance

Informal male dominance is an episodic, tenuous condition occurring in egalitarian hunting-gathering and simple horticultural societies under various forms of ecological, demographic stress and/ or when work and child-rearing practices are segregated and large game is a major resource. Men have more influence and prestige than women, which is socially expressed in semi-institutionalized practices such as polygamy, and tracing lineage and residency patterns along the male line. Women both resist and collude with this. Psychologically, men believe they are superior, but women don't take the men seriously. Men do not control the infrastructure, structure or superstructure of society. Informal male dominance can be either "mild" or "extreme" depending on the socio-ecological context.

Institutionalized male dominance: Stages of submission

A) Enmeshment

Men have power over women in the public economy, but this is countered and tempered by cross-cutting cleavages such as age, skill at work, status of the product made, kinship ties, rank and gender. In many of these contexts women have more influence, prestige and privilege over men. All women have some power within both the public and domestic economy.

B) State Coercion

This subordination is backed by male control over the infrastructure (tools) and structure of society, including the political economy and the military. There are overlapping cleavages in which gender hierarchy emerges. Women are subordinate because of their gender while age, rank, kinship ties, quality of work skills and status of the product become irrelevant.

Upper caste women have great influence, prestige, privilege, and indirect political and economic power in the public sphere. They are subordinate to kings and priests in the domestic economy. Middle and lower caste women disappear from the public sphere and become subordinated within the patriarchal family (waning of kin-group).

C) Legitimation

Superstructural institutions such as the family, education, and sacred traditions are used by those with coercive power to induce those in submissive positions to comprehend their submission as being necessary, socially beneficial to all, part of a cosmic order, inevitable and eternal.

D) Internalization

The forms of legitimation are consciously or unconsciously imported by women into their psychology. This takes the form of low self-esteem, excessive patience, self-destructiveness and passive-aggressive tactics. In this "psychology of subordination" women rationalize their subordination as the "natural order of things". This occurs despite the maladaptedness of the situation and the apparent conflict with their self-interest.

E) Collusion

This is the laboring of women which reproduces the institutions that oppress them. Collusion is the complicity of women in constructing and sustaining their subordination over time through their work. It can exist with or without enmeshment, coercion, legitimation or internalization.

Figure 6.2 Cycles of Female Subordination in the Ancient World

Stages of Submission

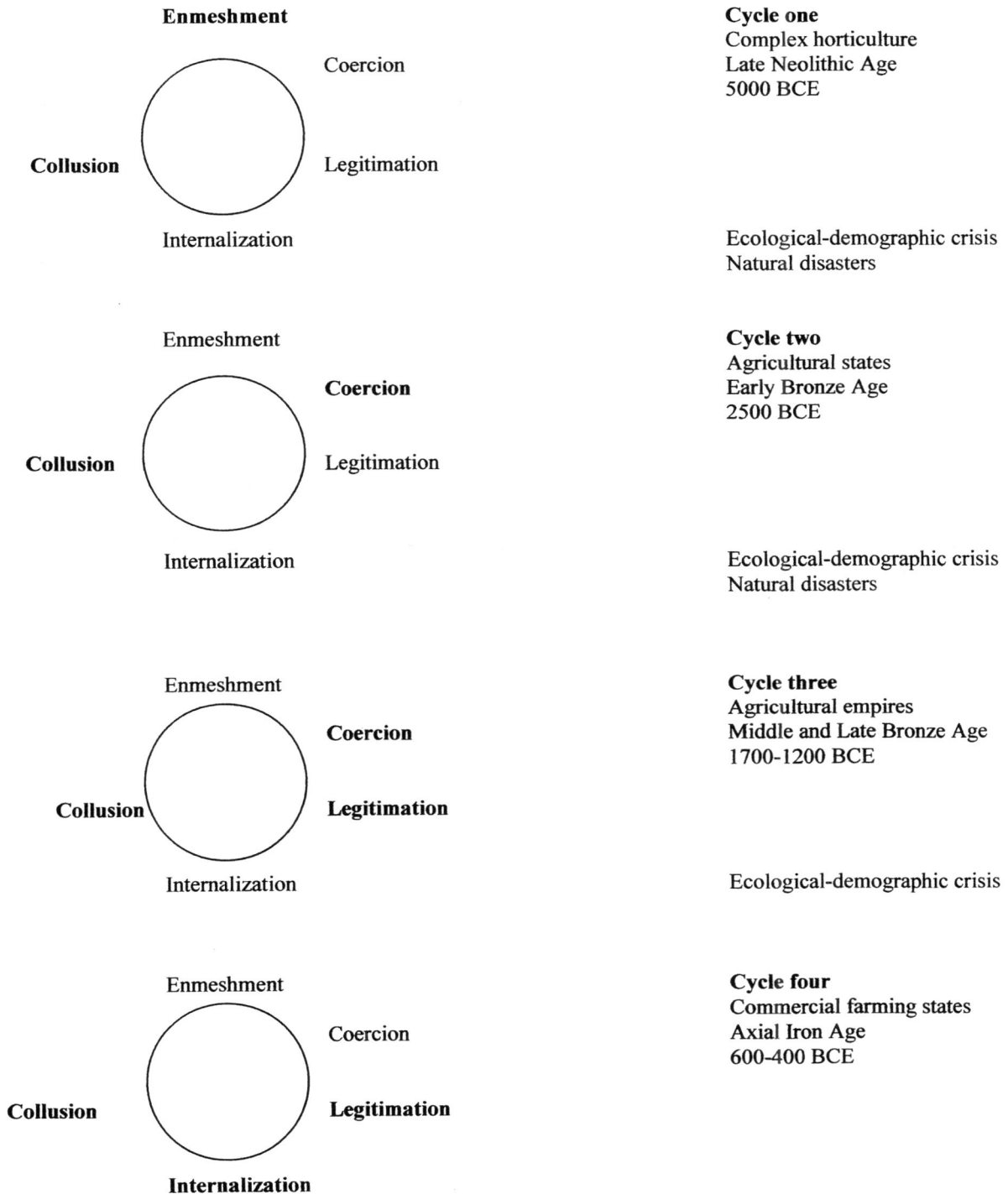

Enmeshment

Coercion

Collusion

Legitimation

Internalization

Cycle one
Complex horticulture
Late Neolithic Age
5000 BCE

Ecological-demographic crisis
Natural disasters

Enmeshment

Coercion

Collusion

Legitimation

Internalization

Cycle two
Agricultural states
Early Bronze Age
2500 BCE

Ecological-demographic crisis
Natural disasters

Enmeshment

Coercion

Collusion

Legitimation

Internalization

Cycle three
Agricultural empires
Middle and Late Bronze Age
1700-1200 BCE

Ecological-demographic crisis

Enmeshment

Coercion

Collusion

Legitimation

Internalization

Cycle four
Commercial farming states
Axial Iron Age
600-400 BCE

relations between genders was mystified as the only possible relation between men and women. Once this was the case, then the seeds for a psychology of subordination were in place. In chapters 13, 14, and 15 we will see that the presence of a vertical collectivist self, a reasoning process called "concrete abstraction", and the use of proximate, as opposed to long-distance senses, contributed to this internalization of subordination.

Notice that collusion is present in all of the cycles. This is because for any vertical power system to continue, the social institutions of dominance must be sustained over time. However, the collusion in which women engaged in the Axial Iron Age (cycle four) was far deeper, more despairing, and objectively worse than the collusion of commoner wives in complex horticulture societies (cycle one). This is because in cycle four collusion was backed by coercion, legitimation, and internalization.

It should now be apparent why informal male dominance is not included in the five stages of subordination and its four cycles: with the possible exception of collusion, none of the parts of the stages were operational in societies characterized merely by informal male dominance.

On the whole, the cycle of subordination follows a movement from social to psychological processes, and then back to a social process. Enmeshment, coercion, and legitimation are all social processes. Internalization is a psychological process, while collusion is again a social process.

Again, regarding changes in the cycle across history: Once state coercion was established in the middle Bronze Age, there was a general movement away from coercion as the major method of inducing submission. Overt coercion became unnecessary in most cases with the growth of explanatory (legitimation) and psychological (internalization) justifications for male dominance and female submission. Coercion was only used when legitimation and internalization broke down.

The reasons why women internalize and collude in social relations in stratified societies depend on the social caste they come from. For example, in agricultural states upper-caste

women were able to exercise more choice than were lower-caste women. Among upper-caste women there was a greater acceptance of subordination in exchange for indirect access to resources, protection, privilege, prestige, and influence. Among the lower castes and classes of women, acceptance had less to do with secondary gains than with lack of alternatives and fear of punishment.

There is a problem inherent in this historical explanation that we have yet to address. I have said that institutionalized male dominance began in complex horticultural societies; but I also said that chiefdoms did not have a specialized military force. So the question arises, how could men have come to power over women without some kind of coercive force in place?

To answer this question, let us begin by examining the life of women in complex horticultural societies. Were there ways by which institutionalized male dominance could have originated without coercive institutions to back it up?

2. The cycle of subordination in the late Neolithic Age: Enmeshed institutionalized male dominance (complex horticulturalists)

In her study on chiefdoms in the Tongan Islands (1987), Christine Ward Gailey describes gender relations there as "ambiguous" rather than coerced (we will use the word "enmeshed"). This means that the primary access to resources, power, prestige, influence, and privileges was never based solely on gender. Age, life experiences, rank, position within the descent group, skill in labor, and the value of products were also factored into who had power, privilege, prestige, and influence in a particular situation.

According to Gailey, there was a multi-dimensional context for determining who was entitled to what they got and when they got it. Many of these dimensions of social life were controlled by females. Within the kin-group as a whole, no one had unlimited authority, even if they were at the top of the rank hierarchy;

and no one at the bottom was ever devoid of power and privilege in every situation. The variation in entitlements based on different contexts acted as a system of checks and balances. Kinship relations involved reciprocal support and obligations throughout the life-span of all people related to each other through birth and marriage.

This did not mean that rights and privileges were equally shared. Chiefdoms were rank societies. Rights and obligations were graded. Overall, chiefly groups had it best, followed by district managers, and then commoners. Since chiefs and distinct managers were males, these men had more power and privilege than anyone else. Yet chiefly power was limited. The chiefly group allocated land and resources to commoners, but the chiefs really could not refuse to do this. The process was a formality. The chief could not deny access to resources to commoners or confiscate their products with no promise of reciprocity. Chiefs had to produce something in return—prosperity, fertility, assurance, and protection.

District managers were low-grade administrators. They also did specialized craft-work, medical healing, house construction, and navigation; they were also part-time warriors. All women, whether members of the chiefly kin group or not, were active in the public domain, and most work could be done by either sex.

Commoners had hereditary use-rights to land. They did the bulk of the fishing, horticulture, and craft production. Male commoners worked on canoes and weapons, while women made carrying devices and storage containers, spun, wove, and made pottery.

Ultimate political and economic power originated from a structural role—the chief—which women never filled. And the male chief had differential access to the labor and products of all men and women.

Despite the overall power of chiefs, in some local contexts women had more power than men. This made women's relationship to power and privilege enmeshed and diffused, rather than diminished equally in all dimensions of society. Perhaps no formal coercive force was required simply because no tribal member was

getting an extraordinarily bad deal. Formal coercion is only necessary when the gap in power between groups is so great that the dominant group can maintain its power only through physical threat.

Let us examine how these "checks and balances" worked in favor of women. As we saw in chapter 2, labor within the village was strictly for the discharge of obligations. There was minimal or no commodity exchange. What few commodities were produced were for export beyond the village. Within the village, there was still the problem of determining the value of the product in terms of reciprocal obligations. The value of a product produced by a woman was determined by the many dimensions of that woman's social standing, not just by the amount of labor time necessary to produce the artifact.

By "social standing" I mean age, rank, gender, and skill. The status of the product depends on the occasion for which it is produced, how old the product is before it is received, and the rank of the person receiving it. Etically speaking, the whole process of production and consumption under chiefdoms is inseparable from the sacred intention of building up a group solidarity through developing the social personhood in each member. This means that at all stages of the laboring process, the participants know where the product is going, and for whom it is destined. They also re-experience the fruits of their labor in the coming ceremony, whether what they produced was a craft or food for the ceremony.

How did these social arrangements affect women? In an absolute sense, women's labor was more highly valued than men's labor because it was sacred. The men did the most demanding physical work, and also the most menial tasks. What they produced were provisions for the culture. For a man not to work was a sign of prestige because work was associated with the profane, mundane world. Work for men had little status. The products of all women, non-chiefly as well as chiefly, were considered special and used for sacred ceremonies—mats and sacred hangings for harvest festivals, rites of passage, and other special occasions. Chiefly women's products were the most sacred of all.

Woman's labor was of the utmost value because it was a magical extension of her powers as a procreator. Women's production as workers was probably thought of as an extension of their production of babies. A woman must have been treated as if she were a goose that laid golden eggs. This was especially true of chiefly women, because without their production, the whole chiefly group would lose its legitimacy as a guarantor of fertility and the continuity of the whole society.

Thus the male chief's power to demand more production was countered and tempered by the higher prestige of women's products. There were many other ambiguities in the status system. Which was more valuable, the product of a non-chiefly woman or that of a male member of the chiefly kin-group? The answer must have been complex. The male member of the chiefly group had higher political status, but a woman's labor had higher status even if she were non-chiefly. This high status of women's labor would have kept male dominance in check. The relations of power between the sexes were no doubt tension-filled and enmeshed. There would, however, have been no tension between the product of a chiefly woman and that of a non-chiefly man; the woman's product would have been superior.

In Gailey's study, there was tension between a woman's role as a wife and her role as a sister. As a wife, she had to defer to her husband; but as a sister, she had authority over her brother. So if a non-chiefly man married a chiefly woman, the woman's inferior status as a wife would have been countered by her superior position as a sister of a chiefly-class man. What she lost in one obligatory context, she gained in another. Further, women were not economically dependent on men. The woman's status as a sister within her kin-group guaranteed her subsistence rights.

Sometimes these cross-cutting cleavages could work against women. We noted earlier that, in an absolute sense, the products of a chiefly woman were valued more highly than those of a non-chiefly man. But this could be an ambiguous power relation if the man were older, had more skill in what he made, or were producing for someone special and for an especially important occasion. So under extreme circumstances, a man's product could have more status than a woman's product.

How did these ambiguities play out in sexual expectations? In this domain ambiguities existed not only between men and women, but between women of different ranks. Prior to marriage, non-chiefly women could do as they pleased sexually, while chiefly women were closely watched. However, non-chiefly women were in danger of being raped, with no kin reprisal. The rape of a chiefly woman, on the other hand, would probably have meant death for the rapist. In fact, the kin group of a non-chiefly rapist might kill the man themselves to avoid the reprisals which would otherwise have been visited on them. Male chiefs had to attract women; they could not bully them into sexual engagements.

Among chiefly people there were other ambiguities. While male chiefs could have more than one spouse, chiefly women had to be formally monogamous. Once married, however, chiefly women often had affairs. Further, chiefly women also had control over secondary wives, and this could make the former's lives much easier.

On the whole, as long as population pressure and resource depletion were relatively stable in complex horticultural societies, institutionalized male dominance was tempered by cross-cutting sets of rights and obligations. But once social stress arose, these checks and balances could have been undermined.

When the soil responded less and less to horticultural methods, the group would naturally seek to respond by moving to a new area. However, if other groups already occupied all alternative sites a crisis would present itself. The villages might go to war with one another; or, under certain conditions, the people might intensify production by switching from horticulture to agriculture. In that case the society might also reorganize itself into a state. No matter which of these strategies was chosen,

Figure 6.3 Life of Women in Complex Horticultural Societies:
Cycle One
Cross-Cutting Cleavages, No Gender Hierarchies

Pros	Cons
Women's labor, both chiefly and non-chiefly, more valuable than men's labor	Chiefly men have power over the political economy
Chiefly and non-chiefly women are active in public arenas	
Women have access to skilled positions	
Chiefly women's labor guaranteed prosperity, crop fertility, succession of generations and protection	
Unmarried, non-chiefly women can do as they please sexually	Unmarried, non-chiefly women are in danger of being raped
Once married, chiefly women have leeway to have affairs	Unmarried chiefly women's sexual practices are closely monitored
Chiefly wives have control over secondary wives	Chiefly husbands may have more than one wife
As kin sisters, women have control over brothers	As wives, women defer to their husbands
Marriage is not an economic necessity for any woman	
Kin-groups give women subsistence rights as sisters	

women's status would have drastically deteriorated.

Even under circumstances when chiefdoms did not turn into states and use other strategies to resolve population pressure and resource depletion, women's status was reduced. For example, if a chiefdom went to war and won, it enslaved its female captives. The experience of being enslaved must have had a disastrous impact on the mentality of the captured women and on that of the women who, as members of the victorious tribe, witnessed this debasement.

We must also keep in mind that chiefdoms were not usually rich in natural resources. When the people were desperate enough, women were offered as commodities for trade. Both a woman's reproductive capacity and her labor became subject to exchange value.

Whether women were offered as concubines to royal households, became slaves in wars between pre-state societies and agricultural states, or were offered as commodities in trade between chiefdoms, the end result was that their multi-dimensional identity became one-dimensional—sexual. And we must remember that these conditions were ultimately due to ecological and demographic stress on chiefdoms.

To summarize this section: The chiefdom cycle of subordination was a shaky one, wherein institutionalized male dominance did not apply in all contexts; it was challenged by a crosscurrent of conflicting reciprocal rights and obligations between kin-groups, and there were many contexts in which women exercised some power and privilege over men regardless of their rank. Women still had power over men in many specific contexts, although, on the whole, men had more power over women, and this power was institutionalized. However, all of this took place under relatively non-stressful circumstances. When stressful ecological and demographic conditions arose, this arrangement broke down and enmeshed male dominance became more severe.

Formal coercion, legitimation, and internalization probably did not occur in complex horticultural societies because no social member had a bad enough existence to be motivated to put these processes in motion.

The power differences between men and women weren't great enough to generate a backlash that would have required an elite group to act with coercive and legitimizing social structures in order to protect its interests.

Legitimation and internalization imply that an oppressed group has rationalized a socially objective loss of power, justifying this loss of power as if it were in the natural order of things. In our own social context, there are many women who deny that there are real objective institutions that hold them back. This kind of legitimation and internalization of oppression never happened in complex horticultural societies.

It takes time for a kind of "collective amnesia" to set in among women, so that they "forget" that they once had some power and privilege. This is why legitimation processes are so important in creating the ground for internalization. If the gods are more powerful than goddesses, then the real social differences in power between men and women in the material world can be legitimized and internalized in women's minds. They then go out and work, producing the next generation of subordinated women.

3. The cycle of subordination in the Bronze Age: Coercive institutionalized male dominance (agricultural states)

If, after a struggle between kin groups within a chiefdom, the victorious kin group led the transformation of their society into an agricultural state, the lower kin groups of commoners would have been transformed into a peasant caste. Kin groups usually retained some of their identity, though in a hybrid form. They usually resisted attempts by the state to break them up. However, the state had far more power than any chief, since it commanded a standing military force rather than part-time warriors. The kin-groups often used their women as bargaining power with the state officials. The head of a village would offer its virgins as potential concubines for the kingly household.

The struggle between kin groups and the state must have gradually undermined the solidarity between kin groups within the former tribe. They began to compete among themselves for who would give the state the best women, increasing the possibilities that their kin group would be granted special privileges. In the process, the average woman must have come to be seen more as an instrument in the struggle between tribes and states, and less as a whole person. Her gender was what mattered. As a kin member in a tribal society, her age, work skill, and position within the kin group were also part of her identity. As a concubine or wife within a divine household of the state, it was only her sexuality that counted. The manner in which women were treated in agricultural states must also have affected male kin group members, who began to treat their women as sex objects or breeding machines.

One of the primary reasons why women's lives deteriorated in agricultural states was that women lost control of the planting. Agriculture is much more physically demanding than horticulture. It involves working with a plow, draft animals, and soil irrigation. Irrigation requires digging ditches, and also breaking draft animals so that the animals take the harness. This is very strenuous work. Manure has to be collected, carried to fields, and spread as fertilizer. These activities take the farmer far from home. None of these requirements is especially compatible with pregnancy or child care.

Women must have gone through an "occupational" crisis comparable to the one men went through when big-game hunting ceased to be a viable form of subsistence. However, for women the crisis must have been much worse, because men went through theirs under egalitarian political conditions. When women stopped tending gardens, it was under conditions in which institutionalized male dominance were already in place. For the first time in human history, women were pulled away from public work and became exclusively involved in the domestic economy. This made them much more exploitable.

In horticultural societies, women in kin groups often ate and worked together; doing so built emotional and economic support and

group solidarity among them. Even though they were the subordinated sector of the population, their unity enabled them to offer resistance to domination. But as the state destroyed the kin-groups, and as women lost their place in the public economy, they also became more isolated from one another: there was simply no place for them to go but back into the cottage industries of domestic households.

The kinds of occupations available to women in agricultural states varied from caste to caste, but in all cases work was in the domestic sphere, and women's place in the hierarchy was mediated by the status of the men they depended on. At the bottom of the social hierarchy was the slave woman, whose sexuality was at the disposal of the elite. In addition to performing sexual services for these upper-caste men, she was a servant for his wife. Other options for the slave were to become a temple prostitute or work in the temple workshops as a mill worker, spinner, brewer, or kitchen worker.

Another possibility was to become a concubine. Concubines were different from slaves. For a concubine, sexual performance could lead to upward mobility, some privileges, and the winning of inheritance rights for her children.

In the middle and lower castes, the status of a wife varied. Though she was subordinate to her husband, a wife still had property and legal rights. Within the home, her husband had complete control over her sexual life. He had the final say over his children, and might even sell them into debt slavery in hard times. The way he related to his wife and children was analogous to the way the state related to him: just as the state allocated resources, made decisions, and enforced punishment within society as a whole, so did he within the family. Thus in agricultural states the family was like a microcosm of the state; just as subjects were subordinate to the king, so within individual families women were subordinate to men. Women in the lower castes had no say whatever in political affairs.

Upper-caste women in agricultural states were in a deeply conflicted position. On one hand, the ruling priestesses or queens shared status, power, and divinity with the kings or priests. They owned and managed property, and they administered the temples of various goddesses. This meant employing as many as a 1000 people per year. Priestesses also had independent power in both the palace and temple workshops. They exercised specialized craft skills, and could be scribes, musicians, and singers. They also had economic, legal, and judicial power to represent their households.

Yet upper-caste queens and priestesses were dependent on kings and priests. They could be used as pawns in their husbands' political designs. Through their marriages, alliances were formed or broken. If there was a palace revolution and the king was overthrown, or a war was lost, these women's lives were completely overturned. They had no independent control over their vertical power and privilege. So on the one hand, they were politically, culturally, and administratively active, exercising power over most men and all women. Yet all of these benefits were inseparable from their marriages, in which they were subordinate to their husbands.

There was no prestigious public identity possible for women in agricultural states. Sexually, they were seen as either reproductive breeders or prostitutes. They could be breeders for elite families or for peasant households. If they worked, it was within the domestic economy. Women could work within the divine households, or at baking, preserving, or sewing in peasant households. With the exception of upper-class women, who comprised just a small fraction of the female population, women's labor was valued far less than it had been in complex horticulture societies.

In the early phase of agricultural states, between 3000-2500 BCE, women were coerced, together with peasants and artisans, into subordination by the presence of a standing military army. These societies were without strong legitimizing institutions or ideologies. But over time, exploitation cannot be sustained solely by force. If nothing else, productivity subsides because people are unmotivated to produce more and have to be supervised constantly.

As we will see in chapter 15, the writing systems of agricultural states were first used for economic, accounting practices. But beginning in the middle and late Bronze Age (the Hammurabi code in 1700 BCE is a good landmark) writing systems began to be used for sacred purposes to legitimize the elites' coercive power. All forms of male dominance must have been strengthened during this period, because coercive institutions were supported and justified by sacred beliefs and dramatizations, along with educational systems. Nevertheless, it took the elites generations to reorganize sacred and secular social institutions to legitimize coercive relations.

Legitimizing institutions did not invent their systems of justification out of thin air. Initially, they appeared to carry on previous beliefs but they did so in a contradictory way. The material content of the lives of those they subordinated had deteriorated, but for a while the customs of more egalitarian tribal solidarities were preserved. The state tried to preserve the appearance of a tradition, even though the substance of that tradition had been subverted. For example, the Divine King might take over many of the dramatization functions of a chief or a big-man, acting as a selfless messenger of the gods. But the gap in material wealth between the king and a typical peasant was incomparably greater than that between a big man or a chief and a commoner. As the state-sponsored dramatizations become hollow, a new mythology was being reworked to justify the rule of the elite, one that paid lip service to the customs and myths of tribal societies. In a later chapter we will discuss much more specifically and in greater depth the forms legitimation took, when we discuss the rise of secondary magic in the Bronze Age and the universalistic religions in the Axial Iron Age.

Robert McElvaine (2001) points out how the story of Adam and Eve can be linked to the history of gender dynamics in the ancient world and interpreted as a legitimizing story for institutionalized male dominance. According to McElvaine, the Garden of Eden is a mythologized reference to hunting and gathering societies in which people lived off of nature and did not work very hard.

As an ecological-demographic crisis ripened, women used their knowledge of roots, nuts, and tubers to help resolve the crisis by gradually switching from gathering to planting fruits and vegetables. This transformation was mythologized as eating from the Tree of Knowledge. Women and men (1) assumed self-conscious control over the food supply and hence had more power, (2) but had to work harder to achieve this power (by the sweat of their brow), and (3) had to take responsibility for the impact of their food production on the ecological environment.

Under these conditions, men's occupational status deteriorated while women's improved somewhat. In addition, since planting lends itself more to child labor, women had more children.

According to McElvaine, men blamed women for the occupational change in affairs, as can be seen in the Gilgamesh Epic. Enkidu, a hunter,

> spends six days having intercourse with a courtesan. She is said to be teaching him 'the woman's art, . . .' The image . . . actually employs intercourse as a metaphor for using her wisdom to tame the natural man and lead him away from his wildness into civilization. [As a result,] Enkidu finds he can no longer communicate with animals and commune with nature. (97).

This parallels Adam cursing Eve and the serpent for eating of the fruit of the tree of knowledge. McElvaine claims that once men began working with women in planting, this caused a rift between men who planted and male hunters and herders. The latter looked down on men who farmed as not real men. As McElvaine puts it, "real men don't fool around with plants."

According to McElvaine, God was also resentful of humanity gaining some independence from him, as he rejected the offering of Cain—the farmer—while looking favorably on the offering of Abel—the herder.

God's rejection implies an accusation directed at Cain, which goes something like, "How dare you bring me the sort of food women produce!"

As we saw in chapter 2, a new ecological crisis grew in especially arid horticulture societies, and more intensive planting was required in order to feed a growing population. The invention of the plow and the use of large traction animals helped resolve the crisis. However, men took over both of these activities and women were banished to the domestic household. This intensive farming required more children to help out, but the nature of agriculture meant that male children were more valuable than female children. As men began selectively to breed large animals, their own agency in birth became clearer. As McElvaine says, "The direct connection is easier to observe in animals that have an estrous cycle than in humans since in these other species the relation between mating and pregnancy is much closer to one-to-one." (McElvaine 2001,122)

Elizabeth Fisher (1979) also argues that it was probably cattle breeding that helped men understand they were partly responsible for the reproductive process. Until this time, men's agency in reproduction was not clearly understood. Intercourse was associated with conception, but not in a directly causal sense. For example, the Australian Aborigines believed that a woman must be opened by a male, but this is only to allow the spirit baby to enter. The male does not co-produce the baby.

The combination of the facts that men's agricultural work was becoming more valuable, and that men were clarifying their agency in birth, tipped the scales and led to the adoption of the seed as a central explanatory metaphor for life: just as men plant seeds in the earth in order to grow crops, men plant seeds in women in order to have children. This metaphor underwent its own evolution and did not appear immediately fully formed:

> One indication that the transition from female emphasis to male emphasis in procreation was underway, but was still a matter of contention in the third millennium BCE, is the Sumerian Myth of

Enki and Ninhursag. According to the story, Ninhursag . . . took the semen of the god Enki out of the womb of another goddess and placed it in the ground, where it grew and produced plants. Apparently seeking full creative power, Enki ate the plants and the power of the semen in them (his own) was so great that it made him pregnant. Because he had no womb in which to carry the offspring, Enki became ill and Ninhursag placed him inside her so that the 'seeds' could develop and be born. . . .(123)

Only after men themselves took over the task of planting seeds and began to place them in plowed furrows that the seed metaphor arose . . . [because] no one could see the *active* physiological processes occurring within women's bodies. Women were . . . indeed like the earth, rich, fertile but empty unless a seed took root in it. (125) [my emphasis]

The pacification of nature and the pacification of women were analogous and linked processes. As intensive planting (agriculture) could produce a larger surplus, states and cities emerged and the distinction between what was wild and "uncivilized" and what was tame and domesticated grew. Nature, like women, became both cultivated and passive on the one hand, and wild or uncultivated on the other.

Where once women were seen as the originators of a departure from the animal world (the Gilgamesh story)—not only with the birth of horticulture, but the cooking of food, the making of clothing, and the spinning of thread and weaving of cloth—women now became the passive receptacle of men's penises, just as the earth was passive to the furrowing by the plow. This was a great reversal. Whereas before the agricultural revolution women brought culture to natural men, after the agricultural revolution men brought culture (not only farming, but states and cities) to female earth mothers.

Further, plowing the ground was a far more violent activity than using digging sticks to

garden, and for members of pre-state societies this was a monstrous activity:

'You ask me to plow the ground! exclaimed a horrified Chief Smohalla of the Wanapun to white men. Shall I take a knife and tear my mother's bosom?'. . . . Now men took control by opening Her and planting seeds in Her furrowed vulva—not natural vulva, but labia that the men were cutting themselves" (McElvaine, 2001,146)

And what did this do to gender relations? According to McElvaine,

the seed metaphor transformed man from little more than a bystander into a godlike creator of life and women from the goddess-like creators into . . . dirt. . . . In Genesis the soil has no creative power (McElvaine, 2001, 128)

But, as McElvaine says, "semen is *not* [my emphasis] seed. It is the equivalent of half of a seed. Neither a sperm nor an ovum gives life, rather each provides a 'half-life.'" (134)

The womb is far more than a container. A woman contributes 50% of the genes to the fetus, as well as an active environment that feeds it. But in the seed/semen analogy, the womb is reduced to a passive gestator receiving a fertile seed, rather than a producer of one of two gametes that must unite, combing reproductive cells in order to produce an embryo.

Human beings' tendency to project changes in human relations onto the sacred world translated into the belief that if men have procreative power over the earth (and women), then (1) the supreme God must also be male, and (2) men are closer to God than are women.

The hierarchy of sacred-human worlds that emerges is:

God
men
women

As McElvaine says, men are the sons of god and women are the daughters of men. The forbidden fruit of planting that Eve offered Adam was in the beginning a boon but in the long-run an inadvertent disaster more for women than for men. Initially it gave women more status in horticultural societies and it depreciated men's status. However when the next round of ecological-demographic crisis occurred it was men who took over the planting and women were subordinated. The discovery and the use of planting is a good example of how the process of discovery is by no means under the control of those responsible for the discovery. This is a sad case of women becoming enslaved to their own creation. This reversal was strengthened by the legitimizing seed metaphor.

4. The cycles of subordination in the Axial Iron Age: Collusion (maritime states, Athens)

The status of women in the Axial Iron Age may have undergone marginal improvement. As we saw in chapter 2, the *material life* in Axial Age societies, as compared to that in Bronze and Archaic Iron Age societies, was more democratic and inclusive of the average person. The Greek polis, the invention of iron tools, the alphabet, and coined money all encouraged more citizen involvement. While women were not citizens, it seems reasonable to assume they acquired indirect benefits because of the improved social status of their husbands.

The more important question is, did women's material and social status *directly* improve or deteriorate in the Axial Iron Age? Despite whatever indirect benefits women may have received, it is probably true to say that, at least in Athens, life was at least as bad for women as it had been for women in agricultural states. In Athens, women continued to have no respectable public identity. Not only could they not run for public office, but they could not even act as jurors in courts or participate in discussions at the polis. Women could not vote or own property.

Women's work situations were just as bad as in agricultural states, and perhaps worse. At

least priestesses in agricultural states managed huge temple households and had major responsibilities. There was nothing similar to this in Athens. All public work for women was seen as unrespectable for one reason or another. For one thing, it was only lower-class women who worked publicly, doing menial jobs like picking grapes or acting as wet-nurses. There were three options for women—wife, prostitute, or concubine, and all were options for slaves.

The life of a wife in classical Greek civilization was bleak. For her entire life she was under the thumb of her father, brother, or husband. She was wedded by age 15 to a man at least twice her age. The marriage was arranged by her father, and often she married a foreigner. She was probably sexually starved, because husbands generally preferred prostitutes, concubines, and young boys to their wives. Husbands and wives didn't even sleep in the same bed or eat together. They occupied separate quarters of the house, and the wife's area of the house was usually dark and damp.

The double standard was deeply institutionalized. For example, if a married woman had an affair, it was legal to sell her into slavery. She could also be barred from public rituals. If she wanted a divorce, she needed the intercession of her father or a male citizen. Meanwhile, for men to be with prostitutes or have concubines was accepted as a matter of course; it wasn't even controversial. In fact, Solon institutionalized state brothels.

Within the household, besides rearing children, a woman's major activities were spinning and weaving wool, grinding corn, and milling wheat. Aside from going to a well for water, she spent most of her time indoors. She didn't even go to the market. It is possible that the lives of upper-class women were somewhat better. After all, since they had slaves, that must have reduced the amount of work they had to do. But the content of their work was not all that different from what slaves did. A woman's upper-class background was undercut by the fact that she was a woman.

It has sometimes been argued that the life of the famous "hetaerae" was enviable. These were prostitutes who were poets and scholars, and who entertained upper-class men. According to Keuls (1985), this way of life was far more the exception than the rule for most prostitutes in Athens. All prostitutes had to deal with unhealthy working hours, exposure to disease, and unwanted pregnancy. They had to contend with being the recipient of violent male actions, from anal sex to being beaten with sticks and sandals. Then there was the likely emotional toll from having to pretend that it was really enjoyable being around such arrogant males. Any meaningful sex life beyond work must have been difficult.

Further, Solon's institutionalization of prostitution included no policies to protect prostitutes. As a young woman, a prostitute might be in demand and have the protection of a pimp. As she grew older, she might be able to negotiate her freedom, but then her age made her less in demand. If she were lucky and made some connection with a former customer, this might lead to a common-law marriage. If not, she was on her own. There were occasions where a hetaerae rose to the status of "madam," and commanded a stable of slave girls, but this was far more the exception than the rule. In the long run, the life of a hetaera was probably worse than that of a wife.

The job of a concubine, on the other hand, was to care for men's bodies. In status, concubines were somewhere in between wives and hetaerae, but they had even less protection. Whereas a wife had a dowry and a prostitute had a pimp, a concubine's only hope was to retain her status with the man into old age. Otherwise she would be forced back into prostitution.

In addition to the mechanisms of coercion, institutions of legitimation were by now well in place in classical Greece. Women were not valued as persons. They received no formal education except possibly in music, and their basic functions were to provide male heirs for their husbands, provide cheap labor, and watch over the house.

Women were included in birth and death dramatizations, but men wanted to be involved as little as possible in the actual birth and death processes. For example, there was a cultivated ignorance among men about female anatomy.

Men still imagined that the womb was no more than an incubator for the male seed. It was midwives who delivered babies, as the doctors wanted nothing to do with the procedure. This cultivated ignorance was rationalized and mythologized to the point that a mother's death in giving birth was raised to the status of a male dying in battle.

Right from birth, girls were taught the habits of submission, the virtues of toil, and the glories of death in giving birth. At a young age they prepared for sacred festivals that praised the virtues of male valor in battle. These dramatizations were supported by a mythology that celebrated the defeat of women (the Amazons). Even the goddesses themselves expressed the fragmentation of the female psyche. There was no female deity who had the multi-dimensionality of say, Apollo or Zeus. Greek goddesses did not combine sexuality, power, wisdom, and skills the way Greeks gods did.

Girls' training in subordination would not have been successful without the socialization of boys to be dominant. Boys were removed from female quarters at around the age of six, and then trained physically and mentally in a gymnasium. A young boy was encouraged to drink and carouse at festivals, and as a young man, he was encouraged to participate in symposiums where he got to abuse older prostitutes. At 20, he received 10 years of military training. By the time he was 30 he was "ready" for marriage, having never dealt with a "free" woman in his entire life. All of his experiences were with prostitutes and slaves. This type of husband was hardly going to treat women in any way other than as second class citizens. It is difficult to respect women when you see them in humiliating situations everywhere you turn.

Meanwhile, as the boy was having all of these adventures, the girl was married at 15, was raising babies, and was expected to be monogamous for life. Yet it was perfectly acceptable for her husband to cavort with prostitutes throughout his adult life and take a concubine in old age. With this kind of socialization in legitimized male rule, girls must have come to imagine that the political-economic forces that were stacked against them were really just an expression of the eternal order of things as reflected in the mythology of immortal gods who abuse goddesses.

As McElvaine (2001) points out, Axial Iron Age sacred life appears to have been less militaristic and brutal than that in Bronze and Archaic Iron Age states. The characteristics of the sacred sage in the Axial Age are softer and wiser than those of the hero in the Archaic Iron Age (Lerro, 2000, chapter 10). While the heroes fought, drank and fornicated, Confucius stressed the importance of being a "gentleman" and showing deference to others. Buddha and Socrates both stressed self-observation and self-knowledge. These sages stressed compassion for the stranger rather than tribal loyalties.

This is a movement from a brash, tough masculinity to another kind of masculinity—that of a philosopher, abstract reasoner, and analyzer. As we will see in chapter 13 on polytheism and monotheism, Judaism did treat women better than did other Axial Age civilizations. But even so, the Hebraic tradition was still male dominated. In India the situation was not much better. The Buddha at first refused to allow women into the Sangha and had to be talked into it by one of his disciplines (Chakravarti, 1987). Further, all universalistic religions excluded goddesses completely, a deterioration from the situation in the Bronze Age.

Of all the Axial Age civilizations, it was Athens that held the deepest contradictions for the lives of women. While Athens had more democratic institutions in place than any other Axial Age civilization, it treated women as if they were another species (McElvaine, 2001). There must have been a great deal of tension between classes when the aristocracy of the Archaic Iron Age had to give up some of its power to the merchants. It was perhaps as a compensation for the intensification of the class struggle (which was essentially between men) that men in all classes found a common bond in their imagined superiority over all non-members of their group—women, foreigners, and slaves. Thus the increased democracy among men was achieved at the price of a decrease in democracy in the relations between themselves and other groups.

A full discussion of the psychological processes that support internalization will have to be deferred to chapters 14 through 16. Nevertheless, let me mention briefly three of those processes now. In chapter 15 we will examine two kinds of selves—the individualist and the collectivist. The collectivist self puts the group before the individual, sees itself as inseparable from the roles it is asked to play, and is most at home in routine situations. The individualist self puts its identity before the group, is more at home challenging roles and situations, and forges connections with strangers beyond the kin group. As you might imagine, women had collectivist selves and thus more readily accepted a subordinate position.

A second psychological process supporting internalization centers on the form of cognition taking place. People in tribal societies think in what I call "concrete abstractions." This means that thinking is practical and rooted in conversations with people and concern with performing actions. Concrete abstraction is more concerned with the present and less with the deep past and deep future.

While all human beings in all societies think abstractly, there was an increase in the level of abstraction beginning in the Bronze Age. With the separation of mental from manual labor, and the invention of writing systems and coined money, certain upper-caste sectors of the population began to think in what I call "hyper-abstract" way. Thinking became self-reflective, sharper, more critical, and more able to see past immediate situations and routine conventions. Hyperabstract thinking is more occupied with thinking about thinking, rather than thinking in reaction to conversations and performing immediate actions. Since women had little opportunity to work in intellectual occupations and administrative positions, to work with writing systems or handle coined money, they were not able to cultivate hyper-abstract thinking. Without this skill it would have been difficult to think critically about their situation; rather, it must have been all too easy to simply internalize what the legitimizing institutions proclaimed.

The last psychological process that contributed to women's subordination was perception. As McLuhan (1969), Ong (1988), Goody (1977, 1986) and Havelock (1963) have pointed out, the leading sense of people in tribal societies typically was hearing. This began to change in the Bronze and Iron Ages when the invention of picture writing and the alphabet challenged this organization of sense ratios and increased the importance of sight. Sight is the most objective of the senses, allowing people to distance themselves from the immediate circumstances, to clarify and separate objects, and to initiate rather than react to events. With the exception of priestesses in the Bronze Age, women's sense ratios were limited to the proximate senses of touch, taste, smell and hearing. For reasons that will be discussed in chapter 14, people who relied on these senses were less likely to challenge legitimizing institutions than they would have been if they were relying more on the sense of sight.

5. Implications for women

In reviewing the patterns of social evolution for women in the ancient world, it is safe to conclude that the more complex societies became, the more the status of women deteriorated. Further, as long as women worked in public and remained in control over the tools they used, women's life varied from relative autonomy (among hunter-gatherers) to a mixture of autonomy and subservience (in complex horticultural societies). The rise of the state and cities in the Bronze Age was a disaster for the status of women. Women ceased to work in public and lost control over the planting.

In hunting-and-gathering egalitarian societies, with the exception of societies living in harsh environments, women's life was good. Though rarely a leader, woman was involved in political decision making processes. Working in public allowed her companionship with other women gatherers. Though gathering was not held in as high esteem as hunting, it was still a respected activity. Marriage and child rearing must have been reasonably enjoyable. A woman was primarily responsible for raising a

small family, marriages were not based on a double sexual standard, and she did not work more than 20 hours per week.

In village horticulture societies women's life became harder. In both simple and complex horticulture societies women worked in gardens, domesticating small animals. The work was still held in high prestige but there was more of it, since, according to Lenski, horticulturists worked 20–30 hours per week. Women were now responsible for raising larger families, but this was countered by the existence of kin groups to help with child rearing. In these societies more work was put into conflict resolution because people were living in close quarters and the option of moving as the result of a conflict carried a higher cost. Tracing lineage became more important in these societies, which meant that virginity became an issue. In both simple and complex horticultural societies there was a sexual double standard and violence against women became more prevalent.

Herding societies and complex horticultural societies were ranked and women lost significant ground compared to their forebears in egalitarian societies. Complex horticultural societies required the raising of more children, but this was done in a much larger community with a far greater division of labor. In herding societies women did not have as many children to take care of, but the nomadic way of life, subsisting in arid environments, was probably more difficult.

With the exception of priestesses in agricultural states, life for women in the Bronze and Iron Ages was far worse than it had been in prestate societies. Women ceased to work in public and instead engaged in cottage industry. This work had low status. The rise of the state weakened kinship ties, while women were still responsible for raising large families. Polygyny was common while virginity for women was expected. In both Metal Ages women were given no formal education.

Is there anything positive to be gained for women with the rise of gender hierarchies? Perhaps there is. Marx argued that, under capitalism, the emergence of the working class from artisan class of the feudal period was in one sense an advance, even though the life of most working-class people was worse. Marx believed that in order for the working class to truly liberate itself it had to free itself from enmeshed loyalties to feudal lords, clerics, and kings. Working-class life was miserable enough so that there could be no illusion about loyalty to the arch enemy, the capitalists.

A comparison might be made between the life of women in complex horticulture societies and the life of artisans in the Middle Ages. Just as artisans' mixed loyalties to various groups inhibited their clear understanding of their subordinate position, so perhaps the enmeshed loyalty of women to kin groups and clans obscured the beginnings of institutionalized male dominance. As long as women's social personhood reflected a combination of her

work skill, the product she produced, her age, and other factors, the more her gender identity was obscured. A precondition for women to build group power to act against gender hierarchy was a clarification of their subordinated status *as women*.

When any subjugated group experiences starkly, in no uncertain terms, that it is subordinated, it is in a better position to do something about it than if its subjugation is mystified or hidden. The intensification and the sharpening of male dominance in ancient civilization created the necessary conditions (but not sufficient, as we will see in chapter 17) for something positive to emerge later on in history—the collective fight against subordination via the women's movement.

Figure 6.4 Comparative Status of Women from the Paleolithic Age to the Late Neolithic Age

Hunter-gatherers	Simple horticulturists	Complex horticulturists
GENERAL CHARACTERISTICS OF SOCIETY		
bands	tribes	chiefdoms
(50-100)	(100-1,000)	(1,000-10,000)
egalitarian	egalitarian	rank
decentralized	decentralized	centralized
situation-specific leadership	episodic leadership	permanent leadership
headman	big-man	chief
generalized reciprocity	egalitarian redistribution	partial redistribution
balanced diet	protein deficient	protein deficient
sacred presences immanent	immanent	immanent
earth spirits	totems, ancestor spirits	totems, ancestor spirits
APPLICATION TO WOMEN		
gathering in public	planting in public	planting in public
baskets	digging sticks	digging sticks
	domestication of small animals	domestication of small animals
		craft production
segregation of labor	segregation of labor	segregation of labor
nuclear families	kin groups/ nuclear family	kin groups/ nuclear family
	brother-sister relationship is the unit	brother-sister relationship is the unit
serial monogamy	some polygamy	polygamy for chief
little sexual double standard		chiefly wives repressive before marriage; permissive after marriage
		commoners permissive before and after marriage; risk of rape
virginity not important		virginity important
two to four children	more children	more children
children raised to be self-sufficient and independent	children raised to be obedient	children raised to be obedient

Figure 6.5 Comparative Status of Women from the Bronze Age to the Axial Iron Age

GENERAL CHARACTERISTICS OF SOCIETIES

Herding	Agriculture	Commercial agriculture
bands	states/cities	states/cities
50-100	10,000-100, 000	10, 000-100,000
rank	stratified—caste	stratified—class
centralized	rigid centralization	moderate centralization
permanent leadership	permanent leadership	permanent leadership
	inherited (King)	inherited (aristocrats)
	authoritarian decision-making	polis—democratic for
		middle and upper classes
partial redistribution	surplus expropriation	surplus expropriation
		commerce within society
		rise of secularized culture
	bronze tools, hieroglyphics	iron tools, alphabet, coined money
transcendent sacred source	immanent sacred source	immanent/transcendent sacred source
god	goddesses, gods	mixed goddesses, gods
vegetable deficient	protein deficient	protein deficient

APPLICATION TO WOMEN

Herding	Agriculture	Commercial agriculture
	men take over planting: plow and domesticate cattle	same
tending sheep and goats	domestic cottage industry	domestic cottage industry
processing animal products:	spinning, weaving, milling	spinning, weaving, milling
milk, animal hides	priestesses run temple	no respectable public identity
some say in politics	no say in politics	no say in politics
		could not own property
	no formal education	no formal education except music
strong kinship ties	kinship ties weakened: extended families	kinship ties weakened; extended families
polygamy common	polygamy common for upper classes.	husband can have concubines slaves and other men. Wife expected to be monogamous
		wife-beating is common
virginity important	virginity important	virginity important
roughly same number of children as hunter-gatherers	more children	more children
encourage independence, aggressiveness, compliance for boys	encourage obedience to parents	encourage compliance for girls, independence for boys

Part III

Phase 1: Biological, Political, and Geophysical Constraints

Chapter 7

Is Origin Destiny?
The Place and Misplace of Biology
In The Emergence of Gender Hierarchies

1. General differences between men and women

At the end of chapter 5, I argued that the emergence of informal dominance in tribal societies can be explained socio-ecologically. But the fact that, if informal dominance emerges, it is always *male* informal dominance and never female informal dominance, cannot be explained socio-ecologically. Further, informal male dominance is just one of the phenomena discussed in this book that require explanation—others include the monopolization of public power and privilege by men in politics, economics, and war. Males also dominate in residency patterns after marriage and in tracing of descent. In addition, men do not have much responsibility for child rearing. In this chapter we will see how many of these problems can be successfully addressed by evolutionary psychology.

Despite the argument by some sociologists that there are no human universals, Donald Brown (1991) has found a pattern of human behaviors that can be characterized as universal or nearly universal. I have grouped and simplified these universals into Harris's classificatory scheme of infrastructure, structure, and superstructure, to which I have added a psychological dimension (see Figure 7.1).

Is it just a coincidence that people in societies as divergent as those of hunter-gatherers and industrial-capitalists exhibit these same patterns? Alice Rossi (1984) argues that a pattern of social behavior can be suspected of

having a biological basis if two or more of the following criteria are met: (Sanderson 2001, p. 212)

(1) there are consistent correlations between behavior and *physiological sex attributes* (body structure, sex chromosome type, hormonal type);
(2) the pattern is *found in infants and young children prior to the occurrence of major socialization* influences, or the pattern emerges with the onset of puberty;
(3) the pattern is *stable across cultures*; and
(4) similar behavior patterns are found *across species*, especially the higher primates.

I contend that some of the universals identified by Brown are "hardwired," because they fill criteria one and four.

Just as there are universal commonalties in human activities across social formations, there are also universal differences between the sexes in labor practices. It is true that pottery making, weaving, and horticulture are done sometimes by men and sometimes by women. However, there are other occupations that are more consistently gender-specific. According to Murdock and Provost's sample of 185 societies, the following occupations are reliably gender-specific in most societies:

Figure 7.1 Universals of Human Behavior *

infrastructure	structure	superstructure	psychological
	structure	**superstructure**	**psychological**
	warfare	gossip	binary distinctions
	politics	non-verbal language:	abstract thinking
		gestures	
		paralanguage	
		body adornment	basic range of emotions
		drugs	
	status distinctions	verbal language	
division of labor by:			
sex		social norms and values	
age			prestige seeking
		religion	
		rituals	
tool-making		art: music, dance	
energy harnessing		symbolism	
food taboos			
discretion in elimination of body wastes			
in-group-out-group antagonisms			
birth control and population regulation		standards of sexual attractiveness	sexual jealousy
		sex as a service provided by women to men	
		husbands usually older	
		incest avoidance	
		group living and cooperation	
		socialization	
		family; marriage and kinship systems	males more aroused by visual sexual stimulus
		families built around mothers/children	
		female monopolization of child-care	
locality/ territory			
concepts of property			

* Adapted to Harris' three dimensions of society. See chapter 1. The list comes from Sanderson (2001, 210-212)

Men
hunting large game
metal working
smelting ores
lumbering
woodworking
making musical instruments
trapping
boat building
stonework
working in bone, horn and shell
mining
quarrying
bone setting

Women
fuel gathering
preparing drinks
gathering
preparing wild plant foods
dairy production
laundering
water fetching
cooking
child-rearing

Quoting Parker and Parker (1979), Sanderson (2001) argues that around the world and throughout history, the work that men do has the following characteristics—

- it involves greater strength and stamina,
- it is more dangerous or risky,
- it is not easily interrupted,
- it requires high levels of skill and training, and
- it requires long periods of time away from home base.

2. The human nature controversy

In what proportion are we biological creatures and in what proportion are we socio-cultural beings? How do biology and society interact through humanity? What is our human nature? Evolutionary psychologists argue that our human nature is essentially biological and that, since throughout most of our existence we have been collector-hunters, our most important predispositions (formed through natural selection) have been adaptations to that activity.

Sociologists traditionally have opposed biological explanations for social behavior, claiming that all social institutions are a product of learning. Sociologists disagree with each other over which social institutions are primarily responsible for why societies are the way they are, but with rare exceptions,

sociologists are on the "nurture" side of the controversy, claiming that everything human beings are is a product of social institutions and can be changed by social institutions. Individuals are more or less blank slates before they become fully socialized.

Biological arguments have had a stormy history among sociologists, in part because the former have tended to be reductionistic, in that they were characterized by attempts to explain all human activities—including art, religion, and even our most everyday choices—by way of drives, genes, or hormones. However, the current proposals by evolutionary psychologists cannot fairly be lumped together with these past reductionistic arguments.

In circles of politically progressive sociologists, it is assumed that human biology has little if anything to do with differences between genders, that all of the important social differences between men and women are socially constructed, and that any biological explanations should be summarily dismissed on ideological grounds. As soon as biology is mentioned, it is assumed that the speaker is (a) saying the ways men and women are different are *inevitable,* and (b) *justifying* whatever differences exist, especially those with regard to influence, prestige, privilege, and power.

There are very good reasons for this current prejudice against biological explanations among progressives. From the late decades of the 19th century at least until the end of World War II, biology was used to justify racist policies against

Native Americans, African Americans, and Hispanics in the United States; against native peoples in South Africa and Australia; and against Jews in Nazi-dominated Europe. Biological explanations were also offered for withholding from women the right to vote, as well as for mandatory sterilization laws and culturally-biased IQ testing. As Deborah Blum points out,

> It was a good three decades after World War II before many people would even discuss the idea again that biology counted in behavior. The whole sorry eugenics episode should warn us against substituting political science for biological science. (Blum, 1997, 260-261)

But then she goes on to say that

> [C]aution is different from refusing to allow honest research, or to acknowledge its results. Let's be vigilant, let's be cautious; let's even be suspicious. . . . But . . . to pretend that the facts don't exist will not protect us. (Blum, 1997, 261)

It is worth keeping in mind that political reactionaries are not the only ones who can use the nature-nurture controversy for political purposes. Between the 1930s and the 1950s the Lysenkoist movement in the former Soviet Union suppressed Mendel's genetics in favor of Lamarck's theory of the inheritance of acquired characteristics. This had disastrous consequences for Soviet agriculture.

In order to defuse the emotional reactions that seem to surround this subject, evolutionary psychologist David Buss names a few of the most common misunderstandings about evolutionary psychology.

(1) Human behavior is genetically determined. According to Buss, genetic determinism is the doctrine that behavior is controlled *exclusively* by genes, with little or no room for environmental influence. In contrast, Buss claims evolutionary theory is a truly interactional framework that acknowledges the role of environmental and social feedback mechanisms. Some genes are *responsive* to the

environment. Gaulin and McBurney (2001) make a distinction between two types of gene-environment relationships—*obligate* and *facultative*. Obligate genes resist environmental interference, while facultative are more responsive. Why? Because obligate genes have evolved to provide for more stable circumstances, while facultative genes have evolved to respond to rapidly changing environments. Obligate genes govern, for example, the body plan—which will remain the same regardless of the environment:

> You would have developed with two arms, legs, and eyes regardless of whether you had grown up in the snows of the Himalayas or sands of the Sahara, regardless of whether . . . you had been fed meat and potatoes or manioc and beetle grubs. (Gaulin and McBurney, 2001, 51)

These genes are passed on across generations. Genes are obligate when they are "relatively insensitive to experience over a wide range of normal environments." (Gaulin and McBurney, 2001, 52)

Genes are facultative when they are more responsive to environmental influences. These arise in two circumstances: (1) when the environment is variable within the lifetimes of individuals, and (2) when the fittest alternative varies from one environment to the next. Facultative traits are not passed down across generations.

More than this, there are some human behaviors that evolutionary psychologists agree *do not* maximize fitness, yet they persist. Joseph Lopreato's "modified maximization principle" states that

> Human behavior maximizes fitness unless its reproductive consequences are subverted by the desire to accumulate resources that engender pleasure, or by self-denying or ascetic tendencies often stimulated by sacred beliefs and practices. (Sanderson, 2001, 208)

This means that people sometimes choose behaviors that seem to contradict biological fitness. The desire to have sex using contraceptives undermines the evolutionary strategy to maximize fitness by spreading one's genes. Religious commitments to celibacy do the same thing.

(2) If it is evolutionary we can't change it. Biological arguments about human nature were formerly inextricably linked with instinct theory—which holds that whatever is biologically driven will show itself regardless of time, place, or context. Instinct theory was largely disproven simply by showing that certain behaviors vary according to various socio-ecological contexts. But this does not mean that human behavior is entirely socially constructed. Between instinct theory and socio-constructionism lies a middle ground that acknowledges biological predisposition. This is the territory of evolutionary psychology. These predispositions are not rigid. Some socio-cultural conditions trigger higher levels of aggression, for example, while other conditions minimize this.

While it is an overstatement inconsistent with social evolutionary findings to say that gender differences are instinctual, it is just as incorrect to say that all gender differences are socially constructed.

Lopreato and Crippen agree that socialization is necessary to become fully human. But some things are easier to learn than others, and this is a fact that many sociologists tend to overlook.

> Experience does not shape the development of behavior without guidance from innate predispositions. Thus we learn some things a great deal more easily than others, some more efficiently at certain stages of development . . . and some not at all. Behaviorist theory focuses at best on the how of learned behavior, on the techniques of learning; it neglects the why, the when, and much of the what. . . . (Sanderson, 2001, 209)

Knowledge of our evolved adaptations, along with the social inputs they were designed to be responsive to, can have a liberating effect, enabling us to change our behavior. However,

changing behavior is not always simple or easy. For example, the knowledge that sexual jealousy is part of our genetic inheritance can help us put this emotion in perspective, but the emotion itself may still be difficult to overcome.

Biology has an influence on our behavior; this is beyond dispute. The only question is, how large is that influence? Men and women are biologically predisposed toward a certain range of behavior, but this range can be constricted, stretched, or suppressed, depending on socio-ecological conditions of time, place, and circumstance. According to Sanderson, "Culture is like the volume control knob on a radio; it can turn predispositions to higher levels or it can tone them down. In a few instances, it might be able to turn them off, despite natural human drives." (2001, 204)

(3) Evolutionary theories require improbable computational abilities of organisms. Though the *rules* for adaptive behavior are complex and their description requires advanced mathematics, the organism does not need complex mathematical computations to *execute* these behaviors. This capacity is built into the organism; it is not a product of conscious calculation. Similarly, an accomplished ballerina or figure skater does not need to mathematically describe an extremely challenging aesthetic performance in order to execute it; neither does a spider require mathematical blueprints to build a web or a beaver to build a dam.

(4) Current adaptive mechanisms are optimally designed. Sometimes it is assumed that evolutionary mechanisms are exactly evolved to match the organism's environment. This might be understood as a projection of the human capacity to design projects according to a plan, or a religious teleological argument for the existence of God as an architect who anticipates all problems from the beginning to the end of time. But nature improvises, it does not design. Many adaptive mechanisms are carryovers from environments that have since changed. For example, we humans continue to retain a strong desire for fat, which was adaptive in a past environment of scarce resources. Today the same craving has negative consequences.

(5) Evolutionary theory implies a motivation to maximize one's gene reproduction.
When we ask people about various projects they are working on, they might mention training their dog, cleaning out their apartment, getting a college degree, or finding work that is a better match to their skills. People do not volunteer, as a motivation, "maximizing gene reproduction." Doesn't this prove evolutionary psychologists are wrong?

The motives of people are only indirectly related to the evolutionary process of gene reproduction and are not a direct expression of it. In the long run, the maximization of gene reproduction provides the framework from which one's motivations ultimately derive, but these motivations are mediated by whether you are a man or woman, the kind of society you live in, whether you are child or adolescent, and the particular situation you happen to be in. In other words there is no universal strategy of fitness that overrides personal identity, age, or the uniqueness of circumstances.

Differences in time scale also preclude any direct correlation between the maximization of gene reproduction and people's individual motives. Maximizing gene reproduction is a project that spans many species over great stretches of time. The overwhelming majority of human projects are limited to the lifetimes of individuals. Still, many of the most important projects that men and women engage in do indirectly increase the possibility of passing on their genes.

(6) Evolutionary theorists' discussions of nature-nurture interaction underestimate the role of the environment. Gaulin and McBurney (2001) critique three different ways of conceiving the nature-nurture relationship. The first is dualism, which holds that some traits are typically characteristic of nature and others are characteristic of nurture. The problem with this formulation is that it fails to identify the *conditions* under which either nature or nurture might be the dominant factor. It implies the causes are due to chance or can never be discovered. But, as we saw earlier, obligate genes are sensitive to rapidly changing environments.

The second way social science conceives of the nature-nurture relationship is more quantitative and interactive. It is often claimed that human behavior is shaped, let us say, 20% by nature and 80% by nurture—or some other percentages. Similarly, one could say that, for the long-term maintenance of human health, it is necessary to consume a certain proportion of protein, fats, and carbohydrates—this is the "nature" part of the health equation; but people's *choices* of proteins, fats, and carbohydrates are a matter of geographical setting and cultural preference. However, according to Gaulin and McBurney, this is still a mistaken understanding because it assumes that the relationship between nature and nurture is mechanical rather than interdependent or mutually constitutional.

> Wouldn't it be ridiculous to claim that bread is 75% ingredients and 25% heat? Bread is what happens when the right kinds of ingredients are exposed to appropriate temperatures. Either one without the other yields nothing useful at all because bread is the product of the interaction. (Gaulin and McBurney, 2001, 80-81)

In other words, bread needs both in order to come into being.

The third and last way the nature-nurture interaction is imagined is that nature sets the limits but experience shapes the trait within these boundaries. This misses the mark because it fails to address the very large problem of exactly *how* experience shapes the trait.

Let me close this section with an analogy that Gaulin and McBurney use to drive home their point:

> Suppose we have a whole bakery full of loaves. And suppose the baker had used several different recipes and several ovens that differed slightly in baking temperature. In this case, it would be reasonable to ask about the flavor differences among these loaves, and in particular whether these differences were more the result of different ingredients or

more the result of baking in different ovens.

Maybe on Monday the ingredient lists were pretty similar, but the oven temperatures varied considerably. Then surely on Monday the oven 'environment' will explain most of the difference in bread flavor. On the other hand, perhaps on Tuesday, the baker was feeling more experimental and added one unique ingredient to each loaf. On Thursday, differences in ingredients may well account for more of the difference in flavor than do any relatively small differences in baking temperature. (Gaulin and McBurney, 2001, 85)

Let us turn now to the history of how human cultures have made sense of human nature. It is likely that people in pre-state societies had no concept of a unified human species as being clearly distinct from other species. In fact, the ethnographic record suggests that they identified more closely with the plants and animals in their immediate ecological environments than they did with members of other human societies. The ecological network of stones-rivers-mountains-humans-plants-animals was the basis of their magical sacred systems. This was also true of the great Bronze Age agricultural states.

It was one of the great struggles of the world religions in the Axial Iron Age, from about 1000 BCE to 650 CE, to try to sever the ecological network that existed between humans and the rest of Nature. The universalistic religions claimed that humanity was *superior* to the plants and the animals, and that people should seek to build links with other humans around the world, specifically strangers. This would constitute a "brotherhood of man." Second, humanity should connect itself with a single transcendental being who exists outside the world. Until the 15th century BCE, whatever concept of "human nature" that might have existed would have been enmeshed with plants and animals in magical systems; alternatively, human nature may have been imagined as unique to humans, but

subordinated to a universal deity in religious systems.

It is only in the past 500 years that the notion has emerged of a human nature that is completely autonomous of any sacred system. Many philosophers, sociologists, and biologists have attempted to define this human nature. Some claimed that we are fundamentally greedy; others claimed that we are altruistic. What is more important for our purposes is that the terrain in which this question was fought was *secular*. Now human nature was deemed either biological or social rather than sacred. To be sure, magical and religious systems continue to define human nature in the present, but they must share the terrain with the social and natural sciences.

McElvaine (2001) names two groups opposed to biological explanations of human nature. One he calls the "Biblical Creationists" and the other the "Cultural Creationists." For the Biblical Creationists, God created people out of formless clay; for Cultural Creationists, humans may be a product of biological evolution initially but biology no longer has any consequence for us. In its extreme form, this view holds that biologically humans are a formless clay from which culture molds socialized people. Biblical Creationists fear that biological evolution leaves no place for a divine purpose; Cultural Creationists fear that biological evolution leaves no place for human purpose and social change. Cultural Creationists treat human cultures as if they were separate species, with no universal characteristics.

McElvaine argues against the notion that culture has nothing to do with biology:

biology provides both the foundation on which cultural systems have been raised and the building materials used in their construction. Cultures are constrained in what they can construct by what building materials are available in the deep structure of the human biogram. (McElvaine, 2001, 33)

McElvaine then uses an analogy to show the relationship between nature and nurture:

Humans at birth may seem to be blank tablets, but they are better viewed as *apparently* blank sheets that have been beneath other sheets on a pad. Evolution pressed hard in writing on those preceding sheets, leaving imprints on the seemingly blank page that we are at birth. Our experiences, many of them specific to the culture in which we are born, then write on this sheet, but with a very soft-lead pencil. The tendency is for some of the loose lead or graphite to slip into the indentations left by evolution. (34)

In addressing the relationship between freedom and determinism he says:

> Our biological inheritance does not determine our destiny: It does restrict our choices. Our human nature is the hand that is dealt to us. What we do with that hand is still up to us. The cards we receive place certain limits on what we can do, and if we hope to do well, we had better look at the cards. We can win at poker with almost any hand, but winning is unlikely to happen without one knowing what cards are held. (41)

3. Sexual selection and adaptation

Evolutionary psychologists believe that human nature was formed in adaptation to an environment very different from the one most people find themselves in today. MacElvaine writes:

> Our distant ancestors had adapted biologically to live in small bands of collector- hunters. The hominid human way of life prevailed for at least 98% of our evolution. It was this process that created human nature. . . . (6) [A]lmost all of the selective pressures that made humans what we are today operated under constraints that were likely to shape creatures to succeed as collector scavengers or collector hunters. (40)

Thus a large part of human behavior is genetically determined by the hunting-and-gathering evolutionary environment in which human nature was formed. According to Buss, natural selection involves three processes: variation, inheritance, and selection. "Organisms vary in ways such as wing length, trunk strength, bone mass, cell structure, fighting ability. Variation is essential for the process of evolution to operate—it provides the 'raw materials' for evolution." (7) Some of these variations are inherited—passed down from parents to offspring. Other variations such as wing deformity caused by an environmental accident, are not inherited.

> Darwin envisioned two classes of evolved variations—one playing a role in survival and another . . . in reproduction. The first he called "natural selection" and the second "sexual selection." Organisms with some heritable variants leave more offspring because those attributes help with the tasks of survival and/or reproduction. More finches who have beaks better shaped for nut cracking survive. But what about the next generation? To pass its inherited qualities to future generations [a finch] must reproduce. (Buss, 1999, 7)

The combination of natural and sexual selection led to differential reproductive success.

> Selection acts as a sieve in each generation, filtering out many features that do not contribute to propagation. . . . Those characteristics that make it through the filtering process do so because they contribute to the solution of adaptive problems of either survival or reproduction. . . . [They can be] direct, such as the fear of dangerous snakes . . . or indirect, as the desire to ascend a social hierarchy which many years later might provide better access to mates. (Buss, 1999, 37)

But what does it actually mean for an organism to "adapt" to its environment? And what is the relationship between adaptation and natural selection? Adaptation involved specific solutions to specific problems—solutions that contribute either directly or indirectly to successful reproduction. For example, sweat glands help solve the survival problem of thermal regulation; taste preferences may be adaptations that guide the successful consumption of nutritious food; and mate preferences may be an adaptation that guides successful selection of mates.

Adaptations can be identified by their low probability of chance occurrence: when we see a reliable, efficient, and economic set of features that could not have arisen randomly, we are justified in assuming that it is adaptive. (If it is reliable, the adaptive mechanism regularly develops in all members of the species across all normal environments.)

But more specifically, what can evolutionary psychology teach us about sexual selection, and how might sexual selection (a) explain some differences between men and women and (b) answer the questions at the end of chapter 2?

Let us start with the most basic problem of all. Why did evolution invent sex in the first place? Presumably, it must provide some survival value. Blum (1997) asks,

What do males do?—the most basic purpose of males in species that reproduce sexually is to provide a means of *remixing genes* to create genetic diversity as a hedge against future environmental changes (72)

In other words, in rapidly changing environmental settings the remixing of genes increases the chance of a variety of adaptive responses arising to meet novel circumstances. Asexual reproduction would work better in slowly changing environments—such as the environments inhabited by most parasites.

According to behavioral ecologist Bobbi Low (2000), at the heart of all strategies of life forms is a single problem: How can effort (calories expended, time spent, and risks taken) be spent optimally? How best to expend effort to replicate genes?

Both men and women seek and use resources for reproductive success, and they do this by (a) striving to mate, (b) investing in children and other genetic relatives, and (c) building genetically profitable relationships with strangers.

However, when a species reproduces itself sexually (as opposed to asexually) there are inherent differences between males and females, because one gender carries the neonate and the other does not. Specifically, men and women differ in (a) what kind of resources they seek, (b) the strategies used for getting them (coalitions), and (c) how resources are used. This helps to explain why men and women have had significant differences in thinking and acting throughout human history. According to Low,

Reproducing in sexual species requires two different sorts of effort: getting a mate (mating effort: striving to gain resources or status, getting mates) and raising healthy offspring (parental effort such as feeding, protecting and teaching offspring). (Low, 2000, 38)

Sexual selection refers to the differences between the sexes in the costs and benefits of mating effort and parental effort. The sex that carries the neonate will make greater parental investment, while the sex that doesn't will make more investment in mating effort. In evolutionary history it was not always the female that carried the neonate. As Buss points out,

There are a few species . . . in which males invest more than females. In some species . . . the female implants her eggs in the male and he is the one who carries the offspring until they are born. In species such as the Mormon cricket, poison-arrow frog, and pipefish seahorse . . . males invest more than females. . . . The male pipefish seahorse receives the eggs from the female and then carries them around in his kangaroo-like pouch. These females compete aggressively with each other for the best males and *the males* are choosy about who they mate with. (Buss, 1999, 42)

In other words, it is not "maleness" or "femaleness" that causes sex differences with regard to choosiness of partners. Rather it is the relative parental investment by the two sexes. Whichever gender invests more in neonate care (in which the process of pregnancy must be included) will be choosier about when, where, and with whom it mates.

Sex differences also evolve in species where females and males are capable of reproducing at *different rates*. In such cases, mating opportunities are not equally valuable to males and females. A woman can produce only one child per year; thus, having multiple mating partners would do little to increase a woman's reproductive rate. Her fertility is limited by the constraints of gestation and lactation, not by any shortage of mates. In contrast, a man's fertility rate is limited primarily by access to mates.

Therefore males focus less on parental effort and more on mating effort. Just as females have costs in parental investment (the process of pregnancy), males have fixed costs for mating effort:

A male must grow large if physical combat is any part of competition; he may have to range far; perhaps he must grow weapons or decoration, like a moose or a peacock; he may have to fight. (Low, 2000, 43)

There are two broad ways of getting more mates: (1) exclude same-sex competitors from mating by force through large size, strength, agility, or a quick temper; or (2) dazzle members of the opposite sex with elaborate ornamentation.

Competition for mates will always be less intense in the sex with the slower reproductive rate and more intense for the sex with the faster reproductive rate. In the case of human sexuality, "when females are the primary care givers they are slow to return to the mating pool and males end up competing for scarce mating opportunities." (Gaulin and McBurney, 2001, 34)

For humans, the pool of fertile males will always be much larger than the pool of fertile females. As you might imagine, and as we will see in more detail later, this problem leads to status seeking and aggression in males more than in females. For the sex with mating-effort strategies, passing on genes has potential for both greater success and greater failure—success, because they have so many chances for offspring; failure, because there is greater danger of injury and death through competition with other males.

Because males can spread their genes without parental investment, they can afford to be more promiscuous. This suggests an explanation for the differences between men and women in the division of labor in hunting and war, as well as differences in social power and in statistical tendencies to take more than one mate of the opposite gender.

Let's take availability for non-domestic labor as an example. Even in hunter-gather societies with a low birth rate, the demands of pregnancy and childrearing reduce the time and effort women have available to learn skills and to work in non-domestic settings. As Sanderson (2001) puts it,

Heavy childcare responsibilities preclude women's being concentrated in roles that require long periods of time away from home. It makes much more sense to leave women at home in charge of children than to disrupt the lives of children by moving them. . . . Moreover, childhood responsibilities make it more suitable for women to concentrate in roles that are easily interruptible, because children are the source of frequent interruptions. Also, roles that are easily interruptible are usually ones that involve lower levels of skill and training. Roles that are dangerous are much better suited for men because of the need to keep children away from danger. . . . (312)

Conversely, since men do not have physiological demands made on them with regard to childbearing and childrearing, they have more time to gather resources. This gives us a clue as to why men have monopolized public life in the areas of politics and economics. If evolutionary psychologists are right, women will be attracted to men who have a high probability of bringing in predictable resources, while men will be more responsive to women who give cues that they are fertile. According to evolutionary psychologists, what men want is not just sex, but fertile sex. What women want is predictable access to resources.

Low lists five traits that contribute to reproductive success: age, body size, dominance rank, early development patterns, and the quality of mates chosen. When women and men decide on a mate, they look for cues in these areas that will increase the probability of making a good choice. Since men and women have different strategies for reproducing their genes, they will not be looking for the same things in potential mates.

Finally, there is an imbalance in the degree of reliability that women and men possess in relation to the passing on of genes. Because women are the carriers of the neonate (newborn baby), they can be confident in their passing on of their own genes. Men, on the other hand, can be far less sure of their paternity. These differences lead women to be more choosy about the genes their offspring will receive from the father, and the non-domestic resources they can be assured of. Conversely, men's strategy is to either spread their genes around by physical display—hedging their bets—or to attempt to control women's access to other men through (a) the presence of abundant, predictable resources, (b) high status and reputation, or, as a last resort, (c) physical violence. These strategies are undertaken by men because for women to have various sexual partners undermines men's confidence that it is *their* genes in which they are investing resources.

These different strategies lead to different assumptions on the part of each gender as to what constitutes a betrayal in a relationship. As Buss has pointed out, men find sexual infidelity more hurtful because they have invested in someone who may be carrying another man's genes. Women, on the other hand, react more strongly to emotional infidelities to other women, because these weaken the commitment to provide resources.

To summarize the ramifications for sexual selection:

Women	Men
slow sex	fast sex
can produce one child per year	can produce many per year
investment in childbearing/childrearing	little investment in childrearing
parental effort	mating effort
more predicable risk	more unpredictable risk: greater chance of success and failure
easy access to mates	difficult access to mates: competition—aggression
	weaponry (vs. men)
	display (toward women)
needs non-domestic resources	need fertility
choosiness as a strategy	promiscuous as a strategy
confidence in motherhood	less confidence in fatherhood
choosiness about genes	spread genes around
	control female sexuality

4. Biological differences in aggression

It has been shown through cross-cultural research that, whether a given society is a tribal or a state formation, its men are likely to be more aggressive than its women. Speaking of the United States and Europe, Deborah Blum (1997) argues:

Aggression, at least as measured by critical statistics, exhibits an enduring gender gap. Government statistics in both the United States and in Europe record between 10-15 robberies committed by men for every one by a woman. (xiv)

According to Blum, men are seven times as likely as women to be arrested for a violent crime. If women's generally smaller physical stature were the *determining* factor in aggressive behavior, then technology should tend to equalize gender differences in violence. But it doesn't.

If women are simply handicapped by size, they should be able to compensate by arming themselves. . . . That hasn't happened. . . . Women are just not drawn to guns in the same numbers that men are. Among women robbers as a whole, only 30% use a gun. Among men as a whole the figure is 50 percent. There is a similar pattern in domestic partner murders: close to 75% of men who kill their partners use a gun. Women kill their partners too . . . but only about half use a gun. (Blum, 1997, xv)

This does not mean that women are never aggressive. According to Blum, females can be competitive and dangerous *when defending their young.*

To what extent is testosterone responsible for gender differences in aggression? Charles Yesalis of Pennsylvania State University, an expert in anabolic steroids, says that synthetic testosterone is effective in children who are lacking in human growth hormone because it adds height and weight. Natural testosterone levels have been linked with competition, status seeking, and violence. However, whatever hormonal differences exist between men and women, they are matters of degree rather than kind. Both men and women produce testosterone; it is not the sole property of men. Further,

There are certainly other strong biological influences on aggressive response. . .

there's the brain's acutely sensitive use of the neurotransmitters noradrenaline and serotonin in regulating the flight-or fight response. . . . Serotonin is essentially the soft voice of reason, calming, controlling impulses, regulating against aggression. (Blum, 1997, 179)

In addition, the competitive, status-driven, and sexual behavior that tends to be linked with testosterone in men is not independent of time, place, and context. It shows itself more in some social settings than others. According to Blum, testosterone levels fluctuate according to daily events. For example, they retreat in reaction to intense exercise and rise with anticipated competition. They retreat after failure in a competitive situation and intensify with success.

Finally, there is no one-to-one relationship between testosterone and violence. As Blum points out, criminals cannot be distinguished from non-criminals by their testosterone levels. But within the criminal population, there seems to be an association between higher testosterone levels and more vicious crimes. Perhaps testosterone is linked to an *attitude*—an edginess, an in-your-face anger, and a desire to strike out. But this propensity can be channeled into sports, debate, or starting one's own business. Moreover, testosterone is not a simple cause of behavior; behavior feeds back and affects hormone levels.

While testosterone is modified by other hormones, while it fluctuates depending on daily events, and while there is no one-to-one relationship between testosterone and its expression in violence, it is nevertheless clear that men's greater tendency toward violence, as compared with that of women, has a great deal to do with testosterone. On the average, men have ten times the amount of testosterone circulating in their blood as women:

In a 1993 study, Alan Booth and James Dabbs looked at T-levels across a range of relationships from dating to marriage to divorce. High testosterone men seemed more likely to make a mess of marriage. They were less likely to marry at all, and if they did, they were far more likely to divorce, often because they were unfaithful or physically abusive. (Blum, 1997, 174).

Do women behave more like men when they are injected with more testosterone?

What we know for sure is that even in adults, testosterone can alter body shape and look. It's the primary difference in appearance between men and women. . . . If a woman receives a lot of testosterone on a prolonged basis, you will see pronounced changes. The clitoris will get bigger. She will often develop a deeper voice, male pattern of hair growth. . . . (Blum, 1997, 165).

But does this translate into similar kinds of behavior? Not according to Kim Wallen: "What I find intriguing . . . is the possibility that a woman's testosterone is not affected by environment in the same way as a male's testosterone" (Quoted in Blum 1997, 165). In other words, the dramatic swings of testosterone relative to competition would not significantly affect women.

If you pump women full of synthetic testosterone . . . they develop a progressive nastiness. . . . [They] became rapidly angrier and more easily irritated by the people around them, but that did not translate to aggressive behavior. They didn't start shoving people around. They just became grouchy and obnoxious. (Blum 1997, 182)

However, the amount of testosterone in the bloodstream does seem to affect career choices. "Women who choose a professional career tended to be higher in testosterone than those who stayed home, and they were less likely to have children." (Blum 1997, 184)

Is there *any* hormone that is subject to fluctuation due to environmental feedback for women the way testosterone is for men? As it turns out, according to Blum, cortisol drives flexible responses in women in *dangerous or*

strange situations, but not competitive ones. These states of arousal in women, however, are complemented by seretonin, which regulates against aggression. Women have an average 30% higher level of seretonin than men.

The reason for male-female differences in aggression may also have something to do with the limbic system of the brain. In a study of the Gurs' live-brain work in early 1995, the following was noted:

Within this system men's brains glowed most brightly in a region linked to a quick physical response. Women's didn't. Their limbic system was more active in another region, linked to a quick verbal response. Equally interesting, the strong male response sprang from a part of the brain considered evolutionarily very old. It also exists in reptiles. But the female response derived from a region called the cingulate gyrus, which appears more recently in evolutionary development and is unusually large in humans. Ruben Gur speculated that this suggested a fundamental physiological difference that would lead women to respond first with words and men with fists. (Blum, 1997, 61)

But how might the differences in aggression be rooted in evolutionary psychology? Blum argues that

Healthy fertile females don't, in general, have to fight to get pregnant. Their chances of reproducing or continuing their genetic line are very high. . . . But males do often have to fight to become a parent. . . . There's been enormous evolutionary pressure on males to be the ones who hustle, who push, who have power who achieve the prize of sexual access. . . . In monogamous species where a long-time mating arrangement happens, the pressure is less. But among polygamous species, competition may be everything and may be brutal. Most of the world's species are polygamous; many scientists argue that early human ancestors were as well. (Blum, 1997, xvi)

Natural selection probably favored those males who would were more aggressive in the hopes of passing on their genes. On the contrary, it doesn't pay for women to be aggressive in competing over sex in order to pass on their genes. Blum asks,

> where in evolution is the comparable incentive for females to become so physically nasty over sex? They seem surrounded by potential and even overeager mates. It makes more sense for the female to be choosy. Pick a mate carefully; go for the good genes. . . . Fighting doesn't seem to give females a strong advantage in terms of carrying genes into the next generation. Early man might have battled his way to several mates and thus several chances for reproduction, but in our species, a women doesn't have more than one successful pregnancy a year. So in terms of reproduction, risking it all for multiple one-night stands might make sense for men, but not women. . . . (Blum, 1997, xvii)

> The number of males a female can seduce has no reproductive gain whatsoever . . . a woman if she chose, could sleep with a different man every other hour and still could have no more than one successful pregnancy a year. What, then, would be the evolutionary advantage of gambling her life in a battle for power that would gain her greater sexual access? 'Throughout evolutionary history, men have been able to gain reproductively by warring behavior; women have not' Low notes. . . . The difference is approach: men seek resources for direct reproductive gain; women, when they are involved, seek resources for themselves and their offspring. (Blum, 1997, 268)

In sum, there is a genetic predisposition for men to be more aggressive than women. But whether this aggression gets expressed or repressed depends on ecological, demographic, and social considerations. Under conditions of ecological and demographic pressures that produce stress, men are more likely to treat other men and women badly than at other times. Evolutionary psychology cannot explain when and where informal male dominance will emerge, but it does explain why, if any dominance emerges in society, it will be men who will tend to dominate and not women.

5. Conflict and power between the sexes: is institutionalized male dominance a conspiracy?

> *If men and women are equal, divided mainly by a few structural nitpicks in the brain and some invisible hormonal tides, why don't women have equal access to the world?*

> —Deborah Blum (1997, 253)

As we have discussed in previous chapters, in the public world, activities involving power—occupational, politics, and economics—men are in the dominant positions. Warfare is also an activity pursued exclusively by men. "In no culture have women ever been observed forming coalitions designed to kill other human beings." (Buss 1999, 302). Men's monopolizing of public activities hasn't changed significantly today. Men command the highest salaries and are paid more for the same work. However, it is important to note that in all the spheres of competition for power, the direct losers in the combat are most often *other men*, not women.

To be sure, not every woman wants to stay home and have babies, and not every man wants to rule the world. Not every woman has been suppressed by society and not every man has been encouraged to compete. In some cases, women rule over men in public settings. A female upper-middle-class manager rules over a working-class forklift driver. But these are far more the exceptions than the rule.

According to Deborah Blum, the reason for differences in public power is that men show more *reproductive gain* from public power than women do.

Status and wealth correlate with male reproductive success. Studies by Low in Sweden and Germany have found that richer men are more likely to marry younger women—raising the possibility of having more children. . . . In the few societies where women wield substantial public power they show no clear reproductive gain from doing so. (Blum, 1997, 266)

The higher up in the class structure a woman moves, the less likely she is to find a mate. This is because her resource investments are divided between the public world and the childbearing world. From the point of view of men, mating with her would be more of a gamble in terms of passing on the man's genes than if the woman were either a full-time mother or worked only part-time. From the point of view of women, biologically it makes more evolutionary sense to attract a wealthy man and have babies than it does to compete in the public world for high status positions.

Women historically have identified more with their families than with their overall sex. They've thus frequently sided with husbands or fathers in supporting 'role definitions' that keep women out of politics and out of traditional male power positions. The failed Equal Rights Amendment . . . was fought against as viciously by women as by men. . . . [F]or many generations women have relied on men to support the household financially. . . . Building an alliance against one's provider would fit right into the old cliché of biting the hand that feeds you. (Blum 1997, 264).

According to evolutionary psychologist David Buss, men and women express their dominance through different actions:

In one study one hundred acts . . . were listed. . . . The first study asked men and women to rate each act for its social desirability or how worthwhile it was in their eyes. Profound sex differences

emerged. Women more than men tended to rate prosocial dominant acts as more socially desirable, including 'Taking charge of things at the committee meeting; taking a stand on an important issue without waiting to find out what others thought. . . . In sharp contrast, men more than women tended to rate egoistic dominant acts as more socially desirable, including 'managing to get one's own way . . . blaming others when things went wrong.' (Buss, 1999, 353)

In another psychological experiment Edwin Megargee tested the effect of dominance on leadership when graded and female dominants *interacted*. After he administered the California Psychological Inventory Dominance Scale he selected only those men and women who scored either high or low in dominance. When the selection was completed he matched up all four pairs.

(1) a high-dominant man with a low-dominant man
(2) a high-dominant woman with a low-dominant woman
(3) a high-dominant man with a low-dominant woman
(4) a high-dominant woman with a low-dominant man.

"The important question . . . was who would become the leader and the follower. . . . He found that 75% of the high-dominant men and 70% of the high-dominant women took the leadership role in the *same* sex pairs. When high-dominant men were paired with low-dominant women, however, 90% percent of the men became leaders. The most startling result occurred when the woman was high- and the man low-dominance.... Under these conditions, *only 20% of the high-dominant women assumed the leadership role* [my emphasis]

The reason for this was neither that the women were suppressing their dominance nor that the men felt compelled to assume their standard role. From the recorded conversations Megargtee found out that "the high-dominant women were *appointing* [my emphasis] their low-dominant partners to the leadership position. In fact, the high-dominant women actually made the final decision about the roles 91 percent of the time." (Buss, 1999, 355)

Why was this? Evolutionary psychologists would claim that women have a biological predisposition to put less stock in public leadership positions.

As easy as it might be to say that men and women simply express dominance in different ways, this really avoids the issue as to who is controlling society. Women may have more power than men in some public situations, or express power behind the scenes, indirectly. But the fact remains that some men have power over all women and most men. Further, all men have some privileges over all women.

Are the privileges and power that most men have over most women a *conspiracy?* According to evolutionary psychologist David Buss, the answer is no. Men and women are in conflict not over *resources* but are in conflict over their differences in sexual *strategies.*

> Members of the *same* [my emphasis] sex are often in competition with each other for precisely the same resources: members of the opposite sex and the resources needed to attract them. Evolutionary psychologists have predicted conflict between the sexes, but not because men and women are in competition for the same reproductive resources. Rather, many sources of conflict . . . can be traced to evolved differences in sexual *strategies* [my emphasis]. . . . The strategies of one sex can interfere with the strategies of the other. . . . (Buss 1999, 313)

Because of this, Buss claims that the phrase "the battle of the sexes" can be misleading.

> [T]he phrase implies that men as a group are united in their interests and

women are likewise united in their interests, and the two groups are somehow at war with each other. (Buss, 1999, 314).

This is untrue because men's loyalty to their wives, mothers, daughters, and sisters is far deeper than their loyalty to non-kin men. As we have seen, it wasn't in most women's interest to side with other women against their husbands and families; similarly, most men also choose the women in their families over other men.

> "Men provide resources to women such as their wives, mistresses, sisters, daughters and mothers. . . . Each individual is united in interests with some members of each sex and is in conflict with some members of each sex." (Buss, 1999, 340)

> "Men deprive *other men* of resources, exclude other men from positions of power and status and derogate other men to make them less desirable to women. . . . Women compete with each other for access to high-status men, have sex with other women's husbands and lure men away from their wives. . . . Women and men are both victims of the sexual strategies of their own sex. (Buss, 1999, 340)

There are, of course coalitions of some men in particular situations. Coalitions are sometimes made by men to exploit women's sexuality, as in gang rape. Men's coalitions may sometimes be used to exclude women from power—as in exclusive men's clubs or lodges in which business is transacted. At the same time, however, these coalitions are often directed against *other men* and their coalitions.

It is easy to become restless with all of this pigeonholing of gender behavior. What about the exceptions? How does evolutionary psychology explain the following instances we are all familiar with?

- Promiscuous women and monogamous men

- Women and men who don't want children
- Men who are jealous of their partners for emotional reasons and women who are jealous for sexual reasons
- Women who are more aggressive and men who are less aggressive or even passive
- Women who want public power and men who don't want public power
- Men who marry older women rather than younger women even though they aren't as fertile

A reminder of Buss's list of typical misunderstandings of evolutionary psychology's theory of human nature can help us. Evolutionary psychology does not predict that *all* humans will conform to its profile. It only claims that most will. The reason? We have an evolutionary history as hunter-collectors far longer than as farmers or industrial urbanites. And the predispositions developed through natural and sexual selection in that hunter-collector environment prevail over those developed in horticultural, agricultural and industrial environments that have emerged relatively recently. However, the modified maximization principle allows for exceptions to the rule where people pursue goals not related to reproduction of genes. What are the conditions where these exceptions take place? Evolutionary psychologists would probably say that in societies with capital-intensive technology and some degree of political democracy, more exceptions to biological predispositions are likely. We will discuss this possibility in depth in the last chapter.

6. Are men and women primarily biological or social beings?

One of the shortcomings of most discussions of male and female differences is a failure to compare these differences against what men and women have *in common,* relative to the rest of the animal kingdom. The issue could be stated

this way: does a man have more in common with a male chimp than he does with a woman? Conversely, does a woman have more in common with a female chimp than she does with a man? In order to answer this question reasonably, we need to be more specific about what men and women have in common compared to our closest biological ancestors. Following the work of Gerhard Lenski (1987) I will address: (a) what we share with all other species, (b) what we share with some other species, and (c) what is virtually unique to humanity.

One thing we have in common with all other species is the need to adapt to the biophysical environment on planet Earth. This includes adapting to physical dynamics of inorganic matter—such as climate, earthquakes, volcanoes—as well as various kinds of organic matter, including other species as well as members of our own species.

The behaviors of any particular species that best enable it to adapt to its niche are selected for reproduction and become part of that species' gene pool. However:

> [Though] the members of a population are fundamentally alike in both appearance and behavior . . . they are not identical. This means that some genes in a population are found in every member, while others are found in varying proportions of the population. (Lenski, 1987, 11)

What we share with some other species is (a) our ability to learn, and (b) our capacity to create and sustain societies. Lenski points out that the social mode of adaptation was one of the most important steps for organic evolution. Associations for mutual benefit go deep into organic evolution and are found in some species of multicellular organisms, and are scattered throughout the rest of the animal kingdom. Within the class of vertebrates, mammals, birds and fish have social qualities; also, many insects—ants, termites and bees—are social. Even colonial invertebrates, such as corals and sponges have social characteristics.

Within the animal kingdom, while cooperation occurs, it is not universal. Alongside cooperation there is competition and conflict. Major activities include nurturing of young, securing food, and defense.

We have even more in common with primates. Lenski names the following characteristics:

- flexible hands with separated fingers and opposable thumbs
- year-round sexual readiness
- prolonged immaturity
- greater reliance on sight than smell
- enlarged neo-cortex
- tool use

Primates have been described as the most curious, mischievous, inventive, and destructive of all mammals.

Learning might be defined as a relatively permanent change in behavior or behavior potential that is made through personal experience with the environment rather than because of genetic inheritance. While learning is common to many species, what makes learning especially important to social species is that what can be learned can be passed on and *shared* with members of the same species within the same generation. While non-social animals learn, whatever they learn is their private experience and skill and is not shared with other members of the same species living on the Earth at the same time.

One of the characteristics that differentiate human beings from other species is the *depth* to which we are social beings. As in other social animals, the emergence, construction, and reproduction of societies over time helps to reproduce our species. As we saw in the first chapter, the essence of human social life is to cooperate—that is, to pool our resources, create a division of labor, and work toward a common goal. By relying on each other and by cooperating we create synergistic results. We can acquire more food while entailing less risk than would be possible for any single member acting alone.

Everything I have said so far about the deep sociality of human beings refers to human beings *within a single generation.* But the emergence of a "socio-culture" involves transmission of what has been learned *across generations.* Culture might be defined as the symbolic systems, and the information they convey, that are transmitted across generations. While there are chimpanzees that use blades of grass as tools for luring termites out of their holes, and which fashion these tools before using them, these tools vanish with the generation that made them. They are not passed down and improved. Further, as long as these tool-making techniques are not passed down across generations and altered based on the experience of previous generations, this behavior remains social and not *socio-cultural* or historical.

A great deal of the difference between animals that have culture and animals that do not has to do with the differences between symbols and signals. According to Lenski, while both signals and symbols convey information, the meanings of signals is much narrower than that of symbols, and the context in which signals are applied is very specific.

Animals signal with movements, sounds, odors, color changes . . . and the signals they produce vary greatly in the amount of information they convey. The simple type of signal [is useful] in only a single context and [has] only one possible meaning—the sexually attractive scent released by the female moth. In contrast, some species . . . are able to transmit more complex information by varying the frequency or intensity of a signal or by combining different signals simultaneously or in sequence. Thus a foraging honeybee returns to her hive and performs the "waggled dance" to direct fellow workers to the food source she has located. (Lenski, 1987, 17)

In the case of symbols, while the ability to create and use symbols initially depends on genetics, the form of the symbol and the meaning that becomes attached to it do not. While chimps and gorillas have learned to use symbols taught by humans, these animals have not yet, to our knowledge, *created* a symbol or system of symbols.

While signals can be used by both social and non-social animals, the use of signals locks these animals into the present, because while some signals can be learned, they cannot be passed down and altered across generations. The use of symbols that can be passed on across generations means we can not only share what we've learned with other humans in the present, but we can learn from previous generations' experience, and plan to help the next generation. The use of symbols not only opens up time, but it opens up space: symbols transmitted between societies make learning non-provincial and potentially global.

Another difference between biological and socio-cultural evolution is that the rate of socio-cultural change is much faster than that of biological change. Biological change occurs through interbreeding and small changes require many generations to appear and become stabilized in the breeding population. Socio-cultural information can be rapidly acquired, exchanged, accumulated, and passed on within a single generation.

Both types of evolution are based on accumulated experience that have been preserved and transmitted from generation to generation in coded systems of information. One is through a genetic code and the other through a symbol system. Both of these strategies address the problem of adaptation to the environment.

To summarize: How human beings differ from other animals in part has to do with the *rate* and the *volume* of learning. In non-social animals, what learning exists is limited to private experience; it is not shared with other members and ends with the death of the individual. In social animals, learning expands because members of a species can pool their learning with other members, thus expanding knowledge for everyone. Finally, with the emergence of culture, learning becomes historicized, linking learning to the past and future through the transmission of symbols not only across time, but across space through a process of diffusion. The question is, *do the commonalties which men and women share as a result of being socio-cultural beings outweigh the biological differences between men and women in terms of mating desires, aggression, competition, and status-seeking, which we have discussed in the first few sections of this chapter?*

Figure 7.2 summarizes Lenski's comparison of socio-cultural with biological evolution. The second part of the chart compares some of the differences between men and women we discussed earlier in the chapter. Are the commonalities between men and women as socio-cultural species (the first half of Figure 7.2) greater than, equal to, or less than the differences between men and women as biological species (the second half of Figure 7.2)? It seems to me that the depth, volume, and rate of learning that results from men and women cooperating to produce a socio-culture unites them to a common fate, far outweighing the biological differences that distinguish them.

But if social evolution determines more of our identity than biological evolution, what does this have to do with gender relations—more specifically, with informal and institutionalized male dominance? As it turns out, evolutionary psychology gives us some good answers to the eight questions posed at the end of chapter 2. These questions and answers address the question of why there was and is no informal or formal *female* dominance.

Here are the questions again, with answers from evolutionary psychology:

(1) Why are there no societies in which informal and institutionalized *female* dominance arose?
(2) Why are there virtually no societies in which women monopolize public power?
(3) Why is it that when privilege and vertical power emerge, women do not have these benefits and men are deprived?

A single response covers the first three questions. The demands on women's physiological resources make them less available to work in the public domain. It is more efficient for a woman to find a mate who already has economic resources and marry "up" than to go into non-domestic work and compete for those resources directly. Men have been selected, because of competition for mates, to seek status more than women in these domains.

(4) Why is it that in no society are women absentee mothers content to "help out" the way men do?

It is a genetic investment for women to take care of their children. For men it is more of a gamble.

(5) Why isn't descent traced predominantly along the female line?

Men are more insecure in their knowledge about their fatherhood than women are. This is why men try to restrict women's sexuality. Women already know their genes are in their offspring

(6) Why don't men usually have to live in women's residency rather than the reverse?

It is easier to keep track of a woman's sexual life in the presence of a man's kin group. If he lives near his wife's kin they are more likely to look the other way if she has sexual adventures.

(7) Why, when mating practices are non-monogamous, do men marry many women far more often than women marry many men?

Men's sexual strategy is to be promiscuous to spread their genes. It does not pay genetically for women to spread their genes.

(8) Why is it that when wars break out women don't do the fighting, and rape and violate men?

Aggression is a selection strategy based on competition for mating opportunities for men.

Evolutionary psychology can explain the absence of informal *female* dominance better than can sociology or the cultural ecology. However, it cannot explain the long-term presence of egalitarian societies without political inequalities and it cannot explain the existence of societies that have minimum or no male dominance. The question of if, when, and where informal dominance emerges is better answered socio-ecologically. Another way to say this is that if, when, and where forms of political and gender inequality will or will not emerge is predictable by socio-ecological considerations. Once these forms of inequality emerge, evolutionary psychology rightly predicts that it is men rather than women who will be at the top of the hierarchy.

Finally, let us examine what all of this means for social change. Which behaviors having to do with gender relations are easier to change, and which are more difficult to change? For reasons we have discussed, informal and institutionalized *female* dominance is unlikely ever to be achieved. Minimizing institutionalized male dominance is a more realistic goal, because the roots of this dominance are socio-ecological. Furthermore, as shown below, I believe the power and privilege that goes with *institutionalized* male dominance are considerably greater than is the case with informal male dominance. Therefore there is greater hope for women today that at other times in history. The institutions necessary to minimize male dominance once it emerged were not present in the ancient world, as we will see in the last chapter.

Here is a comparison of the benefits that accrue for men from informal male dominance (which come from biology), with the benefits men derive from institutionalized male dominance (which has socio-ecological origins). The social benefits men derive from biology-based informal male dominance include:

- more variety in sexual partners
- less responsibility for child rearing
- more meaningful work
- descent traced along male lines
- choice in residency
- fighting in wars

Figure 7.2 Biological vs. Socio-cultural Evolution

BIOLOGICAL EVOLUTION		SOCIO-CULTURAL EVOLUTION
genetic code	FORM OF CODE	symbolic code
signals: Single context, one possible meaning. More complex messages by varying frequency and intensity.		**primarily symbols:** Multi-context, many meanings.
More present oriented.		Past and future oriented. Enables us to deliberate and plan.
In birds and mammals, signals are partly learned.		Humans design form and meaning from scratch.
Some capacity to use symbols created by humans.		
reproduction: No sharing of genetic information.	INFORMATION TRANSFER	**reproduction and diffusion:** Sharing of socio-cultural information within societies and between societies through diffusion.
Slow, takes generations.	RATE OF CHANGE	**Rapid: can occur within a single generation.**

The social benefits men derive from socio-ecology based institutionalized male dominance include:

- economic control over natural resources with the rise of material wealth
- political control over decision making processes with the rise of ranks, castes and classes
- technological control over tools such as hieroglyphics, the alphabet, coined money, the plow, and large domesticated traction animals
- sacred beliefs and practices (discussed in chapters 10 and 11)
- psychological ability to think and sense more abstractly, objectively, and globally with the rise of hyperabstract reasoning, the cultivation of the sense of sight, and the cultivation of an individualist self (discussed in chapters 14, 15, and 16)

In weighing the differences between the benefits derived from informal male dominance and those of institutionalized male dominance, it appears to me that the latter are far greater. Political, economic, and technological control of society is far more important for most human beings than choice in residency (living closer to the husband's or wife's family) or the "right" to fight in wars. Deciding the direction of society (politics), having access to basic resources and finished products (economics), and controlling the machinery of production is more important than how people trace their lineage, residency, variety of partners, and child rearing responsibilities, as important as these may be. While meaningful work is an important benefit of informal male dominance, the control of technology, of the exchange of goods and services, and of who gets what, when, and where, determines the quality of life for the average human even more. Therefore, the most important social institutions requiring change are institutions that have socio-ecological origins and so they lend themselves to socio-ecological solutions. See Figure 7.3 for a summary.

7. Evaluation of evolutionary psychology

I will close with my assessment of the pros and cons of evolutionary psychology. First, here are some positive contributions of this discipline.

Evolutionary psychology has broken past the rigidity of older biological theories, which claimed that *all* social behavior can be explained by biology. It surpassed instinct theory, because its concept of predispositions allows for variation in the *expression* of these predispositions according to time, place, and circumstance. It has established that there are *universal* work patterns that can be traced cross-culturally, and that there is a universal division of labor between the sexes in important work activities. Evolutionary psychology has helped to explain all the characteristics of what I call informal male dominance and some institutionalized male dominance—including men's monopolization of the public realm in politics and economics.

Further, evolutionary psychology has shown the conflicts between men and women as not being primarily over resources but over sexual strategies. This bypasses the simplistic explanation of gender conspiracy. While coalitions between men for political and economic purposes certainly exist, they are cross-cut by loyalties to kin groups, which are generally far more powerful.

Deborah Blum summarizes the contribution of evolutionary psychology in understanding gender relations as follows:

Gender biology has extraordinary promise if . . . we are willing to give it an objective hearing. It opens possibilities; it doesn't close them. And it doesn't segregate men from women. If anything it does the opposite, emphasizing how intricately woven together we are in the design of evolution. We wrap around each other like different-colored threads in an astonishingly complex tapestry. . . . We may use hormones differently, but none of them—not testosterone, not estradiol, none of them—is exclusively a male or female province. Gender biology tells us that we are built of the same materials and that it takes only the barest slip or slide in organization to produce a man with breasts or a women with masculinized genitals. . . . There are very few things that only males or only females can do. That, however, is not the same as saying there are few things that only males or only females are likely to do. (Blum, 1997, 279)

However, while evolutionary psychology's focus on biological differences can explain *why* if informal male dominance or institutionalized male dominance emerges men will be dominant rather than women, it does not predict *if, when, and where* institutionalized male dominance will emerge in the first place. With this in mind, the following are my negative conclusions about evolutionary psychology:

(1) Human society is presented as passive, as essentially the creature of biology. Social elaborations on biological hardwiring are not seen as very significant. I have yet to see an attempt on the part of an evolutionary psychologist to specify what social conditions would have to be shown to exist in order to prove that society is more than just an elaboration of biological evolution. Many of the inventions of the industrial revolution expose the relativity of biology. For example, as long as the plow was the only tool available in farming, women were not able to control their means of subsistence. But with the invention of tractors, almost *anyone* can farm regardless of physical limitations. Another example would be the outer space program and the possibility of colonizing space: how could biological evolution account for our species' preparations to live in environments utterly alien to any that have been known on Earth? Perhaps the most dramatic example is genetic engineering, in which human activity arising from social institutions can actually *change* biological hardwiring.

(2) There is an underestimation of the power of cooperation. To be sure, evolutionary psychologists recognize that cooperation is an important aspect of biological evolution. However, cooperation is not defined strongly enough. Cooperation is not just about sharing

and mutual support. It is about a *division of labor in species activity, and the planning of joint activities to a common end,* which creates synergetic results in the volume and substance produced, the speed in which it potentially can be produced, and the technical skill it allows humans to develop. This form of cooperation is not as old as competition, but it is far more important than competition in promoting human evolution. Further, competition between humans has cooperation as its underpinning. The cooperation of workers on the job is the foundation for capitalists to compete with each other. Far from industrial capitalist society being dominated by competition, it is based on a deeper cooperation: if workers didn't co-operate in order to make goods to be sold at a profit, there would be no competition between capitalists, or any profits.

(3) The qualitative differences between societies are often glossed over and subordinated to an emphasis on our common biological past. There are qualitative differences between hunter-gatherer societies, horticulturalist societies, agricultural state societies, and industrial capitalist societies. Yet all societies are treated by evolutionary psychologists as if they were more or less equal before nature. Because of the tenuousness of their social organization, non-state societies are far closer to nature than agricultural states or industrial-capitalist societies. Whatever biological predispositions continue to be present in state societies, they are increasingly mediated by technological, economic, and political relations. Evolutionary psychologists don't pay much attention to this difference.

(4) Human history is treated as no more than an extension of biological evolution. As I argued in the first chapter, human history overlays the evolution of the biosphere; it interacts with the rest of nature but is also autonomous from it. Over the course of social evolution another layer of natural history, a kind of super-nature, has appeared over the planet, including buildings, tools, and artificial materials. While a dualistic separation between nature and culture must be avoided, this layer of social evolution

deserves special treatment. Human history includes, but is more than biological evolution.

(5) The rate and the volume of learning that social complexity brings to humanity is seriously understated. The volume and the rate of learning due to the division of labor (cooperation) which results in the building and sustaining of socio-culture gives men and women together increased power over the rest of nature, as well as a commonality with each other. This supersedes the biological evolutionary differences between men and women over mating and parenting strategies, aggression, competition, and status seeking. Hence my conclusion, stated at the end of the last section, that we are now more socio-cultural beings than biological beings.

(6) Evolutionary psychologists reduce socio-historical stratification to biological hierarchy. In an earlier chapter I made distinctions between influence, prestige, privilege, and power, and the social formations in which they arise. It seems safe to say that influence and prestige exist in all primate societies; however, privilege and power are missing. These forms of vertical power and entitlement require the building of a whole new type of society; they require much more extensive, systematic, and intensive efforts than other biological species are able to develop. Whatever entitlements exist among social primates are limited to a single generation. There is no chimp chief that passes on privileges across generations. Whatever advantages the chimp has rise and fall within his lifetime. Their is no chimp divine king or priest who accumulates enormous wealth and mobilizes other chimps to fight wars and build monuments while he lives a life of leisure. The forms of stratification that emerge in complex horticultural societies and agricultural states are qualitatively different from anything in the primate world. It is stretching the word "stratification" beyond its usual macrosociological limits to include biological hierarchies in the same category.

(7) The causal relationship between the past and the future is not explicitly stated. Are there any landmarks in human history that signal a change in the dialectic between biology and society? What are the conditions under which

evolutionary psychologists are willing to admit that biology has less hold on human actions now than previously? I am willing to grant that for most of human history people have been governed by a biological fate. I am less willing to grant that this is in any way inevitable. In the last 200 years, beginning with the European Enlightenment, there has been a movement more toward self-determination, a humanly designed destiny. Increasingly, whatever becomes of humanity, it will have economic, political, and technological causes to praise or curse—rather than merely biological ones.

Given all these qualifications, it may be easy to lose track of what I am actually claiming. Let me draw out the implications of what *is* being argued here. First, there *are* universal human work patterns that appear across cultures. Second, in every society known to anthropologists there is a division of labor between men and women in many activities; this is true whether the labor is occurring in a hunting-gathering band or an agricultural state. These differences in work between genders are related to factors such as the amount of strength required, the risk involved, the interruptability of the task, the requirement for skill, and the degree of status attached to it. These differences in both work patterns—and in the status that accompanies them—have a biological basis.

But while biological differences can explain some cross-cultural similarities in tendencies toward male dominance in public institutions, the physical and social environment—including time, place, and context—feed back on biological predispositions and affect when, where, how or even whether these biological differences show themselves. These empirical claims in no way imply that tendencies toward male dominance in any sphere are desirable. The evidence must stand on its own. The question of what can be done about gender imbalances is a separate one that has more to do with politics than with anthropology or history. We first must know what the facts are, before we decide how to interpret and evaluate them, and what to do about them.

Figure 7.3 COMPARING THE BIOLOGICAL AND SOCIAL-ECOLOGICAL LEGACY IN PROMOTING GENDER EQUALITY OR GENDER INEQUALITY

Are the Differences that Separate Men and Women as Biological Beings Greater than, Equal to or Less than the Commonalities that Unite Men and Women as Socio-Cultural Beings?

BIOLOGICAL LEGACY

DIFFERENCES IN SEXUAL SELECTION STRATIEGIES

Women
slow sex
can produce one child per year
investment in childbearing/ childrearing

easy access to mates

needs non-domestic resources
choosiness as a strategy
confidence in motherhood--
choosiness about genes

more sensitive about emotional infidelity

Men
fast sex
can produce many children per year
less investment in childrearing

difficult access to mates: competition--
    aggression
    display

needs fertility
promiscuous as a strategy
less confidence in fatherhood--
    spread genes around
    control female sexuality
more sensitive about sexual infidelity

SPECIFIC SOCIAL RESULTS:

less responsibility for child-rearing
more meaningful work

fighting wars

more variety of sexual partners (polygamy)
descent traced along male lines
choice in residency

GENERAL SOCIAL RESULTS:
Presence of Informal Male Dominance
Absence of Informal Female dominance
Absence of Institutionalized Female dominance

More difficult to change, but less important in determining identity

SOCIO-ECOLOGICAL LEGACY

COMMONALITIES BETWEEN MEN AND WOMEN
Creation of a the most extensive super-organic social system
Depth of social learning
Expansion of shared learning across space
Expansion of shared learning across generations
Speed of social learning

SPECIFIC SOCIAL RESULTS

Economic control over natural resources
Political control over decision-making
Technological control over tools
Sacred control over beliefs and practice
Psychological control over perception, cognition, self

GENERAL SOCIAL RESULTS
Presence of Institutionalized male dominance
Presence of Egalitarian societies
Societies with minimal or no male dominance

Easier to change, and more important in determining identity

Chapter 8

Noble Savage or Brutish Barbarian? Warfare in Pre-state Societies

In chapter 2 we saw that a prevalent way of making sense of social evolution is to characterize it as either "progress" or "degeneration." I criticized both of these lines of theory and suggested a third alternative, which I have called "improvised evolution." Theories of progress and degeneration can also be found when we examine war in pre-state societies. I will contrast both theories to each other, locate the historical time in which they emerged, and draw upon Lawrence Keeley's recent book *War Before Civilization* (1996) to criticize both approaches.

In the second section of this chapter we will discuss Keeley's findings on violence in pre-state societies. One point of this chapter is to counter the romantic claims of the degeneration theorists that pre-state societies were idyllic paradises until they were invaded by pastoralists and hunters in the Archaic Iron Age. In the next section I will rely on the work of Raymond Kelly (2000) to counter claims that warfare is universal. We will specify the conditions under which warless societies become warlike. In the last section of this chapter we will examine the impacts of war upon women.

1. Romantic vs. progressive theories of primitive war

The theory of progress as applied to war begins with Hobbes's claim that life in tribal societies was miserable, brutish, and short. Hobbes assumed that people in such societies were always at war. It follows from this that the presence of colonial civilizations led to an end of feuding and brought relative peace and prosperity. But such a view must contend with evidence of state violence, with which people in pre-state societies did not have to contend. A third notion is that tribal societies lost out against civilizations because their weapons were not technically as effective. Bows and arrows, it was thought, cannot compete with musketry. In addition, tribal ways of war were thought to be inferior to civilized ways because tribal people were far more selective in when and where they obeyed their leaders, as compared with civilized soldiers. Finally, pre-state societies were thought to give their warriors inadequate training, and had few logistical skills, so that they could not sustain military campaigns.

The degeneration theory of war—or, as Keeley calls it, the "golden-age" theory—begins with Rousseau. Rousseau agreed with Hobbes that passions were an important feature of humanity's make-up; but for Rousseau these could be satisfied peacefully without the need for civilized institutions such as private property, laws, and monogamy to constrain them. Second, whatever violent tendencies people in tribal societies had they were overridden by compassion for others. According to Rousseau, except when driven by hunger, tribal people were peaceful and lived in harmony with their surroundings. Peace was their basic way of life while war was an anomaly. Unlike their civilized counterparts, when tribal people fought it wasn't because they were naturally aggressive. It was because they could not control their anxieties or because they had misunderstood the intentions of others. Finally, Rousseau believed that when tribal societies became more warlike it was because they had come into contact with civilization, which corrupted them.

According to Keeley, many anthropologists, especially after World War II, tended to build upon Rousseau's ideas. For example, in comparing civilized to tribal warfare these anthropologists argued that tribal warfare was more stylized and symbolic, and not many people were actually killed. These anthropologists "pacified the past" by calling tribal violence "feuding" rather than war, thus making it appear less serious. It was also claimed that pre-state societies had no fortifications, thus showing that war was not a way of life for them. Anthropologists believed that early tribal peoples incorporated captured enemies into the tribe, rather than enslaving them. Further, romantic anthropologists claimed that tribal societies did not seek to expand their territories, unlike greedy and imperialistic state societies. While civilized warfare arises from political and economic strife and implies the impersonal killing of whole populations branded as "enemy," tribal warfare grew from psychological and interpersonal motives. Pre-state warfare was hot-blooded and passionate, not cold and distant. Finally, romantic anthropologists believed that the exchange of goods and marriage partners between tribal societies tended to prevent war and to maintain inter-tribal peace.

Keeley shows that the claims of both progress and degeneration theorists were either untrue or partly true, as we will see below. But before examining his arguments it is important to ground the claims of both progress theorists and theorists of a golden age in western history and the political and economic climate in which they were formulated.

In the early 19th century, European attitudes toward tribal societies could be characterized as Hobbesian. This provided an ideological justification for subjugating tribal peoples, since it was assumed that their life was being improved by colonial contact. Later in the 19th century, this Hobbesian view came to be supplemented with social Darwinism—an intellectual movement that held that the principles of natural selection and survival of the fittest apply within human society as well as in nature. Social Darwinism had racist implications because it claimed that the differences between industrial and tribal societies in level of social organization were due to the fact that people in tribal societies were genetically inferior. Virtually all industrial societies at that time were white, and virtually all tribal societies were non-white.

According to Keeley, the Rousseauian view of pre-state societies came to be favored after the horrendous European experience of World War II. Europe, unlike the United States, was decimated by the war. Keeley points out that what was particularly disturbing was Hitler's use of a racist ideology against other Europeans, similar to that which Europe as a whole had been using to subjugate tribal societies outside of Europe. Moreover, European anthropologists in the 1950s and 1960s were particularly averse to studying war.

A second major reason why anthropologists and archeologists tended to romanticize war in tribal societies was that such societies were disappearing. Keeley points out how spatial and temporal distance from primitives made them seem all the more noble. This applied to the United States no less than Europe:

> As cynics often observed in the United States during the nineteenth century the nobility of "savages" was directly proportional to one's geographic distance from them. . . . Once the natives were safely reduced to living on reservations, Westerners were . . . inclined to become sentimental about them. . . . It is much easier to admire tribal life once it has been destroyed and little chance remains . . . of its returning. In Western popular culture, Rousseau triumphs over Hobbes only when "man in a state of nature" is no longer a viable competitor and has faded from direct sight. (Keeley, 1996, 167-168)

Keeley closes his book by exposing what both Hobbesian progress and Rousseauian degeneration have in common—the inability to understand tribal men and women as fully human:

Figure 8.1 Progressive and Romantic Theories of Primitive War

Progress (Hobbes)	Degeneration/Romanticism (Rousseau)
Primitive life is ignorant, miserable, brutal, short.	Primitive life is lush and conflict free except when driven by hunger.
Human passions are out of control and need state institutions to suppress them.	Human passions can be satisfied peaceably w/o unnatural civilized institutions interfering.
	Violent tendencies are overcome by compassion.
There are postures of war *between* states but pockets of peace *within* states.	What is called "peace" in state societies is really a more subtle form of war: subjugation.
	Wars are a result of misunderstandings of intentions or due to anxiety.
The presence of civilization introduces peace to tribal societies.	Civilized interference in tribal societies causes tribal warfare.
Tribal societies are technically defective in conducting wars.	Casualty rates are low; tribal war is more posturing and symbolic than serious.
War is a way of life, peace is temporary.	Peace is the basic way of life unless driven by population pressure/ resource depletion or other external forces to war.
	Tribal societies had no fortifications.
Tribal societies are ill-disciplined and selective about obedience to leaders.	
Tribal societies have inadequate training and poor logistics.	
Capture of enemies meant subjugation or death.	Enemies become incorporated into the tribe without subjugation.
Primitives are motivated by territorial expansion.	Primitives are not motivated by territorial expansion.
Primitive war is motivated by economics.	Primitive war is not motivated by economics and politics but by personal and psychological considerations.
	Exchange of goods and intermarriage prevent war.

A previous era refused to acknowledge the intelligence, sociability, and generosity of uncivilized people and the richness, effectiveness, and rationality of their way of life. Today, popular opinion finds it difficult to attribute to tribal peoples a capacity for rapaciousness, cruelty, ecological heedlessness, and Machiavellian guilt equal to our own. Both laypersons and academics now prefer a vision of tribal peoples as lambs in Eden spouting ecological mysticism and disdain for the material condition of life. In short, we wish them to be more righteous and spiritual, happier and less emotionally complicated and less prone to rational calculation of self-interest than ourselves. . . . When we attribute to primitive and prehistoric people only our virtues and none of our vices, we dehumanized them as much as ourselves. (Keeley, 1996, 170)

Figure 8.1 both summarizes these introductory remarks and anticipates differences between the two tendencies to either idealize or denigrate tribal peoples, which we discuss at more length in the next section.

2. Violence in pre-state societies

Keeley challenges romantic notions about the peaceable nature of non-state societies first by pointing out that they do not only fight when driven by necessity:

In the late 1960's a substantial shock to the materialist interpretation of war was administered by Napoleon Chagnon's . . . ethnography on the Yanomamo of Venezuela and Brazil. Chagnon described the Yanomamo as being embroiled in almost constant warfare. . . . Yet Yanomamo villages were surround by abundant unoccupied territory; the fighting between them was apparently motivated only by the desires to exact revenge and to capture women. (Keeley, 1996, 16)

It is also not true that human passions can be easily stopped without state intervention. On the contrary, Keeley argues that the evolution from a non-state society to a state society makes warfare a *less* common practice within these societies. In tribal societies stopping a war is no easy matter. Peace is only considered when warring has reached an impasse and the losses on both sides are roughly equal. Also, in non-state societies (unlike state societies) there must be a consensus within each group to cease hostilities. This is not easy to achieve because some sectors of the population will likely have something to lose if the fighting stops. Warriors, for example, lose status during peacetime, and males who are single may lose the opportunity to gain a wife. Grievers of the dead must give up their vengeance. Young men with little property or status lose opportunities for both. In contrast,

States enjoy a slight advantage over non-states with regard to peace-making because they exercise a much greater degree of centralized control over their populations and economic resources. Because political decision making is in the hands of a tiny minority. . . no complete consensus is needed . . . before a peace can be negotiated. (Keeley, 1996, 149)

Without this state intervention, violent tendencies among primitives are typically not overcome by compassion. While compassion exists in all societies, people in tribal societies could be every bit as brutal and sadistic as people in state societies, as we shall see.

This does not, of course mean that life in state societies is necessarily better. State societies exchange relentless war between societies for caste and class subjugation within society. Further, Keeley has no illusions about the positive impact of state colonization on non-state societies:

Had pacification and the "rule of law," wider trade, and improvements in transportation and communication been the only innovations introduced by imperial agents, imperialism might ultimately have been more of a boon and less of an ordeal for its native subjects. In fact, colonial pacification was not an end in itself, but a means to achieve goals that almost invariably benefited the intruders as much as they harmed the native inhabitants: forced labor, loss of territory, economic exploitation, subordinate social and political status, and lack of legal redress against wrongs or crimes committed by colonists. The price of imperial peace was manifold indignity, dispossession, abject poverty, slavery, famine and worse. (Keeley, 1996, 150)

Another assumption common among those who idealize tribal societies is that wars in such societies result more from anxieties and misunderstandings, rather than from explicit economic motives, such as for territorial expansion. Keeley argues against this in his examination of two of the cross-cultural surveys mentioned earlier: "One of the most persistent myths about primitive warfare is that it did not change boundaries because it was not motivated by territorial demand." (108)

By relentlessly raiding its Dinka neighbors . . . the Nuer tribe of the Sudan expanded its domain from 8,700 to 35,000 square miles in just seventy years. . . . Tribal warfare against other pre-state societies appears to have been just as effective as civilized war at moving boundaries and rewarding victors with vital territory appropriated from the losers. . . . (111)

Both sets of data indicate that the predominant motives for pre-state warfare are revenge for homicides and various economic issues. . . . In New Guinea, for example, where gardening and pig rearing are important, thefts of pigs and garden produce or pigs' depredations of gardens, figure prominently as causes of conflict.... Horses were usually the focus of fighting among the historic Plains Indians. . . . On the salmon-dependent Pacifica Northwest coast, tribes not infrequently warred over river and ocean frontage. In Minnesota, the Chippewa fought for over 150 years

with the Dakota Sioux over use of hunting territories and wild-rice fields. The cattle-herding tribes of East Africa usually fought over livestock. . . . (115)

Decentralized societies focus on pacifying dangerous neighbors by intimidation, expulsion or annihilation and on acquiring additional food, valuables, labor and territory by the direct methods of plunder, capture and physical expulsion. (116)

It is one thing to threaten with words, gestures, and symbols; it is quite another to physically harm or kill. Romantic anthropologists claimed that in tribal societies threats predominated and physical violence was rare. We will see that not only was this not the case, but that the process of stopping violence once it began was more difficult prior to the advent of the state. There is no surrender in tribal societies. There are no white flags, and there are no pretensions to as to rights of humane treatment. Nor are there ground rules to prevent the mutilating and raping of prisoners. Keeley writes:

it is *civilized* [my emphasis] warfare that is stylized, ritualized and relatively less dangerous. When soldiers clash with warriors, [in fighting between civilized states and pre-state societies] it is precisely these "decorative" civilized tactics and paraphernalia that must be abandoned . . . if they are to defeat the latter. (Keeley, 1996, 174)

Speaking of civilization, Keeley says: "They took what had been a nasty free-for-all . . . and turned it into a chess game, with highly specialized units, stylized movements and constrained rules." (176)

Another romantic claim is that tribal societies built no fortifications. This was not true, at least among simple and complex horticulturalists. Keeley notes that

People with very nomadic life-styles and very portable possessions do not waste their time on such labor-intensive projects that they will soon abandon. . . . Judging from ethnographic records, fortifications are most commonly located on hostile borders or frontiers. (Keeley, 1996, 55-56)

He argues that there are four general types of fortifications: fortified settlements, most common in simple tribal societies; fortified refuges, common in chiefdoms; fortified elite residences; and military fortresses, as seen in state societies.

Finally, romantics often depict the exchange of goods and intermarriage as evidence of tribal wisdom in knowing how to avert war. But, according to Keeley, intermarriage does not preclude warfare:

One common assumption made by many people concerning the contexts for war and peace is that if societies are exchanging goods and marriage partners . . . relations between them are likely to remain peaceful. . . . In a brief time frame, this statement is generally true. . . . But in the longer term assuming that intertribal exchanges of goods and intermarriage preclude warfare is a mistake. (Keeley 1996, 121).

Why is this?

Ethnographers have frequently encountered tribes that intermarried and traded with one another but were also periodically at war. . . . The major reason why exchange partners and enemies have often been the same people is simple propinquity. . . . We interact most intensely with our nearest neighbors, whether those interactions are commercial, nuptial or hostile. (Keeley, 1996, 122-123)

In speaking of marriage, Keeley notes that

Any difficulties that afflict such unions are likely to cause ill-feeling between the groups concerned. In cultures where young girls were promised to men in other social groups by their fathers,

violent disputes occurred when the bride was not 'delivered' when she came of age. In situations where payment of the bride-price or dowry was made in installments, failure to deliver a payment as promised could lead to fighting. (Keeley, 1996, 125)

In summarizing, Keeley argues:

Trade, intermarriage and war all have the effect of moving goods and people between social units. In warfare, goods move as plunder, and people (especially women) move as captives. In exchange and intermarriage, goods move as reciprocal gifts , trade items, and bride wealth, whereas people move as spouses. In effect, the same desirable acquisitions are thus attained by alternative (but not mutually exclusive) means. If raiding and trading are two sides of the same coin, the goods and people acquired must be the coin itself. . . . To varying degrees, then, many societies tend to fight the people they marry and to marry those they fight, to raid the people with whom they trade and to trade with their enemies. (Keeley 1996, 128)

If tribal warfare corresponded to the descriptions of neither the progress theorists nor the degeneration theorists, then what was it really like? The answer to that question must inevitably be complex and tentative. Perhaps the best way to approach it is to begin with cross-cultural studies on the percentage of all societies that engage in war. Cross-cultural surveys of recent tribal and state societies from around the world show that 90 percent of the cultures sampled unequivocally engaged in warfare; even the remaining 10 percent experienced occasional violent conflict. (Keeley, 1996, 28)

When I first read these survey results I thought, "yes, but most of these were probably state civilizations." This was not the case. For example, in a study of western North American Indian tribes and bands, only 13% of the 157 groups surveyed were described as "never or rarely" raiding or having been raided. (Keeley, 1996, 28)

From his frank reading of both anthropology and archeology, Keeley makes the riveting point that the relative proportion of homicides compared to the size of population was actually greater in pre-state societies than in state societies. For example, discussing the Bushmen of the Kalahari Desert, he notes that they had a homicide rate from 1920 to 1955 that was four times that of the United States and "twenty or eighty times that of major industrial nations during the 1950's and 1960's." (pg. 29) Similarly, the canoe nomads of Tierra del Fuego "had a murder rate in the late nineteenth century of 10 times as high as that of the United States." (pg. 29) Keeley also notes that "In a recent comparison of casualty rates from ancient and modern battles, it has been calculated that an average of 70% of men engaged in ancient battles were killed or wounded, whereas only 60% of combatants in the bloodiest modern battles have becomes casualties." (Keeley 1996, 53)

In comparing the violent deaths in pre-state societies to state civilizations, we find that the death rates of non-state societies are higher. Moreover, many of the violent deaths caused by state civilizations are not as a direct result of warfare but because their adversaries contracted a disease or because of accidents.

It is sometimes thought that the intensity of tribal warfare increases as a result of colonial contact. Keeley argues for the opposite view:

In another larger, cross-cultural study of politics and conflict, twelve of a sample of ninety societies (13%) were found to engage in warfare rarely or never. Six of these twelve were tribal or ethnic minorities that had long been subject to peaceful administration of modern nation-states. . . . Most of the peaceful societies were recently defeated refugees living in isolation . . . under a "king's peace" enforced by a modern state. (Keeley, 1996, 28)

Further, there is evidence in archeology for massacres among tribal societies long before contact with civilizations. There was no immunity based on age and sex. Time and again

during ambushes, women and children were not spared.

Raids characteristically kill only a few people at a time; they kill a higher proportion of women than do battles or even the routs that follow them. . . . (66)

Whenever modern humans appear on the scene, definitive evidence of homicide violence becomes more common given a sufficient sample of burials. Several of the rare burials of early modern humans in central and western Europe dating from 34,000 to 24, 000 years ago show evidence of violent death. . . . Evidence from the celebrated Upper Paleolithic cemeteries of Czechoslovakia dating between 35,000 and 24,000 years ago implies . . . that violent conflicts and deaths were common. . . . The human skeletons found in a Late Paleolithic cemetery at Gebel Sahaba in Egyptian Nubia, dating about 12,000 to 14, 000 years ago, show that warfare there was very common and particularly brutal. Over 40% of the fifty-nine men, women and children buried in this cemetery had stone projectile points intimately associated with or embedded in their skeletons. Several adults had multiple wounds . . . and the wounds found on children were all in the head or neck—that is, execution shots. (37)

In western Europe . . . ample evidence of violent death has been found among the remains of the final hunter-gathers of the Mesolithic period. . . . One of the most gruesome instances is provided by Ofnet Cave in Germany, where two caches of "trophy" skulls were found, arranged "like eggs in a basket" comprising the disembodied heads of thirty-four men, women and children, most with multiple holes knocked through their skulls by stone axes (38)

The violence did not abate in the Neolithic. Indications of conflict, as reflected by violent death and the earliest fortifications, become especially pervasive in western Europe during this period. Neolithic mass killings occur in Talheim in Germany where:

> The bodies of eighteen adults and sixteen children had been thrown into a large pit; the intact skulls show that the victims had been killed by blows from at least six different axes. More than 100 persons of all ages and both sexes often with arrow points embedded in their bones, received a hasty and simultaneous burial. . . . The villages of the first farmers in many regions of western Europe were fortified with ditches and palisades. Several of these early enclosures in Britain, yielded clear evidence of having been attacked, stormed and burned by bow-wielding enemies. (Keeley, 1996, 38)

At Roaix in France, four millennia ago, "more than 100 people of both sexes and all ages were killed by bow-wielding adversaries and then hastily buried in a mass grave." (pg. 69) At the time, the nearest civilization was Minoan Crete, which was 1,000 miles away.

Evidence of very similar patterns of primitive war is found in the New World:

> Archeology yields evidence of prehistoric massacres more severe than any recounted in ethnography. For example at Crow Creek in South Dakota, archeologists found a mass-grave containing the remains of more than 500 men, women and children who had been slaughtered, scalped, and mutilated during an attack on their village, a century and a half before Columbus's arrival. (Keeley, 1996, 68)

Thus before any possible contact with civilizations, the tribesmen of prehistoric North America, like those of the Neolithic Europe, were wiping out whole settlements. Keeley concludes that

> From North America at least, archaeological evidence reveals precisely the same pattern recorded ethnographically for tribal peoples the world over of frequent deadly raids and

occasional horrific massacres. This was an indigenous and "native" pattern long before contact with Europeans complicated the situation. When the sailing ship released them from their own continent, Europeans brought many new ills and evils to the non-Western world, but neither war nor its worst features were among these novelties. (Keeley 1996, 69)

Up to now we have only discussed the proportion of casualties and the fact that the intensity of the violence was not due to the presence of civilizations. We have yet to discuss the frequency with which war was conducted. Keeley argues that tribal wars, while occurring on a far smaller scale, were far more frequent: "In a sample of fifty societies, 66% of the non-states were continuously (meaning every year) at war, whereas only 40% of the states were at war this frequently. . . ." (32) Keeley goes on to say:

> The high frequencies of pre-state warfare contrast with those of even the most aggressive ancient or modern civilized states. The early Roman Republic initiated a war or was attacked only about once every twenty years. . . . Historic data on the period from 1800 to 1945 suggest that the average modern nation-state goes to war approximately once in a generation. . . . Taking into account the duration of these wars, the average modern nation-state was at war only about one year in every five during the nineteenth and early twentieth centuries. Even the most bellicose, such as Great Britain, Spain, and Russia, were never at war every year or continuously. . . . Compare these with the figures from the ethnographic samples of non-state societies discussed earlier: 65 percent at war continuously, 77% at war once every five years and 55% at war every year. (Keeley, 1996, 33)

He concludes that "There is simply no proof that warfare in small-scale societies was a rarer or less serious undertaking than among civilized societies. . . . If anything, peace was a scarcer commodity for members of bands, tribes and chiefdoms than for the average citizen of a civilized state." (39)

But why was this not previously seen and understood by anthropologists?

The ethnographers seldom analyzed casualties *in relation* [my emphasis] to the small numbers who fought and thus could not compare them on this basis to larger-scale civilized battles. The raids, ambushes and surprise attacks on villages that constituted a major component of tribal warfare were seldom observed and paid little notice. (Keeley, 1996, 9)

So while the absolute number of people killed in state societies is greater, the percentage of the population lost was higher in pre-state societies. Also, the frequency with which war is a routine part of life was greater in tribal societies.

What of the severity and ruthlessness of the violence practiced by tribal societies? Keeley notes that, unlike civilized states, tribal societies rarely permitted a negotiated surrender.

It is extremely uncommon to find instances among non-state groups of recognizing surrender or taking adult male prisoners. . . . When a Mae Enga warrior was seriously wounded by an arrow or a javelin, his adversaries would charge forward to chop him literally to pieces with their axes. . . . Armed or unarmed, adult males were killed without hesitation in battles, raids and routs. (Keeley, 1996, 84)

There were good, practical reasons for not sparing the lives of their captives, such as the cost in manpower of keeping him, including dealing with his resistance. But this does not account for the mutilation and torture that occurred.

At a council, the warrior prisoners who survived these initial torments were distributed to families who had recently lost men in warfare. After these prisoners were ritually adopted and given the name of the family's dead member, they were usually tortured to death over several days (Keeley, 1996, 84)

Those captives who weren't killed were spared, not out of any humanitarian impulses, but because of their trade value—e.g., later tribal societies sometimes traded captives to state civilizations (for their value as slaves) in return for cattle.

Captured women were considered the spoils of victory—and occasionally constituted one of the primary aims of warfare. Women were captured as spouses and also for their labor. Among the Maoris, however, women's fate was far worse: "The Maori sometimes disabled captive women so they could not escape, permitting the warriors to rape, kill and eat them when it was more convenient to do so." (Keeley 1996, 87)

Furthermore, mutilation and cannibalism were an accepted way of life: "By far the most common and widely distributed war trophy was the head or skull of an enemy. The custom of taking heads is recorded from many cultures in New Guinea, Oceania, North America, South America, Africa and ancient western Europe." (Keeley, 1996, 100)

As an amazing example, Keeley cites this record of the words of a Maori warrior taunting the preserved head of an enemy chief :

You wanted to run away, did you? but my war club overtook you: and after you were cooked you made food for my mouth. And where is your father? he is cooked—and where is your brother? he is eaten—and where is your wife? there she sits, a wife for me—and where are your children? there they are, with loads on their backs, carrying food, as my slaves. (Keeley, 1996, 100)

Keeley makes the distinction between ritual cannibalism and culinary cannibalism, both of which were practiced in pre-state societies. Ritual cannibalism involves the consumption

Figure 8. 2 Contrast between Primitive War and Modern War

Primitive War	Modern War
less absolute casualties	more absolute casualties
homicide rates per unit of population is higher	homicide rates per unit of population is lower
war is more frequent (no centralized authority as mediator)	war between societies is less frequent (state mediates conflicts w/i society)
fortified settlements--simple tribal societies fortified refuges--common in chiefdoms	military fortresses--state societies
raids, ambushes, surprise attacks most common	battles and campaigns most common
longer duration: over generations	short duration: intense wars, punctuated by peace
war is more difficult to stop and stabilize with treaties	war is less difficult to stop and stabilize with treaties
not sparing women and children	more sparing of women and children
war mostly to the death: little surrender	war until surrender
captives mutilated, eaten, traded	captives are subjugated
mutilation, torture, cannibalism accepted	ideology and laws forbid torture, mutilation, cannibalism

body—"culinary cannibalism"—is not uncommon:

> Many tribes and chiefdoms in southern Central America and northeastern South America reputedly consumed large numbers of their dead foes and captives. Not withstanding some kind of magical or religious justifications . . . several of these groups seemed to have positively relished human flesh. One record reports that of a Colombian chief and his retinue consumed the bodies of 100 enemies in a single day. . . . In another chiefdom, war captives were kept in special enclosures and fattened before consumption. . . . Several groups in New Guinea admitted to having conducted raids motivated by the desire for human flesh. In many of these Oceania cases, consistent archeological data support the ethnographic descriptions. (Keeley 1996, 103-104)

Both tribal and state societies share a common tendency, when viewing war in retrospect, to suppress the gory detail of what was experienced and to minimize the bloodshed, turning the war into a dramatic story. Also, women are not actively in wars in either type of society. And both modern and primitive wars are largely caused by economic needs and the desire for expansion of territory.

In taking issue with the romantic notions of an idyllic, peaceful non-state society, I am not implying that the Hobbesian assumptions about war are any closer to the truth. Neither am I suggesting that modern warfare is "better" than primitive war. Whether it is or not is not the issue. My aim in this section has been simply to dethrone the notion that tribal societies were inherently peaceful.

3. Beyond peace and war: warless societies

While Keeley's work exposes the violence of pre-state societies, his conclusions about the relationship between violence and war are too sweeping. Raymond Kelly (2000), who has made a similar study of warfare in pre-state

societies, criticizes Keeley's conclusions on the following counts:

- Keeley seems to equate homicide with warfare. Kelly distinguishes between homicide, capital punishment, and warfare.
- Keeley lumps together hunter-gatherer violence with violence in other types of tribal societies. Kelly shows that a significant portion of hunter-gatherers, while certainly violent in some respects, can be characterized as "warless."
- While in some instances Keeley is right in saying warfare in tribal societies could be more difficult to stop than warfare in state societies, Kelly cites peacekeeping devices in pre-state societies that required no state intervention.
- Not all pre-state societies killed women and children as part of warfare. Societies that inflicted capital punishment without going to war killed only men.

All four of these points will be explored in this section.

If the world of pre-state societies was not what Rousseau imagined, neither was it Hobbesian. People were not always at war with each other. In fact, pre-state societies went to a great deal of trouble to maintain peace. Speaking of Paleolithic foragers, Kelly argues:

> The societies that initially spread to all corners of the globe—and passed through the Arctic gateway to the New World— were those that achieved a degree of regional integration through intermarriage, visiting, gift exchange, joint feasting . . . singing and dancing. Such practices fostered a state of positive peace that provided a basis for sharing and cooperation. In other words, it was not merely the absence of war but the presence of positive peace that facilitate Upper Paleolithic migrations. (Kelly 2000, 135)

Even after a war had begun, pre-state societies were capable of reestablishing peace:

the vast majority of societies in which warfare does occur are characterized by the alternation of war and peace; there are relatively few societies . . . in which warfare is continual and peace almost unknown. It is only in this relatively small percentage of cases that something approximating a Hobbesian social condition of pervasive and unending warfare can be found (Kelly, 2000, 124)

According to Raymond Kelly (2000), Fabbro (1978) made an ethnographic study of the characteristics of peaceful societies. Fabbro's criteria for peace included the following:

(a) no wars fought on the society's territory
(b) no external wars
(c) no civil wars
(d) no standing military police
(e) little or no interpersonal physical violence
(f) no structural violence (socially coercive organizations)
(g) the society can undergo change peacefully
(h) there is opportunity for idiosyncratic development.

Melvin Ember's 1978 studies of a worldwide sample of 31 hunter-gatherer societies found that for 64% warfare occurred at least once every two years. Warfare was rare in only 12% of the population.

Fabbro discovered seven societies that were relatively peaceful. Five of the seven satisfied Fried's criteria for egalitarian societies that produced no surplus; these were the Semai, Siriono, Mbuti, !Kung, and the Copper Eskimo. However he compares these societies to two others that do produce a surplus, the Tristan da Cunha and the Hutterites. The point in doing so was to see how powerful a factor having a surplus would be in war-making.

These seven societies were compared across fourteen categories, including habitat, means of subsistence, division of labor, hierarchy, method of socialization, coercive organization, physical violence and conflict resolution. None of these relatively peaceful societies met all of Fabbro's criteria for peace, but they did meet

the first five criteria and partially the sixth. However, according to Kelly:

a reappraisal based on both new sources and a reexamination of the original sources Fabbro employs, leads to the conclusion that the five traditional egalitarian band societies do not for the most part fulfill Fabbro's utopian criteria of "little or no interpersonal physical violence." Most notably they all manifest comparatively high homicide rates. (Kelly, 2000, 31)

As Keeley has demonstrated, pre-state societies are far more violent than many anthropologists have assumed, based on homicide rates. But homicide is not the same as war. As Kelly points out:

The definition of war an analyst adopts can have a significant effect on the conclusions that are reached concerning the prevalence, frequency and antiquity of warfare. For example one could take the position that the killing of a member of one local group by a member of a neighboring group is intrinsically a political act, insofar as it impinges on intergroup relations, and therefore should be considered an act of war. One could then conclude that "war" (defined as lethal violence between spatially distinct groups) occurs in every known ethnographic case as well as among our genetically closest primate relatives. (Kelly, 2000, 122)

Further, in reaction to the loss of a kin member, among the seven societies Fabbro studied the typical reaction was inaction not homicide: "There may be no sequel to an individual homicide in warless societies. The victim's next of kin express their grief and sorrow at the loss but take no action. This is the more typical outcome in these five ethnographic cases." (Kelly, 2000, 41)

Kelly defines warfare as armed conflict that has seven components:

(a) it is collectively carried out (not individually)

(b) it employs deadly weapons (as opposed to non-lethal)

(c) it is envisioned in advance (vs. spontaneous brawls and riots)

(d) it involves making a plan (vs. haphazard action)

(e) it is socially approved of (vs. homicide)

(f) it involves social substitutability (vs. murder, duel, or capital punishment, in which a specific individual is sought); any member of the opposing group will do

(g) it serves instrumental objectives such as defense, revenge, excision, or appropriation rather than being an end in itself.

This more refined definition of war allows other forms of violence to be understood as points on a spectrum. Kelly makes some important distinctions between homicide, spontaneous conflict, capital punishment and warfare. Homicide is different from war in a number of ways, but most importantly it is not supported by the community of the murderer. Spontaneous conflict differs from war in that even though it might be socially approved of it has not been envisioned in advance and there is no plan of action. Capital punishment is closer to war but it lacks one important component—social substitution. This means the target of attack is a specific individual, not the entire group. Whereas non-war forms of violence are universal in space and go deep into the past, warfare is not universal and occurs in only some kinds of foraging societies:

Pongicide (or conspecific lethal violence among the great apes), capital punishment, and war are distinct phenomena rather than members of a unitary category. Pongicide is an analogue of homicide and both are undoubtedly ancient. However, chimpanzees lack both capital punishment and war. While capital punishment is a cultural universal found in all known human societies, war is clearly not universal. All cross-cultural surveys of the incidence of warfare have identified a number of socio-cultural systems in which

war [as defined by Kelly] is considered to be rare or nonexistent. In Ross's (1983) coding of ninety societies in the Standard Cross-Cultural Scale twelve (or 13.3 percent) were so classified. (Kelly, 2000, 123)

We might look at warfare as the most extreme form of a social reaction to killing. The stages of escalation would be: (1) inaction, (2) revenge murder (homicide) and or spontaneous conflict, (3) capital punishment, and (4) warfare. Kelly notes that "The five most peaceful societies line up at different points on the spectrum of violence." (Kelly, 2000, 17) According to Fabbro, physical violence between husband and wife is reported for three of the seven societies (Mbuti, Copper Eskimo and Tristan). Further, according to Kelly, "Homicide is said to be 'quite frequent' among the Copper Eskimo, rare among the Semai and !Kung, and not noted for the Siriono, Mbuti, Hutterites and Tristan. . . ." (Kelly, 2000, 18)

If these societies all shared a common conflict resolution mechanism, perhaps this could explain their warlessness. But apparently they do not:

Among the Mbuti there are a number of categories of individuals who may intervene in a conflict—elders, seniors, kin, neighbors, 'clowns' or the local group as a whole. . . . The Semai are somewhat similar to the Mbuti in that elders may mediate quarrels. However none of the other three warless band societies in Fabbro's sample manifest anything comparable to the Mbuti pattern. Among the !Kung attempts at intervention lead to side fights, and peacemakers are sometimes killed in the general melee that results from third-party intervention. (Kelly, 2000, 38)

Generally speaking, in anthropology it is assumed that the five egalitarian hunter-gatherer societies we studied are less violent than planters. However, as noted in the last section, the homicide rate among hunter-gatherers is greater than that for planters: "Taken together,

Figure 8.3 Contrast between Warless and Warlike Hunter-gatherers

Warless hunter-gatherers   **Warlike hunter-gatherers**

CHARACTERISTICS OF SOCIAL ORGANIZATION

unsegmented societies   **segmented societies**
smaller size, local group varies w/ seasons   larger size, local group steady throughout
family the basic unit.   kin or clan basic unit
relations outside family voluntary   involuntary, interdependence

lack extended families that persist through marriage: extended families persist through marriage:
lack descent groups--egocentric bilateral kin   descent groups

marriage is not exchange between groups: marriage is exchange between groups:
only joins individuals   joins moieties

token gifts   marriage payments
no food storage   food storage--territorial and residential
                                                                 defense.—fortifications

VIOLENCE CHARACTERISTICS

if homicide, next of kin take no action--   if homicide, next of kin take action--
angry feelings, talk, non-lethal violence   feud (internal) or external war

no injury to group, no group liability,   injury to group, group liability
no group responsibility for causing death   group responsibility for causing death

homicide--w/ no social substitution   social substitution
killing limited to men   killing through raids include women and
                                                                 children (worse effects for depopulation)

external war over resource competition   external war over resource competition:
no peacekeeping devices (speak different   no peacekeeping devices
languages)

no internal war because they can withdraw   internal war but have peacekeeping devices

even in circumscribed environments   in circumscribed environments women cannot
women can keep the peace   keep the peace

spirit women as peacekeepers
retaliation by spirits of the dead   retaliation by other groups

armed conflicts between groups occurs   armed conflict between groups if a
if *group* was attacked   *single individual* is attacked.

ECOLOGICAL/DEMOGRAPHIC CONDITIONS

                                                                 spontaneous conflicts
low resource density   high resource density
low resource diversity   high resource diversity
low resource predictability   high resource reliability
populations below 0.2 / square mile   populations above 0.2 / square mile

                                                                 amplified conflict
                                                                 higher population densities
                                                                 environmental circumscription

30–42 per 100,000 per annum for the !Kung, Mbuti, and Semai and ten times this rate for the Copper Eskimo and Gebusi. In contrast, homicide rates for a sample of African agricultural societies cluster in the range of 4.0 6.0 per 100,000." (Kelly, 2000, 21)

However, if we are faithful to the definition of war given by Kelly we can say that hunter-gatherers commit more homicides than planters, yet still preserve the notion that they are less warlike, because homicide and war are two different things.

Another interesting pattern is the relationship between child rearing and violence. All of the non-surplus producing societies noted are permissive in their child rearing practices, while both surplus producing societies, the Hutterites and Tristan, are authoritarian in this regard. But authoritarian childrearing does not necessarily make children more likely to be violent. So too, permissive childrearing does not necessarily make people less violent:

homicide and fighting among adult males are virtually absent in the two cases where the physical punishment of children is most severe (Tristan and the Hutterites). There is an inverse rather than one-to-one relationship between this "authoritarian" socialization (present) and lethal violence (absent). . . . One can conclude that the attainment of societal peace in the form of an absence of war is not contingent upon an absence of other forms of physical violence. (Kelly, 2000, 19)

Both the impulse to express ill-feeling in interpersonal physical violence and the enactment of this impulse in . . . wrestling matches or striking a spouse—are relatively commonplace . . . these societies are not warless as a consequence of . . . enculturation that (1) preclude or diminishes the experience of anger . . . (2) suppress the expression of angry feelings in interpersonal violence (3) effectively limit such expression to nonlethal forms of violence. (Kelly, 2000, 42)

In conclusion:

Violence does not beget violence in a lockstep manner. Female fighting can in fact co-occur with permissive child rearing and absence of physical punishment of children. The same societies that eschew war may be characterized by high levels of interpersonal physical violence. . . . Likewise the same societies that eschew war may evidence homicide rates that are quite high . . . these exceptionally high homicide rates are found in conjunction with day-to day tranquility and the lowest reported incidence of interpersonal physical violence. (Kelly, 2000, 37)

Thus the five warless societies have no conflict resolution patterns in common, their homicide rates are higher rather than lower than societies characterized as warlike, and there seem to be no socialization tendencies that can predict high homicide rates in these societies.

4. Socio-structural, ecological, and demographic conditions for war

What distinguishes warless from warlike societies is not just the means of subsistence. True, if warless societies exist they are likely to be hunter-gatherers. Yet the rates of homicide are higher among hunter-gatherers than planters; thus it is too simple to say that there is something more peaceful about hunting and gathering than planting as a means of production, and that therefore the way people get their food determines whether they are likely to go to war. On the contrary, first impressions would seem to indicate that hunting entails more social violence than planting. We must look elsewhere for an explanation.

Another plausible causal factor is the need to migrate. Perhaps if hunter-gatherers are not biophysically or socially circumscribed they are more likely to be warless because when there is conflict over resources with another society they would have the option of moving. But this seems not to be the case; according to Kelly,

[S]ome of the most warlike foragers are also fully migratory (Aweikoma and Abipon). Moreover, three additional cases of mobile hunter-gatherers exhibit yearly warfare (ie. the Tiwi, Comanche and Chircahua Apache). Thus less than half of the mobile foragers conform to the expectations of anthropological received wisdom regarding warfare frequency while the remainder exhibit unanticipated high levels of conflict in the form of annual raids. (Kelly, 2000, 67)

Neither does a society's tendency to be warlike depend on its ecological setting, since the seven peaceful societies cited inhabit varied ecological settings.

Kelly argues instead that a key predictor in whether pre-state societies are warlike is whether these societies are segmented or unsegmented. In unsegmented societies there is no division of labor within social groups. Families are detachable subunits that perform all aspects of production. Food may be shared with other families, but there is no interdependence in work. The composition of these bands of families fluctuates with the seasons. There is no food storage because resources are dispersed rather than concentrated in one spot.

Segmented societies have a larger population, they are geographically more stable, there is more interdependence in work, and there are more elaborate forms of social organization including kin groups and clans. As we saw in chapter 2, there are descent groups and marriages exchanges between groups. When marriage occurs in unsegmented societies, token gifts are exchanged. In segmented societies, marriage payments are offered. Finally, in segmented societies there is food storage.

Kelly goes on to point out that five of the seven warless societies selected by Fabbro are unsegemented:

Warfare is comparatively infrequent in . . . unsegmented foraging societies but equally infrequent in only one of seventeen other foraging societies. The answer to the critical question of what differentiates

comparatively warless from warlike hunter-gatherers is thus readily apparent. The former lack the organizational features associated with social substitutability. (Kelly, 2000, 51)

What is the connection between segmentation, social substitutability, and war on the one hand, and unsegmentation, individual identification of murder, and capital punishment on the other? A key distinction between capital punishment and war is that of social substitutability and group liability. As noted above, segmented societies are interdependent in the areas of work, marriage, and food storage. This means that an affront to one can be considered an affront to all.

In contrast, because unsegmented warless societies have little group interdependence, and the composition of the band is too unstable to serve as the basis for the feeling that an affront to one is an affront to all. There is no group feeling to avenge the death of an individual member who is killed, but neither do members of unsegmented societies feel responsible of one if their members kills a member of another society. According to Kelly,

the execution of an individual whose criminal responsibilities have been established (i.e., capital punishment) . . . is simply accepted by the killer's kin . . . there is no capacity for violence to escalate beyond a sequence of events in which the homicide is followed by the execution of the killer. Moreover this characterization is uniformly applicable to all the unsegmented societies in Ross's (1983) representative world sample. (Kelly, 2000, 56)

However, "a kin group responsibility to exact vengenance is manifested in 69% of the other segmental foraging societies." (Kelly, 2000, 56)

While the majority of unsegmented societies are hunter-gatherers, there are many hunter-gatherer societies that are segmented. Whether hunter-gatherers are unsegmented or not seems to depend on whether they are nomadic or sedentary. According to Kelly, "All sedentary and semisedentary foraging societies are segmental in organizational design. Conversely all unsegmented foraging societies are either fully migratory or seminomadic." (Kelly, 2000, 67)

Thus the frequency of warfare among hunter-gatherers appears to correlate with the following spectrum:

- low among unsegmented mobile foragers
- intermediate among semisedentary and fully sedentary segemented foragers
- variable among semi-nomiadic foragers (both segmented and unsegmented)
- high among mobile and semi-nomadic segmented foragers (Kelly, 2000, 67)

It is tempting to think there is a direct connection between warlessness, unsegmented social organization, and nomadism. However, the fourth entry above seems to defy that conclusion: warfare is high in mobile or semi-nomadic segmental foragers. Following Kelly, we will explain this shortly.

There are two kinds of warfare—external and internal. External warfare takes place between societies that do not speak the same language. This type of warfare is difficult to stop, in part because of the language barrier. The reason for external warfare, according to Kelly, is resource competition. Internal warfare occurs within a single society in which everyone does speak the same language. This type of warfare is called "feuding" and the reason for this kind of warfare is typically not resource competition but desire for revenge. Enabled by the common language, peace-making techniques usually exist in foraging societies to prevent feuding from getting out of hand.

Unsegmented societies only have external warfare because they are not large enough, interdependent enough, or stable enough to feud. Disagreements among members are likely to be resolved by withdrawal. Segmented societies can have both external and internal warfare. Segmented societies have peacekeeping devices to contain hostilities. External wars are

difficult to stop, whether the society is segmented or not.

The impact of external warfare on the size of the population varies depending on whether foragers are segmented or unsegmented. In unsegmented societies where capital punishment is more the rule, only a specific person is targeted. Since men are the ones who do the fighting, it is mostly men who are the targets and men who are killed. According to Kelly, male deaths in war have little effect on the number of children born to females, as a result of polygyny and widow remarriage.

But in segmented societies where there is social substitutability, women and children are killed as well, and this does affect the population: "Child deaths and reduced births due to adult female mortality decrease the size of the population for two generations because fewer females attain reproductive age fifteen years after the event." (Kelly 2000, 134)

In sum, whether hunter-gatherers are organized in a segmented or an unsegmented manner and whether or not they are mobile or sendentary goes a long way toward determining whether or not they will be warlike. However, this does not account for those unsegmented societies which are mobile and which still are warlike. To explain this we will need to consider not only the form of social organization and settlement patterns, but certain ecological and demographic conditions as well.

The one unsegmented society that is warlike which Kelly closely examined is in the seminomadic Andaman Islands close to the southeast tip of Burma. This island consists of 13 different language groups of people. Though their unsegmented social organization and settlement pattern would seem to work against warfare, they possess three characteristics that, when taken together, appear to predispose them toward warfare:

- their population density is in excess of one person per square mile;
- their seasonal habitat is close to rich aquatic resources; and
- their tropical islands comprise a circumscribed environment (all other

unsegemented societies studied are located upon expansive continental land masses).

The circumscribed environment of the Andaman Islanders and their proximity to rich natural resources mean that they are less likely to make spatial separations between local groups during a good portion of the year. The area is inhabited by the Jarawa, who are exclusive forest dwellers, and the Bea, who inhabit both the coastlines and the forests. The points of conflict between these two groups are the overlaps between coastal and forest niches, where there is resource competition.

The connection between size of the population and incidence of war is more complex. If we group hunter-gatherers together and do not distinguish between segmented and unsegmented groups, then it appears that population density is not a significant factor. However, according to Kelly, "if we restrict the comparative analysis to unsegmented foraging societies a very different picture emerges. Seven of the eight unsegmented foraging societies have population densities of less than one person per square mile and all seven have infrequent warfare. . . ." (Kelly, 2000, 71)

What, then, are the ecological and demographic conditions that promote warfare? Kelly begins by contesting the notion that population pressure and resource depletion drive warfare; instead, the evidence suggests that the important factors are a rich concentration of resources and a circumscribed environment:

It is not the paucity of resources that provides conditions favorable to the origination of war but rather *reliability and abundance* [my emphasis]. It is under the latter circumstances that a society can afford to have enemies for neighbors. (Kelly, 2000, 135)

If neighboring enemies come into deadly conflict, this may produce a reduction of numbers, which in turn will encourage the societies to withdraw from contact, and not to expand further:

It is highly improbable that population decline would engender warfare where none previously existed, since a reduction in numbers produces surfeit rather than shortage; the resources that previously sustained a larger population of hunter-gatherers must necessarily be more than enough for a diminished population. Depopulation clearly provides no impetus to territorial expansion. Inasmuch as hunter-gatherers are prone to move away from conflict, depopulation may engender disengagement along contested borders. (Kelly, 2000, 89)

But if withdrawal is not an option, then more warfare is a likely response. This strategy could lead to extinction for the losers, for existing resources are endangered by avoidance of border areas which become no-man's lands. Thus the area available to continued search for resources shrinks still further.

What, then, are the ultimate conditions for warfare?

Spontaneous conflicts over access to resources occur both within and between unsegmented foraging societies in environments that are: rich in naturally occurring subsistence resources that are characterized by high resource density, diversity, and reliability and that support population densities in excess of 0.2 persons per square mile The incidence and severity of conflict is amplified by higher population densities and/or environmental circumscription. (Kelly, 2000, 136)

Conversely:

Warfare is typically rare to nonexistent within and between unsegmented foraging societies inhabiting environments characterized by low resource density, diversity, and predictability at densities below 0.2 persons per square mile. . . . The absence or near absence of war under these conditions is a product of the critical importance of cooperation . . . rather than an absence of resource competition. Conditions favoring resource competition are . . . likely to be present when there are fluctuations in resource availability at any given location from year to year. (Kelly, 2000, 133)

In chapter 2 we discussed optimum foraging theory and conditions under which people will stay or leave a territory. They were:

- high resource density, low resource predictability—in which case people tend to be highly mobile, to share information, and to exhibit low territoriality;
- high resource density, high resource predictability—in which case people will be less mobile and more territorial;
- low resource density, low resource predictability—in which case people will be highly mobile, but territoriality will be absent; and
- low resource density, high resource predictability—in which case people will be less mobile, and "passively territorial."

The second category would conform most closely to conditions for warfare because resources are concentrated in one area and they are very predictable. This would naturally make this group the most territorial, and though Sanderson does not make this explicit, they would probably be far more competitive with other groups because it is less in their short-term interest to cooperate with other groups. Condition three would be most amenable to the appearance of warless societies, because when resources are dispersed and unpredictable people value territory less, compete less, and cooperate more with other groups because it is in their group's interest to do so.

Figure 8.3 is a summary of sections two and three of this chapter.

If we consider the three ecological and demographic conditions that exist on the Andaman Islands—rich, concentrated resources, a circumscribed environment, and population densities of over 0.2 per square mile—we can see how these conditions might override the fact that both these societies are unsegmented, and

could cause them to move from spontaneous armed conflict to capital punishment to war. Kelly cites the example of the Jarawa:

The majority of incidents of armed conflict are spontaneous conflict over resources, but adaptation to the prospect of this has led to a policy of attacking whenever a Jarawa hunting party has the advantage of surprise. . . . When conditions for an immediate attack are unfavorable the Jarawa may follow the Bea back to their encampment. . . . The central motif continues to be capital punishment of thieving trespassers . . . but the locale has now shifted from the scene of the crime to the perpetrators' encampment. The objective is to shoot one of the perpetrators if possible but the particular Bea individual who enters the tropical forest behind the beach . . . may potentially be any member of the community. . . . The strategic requirement of surprise necessitates social substitution . . . the Jarawa and the Bea provide an in-process illustration of the origination of war in a context of resource competition. (Kelly, 2000, 139).

These are external wars, which are very difficult to stop once they get started, due to the language barrier.

Everything discussed in the chapter so far pertains to modern hunter-gatherer patterns of warfare. How plausible is it to apply this to hunter-gatherers in the Paleolithic period? Kelly points out that there is a contradiction between the archeological and ethnographic literature. If we accept his definition of war and do not confuse it with homicide, the archeological evidence shows few clear-cut signs of warfare among hunter-gatherers prior to development of agriculture. At the same time we have seen that among most modern hunter-gatherers (segmented but not unsegmented) there is considerable warfare. The answer to whether Paleolithic foragers were as warless or warlike as modern hunter-gatherers depends on how likely they were—

Figure 8.4 Impact on Women of Tribal Warfare

Pro	Type of Society	Con
	WARLESS FORAGERS	
Not the target of war		Sudden loss of fathers, husbands, brothers and sons through homicide
Women as peacemakers		
	WARLIKE FORAGERS AND HORTICULTURISTS	
		In internal warfare can be the target of vengeance
		In external warfare can be targeted
Long-distance external war: □ Take over men's work □ Descent traced along female line		**Short-distance external war:** □ Continue to do "women's work" □ Descent continues to be traced along the male line □ Disruption of community life
If the group is victorious: More land, better resources		If the group is defeated: Raped, slaughtered, eaten or sold into slavery

(a) to be unsegmented,
(b) to live in an ecological setting where resources were scattered as opposed to concentrated
(c) to live in non-circumscribed environments
(d) to live in population densities of less than 0.2 per square mile.

Did most Upper Paleolithic peoples live in unsegmented societies?

> The social organization of the societies that existed in the earlier part of the Upper Paleolithic is considered by Gamble (1982) and Whallon (1989). Whallon argues that the expansion of human population into Australia and Siberia allows us to make deductions concerning the human capabilities, communication systems and organizations that would be required to exploit environments characterized by low resource density, diversity and predictability (e.g the Arctic gateway to the New World and the deserts of Australia). In such environments, unpredictable year-to-year fluctuations in resource availability at any given location produce situations of localized shortage that render cooperation [rather than war] between local groups highly adaptive. [This is supported by] the extensive traveling, visiting and intercommunity ceremonial gatherings that are well-developed among ethnographically known hunter-gatherers in desert and arctic environments. (Keely, 2000, 125)

Kelly concludes from this that "the organizational characteristics deduced to be present during the early Upper Paleolithic are fully compatible with the characteristics of unsegmented societies." (Kelly, 2000, 126) Further:

> If all societies in early Upper Paleolithic were unsegmented one would expect war to be limited to circumscribed environments . . . such environments have limited distribution and were in many cases uninhabited in 35,000 BP (due in partly a lack of watercraft). . . . If circumscribed environments . . . were largely unoccupied during the Upper Paleolithic then one would expect that nearly all early Upper Paleoithic societies were warless. (Kelly, 2000, 147)

5. Implications of warfare on women

From what has been said in this chapter it would seem that women fare better in the conditions existing in warless societies than in societies that are warlike. In warless societies when capital punishment or homicide is prevalent, women can expect not to be targeted because since those suspected of committing homicide are likely to be men. However the frequency of homicide in these societies means that women could lose their husbands, fathers or sons unpredictably. Another reason women would do better in societies that are warless is that when these societies do go to war women are the leading peace-makers. In unsegmented societies, such as those in the Andaman Islands, even when warfare is prevalent women can play an important role as peacemakers—a role that would not be possible in segemented societies.

In societies that are segmented—whether they rely on hunting and gathering or simple horticulture—women are far more endangered because of social substitutability. Because of substitutability, women are more likely to be victims of external warfare or the internal feuds of their own society. Effects of warfare on women's occupational status depend on whether the war is a short-distance or long-distance affair. When men leave their hamlets or villages for a short time to fight, this disrupts community life but women may benefit from the new resources and land if the men are victorious. If their men lose the war they are in danger of being raped, eaten, slaughtered, or sold into slavery. It is when men go away for a long time to fight in wars that women benefit considerably. Women are forced to take on some of the roles and jobs left by men, and these are often highly prestigious. It is no accident that societies that trace their descent lines through females (i.e., that are matrilineal) are, according to Harris (1977) societies in which men are engaging in long-distance wars.

Figure 8.4 summarizes the conditions for women under warfare in pre-state societies.

We can be confident that most of the agents in carrying out the horrendous deeds described in this chapter were men. We are now faced with the question, *How responsible were women for this state of affairs?* In view of the fact that women did not directly fight in wars, did they bear any responsibility for what occurred? Were women simply victims of circumstance?

At the end of chapter 1 we discussed men and women as history shapers. They are in fact *interdependent* history shapers. This means that there are no activities in history in which one gender bears sole responsibility. Warfare entails far more than simply the effort involved in killing or attempting to kill. What are women doing during the preparation for war? How do the women treat the men after they return from war? Do they withdraw to another part of the village shaking their heads and saying to themselves, "Oh, that's men's business?" Hardly. Women prepare the costumes for war, assist men in putting on war paint, and encourage them.

As Carol Tarvis (1992) points out, women boosted morale by supporting departing warriors. Richard Nisbett (1996), in speaking of Wyatt-Brown's depiction of women in the Old South, points out that: "women of the southern highlands did not shrink from the suffering and sacrifice involved [in feuds] but rather [would] excite and cheer their husbands to desperate deeds. They would hate a man who took insult or injury without revenge." (Nisbett 1996, 86) Of the American civil war he writes: "An old veteran . . . was once asked why southern soldiers had fought so bravely and so long after it had become apparent that they would be crushed by the North. 'We were afraid to stop . . . afraid of the women at home. . . . They would have been ashamed of us.'" (Nisbett, 1996, 86-87)

There is no question that it is men in power who decide to go to war and it is men who most often carry this decision out, but

we overlook the women who support and endorse war [and] we overlook the men who promote pacifism and negotiation . . . most of the greatest pacifists and reformers in history have been men . . . throughout history women have been just as militant in wartime as men. Women have always participated in wars, in whatever ways their societies permitted—as combatants, as defenders as laborers in the work force to produce war materials. . . . Women are the unindicted co-conspirators in the making of war. (Tarvis, 1992, 66-67, 71)

It might be argued that these examples do not paint an accurate picture of women and war because the examples used were from stratified state societies, not egalitarian or ranked tribal societies. But this chapter has shown that men in tribal societies were every bit as violent as conscripts fighting in state societies. It would hardly be realistic to assume that women in tribal societies behaved toward war in ways that were radically different from ways women in state societies behave.

Chapter 9

Chariots, Infantry and Nomadic Invasions: War in the Bronze and Iron Ages

This chapter has two aims: first, to show how warfare changed over time; and second, to show that, if Neolithic horticultural societies were in fact invaded by more warlike pastoral societies, such invasions occurred too late to be considered a possible cause for the deterioration of women's status in those early complex societies.

At least five major transformations in the nature of warfare occurred during the transition from pre-state to state societies:

a. warfare became a specialized activity of a standing army;
b. warfare became less frequent;
c. the specialized army supported the power and privilege of the upper castes *within* society as well as fighting wars externally;
d. subjugation stemming from the perpetual *threat* of violence became predominant over direct killing;
e. the weaponry of warfare became more lethal.

In pre-state societies the activities of a warrior did not constitute a full-time occupation. Warriors were also workers in other specializations. This meant that, if a conflict arose, most men would have to fight. They would also be the perpetual targets of ambushes or wars initiated by other societies. In contrast to this, most males in Bronze Age societies were not obliged to fight, as these societies had specialized groups of aristocrats.

The frequency of warfare in Bronze Age civilizations was less than in pre-state societies, in part because subjugation replaced killing.

Like modern state societies, the civilizations of the Bronze and Iron Ages were stratified. A full-time military acts as a coercive force that protects the power and privilege of the upper castes against any challenges from the lower castes. The means of coercion was now monopolized by the state. War between societies was supplemented or replaced by caste tensions within these societies.

Unlike modern states, ancient state societies did not spare women and children in wars. As with segmented hunters and horticulturalists in pre-state societies, there were minimal or no laws or customs forbidding torture, mutilation, or cannibalism. Captives were more likely to be subjugated if possible (rather than killed), because ancient states had the military power with which to force captives to work as slaves. Like modern states, ancient states had greater numbers of causalities when they did fight, because their weapons were more powerful than those of pre-state societies. The last of these five changes in warfare will be the subject of sections one and four of this chapter.

The second major point of this chapter has to do with the one of the contentions of Goddess theorists, which we touched on in chapter 3, concerning the origins of male dominance. These theorists claim that "pastoralist invasions" of Neolithic societies occurred as early as 4400 BCE and explain the origins of institutionalized male dominance. If these invasions occurred as early as Gimbutas has claimed—that is, *before* the rise of state civilizations—then these invasions can be interpreted as the *cause* of the rise of state societies and the consequent deterioration of women's status. I will argue that these invasions occurred beginning in the 18th century BCE, after the state and institutionalized male dominance had already emerged within these societies. Whatever invasions occurred cannot explain the deterioration of women's status. Such deterioration cannot be blamed on an external social force. Causes *within* tribal and state societies (which have been discussed in chapters 4 through 8) will have to be considered.

I will close the chapter with a chart comparing the lives of women under pre-state warfare conditions with those under state warfare conditions.

1. Chariot warfare in the Bronze Age

Chariot warfare in the Bronze Age differed from warfare in pre-state societies in a number of ways. Chariot warfare involves at least four separate processes: the invention of the wheel, the invention of a spoked wheel, the domestication of the horse, and the invention of the bit. These innovations together resulted in warfare that was less labor-intensive, more lethal, and less frequent than warfare in pre-state societies.

Drews (1993) argues that the linking of horses to spoked wheels and chariots was preceded by other means of harnessing energy. Oxen had been hitched to solid-wheeled wagons in Mesopotamia from the beginning of the third millennium BCE. Early in the second millennium the heavy wooden wheel evolved into a lighter two-, four-, and six-spoked wheel. The spoked wheel exploited the speed of a horse as both a draft animal and later as an animal of war. Drews writes:

> The chariot was a technological triumph of the early second millennium. [It was] made of light hardwoods with a leather-mesh platform on which the driver could stand. . . . The wheels were . . . the revolutionary element: the heat-bent spokes provided a sturdy wheel that weighed only a tenth as much as the disk wheels of the third millennium. With such a vehicle one could begin to exploit the

> horse as a draft animal: whereas an ox cart traveled only two miles in an hour, a team of chariot horses could cover ten. (Drews, 1993,104)

He further notes that "The horse's walking speed was almost twice that of the ox. . . . [T]he horse unlike the ox had gaits other than a walk: at a trot the horse can cover almost ten miles an hour; at full gallop it can for a few minutes move at a speed of over 30 mph. Use of the horse as a draft animal revolutionized transport and travel in the ancient world." (Drews, 1989, 84)

The number of chariots grew as they became more feasible to produce:

> Chariot forces in the middle of the seventeenth century [BCE] were relatively small and possibly numbered no more than a hundred vehicles. At this time, chariots were presumably used against *infantries* of the old style. As charioteers proliferated, the target of a chariot archer was increasingly the horses and crewmen of the *opposing chariotry*, [my emphasis] and it became important for a king to have more chariots than his opponent hand. Thutmose III's account of his victory at the Battle of the Megiddo shows that by the middle of the fifteenth century B.C. a Great King could deploy at least a thousand chariots. At the beginning of the next century the Great Kingdom of Miranni seems to have had at its disposal a chariotry numbering several thousand. (Drews, 1993, 106-107)

The power of the composite bow considerably increased the lethality of chariot warfare.

> The typical military chariot carried two men, a driver and a fighter. . . . In Egypt, the Fertile Crescent, and India the chariot fighter was normally an archer . . . armed with a composite bow. This weapon was far more deadly than the self bow, which was made all of wood. . . . [The composite bow] was more difficult to string but had a much greater range and effectiveness than

the self bow. Although most accurate at a range of about 60 meters, the composite bow could shoot as far as 160 or even 175 meters. (Drews, 1989, 86)

However, the cost of maintaining a military of chariots was high. For example, though the composite bow had double or triple the range of a self bow, it was very expensive to produce. Then there was the feeding of the horses. Stuart Piggott claims that it took between eight and ten acres of good quality grain-land to feed one team of horses. In addition to the cost of weapons and armor, there was the added cost of paying all the specialists—which included warriors, trainers, grooms, veterinarians, and carpenters. Charioteers and warriors were not drawn from the class of commoners. They had to be strong and athletic, with good eye-hand coordination. They were privileged men who were given land by the king. Then there was the added cost of paying a bureaucracy of clerks to keep track of the system as a whole.

Drews takes issue with conventional historians who believe that the infantry was predominant in the Bronze Age. Drews claims that the infantry played a *subordinate* role to that of the chariots. As we shall see, it was only in the Iron Age that the infantry and cavalry played the dominant part; Drews puts it thus: "If one is looking for the kind of battle familiar from classical antiquity—heavy infantries fighting hand-to-hand in the center, with horse troops engaged on the wings—one will search in vain the documents and pictorial representations that have come down to us from the Late Bronze Age kingdoms." (Drews 1993, 137) Instead, "Battles between eastern Mediterranean kingdoms of the Late Bronze Age . . . must have consisted primarily of two chariot forces charging against and past each other and then circling back to charge each other again, the archers all the while shooting against the opposing squadrons." (Drews 1993, 136)

This does not mean that infantries were not used in the Bronze Age, but that they were arrayed primarily against *non-civilized* societies.

A contrast emerges . . . between warfare against civilized enemies and warfare against men from the hinterland. . . . The kingdoms, and cities generally, were sited in fertile plains, which could be dominated and defended by chariots. When one king attacked another the confrontation was . . . a chariot battle. Similarly, a kingdom could depend on its chariots against barbarians who raided its perimeter. . . . On the other hand, in order to carry the battle to mountainous or rough terrain, where chariots could not go, a king necessarily depended on an infantry. . . . Only on those occasions when a kingdom fought against barbarian tribesmen *in the tribesmen's own habitat* [my emphasis] would foot soldiers bear most of the weight. (Drews, 1993, 138-139)

Summarizing:

warfare against civilized enemies—chariots
warfare against barbarians—on perimeter of kingdom—chariots
warfare against barbarians on mountainous terrain—infantry

Infantries in the Bronze Age were predominantly active only in places where chariots couldn't go.

But this does not mean infantries were used only when chasing guerrilla tribesman into the hills. According to Drews, they had the *auxiliary* function, within the context of chariot warfare, as "runners"; moreover, they acted as an escort for chariots, and, in the aftermath of a success, pursued fleeing enemies. They also besieged cities and engaged in hand-to-hand combat alongside chariot encounters. Infantries performed tactical functions like

. . . screening the chariotry; following up a charge to detach or capture fallen enemy crewmen; clearing and holding any terrain impassable to chariots and rescuing wounded friendly crewman. A body of runners following some distance behind their chariotry could also engage enemy chariots who had passed through them

Figure 9.1 Pastoral Invasions in the Bronze/ Iron Ages

Conventional View about Indo-Europeans	Category of Comparison	Drews, Piggott, Mallory
Intruded in three waves: ☐ 4400 BCE ☐ 3400 BCE ☐ 2800 BCE	**Time of habitation**	Did not inhabit West Asian lands before 1700 BCE
Inhabited a vast territory of steppes the Black Sea	**Place of habitation**	Inhabited eastern Anatolia, if anywhere
Evicted from homeland: Migration Improvised on arrival	**Reason for leaving homeland**	Invasion Planned attack
Massive wandering	**Size of the population**	Came as a minority, no more than 75,000
Came from far away	**Distance traveled**	Came from nearby—Palestine, Sicily
Horses, wheel and chariot introduced simultaneously	**Timing in use of animals, tools and artifacts**	Horses, wheel and chariot are introduced at different times
Introduced horses, wheel and chariot ☐ Wheel introduced about 4500 BCE	**Initiator in use of animals, tools, and artifacts**	Latecomers in the use of horses, wheel and chariot ☐ Horses were introduced by many cultures ☐ Chariot introduced in eastern Anatolian highlands in about 1700 BCE ☐ Wheel introduced at the end of the 4th millennium and the beginning of the 3rd millennium (Piggott)
Wheel first hitched to horses	**Relationship between wheel And animals used**	Wheel first hitched to oxen
All Indo-European	**Composition of the population**	International
Dorians were the first invaders of Greece	**Relationship to Greece**	Seaborne raiders from Thessily precede the Dorians (Drews)
Dorians subordinate all classes on Mainland Greece	**What social class was Subordinated?**	Dorians only subordinate the working classes The higher classes were either killed or fled from the previous inv: (Drews)

and were attempting to rally for a second charge (Drews, 1993, 139)

In the Iron Age, horse troops supported the infantry; in the Bronze Age, what infantry existed supported chariot warfare with horses. Furthermore in the Bronze Age, when infantrymen were recruited, there was no general call for all male-citizen militias, which characterized the Iron Age.

The recruitment of footsoldiers by the eastern Mediterranean kingdoms is consistent with the secondary role that infantry played in the Late Bronze Age. There is . . . no evidence for a general call-up of adult males in these kingdoms: nothing parallel to citizen militias of Archaic Greece and Italy, or the tribal militias of Israel and Judah in the early Iron Age . . . kings depended upon professionals rather than upon mobilized civilians. . . . (Drews, 1993, 147)

Where did the infantrymen come from?

In the thirteenth century [BCE] . . . many kings preferred to secure the services of valiant barbarians on a permanent basis. In return for a plot of land . . . the warrior would be available for annual campaigns and might perform guard and sentinel duty at other times of the year. (Drews, 1993, 152)

Some kings ordered conscription, but the number of men called was small and they were not expected to engage in hand-to-hand combat.

2. Pastoral invasions in the late Neolithic? Domestication of horses; wheels and chariots as diffused inventions

What are the implications of how chariot warfare developed for Goddess-theorist claims for early invasions of Neolithic societies by Indo-European pastoralists? There is a problem in explaining how Indo-European languages became so widespread throughout the world. The earliest distribution seemed to range from

what is now Spain and England in the west to the Baltic in the northeast to India. Did the cultures that originally spoke the forerunners of modern Indo-European languages invade other societies? Did they migrate? Goddess theorists argue that not only did the Indo-European-speakers invade other societies, but they were primarily responsible for the emergence of institutionalized male dominance.

According to Drews, the conventional portrait of Indo-European-speakers is as follows. Between 4500 and 2000 BCE, Indo-European-speaking pastoral nomads— who already made up a fair portion of the world's population and inhabited a vast territory from eastern Europe to the Eurasian steppe—were evicted from their homeland and set out on a massive folkwandering, settling in most of the areas of the Old World where Indo-European languages are currently spoken.

While only partly identifying with this conventional view, Maria Gimbutas's "Kurgan hypothesis" adds that Indo-European pastoralists from their Kurgan Culture migrated into Europe in three massive waves:

4400 BCE
3400 BCE (the Hittite invasion of Anatolia)
2800 BCE (when proto-Greeks arrived)

According to Gimbutas, these Indo-European speakers pioneered the taming of horses and introduced wheeled vehicles in mid 5th century BCE. In her view, wheeled chariots driven by horses originated around 4500 BCE, and the innovation was introduced into Europe by invaders from steppes above the Black Sea.

The problem with Gimbutas's hypothesis is that, in order for chariot warfare to be a coherent force, the invention of the wheel, spoked wheel, the domestication of the horse, and the invention of the bit would already have had to have occurred. According to reputable archeologists Robert Drews (1989) and J.P. Malory (1989), these inventions *did not* happen all at once and they did not appear this early. They were diffused in space and time. The following is a summary of how horses, spoked wheels, and chariots first emerged from the

Paleolithic Age to the middle of the Bronze Age, according to Drews and Malory:

horses eaten in the Ice Age
  horse domesticated—in steppes
  horses domesticated from France to Asian steppes at end of 3rd millennium
  horses used as pack animals and riding animals 2000 BCE
wheel invented in 3000 BCE
  used as a wagon
  used as ox driven wheeled carts
  spoked wheel used with horse drawn chariots—recreation, light transport (2000 to 1800 BCE)
bit used with horse-drawn chariots (1800 BCE)

All of these inventions did not converge in the phenomenon of spoked-wheeled chariots powered by horses and used for warfare until roughly 1700 BCE.

Horses were first eaten during the Ice Age. By the end of the third millennium BCE, horses were being domesticated in the region from France to the Asian steppes. By 2000 BCE, the horse was being used as a pack animal and riding animal. While it was linked to wheeled carts it was not hitched to chariots until later. Horses are not native to the Near East, as they thrive on the steppes. It did not pay for people from the Near East to import them because the climate was too warm and there was nothing horses could do that oxen could not do as well or better. As a result, horses were rare in the Near East in the fourth and third millennium.

Until the invention of the bit, horses could not pull heavy loads. The horse pulled against a neck strap, which made breathing difficult. Also, riding a horse was difficult. Horses' superior speed relative to oxen could only be exploited with the help of the bit. Without it, speed and control of the horses for military warfare was limited to the use of a nose ring. The bit allowed horses to breathe easier, and allowed them to carry heavier loads when spoked wheels were invented.

According to Drews, most 19th century European philologists and historians believed that Indo-European speakers had introduced both horses and wheeled vehicles into the Near East. This idea was undermined by the work of Victor Hehn, who argued that the horse did not become important until the invention of the chariot. Hehn also supported the claim that early wheeled vehicles were driven by oxen, not horses.

Not only was the horse linked to drawing chariots much later than Gimbutas suggests, but Indo-European speakers were not the first to domesticate the horse. As Drews notes,

> Throughout the immense area to which the wild horse was native, the domesticated horse is attested in the Neolithic and Chalcolithic periods. By the end of the third millennium, the domesticated horse was so common that in a number of sites, from central Europe to central Asia, more than half of the bones recovered by archaeologists were horse bones. That the PIE (Proto-Indo-European) speakers had a word for horse is of almost no significance, since *every* [my emphasis] people living in or near the horse's natural habitat must have had such a word. There is . . . no reason to believe that third millennium PIE speakers were any more dependent upon the horse than were other Eurasian societies. . . . Nor is there any reason to suppose that the 'tamed' horse, or a horse controlled by a bit, was peculiar to Proto-Indo-European society. (Drews, 1989, 132-133)

On the contrary, the *riding* of horses (as opposed to using them as draft animals) was not characteristic of any known PIE society in the second millennium, including the Bronze Age Greeks or the Aryans of India.

Turning from horses to origins of the wheel, Stuart Piggott takes issue with Gimbutas's claim that wheeled vehicles originated in the Eurasian steppes as early as 4500 BCE. He argues that the diffusion of the wheeled vehicle to Europe occurred at the end of the fourth millennium or the beginning of the third. Piggott makes a case that it was in the steppes of Georgia that wheeled vehicles were first used, spreading from there to Mesopotamia and central Anatolia. The first use was not in the areas to the north, where Gimbutas claims the pastoral invaders originated:

> Further evidence for the primacy of the lands south of the Caucasus in the development of the chariot comes from thousands of rock carvings found in the Syunik region of Armenia . . . and they seem to show a development from wagons, to spoked wheels carts (many of them ox drawn) and horse-drawn 'chariots'. . . . Perhaps the spoked wheels originated here, as an improvement designed for the ox cart; and perhaps only after light spoke wheeled vehicles had been developed did the cart drivers begin to substitute horses for oxen, and to breed horses on a scale that until then had been found only north of the Caucases. We may tentatively conclude that the chariot was developed in Armenia, and that the reason why it was developed there is that the making of wheeled vehicles was all along . . . a specialty of that region. (Drews, 1989, 118)

Turning from the horse and the wheel to chariots, we find that the first use of the chariot was *not* for warfare. Drews writes:

> The era of the war chariot . . . began in the 17th century B.C. Before that time, chariots seem to have been of little or no importance on the battlefield even though they had been used for rapid transportation, for amusement and for royal display as early as 1900. It is likely that in Mesopotamia . . . kings had all along ridden to the battlefield—on stately heavy wagons in the third millennium and in chariots after the development of the spoked wheel. (Drews, 1993, 105)

Chariots first appear in southern Russia and Eastern Europe in the 16th century BCE, about the same time that they first appeared in the Near East. Effective chariot warfare began two centuries after the appearance of the first chariots.

The place where horses, wheels, and chariots first came together was Armenia. According to Drews, Armenia was excellent horse-pasturing country and archeologists have found bronze bits, vehicles of various types, and ancient harnessing devices. The Armenians had a long tradition of wheeled transportation. Drews concludes as follows:

> Perhaps it is theoretically conceivable that PIE speakers pioneered rapid and comfortable transportation by 'chariot' in a homeland located in the forest-steppe or the open steppe above the Black Sea, [but] there is no direct evidence for the spoked wheel north of the Caucasus before the middle of the second millennium. (Drews, 1989, 149)

However,

> that chariot *warfare* [my emphasis] was perfected in the lands north of the Caucasus is not suggested by any evidence . . . since there is no period in which chariot warfare is attested for the Eurasian steppe. Our earliest evidence for chariot warfare comes from Anatolia. If the PIE speakers were in large part responsible for the development of chariot warfare, eastern Anatolia is far more likely Indo-European homeland than either the Carpathain Basin or the Pontic steppes. (Drews, 1989, 149).

The Carpathian Basin or the Pontic steppes is much closer to the area Gimbutas located Indo-European invaders.

3. Pastoral warfare and invasions in the middle Bronze Age?

Drews makes a nice distinction between a "raid" and a "takeover." A "takeover" is executed to establish control over a society through a violent coup against a rival king and his army. It does not imply plundering and the destruction of an infrastructure nor extending an imperial network. Raids, by comparison, are more destructive of infrastructure. Those who "took over" presented themselves as champions of local gods, aligning themselves with the general population. A takeover keeps the infrastructure in place and those at the top try to govern it. A takeover entails a commitment on the part of a conquering group to put itself in a governing position *for generations.* This requires the managerial skills necessary to reproduce a society over time.

The relationship between herding and planting societies has *always* vacillated between trading and raiding. Under normal conditions herding societies cannot *take over* complex horticulture societies or agricultural states. Why is this? There are five principal reasons.

The first is numbers. A typical herding society consisted of roughly 50 people, while simple horticultural societies averaged anywhere from 100 to 500 people. Complex horticultural societies consisted of 1000 to 50,000 people. Agricultural civilizations numbered tens of thousands.

Second: If herding societies had had access to wheeled chariots driven by horses, along with the type of weaponry described above, it is possible they might have conquered simple horticultural societies. But as we have seen, agricultural states developed these technologies first.

The third reason has to do with organization. Complex horticultural societies were themselves centralized and warlike; agricultural states were even more organized, with a specialized military. When faced with such a foe, the best a herding society could probably have done was to engage in simple raids.

Fourth: even though a herding society might occasionally overcome these obstacles and conquer a planting society, the former would have no experience in managing a centralized chiefdom or agricultural state. Even if it conducted successive takeovers and had intentions of staying, it would have to "rehire" the existing authorities to manage the society. These managers would have little incentive to do a good job. The overall wealth of society would deteriorate. Besides, the herders would have to watch over these managers, and they would not have had the numbers to do this.

Finally: Even if a herding society had somehow taken over a planting society, it would be difficult for the former to legitimize its rule without a writing system. Herders, like people in all other pre-state societies, did not write or read.

In short, before the widespread use of bronze, there was nothing extraordinary about the power of pastoralists. As Malory says, "Indo-Europeans did not burst into history; they struggled in over a period of 3500 years. . . ." (Malory, 1989, 24)

Furthermore, the way the Indo-European languages were spread seems to have depended upon local circumstances. As Mallory points out, if Indo-European speakers moved into a sparsely occupied open steppe area, their language became quickly predominant. But when they encountered agricultural societies, the process was much slower.

It appears, then, that there was no Indo-European invasion until at least the middle of the Bronze Age. While Indo-European speakers (and other pastoralist peoples) existed at the same time as horticultural societies, mutual contacts were probably limited to periodic raids by the former against the latter. Pastoralists did not acquire the power to take over more complex societies prior to at least 1700 BCE.

Around that time, certain herding societies began coordinating their activities *internationally.* The cultures that have been identified with the Indo-European takeover— the Hurrain, Sumerian, Hattic and Proto-Anatolian—had a combined population of only about 75,000. Rather than an improvised wandering (as the conventional model would

Figure 9.2 Bronze Age verses Iron Age Tactics and Weaponry

BRONZE AGE	ARCHAIC IRON AGE
chariot corps predominant (mobile platforms for archery)	**infantry predominant**

BRONZE AGE

chariot corps predominant
(mobile platforms for archery)

3000 BCE:
 carts drawn by oxen traveled at 2 mph

1700 BCE:
war chariots drawn by horses traveled at 10 mph

100 chariots per average Bronze Age society
warriors shot arrows to a stationary enemy

1500 BCE:
1000 chariots per average Bronze Age society

cost to maintain chariots is high

 combat between 2 kingdoms: chariots
 combat against barbarians on perimeter of kingdom:
      chariot, infantry as runners only in
 combat against barbarian in hills: infantry

composite bows and lances

bronze rod not as lethal
javelin used by hunters and runners

warriors--used composite bow

large shields covering most of body fighting
from a chariot

professional warriors: hired barbarians
civilian conscripts used only for defense

no cavalry because no saddles or stirrups

ARCHAIC IRON AGE

infantry predominant

used tactics of hill people:
    in mass
    on plains

javelins, spears, swords

swords more lethal
    javelin used by runners
spears for infantry
rapier used for hand to hand combat

round shield--more economical for fighting
close-in

citizen militias

cavalry 12th century

advantages of cavalry over chariots:
1) could operate in terrain too rough for
wheeled vehicles
2) chances for flight was better
3) less costly
4) saddles and stirrups increase accuracy

have it), Drews claims Indo-European speakers planned and organized takeovers of more vulnerable societies.

But who were these invaders and where and when did they invade? Drews identifies the following groups:

Hyksos = Egypt in 1785 BCE
Kassites = Babylon, Mesopotamia, 1595 BCE
Aryans = northwest India, late 17th and early 16th centuries BCE
Hurrian princes = Levant, southern Greece, 1225-1200 BCE
Dorians = southern Greece, 1075-1050 BCE

These invaders were not isolated bands of herders. They were internationally coordinated groups that were less provincial than the Mesopotamian and Egyptian kings.

> The Indo-European and Hurrian princes in the Levant maintained surprisingly close connections with each other over distances of hundreds of miles, exchanging not only lavish gifts but also daughters and sisters in marriage. Similarly, the Kassite aristocracy of southern Mesopotamia held together by gifts, correspondence and an interest of chariotry was also assiduous in cultivating personal and diplomatic relations with the rulers of lands as far away as Egypt. The Hyksos rulers in Egypt . . . seem to have been in touch with Crete as well as with Mesopotamia and . . . the Levant. . . . James Breasted fittingly named the Late Bronze Age 'The first International Civilization.' (Drews, 1989,179)

4. Pastoral invasions in the Iron Age? Infantry and cavalry

Turning to the Archaic Iron Age, Drews (1993) argues that the abrupt end of the Bronze Age that occurred in the ancient world in Greece, Crete, Anatolia, Cyprus, Syria, and the Southern Levant around 1200 BCE was directly related to changes in tactics of war in the Archaic Iron Age. This new style of warfare "opened up new and frightening possibilities for various *uncivilized* populations. . . ." (Drews 1993, 33). What were these frightening possibilities?

The revolution in Iron Age military fighting was due to advances in technology, and also to a change in who got access to the new tools. The revolution included the invention of saddles and stirrups, changes in the use of armor, and the increasing use of weapons such as javelins, spears and swords.

In the Iron Age, cavalry replaced chariotry as the dominant military arm. In the Bronze Age there was no cavalry because, as Drews points out,

> Without saddle or stirrups riding a horse was difficult enough, and the Bronze Age rider was not yet able to control his mount and shoot a bow at the same time. . . . The earliest representations of archers shooting from the backs of galloping horses are ninth-century Assyrian reliefs. These reliefs show the cavalry archers operating in pairs. One cavalryman holds the reins of both his own and his partner's horse, allowing the partner to use his hands for the bow and bowstring. The early cavalry teams thus parallel exactly the charioteer and chariot archer. The cavalry archer was undoubtedly less accurate than his counterpart on a chariot (bouncing on a horse's back was less conducive to a good shot than standing—knees bent on the leatherstrap platform of a chariot). But in other respects the cavalry teams were surely superior. They were able . . . to operate in terrain too rough for wheeled vehicles and their chances for flight . . . were much better; when a chariot horse was injured both crewmen were in immediate danger, but if a cavalryman's horse was killed or injured the cavalryman could immediately leap on the back of his partner's horse. . . . (Drews, 1993, 165)

In short, the saddle and the stirrup increased accuracy in shooting, the calvary expanded the terrain for fighting, and the use of mounted horses allowed for quicker recovery and getaway. For all these reasons the cavalry began to replace chariots:

It appears then, that the use of cavalry began in the twelfth century, that by the tenth century some kings employed thousands of cavalrymen, and that the ninth-century Assyrian kings had at least as many horses in their cavalry as in their chariotry. The final obsolescence of chariotry came with the discovery, in the eight century of new techniques for reining a ridden horse. . . . The new method . . . allowed cavalrymen to operate independently rather than in pairs. . . . With every rider an archer, the firepower on the backs of a hundred cavalry horses was *double the firepower drawn by a hundred chariot horses.* [my emphasis] (Drews, 1993, 166)

During the Archaic Iron Age the infantryman's corslet emerged. This gave him more substantial body protection. In addition, the invention of the rounded shield at the end of the 13ᵗʰ century gave the infantryman more agility and mobility in fighting.

Perhaps the most important item of defensive armor that comes into use at the end of the thirteenth century is the round shield. . . . Until the introduction of the round shield, footsoldiers of the eastern Mediterranean kingdoms carried large shields of various shapes . . . [such as] the huge 'figure eight' shield which enveloped the warrior on three sides from neck to ankles, while providing some freedom of movement for the arms. . . . The size and design of these . . . shields are quite understandable if they were intended for defense primarily against missiles, and only occasionally against hand-to-hand weapons. . . . The round shield, on the other hand, was certainly meant for a hand-to-hand fighter. For him, agility and mobility counted for much and he sacrificed the security of a full-body shield in order to be fast on his feet and to have free use of his offensive arm. . . . With one

exception, there are no round shields attested anywhere in the eastern Mediterranean kingdoms before the late thirteenth century. (Drews, 1993, 178)

There was also a proliferation of lethal projectiles and thrusting instruments during this period—such as a small long-range javelin (about one-half to one-third the length of today's javelin used in sporting events). In the late Bronze Age, javelins were used only by hunters. In the Archaic Iron Age, according to Drews,

Composite bows were appropriate for the chariot warrior but for a runner a far preferable long range weapon was a javelin . . . thrown on the run whereas an infantry bowman would have to shoot from either a crouching position or a flat-footed stance. . . . [Javelins were] used against chariots in the late Bronze Age. (Drews, 1993, 182)

Another advantage of a javelin over an arrowhead was that it lasted longer:

A military arrowhead was normally barbed, so that the victim could not retract it without tearing his flesh; but these heads are elliptical, designed for easy retraction. The possibility that an archer could or would wish to retrieve a spent arrow is unlikely, but a warrior with only two or three javelins would perhaps have retrieved each of them several times during a skirmish. (Drews, 1993, 189)

Javelins were also used as a screen for heavy infantry. They played a key role in bringing chariot warfare to an end.

Changes in the use of spears also contributed to the military revolution:

[E]vidence indicates one change in the manufacture of Aegean spears: the twelfth century spearheads had solid-ring sockets, whereas earlier sockets had split rings. That difference resulted from a change in the technology of bronze working: instead of forging the spearheads in smithies, twelfth century bronze workers cast them in foundries. The solid-ring socket seems to have had no military significance although the development of foundries does suggest that *mass production* [my emphasis] of bronze artifacts was suddenly important in the Aegean. (Drews, 1993, 191)

In Israel the spear seems to have been the militiaman's primary weapon during the period of 'the Judges' . . . It is undoubtedly safe to say that in the early Iron Age hand-to-hand fighting throughout the eastern Mediterranean was a contest of thrusting spears. This weapon was appropriate especially for infantrymen in close order formations. (Drews, 1993, 192)

Finally, we come to the sword, the most revolutionary of all the new weapons. According to Drews, ordinary swords were between 14 and 20 inches in length, with a long sword being 28 inches. Swords were designed to keep from bending, making them more lethal. About 1200 BCE a particularly deadly sword called "Naue Type II" appeared in the Eastern Mediterranean. While still made of bronze it was difficult to bend no matter how violent the slash. With this rigidity, a warrior could cut off an enemy's extremities in one swipe, rather than merely inflicting a thrusting wound. The bronze rod broke bones and could be used to beat an opponent to death, but this was far less efficient. The earlier sickle sword had a narrower range, it wasn't big enough to cut off an opponents limbs, and a soldier carrying it would never have two hands free.

After its introduction ca. 1200, the Naue Type II quickly established itself. By the eleventh century it was virtually the only sword in use in the Aegean and excavated specimens show that it was also the standard sword in the Near East in the early Iron Age. The only improvement required was the substitution of iron for bronze . . . iron could provide a sharper,

stronger and more durable blade. (Drews 1993, 194)

Italy was important in production and diffusion of these Greek weapons. This change in military technology implied that infantries were now being trained and armed with the weapons.

Finally we should note that iron oxides are widespread on the Earth's surface, whereas copper and tin—the two metals which when alloyed make bronze—are relatively rare. This means that herding societies would have had easier access to the raw material for iron than the raw materials of bronze. And this in turn would have put them on a more equal footing with more complex societies. As a result:

Within a period of forty or fifty years, at the end of the thirteenth and beginning of the twelfth century, almost every significant city or palace in the eastern Mediterranean world was destroyed. (Drews, 1993, 4) [This] seems to have begun with sporadic destruction in the last quarter of 13th century [BCE], gathered momentum in 1190's and raged in full fury in the 1180's. (Drews, 1993, 7)

The Hebrews are a good example of a pastoral society that benefited from the new weaponry and military tactics:

David won his victories with foot-soldiers. The traditions about him quite consistently present him as making no use of chariots in battle and as fighting under the aegis of the infantryman's god, the Lord of Hosts. The further back one goes in the history of the Israelite monarchy the greater the role that one finds the militiamen of the infantry. Saul seems to have no regular army of professionals and no horse troops. . . . Finally before the creation of the Israelite monarchy, the people of Israel, as of Judah, depended for security entirely on a militia. (Drews, 1993, 172)

Moreover, according to Drews, ". . . the 'Conquest of Canaan' had been effected by Israelite footsoldiers against the chariots of the Canaanite cities." (Drews, 1993, 212)

Greece, like other places in Western Asia, was taken over as a result of chariot warfare. There were not many wheeled vehicles in Greece before Indo-European attack because the Greeks lacked the wood to build them. The Dorians are the group generally identified as the invaders.

There are two extreme views about this group. Some hold them responsible for destruction of the Mycenaean world and the creation of historical Greece. Others, however, go so far as to deny that any invasion took place. It is now well established that Mycenaean civilization was suddenly destroyed at the end of the 13th century BCE. Drews agrees with Anthony Snodgrass that the Dorians came from a nearby province (not far away) and had a material life similar to that of the Mycenaeans. However, Drews does not agree that the Dorians were the ones who destroyed Mycenaean civilization. He argues that if the Dorians were the first invaders of the Greek mainland, and if they were so much like the Greeks themselves, why should they not not have just taken over Greek society? Drews reasons that only a less-civilized society would be content to live among the ruins and not want to take over the social system they had conquered.

Drews argues that two adjustments are necessary to the common view. The first is *more time* must be assumed to have elapsed between the fall of the Mycenaean civilization and the conquest of Greece by the Dorians. The second is to consider the possibility that by the time the Dorians had entered the region of southern Greece, many of the former inhabitants had already departed.

Drews claims that the destructions that occurred were gradual, occurring between 1225 and the end of the 12th century BCE. The Dorians did not arrive until 1075 to 1050 BCE, long *after* the Mycenaean civilization fell. He argues that, by the time the Dorians arrived, the land was already half emptied, meaning some other group had already been there. Drews

suggests that southern Greece had already been conquered by seaborne raiders from the Thessely coast of Northern Greece. The upper and middle classes scattered, leaving the rural working-class, non-Greek-speaking Helots. The Dorians thus subjugated only the rural working classes, which were left from the previous invasions. Figure 9.1 contrasts the differences between the conventional model of the origins of Indo-Europeans and those of Drews, Piggot and Mallory.

The extent to which warfare had changed can be seen in that, even when Bronze Age civilizations were able to defeat pastoral invaders, this was not accomplished with chariots. In the case of the Egyptians, this was done from the sea. "The Egyptian archers . . . were able to shoot their bows far more effectively from the deck of a ship than from the platform of a bouncing chariot." (Drews, 1993, 223) In general all agricultural states had abandon chariots:

No civilized society could defend itself without putting into the field infantrymen equipped for hand-to-hand combat. Against the new peril new weapons were required and new pieces of armor. In Greece especially . . . [these changes] created the armored foot soldier, protected by a helmet, corslet, greaves and a round shield. (Drews, 1993, 224)

Because of the power of the infantry and the new weaponry, the use of the chariot declined:

. . . all over the eastern Mediterranean the principal role in battle was now borne by offensive infantrymen. Thus chariot warfare, which in the Late bronze Age had distinguished cities and kingdoms from the barbarous hinterlands, did not survive into the Iron Age, and even the wealthiest kings had now to depend primarily upon footsoldiers. . . . With a long sword as his primary weapon for hand-to-hand warfare, the raider required an 'open' space in which his agility and fleetness could be exploited. But before the hand-to-hand fighting began, the chariots had to be overcome, and it was surely for this purpose that the raiders brought their javelins . . . the javelins suggest a swarming tactic, the javelineer running forward and then hurling his weapon at a team of chariot horses. (Drews, 1993, 210)

According the Drews, the democracy of the polis in the Axial Iron Age was built from the democracy of citizen militias.

[P]olitical power belonged to those societies in which warfare was every man's concern, the adult males of a community serving as its militia . . . The solidarity of an Iron Age community, whether of a polis or of a nation, stemmed from the recognition that in war the fortunes of the community would depend on every man playing his part. . . ." (Drews, 1993, 225)

In contrast, in the Bronze Age:

The kind of solidarity required in the Iron Age was . . . unnecessary and therefore unknown in the Late Bronze Age, since . . . the king's subjects were amply protected by the king's chariots and chariot runners. The military revolution that occurred . . . was . . . a prerequisite for the social and political changes that made the world of the Iron Age so different from that of the Late Bronze Age. (Drews, 1993, 225)

The infantries . . . used weapons and guerrilla tactics characteristic of barbarian hill people but never had been tried *en masse in the plains and against the centers* [my emphasis] of Late Bronze age kingdoms . . . a long slashing sword had been available in temperate Europe for centuries and the javelin everywhere for millennia. Until shortly before 1200 B.C., however, it had never occurred to anyone that infantrymen with such weapons could outmatch chariots. (Drews 1993, 97)

In classical Greece chariots reassumed the primarily decorative function—in parades and for recreation—they had prior to their use for war in the Bronze Age. Figure 9.2 contrasts Bronze Age and Iron Age military technology.

5. Pastoralism as the supreme "culture of honor"

In a previous chapter on the impact of biology, we studied some of the reasons why men are more aggressive and violent than women. We have also identified some of the ecological conditions under which male violence is likely to surface. But what about differences in the predisposition toward violence among men in *different* societies?

According to Richard Nisbett and Dov Cohen (1996), men in some societies are more "macho" than men in other societies, and the reason has little to do with either biology or population pressure. In their study of violence in the U.S. South, Nisbett and Cohen identified a "culture of honor"—by which they mean the predisposition to solve problems with the use of violence, the tendency to intentionally build a reputation for toughness and strength, and the tendency to interpret ambiguous signals from other men as a threat to that reputation.

Nisbett and Cohen have identified four conditions under which this culture of honor is be maximally developed:

(1) when resources are *scarce or unpredictable*
(2) when these resources are *sufficiently portable* and theft is possible
(3) in low population densities
(4) the *absence of a state* to regulate law.

What type of societies are most likely to posses these conditions? Hunter-gatherer societies at certain times may have all these conditions, except that of having resources that are portable.

Hunting-gathering economies rarely have a large enough surplus from another group of hunter-gatherers to be willing to risk death to obtain it. . . . [T]he energy of a hunter-gatherer would be better expended finding food from himself than in trying to take the meager portion of another hunter-gatherer. (Nisbett and Cohen, 1996, 29)

Simple and complex horticultural societies sometimes have a predictable resource and their resources are not portable, though there is a absence of the state.

If that means of production were always successful there would be no need to try to steal the output of other people, but it is not always successful. . . . If the weather is too hot and dry or too wet, there may be a very poor harvest. But one's neighbor may well have enough food stored—because of the local terrain, or greater industry or better luck—to make a raid reasonable. . . . (Nisbett and Cohen, 1996, 89)

In agricultural societies none of these conditions would exist, because in addition to the conditions of horticultural societies these societies have states to regulate violence.

Farmers in stable agricultural communities have a greater investment in remaining peacefully on their land than in stealing their neighbor's surplus. Moreover, farmers usually have granaries that provide enough surplus for them to survive a number of poor harvests in a row. They would literally have to be starving to make it rational to steal bread from their neighbors—with whom a peaceful coexistence is essential to productive economic activity. In addition, the very stability of such societies often supports a state powerful enough to protect against theft and raiding. (Nisbett and Cohen, 1996, 89)

One very important exception for agricultural societies is the caste location of the group. Even though there is great material wealth, for peasants resources are scarce. However this by itself does not make peasants predisposed toward a psychology of honor.

The societies that consistently meet all four conditions are the pastoral societies we have been studying.

Herdsmen the world over tend to be capable of great aggressiveness and violence because of their vulnerability to losing their primary resources, their animals. . . . In such regions the state often has little power to command compliance and citizens have to create their own system of order. The means for doing this is the rule of retaliation. If you cross me, I will punish you. (Nisbett and Cohen, 1996, xv)

To maintain credibility, the individual communicates a willingness to be violent or take high risks to protect his portable resources, and he is especially on guard against any signs of disrespect.

Nisbett and Cohen believe that their findings about parts of the U.S. South can be applied cross-culturally and historically. If this is the case, then there is no question that societies in the ancient world that were taken over by herders would have had the most severe "culture of honor" syndrome to contend with. It might be fair to say that in those instances where herding societies had initiated successful takeovers of egalitarian hunting and gathering societies, the former might have *initiated* institutionalized male dominance. But herding societies would not have had the institutional power to *sustain and transmit* their culture of violence to the subjugated population, unless that subjugated population *already had* its own form of institutionalized male dominance already in place. This is what probably happened during the Bronze and Iron Ages.

What was the impact of state warfare on women? In one sense warfare organized at the state level must have been preferable to the relentless danger of ambush, raids, and homicides that existed in segmented pre-state societies. However, the extent of violence on women and their husbands if war broke out was potentially greater. Since not all men were called to fight in the Bronze Age, as they were in the Iron Age, more married Bronze-Age couples could enjoy the security of knowing that the husband would not be called away to fight. However, the *threat* of the use of advanced weapons on the subjects of states would likely have discouraged thoughts of dissent and reduced the likelihood of rebellion. All women who were victims of a herding invasion would have to deal with the "culture of honor" syndrome, which is a superstructural addition to institutionalized male dominance.

At the beginning of the section on pastoral invaders we noted that one of the conditions under which pastoralists might be able to *take over* a more complex society rather than raid or trade with it was one in which the former had access to more lethal weaponry. But was this the only possible basis for the pastoralist invaders' success? Some archeoastronomers and climatologists say no.

Figure 9.3 Women in Ancient Warfare

Pro		Con
	WOMEN IN PRESTATE WAR **Warless foragers**	
Not the target of war		Sudden loss of fathers, husbands brothers, sons through homicide
Women peacemakers		
	Warlike foragers and horticulturalists	
		Internal warfare can be the target of vengeance
		External warfare—can be targeted
Long-distance external war: take over men's work		Short-distance external war: continue to do "women's work"
Descent traced along female line		Descent continues to be traced along female line
		Disruption of community life
If group is victorious, more land, better resources		If defeated, raped, slaughtered, eaten, sold as slaves to states

WOMEN IN ANCIENT STATE WARFARE

Pro		Con
	Bronze Age	
Coercion an internal *threat,* not a constant reality		More systematic coercion
Most males not obliged to fight		More lethal weaponry
		More males die if wars occur
		"Culture of honor" to contend with

Figure 9.4 Composite Figures for Biology (Chapter 7) ; Wars (Chapters 8, 9)

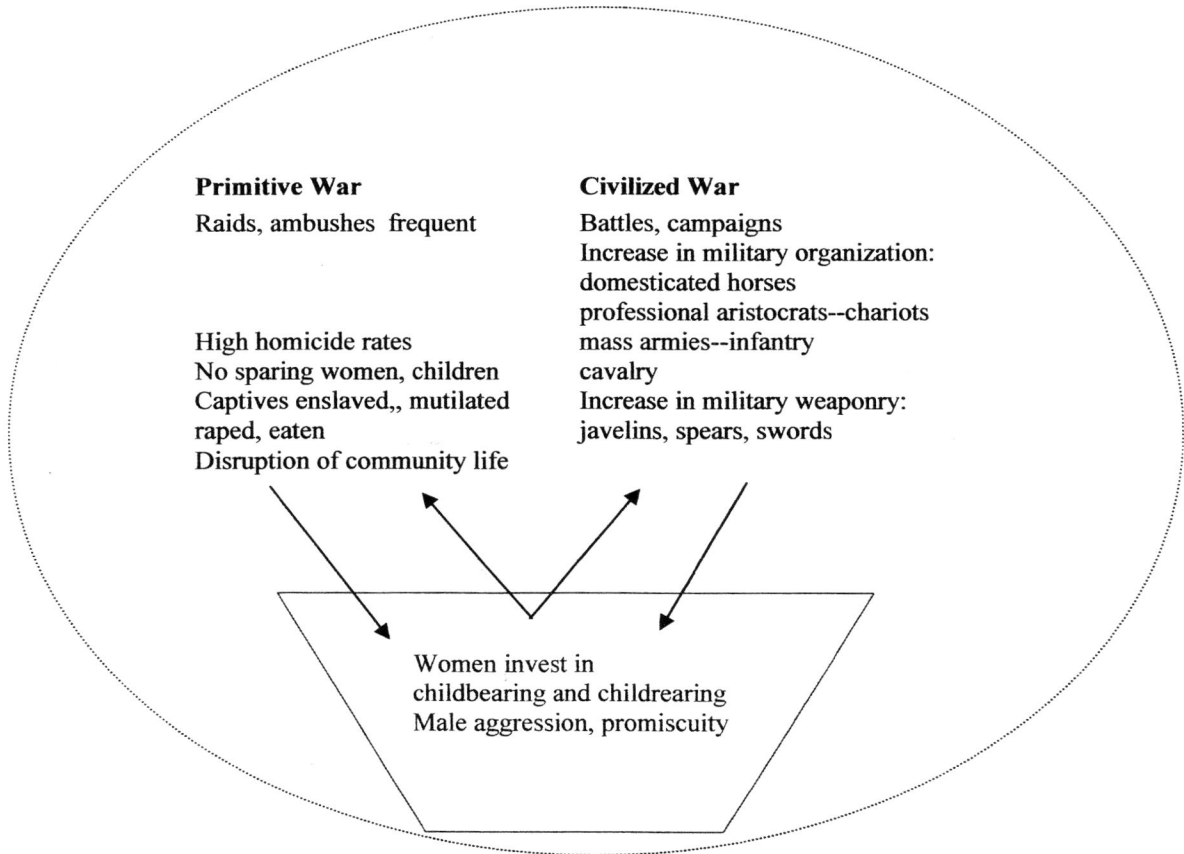

Primitive War
Raids, ambushes frequent

High homicide rates
No sparing women, children
Captives enslaved,, mutilated
raped, eaten
Disruption of community life

Civilized War
Battles, campaigns
Increase in military organization:
domesticated horses
professional aristocrats--chariots
mass armies--infantry
cavalry
Increase in military weaponry:
javelins, spears, swords

Women invest in
childbearing and childrearing
Male aggression, promiscuity

Fire, Water, and Comet Debris: Climatic Crisis and Natural Disasters in the Bronze and Archaic Iron Ages

The purpose of this chapter is to present, analyze, and evaluate the plausibility of claims made by an interdisciplinary group of astronomers, geologists, and climatologists who argue that natural disasters in the Bronze and Archaic Iron Ages may have been caused by the impact of comet debris. After weighing this evidence, in the next chapter I will discuss how the social stress caused by these disasters might have contributed to institutionalized male dominance.

1. Catastrophism old and new

Just as the theory of progress has dominated western history and social science up through the past century, so the theory of *uniformitarianism* held sway in the geology and astronomy well into the second half the 20th century.

According to Huggett (1997), uniformitarianism as developed by the geologist Lyell implies four basic assumptions about the evolution of the Earth:

(1) uniformity of law—that all natural laws are constant throughout space and time
(2) uniformity of process—that processes now operating to mold the Earth's surface can be used to explain the events of the past (this is called *actualism*)
(3) uniformity of rate—that geological changes are gradual and incremental, rather than sudden and qualitative
(4) uniformity of state—that the Earth has been fundamentally the same since its formation, that it operates as a steady-state, rather than changing in a directional fashion.

Uniformitarians also believe that catastrophic natural events, when they occur, tend to be localized and do not have global effects.

The opposite of uniformitarianism is *catastrophism*—the view that Earth history has been shaped to a significant degree by overwhelmingly violent natural events, sometimes on a global scale. Until recently, catastrophist ideas were unwelcome in serious scientific discussions because, in the 19th century, opponents of Lyell's geology and Darwin's evolutionary science appealed to a literal interpretation of the biblical Deluge as an explanation for the geological. This "old" catastrophism assumed changes in nature to have been lawless, sudden, governed by divine intervention, and global in magnitude. Early catastrophists believed God violated natural law by intervening in nature. Thus it is easy to understand why uniformitarianism held sway in secular academia for so long.

Until the last decade or two, uniformitarian astronomers held, on good evidence, that the motions of stars and planets are relatively stable and are governed by gravitational fields. The place of comets and asteroids in this scheme has, however, become more controversial, and it is with regard to these objects that a new catastrophist attitude has begun to take hold among astronomers, geologists, and evolutionary biologists. Interest in comets and asteroids goes back to the time of Aristotle; Isaac Newton was likewise fascinated by the subject. (Clube and Napier, 1982, 1990) Throughout most of the 20th century, until about 20 years ago, comets and asteroids and meteorites were thought to be unpredictable but harmless because meteorites were too small to do damage, asteroids were only known to orbit between Mars and Jupiter, and comets consisted of ice that would be melted by the Sun before it could enter Earth's atmosphere.

Photographs from recent space probes document craters on the Moon, Mars, Mercury, and Venus that cannot be explained as the result of volcanism. On Earth, astronomers have identified at least 150 impact craters around the world, with much of South America, Asia, and Africa still unexplored in this regard. As a result, the scientific community is today more willing than previously to grant that cosmic impacts from space have profoundly shaped Earth history.

However, the neo-catastrophist revolution has for the most part been confined to discussions of the pre-human past. Human history is still presented to us as being either the work of God or the work of humanity, with nature as merely a backdrop. But an interdisciplinary group of historians, physiologists, and archeologists (McNeill, 1976; Diamond, 1997; Fagan, 1999) argues that history has been shaped largely by climate, geography, and plagues.

Historians have long known that Bronze Age civilizations were beset by periods of unexplained drought, famine, and plague, in which societies collapsed for reasons that are unclear. Many historians are willing to grant that earthquakes and volcanoes were responsible for the collapse of a few civilizations. But the notion that ancient societies fell victim to *extraterrestrial* agents of destruction—comets, asteroids, or meteors—is as yet entertained by only the most intellectually daring.

Recently, a growing number of astronomers (Clube and Napier 1982, 1990; Steel 1995), dendrochronlogists—those who study tree-ring evidence to track human history (Baillee 1999), geologists (Schoch 1999), and popularizes of science (Lewis 1996; Gribbin and Gribbin 1996) have argued that the Earth has been subjected to the impact of comet and/or asteroid debris during the period of recorded history.

Where do the Earth-threatening objects and debris come from? According to Clube and Napier, as the solar system passes through the Milky Way galaxy, it is subjected to strong gravitational forces which destabilize the smaller comets in the Oort cloud (which lies beyond the orbits of Uranus and Neptune). It takes comets some 3 to 5 million years to travel from the Oort cloud into the solar system and establish themselves in long-range, periodic orbits. As a result of this process, giant comets enter in Earth-crossing orbits at intervals of about 100,000 years.

More specifically these Near-Earth Objects can come from the following sources, which I have paraphrased from Napier (1998):

(1) The zodiacal cloud—the most massive entity in the near-Earth environment—which is a flattish system of dust and boulders in the plane of the planets. Its mass is highly variable over short time scales of 10,000 years.
(2) The Oort cloud, from which rare giant comets come. Objects from this source will dominate others, but they appear only sporadically—say, every 100,000 years.
(3) The dust of comets, encountered in the passage of Earth through comet trails. In this case, impacts persist periodically for a century or so and produce meteor storms.
(4) Apollo asteroids, which orbit the Sun in paths outside the asteroid belt, sometimes intersecting Earth's orbit. Some are more than 10 kilometers across.
(5) The dust of asteroids within the asteroid belt that collide with one another and emit debris.

Clube and Napier argue that cometary *debris* has caused terrestrial effects more frequently than has the *direct impact of comets or asteroids.* This debris has been a recurring hazard from the last Ice Age to the present day. Clube is clear on this point:

Figure 10.1 Catastrophism Old and New

Category	Uniformitarian	Old Catastrophists	Neo-Catastrophists
Law	Natural laws are constant in space and time. When laws don't apply, claim ignorance.	Divine intervention	Natural laws are constant in space and time.
Process	Actualism	Non-actualism	Non-actualism
	Processes now operating to mold the earth's surface should be invoked to explain past. If they don't, it is a sign of human ignorance.	Divine intervention overrides natural laws	If current laws don't apply, search for new laws.
Rate	Geological changes is slow	Change is sudden	Change is sudden, complex regularity
	Predictable	Random	Periodic (semi-predictable)
	Ongoing	One-time (rare)	More frequent--episodic
State	Steady-state configuration-- the earth has been fundamentally the same.	Directional--God's will	Ancient world was different from the modern world
Magnitude	Local events	Global events	Local, regional, global

It is really quite implausible to suppose that direct cometary encounters could have continued for millennia to be perceived as a common apocalyptic threat or that direct asteriodal encounters will be so perceived today. . . . On the other hand, comets which travel in association with . . . invisible sub-cometary debris and whose orbits are such as to bring about an occasional close passage by the Earth may give rise to lesser apocalyptic events whose effects are less likely to be global in extent. Under these circumstances, the range of phenomena known as blazing stars, providences or fireballs will sometimes be associated with cometary apparitions and it would be reasonable—without any knowledge of cometary orbits—to regard all comets as potential signs. (Clube, 1998, 237)

Comets may themselves initiate an Ice Age, through a hypothetical series of events described by astronomer Fred Hoyle. But comets are not directly responsible for the natural catastrophes that have occurred in human history *since* the last Ice Age. Cultural anthropologist Benny Peiser agrees:

Most environmental disasters which have been witnessed and studied by modern humans occur on a strictly local or regional level. Such calamities are triggered by natural agencies such as volcanic eruptions, seismic activity, catastrophic storms, or giant floods, which affect only relatively small geological areas. (Peiser, 1998, 120)

Astronomers Clube and Napier distinguish their "neo-catastrophism"—or "coherent catastrophism"—from earlier catastrophist theories in several ways. Unlike Ignatius Donnelly and Immanuel Velikovsky, whose popular books in the late nineteenth and mid-twentieth centuries appealed to wide audiences, Clube and Napier do not suggest that a comet or an asteroid *directly* impacted the Earth during human history. Instead they argue that a huge comet (100 km) circulated through the solar system several thousand years ago, and the Earth periodically passed through its train of debris. Clube and Napier do not argue that the impact of this debris was always global in scope. Damage from impacts would have varied in magnitude depending on the size of the debris and where the objects hit (land or sea). Thus some of the resulting catastrophes would have been local, some regional, and some global. Neocatastrophist and traditional catastrophist theories agree that such impacts represent a sudden departure from normal geological processes and that the processes that govern geological phenomena today might not be the same as those that did so in the ancient world. See Figure 10.1 for a comparison of uniformitarianism, the old castastrophism, and neo-catastrophism

2. Natural Disasters in the Early Bronze Age

Exploration of the possibility of comet and asteroid impacts in human history has begun and the results so far have been disturbing. According to W. Bruce Masse, "Planetary scientists and astrophysicists recently have begun to model the potential hazards on Earth from impact by asteroids and comets. These models suggest that some 25 at least locally catastrophic impacts likely occurred in various portions of the world during the past 5000 years." (Masse, 1998, 53)

What are some of the typical effects of such impacts? Napier writes:

Land impacts are less common than ocean ones and their potential for destruction appears to be smaller . . . a land impact will generate blast, heat, earthquake and dust. . . . Blast air pressure momentarily increases as the shock passes. . . . Corresponding to this overpressure is a wind speed of 160 mph. Heat—everything combustible along the line of sight of the rising fireball will be ignited.... Earthquake[s] . . . will cause devastation over a region 500-1000 km across. Dust—the greatest volcanic outbursts yield measurable climatic coolings of duration of a year or more. A 10,000 megaton impact represents a threshold beyond which the cooling may begin to exert agricultural and biotic effects on a global scale. (Napier, 1998, 25-26)

According to Baillie (1999), the extraterrestrial-terrestrial dynamics look something like this:

(1) Cometary debris enters Earth's atmosphere
(2) causing explosions in the atmosphere
(3) which in some cases trigger Earthquakes.
(4) Earthquakes in turn cause tsunamis.
(5) Increased levels of dust in the atmosphere lead to
(6) colder weather and poor growing conditions.
(7) For planting societies this leads to crop failure, famine, and disease.

Bruce Massey (1998) developed a table of the physical effects of the occurrence of large-scale catastrophic environmental events, including earthquakes, monsoon floods, volcanic eruptions, terrestrial impacts, and oceanic impacts. Earthquakes registering between 7.0 and 8.5 on the Richer scale would result in tsunamis along the coasts and lake margins, and occasional low dense smoke from fires. The impact of monsoon floods might be coastal storms, intermittent torrential rainfall over several days, thunder and lightening, and intermittent hurricane force winds.

Effects from volcanoes may include forest fires and house fires from pyroclastic flows, incendiaries and lava; tsunamis with underwater eruptions and earthquakes; high altitude ash plumes, massive electrical discharges and thunder. The terrestrial cosmic impact would include fires by thermal radiation, black rain, high-altitude clouds of debris, air-pressure blast waves, and large storm fronts. Lastly, oceanic comic impacts would result in thermal radiation and major cyclonic storms of super hurricane force.

The sound effects people would experience would be structural collapse noises, claps, booms, whistles, hisses and roars, and wind shreaks. Visual effects would include brilliant

sunrises and sunsets coupled with darkness for days or months from periodic ash plumes and cyclonic storms. There would appear a high altitude fireball before and after an impact.

Tree-ring evidence provides a yearly record of past growing conditions. Evenly spaced tree rings give evidence of stable weather patterns. However, when rings show *irregularities* in growth and damage scars, this may indicate major disasters—earthquakes, floods, fires, or volcanoes. The comparison of tree rings can also enable us to date these ancient disasters quite accurately and to measure their geographical scope. Thus it is possible that the study of tree rings—dendrochronology—could help us not only identify ancient catastrophic events associated with comet or asteroid debris, but to determine exactly when and where these events occurred.

Dendrochronologist Mike Baillie has compiled a list of dates that various authors claim to be associated with catastrophes in the ancient world:

9600 BCE—floods (Allan and Delair, 1995; Masse, 1998);
7500 BCE—comet debris (Clube and Napier, 1982, 1990);
3100 BCE—comet Encke (Steel, 1995; Baillie, 1999);
2807 BCE—flood (Masse, 1998; Pellegrino, 1995);
2700 BCE—comet debris (Clube and Napier, 1982, 1990; Masse, 1998);
2300 BCE—flood (Schock, 1999; Peiser, 1998; Peligrino, 1995; Courty, 1998; Baillie, 1999; Masse, 1998)
1628 BCE—earthquake at Thera (Baillie, 1999; Pankenier, 1998; Pellegrino, 1991; Greene, 1992)
1159 BCE—comet (Baillie, 1999; Nur, 1998; Drews, 1993).

See Figure 10.2 for an overview.

The most thoroughly attested dates appear to be 2300 BCE, 1628 BCE, and 1159 BCE. These roughly correspond to the beginning, middle, and end of the Bronze Age.

Geologist Robert Schoch argues that there is clear evidence that around 2300 BCE there was a major climatic downturn in areas near the edge of the Sahara; places that had been farmed turned into deserts. Across Europe and Africa there was a drop in water levels. Large areas of present-day Iraq were either flooded or burned. This event affected civilizations in Israel, Anatolia, Egypt, Mesopotamia, and the Indus Valley. The climatic changes appear to have been associated with volcanos, earthquakes, and floods. But were these proximate or ultimate causes?

Benny Peiser (1998) synthesized some 500 research papers that provide sedimentary, climatological, and geological evidence for natural disasters around 2300 BCE, and collaborated in Schoch's assessment. He concludes that only extraterrestrial impacts could produce such a wide range of effects.

Let us review this evidence briefly.

Since lakes alter their size in response to variations in the water budget, their sediments are perfect indicators of past climate change. If many lakes in certain regions and continents display similar stratigraphic signals in their sediments, these are clear indications of past climate changes. Peiser writes:

It has been known for some time that the water level of many African lakes dropped abruptly during the 3rd millennium BC. . . . Lake Bilma, Lake Fachi and Lake Dibella are three paleolakes . . . in the western Sahara which dried out during 4000 BP . . . a time which also witnessed expansion of the Sahara and the demise of the Saharan Neolithic. . . . At exactly the same time, 3800 BP, the water level of three salt lakes in the Thar desert in north-west of India . . . dropped abruptly (Peiser, 1998, 121-122)

Comparisons with data from Europe provide corroboration:

Harrison, Pretice and Guiot analyzed the sedimentary stratigraphy of 37 European lakes. . . . One of the main findings . . . shows a spectacular low stand of water levels of almost all of the 37 North and South European lakes in question. At that time the European lakes had dropped to their lowest level during the entire Holocene period, indicating a dramatic dry spell at around 4000 BP. (Peiser, 1998, 122)

A series of palaeoenvironmental investigations indicate the occurrence of similar fluctuation of lake levels in South and Central America. (Peiser 1998, 122)

Peiser concludes: "Since most of the lakes and lake systems mentioned . . . are not interconnected geographically, it would appear likely that the abrupt fluctuation of their water regime in different parts of the globe was more or less synchronous." (Peiser, 1998, 123)

Turning to sea level changes, Peiser notes:

When the ice-sheets of the last glaciation at the end of the Pleistocene began to melt, due to an abrupt warming period starting at around 10,000 BP, it triggered an immense rise of the world sea-level. This upsurge continued for more than 5000 years and came to a hold at the end of its mid-Holocene highstand some time between 4500 BP and 4000 BP. . . . The mean sea-level of the world oceans suddenly began to drop, a phenomenon which has been associated by many researchers with an abrupt downtown of temperatures which triggered an episode of glacial resurgence around 2300 plus or minus 200 BC. . . . Mandelkehr has listed some 20 scientific reports about sudden decrease of sea levels in many different continents which investigators have dated between 2500 and 2300 BC . . . such as Florida, Brazil , the Netherlands, the Pacific coast of the United States, Panama, France, England and the west coast of Africa, Japan, Hawaii, Australia and New Zealand. (Peiser, 1998, 124)

Peiser concludes that this is definitely not a local or even regional event or series of events. In parts of Africa, northwest Greece, and southwest India forests disappeared and glaciers reappeared which reached a peak about 4000 BP. (Note: BP stands for "before the present."

To translate BP dates to BC or BCE, subtract 2000 years from the former. For example, 4000 BP is equivalent to 2000 BCE.)

Peiser argues that the fossil record for plants and animals shows that many of the desert areas of Africa, the Near East, and the East were once fertile: "The moist period of the Mid-Holocene which had a beneficial effect on the natural and cultural environment of the Sahara for almost 2000 years came to a sudden end with the onset of the severe Post Neolithic Arid Phase which struck the central Sahara between 2500 and 1000 BC." (Peiser, 1998, 128)

In addition it appears there was significant volcanic activity at this time. In her analysis of the soil record, Marie-Agnes Courty states:

Comparison of natural soil sequences and 3rd millennium BC archeological deposits across northern Syria have allowed us to identify the regional trace of this exceptional event that is represented by a thin dust layer. . . . Deposition of the dust layer occurred just after a disruption of surface soils possibly caused by a shock wave well documented in archeological sites with rapid propagation of a wild-fire and was synchronous with the fallout of black carbon originating from major forest fires in other regions. The effect was immediately followed by exceptionally heavy rain storms. Its petrographic assemblage indicates ejection of rock fragments from various exogenous geological formations. (Courty, 1998, 93)

Earthquakes were also common during this period:

Claude Schaeffer . . . was the first researcher to present evidence of widespread seismic catastrophes in large parts of Asia minor and the Levant around 2300 BCE. . . . Evidence for major Earthquake damage in Early Bronze Age strata has been detected in many Anatolian and Near Eastern settlements. . . . Most researchers would agree that there seems to be no natural phenomenon capable of triggering abrupt climatic

change and extensive seismic activity at the same time. Yet almost 35 years ago, Rene Gallant . . . focused on this apparent anomaly . . . and suggested that cosmic impacts would easily account for the synchronicity of climate change and seismic activity. (Peiser, 1998, 131)

Finally we turn to the most cross-culturally attested kind of catastrophe—flooding. Peiser hypothesizes that widespread floods could have been caused by impact of an asteroid in the ocean: "An impact by an asteroid 300-400 meters in diameter anywhere in the Atlantic would cause rampant flood disasters and would devastate the coasts on both sides of the ocean by tsunamis over 1000 meters high." (Peiser, 1998, 130)

In China:

Particularly well attested is the flood catastrophe which destroyed many Neolithic villages along the Yellow Sea coast in China. . . . At around 2300 BCE most of these coast line settlements were submerged by the sea. . . . New villages established shortly after this disaster were consequently founded on much higher terraces. Later sites of four to three thousand years ago, that is late Neolithic to early Bronze Age, are mostly located on comparatively higher terraces or even several hundred meters higher on top of hills (Peiser, 1998, 130)

In India:

Extraordinary floods also devastated a number of settlements and cities of the Indus Valley civilization during the late 3rd millennium. In one of the major centres of this high culture, Lothal, five major flood layers sealed the cultural remains of consecutive settlements, the first of which is dated . . . to 2350 BC (Peiser, 1998, 130)

3. Natural Disasters in the Middle and Late Bronze Age

In his work on early Chinese dynasties, David Pankenier argues that the Shang dynasty may have commenced during a time of celestial bombardment:

There appears to have occurred a series of related astronomical/meteorological phenomena between 1610 and 1550 BCE contemporaneous with the dynastic transition from Xia to Shang. Assuming they are factual, accounts of these phenomena in the Bamboo Annals may point to repeated multiple cometary apparitions, meteor storms and possible impacts leading to anomalous weather-related consequences on a wide scale in north China, most notably one of the severest droughts in cultural memory. Second, accounts of a cosmic conflict between the Yellow Emperor and Chi You, that is between an established sky-god and order giver and a fearsome, chaos-bringing intruder bear all the earmarks of a mythicized version of such events that is the sudden appearance of a spectacular comet, possibly with multiple companions. . . . (Pankenier, 1998, 194)

We will hear more about the relationship between Chi You and the Yellow emperor in our chapter on Axial Age religion.

Mike Baillie suspects that both the start and the end of the Shang dynasty were caused by the impacts of comets in 1628 and 1159 BCE. In fact, for Baillie, the concept of the Mandate of Heaven *literally* had to do with justifying one's rule before celestial forces. When dust blocked the sun, causing cold and the failure of crops, this was a sign that the Mandate of Heaven had been withdrawn.

The beginning of the Shang dynasty was contemporary with the volcanic eruption that devastated the island of Thera. In the middle of the second millennium BCE, possibly the most destructive volcanic eruption in human history occurred off the Island of Crete. This eruption destroyed Minoan civilization, one of the most impressive of the ancient world. The eruption produced tsunamis and cast an ashen pall that shaded most of the planet for years. The air shock waves from this event may have been as much as 350 times more powerful than those produced by a moderately sized hydrogen bomb. Temperatures plunged all over the Northern Hemisphere, leaving summer freeze scars in trees from Turkey to California. According to paleontologist Charles Pellegrino, "Fifty cubic miles of rock hurled into the heavens. . . . There were cracks in the Earth, radiating out from the island. One of them was more than a hundred miles long. . . . [T]he noise shot around the world sixteen times." (Pellegrino, 1994, 199)

Imagining himself on the moon, Pellegrino describes what the process might have looked like:

Even from a vantage point on the lunar highlands you could have seen it without the aid of telescopes or binoculars. A black spot had appeared on the Aegean Sea, vast and cloudlike. It swelled on the planet below, burst up through the atmosphere and started to rain fire down upon Melos, Naxos and Crete. . . . White clouds formed and vanished on its edges. In less than an hour it widened to two hundred miles, and then to four hundred miles. It rolled over Turkey and Egypt, turned day into starless night. . . . The stain thinned over Syria and Iran, pulled itself apart into long streamers, thinned still more and spread across Asia like ink poured into a saucer of water—except that this ink stain was laced with sheets of brilliant blue lightning. . . . Within hours of the Theran upheaval . . . death rolled into southern Turkey on the tongue of a tsunami . . . funneling it thirty miles inland. To penetrate so far, it had to be eight hundred feet tall when it hit the shore. (Pellegrino, 1991, 13–14)

Thera is a flooded crater 150 miles south east of Athens. It is about eight miles wide and half a mile deep.

While historians agree that Minoan civilization came to an abrupt end, they don't all agree on the cause. Some think it collapsed as a result of raids. Pellegrino argues against this:

Marinatos had seen walls that seemed to have collapsed in an unusual way. Rectilinear blocks more than six feet long had been moved about in a manner that suggested the sucking and dragging motion of water receding in a huge mass. The whole upper part of a vertical blocks was missing. It appeared to have been snapped off. Recently, a digger had discovered a missing piece jutting out from under a bush. The two-broken halves matched perfectly; but the upper part had been deposited more than three hundred feet away from its foundation. . . . Invading people don't do that . . . they do not go to the trouble of breaking ordinary stone walls apart, and hauling half-ton pieces three hundred feet. . . . There was also a great deal of carbonized wood in the house—evidence of extensive fire damage. (Pelligrino, 1991, 48-49)

From the eastward spread of the ash cloud, we know that a gale must have been blowing in the general direction of Turkey when the island exploded. Oceanographic core drillings have revealed ash deposits two feet deep on the sea floor near the Turkish and Cypriot coasts . . . recent excavations suggested that at least a quarter inch of dust fell out of the cloud as it rolled over Egypt. The dust was rich in sulfur and some of it appears to have fallen as acid rain. Doubtless it blacked out the sun for several days. . . . Megatons of ultrafine dust had been hoisted fifty miles high into the stratosphere, where it shaded out some of the sun's radiation, absorbing its heat long before it reached the ground. (Pelligrino, 1991, 77)

Across parts of Turkey, and two hundred miles east of Thera . . . drifts of volcanic ash several feet deep were deposited. The dust cloud spread fewer than one hundred miles west, suggesting

that a powerful squall, blowing from the west, stopped it and hurled it east. (Pellegrino, 1994, 208)

In comparing the Thera explosion to Mt. Vesuvius and St. Helena, Pellegrino says:

The death cloud from Vesuvius according to an eyewitness account . . . was barely twenty miles wide. Thera's black shroud spread over much of the Aegean, and appears to have had lethal effects even hundreds of miles away. . . . Vesuvius and St. Helens combined added up to only one cubic mile of airborne debris. Thera ejected almost thirty times as much. (Pellegrino, 1991, 62)

The eruption of Thera released roughly 15 million times more energy than did the eruption of Mount Pelee on Martinque in 1902, blowing a thirty cubic mile hole in the Earth. Referring to another relatively recent spectacular eruption, that of Krakatoa in 1883, Pelligrino notes:

The blast wave from the explosion caused permanent damage to people's hearing more than 500 miles away and was powerful enough to shatter windows and crack walls at a distance of 100 miles. More than thirty thousand were killed by tidal waves as far away as 2000 miles. Thera was as much as fifty or even a hundred times more powerful. (Pellegrino, 1991, 213)

Geologist Mott Greene explains why the Thera eruption was so catastrophic:

When the eruption climaxes with the formation of a caldera, as in the case of Krakatoa and Thera, the roof of the magma chamber actually caves in. . . . If the volcano . . . is an island, and if the magma chamber is breached while the magma is still being erupted, the violence of the explosion can be many times magnified by the vaporization of the inrushing sea-water coming into contact with the incandescent magma, in a so-called phreatomagmatic eruption, akin to the explosion of a gigantic steam boiler. (Greene, 1992, 60)

Greene believes that Hesiod's *Theogony* contains descriptions in metaphorical language that correspond precisely to geological processes that occurred in the middle of the second millenium BCE. According to Greene, mythological literature like the *Theogony* cannot be understood unless supplemented by archeology and natural history. He argues that the classicists who study myth are trained only in the humanities, not in the physical sciences, and are thus poorly equipped to discern the real meaning of many ancient texts. His view goes against both sociological and psychological schools of interpreting myth, which assume that myths have nothing to do with the natural world:

> The 'ancients' . . . lived and worked outdoors and did most of their thinking there. . . . Because we have come indoors in the last hundred years, much that was obvious to earlier generations of scholars about ancient mythology is no longer obvious to us. The myths are to a large extent stories about nature. (Greene, 1992, xii)

The *Theogony* is Hesiod's story of the lineage of the Greek gods and their struggles over the control over the cosmos. Hesiod focuses on the battles between the Olympian gods, headed by Zeus, and the Titans (the previous generation), led by Kronos, Zeus's father. For Greene, these mythological battles were mot merely the stuff of fancy:

> Close attention to the sequences of events in the battles, to their appearance, sound and their effect on the physical world leaves no doubt that the phenomena described are volcanic eruptions. Not only that, but eruptions described so carefully and in such detail that the volcanoes in question can be identified and the particular eruptions . . . dated. The battle

of Zeus and the Titans recounts the eruption of the volcano at Thera. (Greene, 1992, 47)

In the *Theogony*, we read the following:

> There had been a long war with much suffering on both sides and many bloody battles between the Titan generation of gods and the children of Cronus. The mighty Titans fought from the top of Mount Othrys, while the Olympian gods . . . the children of Cronus . . . fought from Mount Olympus. . . . They [the monsters in the service of Zeus] grasped massive rocks in their sturdy hands and took their place in the bitter battles against the Titans.
> The limitless expanse of the sea echoed terribly; the Earth rumbled loudly, and the broad area of the sky shook and grounded. . . . While the weapons discharged at each other whistled through the air both sides shouted battle cries . . . till the noise reached the starry sky.
> [Zeus] advanced through the sky from Olympus sending flash upon flash of continuous lightning. The bolts of lightning and thunder flew thick and fast . . . forming a solid roll of sacred fire. Fertile tracts of land all around cracked as they burned and immense forests roared in the fire. The whole Earth and ocean streams and the barren sea began to boil. An immense flame shot up into the atmosphere so that the hot air enveloped the Titans, while their eyes . . . were blinded by the brilliant flash of the lightning bolt. The prodigious heat filled the Void. The sight there was to see and the noise there was to hear made it seem as if the Earth and vast Sky above were colliding. If Earth were being smashed and if Sky were smashing down upon her the noise would be as great as the noise that arose when the gods met in battle. The winds added to the confusion, whirling dust around together with great Zeus' volleys of thunder and lightening bolts . . . so that the uproar was deafening.

They attacked relentlessly, throwing showers of three hundred stones one after another . . . till they darkened the Titans with a cloud of missiles. (Greene 1992, 49-51)

Greene claims that the story in the *Theogony* follows fifteen stages that match the geological stages of the Thera eruption. Here is a paraphrased version of Motte's geological interpretation of this story:

<table>
<tr><td>Hesiod</td><td>Thera</td></tr>
<tr><td>(1) a long war between Olympians and Titans</td><td>(1) premonitory seismicity</td></tr>
<tr><td>(2) both sides gather strength; Zeus's allies grasp massive rocks</td><td>(2) increased activity</td></tr>
<tr><td>(3) terrible echoes over sea</td><td>(3) first-phase explosions</td></tr>
<tr><td>(4) ground rumbles loudly</td><td>(4) tectonic earthquakes</td></tr>
<tr><td>(5) sky shakes and groans</td><td>(5) air shock waves</td></tr>
<tr><td>(6) Mt. Olympus trembles</td><td>(6) great earthquakes</td></tr>
<tr><td>(7) steady vibrations of ground like stamping of innumerable feet running</td><td>(7) earthquakes</td></tr>
<tr><td>(8) weapons [massive rocks] whistle through air</td><td>(8) pyroclastic ejecta</td></tr>
<tr><td>(9) loud battle cries reaching up to the high heavens</td><td>(9) explosive reports</td></tr>
<tr><td>(10) Zeus arrives: lightning, thunder; fields and forests burn</td><td>(10) volcanic lightning</td></tr>
<tr><td>(11) Earth and sea boil</td><td>(11) magma chamber breach</td></tr>
<tr><td>(12) immense flame shoots up into the air enveloping the Titans</td><td>(12) phreatomagmatic explosion and heat</td></tr>
<tr><td>(13) enormous sight and sound, one would think the sky had collapsed onto the Earth</td><td>(13) sound of above</td></tr>
<tr><td>(14) arrival of windborne dust, with lightning, thunder, with deafening uproar</td><td>(14) final ash eruptions</td></tr>
<tr><td>(15) Titans buried under missiles and bound beneath the Earth</td><td>(15) collapsed debris</td></tr>
</table>

Greene's commentary on this comparison is as follows:

We should note that there is a complete one-to-one correspondence with no missing elements and that they are all in the correct order. . . . Zeus' weapons are thunder and lightning and they appear in the poem as the instrument of the Titans' downfall. . . .

Any volcanic eruption that forcibly ejects large quantities of ash and gas at high velocity into the atmosphere will, of necessity, create turbulence and static electricity manifest as lightning discharge. . . . [I]n a volcanic crater flooded with sea water, eruptions of steam and tephra (pyroclastics) greatly increase the electric potential gradient and eject a huge amount of material carrying a large positive charge, which is then repeatedly discharged back into the mouth of the crater from which it emerged, giving the appearance of lightning bolts being hurled into the mouth of the crater across a distance of several kilometers. In other words, at the climatic breach of the integrity of the magma chamber at Thera, huge volleys of volcanic lightning immediately preceded the final phreatomagmatic collapse of the caldera and its associated heat and noise—and the end of the Ttitans, giving rise to the interpretation . . . that Zeus's intervention was decisive. The volcano exhausts itself and disappears beneath the ocean, the Titans are bound beneath the Earth. (Greene, 1992, 62-63)

A reasonable skeptic may ask how we know it was Thera that was being described and not some other volcano. Greene insists that one volcano *can* be distinguished from another:

Each of the Earth's volcanoes also has an 'eruptive signature." . . . This uniqueness is expressed in the pattern and frequency of its eruptions, the kind of material it throws out and even the chemical composition of that material, which allows geologists to trace layers of volcanic ash on land or on the seafloor back to the volcanoes that spawned them, to compare ratios of specific minerals within other volcanic products and use a variety of techniques to date the eruptions. . . .
These eruptions may be graded in severity based on a number of criteria-the height of the volcanic cloud and whether it entered the stratosphere, the volume of material ejected. . . . These criteria are folded into something called the Volcanic exploisivity Index (VEI)-an attempt to do for volcanic eruptions what the Richer and Mercalli scales have done for the study of Earthquakes (Greene, 1992, 56-57)

After reviewing the data on earthquakes around the world and specifically the Mediterranean, Greene concludes that while the eruption of Etna in Sicily was also very violent the eruptive pattern was very different. Furthermore, it was not as violent an eruption as Thera: "Thera was somewhere between 1,000 and 10,000 times more powerful than the greatest recorded eruption for Etna. . . . The explosion at Thera was the only VEI 6 in the last 10.000 years in the Mediterranean." (Greene 1992, 58)
Charles Pellegrino believes that Egyptian and Hebrews sacred sources describe the same

disaster: "Egypts's Ipuwer papyrus and the Old Testament seem to be describing the same event. 'Blood everywhere' could be a reference to people coughing up blood after inhaling the ash of Thera or to the Nile River, polluted with acidy, sulfuric ash." (Pellegrino, 1991, 79)
More specifically we find:

For nine days there was no exit from the palace and no one could see the face of his fellow. Towns were destroyed by mighty tides. Upper Egypt suffered devastation . . . blood everywhere . . . pestilence throughout the country . . . Ra has turned his face from mankind. If only it would shine even for one hour. No one knows when it is midday. One's shadow is not discernible. The Sun in the heavens resembles the moon. (Pellegrino, 1991, 78). Life is no longer possible when the Sun is concealed behind the clouds. (Pellegrino, 1994, 214)

The Old Testament refers to plagues of frogs, flies, and locusts. Pellegrino explains this naturalistically using the aftermath of the Mt. Pelee explosion as an example:

Those creatures who were not killed outright by the ash were 'made bold by hunger'. Ants were driven by Pelee from the banks of Martinque's Blanche River. With them came centipedes more than a foot long. . . . They swarmed into barns, up the walls of parlors, into bedding and night clothes. Rats attacked children on the streets. . . .
The Old Testament tells us of hail mixed with flames raining from heaven, and peals of thunder, and lightening flashing down to Earth. Such things were witnessed as Mount St. Helen's cloud . . . passed over Yakima (Pellegrino, 1991, 80-81)

Putting the Exodus into the naturalistic terms of a tsunami, Pellegrino reasons:

The shore is the worst place to be, for here the wave is reflected, compressed and enhanced by the ever-diminishing distance between the bed of the sea and its surface. Its first breath is felt as a sudden retreat of the water plunging over a matter of minutes deeper than any tide can ebb. Tuthmosis III's north shore sentries could not have known what was happening to them. Such things are rarely seen in a human lifetime. Because they did not know what they were seeing there was no cause for fear, only astonishment and curiosity. . . . Mud dunes that had lain under thirty feet of water were suddenly climbing into open air. . . . Driven by wonder and curiosity at least some of Tuthmosis III"s sentries must have followed the retreating coastline. Then the sucking noises abruptly cease, and a new sound was in the air, and even those who had remained on the higher shore knew suddenly and too late . . . their high ground was but an illusion. It rippled away in that moment of awful realization when they saw the black shapes stirring . . . rising upon their haunches. When the sea returned-faster than any charioteer could hope to flee-it was forty feet above the high-tide mark (Pellegrino, 1994, 238)

In assessing the reliability of sacred texts, Pellegrino comments that while the actual existence of specific biblical characters may be questionable, the processes the texts describe have a geological foundation: "We do not know that a man named Moses ever existed, but black, ground-hugging clouds, easterly winds, walls of water and dust there were, in great abundance. The rocks tell us so." (Pellegrino, 1994, 239)

We must be very careful with the naturalistic interpretation of mythology. As I have shown previously (Lerro, 2000), there are many reasons why myths are often not historically reliable. In reconstructing events of the distant past we should rely primarily on physical evidence like cratering or computer simulations of the ancient skies and the ancient climate. Myths should serve only as supporting evidence.

Was there a causal relationship between the impact of comet debris, the eruption of Thera, and the Exodus? We don't know yet. But what has changed among some geologists and astronomers is the view that this is no longer wild speculation, but a plausible hypothesis.

Let us now turn our attention to the late Bronze Age. At the end of chapter 9 we discussed how the new Iron Age weaponry and military strategies were instrumental in allowing pastoralists to take over some agricultural states. Baillie believes that the period between 1250 BCE and 1150 BCE (the Archaic Iron Age) was also deeply affected by the impact of comet debris.

According to Baillie, experts in climatology do not think volcanoes *by themselves* could cause such dramatic changes for so many years, because dust washes away quickly and modern volcanic eruptions have lasted, at most, three years.

Could earthquakes have been the cause of the evident devastation? In speaking about Greece and the Islands surrounding them, Drews (1993) gives five reasons why earthquakes *by themselves* could not have been responsible for the disasters that overcame these lands. In my previous book (Lerro, 2000) I summarized these reasons:

(1) *Damage must be distinguished from destruction.* Very few cities are known to have been destroyed by earthquake alone. After the quake, damage is repaired and the city rebuilt. At each site surveyed by Drews, buildings clearly collapsed, but at none of these sites was there any displacement of *surface* levels.

(2) *Earthquakes do not explain the evidence of fires.* The fires that accompany *modern* earthquakes are due to broken gas pipes and snapped electrical cables. Neither gas nor electricity was harnessed in the Bronze Age.

(3) *In none of the six areas Drew studied were there any casualties.* There was an absence of skeletons. In earthquakes of serious consequence, victims are interred at the site and casualities are numerous.

(4) *Nothing of value was buried by the collapsing buildings.* Places instantaneously

Figure 10.2 Contending Claims for Natural Disasters from Neolithic to Late Bronze Ages

Who	When	Where	Cause	Effect on Earth
Allan and Delair	9600 BCE	global		flood
Masse	9300 BCE	cosmic impacts		flood
Clube and Napier	7500 BCE			
Ryan and Pittman	5000 BCE	Near East		flood
Ryan and Pittman	3100 BCE	Eastern Mediterranean		flood
Steel	2807 BCE	Stonehenge I	proto-Encke comet	meteoric Storms
Masse	2700 BCE	oceanic comet impact		flood
Clube and Napier				flood
Masse		Set kills Osirus--Egypt	Taurid meteor storm	
Masse	2345 BCE	Gilgamesh--Mesopotamia		
		Near East/ Western Asia		
		Old Kingdom Egypt		
		Akkadian Empire in Mesopotamia		
		Anatolia, Greece		
		Israel Abraham		
		Indus civilization		
Pellegrino	2216-2156 BCE	Sodom and Gomorah	comet apparitions	meteor storms
Pankenier	1610-1550 BCE	Xia to Shang dynasty		
		(Yellow Emperor--Chi You)		
Pellegrino	1628 BCE	Island of Thera		Santori volcano
		Exodus from Egypt		
Baillie	1159 BCE	Near East, Eastern Mediterranean Europe	comet Troy, comet Babylon, comet Jerusalem	Earthquakes, tsunamis, increased dust leads to colder weather, poorer growing conditions, crop failure, famines and disease.

Figure 10.3 Interaction of Natural Disasters and Ancient History:*

Tree Ring Events	Europe	Near East	Hebrew	China
3195 BC		Start Egyptian civilization		
	Henge at Stonehenge constructed			
2354 BC	Bronze Age starts Britain, Ireland	Akkad	Flood of Noah (Ussher date)	Emperor Yao famous for floods
		Middle Kingdom		Start Xia Dynasty
1628 BC	Stonehenge abandoned	Start Second Intermediate Period	Exodus of Moses Plagues of Egypt	Comet Ends Xia Dynasty (King Chieh) start Shang Dynast (King T'ang)
		New Kingdom		Shang Dynasty
1159 BC	Comet Troy ends Middle Bronze Age	Comet Babylon Start of 3rd Intermediate Period	Comet Jerusalem David Plague	Comet End Shang Dynasty (King Chou) Start Chou Dynasty (King Wu)

* adopted from Baillie (1999)

destroyed by earthquakes should show evidence of gold, silver, or bronze. There was nothing of this nature in the debris of any of the six sites studied. Whatever valuable items were found had been stored in secret places.

(5) *Resettled communities located themselves in areas that would put them in danger of earthquakes, not in safety from them.* When people later recovered from the catastrophe, a great many of their new settlements were sited *on the coast.* This is hardly the best place to settle after an earthquake, given that earthquakes under the oceans or the Mediterranean Sea could result in tsunamis which would *destroy* coastal settlements.

Drews and Baillie agree that earthquakes by themselves could not have caused the end of the Near Eastern Bronze Age civilizations, but their conclusions differ in other respects. Drews points to the nomads' new weapons and military strategies as a subsidiary cause for the civilizations' collapse. Baillie argues that the destruction came ultimately from the impact of comet debris, which then catalyzed geological processes such as earthquakes and volcanic eruptions.

Baillie's overall thesis is that

> At or around 2354, 1628, 1159, 208 BCE and 540 CE the Earth was subjected to environmental dislocation either by the effects of close-passing comets, by dust loading from such comets and their components, from direct bombardment or dust from the trail of dead comets, that is, some combination of close approaches, impacts and dust. (Baillie, 1999, 215)

Baillie links tree-ring evidence for natural disasters to the troubles of many Bronze Age societies. Please see Figure 10.4. For those who are familiar with ancient history some of the dates cited in this chart may seem odd. But keep in mind the fact that the traditional dating for the rise and fall of many ancient civilizations is based on Egyptian chronology. This chronology has become controversial in recent years, with various revisions offered. The tree-ring evidence Baillie offers is considerably more reliable. The dates traditionally given to events in ancient history will have to be reorganized in the light of tree-ring evidence. It will take interdisciplinary cooperation among archeologists, geologists, astronomers, and historians to sort all this out.

For our purposes the exact dates aren't as important as the knowledge that at the same time that institutionalized male dominance was being consolidated in Bronze Age agricultural states, people lived through the impact and aftermath of natural disasters whose effects lasted hundreds of years. Though I am arguing, with Baillie, that the primary cause for these disasters was comet debris, for purposes of this chapter it is not necessary that the reader be convinced of this. It is sufficient to show that—whatever the primary cause—there were natural disasters, that they caused a considerable amount of environmental and social stress, and that this stress impacted institutionalized male dominance, as we will see in the next chapter.

The idea that comets caused catastrophic terrestrial events within the past few thousand years will be more important for my argument in the chapter on magic and religion (chapter 13), because there I attempt to show that there was a movement in sacred traditions from Earth spirits to sky gods. The rain of death coming from comets in the sky and the association of the sky with males then helped to *legitimize* institutionalized male dominance.

4. Evaluation of the plausibility of cometary encounters in the Bronze Age

Did comet debris cause the natural disasters in the Bronze Age? As most or all of the researchers admit, we have only circumstantial evidence. Moreover, neither I or any of the other neo-catastrophists claim that comet debris caused *all* natural disasters during this period, only the biggest ones. But we can be reasonably sure that (a) the Earth and other planets have be bombarded by comets and asteroids, both in the deep past, and (in the case of Jupiter) in the very recent past; and (b) that there were natural disasters throughout the Bronze Age—as has been confirmed by geologists, archeologists and historians.

It seems unrealistic to think that, even though Earth was bombarded in the geologic past, such events ceased when *Homo Sapiens* came on the scene. I repeat the conclusions of my previous book:

(1) From the evidence of both astronomy and mythology it seems plausible to believe that there *have* been impacts from space *throughout* human history.

(2) From both simulations of the ancient skies by astronomers and from ancient mythology it appears that the effects of celestial impacts and their aftermath on *ancient* civilizations were far more devastating than anything that occurred during the Axial Age or any other more recent historical period.

Figure 10. 5 shows the interaction of the forces of coercion and stress in the Bronze Age.

Figure 10.4 Interaction of Forces of Coercion in the Bronze Age

Date*	Technology	Natural Catastrophes	Social-Cultural	Migrations/ Invasions	Likely Impact of War on Women
3195	proliferation of the domesticated horse increased use of riding horses in Eurasian steppe riding horses imported into Mesopotamia	proto-Encke comet	Stonehenge		
2800- 2700		flood/comet	beginning of Egyptian/ Mesopotamian civilizations		
2354			beginning of Chinese states Xia dynasty		
1900	invention of the spoked wheel development of a light horse-drawn chariot chariot used for recreation and transport Anatolia–possible experiments with chariots in battle				
1800-1700	introduction of bit into the Near East chariots used in battle in Bronze Age states				
1623-1628		comet apparition parting of Red Sea Santori volcano	end of Indus civilization end of Xia dynasty end of Minoan civilization Exodus		most males not obliged to fight. higher percentage of males die who do fight
1550				Hyksos chiefs make themselves kings with chariot warfare. expelled by Egyptians	
1300			end of Mycenaen civilization	Kassites, Hurrainas, Aryans invasions	
1225 to 1200	rise of cavalry and infantry decline of chariots javelins, spheres, swords			Greece invaded by people of Thessily	subjugation replaces direct coercion
1159	weaponry more lethal citizen militias	eruption, Hecate event	end of Shang dynasty	Dorian invasions	males obliged to fight

* all dates are BCE

Chapter 11

Natural Disasters and Gender Stress: Did Floods, Earthquakes and Volcanoes Undermine or Intensify Institutionalized Male Dominance in Bronze Age States?

How did the natural disasters described in the last chapter impact gender relations? If institutionalized male dominance was already in place, did floods, volcanoes, and earthquakes provide women with an opportunity to improve their condition—or did natural disasters reinforce institutionalized male dominance and make matters worse for women than they already were?

Here are some specific questions that need to be addressed:

1. *How different were natural disasters in the ancient world from disasters in the modern world?* Were Earth dynamics or the climate significantly different then? Were there more floods, volcanic eruptions, or earthquakes than today?

2. *How different were human responses to the disasters in the ancient world compared to those in the modern world?* Did people panic and act more irrationally than do contemporary people? Would the ancients have had more reason to abandon their sites of habitation than do people today?

3. *Was the tension between city and country as severe in the ancient world as in the modern world?* Were mobility patterns more or less in flux in the ancient world as compared to those in modern cities? Was there a more or less developed linear sense of time in the cities? Were urbanized people more or less attached to the land? Was there more or less competition between groups?

4. *How similar were the psychological reactions of the ancients to those of modern people?* As we are about to see, psychologists have identified reactions typical of modern traumatic stress victims—including changes in cognitive patterns. If natural disasters in ancient times were more intense and widespread than those in modern times, would post-traumatic stress reactions have been widespread throughout entire populations? Most importantly for our purposes:

5. *Did men and women deal with stress from natural disasters any differently in the ancient world than they do today?* Would men and women have differed in their exposure to risk and in their perception of risk? Did men and women prepare for a disaster any differently than they do today? Did volcanoes, earthquakes, and floods have the same effects on men as on women in the ancient world, or were men more susceptible to lightning and women to earthquakes—since men were more likely to be outdoors and women indoors? Did men and women differ in their response to emergencies? Was there more or less of a

division of labor under hazardous conditions?

6. *How did men treat women during natural disasters in Bronze Age states?* Would there have been an increase or decrease in domestic violence? Was there any difference in men and women's coping mechanisms under these conditions?

We will not find direct archaeological or textual evidence from Bronze Age states to answer our questions. Ancient agricultural states recorded stories—often framed in myths—about natural disasters, but they did not preserve descriptions in modern scientific language. Neither the Egyptians nor the Mesopotamians performed cross-cultural studies comparing their own psychological reactions to stress with those of members of the Indus civilization or the Shang dynasty in China. Nor do we have any explicit commentary, dating from the Bronze Age, on changes in gender relations. However, it is possible to assemble research findings from various fields in order to piece together a believable view of how gender relations were affected by natural disasters in those times.

This chapter is divided into five parts. In the first section I examine people's response to natural disasters *today,* without regard for gender differences. In the second section I compare modern to ancient natural disasters in terms of their power, scope, and duration. In the third section I examine research on how men and women respond differently to "normal" stress in *modern* society. In the fourth section I explore how men and women are treated differently during natural disasters in *modern times.* In the last section I synthesize the work of the first four sections by addressing the question of how natural disasters are likely to have impacted the levels of stress in men and women in the ancient world. I also draw out the implications for institutionalized male dominance.

Section two answers four of the six questions posed above and section five answers the last two questions.

1. Natural Disasters and human response in modern times compared cross-culturally

In his book *The Stress of Life,* physician Hans Selye greatly advanced the study of stress by pointing out how influences from our environment—toxins, viruses, heat, and cold—can throw the body out of balance. Environmental stress forces the body to mobilize its resources to either restore balance or, in extreme cases, to fight or flee. Importantly, he pointed out that not all stress is bad. What he called "eustress" requires the body to mobilize energy to attain goals that are under the organism's control—such as giving a public speech or running a marathon. Selye concluded that it is not realistic or desirable to try to lead a stress-free life, but it is possible to minimize wear-and-tear on the system. Selye also argued that there are a number of forces working on the human organism that counterbalance each other. For example, living in a comfortable climate and eating well can lessen the impact of environmental pollutants.

Tavris and Wade (1998) point out that there is seldom a simple, causative, one-to-one relationship between stressful events and illness. Biological, psychological, and social mediators make an individual's response to stress variable. People's responses to stress depend upon the strength of their immune systems, their personalities, explanatory styles, and coping techniques. Social factors—the economy, social class, ethnicity, and gender—also shape responses to stress.

Tavris and Wade divide all stressors into four types: recurring conflicts, such as family fighting; traumatic events, such as the sudden death of a loved one; continuing problems, like working two or three jobs just to get by; and daily hassles like losing your keys or daily planner. Despite their vast differences, what all these types of stressors have in common is they are made worse when the stress is *continuing* (rather than occasional) and *uncontrollable* (rather than partly or totally under an individual's control). This is important for our study of natural disasters in the ancient world, since—as we are about to see—these sources of stress were both continuing and uncontrollable.

Most discussions of stress assume that the individual is living in a stable society—no wars, revolutions, or economic depressions. Neither does the typical clinical discussion of stress touch upon the impact of natural disasters—floods, famines, droughts, earthquakes, or sudden changes in climate.

Natural disasters are events in biophysical nature that are not under human control, and that cause havoc and damage to the environment and injury or death to human beings. Disasters can be usefully distinguished from emergencies. In an emergency the traditional and existing social arrangements are sufficient to overcome the problems posed by the events. In a disaster, the infrastructure and structure of society are significantly weakened or destroyed and people have to collectively improvise their responses.

In *Environmental Disaster and the Archaeology of Human Response* (2000), Bawden and Reycraft name several indicators for natural disasters, which they divide into environmental parameters and social variables. I have combined these with similar factors discussed by Veitch and Arkkelin in *Environmental Psychology* (1995).

Environmental Parameters:

1. Event magnitude—the more powerful the event, the less adequate the technology available is to mitigate it.
2. Event frequency—the more frequent the extreme events, the greater the need for response.

3. Event duration—the shorter the event, the less time available for cultural response. If the event is longer, there are mixed possibilities: it allows more time for implementation of counter strategies but the event tests society's capacity for endurance.
4. Event speed at outset—length of time between first appearance and its peak. Extreme events with slow onset times—drought or soil erosion—may be predicted and mitigated.
5. Areal extent of event. The larger the area affected, greater the loss to society
6. Spatial dispersion—distribution pattern of damage effects. Does the event homogeneously affect the landscape or are some areas left intact?
7. Temporal spacing: Some hazards have random time distribution; others (tornadoes) are seasonal and cyclical.
8. Timing of event—does it occur, for example, during planting season?

Social variables:

9. Resource distribution—whether resources are concentrated or dispersed.
10. Level of capital investment in resource exploitation: cattle herding or irrigation agriculture directly affect potential damage. Capital investments tend to be concentrated and difficult to replace.
11. Level of technological efficiency—the more advanced the technology, the greater the capacity for response to the disaster.
12. Type of economic system—dependence on monocropping versus less productive but diverse drought-resistant crops.
13. Experience with event—whether the event occurs within a lifetime or a single generation may affect the type of response.

14. Population density—the greater the population density the greater the damage, and the more individuals forced into areas of greater risk. The relative as opposed to absolute size of the population must be considered—Veitche and Arkkelin (1995) give the example of a nursing home fire being a far greater disaster if it is the only nursing home in town, than if it is one in fifty.

15. Stratification patterns—poorer individuals are forced into risk-prone areas.

16. Level of sociopolitical complexity—amount of energy, labor, and resources that can be brought to bear on the event.

17. Areal extent of a given polity—this determines the geographical extent from which labor and resources may be taken.

Psychological variables:

19. The visibility of the effects—how badly have attachments been severed? A deep impact can be invisible and a minor impact can be very visible.

20. The existence of an identifiable low point, where people can say to themselves "the worst is over."

21. Perception of control—how much do people feel they can do to alleviate the situation?

Figure 11.1 (a simplified list of the parameters and variables stated above) shows the best-case and worst-case scenarios for these variables. We will come back to this list in the next section to assess how many conditions are likely to have fallen under "worst-case scenario" in the Bronze Age.

Bell, Fisher, Baum, and Greene, in their text *Environmental Psychology* (1996), name six typical "myths" about how people react to disasters that need to be dispelled:

- disaster victims panic
- disaster victims act irrationally
- there is looting if homes are destroyed
- there is rampant individualism
- disasters are followed by epidemics
- people flee from the disaster site.

Contrary to these "myths," Bell *et al.* argue that research shows that disaster victims rarely panic or display mass hysteria; that most behavior is highly rational and adaptive; and that looting occurs only if there are huge economic differences and there is an authoritarian government. Further, far from bringing out individualism in people, disasters typically evoke community spirit. There is a temporary reduction in social differences and people often forgo, at least in the short run, notions of private property and share whatever resources are available. Few disasters are followed by epidemics. Last, people do not flee from the site; on the contrary, it is difficult to get them to leave the scene of the disaster, partly because they are attached to the land.

Bell *et al.* (1996) name five typical *effects* of disasters:

- they cause substantial distress and mental health problems immediately after their impact;
- this distress is short-lived and, by a year or two after disasters, most victims have adjusted;
- severe chronic stress is unusual and limited to those victims who have psychological problems prior to the disaster;
- there may be a positive effect because of the social cohesiveness which follows when victims bond;
- the shared sense of the basic meaning of life is challenged.

In his book *Environmental Disasters in Global Perspective* (1994), Lewis Aptekar argues that the more damage is incurred by the social infrastructure, the more the basic cultural meanings and sense of order are challenged.

Aptekar cites Barkun's historical analysis of disasters in a global context, which found that *single* disasters rarely break the existing faith of people or change society; only a *series* of disasters can do this. (Aptekar 1994, 86)

Two other characteristic effects of disasters might be added to the list above, according to Aptekar:

- avoidance of cognitive ambiguity, and
- a tendency to go to war.

Aptekar claims that during times of disasters, people avoid cognitive ambiguity, preferring to reorganize their perceptions of the environment than to reorganize their thinking. Yet "People also reorganized their thinking. They distorted the memory of the disaster, they forgot parts of what happened and most important they denied the magnitude of the disaster's impact and their reactions to it." (Aptekar 1994, 107)

Regarding evidence of increased bellicosity accompanying disasters, Aptekar has this to say:

[Melvin and Carol Ember] . . . have pointed out that the unpredictability of natural disasters is strongly correlated with societies going to war. The authors used the Human Relations Areas Files to examine the ethnographic findings of 186 mostly pre-industrial societies.

It was not the actual scarcity produced by the disaster as much as it was the fear of the unpredictable scarcity of food that lay behind the aggression. Societies invaded other groups, not because they were fearful of having no food as a result of a predictable disaster, but because they were afraid that at some unknown time they might not have food. Therefore they attacked other groups to gather enough food to store for possible scarcity. The

possibility of being invaded increased people's fear of each other.

Cross-cultural data illustrate how nomadic and pastoral peoples in large part are forced by environmental disasters to leave their traditional way of life and homelands. (Aptekar, 1994, 60)

Until now, we have not distinguished between societies in terms of how they actually deal with natural disasters. Do hunter-gatherers and herders deal with earthquakes, floods, and volcanoes any differently from the way planting societies do? And how are planting societies' coping methods different from those of industrial capitalist societies?

According to David Miller (2000), simple nomadic societies composed of hunter-gatherers or herders are not severely impacted. This is because people in these societies do not build permanent dwellings; thus storms, droughts, fires, or floods minimally affect their way of life. Their high mobility serves to minimize the impact of local weather conditions. It is relatively easy to flee from present dangers or leave regions that cause persistent, severe, or recurring problems.

At the other extreme end of the scale of social complexity are industrialized societies. These are cleaner and safer than were their counterparts of 200 years ago, and most people no longer live in constant fear of mass epidemics or deadly contagious diseases. In addition, buildings in industrial societies are today more securely built to minimize the impact of earthquakes or floods. Many local, regional, and national agencies in these societies have direct roles in disaster response.

It is the societies between these extremes—horticultural villages and especially agricultural states—that are the most vulnerable to natural disasters. In the largest agricultural states population densities are even higher than those in modern industrial cities, and many cities in agricultural states lack sewage systems, running water, and industrial medical practices. This

Figure 11.1 Impact of Natural Disasters on Societies

Worst case scenario	Minimum damage

ENVIRONMENTAL PARAMETERS

Worst case scenario	Minimum damage
frequent or multiple impact	infrequent and single impact
short duration—no preparation	
long duration if society has little endurance reserves	long duration if society has endurance reserves
scope of damage is more: greater loss of resources	scope of damage is less: resources preserved
intensity of damage---evenly distributed	intensity of damage uneven—either left in tact or some areas benefit
random distribution	seasonal or cyclical distribution
bad timing—during planting season	good timing—when a society is less vulnerable

SOCIAL VARIABLES

Worst case scenario	Minimum damage
concentrated resources loss of technology less investment in technology affects capacity to respond	dispersed resources large investments for mitigation technologies
non-subsistence production: cash crops	subsistence production
within a single lifetime: no basis of comparison	over generations: some basis of comparison
greater population density	less population density
socially central population affected	socially peripheral population affected

PSYCHOLOGICAL VARIABLES

Worst case scenario	Minimum damage
damage more visible	damage less visible
no low point	identifiable low point
no perceived locus of control	perceived locus of control

makes agricultural states breeding grounds for diseases. Further, even *modern* agricultural states do not have well integrated mass communication, transportation systems, or much in the way of state services for their population. The lower classes in the cities and the peasants in the outlying areas can expect little help from these states. Last, the buildings in the cities of agricultural states are typically far from being earthquake proof. According to Miller, "Early farming societies were established in flood plains where floods could destroy both crops and settlements." (Miller 2000, 314) The combination of city-rural interdependency with a lack of well-coordinated response systems makes these societies the most vulnerable to natural disasters.

Michael Barkun (1974) argues that cities and rural areas—whether agricultural or industrial—don't react to a natural disaster in the same way. Cities have a wider mix of people without subgroup loyalties outside the family. This, combined with their influx from other societies, undermines group solidarity. Cities are also more likely to have developed a linear rather than a cyclical sense of time. This means the disaster will be perceived as more threatening, because the future is open, rather than just a point on a predictable cycle that will return to stability. In addition, people living in cities are less identified with the land than are people in rural areas, in part because they are not bound to the land by their work habits and leisure patterns to the same extent. Last, people in cities are less likely to relate to disasters as globally disruptive to all. The heterogeneity of interests makes one group's misfortunes another group's windfall.

So far we have discussed the impact of disasters on societies in general and touched upon cross-cultural variation. But this cross-cultural variation is *modern*. It says nothing about the ancient world. After all, the hunter-gatherer bands and agricultural states that exist today are not the same as those that existed

thousands of years ago. This is largely because of the impact of global capitalism on all non-capitalist societies.

2. Natural Disasters and human response in Bronze Age agricultural states

Figure 10.4 summarizes how the social impacts of technological changes in weaponry plus invasions (chapter 9) and natural disasters (chapter 10) might have interacted. In chapter 9 we saw that civilizations in the Bronze and Iron Ages were not in a constant state of warfare. However, when they did go to war killing was more lethal and greater in scope than previously, thanks to the invention of chariot warfare, the use of infantry and cavalry, and the use of iron swords.

Natural catastrophes by themselves probably did not cause pastoralists to attempt a takeover of agricultural states. Such attempted takeovers in the early Bronze Age were not successful. However, when the occurrence of natural disasters coincided with pastoralists gaining access to lethal weaponry, in the 16th or 17th century BCE, the balance of forces may have tipped in favor of the herders. Notice how most of the invasions on record were concentrated between the seventeenth and the 11th centuries BCE, when chariots and new iron weaponry were accessible and also when natural disasters occurred.

I will begin by assessing the possible impact of these disasters on Bronze Age civilizations, using the criteria developed in Figure 11.1. Let us return to the six questions posed in the introduction to this chapter: As we will see, the answers to these questions are closely interwoven with the criteria developed in Figure 11.1.

1. *How different were the natural disasters in the ancient world from those that occur in the modern world?*
As we saw in chapter 10, the natural disasters in the Bronze Age had an impact that

was greater in scope, duration, and intensity than that of any disasters that have occurred since then. Agricultural states had no earthquake retrofitting for buildings and no special agencies within the state to prepare for natural disasters. Whether the damage to society was homogeneous or heterogeneous probably varied. That these events were probably not random but cyclic is suggested by the stories told in these societies of *world ages* that ended in periodic destruction. The disasters described in the last chapter lasted far beyond a single planting season and so, when the disaster struck, its effect would have carried into the next season and perhaps the next few years.

2. *How different were human responses to the disasters in the ancient world as compared to human responses in the modern world?*

Agricultural civilizations had resources concentrated in urban areas as opposed to the dispersed resources of foraging societies. Unlike industrial capitalist states, these societies had peasant populations who produced for subsistence. There was no cash-crop farming, except in Greece. This must have somewhat lessened the impact of natural disasters, because peasants at least had the option of growing their own food.

Furthermore these Bronze Age societies traded with other societies, so they could have received support in recovery through trade. However, the three principal periods of disaster—in the early, middle, and late Bronze Age—affected *all* the major civilizations of the Old World, so all were more or less in the same boat. Agricultural civilizations had high population densities, and many civilizations of the Near East were located near coasts. It is possible that those with the most wealth concentrated in the cities were most severely affected by disasters such as earthquakes, because of the danger of collapsed buildings. Among the peasants this was less of a problem. At the same time, peasants would not have been spared the effects on crops and the death

of their cattle. The disasters were most likely followed by epidemics, because of the conditions already present in these societies:

> Archaeological digs reveal that settlements were abandoned while still intact. This and the predominance of burned villages suggests that epidemics may have been responsible for the extinction of many ancient villages. . . . The population density usually exceeded that of the worst slums of modern cities. This very high population density, coupled with near total lack of sewage facilities, created ideal conditions for the spread of plague, cholera and smallpox. (Miller, 2000, 307)

3. *Was the tension between city and country as severe in the ancient world as it is in the modern world?*

The population of ancient cities was small by today's standards—between 10,000 to 100,000—and the average individual lifespan was half what it is in modern industrial societies, with the mortality rate being much higher: Ancient cities had fewer people and the turnover rate was far higher.

Cities in the ancient world preserved the cyclic sense of time common in the rural zones. While under Judaism and Islam sacred time began a shift toward linearity, at the time of the natural disasters a cyclic sense of time was still in place. Speaking of the relationship between city and country in the ancient world, Murray Bookchin (1987) points out:

> Prudent estimates of the number of rural workers needed to sustain a single city dweller have been placed at a ratio of ten to one. Hence any serious agricultural catastrophe like a drought, floods or pest infestation . . . that devastated agriculture could lead to a breakdown. . . . If they expanded beyond the capacity of their agricultural base they direly needed

tribute from other city-states to sustain themselves. (Bookchin, 1987, 87–88)

The people of the cities were far closer to those in the country than is the case today:

The ancients never doubted that these 'bumpkins' were their 'country cousins' in a very real cultural and material sense. The ancestral farm, if an urban citizen owned one, or the family village where the bones of his ancestors lay, was a place to which he repaired from the demands and stresses of city living. It was there that he found his 'roots' and from there that he carried his household deities into the very confines of the city. (Bookchin, 1987, 90)

This contrasts with the situation in medieval Europe:

From the thirteenth century onward, particularly in Italy and the lowlands of modern Belgium and Holland, city-states began to emerge that were structured around uniquely urban tasks, artisan oriented, financial, commercial and industrial—that slowly loosened urban life from its traditional agrarian matrix and provided the town with an authentic civic life and momentum of its own. (Bookchin, 1987 92)

In the ancient world those who made a profitable income from trade and workshops did not reinvest it in city life. If they could accumulate enough to retire, it would be on property in the country. It the medieval world both artisans and merchants identified with city life and were not embarrassed by their vocations.

The medieval city was not just a sacred and administrative center. European cities, unlike the great agricultural states of the ancient world, were not located in river valleys that lent themselves to centralized irrigation. In Europe, cities were surrounded by forests, which made agriculture decentralized. As Bookchin says, in Europe feudalistic agriculture was too disorganized to be a permanent fetter on city development.

4. *How similar were the psychological reactions of the ancients to those of modern people?*

In agricultural states there was much less likelihood of an individualistic reaction to the disasters. These were collectivist societies, as we will see in chapter 16. It is more likely that people would have been psychologically devastated in collectivist societies than in industrial societies because, as we will see in chapters 12 and 15, in the former people were far more attached to their environment and the effects on the environment were unmistakably visible. A disaster that drove them from that environment would literally drive them out of their minds.

Because the scope, intensity, frequency, and duration of these disasters were extreme, the need for the avoidance of cognitive ambiguity was probably acute. However there are at least two processes working against this. One is that decontextualized, dualistic abstractions in thinking which began in the Axial Iron Age with the development of coined money and the alphabet were not yet in operation (see chapter 15 for more on this). This meant that people saw cognitive opposites as *polarities,* not dualities—which go with a cyclic notion of change. This way of thinking would have worked against dualistic scapegoating, which must have flourished more readily following the emergence of a monotheistic god and an absolutely evil devil. The other factor that worked against cognitive ambiguity was the mythology of the ancients, which had built into its cosmology an *anticipation* of natural disasters. This probably lessened the trauma.

Totaling up all the parameters in Figure 11.2, there are at least 10 factors present in the ancient world that could be considered as

Figure 11.2 Impact of Natural Disasters on Bronze Age Agricultural States

Worst case scenario   **Minimum damage**

ENVIRONMENTAL PARAMETERS

frequent or multiple impact--**yes**	infrequent and single impact
short duration—no preparation	
long duration—if society has little endurance reserves-- **yes**	long duration if society has endurance reserves
scope of damage is more: greater loss of resources--**yes**	scope of damage is less: resources preserved
intensity of damage—evenly distributed--**both**	intensity of damage uneven
random distribution	seasonal or cyclical--**yes**
bad timing—during planting season—**yes**	good timing—when a society is less vulnerable

SOCIAL VARIABLES

concentrated resources--**yes**	dispersed resources
large investment in technology. If lost less investment in technology affects capacity to respond	large investments for mitigation
non-subsistence production: cash crops	subsistence production--**yes**
within a single lifetime: no basis of comparison	over generations: some basis of comparison--**yes**
greater population density--**yes**	less population density
socially central population affected--**yes**	socially peripheral population affected

PSYCHOLOGICAL VARIABLES

damage more visible--**yes**	damage less visible
no low point--**yes**	identifiable low point
no perceived locus of control--**yes**	perceived locus of control

leading to the worst-case scenario, three that would have led to minimum damage, and one that could fit in either category.

3. Women, men, and stress in modern times

Before addressing the possible differences in how men and women handled stress in the ancient world we must first survey how women and men handle stress *today*. In their research work *Gender and Stress*, Barnett and Biener *et al.* (1987) argue that gender differences in physiological reactions to stress are minor compared to the similarities. They summarize their findings by pointing out that:

Relative to females, males show exaggerated reactions to stress in some, but not all of the variables measured. It has been observed consistently that both the plasma and urinary excretions of epinephrine rise more appreciably in males than in females during subject's exposure to achievement-oriented laboratory tasks or stressors. Other neuroendocrine reactions either do not differ between males and females (e.g., norepinephrine) or show no consistent pattern related to gender (cortisol). (Barnett and Biener, 1987, 31)

However, this does not mean that under all circumstances women have less exaggerated reactions: "[I]n a situation likely to be equally if not more involving for women—accompanying one's child to the hospital—epinephrine excretion was as high in mothers as in fathers." (Barnett and Biener, 1987, 356)

The bulk of this section will deal with the differences between how women and men deal with stress in three primary settings—at work, at home, and with social networks. Lastly I will touch upon coping mechanisms.

According to Barnett and Biener, three theories shape research on the impact of gender on social roles:

The first, the 'social-role' hypothesis asserts that there are *no* gender differences in the nature of social roles . . . both employment and marriage confer many mental health advantages; since men more often than women occupy *both* roles, they therefore more often enjoy their benefits. By implication, as more and more women enter the labor force the health advantage currently enjoyed by men will disappear. This formulation assumes that the differences between the role of female employee and male employee as well as those between husband and wife are of negligible significance. (Barnett and Biener, 1987, 137)

The social role hypothesis states that (a) *health* is improved by occupying more than one role, (b) the roles are separate but *equal* in status, and (c) the roles are *interchangeable* in status—meaning that a woman playing a traditionally male role would be treated essentially the same as if she were a man.

The second theory, the "scarcity hypothesis," claims that the occupation of a variety of roles by an individual does not improve mental health; instead, *roles drain energy*. Thus the more roles a person plays the less energy that person has and the more conflicts he or she will have to endure. This will result in more stress. One way of explaining the difference between men's and women's stress level is to argue that, since men formerly occupied more roles, they were therefore more drained and were exposed to higher rates of occupational hazards. The assumption is that with women's increasing participation in paid employment they too will experience role-drain, and be subjected to the same occupational hazards—which will cause a *decline* in women's mental health. The scarcity hypothesis assumes that the home life (which was traditionally more women's domain) is less stressful than the world of work.

The third theory, the "sex role hypothesis," agrees with the social role hypothesis that a variety of roles is healthy rather than draining, but that claims that the traditional roles that men and women play are not equal in status; when women play traditional male roles they are not treated in the same manner. Further, traditional female work in the domestic sphere is held to be *more*, rather than less stressful than work in public.

Of the three theories, the sex role hypothesis appears to be most supported by the available research.

Studies show that the playing of multiple roles at both home and work yields a positive effect on health—but not all roles have equally positive effects. House (1974) compiled the following objective criteria that determine whether jobs are conducive to health or stress-producing: (a) occupational status, (b) income, (c) self-employment, (d) hours worked, (e) whether the work is machine-paced, (f) authority over the work of others, and (g) job complexity.

Karasek *et al.* (1987) defined *psychological workload* as having the following components: (a) time pressure, (b) deadline stress, (c) excessive workloads, and (d) conflicting demands. Measures of job control included: (a) routinization verses variety of job content, (b) control over decision making, (c) control of skill utilization and pace of work, and (d) clarity of working roles versus role ambiguity.

Several investigators have examined multiple roles in relation to perceived and objective health measures. Barnett and Biener, summarizing Verbrugge 1983, and Verbrugge and Madans 1985, write:

[T]he *more* [my emphasis] roles a women occupies the healthier she is likely to be. In addition, much of their evidence suggests that the employment role is the strongest correlate of good health for women. . . . Women who were employed and married, with or without children,

had the most favorable health status. Non-employed, nonmarried women with no children reported the worst health profiles. (Barnett and Biener, 1987, 103)

The evidence appears to show that women are healthier with more, not less on their plate, provided that what is on their plate includes working in public. Besides the diversity of work, benefits include "an increase in available social support from co-workers or supervisors, the socio-economic benefits of working outside the home and greater access to and use of health services." (Barnett and Biener, 1987, 103)

It is important to be clear that an increase in health does not imply that women have it *easier* than men at work. As we will see, they have it harder. But the research indicates that paid employment, *regardless of social class and difficulty of the job,* when compared to being a homemaker and nothing but a homemaker, is a predictor of health. "[D]espite the belief that the more high-powered a woman's career, the more danger to her well-being, the advantage is *greater* for women in higher occupational statuses. . . . [In addition,] being employed is beneficial even to women in low-level jobs." (Belle 1982, Ferree 1976, quoted in Barnett and Biener 1987, 134)

The life of a full-time homemaker contains more stress because "The homemaker role is unstructured and invisible, involves women in boring, repetitive and unskilled tasks, affords little prestige, and is enacted in the context of isolation from adult interaction." (Barnett and Biener, 1987, 83)

The intensity of homemaking strains does not vary with women's status aspirations, their formal training, previous occupational experience, or social class. These strains emerge because of the demands encountered *within* [my emphasis] the home rather than because of unfulfilled dreams outside the home (Barnett and Biener, 1987, 84)

If men are fathers and they work too, they should also be experiencing great stress. But this assumes that the roles of father and mother are separate but equal. Barnett and Biener challenge this:

Married women more than married men experience extensive family role demands. Due to different normative expectation . . . the roles of wife and mother are likely to be more time consuming and expansive, to involve more areas of responsibility, and to be more disruptive of other social roles than the roles of husband and father. (Barnett and Biener, 1987, 87)

Being a mother is rarely associated with psychological well-being and is often associated with psychological distress. Findings from recent studies indicate that being in the role of mother did not predict any three well-being indicators—that is self-esteem, pleasure or low levels of depressive symptomatology. With respect to physical health, mothers compared to nonmothers have a small advantage. This health advantage, however, is dependent on the ages and number of children. The combination of little control, relentless demands, and great responsibility exposes wives and mothers to many frustrations and failure (Barnett and Biener, 1987, 132–133)

In contrast to the belief that women's occupancy of family roles is critical to their psychological well-being, evidence suggests instead that women's mental and physical health is *not* dependent on their being in the role of wife or mother.

What about the role of husband? The traditional husband role typically combines low demands and high control, thus perhaps accounting for the beneficial effects of marriage on health outcomes for men: "Because men define their work role as fulfilling their family

roles they are less likely to experience inter-role conflict if their work cuts into their family time." (Barnett and Biener, 1987, 131)

In short, the roles of husband and father are understood by men as being subordinate to work. The role of wife and mother is understood by women as being more important than work, so there is a built-in conflict whenever a woman works.

The imbalances in the expectations in the roles of husband and father versus wife and mother can be seen in the differences in health between men and women who are married. Several studies of psychological health indicate that men benefit more than women from being married. (Gove, 1972, 1973, 1978; Cheary and Mechanic, 1983).

With respect to physical health too, there are indications that men benefit more from the role of spouse than do women. Whereas disease morbidity and mortality rates tend to be lowest among the married, they are lower among married men than married women. . . . Overall, findings suggest that marriage is more productive for men than it is for women. (Barnett and Biener, 1987, 128)

The range of stressors for women, from the least to the most, looks something like this:

1. women with middle or upper middle-class occupations who are married with children
2. women with working-class jobs who are married with children
3. women who are married but who do not work in public
4. women who are unemployed and not married.

I did not find any research that compared the differences in health between married middle- and upper middle-class women with children who were not working with married working-class women who were working.

Today, though the majority (60 percent) of women with family responsibilities are choosing to work, the percentage of jobs that have been traditionally male that are really open to them is still low. Women are concentrated in clerical and helping professions rather than in executive or blue-collar jobs. Further, the roles that women do occupy are far from conforming to the "separate but equal" scenario of the social role hypothesis: "Jobs traditionally held by women are often characterized by tedious and repetitive tasks, low authority and autonomy, limited upward mobility, rewards for vicarious rather than direct achievements, and under-utilization of skills and talents." (Barnett and Biener 1987, 98)

The most stressful job conditions are those that combine a low level of decision-making latitude—for example, having little control over the pacing of tasks or the allocation of resources—with tasks that are psychologically demanding, such as those that have time pressure, deadlines, large workloads, and conflicting or heavy emotional demands. "This 'high strain' combination is related to elevated risk for such negative health outcomes as coronary heart disease and ulcers. . . . [T]o illustrate, a surgeon and a nurse may face similar levels of psychological demands, but they differ greatly in their power to control how they deal with these demands." (Barnett and Biener, 1987, 131)

Occupations in which there is high demand on the one hand and low control on the other have the highest coronary-vascular disease outcomes.

In contrasting the difference between "male" and "female" jobs, Barnett and Biener report:

Men and women are likely to differ in the nature of problems typically encountered in the workplace. [In one study] only one of four general types of role strain examined in this research did women and men have similar experiences: encountering noxious environmental conditions in the work setting, such as the presence of dust and direct, or exposure to injury or illness. . . . Men were more likely than women to encounter strain from job pressures and the time demands of the work task. Problems of this type include having too much work to do, working too many hours, doing tasks that no one else wants to do. . . . In contrast women were more likely than men to experience difficulties related to receiving inadequate rewards, such as earning insufficient income, lack of job security, inadequate fringe benefits and limited opportunities for future job advancement. (1987, 85–86)

Finally, women do not have the same powers within traditionally male jobs even when they do manage to occupy them: "Women have been found to have less control over the work of other people than men, even in positions of similar educational and occupational status." (Barnett and Biener, 1987, 98)

In summarizing the relationship between work and home, Barnett and Biener state: "It is ironic that the roles that appear to be most predictive for women's and men's well-being are those ignored in the core role models. *For men the role of husband seems central for psychological well-being; for women, it is the role of paid employee.* [my emphasis] (Barnett and Biener 1987, 134)

I will now turn to the impact of social networks on men and women. According to Barnett and Biener (1987), women are more impacted by events that are stressful to people about whom they care. Men, despite their ability to empathize, live lives that are less involved with the emotional concerns of others. Men's concern for others may show itself in particular relationships, but does not extend as far into their social networks. (Barnett and Biener, 1987, 149)

But not only is women's experience of stressful events that happen to kin and neighbors somewhat different than that of men, women's roles imply a greater expectation of obligation to *respond* to the problems of kin and neighbors than do men's roles. This leads to role overload, because both men and women look to women for support:

Women are more likely than men to be named as helpers in a crisis situation. For each of four types of problems—economic and work-related, interpersonal, death and health—the proportion of female helpers exceeds that of male helpers. Women are somewhat more likely than men to seek the support of other women, but men also report more female than male helpers. Women report having more helpers than men for all four types of problems. . . . [W]omen were 30% more likely than men to provide some type of support. (Barnett and Biener, 1987, 148-149)

Furthermore, providing support on one occasion can be interpreted as an obligation to provide *ongoing* support, which is a further energy drain.

Finally we turn to coping techniques for stress. Problem-focused coping is action oriented. The individual goes directly to the perceived source of stress and tries to either dissolve or modify it. She or he does this by developing plans, strategies and tactics. Emotion-based coping does not try to change the situation but looks for emotional support from others; the existing situation is accepted as given. Research indicates that men use problem-focused coping more, while women use emotion-focused techniques more.

This difference in coping strategies can be meaningfully connected to gender stratification. It makes sense that because men in general have more power and privileges, men will have more

experience and hence confidence that many problems can be resolved by taking action; after all, they have had success in the past. Conversely, for women with less power and privilege, problem-focused coping doesn't pay. It makes more sense to accept the situation and change how one feels about it, because one's emotional reaction appears to be more under one's control.

Whether one strategy or another is adaptive greatly depends on whether the situation itself is easy or difficult to change. Problem-focused coping is more adaptive in situations that are not difficult to change. However, in situations that are too big for individuals or groups to change, problem-focused coping will be maladaptive. (This is important in considering how men are likely to cope with natural disasters). Emotion-based coping works better in situations that are uncontrollable.

Using a problem-focused strategy in uncontrollable situations will add to stress and may trigger an emotion that research suggests men experience far more than women—anger.

There is one negative emotion that is expressed more by men than by women and is consistent with male gender norms—the expression of anger. . . . It may be . . . that anger is the one emotion that yields no physiological benefit in its expression. While there is evidence that suppression of anger is related to elevated blood pressure for men as well as women, it is not necessarily true that anger expression is associated with *decreased* [my emphasis] physiological or cardiac reactivity. . . . [H]yperassertion, in addition to lacking physiological benefit may push people away, leaving the enraged person isolated and cut off from confidant relationships. (Barnett and Biener, 1987, 358)

Barnett and Biener summarize their research on stress by claiming that it is in *moderately* stressful situations that gender differences are most likely to show themselves. In extremely stressful situations the *commonality of humanity* overrides gender differences. In low-stress circumstances *personality* differences are the leading factor. It is in the middle range of stress that socialized gender differences are most likely to be decisive.

4. Natural disasters and gender stress in modern times compared cross-culturally

I will begin this section by presenting research on the impact of *modern* disasters on gender relations. In the last section I will bring the first four sections of this chapter into a synthesis in order to show how natural disasters might have impacted gender relations in Bronze Age civilizations.

Alice Fothergill synthesized over 100 studies of populations in the United States and other industrialized nations, with some research on industrializing countries, that addressed gender issues in disasters. She developed a nine-stage typology based on stages of natural disasters. I paraphrase her results below, interspersed with quotes and conclusions from other anthropologists.

(1) *Exposure to risk*

In their text, *The Angry Earth,* two anthropologists who study natural disasters (Oliver-Smith and Hoffman, 1999) argue against what they consider to be a naïve environmental determinism. They claim that the social structure already in place before disasters mediates how the disaster will be dealt with and how the disaster will be experienced.

Because women in general have less power than men before a natural disaster occurs, they are more vulnerable to hazards during and after a disaster.

Gender is a pervasive division affecting all societies, and it channels access to social and economic resources away from

women and towards men. Women are often denied the vote, the right to inherit land and generally have less control over income-earning opportunities and cash within their own households. Normally their access to resources is inferior to that of men. Since our argument is that less access to resources, in the absence of other compensations to provide safe conditions, leads to increased vulnerability, we contend that in general women are more vulnerable to hazards. (Enarson and Morrow, 1998, 2)

This means that, in societies with rigid female subordination structures, if caretakers have to make a choice between children as to which to save and which to let go, boys will have preference.

One "myth" about how women and men behave during natural disasters is that women become "damsels in distress" to be rescued by heroic men: "Typecast as hapless victims protected and rescued by vigilant men, women are in fact also present in every disaster response as mitigators, preparers, rescuers, caregivers, sustainers, and rebuilders." (Enarson and Morrow, 1998, 6)

In "normal" times, women experience more stress than men in both home and work; so too, in times of natural disasters women do double duty in the public and domestic worlds. Women are frontline participants during the crisis and they are long-term caregivers to those in their social network who are affected by the disaster.

Seventy percent of those in poverty in the world are women. These means that before a disaster strikes they have less food; they are living in more dangerous shelters due to inadequate construction materials; they are located in areas where disasters have been known to hit before, because they have no other place to live; and they have less access to "official reports" because they have less consistent access to mass media.

(2) Risk perception

Women perceive disaster events or threats as more serious and risky than do men: "women may show more concern with danger, human suffering and loss of life, while men were more preoccupied with knowing the specific technical aspects of protective measures." (Enarson and Morrow, 1998, 14)

(3) Preparedness behavior

Official disaster management organization is male dominated and organized in a military top-down manner. Men manage the operations and women deliver provisions, if they are present at all. In societies where the state has disaster organizations in place women are more limited to the domestic world where they prepare family members, build up supplies and prepare the inside of the house for the storm. If men were present they shore up the outside of the house.

(4) Warning communication and response

Women are more likely to receive risk communication due to their *social networks* and to respond with protective actions such as evacuation. Men are more distrustful of information coming from peers and are more likely to deny that there is a problem and to stay longer on the site.

(5) Physical impacts

It is difficult to say whether more men or women, proportionally, are likely to die in disasters. This would depend on the kind of disaster and whether it is men or women who are likely to be outside their house at the time. Lightning and hurricanes are much more likely to be lethal to people who are outdoors during the event. On the other hand, an earthquake may be more lethal to those indoors. Women may be more vulnerable in this case because child care often requires staying indoors.

There are socio-cultural reasons why disasters may be harsher on women than on men: "Several recent studies also show increased rates of domestic violence in terms of disasters. Women in 'developing' countries are more likely to die in disasters due to discriminatory practices, women's location in a disaster and childcare responsibilities. (Enarson and Morrow, 1998, 17)

(6) psychological impacts

Men and women internalize their experiences differently. Fothergill found that, following natural disasters, women had more mental health problems—depression, post-traumatic stress disorder, and anxiety. Men had more behavioral problems such as drinking and attention problems. Men seem to cope well with extreme events in the present but have difficulty expressing anxieties. This difficulty may come back to haunt them later, since men have a delayed reaction to stress that may come two years or more after the event.

During and after natural disasters, men tend to rely on the problem-focused coping techniques discussed in the previous section on stress.

Men appear often to look for practical, not emotional, solutions to disaster and when there is no role for practical help (perhaps because this role has been assumed by official agencies) or because the damage is such that the level of help necessary is beyond their capacities they can suffer anxieties and emotional disturbances. (Enarson and Morrow, 1998, 92)

If we consider that this anxiety is likely to be compounded with loss of perceived control and with men's general tendency to become more angry than women, it is not far-fetched to assume that women, as a visible and subordinated group, will likely be the recipient of this anger: "These emotional impacts of disaster can ripple outward from those directly involved to others in their family or in the community." (Enarson and Morrow, 1998, 92)

Women, on the other hand, are in danger of losing their sense of self:

> Women often suffer from physical and emotional exhaustion in post trauma period . . . and women in the traditional role of homemakers and caretakers are most at risk of losing their sense of self after a disasters as they always put the family needs before their own. Women caregiving roles expand dramatically after a disaster and the demands on women are an extreme version of their predisaster obligations. (Enarson and Morrow, 1998, 19)

(7) *Emergency response*

In his text *Social Psychology* (1998), Fathali Moghaddam challenges the notion that in emergency situations men are more helpful than women. He defines altruism as behavior intended to help another without regard for benefit to oneself. He claims that there are two kinds of altruism—heroic and nurturant:

> Heroic altruism is often short term, requires physical action and is public or 'visible" Most important heroic altruism does not commit the helper to a long-term relationship. A person who runs into a smoke-filled house to save some strangers is not committed to stay and develop long-term relationships with the fire victims. Nurturant altruism . . . requires a longer involvement, tends to be private rather than public and is passive in the sense that the help-giver may spend more time listening and sympathizing than taking decisive action. In the context of traditional values, heroic altruism tends to fit a more masculine gender role, whereas nuturant altruism is a closer fit for the traditional female gender role. (Moghaddam, 1998, 298)

According to Forthergill, most studies address helping behavior in the public sphere, which corresponds to heroic altruism, thus ignoring nurturant altruism.

> Men are more likely than women to volunteer and participate in certain response work such as search and rescue, while women are more likely to help with the provision of supplies. . . . Women often do the unheralded clean up duty, sweeping up glass, and doing minor repairs—work that is not visible, receives no media attention and remains largely unrecognized. (Enarson and Morrow, 1998, 20)

(8) *Recovery*

The recovery phase is defined as about a one-year timeframe following a disaster. Forthergill reports that women may be more likely than men to receive help from their families and to seek and receive aid from public assistance. A significant number of men interpret aid from public agencies as a stigma that threatens their role as "provider."

In "developing" countries, women's low status guarantees that they won't receive as much food as men to begin with. Women will have less access to jobs and resources and the loss of a husband will guarantee descent into poverty if a woman does not have an older son to take over. The cost of hiring labor for help is beyond the means of most woman-headed households. On the average, women marry men who are ten years older. When women reach middle age and the husband dies, prospects for remarriage are slim.

Women's attempts to do traditional male work raise other problems:

> Women headed households in a male dominated rural society present special problems. The cultural division of labor does not permit a man to do women's work without suffering loss of face. Women often do men's work but the reality of this fact is distorted or ignored since by prevailing ideology women do 'unproductive' domestic labor. . . . Women lose status by carrying out male tasks in a peasant family. (Enarson and Morrow, 1998, 68)

(9) *Reconstruction*

Fothergill's synthesis of research shows that the poor or women have the most difficult time returning to the normal routines of their lives in the wake of a natural catastrophe. This includes the return to domestic life.

It should be mentioned that for some the temporary accommodation following a disaster was a respite or even seen as a holiday before the more stressful return to the home:

> I was happy at the caravan. . . . It was summer. It was a proper caravan site. The kids had got the playground and we'd got the laundry where we could go and do the washing. We'd got to shop if you ran out of anything. . . . I could have quite happily stayed in that. . . . [T]hat time in the caravan site to me was breathing space. (Enarson and Morrow, 1998, 88)

For emergency planners, the ultimate goal was to get people back to their homes. For a significant portion of the population, this was not experienced as a relief:

> Utopia for them would be getting the keys to their houses. . . . I don't think there was one person who coped with that. When they got their keys, that was when they collapsed. We had people collapsing on the pavements, on the path going up to their houses, getting the key in the door but couldn't turn the key (Enarson and Morrow, 1998, 89)

Fothergill concludes that:

> The disaster data presented here advance the notion that women's lower status and lack of economic power in society in so-called 'normal times' has serious ramifications in a disaster situation . . . such as women's lack of decision-making power in evacuation, their dismissal by officials as 'hysterical,' the denial of leadership position to women in emergency management, women's subjection to domestic violence, and the devaluation of women's work throughout the disaster process. Disasters, like non-disaster periods, are a time and place where gender inequality is maintained and reproduced. (Enarson and Morrow, 1998, 23)

Figure 11.3 Comparing Effects on Women in Modern vs. Ancient Natural Disasters

Stage of Disaster	Modern		Ancient Bronze Age States
	Core	Non-Core	
1) Exposure to risk	Deskilled domestic work Less children, less adult help.	Women exposed more than men: less land, less opportunity for public work Live in shoddy shelters on dangerous land Preferential treatment for boys. Less access to official reports Similar to Bronze Age states	No opportunity for public work Less dangerous land Same as Non-Core No official reports by state Creative cottage industry work More children, more adult help
2) Risk perception	Women show more concern for people, men with technical aspects Women more attached to children Men internal locus of control; women external	Similar to Bronze Age states	Women less attached to children because of high death rate Men and women, external locus of control
3) Preparedness behavior	Women excluded from state controlled disaster agencies	Similar to Core	No state-controlled disaster agencies for anyone
4) Warning communication	Women trust network of peers; men distrustful of peers and stay on the site longer	Similar to Bronze Age states	More dense but limited network. No mass communication
5) Physical impact	Less severe in scope, intensity and frequency	Similar to Core Peasants vulnerable–grow cash crops More people die in absolute numbers (larger population) Same as Bronze Age states	More severity in scope, intensity, frequency Peasants less vulnerable—grow own crops More people die in relative numbers (smaller population) Domestic violence more severe. No state institutional constraints
	Rise in domestic violence towards women State institutional constraints		

Figure 11.3 Continued : Comparing Effects on Women in Modern vs. Ancient Natural Disasters

Stage of Disaster	Modern		Ancient Bronze Age States
	Core	Non-Core	
6) Psychological impact	**Women** Mental distress Emotion-focused **More adaptive** Recipient of anger Loss of self Split between public and domestic identity **Men** Behavioral distress Problem-focused **Less adaptive** More prone to anger	No loss of self No split between public and domestic identity	Problem-focused maladaptive
7) Emergency response	Nurturing altruism Heroic altruism Media attention		No heroic altruism for anyone (marginal public space, few strangers)
8) Recovery	More accepting of public help Public help a stigma	Similar to Bronze Age states	No public help for anyone
9) Reconstruction		Similar to Bronze Age states Similar to Bronze Age states Similar to Bronze Age states Similar to Bronze Age states Similar to Bronze Age states	Women less likely to remarry (women marry men 10 years older) Men more likely to remarry **Infrastructure damaged?** Women have less access to food and work Men stigmatized for doing "female work" Women stigmatized for doing "male work" Women have difficulty resuming routines

5. Natural disasters and gender stress in Bronze Age agricultural states

In this last section I will again discuss Fothergill's nine stages of disaster, this time integrating the following material:

- Figure 11.2 on the impact of natural disasters on Bronze Age states
- Differences between men and women in stress levels as applied to work, and home settings, social networks. Differences in coping mechanisms
- How men and women differ in response to natural disasters in modern times.

After reviewing the nine stages we will be in a position to conclude the chapter by answering the last two questions posed at the beginning of the chapter:

5. *Did men and women deal with stress from natural disasters any differently in the ancient world than they do today?* and,
6. *How did men treat women during natural disasters in Bronze Age states?*

Before beginning our comparison of modern to ancient responses to natural disasters we must distinguish three types of modern societies. This way we can properly target *which* modern societies we are comparing to the ancient world. World-systems theory proposes that modern societies are now interdependent parts of a single world-capitalist system. Within this system there are three zones:

(a) Core countries with an industrial-electronic energy base; these include the United States, Western Europe, and Japan. These are the most powerful countries.

(b) Semi-peripheral countries with an industrial-agricultural base; these exist primarily in Eastern Europe, Asia, and Latin America. These societies have less power than core countries.

(c) Peripheral countries with a horticultural base; these exist principally in Africa. These countries have the least power.

It is the semi-peripheral and peripheral countries that, in modern time, most resemble Bronze Age agricultural states, and it is these modern zones that will be used as a basis for comparison, for the most part.

(1) *Exposure to risk*

Exposure to risk in ancient societies, as in comparable modern societies, was and is relative to women's existing place before natural disasters hit. In Bronze Age agricultural states institutionalized male dominance was in place without a competing ideology that men and women were in any way equal. This meant that it was easily justifiable for women to receive less food. While women in peripheral and semi-peripheral societies today have limited access to communications media, women in agricultural states (like the men) had none.

To what degree did the causes of stress discussed in the sex role hypothesis (according to which traditional female work in the domestic sphere is held to be *more*, rather than less stressful than work in public) apply to the working conditions and marriages of women in agricultural states? If indeed women do better when they move back and forth between the public and domestic roles, this means that women in both the ancient agricultural states and in modern non-core countries must be seen as disadvantaged.

In Bronze Age states there was very little variety of experience in public for women, a lack of social support on the job (outside the extended family), no economic independence, and there were no health care services (these were not available to anyone). However, while the traditional work roles at home were more stressful than the work that men did, there was no split between public and private identity for women. The traditional roles were not equal, and there were no opportunity for women to play male roles.

However, in some respects the home-life activities of women in the ancient world were more advantageous than those of women in modern non-core societies. For instance, unlike working-class women on the job in modern societies, stress did not come from time pressures or conflicting demands. The main stressor was simply the heavy workload.

Compared to women in modern core countries, women in agricultural states deferred more to male decision-making, yet the process of work in cottage industry did involve more creativity. The adoption of advanced technology in the home has deskilled modern core women, just as the invention of machines deskilled men who worked in factories. Furthermore, like other artisans, women could control the pace at which they worked. While ancient women had more children, they also had more adults around them to help with child-care duties.

Last, as social networkers, women in the ancient world were probably under more stress than modern core women, because there were no state institutions to lift the burden of listening to problems and supporting others. There were no social workers or therapists.

The comparison of Bronze Age agricultural states to *core* countries in modern times yields somewhat different results. A large portion of the population in core countries occupies intermediate positions between the very rich and the very poor. No women in the upper-middle middle classes live in poverty, and even most working-class women enjoy adequate housing conditions and live in geographical areas that are not environmentally dangerous. Also women have access to media reports. This is not to say there are no poor women in industrial core societies, but only that they constitute a smaller section of the population than Bronze Age agricultural states.

(2) *Risk perception*

I suspect that the gap between men and women in risk perception was *less* severe in ancient times and in semi-peripheral and peripheral countries today than it is between men and women in the core countries today. Both women and men in Bronze Age agricultural states had much less of a sense of being in control of their environment. In psychological terms, they had an external locus of control. Furthermore, because of the shortness of life and the high mortality rate, women as well as men were less psychologically attached to their children and kin groups.

(3) *Preparedness behavior*

In Bronze Age societies men could not monopolize formal disaster-management institutions because such institutions did not exist. The state did deliver periodic prophecies based on oracles, but there was nothing like the capacity to predict the coming of hurricanes or tornadoes that we have today. Thus there was far less preparedness in the ancient world than in any modern society. While semi-peripheral and peripheral modern countries do not have the wealth that core countries have to invest in meteorological projections, the United Nations provides some rudimentary help.

(4) *Warning communication and response*

In Bronze Age agricultural states the kin groups of tribal societies had weakened and, in the cities, social groups were divided into castes. While social castes did not discuss warning communication with each other, people had social networks within their social castes that could have served this function. While peasants in the rural areas of agricultural states must have had social networks, these networks were more limited than those in semi-peripheral and peripheral countries today. This is because in ancient times there were few roads between peasant households.

(5) *Physical impacts*

As discussed in section 2, in duration, scope, intensity and frequency the natural disasters discussed in chapter 10 were considerably more powerful than natural disasters in modern times. This means that in *relative* numbers far more men and women died then as compared to those who die in disasters in non-core countries today. However, in non-core societies today, many more people die in *absolute numbers* because the overall size of the population is greater.

Nevertheless the manner in which Bronze Age societies coped with these disasters had some advantages compared to the way non-core countries cope with disasters today. For example, the fact that peasants grew their own food no doubt helped them get by: unlike peasants in current non-core countries, they were not growing one crop for exports, thereby making them more vulnerable for help and dependent upon food aid.

I suspect that domestic violence would have been at least as bad in ancient times as it is in non-core countries today. For one thing, wife beating was prevalent in Bronze Age societies and the occurrence of natural disasters was likely to have made things even worse for women than they already were, for reasons we will take up in the next section. The absence of domestic violence centers would have meant that there were fewer external constraints operating.

(6) *Psychological impacts*

The gender difference in coping mechanisms would probably have implied worse consequences for women in the ancient world than it does for their modern counterparts, because natural disasters were so much more powerful then. Men would have felt they had less control over the situation than they do in modern times. If it is true that men in Bronze Age agricultural states expressed anger more readily than women did (and I see no reason why they wouldn't have), and we combine that increased expression of anger with a sense that the natural disaster is beyond their problem-focused capacity, it is not far-fetched to assume that men would have frequently taken out their hostility on a target that was both subordinate and visible—women.

As we will see in a later chapter on the self, women tend to have vertical collectivist selves. Because of this, it makes sense that women would have subordinated themselves in relation to husbands, brothers, and children in Bronze Age states, as they continue to do in non-core countries today. A natural disaster might intensify this tendency. Yet in the context of the ancient world this would not have seemed a "loss" of sense of self.

As we will see in the next subsection (on emergency response), natural disasters can result in a definite loss of sense of self in women in core countries in the modern world. However this is the loss of an *individualist self*, one that is capable of choosing to put oneself before one's husband or family. This was not an issue for women in the Bronze Age states.

(7) *Emergency response*

In considering Bronze Age societies the distinction between heroic altruism for men and nurturant altruism for women must be significantly tempered. In order for heroic altruism to exist there must be a critical mass of strangers to rescue and these strangers must inhabit an area of a social space defined as "public." As we will see in later chapters, the number of strangers in agricultural states was relatively small compared to the situation in all modern societies. Furthermore, the zones that can be characterized as "public" were small compared to those in modern societies. While it is probably fair to say that women in Bronze Age societies were more nurturing than men, and that men would be more preoccupied with the impact of disasters outside the home, it should not be assumed that men spent much of their time helping strangers in public. It is a stretch to credit men in these societies with heroic altruism.

A natural disaster can throw the existing order into question. At least two responses are possible. One is to challenge the existing institutions and agitate for forms of social life that have not been tried before, which are more democratic and, to use a modern political term, "progressive." It is tempting to argue that the impact of natural disasters might cause women to question their status relative to social influence, prestige, privilege and power during these times. It is certainly true that in modern societies with extreme inequality and dictatorial governments, people do sometimes take advantage of a natural disaster as a catalyst for economic and political revolution. However, in

order for this to happen, an opposition movement must be in place before the disaster occurs. Without this there may be rioting, but the rioting will not lead to political and economic change. There was no women's movement in the ancient world (the reasons for this are discussed in the last chapter); thus there was no possibility for a revolution in gender relations.

Where there is no preexisting progressive movement, following a disaster the existing order may be challenged by conservative groups that agitate for more rigid social structures and traditional roles for men and women. Thus it is far more likely that, in the ancient world, institutionalized male dominance was *strengthened* by the presence of natural disasters.

The power of natural disasters to "conservatize" people can be seen in Susanna Hoffman's description of her involvement in the Oakland firestorm of 1989 (Oliver-Smith and Hoffman, 1999). The Oakland firestorm was the largest firestorm in United States urban history, leaving 6000 people homeless. Ninety-five percent of this population lost every possession. This case study is especially important because of where it happened, who it happened to, and how women responded. The firestorm occurred in a core industrial capitalist country; to women who were middle- to upper-middle class, who were politically progressive, and for whom feminism was a very important movement. If ever there could be a situation in which women might be expected to break out of the traditional gender roles during a natural disaster, assume public roles, and help strangers, this one would seem to be the best candidate. However this is not what happened:

> But for many, progress in carving out new gender behavior suffered a fifty-year setback after the firestorm. In the shock of loss, both men and women retreated into traditional cultural realms and personas. Men launched into command and took

action. Assuming the family helm, they proceeded to exercise autonomous decision making. For example the husband of one woman . . . would not let her speak to the insurance adjuster, architect or contractor and refused to allow her input on the design of their new home.

Women found themselves thrown into utter domesticity. Whether they worked in the outside world or not, women drowned in a veritable sea of . . . homely detail. . . . Women's caretaking roles expand dramatically at all stages of disaster response. . . . To women, immediately and for the course of several years of the recovery, fell almost all the child-care chores, the soothing, clothing, feeding, tending and chauffeuring of the young. . . . Women . . . fell unwittingly into old habits of compliance. As men picked rental houses and very often commandeered family finances, money allocation, the filling out of paperwork, the choice of professionals . . . women retreated in silence and acquiesced. (Oliver-Smith and Hoffman, 1999, 177)

Unlike many men who went back to work, "Many women quit their jobs or took extensive leaves. Women could not reconcile their now-massive domestic chores with their outside occupations. . . . They retreated from careers such as social work and hospital administration." (Oliver-Smith and Hoffman, 1999, 179)

Women took up small tasks while the men took on the larger-scaled projects such as attending meetings and hiring crews. Thus old gender patterns translated into the claiming of space and the buying of equipment: "Extra room became men's exclusive workspace, with the first objects bought frequently beings men's computers and equipment. . . . Many insurance companies issued checks for homes in men's

names alone." (Oliver-Smith and Hoffman, 1999, 179)

Hoffman sums up by saying that "the return of old behaviors and the loss of new was so swift, so engulfing and so unconscious that few understood what occurred." (179)

If this post-disaster conservatizing of women could happen in an industrial society with the clear presence of a women's movement, to middle and upper-middle class women with sound resources and good jobs, what chance would poor, illiterate peasant women (who constituted 90% of the population of agricultural states) have to challenge institutionalized male dominance in the absence of a women's movement—and the presence of much more extensive and prolonged disasters such as floods, earthquakes, and volcanic eruptions?

(8) *Recovery*

Whatever recovery went on in the ancient world, there was no issue of receiving aid from the state, as state institutions were not set up to provide systematically for citizens in the event of a disaster. If the disaster made institutionalized male dominance worse than it was before the disaster, the "recovery" period would have presented essentially the same problems for women as were outlined in section 4 of this chapter.

(9) *Reconstruction*

Since the state provided no alternative services, there was no respite from the return to the domestic household.

Figure 11.3 summarizes this section into a chart showing the similarities and differences in gender relations in Bronze Age agricultural states as compared to Modern core and non-core capitalist states.

Finally we are in a position to answer the last two questions posed at the beginning of this chapter:

5. *Did men and women deal with stress in natural disasters any differently in the ancient world than they do today?*

Yes, responses were different. The intensity, scope, frequency, and duration of the disasters were far greater than those of disasters today, and so a much larger percentage of the population was affected. The people had no state agencies to warn them, to help prepare them, or to assist them with recovery. Though state disaster centers for preparedness and recovery in the modern world may be male dominated, this is better than having nothing in place. Bronze Age peasants had one advantage over non-core peasants in modern societies, in that it was easier for the former to grow their own crops. However, since the damage from the disasters in the Bronze Age was so extensive, the growing of food crops might have been virtually impossible for several seasons at a time in any case.

6. *How did men treat women during natural disasters in Bronze Age states as compared to modern times?*

The short answer: probably worse. At the time natural disasters struck in the early, middle, and late Bronze Ages, institutionalized male dominance was already in place. This meant that women were more exposed to risk because they already had less political, economic, and technological power. Women in Bronze Age states had some advantages over modern women homemakers in core countries, in that they enjoyed skilled, creative labor in cottage industry; less attachment to children; and less of a split between public and domestic identity. But the split that modern women feel implies a possibility of using natural disasters as opportunities to make gender relations more equal.

Even prior to the disasters of the Bronze Age, domestic violence against women was quite common. It is hard to imagine that matters did not deteriorate when there were no state interventions to help women against domestic violence or to provide a support network. If men's problem-focused coping mechanism does not work well in modern disasters, it would have worked even more poorly during ancient disasters, when events were even more out of human control. This would have led to less adaptive behavior on the part of men, and hence more anger, some of which would probably have been directed at women.

At the end of section 3 on gender stress, I quoted the conclusion of Barnett and Biener (1987) that in extremely stressful circumstances gender differences wouldn't be very great because men's and women's common humanity would override gender differences. They argue that it is under moderate stress that gender differences reveal themselves. But, as stated earlier, the example they use for extreme stress is a fire—a relatively short-term event. The events in the ancient world were of far longer duration. I propose that in the short run, during the most immediate and severe aspects of fires, floods and earthquakes, the feeling of 'common humanity' would have been present. In the long run, however, during the aftermath, as people adapted to the change in climate, the failed crops, famine and disease, this "common humanity" would have waned and the gender patterns that existed before the natural disaster, in the absence of a women's movement, would have returned in greater force.

Therefore, to answer the question posed at the beginning of the chapter, floods, earthquakes, and volcanoes probably *intensified* institutionalized male dominance. This only eased up in the Axial Iron Age when natural disasters ceased, and when economic, political, and religious changes softened the worst aspects of institutionalized male dominance. This is the subject of chapter 13.

Figure 11.4 Composite Figure of Natural Disasters and Gender Stress
(Chapters 10 and 11)

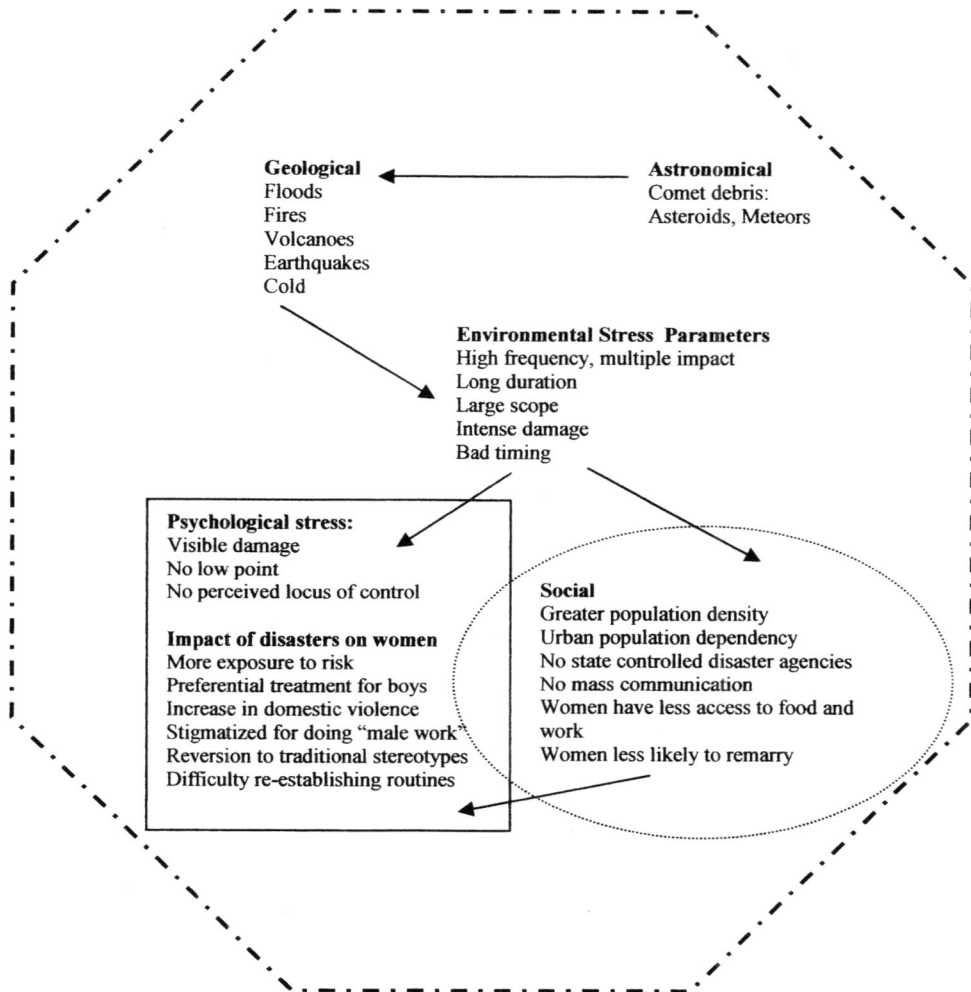

Geological
Floods
Fires
Volcanoes
Earthquakes
Cold

Astronomical
Comet debris:
Asteroids, Meteors

Environmental Stress Parameters
High frequency, multiple impact
Long duration
Large scope
Intense damage
Bad timing

Psychological stress:
Visible damage
No low point
No perceived locus of control

Impact of disasters on women
More exposure to risk
Preferential treatment for boys
Increase in domestic violence
Stigmatized for doing "male work"
Reversion to traditional stereotypes
Difficulty re-establishing routines

Social
Greater population density
Urban population dependency
No state controlled disaster agencies
No mass communication
Women have less access to food and
work
Women less likely to remarry

Part IV

Phase 2: Legitimization, Superstructural Justification

Chapter 12

Primitive and Secondary Magic: From Animism to Polytheism

I have completed my description of all of the forces of coercion and stress that affected ancient societies and contributed to the rise of institutionalized male dominance (chapters 8 through 11). In the next two chapters we will look at the sacred forces that *legitimized* institutionalized male dominance (the third stage of female submission of the cycle of coercion, internalization, and legitimation). We will see that primitive magic justified egalitarian relations between women and men while secondary magic legitimized the rise of men over women. The emergence of sky-god religion consolidated and deepened gender hierarchies in some Axial Age civilizations and softened them in others.

In the first two sections of this chapter I will provide a quick overview of the differences between magic and religion. Then I will proceed to define primitive and secondary magic more precisely, and will close with a discussion about the role of magic as a legitimizing force. I will postpone to the next chapter an in-depth discussion of religion, where it will be connected with the social effects of natural disasters in the ancient world, resulting from the impact of debris from comets and asteroids, as discussed in chapter 10.

1. Commonalties between magic and religion

In my previous book (Lerro, 2000) I argued that a distinction must be preserved between the terms *magic* and *religion*. Some of the first anthropologists, such as Frazer, distinguished magic from religion, but this distinction was often used to suggest that religion is superior, less superstitious, and more reasonable. In addition, the distinction was preserved to legitimize missionary work and colonization originating from Europe and the United States. Today historians of religion include tribal sacred systems under the category of "religion" because doing so is more respectful of tribal societies. While respectfulness of sacred traditions is a good thing, calling the sacred practices of pre-state societies "religion" obscures some very important distinctions. For example, the word *magic* originally meant, "to make or be vigorous." The term *religion* has been translated in various ways, one of which is "to bind back," implying something has been lost. These are very real differences in imagining the way the world works, and are worth preserving.

I will use the terms *primitive magic* and *animism* to refer to the sacred systems of tribal societies. Animism implies that the world is oozing with forces and spirits. The terms *secondary magic* and *polytheism* will be used to designate the sacred systems of Bronze Age agricultural states. With polytheism the infinite plurality of forces and spirits characteristic of animism has been concentrated into a finite and systematized pantheon of gods and goddesses. *Religion* will be used to describe the sacred practices of the Axial Iron Age agricultural and commercial states. Here the finite pantheon of polytheism has been concentrated even more into a single monotheistic force. The previous deities are either cast out or subordinated to a Supreme Deity. The implication is that, previous to the rise of religion (monotheism), there was no religion; there was magic, an alternative sacred system.

All sacred systems contain at least seven dimensions: beliefs, myths, morals, dramatizations, techniques, a scope of inclusion, and transmission methods. All human societies must have answers to the great mystery questions about the origin of the world—where did we come from, and where are we going? Beliefs are simply rational commitments to particular answers to these mystery questions. People in all societies internalize the answers their society gives them about these questions, whether or not they ever have themselves thought through the answers.

People do not live by intellect alone. We also respond imaginatively to stories about the origin of the world—where we came from. In addition, myths give us guidance regarding the most general dilemmas that human beings must face—loyalty-betrayal, selfishness-community, risk-security, and success-failure. Strategies for resolving these problems were projected onto the sacred realm of conflicts and struggles among sacred beings, as well as between sacred beings and humanity.

Both magic and religion also provide symbols that are highly concentrated reminders of the sacred world and that act as cues to remember the sacred world in everyday life. These symbols are emotionally compelling and can be used to organize and motivate people quickly—whether for good or for questionable purposes.

Myths, symbols, and beliefs need to be grounded in actions and rooted in rhythms, which implies enactment in particular times and places in order to increase the chances of remembering the individual or group identity amidst the struggles of daily life. Dramatizations give perspective, especially regarding the issues of beginnings, endings, and changes in boundaries. Such issues may concern the biophysical world, the human community, or milestones in an individual's life such as marriage and death.

In everyday life, the sensory, imaginative, and emotional dimensions of the psyche are only moderately engaged, because an individual cannot afford to "get lost" in a specific psychological stimulus. During these dramatizations, however, specific techniques are employed to alter the participants' states of consciousness beyond everyday moderation, by either expanding or contracting sensual, emotional, and imaginative experience. The purpose is to help remind people of the "big picture" amidst the detail of everyday life.

Sensory saturation involves systematically filling sacred drama with vivid colors, sounds, smells, and movements that alter consciousness by linking the participants to the mythological beings to whom the group is appealing. Sensory saturation may also involve isolating some senses, with the effect of accentuating the experiences with the one sense that remains open. Sensory deprivation (as in meditation or prayer) is used to alter consciousness by minimizing all sensory contact with the world.

Beliefs, myths, symbols, dramatizations, and techniques deal either with ethereal matters, or with periodic processes such as harvests, seasonal hunts, etc. But people also need codes for how these beliefs and myths can be brought into everyday life. All societies have a way of classifying actions or intentions as right, wrong, or in-between. Morals are designed to help people to deal with ambiguous situations in everyday life.

All sacred traditions appeal to many dimensions of the human being—intellectual, imaginative, emotional, experimental, and practical.

Finally, a magical or religious system must develop a way to pass on all of the dimensions mentioned to the next generation. This can be done by oral or written means, by storytelling, or by book-reading.

1. First-order tensions between magic and religion

Figure 12.1 gives both an overview of the different questions that arise as a result of engaging the seven dimensions of sacred culture, and the different answers magic and religion give to each of these dimensions. I call these "first-order differences" because they are foundational preconditions for understanding the "second-order differences" that are discussed later in this chapter and in the following chapter.

In the beginning, forces mattered more than beings. It is as if sacred power was understood as a liquid or a gas capable of permeating anyone or anything. To the extent that beings existed, they were many and they tended to be subordinate to forces. With animism, sacred forces came from many places. With the rise of secondary magic, forces came to be subordinated to beings, which manipulated these forces. With the rise of the great religions a single being was believed to give humanity relative control over these forces (dominion over nature) and only intervened when humanity did something drastically wrong.

In magical traditions, forces or beings were sensuous, present mostly on earth, and located in concrete places. Differences between these presences and humanity were more a matter of degree rather than of kind. In contrast, the deity of the universalistic religions was non-sensuous, abstract, and celestial. On earth he was either everywhere or nowhere, but in no specific place.

All magical traditions regarded their myths and symbols as literally true, in part because the relationship between the sacred world and the mundane world of everyday life was understood as a distinction, not a separation. Since the myths and symbols were understood as coming from the sacred world and the distinction between sacred and secular was not severe, myths were regarded as stories about what could literally have occurred. Because in religion there is a clear separation between the human and divine worlds, there are other separations such as truth vs. illusion, appearances vs. reality, and myth vs. history (especially in the case of the Hebrews). When the great religions first emerged, the philosophers and sages related to these stories as opportunities to teach morality by presenting dramatic but difficult ethical dilemmas. The symbols and myths were representational reminders. They became figurative; they were metaphors, not literal truths.

Just as magical traditions saw their stories as being literally true, so too did they understand their rituals as *directly* changing reality without any intervention by spirits. Just as the great religions understood myths and symbols as representational, so too did they view religious dramatization as a supplication to a divine watchman thought to have power independent from the ritual itself. In other words, in religion it was not the ritual that changed reality, it is the deity who chose to change reality after witnessing the ritual. In religion, sacred dramatizations are representational; in magic, sacred dramatizations are presentational.

The shift from magic to religion also brought changes in morality. Magical morality is situational and provincial, while religious morality is universal. The reasons for this shift have to do with society's ecological setting and social organization. In magical societies the relationship between the tribe and the local animals and plants matters far more than moral relationships with people in other societies. This is partly because few tribal societies engage in trade in a systematic way that might require a more generalized morality that applies across groups.

Religion, on the other hand, builds a universal morality by first suppressing humanity's bond with its local ecology and then by encouraging humans to spread its connections to *other humans* in other societies—strangers. Just as humanity should aspire to globalize its morality, it simultaneously discovers a universal morality that has always existed through a universal deity. Just as God is everywhere and beyond particular situations, so is religious morality.

For the universal religions, both the world and humanity have fallen from a divine state and badly need reform. Therefore learning to become a better person is part of a cosmic transformation. For magical people the invisible world is on a moral par with this one. Therefore, to them there is no burning desire for self-improvement. Morality is strictly linked to resolving local situations within society. Daily practices of self-improvement are far less common in magical societies.

Magical traditions placed more emphasis on using techniques in association with dramatizations to *saturate* the non-rational faculties to alter states of consciousness than do the great religions. When the great religions invite humanity to renounce their ties with *external* reality (plants and animals), they also encourage the renouncing of our *internal* nature, which includes any non-rational psychic states tied to the senses, such as imagination and emotion. What is encouraged instead is sensory deprivation.

Primitive magical *group* experience went unmediated by any sacred specialist (*individual* magical experience was mediated by a shaman). It was this group process that was thought to change reality. With the rise of secondary magic and then religion, sacred group experience became mediated by priests, priestesses, or sages who interpreted and evaluated experience. In universalistic religion,

the experience itself is between God, the priest, and the individual. The group becomes background.

Lastly, primitive magical traditions were transmitted orally through storytelling. In secondary magical societies, hieroglyphics made it possible to translate some magical stories into written myths. When religion emerged, the simultaneous invention of the alphabet made written myths more available to the general populace.

To summarize the differences between magic and religion I offer the following "first order" definitions of magic and religion from my previous book (Lerro 2000). For purposes of contrast I have temporarily collapsed the differences between primitive and secondary magic, which I will discuss shortly.

> Magic is a sacred system prevalent in tribal and early state societies in which a plurality of earthly, concrete sacred presences can be directly influenced through group rituals and through techniques. The techniques emphasize filling the participants' senses, imagination, emotions, and kinesthetic faculties . . . and are transmitted orally through storytelling. Magic is exclusive and makes no attempt to include members of other societies. (Lerro, 2000, 6)

> Religion . . . is a sacred system prevalent in state societies . . . over which a single, abstract and celestial deity presides. This deity cannot be compelled through dramatization but can be influenced by more austere or intellectual practices. Religion is usually transmitted through the written word, and strives to include members of other societies. It has universalistic intentions. (Lerro, 2000, 6)

Several perfectly reasonable objections could be raised regarding these distinctions.

Figure 12.1 First Order Differences Within All Sacred Systems*

MAGIC		RELIGION
	Beliefs: **1) animistic, polytheistic or monotheistic?** (Is the ultimate source singular or plural?)	
animistic, polytheistic		**monotheistic**
	2) How **concrete or abstract** are the sacred presences? (Are they close, earthy and immanent or far away, austere and transcendental?)	
concrete, earthy		**abstract, celestial**
	Myths: **3) Literal or metaphorical** treatment of founders, sacred texts or stories?	
literal		**metaphors**
	Sacred dramatization: **4) Literal or representational** treatment of dramatization, props or gestures?	
presentational		**representational**
	Moral outreach: **5)** Is the system **exclusive and local or inclusive** **and universalistic** in the treatment of other people and sacred systems?	
local, exclusive		**universalistic, inclusive**
	Techniques: **6) Saturation or austerity?** (Are altered states achieved by filling or emptying human psychology like the senses, emotion, imagination, and body movement?)	
sensory saturation		**sensory deprivation**
	7) Mediated or unmediated access to sacred experience? (Is higher truth revealed through earthly intermediaries or experienced directly?)	
unmediated		**mediated**
	8) Private or group? (Are altered states achieved primarily through isolation or through community?)	
group		**private**
	Transmission: **9) Oral or Written?** (How are these traditions passed on across generations?)	
oral, storytelling		**written, scriptures**

*modified from Lerro, 2000 (pg. 3)

- People in ancient societies didn't have categories "magic" and "religion" for what they were doing. In my summary above, I am imposing these categories where they never existed.
- There are some religious traditions that have many characteristics categorized above as magical. For example, Hinduism is considered a world religion and yet has *many* gods.
- Catholicism is a universalistic religion, yet uses sensory *saturation* to alter states of consciousness.
- Finally, even within a given religion different social classes will practice religion differently. All people do not practice a religion in the same way.

I would answer these objections as follows.

(1) The categories "magic" and "religion" are indeed modern rubrics. But this does not negate their usefulness. If these labels can give us more insight into the phenomena under discussion, why not use them, even if the participants didn't? When it comes to understanding how people construct meaning, sometimes it is useful to use the emic categories of the participants, while other times it helps to import etic categories the participants themselves have never used. Distinguishing magic from religion is one such etic interpretation.

(2) Some religious traditions are more magical than others. Hinduism and Catholicism are far more magical than Buddhism and Protestantism. The contrast between magic and religion is really only valid in discussing the period prior to the Axial Iron Age. Discussions of magical or religious traditions after about 400 BCE require a different framing. We are here concerned only with the traditions of the great religions—Judaism, Buddhism,

Confucianism—when they first emerged as *reform* movements and before they acquired state power.

(3) We are discussing the religious ideas of the reformers, many of whom were of the *upper classes*. These reformers were not able to appeal to all social classes, and to the extent that they appealed to the lower classes, they could not convince the latter to practice these traditions the same way that they themselves did.

The third objection assumes a convolute as opposed to an evolute theory of social change (please see the Introduction under "qualifications"). I am not arguing that once religion emerged, magic simply vanished. When the great religions emerged, they may have been practiced in earnest by the sages and prophets, whereas the priests, artisans, and merchants of agricultural states practiced a combination of religion and magic. The peasants in the country, on the other hand, were only barely touched by the great religions and continued their traditional ways, which were closer to tribal magic.

3. Diffused psyches and spell-casting

One important way in which magic and religion differ is in where people practicing these two sacred systems tend to believe that the *psyche* is located.

I usually begin my lectures on the differences between magic and religion by asking students to identify all of the activities that occur in the psyche—thoughts, feelings, dreams, memories, and fantasies, to name a few. When I press my students to define what the psyche is, after much struggle they say it is everything that goes on inside of people that no one else can see. In other words, the psyche begins *inside* of us—in the brain or the heart— and ends with our skin. In between one individual's psyche and another is dead matter—the classroom tables, chairs, and blackboard. This is not far from both a scientific and a religious conception of the psyche, but it is not a magical conception.

In magical systems the psyche has its origin in the world (what we would call "nature"), comes through the individual, and returns back to the world. The psyche is diffused into the world; it is not held captive in the bodies of individuals. Therefore, people in magical societies are far less responsible for their psychological states than are people in religious societies. Activities that are unusual or disruptive of the community are often attributed to various earth spirits. The individual responsible for these activities is believed merely to have been possessed. Contrary to modern western psychology, where an individual is held responsible for more or less everything psychological, in primitive magical societies forces beyond the individual are primarily responsible. Tribal people do not originate their own dreams; dreams come to them. Uncontrollable sexual urges are blamed on sacred presences in charge of erotic processes, such as Aphrodite. In short, in magic the division between our inner states and the world is a *permeable membrane* rather than a barrier.

While at first thought it may seem that the magical way of imagining the relationship between the inner and outer worlds would make people passive, this is not the case. If the psyche is diffused and the relationship between the inner and outer worlds is a permeable, then just as the world can affect us, we can affect the world. The belief that groups of people can change the psyche of the external world is the real justification for magical practices.

This influencing of the world psyche is accomplished through ritual. Though the psyche is diffused throughout the world and through the individual, psychic energy must be focused in a particular time and place in order for people to use it for a specific purpose—such as to achieve a successful hunt or harvest. The force that must be harnessed has been given the name "mana" by some anthropologists. "Mana"

could be considered the rough magical equivalent of gravity or electromagnetism, in that it is regarded as a force or element of nature. It can be used for good or evil, and tribespeople vie with the earth spirits for its control.

The celestial world is divided into the four directions, and these divisions are further broken down into provinces ruled by various presences. For example, among the Greek gods, Aphrodite is the goddess of love and creativity, Demeter is the goddess of planting, and Mars is the god of war—or, more generally, of setting limits. These presences must work together in order for the celestial world to function harmoniously. Each god or goddess has a number of "correspondences." Mars corresponds with the color red; typically each god or goddess corresponds also with a particular animal, plant, mineral, musical sound, and so on.

In the center of the camp or village is a magical circle or a square in which the four directions are aligned with the heavens. The area is further divided into the departments of the sacred presences that reflect the heavens. In a magical ritual for a particular purpose a certain goddess or god is appealed to for assistance. Since the heavens are a macrocosm of the Earth, everything on Earth—each of the plants, animals, aromas, minerals, and colors that surround people—has a correspondence with what goes on in the heavens.

The sacred presence is invoked first by gathering together all of the correspondences associated with that presence. Prior to the ritual, people place the corresponding materials in the sector of the magical circle that goes with that presence. During the ritual, the people gather together and work up their collective emotions, imaginations, and memories; this is thought to affect the emotions, imagination, and memories of the sacred presence in charge of, say, hunting or harvesting. When the people's mythology is acted out and the participants' states of consciousness are altered, they believe both the celestial world and the earthly world have been altered.

People believe that when they enter this magical zone and the ritual begins, *time stands still and space becomes non-local.* Whatever happens in a ritual can instantaneously affect, for better or worse, whatever they are trying to influence— especially the part of the landscape within the province of the sacred presence. Once the department of the sacred presence is called upon in the sky, it is first drawn down to the magical circle and then projected out to that area of the land that directly extends from the part of the circle the sacred presence occupies, and to the land that surrounds the campsite or village. The "target" animal or plant is immediately affected depending on how powerful and coherent the ritual was.

This instantaneous sense of time is related to what Jung called "synchronicity." When performing a magical act there are no chance events. All activities are full of meaning. What takes place in the ritual is not a representation of reality; neither is it a cause of a reality that will show itself later as an effect. It is a *presentational recreation* of reality.

Because the psyche is diffused and there is a reciprocal relationship between the inner and outer worlds, rituals can compel the world to change. A magical ritual casts a spell. A spell is somewhat like a recipe. If it is followed, certain consequences must occur. For this reason primitive magicians do not worship sacred presences. The relationship between earth spirits and tribespeople might be characterized as "respect." It is something like the relationship between brothers and sisters: sometimes you cooperate and sometimes you compete—in this case, for the manipulation of mana. All sacred presences are somewhat *dependent* on the rituals of tribespeople for their existence.

4. Second-order tensions: primitive magic, secondary magic, and religion

In the second section of this chapter we contrasted the difference between magic and religion. In the last section we went into more specifics about magic. Until now I have temporarily collapsed the distinction between primitive and secondary magic. This distinction is very important for understanding the change in the status of women that occurred with the rise of stratified societies. Primitive magic took place in Paleolithic hunting-gathering societies and in Neolithic simple and complex horticultural societies. Most hunting-gathering societies and simple horticultural societies are egalitarian politically and there is no institutionalized male dominance. The rise of secondary magic accompanied the emergence of institutionalized male dominance, and so understanding the differences between primitive and secondary magic may give us some insight into how male power was legitimized in secondary magic. This will be the subject of the next three sections of this chapter.

The rise of stratified societies and the increased control over the natural environment affected how magic was practiced. As I said in my previous book (Lerro, 2000) there are subtle changes in the movement from primitive magic to what I call "secondary magic."

(1) Primitive magical practices emphasized dramatization acts more than myths. Myths and storytelling supplemented the ritual. In secondary magic, the relationship between myths and drama was reversed. Now *myths became the main source of inspiration* and rituals acts supported the stories. Secondary magic was the source from which polytheistic deities emerged.

(2) Primitive magical acts had more to do with harnessing the force of mana than with divining or influencing what other beings were up to. The basic assumption of animism is that everything is alive; but it is alive with forces

more than with beings *per se*. In secondary magic, this relationship was reversed. *Beings, specifically gods and goddesses, became more powerful than forces.* In polytheism there were many gods and goddesses, but there was no longer an infinite number of sacred beings.

(3) In primitive magic, earth spirits, ancestor spirits, and totems were essentially equal and interdependent with human beings. In secondary magic, *gods and goddesses were more powerful than human beings,* reflecting the new political and economic relations of rank and stratification. In addition, there were fewer goddesses and gods than earth spirits and they were responsible for larger provinces of human concern.

The goddesses and gods of the Bronze Age were a hybrid of the earth spirits of primitive magic and the sky gods of the Iron Age. They definitely had more power over humanity than the earth spirits did, but not as much power as a transcendental god has over religious people.

(4) Earlier in this chapter I said that one difference between magic and religion has to do with the co-creative power of the people in the ritual. In primitive magic, people believed they *recreated reality* whenever they did a ritual, and reality was the result of collaboration with the earth spirits. In religion, people are a passive audience and the work is done by a priest. In secondary magic, there was still interdependence between sacred beings and humanity, but sacred beings took the lead. Mythological beings were primary and human beings merely helped them out.

(5) One of the few characteristics primitive magic and the universal religions had in common is they both discouraged elaborate image-making, but they did so for different reasons. In nomadic hunting and gathering societies, the lack of images was mostly due simply to the inconvenience of traveling with large images. Also, the materials available to build such images were not nearly as durable as bronze. In the case of the great religions, the reasons for discouraging image-making were

ideological. The building of large images appeals to the non-rational imagination, of which religions are suspicious. For universalistic religions, god is inclusive of everything sensual, but there is more to him than the senses. To build images is to risk confusing a specific sensual image with the whole. Secondary magical societies, in part because they were more stable than nomadic societies and in part because they had more durable materials available, built large images of gods and goddesses.

I would now like to make explicit what so far has been implicit in my discussion of the social evolution of dramatization. Primitive magical societies performed sacred dramatizations—I will call these *rituals*—to express the belief that they recreated reality through their actions. Since the people involved in religious practice were more passive and often constituted merely an audience, I will call their dramatizations *pageants*. Secondary magical traditions fell somewhere between these two categories. I will call the dramatizations in these societies *ceremonies*, to show that people's involvement included elements of both participation and passivity, recreating reality while also being submissive to reality. In secondary magic, people co-created with gods and goddesses.

(6) Hunting is a far less predictable vocation than planting. With planting, a cultivator may not be able to control the quality of the crop, but if the timing is right they will be assured of having some sort of crop every year. Hunting is a more fickle affair. Hunters either catch something or they don't. Thus hunting peoples must accept a greater element of chance in their lives. The degree to which a society is comfortable with chance or relies on control affects its concept of time.

In planting societies, unlike hunting societies, time was not instantaneous; it was cyclic. Planting and harvesting lent themselves to understanding time as comprised of polar rhythms. This does not mean that nomadic

Figure 12.2 Second Order Differences Between Magic and Religion

Primitive Magic	Secondary Magic	Religion
Paleolithic and Neolithic tribal	Bronze Age agricultural states	Axial Iron Age commercial states
psyche diffused in nature	psyche diffused in nature	psyche compressed w/i the individual
animistic	polytheistic (gods, goddesses)	monotheistic (one god)
dramatization predominant over myth	myth predominant over dramatization	history over myth and drama
forces predominant over beings	beings predominant over forces	one being predominant over all forces and beings
sacred presences equal to humanity	sacred presences superior to humanity in degree	sacred presence superior to humanity in kind (transcendental)
many spirits, small domains	fewer goddesses and gods, larger domain	one god, everywhere
humans recreate reality: participants	humans co-create reality with more powerful deities, helpers	reality created before time humans an audience
forces, small images	large images	imageless
rituals	ceremonies	pageants
instantaneous time	cyclic time	linear time
polarities fused	polarities differentiated	absolute dualities
spaces are diffused, temporary home	spaces are crystallized, permanent home	spaces decline in importance

hunter-gatherers have no sense of rhythm and timing, because they do. But they travel too much to be able to work out a cosmology of rhythms—based on the solstices and equinoxes—in the kind of detail that planters did, with their sedentary life-ways. The latter had more tools with which to track their experiences, and, importantly, writing systems with which to objectify their discoveries in a relatively permanent way.

In all magical societies—primitive or secondary—the universe was regarded as eternal, but as constantly requiring itself to be ensouled or reproduced in time. Nature replenished herself in the movement across the four seasons, so that Spring could not exist without Winter nor Winter without Fall. These opposites were complementary. So, too, did the goddesses and gods have polarities built within them—strengths that could become weaknesses, and weaknesses which, in certain situations, could become strengths.

For the universal religions—western more than eastern—nature was created by God *before* time began. Religious people are expected not to be fooled by the lure of nature's cycles, but to create a new social world with other non-kin human beings *in history*. Historical events are non-repeatable and irreversible. Religious time is a linear, one-way arrow—from past to present and future—that is open-ended.

For universalistic religions, polarities are no longer seen as necessary in order for life to continue. Polarities become dualities, mutually exclusive opposites. Whereas opposites in magical societies are understood as relative, necessary, and interdependent, for the great religions (again, especially the western ones) opposites are absolute, voluntary (the result of a mistake or an evil deed), and independent of one another. A single deity becomes the focus or repository of all that is good. The devil becomes the absolute focus or repository of evil. Human beings are caught in the struggle between these two cosmic forces.

(7) In hunting-and-gathering societies, biophysical nature was diffused, as were the forces that governed the sacred world. The boundaries between areas that surrounded the hunting camp that were sacred and the areas that were secular were porous and easily changeable, as were the psyche and nature. In centralized complex horticultural and agricultural societies, there was a more rigorous division of labor. This was reflected in sacred beliefs, in which sacred beings became more crystallized and sacred places became a more concentrated, permanent domain for these gods and goddesses.

The emergence of astrology in secondary magical societies illustrates how both time and space were systematically organized according to the cycles of the year. Every place in the heavens had a specific meaning because of its location. It was thought that events in the year could be predicted based on time of the year when the events occurred.

The differences between primitive magic secondary magic and religion are summarized in Figure 12.2

5. Goddesses in secondary magic: from subordination to marginalization

There are a number of claims or assumptions that neo-pagans make about the goddesses, some of which we addressed in chapter 3. It is important that we elaborate on these assumptions—that

(1) goddesses had high status in polytheistic societies, and with the rise of monotheism, goddesses' status declined;
(2) women's relationship with goddesses was primarily mediated by secret societies;
(3) there was a direct correspondence between the status of goddesses and the status of women.

Sumerologist and Assyriologist Tikva Frymer-Kensky (1992) contests all of these assumptions or claims. According to Frymer-Kensky, the presence of goddesses in Mesopotamia did not imply the existence of a secret women's cult separate from society as a whole. Instead, gender categories were immanent in the cosmos, culture, and society. The gods and goddesses engaged in the same activities that men and women did, but writ large. The natural elements controlled by goddesses were *specific to their gender*. Goddesses in Mesopotamia were not self-determined by secret societies of women. The activities of goddesses had to make sense to all members of society, including the priests who were writing, reading, and teaching the sacred texts. Therefore, "Goddesses are the 'women' of the divine world and behave much as women are expected to behave. They are not role models that women devised for themselves." (Frymer-Kensky, 1992, 14)

What were the goddesses expected to do?

Cosmic geography was divided along gender lines and control over the geographic realm and their power elements was not in female hands. The sky was in the hands of a male god (the god An) as were the air (Enlil) and the waters (Enki). Meteorological and astronomical phenomena, such as sun, moon, stars, and storms, were also in the hands of males. . . . Events on the surface of the earth, humans, and animals were the domain of the god Enlil. So too, the seas, particularly the fructifying subterranean seas, may once have belonged to the goddess Nammu; but in historical times, Enki is in full control of these waters. The further down we go into the terrestrial realm, farther removed from public activity and human power structure, the longer goddesses could maintain their control. Throughout Sumerian times, the netherworld from which things grow and to which they return, where even humans are fashioned before birth and spend their

life after death, was the domain of a goddess. The goddesses are in control of reproduction, fertility, and sexuality (Frymer-Kensky, 1992, 46-47)

Kingship and lawgiving were activities of male gods while other activities were women's domain. Women's domestic activities (and the corresponding goddesses) included:

the weaving of cloth (wool being represented by the divine Ewe)—Uttu
the growing of grain—Nisba
the drinking of beer—Ninkasi
the making of pottery—Ninurra

What all these activities had in common was storage and transformation. Women were the bringers of culture, "transformers of raw into edible, grass into baskets, fleece and flax into yarn and then linen to clothes, and babies into social beings." (Frymer-Kensky 1992, 110)

But the storage of baskets, yarn, and linen demands retrieval and a system of keeping records of consumption patterns. This was also the role of goddesses in managing the temple household. The range of roles goddesses performed was not limited to domestic activities; other activities included dramatic performances, singing at ceremonies for the dead, dream interpretation, medical healing, wisdom writing, and surveying.

What must be kept in mind is that right from the beginning of agricultural states the place of goddesses was subordinate to that of gods, and in these worlds it was only with rare exceptions that goddesses did anything different than women in agricultural states did. We have concrete evidence that women's status in these societies was subordinate to men's, and this is reflected in the goddesses' subordination to gods. The fact that goddesses played very similar roles in the sacred world to those that women played in the material world gave a sanctity to those activities, while it discouraged women from engaging in activities outside these realms.

The goddess Innana is often presented as the archetype of the liberated goddess. There is no question that she breaks many of the rules—she marries and fails to assume any of the economic responsibilities of a wife; she refuses to spin, weave or dye cloth; she has a role in war and can turn men into women and women into men. She stands at the boundary of differences between men and women. But before we jump to any conclusions about the power of Innana to act as an inspiration for women to break out of traditional roles, two points are worth noting.

First: "As in all rituals and occasions of rebellion, the socially approved, scheduled and regulated breaking of a norm actually serves to reinforce it." (Frymer-Kensky, 1992, 29) In other words, when rebellion is understood as a small part of *a closed system* of dominance, the rebellion is simply part of the cycle in which the dominant order is sustained. It serves as an outlet, rather than as a serious challenge to the existing order. It would be a serious threat if the system were conceived as open—that is, linear—where the future is undetermined. Rebellion would also be a threat if it were unpredictable rather than regulated.

Second: Inanna's power is not direct power, it is indirect power:

> Inanna gets her power directly from An and Enhil. But this is a reflected form of authority. It is not independent power. In the ordering of the pantheon, An and Enlil are the heads of government. Inanna/Ishtar has no position of power among the gods, no political authority over them. She is sheer force, rage and might, with a physical power that exists in a somewhat uneasy relationship to the orderly world of the hierarchical pantheon. (Frymer-Kensky, 1992, 65)

Inanna remains outside the direct chain of authority. She has no niche in the state political system of the gods. (66)

As a female, she has no real place in the hierarchy of power among the gods . . . and thereby seeks her power in the upper reaches of human society in the company of the king. (69)

One of the functions the goddess Inanna performed was to create a bridge between the human and divine worlds. Frymer-Kensky notes: "amorous and available, she brings the king into the world of the gods, shrinking the distance between the divine and the human, providing a bridge" (Frymer-Kensky, 1992, 69). Frymer-Kensky goes on to describe this liaison:

> The sacred marriage began with a journey and procession by the king to the *giparu* of Inanna's temple . . . the core of the ritual was an act of sexual congress between king and goddess figure. To the 'holy lap' of Inanna, the king went 'with lifted head' (proudly) as a desired awaited partner . . . Inanna gazed at him with her shining countenance, caressed him and embraced him. This sexual union was intended to promote the fertility of the land . . . the king played the male role, and in which he figures as the god Dumuzi, the spouse of Inanna. The texts do not mention what woman played Inanna. (51)

While the purpose of the sacred marriage was to promote fertility, Inanna was not the sole determinant in this process. Insuring fertility was about the convergence of many activities that involved not only goddesses and women, but gods and men as well. Fertility was not understood in Mesopotamia as the monopoly of females:

> It is through the concerted effort of gods and humans that the fertility of the world is assured. The gods bring fertility

through their control over rain, air, sun and soil; humans bring abundance through their work in fields, canals and storehouses. The sacred marriage of the king and the goddess is a dramatic expression of this divine-human partnership. (Frymer-Kensky, 1992, 56)

The mother goddess controls human and animal reproduction but she is not a fertility goddess in the conventional sense for she has no power over agricultural fecundity. (Frymer-Kensky 1992, 50)

And finally:

The historical evidence, from the writings of Sumer and Babylon indicates that the conceptualization of fertility was much more complex than the simple idea of earth mother and her womb . . . more common are the many indications that fertility required many gods and that no one god was able to insure it. (Frymer-Kensky, 1992, 92)

Though goddesses had an important role in insuring fertility, this does not necessarily mean that women in agricultural states were sexually liberated.

The Mesopotamian temples contained all kinds of women functionaries, long translated "priestesses" or "hierodules." Once again, serious study of the documents relating to these women shows that there is no evidence that any of them performed sexual acts as part of their sacred duties. The only form of sexual service that we do not have to doubt was the sacred marriage of Sumerian times. There we have unequivocal statements that the king slept with the goddesses. But even this one sexual ritual disappeared after Sumerian times as the sacred marriage underwent a radical

transformation: instead of being played out by human beings, it was represented by placed statues of the god and goddess in a garden for the night. (Frymer-Kensky, 1992, 202)

Frymer-Kensky concludes: "The whole tradition of considering ancient pagan religion sexy and its women cultic functionaries as sex partners is a myth. It speaks more about its adherents than it does about the ancients. It is born of conflicted attitudes towards sexual activity in Western civilization." (202)

There is a dialectical relationship between how the gods and goddesses interact and how actual men and women in society interact. In times of stable social relations there is a general congruence between the two. When there is social instability and men's and women's roles are changing, the relationships between gods and goddesses also begin to change. The first few centuries of the Bronze Age were socially stable, but the middle and late Bronze Ages were characterized by many instabilities described in chapters 10 and 11. These changes were reflected in the changes in goddess-god responsibilities. Three stages of change in the relationship between men and women's roles and the domains of gods and goddesses can be seen across the Bronze Age:

performance of roles by women—domain of
    goddesses
performance of roles by men—domain of
    goddesses
performance of roles by men—domain of gods

In the early Bronze Age (which we have been discussing), the roles of women and the domain of goddesses went together. But in the middle Bronze Age there was an interesting contradiction. Men took over many female roles, but did so in the name of goddesses. Finally, in the late Bronze Age, men performed these roles in the names of the gods. We will now turn to the latter two stages.

As we have seen, in the early Bronze Age, goddesses were subordinate to gods, but goddesses still had important roles to play. But between about the 1900 BCE through to the end of the Bronze Age in the 12th century BCE, the roles of goddesses went from being merely subordinated to being marginalized.

In the middle Bronze Age, the roles of men and women began to change. Frymer-Kensky argues that first men and women's *roles* changed in favor of the male, but for a while the doings of the gods and goddesses did not reflect these changes. In this middle period men took over more functions of women but did so in the name of *goddesses.*

Male professional practitioners continued to attribute their activities to goddesses. This was a form of culture lag, in which men had taken over the roles that women formerly women played, but preserved the cultural memory of women's contribution by projecting their own role onto a goddess figure.

The activity of lamenting will illustrate:

Private laments continued to be preformed by women, but the public congregational laments written after the Sumerian period . . . were performed by a special kind of male singer . . . not by women. These professional male singers ascribed their activities to goddesses. . . . The name of this dialect is an indication that the . . . priests sang in a special, thin probably falsetto, voice. (Frymer-Kensky, 1992, 43)

There was not always a direct correspondence between what the gods and men did or what the goddesses and women did:

Although these cultural contributions of goddesses derive from the actions of women, the relationship between the activity of goddesses and that of women in cultural life is not a direct one-to-one match. At any given moment the

portrayal of goddesses in culture reflect both the actual role of women at the time the literature was written and the cultural memory of the contribution of women to the development of civilization. (Frymer-Kensky, 1992, 42)

Later in the Bronze Age, the roles of goddesses themselves became marginalized just as the roles of women already were:

There is a constant direction to the movement, one in which the areas under goddess control are shrinking, with more and more occupations taken over by male gods. [For example] Ninurra, goddess of pot making, was transformed into a male god and ultimately absorbed into the figure of Enki. . . . Ningirim, who appears prominently in the incantation literature as the exorcist of the gods . . . in later Sumerian times, exorcism and incantation are in the hands of Enki and his son, Asarluhi. (Frymer-Kensky, 1992, 43)

Why should this be? According to Frymer-Kensky, "The dramatic decline of women's visibility does not take place until well into the Old Babylonian period (circa 1600 BCE) and may be a function of the change from city-states to larger nation-states and the changes in the social and economic systems that this entailed." (Frymer-Kensky, 1992, 80)

The change to stage three, in which gods dominate in the sacred just as men dominate in the material, can be seen in the myth of Tiamat and Marduk:

Ti'amat, the primordial mother 'she who gave birth to all' . . . for she represents the ancient order which Marduk must defeat in order to become king of the gods . . . Marduk defeats Tiamat . . . and becomes king of the gods. From her body Marduk creates the world and organizes the cosmos as a divine state. (Frymer-Kensky, 1992, 76)

The functions of goddesses became passive and sexuality was no longer the method of uniting the human and the divine:

We live in the body of the mother, but she has neither activity nor power. . . . The later kings took part in a ritual that celebrated stability rather than fertility, order rather than union, monarchy rather than renewal. The royal sacred marriage did not entirely disappear. . . . But this cult as a whole was no longer state-centered or run, and became a matter for private rather than public worship. . . . In these later sacred marriages a king no longer played the part of the god. Indeed no humans were involved in the conjugal union. . . . Human sexuality has lost its power to express the congress of the gods . . . and interchange between divine and human is completely lost. (Frymer-Kensky, 1992, 76)

As Frymer-Kensky says: "the world by the end of the second millennium was a male's world, above and below." (80)

By the time we reach the outlands of the universalistic religions, we are not confronted with a battle between a polytheistic matriarchy and a rising patriarchy; from here on, sacred battles that reflect crisis are battles between *male* gods, not between male gods and female goddesses:

The religion of Israel's contemporaries was not one in which gods and goddesses had equal roles and import. There was no longer possible a choice between monotheism and the goddesses, but rather one between monotheism and a male dominated polytheism. (Frymer-Kensky 1992, 6)

The early struggle of Israel was against the gods of Canaan—Baal and El. . . . Biblical religion did not pit a sole god against goddess-worship. On the contrary, its struggle was to win and keep the allegiance of the people . . . for YHWH . . . vis-a-vis the male Canaanite gods. (Frymer-Kensky, 1992, 157)

We will continue this story with the rise of Archaic Iron Age religion in the next chapter.

In summary, Neo-pagans are right to claim there is a change in the status of goddesses as we move from the early Bronze Age to the middle and late Bronze Age. However, the movement is not one in which Goddesses go from being *superior* to or even *equal* to male gods to becoming subordinated. Rather, goddesses move from subordination toward marginalization. It is not the case that the deterioration in the status of goddesses occurred concurrently with the shift from polytheism to monotheism. Rather, the entire process, both subordination and marginalization, occurred *within* a regime of polytheism and secondary magic. While monotheism continued to legitimize the subordination of women, it did not initiate it. Further, in some places the suppression of goddesses under monotheism actually went with a slight *improvement* in the status of women.

6. How did secondary magic legitimize women's subordination?

From a Marxian and Neo-pagan feminist point of view, it would be easy to suppose that magic supported women while religion undermined women, because earth-spirit magic took place in egalitarian societies and sky-god religion occurred in stratified societies where women had lost significant status. If all we were dealing with were tribal egalitarian societies on the one hand and commercial class-stratified societies on the other, this would be a good assessment. However, when we examine agricultural states and the secondary magic that went with them, the picture becomes more complex.

If we re-examine Figure 12.2, we see the following trends from primitive to secondary magic:

- Predominance of forces to predominance of beings
- Predominance of forces to predominance of images
- Movement from many spirits covering a local terrain to few gods and goddesses responsible over a wider domain
- Emphasis of storytelling myths over dramatization
- Co-equal relations between humanity and spirits to superiority of gods and goddesses over humanity
- Movement from creation to co-creation, from participants to helpers
- Movement from rituals to ceremonies
- Movement from instantaneous to cyclic time
- Movement from fused polarities to differentiated polarities
- Movement from spaces being fused to spaces being crystallized

How do these changes in magic legitimize the rise of institutional male dominance? How direct is the connection between the rise of secondary magic and the deterioration of women's status? Is there a one-to-one relationship? Is the relationship indirect? Is there no relationship?

Broadly speaking, primitive earth magic did support women's egalitarian status. Ideally, in small-game foraging societies in lush conditions, these societies were egalitarian politically and informal male dominance was at a minimum.

Primitive magic was a sacred tradition that ideally expressed these social relationships. To begin with, when the psyche was understood as diffused in nature this meant that "mana" could flow between humanity and the sacred world. The interdependence of the earth spirits on humanity, the confidence that people felt in casting spells, the belief that rituals literally recreated the world, would support women's perception that they as well as men could transform the world. There was some asymmetry in that shamans were more frequently men than women, yet it is still safe to say that, to the extent that earth-spirit magic supported egalitarian relations for men, it did the same for women.

When we examine the trends listed at the beginning of this section, we see a number of direct connections between the emergence of secondary magical characteristics and the rise of stratification. For example, the fact that gods and goddesses are superior to humanity is a projection into the sacred world of the relationship between the upper castes and the lower castes, along with the privileges of all men over all women. The fact that humanity no longer creates, but co-creates with these deities shows social alienation between most groups and the product of their labor. The movement from rituals to ceremonies also indirectly shows people's loss of confidence that they can change the world without first checking with the sacred presences.

Other trends are not easily analyzed in terms of politics and economics. The movement from many presences to a few presences seems to reflect a more complex social organization with specialized tasks. The tendency of the domains of gods and goddesses to spread further across the world seems to correspond to agricultural states becoming less provincial and even developing empires. The movement from an emphasis on dramatization to storytelling is a reversal of the relationship between action and speaking: Storytelling is more abstract and people are less confident about changing the world and more comfortable speaking about it. As the sacred presences become more powerful, their actions begin to undermine the dramatization rituals performed by humans. Humans become more passive and tell stories about what these sacred presences are up to.

Lastly, the movement from forces to beings and from forces to images seems to express the movement from hunter-gatherer mobility to a more settled way of life. It is difficult to make elaborate images, especially those that require firing, if a society is nomadic. The change in the sense of sacred time from instantaneous to cyclic, of fused to differentiated polarities, and from fused to crystallized space reflects a settled, specifically agricultural way of life.

As we saw in chapter 2, when secondary magic emerged agricultural states were divided into the following castes:

Divine King and Queen
Priests and Priestesses
Military
Merchants
Artisans
Slaves
"Expendables"
Peasants

Priests and priestesses were the main practitioners of secondary magic. The other social castes in the cities, such as the merchants and artisan groups, were probably practicing a hybrid of secondary and primitive magic. The peasants on the outskirts of society were probably least affected by secondary magical practices and probably continued to practice an "alloy" that was predominately primitive magic.

For priestesses in the city, secondary magic must directly have supported high social status, with few contradictions. The mythic stories about the exploits of goddesses are similar to the activities that priestesses performed in managing temples. That sacred presences had

power over humanity was not such a bitter pill to swallow, because the priestess's caste position gave her indirect power over most men and all women (though she was still subordinate to the priest). She could identify with specific goddesses and the domains they oversaw, because she was herself in charge of many activities in the temple household. The priestess had a sense of co-creating with gods and goddesses, because she had a managerial sense that her work reproduced society.

While she did not make the images of goddesses, the priestess could certainly identify with them, since in seasonal rituals she temporarily embodied one of the goddesses. She must have felt great power in sacred ceremonies, because the group participatory process in magical traditions was concentrated in her hands. The high structural content of cyclic time and of large structured places must have given the priestess a great deal of reassurance that her location in the universe was secure. The understanding that goddesses were immanent in the earth must have made her feel quite at home in what she was doing, since the goddesses were right beside her, justifying what she was doing. Interdependence with goddesses was quite comprehensible, since goddesses were somewhat akin to older sisters.

For most women in the city, *secondary magic must have been both a consolation and at the same time a legitimization of their low status.* On the one hand, while goddesses had high indirect status in Bronze Age states, women had little direct power. The myths that became prevalent over dramatizations were stories that she herself had little hope of living out. The domains that goddesses ruled over were ones the typical woman was familiar with, but she herself could never aspire to having charge of those domains. The large images of goddesses and gods were made of bronze, and their manufacture was the province of male artisans. As anyone knows who has practiced magic, the process of making a sacred being is at least as important as the result. This was not anything most women did. The dramatization ceremonies were contradictory: on the one hand women believed they were co-creating the world with gods and goddesses. But in their material life, they were denied the opportunity to work in public. They could hardly have the experience of co-creating the social world in any real sense.

The reorganization of time and space also had mixed effects. On the one hand, cyclic time and crystallized, structured places and divination systems like astrology provided a comfortable assurance that there is a time and a place for everything. But for the typical woman position this structure would probably have been experienced as a fatalistic straitjacket. Secondary magical traditions sustain the notion that the goddesses and gods are immanent. This must have been a painful contradiction for women in the city to live with. How could goddesses be in the world, powerful in their own right, and yet allow the status of women to be so low?

For peasant women living in the outskirts of agricultural states, the contradictions between sacred beliefs and their material conditions were probably played out in how *primitive magic* was transformed, since secondary magic probably never become a significant part of their beliefs.

Peasant women had the lowest status in all of society. Let us look at the enormous contradictions the peasant woman would have had to face to reconcile her miserable material life, compared to a woman living in a society with the egalitarian cosmology of primitive magic. Please see Figure 12.3

The result of these contradictions led to the bastardization of magic. It became superstition, and superstition in turn sowed the seeds for the appeal of the great religions.

In conclusion: It is simplistic to assume that magic and/or goddesses always supported women and lower classes, while religion always supported the upper classes and men. Broadly speaking, primitive magic was a meaning-making system that supported egalitarian political and economic relations between men and women. Secondary magic involving goddesses, however, was from the beginning an ideology that justified institutionalized male dominance.

Figure 12. 3 Contradictions of Practicing Primitive Magic
for Peasant Women under Conditions of Institutionalized Male Dominance

primitive magic	material status of peasant women
symmetrical relationship with the earth spirits	exploited by the upper castes in the city; husband has many privileges over wife
dramatization has more power than myths	work is long, hard, and routine; cottage industry with some diversity in activities
forces more powerful than beings	the forces that appear to control her life are completely beyond her power to change
sacred presences are equal to humanity	other social classes are all above her. Subordination is a way of life
many spirits, small domains	this seems to go with the state of their home and village (this would be more of a contradiction if they were identified w/secondary magic)
humanity recreates reality with sacred presences	this is inconceivable since her whole life involves reacting to abuses from higher castes and her husband
forces, small images	this would seem to go with being poor, having little access to bronze
rituals recreate reality	this is where superstition may come in and obsessive-compulsive behavior
instantaneous time	this would contradict the seasonal nature of agriculture which goes with a cyclic sense of time
space is diffused and temporary	this would contradict the nature of agriculture which is structured and permanent
earth spirits immanent, like a brother or sister	this would contradict the sense that the earth spirits, though close at hand, are of no help in alleviating her situation

Chapter 13

Archaic and Universalistic Religion: From Polytheism to Monotheism

At the end of the last chapter we discussed how women's subordinate status was justified in the Bronze Age by secondary magic. In this chapter we will turn to the various aspects of religion. How did the following changes from primitive magic to religion legitimize institutionalized male dominance?

- from animism to monotheism;
- from myth to history;
- from envisioning the sacred presence as a variety of forces to worshiping it as a single being;
- from equality among sacred presences to inequality;
- from many spirits each with its own domain to one God who is everywhere;
- from recreating reality in time to a God creating reality before time;
- from images to imageless metaphors;
- from rituals to pageants;
- from cyclic to linear time;
- from diffused spaces to a decline in the importance of spaces.

These are some of the trends I will attempt to clarify in this chapter. In addition, I will discuss other aspects of religion that are related to the legitimation process:

- a change in the psyche from diffused to compressed;
- the marginalization of the use of the non-rational mind, and increased use of the rational mind;
- a change in the image of a sacred earthly archetype, from hero to sage;

- the democratization of the afterlife to include everyone;
- effects from comets and/or asteroids.

Between late Bronze Age polytheism of the 12th century BCE and the emergence of Axial Iron Age monotheism between the 8th and 5th centuries BCE, there occurred a transitional period known as the "Archaic Iron Age." The timing of the Archaic Iron Age varied from one civilization to another, because civilizations did not all acquire iron at the same time. We will contrast the growth of the universalistic religions during the Axial Iron Age to the religion of the Archaic Iron Age. Figure 13.1 shows an overview, along with some of the similarities and differences.

The plan of this chapter is to begin by describing some of the new characteristics of universalistic religion and then to survey how these new characteristics were expressed among the major Axial Age peoples—the Chinese, Indians, Greeks, and Hebrews. Then we will return to a discussion of the social impact of natural disasters of cometary origin, begun in chapter 10. In this instance I will discuss these disasters' impacts on the process legitimizing male domination. I will close the chapter by answering the questions above and will discuss their relevance to the legitimation of institutionalized male dominance.

1. Universalistic religions

Let me begin by gathering together some of the characteristics of universalistic religions of the Axial Iron Age that were mentioned in the

Figure 13.1 Comparison of Archaic and Axial Ages

Country	Archaic Iron	Date	Axial Iron	Date	Universalistic Religion
China	Zhou dynasty	1046 BCE	Warring States	500 BCE	Confucianism/ Taoism
India	Vedic-Brahmin	1500 BCE	Middle Ganges plain	600 BCE	Buddhism
Greece	Mycenaean-Homeric	1500 BCE	Classical civilization	600 BCE	Pre-Socratics Orphics
Near East	Hebrews (Moses)	1400 BCE	United Monarchy	600-400 BCE	Judaism (Middle prophets)

Archaic (1400-600 BCE)	Axial (600-500 BCE)
Feudal: aristocratic herding or monarchies	Urban- secular states
Ruled by warrior or priestly aristocracy	Ruled by landed aristocracy; rise of merchants Secular subculture expands
Society embedded in a spiritual cosmos--theocracies	Society governed by autonomous laws--republics
Economic constriction in circulation limited to ruling class	Revolution in economic circulation of goods through coined money and alphabet to include more social classes
	Trade in more subsistence goods
Rule by birth or appointment	Rise of formal democracy in Athens Buddhism challenges social castes, promotes alternative spiritual community--sangha Confucius includes peasants in "Heaven"
Sky-Gods of mountains, storms sensual, worldly	Transcendent, monist God. Non-dualism non-sensual, otherworldly
Olympian heroes, Brahmins	nature philosophers: universal element idealists--Orphics, Pythagoras, Parmenides , Plato Confucius, Mo-tzu, Mencius Buddha
Parochial special groups	Universalizing: towards nature, towards humanity
Sacred archetype: Hero or Priest	Sacred archetype: Sage
Good and evil is the province of the Gods or Goddesses Either no afterlife or afterlife for few individuals	Good and evil is the responsibility of individuals Afterlife for all individuals
External laws: Fate, Vedas fear, obedience	Internal dictates: conscience, morality
Hero : energetic feats of prowess, bravado, conquest, adventure seeks honor, and glory	Sage: introspection, self-awareness, impulse control, humility, persistence, love of the stranger, suppression of body and aggression
Life is more than survival: adventure	Life is more than survival: self-improvement, humanity has a special destiny

* Modified from Lerro (2000)

previous chapter but not described there in any detail. In the first section of chapter 10 we defined religion as "a sacred system prevalent in state societies . . . over which a single, abstract, and celestial deity presides. This deity cannot be compelled through dramatization but can be influenced by more austere intellectual practices. . . . Religion is usually transmitted through the written word and strives to include members of other societies. It has universalistic intentions."

Later in that chapter I said that universalistic religion denies that cosmic creation takes place *in time* through the participation of humanity. On the one hand, cosmic creation is God's business before time began. On the other, humans are separated from sacred time by being expected to create their own history. Finally, universalistic religions renounce the polar nature of the sacred, in which opposites are interdependent, necessary, and complementary, in favor of an absolute separation of mutually exclusive dualities.

As I mentioned at the end of chapter 2, in the Near East and the East the period around 500 BCE was called the "Axial Age"—meaning that it was a pivotal point in history. It was then that what have been called "the great religions" emerged, in part as a reaction to the inability of secondary magical traditions to resolve the new problems of the more urbanized and commercial civilizations. The prophets or sages of these new religions included Amos, Isaiah, Zarathrustra, Confucius, Lao Tze, Buddha, and Socrates

Monotheism arose temporarily in Egypt approximately 1400 BCE, with the worship of the sun; it arose in the Near East when, as we saw, the Hebrew god Yahweh was transformed from a tribal god into a monotheistic god between 900 BCE and 600 BCE; and it arose in Persia with the worship of Ahura Mazha. The teachings of Confucius in China and the Buddha in India developed ethical systems as opposed to religions, but these were built on universalist, anti-magical, or non-magical principles. Lastly, the Greek "nature philosophers" tried to explain how the world worked not on the basis of appeal to a single deity, but from the transformations of a single

element; while the Orphic prophets and Pythagoras described a transcendental world beyond anything tangible.

In the period between the Archaic and the Axial Ages the following four processes occurred, which I have described elsewhere (Lerro, 2000):

> 1. The psyche became *focused and subjective* rather than diffused and objective. This meant:
> > (a) The psyche became compressed within individuals.
> > (b) Nature no longer was regarded as having any psyche, and earth spirits became insignificant. Nature was understood as only physical, material, and secular.
> 2. There was a change in value between the soul and spirit functions within the psyche. This meant:
> > (a) The soul-like qualities of the individual were looked upon with suspicion.
> > (b) The spirit-like qualities of the individual acquired high status. Spirit-like qualities were also projected onto a new transcendental realm and became properties of a sky god.
> 3. There was a new union between the little spiritual qualities of the individual and the big spiritual qualities of the supreme presence in the sky.
> 4) Religious individuals now had dominion over nature rather than participating as part of it.

The soul-like qualities are typically identified with the non-rational side of the brain: imagination, intuition, emotion, dreams, fantasies, memories, impulses, and the senses. The spirit-like qualities include abstract reasoning, analysis, self-reflection, and suppression of gratification.

I will describe processes one and three first. As we saw in chapter 11, when the psyche was diffused in nature this gave individuals in magical societies an excuse for anti-social

Figure 13.2 Third Order Differences Between Magic And Religion*

Primitive Magic	Secondary Magic	Religion
egalitarian/ rank	stratified: caste	stratified: class
Paleolithic Neolithic Ages	Bronze Age	Iron Age
psyche diffused in nature	**psyche diffused in nature**	**psyche focused in individual**
soul functions	**soul functions**	**spirit functions**
imagination, intuition, emotion, dreams, fantasies, memories, impulses, senses		abstract reasoning, analysis, self-reflection, will-power sensual suppression
individual responsibility external: other groups, forces, spirit beings	individual responsibility external	individual responsibility internal: personal conscience
sacred presences immanent:	**sacred presences immanent**	**sacred presences transcendent:**
spells		prayer
confidence		faith
organic, symmetrical interdependent		contractual, asymmetrical independent
consciousness interdependent w/matter		consciousness independent of matter
respect: brother/sister metaphor	reverence: older brother/ sister metaphor	worship: father metaphor
universe is improvised		universe is planned w/ purpose
animals equal to/ higher than humans		humans higher than animals

---

* modified from Lerro (2000) pg.116-117

behavior: they could claim that they had been duped by external spirits. Religious individuals in the Axial Iron Age could no longer refer to *external* processes to account for anti-social or unspiritual behavior. They were now responsible for everything they did. Each individual's psychological states became his or her private property, for better or worse.

As the psyche was withdrawn from the natural world, people began to relate to nature as a means to an end, not an end in itself. As the monotheistic god would tolerate no competitors, the earth spirits (and other sky gods) became discredited. As nature became secularized, there was nothing to stand between the religious individual and the transcendental God. This also debilitated people's confidence in the power of their rituals to change the world.

Because the props used in dramatic actions were no longer a part of a diffused psyche, the dramatization was now understood as a *symbolic* representation; it did not directly change reality. In part this was because God was now out of the world and could not be compelled to respond in a particular way. Whatever "psyche" this God had, it had nothing to do with the inner states of individuals. The relationship between the religious community and God resembled a *contract,* rather than the organic interdependence of the earth spirits with humanity. Though humanity was ultimately dependent on God, humanity also had free will.

Part of a religious dramatization is a submissive act of prayer, which God may be moved to answer. Prayer requires faith. Magical people do not have *faith,* they have *confidence.* Religious individuals do not *respect* their deity, they *worship* him. Worship is an asymmetrical relationship in which humanity is completely dependent on God and God is completely independent of humanity. Religious followers are much less participants in their ritual and more of an audience for a religious specialist, a priest, who does most of the work.

Now let us turn to the second process unique to the universalistic religions: that whereby the spirit qualities become more important, the soul qualities are de-emphasized,

and humanity acquires domain over nature. This can be seen in the use of spirit-like abstractions to distance oneself from the concrete. There are at least three ways this operates:

> (a) the de-sexualization and rationalization of creation myths
> (b) the depiction of our ultimate home as being in the stars, not the earth
> (c) the movement toward a globalization of the human community.

One arena in which religious traditions reveal their preference for spirit functions is in the telling of creation myths. In magical myths the world is birthed as the result of love-making or some other sensual process. In religious traditions the world comes into being without human-to-human or natural action; it is created by a word, by breath, or by light. These are all relatively abstract phenomena. In the Western traditions, God labors for six days showing the spirit-like quality of perseverance. Creation is accomplished through planning, another analytical "spirit-like" function. For the great religions there is first consciousness, then there is matter. First there is thinking, then there is doing. First there is God, then there is nature. This is very different from the pattern of magical myths, in which consciousness is portrayed as being embedded in matter. Neither thinking nor planning is separate from immediate action.

Universalistic religions claim that the earth is a kind of reform school for humanity. It is not our ultimate home; it is merely a training ground for cultivating a spiritual life. A religious individual is expected to work on him- or herself, with the ultimate goal being to return to our home in the stars or a transcendental plane. Though magical people believe in dimensions beyond the physical, this earth is considered not to be very different from these invisible worlds. There is no fallen state for humanity or the earth.

Nature is both external and internal. When the first religious prophets attempted to point beyond the earth toward the ultimate home of humanity in the stars or other dimensions, the status of non-human creatures who live on earth deteriorated. Whereas in magical societies animals are usually understood as superior to humanity, with the rise of the universalistic religion this relationship was reversed. It was now assumed that human beings should renounce kinship with animals and embrace a relationship with an expanding community of strangers.

For religion, the soul-like qualities of the human psyche are suspect because they might drag humanity down to the fleshy world of the now depreciated animal kingdom. The project of all universal religions is to rescue humanity from animality. See Figure 13.2 for a summary.

In the sections that follow I will discuss the details of these historical processes as they played out in the Axial Iron Age in the Near East (Judaism); India (Buddhism); Greece (the nature philosophers and the Orphics); and China (Confusianism).

2. From Bronze Age Polytheism to Archaic Iron Age religion: the Hebrews

In this section we will resume with Frymer-Kensky's account of the movement of the Jewish people away from the polytheistic, male-dominated tendencies of late secondary magic towards monotheism.

For Hebrews (unlike the Chinese, as we will see later in this chapter), there were no mythological heroes, there were instead prophet/sages. However the early prophets more closely relate to heroes than did the late prophets. For example, Moses heard voices. By the time of the middle prophets of the Axial Iron Age such as Amos, there were no more voices to be heard. The psyche was firmly located within the individual.

In this section we will discuss changes in gender dynamics of the Hebrews and how those changes affected dynamics between gods and goddesses. For Hebrew women the rise of monotheism was a slight improvement in their previous state.

To study the religious history of the Hebrews requires a reliance on the Bible. But of course the Bible, like virtually all writings of the ancient world, has an ideological component. It reflects the needs, hopes, and politics of those who did the writing, and of the historical period in which they wrote. In later periods of history these books were reworked in the service of new political aims. Because these texts changed, our contemporary impressions of the Israelites may be derived from the *later* writings of the Bible which have been reworked, rather than from the writings of the Bible recorded during the actual times we are studying—namely from about 1400 BCE to 600 BCE. Frymer-Kensky points out that there are no independent contemporaneous texts, no marriage contracts, bills of sale, or court transactions.

According to Frymer-Kensky, ecological and demographic factors explain why the leading god for the Canaanites and the Hebrews was different from the deities of the river valleys. Unlike the Mesopotamians, Egyptians, Chinese, and Indians, the Hebrews had no large body of water from which to build irrigation systems. Direct rainfall was all they had. Hence rain gods were especially important. Secondly, unlike the civilizations of the river valleys which were overpopulated, Hebrew society was underpopulated and needed laborers. Therefore the Hebrews treated motherhood as more important than did Bronze Age civilizations.

For the Jews, Yahweh did not spring out of thin air; he began as a leader of a council of gods. It was only over time that all the other gods vanished and he was left to rule alone. But what became of Hebrew goddesses? Was it their fate to be marginalized, as the Mesopotamian goddesses were?

As we saw in the last chapter, the goddesses of ancient pagan religions had subordinate functions. Gradually male gods took over more and more of their functions. Even though the functions of goddesses became marginal, they were still divine and sexuality was still part of the cosmic order. Israelite sacred traditions took a different route: Their divine world no longer had sexual polarities built into it. Sexuality was exclusive to the *human* world. Frymer-Kensky points out that Yahweh was not male in either virility or sexuality. He was not imagined below the waist. Neither did God express physical affection for Israel. In the Bible:

The sexual and divine realms have nothing to do with each other. Indeed the Bible is concerned to maintain their separation, to demarcate the sexual and sacred experiences and to interpose space and time between them. (Frymer-Kensky, 1992, 189)

Furthermore, *the functions that used to be played by both gods and goddesses is taken over by humanity.* Unlike the Bronze Age civilizations, for the Hebrews humanity is not subordinate to nature but has dominion over it. The process by which this came to be is very interesting:

God had a council of divine beings who were charged with upholding social justice. When they did not do so, the whole world began to totter. As a result, God made these gods mortal. . . . [T]here are no longer any gods—and it is up to humanity to ensure that the foundations of the earth do not totter. The way to do this is right behavior and social justice. (Frymer-Kensky, 1992, 106)

When humanity did not do its job, God intervened. This means that God does not have absolute power. He intervenes in *reaction* to human behavior.

Biblical monotheism is essentially anthropocentric. . . . [I]n the absence of other divine beings, God's audience, partners, foils and competitors are all human beings, and it is on their interaction with God that the world depends. (Frymer-Kensky, 1992, 107)

Humanity's dominion over nature, and the dependence of nature on human actions, is fraught with immense consequences:

Human failure could result in the destruction of everything. The very existence of nature, the people of Israel are told, depends on their observance of laws of social behavior which have ostensibly nothing at all to do with the natural order.

We can only imagine the bewilderment of farmers who are told that the earth will be fertile so long as farmers remember to treat the poor correctly. Such a theology places the responsibility for fertility on human beings, but it provides no ritual to help assure fertility, no rite by which to celebrate abundance, no way to participate in the mystery of regeneration. It seems impossible that the farmers of Israel could have adhered to a system so abstract, so devoid of symbols. . . . (Frymer-Kensky, 1992, 153)

This new arrangement is momentous in human history, for it separates the sacred from the natural world and gives humanity responsibility for bridging the gap. This means that the occupations, inventions, and functions of society are understood as *human* in origin, not given by divine powers. Yahweh does two things: He takes away the powers of the other gods, and he gives those powers to humanity.

The result of this is that Hebrew women take on some of the functions of the vanquished goddesses—hence their somewhat improved position compared to women in Bronze Age civilizations:

There is always a tension between the central importance of humankind, on the one hand, and its insignificance compared to the magnitude of the unknown universe and the immeasurable God. The gap is enormous and the tension almost demands a mediating figure through which humans can attain the knowledge they require, through which they can avoid the pitfalls of wrong decisions. . . . The very importance of humans in the biblical philosophy of culture creates a flight from the human and a reemergence of females to do some of the work of the ancient goddesses. (Frymer-Kensky, 1992, 117)

While men retain technological, economic and political power over women, both are more equal before God in their basic powers.

Figure 13.3 From Bronze Age Polytheism to Archaic Iron Age Religion: Near East

Bronze Age	Archaic Iron Age
Polytheism	**Proto-monotheism**
Mesopotamia (agricultural states)	**Israelites (pastoralists)**
nature an interplay of divine forces Gods may battle each other or join together Goddesses subordinate or marginalized	**no interplay of divine forces** no more divine battles; both Gods and Goddesses vanish
sexuality part of divine order sex makes people more like deities	**sexuality not a part of the divine order** no sexual dimension to divine experience part of human order
space and time integrates sexual and sacred	space and time separates sexual and sacred God is not phallic; not imagined below waist
humanity subordinate to deities	**humanity grows at expense of deities** (God and humanity the major players)
fusion of divine with humanity	**separation of divine and humanity**
nature is self-determining	**human interaction determines nature** God mediates the relationship between humanity and nature
humans determine what Gods do through manipulation of them	humans determine what God does through ethical or unethical actions
focus on deities fluctuates depending on a crisis	**focus on deity a permanent demand**
fertility rituals necessary ritual can facilitate the union of natural forces to create fertility	**fertility rituals are faithlessness** fertility lies in God's power over the rain nature already fertile let God take care of it unless--- land can be polluted by murder, sexual activity, idolatry
deities provide humanity with culture stories about Gods and Goddesses exemplify relations between humans	**humanity develops its own culture** stories about men and women teach lessons
men and women inherently different --no solidarity between them	desires and action of men and women are more similar than different-- more solidarity
women are more globally subordinate	**women are less subordinate** women engaged in rational argumentation; nagging; lying and deceiving not condemned by Yahweh no law sanctifying wife-beating rape seen as murder
right to beat wives under the law rape accepted	
women cannot inherit property double standard about adultery expected to be domestic	women and men equally bound by law no penalties for wifely insurrection double standard about adultery expected to be domestic but women as composers and writers female deception is acceptable

Beyond the realities of Israel's social structure . . . the stories show women having the same inherent characteristics as men. . . . The circumstances of their lives are different from those of *some* men (those with power) but there are no innate differences that precluded women from taking men's roles should the occasion arise. In their strengths and weaknesses, in their goals and strategies, the women of the Bible do not differ substantially from the men. This biblical idea that the desires and actions of men and women are similar is tantamount to a radically new concept of gender. (Frymer-Kensky, 1992, 120-121)

To be sure, Israelite women were not equal to their men. Their property rights were limited. Women did not inherit property except when their husbands died and there were no sons. There was also a double standard regarding adultery. Moreover, women were expected to preoccupy themselves solely with the domestic world:

Men and women were equally bound by the laws, but the laws revolve around the sexual activity of women. . . . [F]or a married man to sleep with an unattached woman is not mentioned as an item of concern. However, a married woman could not be approached sexually by anyone but her husband. (Frymer-Kensky, 1992, 191)
The public arenas of palace, temple and low court were normally male preserves and women . . . operated in the domestic sphere. (Frymer-Kensky, 1992, 120)

Generally the biblical laws accept the various structures of power as given. They merely wish to curb *abuses* of this power. It is in curbing abuses of power that Israelite traditions are an advance for women compared to life for most women in the Bronze Age. For example, the Bible recognizes that rape is a crime of violence and the woman is a victim. It compares rape to murder. Secondly, there were no penalties for a wife's insurrection against her husband. In fact, God accepted female

deception. Yahweh himself does not have an absolute standard for honesty. For example, God sends Moses to misinform Pharaoh about the Israelites' intentions. Most or all the prophets of Israel deceive. Because Israel is up against much stronger Bronze Age state civilizations Yahweh understands that trickery and deception are the tools of the underdog. And he doesn't draw the line at gender relations. Lastly, despite an insistence that women's main concern was domesticity, women did work beyond the household. "We hear of women signers, musicians, composer/writers, prophets, midwives, lamenters" (Frymer-Kensky, 1992, 129).

In conclusion, the early version of the Hebrew bible is neither anti-women nor anti-sex. According to Frymer-Kensky, the prophets of Deuteronomy are responsible for perpetrating these stereotypes. Deuteronomy was a product of the *Axial Iron Age*, not the Archaic Iron Age. Frymer-Kensky suggests that the stress of being conquered and the destruction of the Temple in Jerusalem by the Babylonians in 586 BCE might have been a displacement reaction of Hebrew men against the powers of women in the earlier periods.

Figure 13.3 is a summary of the differences between Mesopotamian polytheism and the Archaic Iron Age religion of the Hebrews.

3. From Archaic Iron Age religion to Axial Iron Age religion: Greece and India

Greece and India, during the Axial Iron Age, had many similarities. Since we discussed Greek society at the end of chapters 2 and 6, I will focus on India here. As in Greece, iron had an important impact on Indian society. During the Archaic Iron Age, iron was limited to the making of weapons and hunting implements. But this changed. According to Sharma (1983), parts of India became centers for the manufacture of wrought iron when its use was extended to crafts, clearance, and cultivation. As in Greece, iron implements were helpful in making land available that was normally not suitable to cultivation with wooden plows.

Economics constituted a second major commonality between Greece and India. A wider range of goods, textiles, refined pottery, and woodwork became available in both regions, and wage labor expanded. Unlike the Brahmins, Buddhists were sympathetic to trade and encouraged it in a number of ways:

In certain respects the behavior pattern of an ideal trader is recommended in Buddhist teachings as a model for a monk. . . . Early Buddhist teachings seem to recommend a number of tips for success in trade. A trader needs three qualities: vision, shrewdness and ability to inspire confidence. Vision enables him to judge the nature of the commodity, the price at which it arrives and the price which will give him profit. Shrewdness consists in his skill in selling and purchasing commodities. Confidence is inspired not only by trading with borrowed money . . . and also by repaying the borrowed money with interest on time (Chakravarti, 1987, 126)

While evidence of the activity of borrowing can be found found in Vedic texts, the idea of *interest* does not clearly appear until the invention of metal money. Moneylending and usury were not condemned in Buddhist texts. Further, the Buddha encouraged the householder to repay debts, freeing him from lifelong reciprocal obligations and allowing him to wander. (Chakravarti, 1987)

Prior to the Axial Iron Age, debt between people was a method of holding people together in kinship obligations and keeping them rooted in one place. When the Buddha encouraged people to pay off debts, he was encouraging them to be less bound to places and kinship obligations, to be more mobile, and to connect with strangers. These are all characteristics of universalistic religions that have economic underpinnings.

The commercial values of the Buddha resemble Puritan, early capitalist values. Buddhists were against the ostentatious display of the Brahmins, as well as their cavalier dismissal of the lower classes. The Buddha applauded hard work and saving for a rainy day.

The use of coined money by a broader range of social members weakened status distinctions. Under the Brahmin system, receiving services was dependent on the status of the group. In Buddhist times, receiving services was dependent on having money *regardless of social status*. The system was broadened to include strangers. As noted earlier, in order for trade to proceed smoothly people needed to be able to tolerate strangers. Buddhists supported this.

Tolerating and even extending hospitality to strangers made it easier to develop schools of philosophy. Debating halls were built along with special parks or orchards where philosophers stayed in the course of their travels.

A fourth area of similarity between India and Greece (and also China) was the softening of caste hierarchies. The emergence of republican territories in India was a reaction against the growing power of the monarchies and the theocractic attributions of the king during the later Vedic period. Like the Confucian vision of the emperor (as we will see later), the King under Buddhism was not despotic. He was expected to be just both within society—protecting people's property and the family—and in fighting wars abroad. The emergence of a standing army of peasant militia along with a regular taxation system insured that the king had the resources to do this.

This move towards democratization had spiritual implications. Unlike the Brahmins, for the Buddhists birth and occupation were completely irrelevant for spiritual development. Theoretically craftspeople could become enlightened. Defilement did not come from eating and touching the wrong things, but from evil actions and thoughts. Within the spiritual realm there was equality across castes, but within the socio-political world social distinctions remained important.

The Buddhist vision of a just social order meant providing for the basic needs of everyone. The Buddha went so far as to say that providing for these needs was a *precondition* for a just moral order. He claimed that theft and violations of property would only cease when everyone's basic needs were satisfied. These democratizing intentions should not be interpreted as meaning that the Buddha was a social revolutionary. He denied the superiority of the Brahmins, but he did not preach explicitly against the structure of the caste system. He merely wanted to curb its abuses.

The following is a summary of the major innovations Buddhism made to Indian society:

(1) Houselessness—wandering with the objective of meeting distinguished teachers and philosophers, having discussions, and collecting alms (this is in contrast to the Upanishad seers, who retreated into the woods accompanied by their wives);
(2) Opposition to the Brahmin acquisition of wealth and possessions;
(3) Opposition to Brahmin sacrifice;
(4) Claims of social pre-eminence now seen as requiring a basis in humanly made laws that are distinct from the natural order;
(5) Society based on rational principles (as opposed to Brahmin privilege), with the king responsible to rule for the good of society;
(6) Opposition to the idea of special knowledge and revealed teachings tied to a hereditary caste;
(7) Higher value placed on economic functions than on religious ones (via Brahminism);
(8) Separation of political from spiritual institutions (as opposed to their being united under the Brahmins).

A summary chart of the characteristics of the Archaic and Axial Ages in India is provided in Figure 13.4

On the whole, Axial Age cities were more cosmopolitan than their Bronze Age counterparts, and the people who lived in them were largely detribalized. Buddha supported traders and artisans against the aristocrats, and advocated charity, money-lending, and hospitality to non-kin. As mentioned in chapter 2, in Greece the institution of the polis promoted rational discussion as the basis for political decisions, rather than the authority of kings or priests. (Ober 1989).

Like their Bronze Age brethren, the Archaic Iron Age Homeric Greeks and the Indian

Brahmins understood society as embedded in and subordinated to nature. In both Greece and India this was challenged. Society was said to be governed by its own laws distinct from the natural order. Support for commercial relations with strangers weakened or severed kin obligations and, by extension, loyalty to plants and animals. In the Bronze Age, kings, queens, priests, and priestesses were the vessels through which the gods and goddesses of nature spoke. Theocracies were challenged when Divine government, seen as rooted in nature, was no longer accepted as given.

In short, because relationships within society and relations between society and nature were shaken, a new basis of morality had to be found. People living in these cities could no longer rely on membership in an animal or plant clan (as in tribal societies) or in membership in a caste (as in agricultural states) to guide their behavior. Understood sociologically, the universalistic credos of Confucius, Buddha, Socrates, and the Hebrew prophets were attempts to resolve this problem.

Like the Hebraic religion, Greek and Indian religion and philosophy went through a major transformation between 1500 BCE and 500 BCE. For the Greeks this stretched from the end of Mycenaean civilizations through the "heroic" Homeric times to the Pre-Socratics and Orphics in 600-500 BCE. Unlike the Hebrews' deities, the Greeks gods and goddesses never vanished to be concentrated in a monotheistic God. During the Greek Axial Age there was a two-fold movement away from the Archaic Iron Age. On the one hand Greek philosophers (the Pre-Socratics) moved away from any sacred explanations for natural phenomena: When they searched for the causes of things, they sought a universal element—whether it be water, air, or fire. On the other, the Orphics, Pythagoras, Parmenides, and Plato sustained a sacred tradition but in a new form: they introduced a single spiritual source that was desensualized and otherworldly but not really a monotheistic deity.

Like that of the Greeks but unlike that of the Hebrews, the Indian "Axialization"

Figure 13.4 Archaic vs. Axial Iron Age in India

Before 1500 BCE	1500–500 BCE	500 BCE
	Archaic Iron	**Axial Iron**
Vedic Rig Veda	**Later Vedic** Brahmins: Hindu	**Upanishads** Buddhism
thin forests, lack rainfall	Upper Ganges plain forests easier to clear	Middle Gangetic thick forests close to mineral resources
pastoral (cattle, sheep and goats for meat and milk) horses for chariots, not domestication	**pastoral- horticulture** **barley (no rain required)**	**agricultural state** **wheat and rice** **paddy transplantation**
large sacrifices of cattle and killing for meat	sacrifices of cattle and meat consumption	non-injury to animals
king first among equals (chiefdoms?)	autocratic **monarchical kingdoms**	kingship should be just **republican territories**
		rise of territorial units (Kosala and Magadha) decline of clans growth of individualism
	no state **no standing army**	**state** **standing army** (peasant militias)
	no taxation system	taxation system
no iron	**iron for weapons** (war and hunting) wheels and chariots **pre-field, hoe and wooden ploughs** used lance, sphere	**iron for clearance, cultivation,** (handicrafts, manufacturing) **iron ploughs** used axes, saws, chisels
	Brahmins: anti-trade	**Buddhists: pro-trade** 3 virtues of trader: vision, shrewdness, confidence
	disapproved of sea voyages debt encouraged (generalized reciprocity)	sea voyage are acceptable paying off debts (free to trade abroad)
	pre-money debt w/o interest	encouraged money lending debt w/ interest lay converts--traders emergence of wage labor
	prostitution not tolerated	prostitution tolerated hospitality and charity to non-kin encouraged debate
	householder identity acquisition of wealth	identity beyond the householder renunciation of wealth preeminence of society
	society based on charisma sacred knowledge based on birth unity of king and sangha	society based on rational principles no sacred knowledge based on birth separation of king and sangha

movement, namely Buddhism, was more a philosophy than it was a religion. But in the way it conceived of an ultimate source, it was otherworldly and non-dualist.

Both the Homeric gods and goddesses of the Greek Archaic Iron Age and the Vedic gods and goddesses were sensual, brawling bands of conquerors, preoccupied with a local piece of land. The Orphics, the Pre-Socratics, the Pythagoreans, and Buddhists all shared a more cosmopolitan outlook, both towards nature (this was especially true of the Pre-Socratics) and towards humanity in general (the Buddhists and Pythagoreans).

Many of the differences between Archaic and Axial Age religion had to do with the type of societies that gave rise to them. Both Homeric Greece and Vedic India were pastoral societies with a provincial form of social organization, so it makes sense that the sacred presences of these peoples would jealously guard a particular piece of land. Conversely, the cities of the Axial Iron Age were cosmopolitan, in some cases with empires. It makes sense that their gods would be more global and universalistic.

The Archaic and Axial periods each had a sacred archetype—the hero and the sage. These archetypes shared a restlessness with the obligations to family and kin-group that had been characteristic of Bronze Age agricultural states. As different as the Brahmins were from the Buddhists, both agreed that there are more important matters to attend to in life than merely the fulfillment of the obligations of being a householder or the expectations of your kin group.

While the hero was a land-based man of action, the sage was an urban-based man who spent his time in discussion with strangers (being a wandering scholar) and in reflection. The sage thrived on diversity in order to discover commonalties across differences. Partly because Socrates and Buddha believed in an afterlife for all, they were less pressed to find meaning in facing great danger and overcoming it, as the hero did. The sage looked upon the seeking of fame and honor as shallow and a distraction from real spiritual development. Because the sage was far more introspective

than the hero, he was less subject to mood swings, had more perseverance, and saw further into the past and future.

As Hatab (1992) points out, the Orphics of the Axial Iron Age developed a "puritan psychology" in which the mind is not only separated from nature but from the body as well. The world is understood as a reform school in which to learn lessons. When the right lessons have been learned, the mind can detach itself from the world of rebirth and attain its ultimate state of oneness with all existence. This is both a Platonic and Buddhist argument as well.

Lastly, just as the Hebrews desexualized the divine, so did the Orphics, Pythagoras, Plato in Greece, and the Buddha in India. In all three traditions the Axial Age sacred source is non-sexual, abstract, and universal. So too, the later sages in India and Greece are more uncompromising that the Indic Brahmins or the warrior-heroes of archaic Greece.

The Archaic Iron Age religion still dripped with the magical sense that the psyche is diffused in nature. Hence the early Hebrew prophets heard the voice of Yahweh; and the Greek hero, according to Dodds (1951), had no unified sense of willpower, soul or personality. Morality was driven by external commands. Just as the Hebrews had the Old Testament, so the Brahmins referred to the Vedas to give them answers to moral questions.

In short, the Archaic Iron Age was caught in the nether world between the polytheism of the secondary magic of Bronze Age agricultural states and the monotheism of universalistic religions in Axial Iron Age commercial cities. Its characteristics were neither wholly one or wholly the other.

4. Archaic to Axial Age religion in China

Social Mobility and The Rise of Territorial States

In ancient China we can identify four periods of transition from the Archaic to the Axial Iron Age. The Archaic Iron Age begins with the Chou Dynasty, dated from 1046 BCE, while the Axial Iron Age is clearly manifest in the Han empire, beginning in 221 BCE. During this 800-year period there were two transitional periods. The first was the Chun-Chiu dynasty, which lasted from 722 to 464 BCE; the second is the Warring States period of Confucius, Mo-Tzu, and Mencius, which is dated from 464 to 222 BCE. Our focus will be the contrast between the Chou dynasty and the Warring states period. For readers who prefer to see the big picture first, Figure 13.5 is an overview chart.

The Chou dynasty had many of the characteristics typical of the Archaic Iron Age elsewhere. There was a plurality of small states, approximately 71 of them, governed by a hereditary nobility and a weak ruler. Merchants were few; people relied on local markets and small fairs. The aristocracy was satisfied with limited imports from outside areas of jewelry and salt.

The Chou dynasty was composed of city-states in which each capital city was a political base with its own capital, temple, and military force. Though aristocrats lived off the work of peasant farmers, hunting was still an important activity, providing animals to be offered up to the ancestors in the temples. Hunting was inseparably identified with combat. To assure success, every military campaign of the aristocrats began at a temple, where divinations were performed.

One of the major characteristics of the transition from the Archaic to the Axial Iron Age was an increase in social mobility. During the Chou period and the Chun-Chiu times, the state was run in a familial manner, being organized like a large household, with the closest relative of the ruler playing the most important part. Respect for rulers depended not on the institution of state but on the personality of the ruler. Further, the ruler was always a co-ruler with his brothers. This meant he could not discharge his ministers for incompetence or treachery because they weren't elected or even appointed by him. They were *born* to help him rule.

The ministers constituted the second social caste, an upper aristocracy holding fiefs and serving the ruler as vassals. They inherited their positions and fiefs from their fathers.

The third caste consisted of the "shih," a conglomerate of all non-aristocratic groups. The Chou state was *not* run bureaucratically. The development of a territorial state during the Warring States period was inseparable from the building of a bureaucracy. According to the great sociologist Max Weber, this required a transition from familial relationships with role ambiguity, no formal training in skills, and no screening process, to impersonal relationships with clear definition of roles, formal training to acquire skills, and a screening process to test these skills. A larger, more complex territorial state needed administrators of higher ability. Those of non-aristocratic origin (the shih) would have been safer to train because their loyalty was more reliable. Having none of the land and privilege of the aristocracy, they had little to gain by betraying the ruler. By contrast, a courtly aristocracy was more unreliable because it had land and privileges to fall back on.

The story of upward (and downward) mobility can be demonstrated with rise of the ministers and shih and the decline of the sons of rulers. According to Cho-yun Hsu (1968), before 464 BC the shih held 26% of government posts. After that time their share more than doubled to 55%. What caused this change from feudal monarchies to territorial states?

The decline of the Chou monarchies coincided with great battles between the aristocratic classes within these monarchies ("the Spring and Autumn period"). Weak rulers seized the opportunity to increase their power by *not* intervening in the conflicts of the aristocracy. This resulted in some lineages being destroyed. One of three results followed:

1. A state was allowed to retain identity, but only as a satellite of the conquering state;
2. The residents of states might be given to other states as slaves. If a man of noble birth emigrated to another state, his rank in the new state depended strictly on his own character and ability. There was no recognition of privilege across states;
3. The population of the conquered state might be resettled in territory belonging

to the victorious state. Our focus will be on this political strategy.

As a result of aristocratic warfare, the 71 states of the Chou period were incorporated into the 21 victorious states during the Chun-Chiu period and into 7 states in the Chan Kuo (Warring States) period. This meant that the territorial rulers of the more centralized Chinese society had to expand their military on the one hand, and develop new military technology on the other. In speaking about the difference between the Chou and later periods, Mark Edmund Lewis (1990) argues that the number of chariots in use went from about 800 before 530 BCE to 4,000 after 530 BCE.

But while the number of chariots grew, the days of using chariots at all were numbered. For one thing, chariots were too expensive for use by an expanding army. For another, chariots were not very flexible, being useless in mountains or in swamps. Finally, they were always in danger of being stolen. An infantry headed by peasants was cheaper and more geographically efficient, while a cavalry was superior to chariots when high speed was needed. Mass infantry composed of peasants complemented mounted cavalry and replaced the chariot armies of the aristocrats. Mass infantry required less skill and less expensive equipment. The invention of the crossbow and the increasing use of iron weapons made the infantry formidable.

As the state began to reorganize itself, there was more opportunity for upward mobility for peasants in joining the new standing army. Many peasants found army life more attractive than life as a peasant. Moreover, the state had to pay more attention to peasants if it expected the standing army to be more efficient. For example, the state responded to famines by distributing rice to every family. Further, peasants were bestowed titles for bravery and received rewards in the forms of land or position in government. Fighting slaves were freed after military service. People of non-aristocratic origins were able to move into positions such as chiefs of staff, commanders of armies, ambassadors, and chancellors.

In the Chou period, fighting had occurred at any time of the year. In the Warring states period, fighting was postponed until after the crops were planted. This was because those who fought and killed were the same as those who sowed and cultivated. Whereas in the Chou period only the aristocracy fought, when the peasantry was responsible for war accommodations had to be made. Thus increased military power required more coordination and strategizing than ever before.

Unlike during the Chou dynasty, during the Warring States period military service was required for all, and for this service each family was granted a holding of state land in accord with merits earned in battle. According to Mark Edward Lewis (1990), between 543 and 539 BCE the fields of Zheng were reorganized into a grid and rural households were organized into units of five. This reorganization helped to break down the barriers between urban and rural areas.

Just as the military forces grew, so the government expanded its control over wider areas of land, including the reclaiming of wasteland. Laborers were hired to drain swamps. New methods of irrigation using the wellsweep could increase the volume of water drawn. Useless soil was made more fertile. These improvements in the land, combined with the death of many aristocrats in war, meant that there was more land available for cultivation. Distinguished soldiers got grants of lands. These lands were no longer fiefs but became purchasable commodities.

Private ownership of land existed during the Chou dynasty but land was acquired by the use of force rather than through economic transactions. In wars among states territory was freely ceded, annexed, and conquered without consulting its official owner, the Chou king. Based on the criteria of might, peasants never owned the land they worked on. Therefore, there was no need for the state to tax peasants.

A reform in the tax system was a mixed blessing for peasants. On one hand it became possible for a typical peasant to own a piece of land; but on the other, if he lost out in the competition for new lands he would become a tenant of the remaining lords. As a tenant, the peasant did not have the protection of the lord, as he did in the Chou Dynasty.

While a proportion of peasants might have been successful in gaining new land to farm, for most the breaking up of the traditional land system made life worse. Anyone who could not maintain land lost out to whoever could pay the price of the land. The newly developed merchant class (see below) bought up much of the land, concentrating the wealth once again. Former peasants became landless plebeians rehired to work the land as tenants. Some traveled to the cities and sought careers as scholars, public servants, artisans, or merchants.

States during post-Chou times were expanding on the one hand and becoming more centralized on the other. They were also becoming more interdependent. The rural manor in Chou times was self-sufficient, the farmer hunting for meat and fur, repairing his own house, and making his own rope. His wife spun and weaved their clothes. Vegetables were grown in gardens and sheep were raised in pastures. But by the time of the Warring States, the peasant economy was no longer self-sufficient. A farmer could no longer supply his own cloth, cooking pots, or implements, but depended on people in other occupations, whom he supplied with grain. Different states specialized in different industrial products. In order to coordinate this interdependency a fluid medium of exchange was needed.

According to Cho-yun Hsu, cowrie shells, cloth, hemp, and silk were used as primitive media of exchange. But during the 4th and 3rd centuries BCE, bronze money came to be used. The coins were made in different weights, sizes, and denominations.

As in other societies, the first cities in China were fortresses and ceremonial centers, not administrative or commercial centers. Whatever industrial, commercial quarters existed were outside the city walls. Cities of the Warring State period were larger and less militarily and spiritually dominated. The new outer wall of these cities *included* industrial and residential areas.

Prior to the warring state period, states collected tariffs and cities could require travelers to pay tolls. This obstructed commerce: "In a China so compartmentalized a merchant would have found it hard to carry on any large scale trade if each state and city insisted on having its own customs house to stop the passing goods." (Cho-yun Hsu, 1968, 116)

As the concentration of power reduced the number of states and the specialization of labor required more contact between the states remaining, it was advantageous for the larger states to improve highways and waterways to facilitate commercial travel, making transport safer and bypassing tariffs and tolls. The expansion of land controlled by states gave merchants more territories in which to trade. A traveling merchant could feel secure within the territory of any single state. Improvement in travel facilitated upward opportunities for mobility among peasants who wanted to try becoming merchants.

Easier and safer conditions of travel benefited not only merchants but scholars and their students, who were able to walk from one state to another. Shih intellectuals could have interstate friendships.

To summarize, the Warring States period saw many new breakthroughs, including a significant rise in population, an increase in scale and diversity of urban centers, the appearance of irrigation systems, the use of iron weapons, the expansion of handcrafts, an increased use of money, and an expansion in wage labor. The government became increasingly centralized. The state came to be staffed by salaried officials, and formerly autonomous local governments came to be controlled by the courts. The cavalry, infantry, and the crossbow replaced chariots, just as they did in the Near East. Upon the ashes of collective kin property of the Chou dynasty arose both an expansion of state property and the contraction of private property of the household. This Axial Age society is called "Warring States" not because its political units were always at war, but because the states were created through progressive extension of military service and the reorganization of society along militaristic lines.

During the change from Chou to the Warring States in China there was also a transformation in how the military was run, a change that ultimately had religious implications. The attitude toward fighting during the Chou dynasty is characterized by Lewis as "heroic." This means that the warrior valued daring and sought glory among his fellows. He fought for vengeance and to appease the ancestors. This "hero" had no sense of fighting for a sense of justice as represented by any state administration. Killing or risking one's life was the only way glory could be achieved.

With the rise of the Warring States and a centralized army, the values of heroism began to decline. The rule of the state meant the crushing of rebellions within the upper classes, specifically the aristocracy, and championing the peasants. According to Lewis, the art of command changed to emphasize

(1) the mastery of written texts,
(2) mental effort to organize and coordinate the action of masses,
(3) the discovery and creation of pattern in the chaos of battle, and
(4) its relations to political authority and social order (Lewis, 1990,97)

As we saw earlier, in the Chou period there was no formal training for generals apart from the usual training received by all nobles. The new military commanders were trained with military texts that taught the necessity of formulating strategic battle plans *before* entering into battle. What mattered to the new commanders was not physical prowess, but the *mental* capacity to calculate. This included assessments of degree of harmony between rulers and people, and of the strength and social coherence of the opposition; the timing of the season; the skills of the opposing commander and the state of the terrain. *Dependence on reason forbade any reliance on divination* because the latter would introduce doubt into the strategy.

For the sage, success meant having to fight *as little as possible*. After calculations the leader would only fight if victory was more or less assured, therefore saving wear-and-tear on his forces. This type of leader could be *deficient* in military skills and still succeed.

On the other hand, since all people in the military could not be commanders, the renouncing of heroism also involved discipline (i.e. submission) on the part of the population. The work of a hero involved both skill and improvised mental effort. With his decline, military action was increasingly characterized by a division of labor. The work of the commander involved *deliberative mental* effort and the work of the population involved *less skill and more obedience.*

Passivity was the norm for the peasant army. The commander was encouraged metaphorically to "block up" the eyes and ears of his men so they would have little knowledge of what was going on. The commander had to use various devices such as banners, bells, and drums to keep his soldiers from taking initiative and advancing on their own. If they were tempted by the values of the heroic warrior they could more easily be goaded by insults to engage in battle prematurely.

In order to make the army more accepting of passivity, the image of the fighter had to be altered. While the heroic warrior had a virile image as an aggressive, impulsive risk taker, soldiers were now encouraged to be more passive by directing them to follow the Tao— the way of nature, in which superior strength is paradoxically shown by yielding.

The following seven points summarize the changes in the military with the emergence of the Warring States, according to Lewis:

(1) The army is unified as a single body. During the Chou period, each lord marshaled members of his fiefdom to fight. Since there was no centralized state to coordinate their efforts, the army under the Chou dynasty had no specialization of labor. This, combined with the values of heroism, would make efficiency of efforts highly problematic.

(2) The behavior of soldiers was made more standardized and predictable, and the *integrated squad* was the lowest independent fighting unit. During the Chou period the lowest unit for independent decision making had been the individual soldier. In the Warring States period, the individual had to follow the squad leader.

(3) Combat became a duel between opposing *minds* of commanders. Creativity could only be exercised at this level; soldiers themselves simply followed orders.

(4) Commanders were held responsible under law, and had to account to the head of state for their action. In the Chou period the commander and the ruler were the same.

(5) Soldiers came to be referred to metaphorically as natural objects, children, or animals.

(6) The ideal of masculine strength was replaced by that of Taoist obedience.

(7) Individual initiative was punished. In the Chou period initiative had been rewarded.

The socialization of nature and the naturalization of society

As in other agricultural civilizations, the actions of divine kings and queens in China were rooted in nature through an elaborate set of magical correspondences. The cosmos was understood as an alternation of yin and yang that cycled through the five elements. A key mediating force between Heaven and Earth is the wind, or *qi*. While in part based on an analogy with human breath, this was also linked to the monsoon wind in North China. The "temperament" characteristic of each region was shaped by the wind. This in turn shaped the characteristics of the people who lived there.

> The qi of mountains will produce many males; the qi of swamps will produce many females; the qi of places with obstructed access will produce many mute people; the qi of windy places will produce many deaf people. . . the qi of stony places will produce many strong people (Lewis 1990, 216)

As we saw in chapter 1, all political elites must legitimatize their monopolization of the means of violence. In the case of China, the Chou aristocracy justified their political power by claiming to serve the ancestors. The new territorial lords of the Warring States justified their power by claiming it was merely an expression of what was *already going on* in the cosmos.

All societies are limited in the degree to which they can see the world objectively. Mostly worldviews are organized as an unconscious projection of the predominant form of social organization. All societies also have to explain the relationship between the social world and the rest of nature. In Axial Age China, the social phenomena of coercion were unconsciously projected on to the physical world (nature). Then, thinking they had found something objective, philosophers "discovered" the laws that should govern the structure of their society by studying the natural environment. Nature was shaped into a social image, and then reused as a model for social relations.

In the case of ancient China, the threat of violence was necessary for the elite to maintain its power. As a way of legitimizing their rule, the elite searched the natural world and "discovered" violence at every turn (failing to see cooperation as well) and then justified the continued use of violence and the threat of violence in society as merely an effort to follow the path of nature (Heaven). The actions and powers of the ruler become inseparable from Heaven itself.

The logic went something like this:

Monarch = head of social order
Human community = natural order (Heaven)
therefore
Powers of monarchs = powers of Heaven

The elite presented themselves as mediating the forces of Heaven and Earth using magical correspondences to sanctify their violence. So just as the punishing power of nature was strongest during autumn and winter so was the punishing power of the Emperor as the Son of

Heaven also at its peak in wars during this season. More specifically:

> Qi stood in the same relations to the Earth as the stars and other astral phenomena did to Heaven. Each was the dynamic, moving element in its own region, and as such they were . . . natural . . . for human action linked to society in a great triad of sympathetic resonance. And just as the reading of qi . . . was primarily of importance in military affairs, so a large share of . . . divination . . . dealt with war and peace. The basic dynamic patterns of the universe were integrated into a grand vision of a systematically interacting cosmos in which human violence became part of the motions of heaven and the pulsation of Earth. (Lewis, 1990, 144)

Qi in the human world was identified with the undisciplined violence of the discredited aristocracy, and needed to be harnessed by the controlled mental effort of the ruler:

> Violent men or fighters were identified with the unthinking impulses of this 'configured energy' (Lewis 1990, 214). Not only was qi linked with physical strength and bellicosity but it was explicitly contrasted with the mental acuity and reflective capacities of the commander and with the potency of the sage. . . . Qi was linked with unthinking youth and physical strength. (Lewis, 1990, 224)

The outer world of nature (the beasts) is violent and the inner nature of man is violent through the expression of anger. This would normally impel men to fight. But a sage could use violence to create order:

> Separation and division were the root of humanity. Sages were mythic prototypes of territorial rulers. Rulers . . . created and maintained humanity through mastery of division and appropriate pattern. . . . Having banished violence to the realm of undifferentiated nature, they claimed authority through their bestowal of

intelligible pattern on brute masses. (Lewis, 1990, 241)

This struggle to control qi is expressed in two images of the peasant: one as a diligent farmer, harnessing energy productively in peacetime; the other as the savage rebel in the army. In the latter case qi becomes destructive because it is not sublimated in obedience to military commanders.

This new relationship between society and Heaven was further legitimized in games of kickball and in animal park pageants. Again these are legitimizing activities because they move away from direct violence and toward rationalized, symbolic, and indirect violence.

In Chou times kickball was a mock battle and a form of military training. During the Axial Age this military training became outdated but the activity lived on in the form of entertainment. Still the legitimizing connection with Heaven remained. The round ball stood for Heaven and the square walls for Earth. The field had two sides, yin and yang. As the teams interacted the patterns of Heaven were reproduced on Earth.

The belief that violence is natural goes back at least to the Chou dynasty in their notion of hunting as a form of warfare and warfare as a form of hunting. There was an analogy between animals sacrificed in the hunt with prisoners captured through war. For the Chou, hunts were training grounds for war and a means to capture prey for sacrifices.

The official hunts in the great parks during the Han period were *pageants* that portrayed the violence of an imperial state not only against its social enemies but toward the realm of beasts and plants. Just as animals were seen as natural soldiers subordinate to humanity, soldiers were seen as social animals not only subordinate to the commander, but *made human* through the power of the sage and the commander.

> In all these rituals and contests the participants were servants, barbarians, criminals and even beasts, while the emperor and his agents appeared as the human images of Heaven incorporating

violence and death into the overarching patterns of the cycle of calendrical time (Lewis, 1990, 138)

Mythology as Politics: Triumph of the Yellow Emperor

Part of the ideology of Axial Iron Age China was the notion of the birth of humanity in this period, in contrast to the bestiality of human beings during the Chou period. This political legitimation is expressed in myths of the victory of the Yellow emperor over various foes, including the Divine Husbandman, the Fiery Emperor, and Chi You. These ancient forces were then recruited and used as raw material for a new history of Chinese civilization, one that justified the rulers of the territorial state.

This ideology begins with the notion that in earliest times humans were not separate from animals, but that this separation had occurred because (a) superhuman sages had given human beings technology that (b) separated humanity from animals physically, expelled the animals from their habitats and (c) introduced moral practices that made a civilized existence possible.

The following passage from the Confucian Mencius gives a clear depiction:

In the time of Yao, the world was not yet stabilized. Floods ran rampant and inundated the world, grasses and trees grew in profusion, birds and animals multiplied wildly. . . Yao, in his solitude, worried about this, and he raised up Shun and sent him to rectify it. Shun commanded Yi to take a fire and set the mountains and highlands ablaze so the animals fled and hid. Yu then channeled the nine rivers and led them, rippling and swirling to the sea. . . . Hou Ji taught the people husbandry, the planting and reaping of the five grains. (Lewis, 1990, 171)

Yet humanity still contained all the elements of nature, so that under certain conditions it could *degenerate* to an earlier stage of evolution. The warrior of the Chou period, by his heroic methods, was one example of this. The Chou aristocrats were linked with one of the mythological figures whom the Yellow Emperor defeats, Chi You.

The Yellow emperor was a lord of rain, storm, and fog, but his relationship to Chi You is complicated because Chi You was also a storm god, and because both were involved in sacrificial rituals of the new year, which occurred during the second half of the dry season. In the monsoon climate of North China there was concern over the coming rain, this concern was linked to the coming violence of the government.

At first the Yellow Emperor and Chi You were not adversaries but master and servant. Later Chi You became demonized. He plunged the world into chaos and then was slain and eaten in a sacrifice that restored the world. The means by which the Yellow Emperor defeated Chi You was by following a *military treatise* given to him by the Queen Mother of the West. Two things are important here. We see the introduction of writing to overcome the physical power of Chi You, and that the source of this knowledge is a woman, not a man.

Before the Yellow Emperor began to carry out the role of ruler, there appeared Chi You and his eighty brothers. They had the bodies of beasts, the speech of men, bronze heads and iron brows. They ate sand and stones . . . they terrorized all under Heaven and slaughtered barbarically. . . . [T]he people desired for the Yellow Emperor to carry out the tasks of the Son of Heaven, but he practiced love and virtuous potency and could not make forcible prohibitions, so no one could oppose Chi You. (Lewis, 1990, 203)

It was the military treatise that made the difference in the Yellow Emperor's victory.

Chi You and the Yellow Emperor both proclaimed violence and punishment as necessary. But under the violence of Chi You, punishments *destroyed* social order. The Yellow Emperor instituted punishment which was not arbitrary, but legal and based on human justice. Whereas under Chi You, punishments turned humans into beasts, the violence (or the threat of violence) of the Yellow emperor turned beasts into humans.

Lewis applies a sociological analysis to this myth and its meaning for the politics of different classes:

In the Warring States the *cultic* [my emphasis] roots of the tales of the Yellow Emperor were gradually suppressed as part of the general reinterpretation of ancient divinities as historical figures. . . . Among the common people shamanic rituals devoted to a host of anthropomorphic spirits continued to flourish throughout the Chou and . . . the entire history of imperial China, but elite religion and the state cultus focused increasingly on ancestor worship, [and] official sacrifices to abstract natural forces or spirit analogies of the bureaucracy. . . . [T]he devotion of state cultus entirely to abstract deities such as Heaven, Earth or the Supreme Unity was part of a general re-creation of the spirit world by the emerging elite. . . . It was the first round in a battle for control of the realm of the spirits that would span the history of imperial China, a battle between the historicizing, philosophical intellect of the literate elite and the protean religious practices of the local, peasant communities. (Lewis, 1990, 195)

Chi You is a mythological projection of the heroic mentality of aristocracy of the city-state Chou dynasty, while the Yellow Emperor is a projection of the legalist bureaucracy and military commands of the territorial lords of the Warring States period:

Specifically they constituted a mythology of statecraft; they dealt with the interest and concerns produced by the gradual destruction of the city-based world of the Chou nobility at the hands of the rising territorial lords. The tales of Yao and Shun dealt with the competing claims of virtue/talent and heredity that became an issue as dependent ministers recruited for their skills and linked to the ruler through

hierarchical bonds replaced the nobility that had held office as a hereditary privilege. The myths of . . . the taming of the flood reflected the transformed relation of the political order to the land in a state that was created through the progressive extension of direct control into the countryside. . . . The stories of the Yellow Emperor and his battles offered a dramatic representation of the reorganization and revaluation of political violence where mass, peasant armies under the command of the court were replacing the chariot armies of a warrior aristocracy. (Lewis, 1990, 169)

To this absolutist state of the Yellow Emperor, humanity owes everything, thus legitimizing this state's existence:

[H]umanity had been created by rulers through their superhuman powers . . . if men were made by men solely by a set of technologies and moral teachings created by former kings and maintained by present rulers then subjects were human only through the authority of their masters. Without the controls institutions imposed by the elite, the common people would be nothing but beasts. In accounts of ancient history the Warring States elite thus justified their political power as a very definition of humanity, the only barrier or dividing line between civilization and the savage world of the beasts. (Lewis, 1990, 212)

Democratic and skeptical tendencies
To a certain extent, the changes in Chinese rulership from aristocracy to rule by a benign emperor resulted in more democracy and skepticism. This change was supported by two of the most important ideological schools of the Warring State period, the Confucian and the Legalist schools. Both believed that there is a relationship between how well governed the population is in peacetime and how difficult it will be to control them during wartime. The more fairly they are governed, the better fighters they will be. The virtues of the ruler

Figure 13.5 Archaic and Axial Iron Age in China

Zhou Dynasty **1046 BCE** **Bronze Age**		**Warring states** **464-222 BCE** **Axial Iron Age**
feudalism 21 states; non-bureaucratic and familial city-state aristocrats state or group ownership little social mobility self-sufficiency for peasants small cities served as military strongholds	**politics**	territorial states **7 states; bureaucratic w/qualifications** **necessary** territorial lords private ownership of land upward and downward mobility peasants less self-sufficient: must import tools large cities are administrative and commercial improved irrigation systems, highways, waterways
little demand for merchants small fairs, local markets, tolls, tariffs barter with hemp, silk	**economics**	merchants rise: state interdependency arises lifting of tolls and tariffs bronze money
chariots long training state has decentralized army only aristocrats fought heroic deeds by individuals war as means to glory	**technology/military**	cavalry, mass infantry, cross-bow less skill, more soldiers state centralized army entire population conscripted by state uniform action by troops war as response to a murder war sometimes overridden by ritual
hero (aristocrat) physical daring killing for glory authority from ancestors physical-practical intentions hunts as training	**sacred archetype**	**sage (autocrat)** wisdom, mental skill killing for justice, persuasion direct mandate from heaven imitation of heavenly violence symbolic, legitimizing intentions great parks, pageants--extend violence into nature--kickball
humans undifferentiated from animals disorganization of nature morality based on arbitrary force	**humanity-nature**	culture sages give civilization humanity separating from animals technology morality based on ritual
Chi You Chi You: rain, storms, comet punishment, all social order collapses butting: bestial justice turned humans into beasts undisciplined qi reckless youth natural disturbances result from magical practices	**mythology**	**Yellow Emperor** Yellow Emperor: rain, storms, fog punishment, social world becomes stable legal procedures: human justice turned beasts into humans disciplined qi wisdom of sage natural disturbances a reflection of social organization (Confucius)
aristocrats rule by semi-divine government mandate from heaven (charismatic right) right to govern: blood, heredity kinship bonds respect for past	**skeptical ideology**	secular government mandate from heaven to serve people right to govern: virtue, competence qualifications contract: calculated self-interest accepted less respect: for the past, more democratic, skeptical

during peacetime could ultimately *eliminate* the need for military wisdom. "The techniques that preserved social order also maintained discipline in the army and no separate military arts were needed." (Lewis, 1990, 131)

> [T]he Confucian identification of Heaven with the people was basically a criticism of belief in a personified heaven or spirits who could be bought with sacrifices and who revealed their will in omens and natural prodigies. . . . The people as heaven manifested themselves in the world not in cosmic pattern or order but in negation of that order expressed through . . . monstrosities and disasters. Their equivalents or doubles in the natural world were floods, the raining of blood, two-headed calves and any other freak or abortion of conventional nature that signaled the breakdown of proper order. (Lewis, 1990, 237)

There is a great deal we can learn from this passage. In the first place we see the Confucian disdain for magical cosmic powers and divination practices. In his conception of Heaven as reflected in the organization of society, Confucius taught that no society was worthy unless it takes the needs of the peasants into account. Insofar as rulers are unjust, Heaven will show its displeasure by bringing natural disasters. Confucius, like all Axial Age philosophers, wished to soften the caste hierarchies of both the Bronze and Archaic Iron Ages while maintaining class distinctions.

Similarly, the Mohists claimed that Heaven is equally concerned with *all* mankind (instead of just the ruler or the aristocrats). Because all men are created equal, no one man had a mandate from heaven. Mencius claimed that the sovereign's dignity is determined by the *environment*, not by inner charismatic qualities. Further, he claimed that the people, not the ruler or emperor, constitute the most important element in a nation. Hsun Tzu taught that Heaven does not create people for the sake of the sovereign, but the sovereign for the sake of people.

In addition these reformers ceased to glorify the past. Shang Yang argued that there is more than one way to govern the world and no need to imitate antiquity. Skeptical philosophers derided traditional values. For example, Man Kou Te said that "small robbers are put in prison, the great robber becomes a feudal lord."

Conclusion

All of this displays the four characteristics of the Axial Iron Age religion. The expansion of the land in space supports a religious desire to incorporate strangers into society and break away from provincialism towards universalism. The change in attitude towards war also shows a transition from a spontaneous, courageous imagination (soul qualities) of the hero to the calculating, reasoned military strategy of a sage (spirit quality). The Confucian protest of the exclusion of peasants from the concerns of Heaven shows a desire for the inclusiveness and kindheartedness characteristic of the universalistic religions. The movement from military training exercises to games of kickball and animal pageantry in parks shows how dramatization is weakened into entertainment or passivity, while being symbolic of something that was once real. The battle between Chi You and the Yellow emperor is the mythological counterpart to the battle between the hero and the sage as a model for society.

The description of the use of the magical correspondences of qi to the legitimation of the powers of rulers and the need for submission of the population is something that is closer to a secondary magical legitimation strategy than a religious one. While this section does not discuss the impact on women, the legitimizing tactics for the subordinate of peasants can be seen as applying to women.

5. Comets and the origin of sky-god religion

Until now we have talked about the polytheistic, secondary magical tradition in the Bronze Age (chapter 12) and the movement from Archaic to Axial Age religion as if the entire process was unaffected by the presence of comets, asteroids, and their debris. When we discussed the characteristics of the sky gods in the Archaic Iron Age and compared them to the monotheistic deity in the Axial Iron Age, it appeared that God has evolved—moving from a tempestuous, jealous, adolescent to a wise old man. The model for humanity follows a similar pattern. The hero is very much like the sky-gods in the Archaic Iron Age while the sages resemble the monotheistic deity in their characteristics. For both the sacred and secular world there is a movement from externally driven, physical motives, to internally driven rational motives; from external laws to internal conscience; from storm and stress to universal light. Might this trend have something to do with the presence or absence of celestial disturbances?

As we saw in chapter 10, natural disasters peppered the Bronze Age. If they were caused by comets, asteroids, and their debris, then the changes in sacred tradition that began around the time of Hammorabi in the 19th century BCE culminating in the Axial Age religion may have been driven by an astronomical-geophysical process to which humanity had to adapt.

To be more explicit, while there does not seem to be a correlation between the natural disasters around 2300 BCE and changes in polytheism, there are definite connections between the natural disasters in the middle Bronze Age and the movement from the subordination to the marginalization of Goddesses. Further, the natural disasters of the late Bronze Age go very well with the tempestuous nature of the sky gods in the Archaic Iron Age. Lastly, there is no record of cometary activity or natural disasters between 1000 and 500 BCE. It is perhaps no coincidence that the idea of a universalistic, gentle loving god arose at this time.

In other words, in the last Bronze Age or early Archaic Iron Age the characteristics of the gods are arbitrary and cruel because real events in the sky were capricious and caused misery on earth. The authoritarian laws during this time perhaps came about as a way to impose order in a situation that was out of control. Perhaps the thunderbolts hurled by Zeus, the fire and brimstone cast down by Yahweh, and the violent chaos induced by Chi You were not just metaphors.

Conversely, after centuries of chaos the ceasing of cometary activity would have seemed merciful, and perhaps the work of a new kind of caring divine presence. When the workings of nature appeared to be more self-regulating, human beings (at least those in charge of the superstructure of society) would then project what they experienced in the world into their own psychology. They imagined their internal world could be contained and self-managed.

All ancient societies have sacred presences that inhabit the sky (though not all are male and not all seem to correlate with comets). Whether sacred presences were male or female, whether they were sky gods or sky goddesses, prior to the Bronze Age sacred presences of the *earth* were understood as more important for people's everyday concerns. It is my contention that the shift in emphasis from earth to sky in the Bronze Age can be partly explained by cometary activities and its aftermath on earth. However, while cometary activity can help explain the rise of an orientation toward polytheistic sky gods, and away from animism, this is *not* enough to explain the movement from polytheism to monotheism.

On the surface it would seem that the focus on events in the sky—comets, dust, storms and hail, and the resulting disasters on earth—earthquakes, volcanoes, cold, crop loss—would be directly connected to the movement from earth spirits to sky gods. In other words if events in the sky are causing earthly disasters, then the beings who inhabit the sky must be more powerful than those on earth. A new mythology would favor the sky gods and goddesses over the earth deities. Clube and Napier (1990) argue that it is not quite that simple.

On the basis of a cross-cultural comparison of mythologies, Clube and Napier argued that good and evil forces are an expression of standing and fallen comet debris. They argue that first order conflicts are *not between sky and earth, but between competing sky gods*—a god and a dragon, or two dragons. The *outcome* of the battle consisted of geological disasters. In other words the battle is between comets and their celestial debris. The celestial object that fell to earth lost the battle and became a devil. The comet or piece of debris remaining in the sky became a sky god who was worshipped.

And what is the relationship between the *fallen sky god* and the existing earth spirits? What seems reasonable is that the fallen comet (sky god) at first dominates the earth spirits. After the remaining victorious comet fades, the sky god becomes invisible, assuming a transcendental status. Many of the earth spirits come to merge with the falling comet or asteroid debris and add to the characteristics of what becomes the devil, counterpoints to the monotheistic gods in the Axial Iron Age.

The emergence of monotheism can be summarized in the following steps:

Bronze Age and Archaic Iron Ages
>   (1) there is a celestial struggle in the sky between sky gods (comets or comet debris)
>   (2)
>   a) some of the debris remains in the sky—the victorious sky god.
>   b) some of the debris falls to earth causing natural disasters. The fallen comet (a demon) rules over the earth spirits

Axial Iron Age
>   (3) a ceasing of comet or asteroid activity relative to the earth
>   a) sky gods become singularized into a monotheistic deity which then fades away
>   b) the fallen sky god merges with some of the earth spirits and becomes the devil.

It seems naive to argue that comet activity directly *caused* the movement from earth spirits to sky gods. I'm convinced that these astronomical events *supplemented* the effects of political and economic stratification that predated these events which we've discussed in earlier chapters. If the evolution of Bronze Age civilizations would have continued into the Iron Ages *without* any interference from comets or asteroids people in these societies still would have come to believe in the predominance of

polytheistic sky gods for political and economic reasons. In other words, cometary activity is neither a necessary nor sufficient condition for the emergence of sky-gods from earth spirits.

If the comets or asteroids *by themselves* were enough to cause a predominance of sky god religion then all peoples around the world, whether they were hunter-gatherers, simple and complex horticulturists, or herders would have instantaneously overthrown their previous beliefs in earth spirits, ancestor spirits, and totems in favor of sky gods. Political centralization, economic stratification, empire building, the use of writing, and access to bronze all contributed to the rise of sky god religion. We know that egalitarian and rank societies didn't become sky god worshipers despite having experienced the same celestial fireworks. Their respect for their earthly sacred presences remained because these sacred presences were a better reflection of their form of social organization despite the physical events they witnessed.

If comet intervention was a contingent rather than a necessary or sufficient condition for the rise of the sky gods, then the *ceasing* of this unpredictable celestial events must have been *necessary* in explaining the consolidation of the sky gods into a single monotheistic deity. The characteristics of the Axial Iron Age—the notion that social organization has its own laws independent of deities; that humanity is a single species that must unite in a universal brotherhood; that good and evil are the responsibility of each individual; that people should learn to love strangers—all these values would not have emerged if comet and asteroid activities continued into the Axial Iron Age. The change in the sky from tempestuousness to calm contributed to the transformation of the deities from jealous, unpredictable, and cruel to forgiving, predictable, and loving.

However the absence of cometary activity by itself is not a sufficient condition for the rise of monotheism, because there were many times both before and after the Bronze Age when there was no cometary activity and the existing societies were not monotheistic. For monotheism to emerge there must be specific inventions—coined money, the alphabet, the discovery of iron, and hyperabstract reasoning (as we will see in chapter 15) besides the absence of comet debris. To summarize: *the presence of comet debris was a contingent, supplementary force in the movement from earth spirits to polytheistic sky gods, and the absence of comet debris was a necessary but not sufficient condition for the movement from polytheistic sky gods to a monotheistic sky god.*

Until the Axial Iron Age, the stories or myths of fires, floods, and other natural disasters were assumed to be literally and historically true by all Stone and Bronze Age societies. In addition these disasters were believed not to have been arbitrary. They were connected to a cycle of world ages, which included a golden age, a fall, a disaster, and a restoration.

In the first millennium, as the skies became more stable, the notion of world ages began to weaken and the tales of natural disasters lost their sense of literal truth. As individuals came to understand their psyche as compressed within their body, and as they came to take more responsibility for their inner states, the stories of natural disasters tended to be seen as *allegories* for the psycho-spiritual conditions of humanity, rather than descriptions of real events.

But like most of the new elements in the Axial Iron Age, the linearization of time and spiritualization of the material heavenly bodies only applied for the some of the civilizations of the Near East, and only among the middle and upper classes. The remaining agricultural and tribal societies and the lower classes within Axial Age civilizations *continued* to believe in world ages and the literal truth of the myths.

While I do not deny that people create myths for psychological, sociological, and spiritual reasons, that does not mean that these myths may not sometimes describe actual historical occurrences.

In its attempt to psychologize or spiritualize the memory of natural disasters, Axial Iron Age religion denied that humans are helpless before nature. We are really the custodians of a passive nature over which God has given us dominion. The theory of progress also lurks behind this Axial Iron Age effort to dismiss the catastrophes: People in Bronze Age civilizations were too ignorant and superstitious to simply report what was real.

6. To what extent did religion legitimize women's subordination?

In the first chapter, I defined legitimation as the set of superstructural institutions used by those with coercive power to induce those in submissive positions to comprehend their submission as being necessary, socially beneficial to all, as part of cosmic order, as inevitable, and as eternal. How did universalistic religions support or contradict these five characteristics of legitimation? In order to answer this question we return to the questions posed at the beginning of this chapter.

The drastic changes in the psychology of humanity—the compression of the psyche in the body of the individual and the rise of the spirit functions over the soul functions—were novelties for a few men, mostly middle- and upper-class traders and aristocrats. The emergence of a personal conscience, the sense of individual responsibility for psychological states—these were for men, not women. The soul qualities that men and women shared in previous ages became depreciated, and these were the only functions women could develop. These will be topics taken up in the next three chapters as we discuss the internalization phase of women's subordination.

What is important for now is that men in power projected their new spirit-based psychological characteristics onto the monotheistic deity. God was transcendent—abstract, celestial, and independent. This God planned the universe and went through a rational process—breathing and pronouncing words—rather than a non-rational process such as love-making to bring the world into existence. This God broke with the cycles of nature in time and was everywhere and nowhere in space. The soul qualities of goddesses were opposed to all of this, but the goddesses of agricultural states had little or no place in the universalistic religions.

The movement from hero to sage did not impact women *per se*. The image of the sage did reflect attempts in the Axial Iron Age to curb some of the abuses against peasants and women that occurred in the Bronze and Archaic Iron Ages. However the promise of an afterlife for non-elite groups meant non-elite groups of men.

The celestial phenomena of comets and asteroids legitimized the power of sky gods over earth deities, and were reflected in the characteristics of the hero. When the activity of these celestial bodies ceased, people's focus of attention remained in the sky, but the characteristics of the god became calmer and more invisible. The quality of calmness also typified the sage, and indirectly softened men's relationship to women.

In monotheism, God is worshiped rather than respected. Sociologically, this can be read as projection of the lower classes' seeming helplessness before the upper classes and indirectly of women's relationship to men. When God created reality before time, this also expressed the alienation of women from the creative process of work. The movement from rituals to pageants further showed the loss of women's power and the ability of the lower classes to connect with the sacred source.

The movement toward linear time and away from cyclic time is characteristic of the Hebrews more than any other Axial civilization. It was both a blessing and a curse. Moving away from myth and cyclic time was a moving away from the subordination of women in the Bronze Age. In the case of the Hebrews, moving from myth to history was a step up from being the plaything of nature to having dominion over her. This involved enormous responsibility; but for Hebrew women, in spite of still being subordinated to men, it contained more hope than anything the Bronze or Archaic Iron Age had to offer.

The movement from polytheism to monotheism, the movement from provincial deities to a globalizing deity, and the movement from diffused space to a decline in the importance of space, probably reflect the empire-building tendencies of Axial Age civilizations, where expansion demanded that people not become too attached to a particular area. Indirectly, empire building was also an attempt to globalize women's subordination. As a movement from concrete to abstract deity, this was a reflection of hyper-abstract thinking processes which came into use during this period. This is the subject of chapter 15.

The God of the great religions was far away, for men as well as women. From the point of view of lower-class women, there was at least a *consistency* between their subservient relationship to the deity—typified by worship and prayer—and their subservient political and economic relationship to men in society. There was also a consistency between major changes in psychology and sacred beliefs and the discomfort in women's material status. While the great religions promised a better life in the *next* world, this world was presented as a vail of tears—which it certainly was for women. In a sense, secondary magic must have been more painful and have created more of a mystification than the universalistic religions did. This might be one reason universalistic religions had some appeal for women.

Like secondary magic, universalist religion, at least until 500 BCE, was an upper-class movement. It presented women in these societies with a new set of contradictions.

The status of women in the Axial Iron Age varied from society to society, but some generalizations can be made. Priestesses from the upper castes lost their sacred power in the Archaic and Axial Iron Ages. The lives of women in India were not significantly improved as a result of the emergence of Buddhism, as the Buddha denied women a place in his spiritual community. The Buddhist disciple Ananda was women's only champion and it was only because of him that women were allowed into the Buddhist *sangha*:

Considerable distrust of women is displayed in the Buddhist texts. They are likened to black snakes, treated as evil smelling and adulterous; they are accused of ensnaring men, and are labeled as secretive . . . they are full of passion, easily angered, stupid, envious and have no place in public assemblies. . . . Women were expected to be like slaves, obedient to husbands. (Chakravarti, 1987, 33)

Women could not be heads of the social world or the Buddhist spiritual community.

There also seems to be exclusion of Chinese women in the philosophy of Confucius or Lao-Tze. As in Greece, women were expected to marry between the ages of 13 and 17 and were forbidden to remarry.

By the time of the Han dynasty in China, polygamy and wife-beating were prohibited, and women's new roles in the empire were debated. But even here the traditional ways of seeing women were well represented. Ban Zhao, the daughter of a famous philosopher, was granted certain privileges in the writing of texts—which were reserved for men. In spite of her position, the instructions she offered to women were anything but liberating:

Ban Zhao advocates for women the virtues of humility, meekness, chastity, cleanliness, solemnity, industriousness, deference to one's husband, obedience to one's in-laws, harmony with one's husband's younger siblings, and devotion to religious duties of the ancestral cult . . . she urges women to refrain from assembling in groups. . . . Condemnation of a husband's physical abuse . . . and support of women's literacy are the only issues on which Ban Zhao expresses fairly progressive views. In her advocacy of women's literacy, Ban stresses the need for women to be as learned . . . if only to understand how to serve their husbands better. (Vivante, 1999, 16)

As we have seen, Jewish women were the exception, having it better in the Archaic Iron Age than in the Axial Iron Age. Life for Jewish women from the time of Babylonian captivity deteriorated, if we take the writings in Deuteronomy as any indication. In spite of all this, the rise of universalistic religions tended to loosen the caste hierarchies compared to agricultural states, as they became class hierarchies. Indirectly this may have improved the status of some middle-class women.

In sum, the loosening of stratified hierarchies and the absence of natural disasters in the Axial Iron Age provided women with some indirect benefits as compared to women in the Bronze and Arachic Iron Ages. Yet the virtual disappearance of goddesses, and their subservient relationship to a male god, legtimized the rule of some men over all women and men. This was further internalized when women were excluded from the spirit functions that men used, along with the development of an internalized psyche that was the sole property of men.

This internalization process is the subject of the next three chapters.

The Greeks treated women as though they were of a different species.

Part V

Phase 3: Internalization—
The Psychology
of Oppression

Chapter 14

Environmental Psychology and Sense Ratios:
From Camps to Villages to Cities

The next three chapters focus on the process of how women (and most men) might have internalized their oppression. The rise of sight as the leading sensory mode and "space" as the leading metaphor for interpreting the relationship between humans and their environment (discussed in this chapter), as well as hyperabstract reasoning (chapter 15) and the individualist self (chapter 16), constituted faculties developed by a few elite men—faculties that created more distance between social groups. The continued perception by women of geographical zones as "places," along with their continued use of the proximate senses, left women less engaged. So too the continued use of concrete abstraction and the cultivation of a collectivist self made women less likely to question their subordinate status.

The purpose of this chapter is to show:

- how the built environment impacted which senses were deemed important and which were depreciated;
- how the environment-sense ratio reciprocally evolved in the ancient world;
- how these built environments and sense ratios changed to legitimize institutionalized male dominance and to encourage women to internalize that domination.

Environmental psychology is the study of how the natural and built physical environment impacts the human psyche—including memories, imagination, emotions, perception, and cognition.

The objects of the world serve to stabilize human life. They provide order and continuity over time. The things that we build, use, and surround ourselves with are inseparable from who we are. The material objects that we use are not just instruments we pick up and discard at our convenience; the qualities of these objects rub off on us. Objects affect what we can do, by either expanding or restricting the scope of our actions and thoughts. Tools, buildings, and furniture influence our identity. Objects in their natural state have inherent properties independent of human meaning; but once objects become socialized through human labor they become artifacts under human control. We become attached to them, and they affect us.

As we saw in chapters 11 and 12, for most of human history people believed that dreams, emotions, and memories originated in nature, went through people, and reconnected back to nature. Further, the ancients believed that this "psyche at large" was concentrated in huts, houses, and temples.

According to some geographers, all societies designate some areas as "places" and others as "spaces." Some areas invite a feeling of coziness and security while others invite an adventurous spirit. Some physical environments suggest equality, while others invite subordination. Further, some physical environments lend themselves more to sight while others lend themselves to sound and touch.

As we will see, these effects are important in understanding how male dominance became legitimized and internalized.

1. Physical locale as psycho-physical "place" or "space"

Lyn Lofland (1998) proposes that the social terrain can be divided into three areas—private, parochial, and public. The private realm is governed by ties of intimacy among primary groups which are located in households. The parochial realm consists of areas where kin groups, friends, and enemies (with whom each member has a culture and history) congregate. This is typically called a "community." The public realm is the area of society where strangers meet.

In hunting-and-gathering societies dwellings were makeshift and not permanent. According to Wilson (1988), because everyone could see what everyone else was doing in such societies, the boundary between the parochial and the private was very weak. With the rise of settled villages and more long-lasting architecture, the distinction between the parochial and the private grew much stronger. The public realm did not exist *within* egalitarian societies; it existed only in the buffer zones *between* societies, as either trading zones or war zones. In complex horticultural societies a public zone existed in the peripheral markets where commodity production took place.

It was not until the rise of agricultural states that the public realm came into its own. Lofland argues that in agricultural states the public realm was far more occupied than the private realm, because the housing in cities was so bad that it was better to occupy one's free time in public. Once in public, without mass transportation the major way to get around was by walking. Many activities such as securing water or disposing of body wastes were also part of public life, along with amusements and religious devotion. It wasn't until the industrial revolution that the private and parochial realms were once again enlarged and the public realm weakened.

The proportion of society that is devoted to each of these realms correlates with social evolution as follows:

- hunter-gatherers: private and parochial realms fused—no public realm inside society;
- simple horticulturalists: private and parochial realms differentiated—no public realm inside society;
- agricultural states: private and parochial realms decline—public realm inside society.

Within the field of geography, phenomenological (Casey, 1997) and humanistic (Tuan, 1974, 1977, 1982) traditions make a case that, after a repeated experience with a location, people become attached to it, "planting" emotions and memories there, thus making it a "place." When people form less of an attachment to an area and they treat it as purely physical, it becomes a "space." What is it that makes people divide up their world into places and spaces to begin with?

People in all societies experience a tension between the known and the unknown. On the one hand we need a predictable rhythm of activities that allows us to be productive. But at the same time, too much rhythm without variation becomes monotonous. We also need some degree of novelty, adventure, and change. The relationship between the physical environment and human societies is dialectical. In a very real sense people must shape and sustain societies by adapting to the physical ecological setting and its constraints. But to the extent that people can be creative in their environment they project their collective needs for security and adventure onto the socio-ecological zones they inhabit. It is these zones that get divided into spaces and places.

Whereas places repeat the known and predictable, giving rhythm to life, spaces present us with the unknown or unpredictable and give novelty to life. While places tend to be cozy and warm and to produce continuity, spaces tend to be expanding and cold, and to invoke destabilization. Where places invite a consolidation of tradition based on the past, spaces invite us to consider future possibilities. Places are like tried-and-true paths that people follow, while a space challenges us to blaze a trail. When people are in spaces they are freer to wonder and dream. For modern society, *outer space* is probably the most awe-inspiring space we can imagine because it is the realm least known.

Places provide a terrain to plant and sustain memories, stories, and emotions. For example, let us suppose I have just moved to a new neighborhood. One of the first things I may do is stroll down to the local avenue. I walk past a restaurant. The smell of garlic and tomato sauce lures me through the door. The waiters seem friendly and the music is Italian opera, which I like. I decide to try it out. The food is terrific and two weeks later I return, try a different dish, and have another enjoyable time. The next couple of occasions I come in, the waiters remember me and learn my name. I begin to think of this as "my place." The ups and downs of my life become associated with this physical environment. The emotions and memories in which I experience life are "planted" and "watered" when I enter this restaurant.

Let us suppose that after four or five months I become romantically involved with someone. After a few successful dates I decide to take her to "my place"—the Italian restaurant. This is risky business. Why? Because if I go there enough times with this person, it may become "our place." Probably it will be harder for me to make a distinction between the memories and emotions planted as "my place" and whatever memories and emotions built as a result of going to "our place."

Now let us suppose that after a year of dating, we break up. What will become of my association with the restaurant? If the psyche were *completely* compressed within the individual, as the psychology of the modern age tells us, and people never became attached to their physical terrain, then I could simply return to the restaurant and start over. But in fact it will be difficult to associate new experiences with that restaurant, because these will be mixed up with my emotions and memories of "my place" and "our place."

Not only do people become attached to places, they become attached to a *particular configuration of the objects* within their physical environment. Every time we move a piece of furniture to a new location within a room, we

affect our psyche. *Time is experienced cyclically in both places and spaces.* When we return to a physical location that was a source of comfort and security, where memories and emotions have been housed—say, an old neighborhood or a school—we usually want it to be the same, not altered. If the place has changed too much, it is as if our emotions and memories are pulled from their psychophysical roots and become homeless for a time.

People's emotional investment in the configuration of objects in a room can easily be seen when one of the members of a couple decides to change the arrangement of a living room, kitchen, or other common area. The argument that follows is only partly related to aesthetics! The specific locations of the artifacts of an area become a part of a whole experience. To rearrange any part of the room tampers with the emotions, memories, and stories people have planted in these areas. People become disoriented. This is one reason why it is so important that, if people want to get a fresh start in a new house, they change the organization of their artifacts within the rooms of the home.

Spaces are areas of social life where high adventure is expected. Mountain-climbing regions, amusement parks, areas for playing and watching games of chance (including the stock market), pick-up bars, masquerade parties, and carnival or Mardi Gras festivals are all areas or times in which people seek thrills as a result of unpredictable outcomes. Unlike places, spaces can be created either on a one-time basis or upon repeated visits.

Spaces and places are interdependent. Too much of one calls forth a need for the other. A society that is organized around too many spaces creates an experience of chaos and lack of shelter. Conversely, a society that does not have enough spaces will invite conformity and inertia.

Place-space conflicts emerge when a single physical area is experienced by one person or group as a place while for another it is a space. For instance, let us say that every day after work I go to a particular bar. At this bar I have my favorite pool table, the jukebox has songs I especially like, and my long-time friends are there. This is "my place." But let's say I have to work one Saturday. After work I stop at the bar. It has now changed from my place to a space. None of my friends are there. There is a new crowd of people, and a new bartender is serving different kinds of drinks. The jukebox has been replaced by a disc jockey and the pool table has been moved out of the way for dancing. For this crowd, the bar is a space for erotic possibilities. For me the bar is a place where I build continuity with the rest of my life. My irritation can be understood as a contest with the weekend crowd over what kind of bar this is.

As we will see later on in this chapter, places and spaces are inseparable not just from memories and emotions but from the senses as well. As it turns out, the proximate senses of touch, taste, smell, and sound are more often stimulated by places. Every area we identify as a place has its own sensual symphony of smells and sounds. Spaces appeal more to our "long-distance" sense of sight. So too, we will see that men's and women's access to spaces and places is not interchangeable. Men are more encouraged than women to inhabit physical locations that are spaces, while women are encouraged to inhabit places. The reasons for this will be discussed at the end of this chapter.

In section one we named three realms of habitation—private, parochial, and public. What is the relationship between these realms and spaces and places? While spaces and places can be seen as polar tensions within each of the three realms, they are not equally distributed. In the private and parochial realm, places are more important than spaces; while in the public realm spaces predominate.

The following is a summary of the differences between spaces and places, together with the three realms described by Lofland. I have included the sense ratios and gender differences which *anticipate* sections later on in this chapter.

Place	Space
	ALL SOCIETIES	
has psychic properties (memories, emotions)	**has psychic properties (thrills, expectations)**
known	unknown
predictable	unpredictable
bounded (cozy)	expanding
warm	cold
security (nurture, support) claustrophobia	opportunity (adventure/risk) delirium
monotony	chaos
continuity	change
reality (where you are)	wander, dream (where you could be)
familiar, path, discovered	unknown/ no paths or trail blazing, foreign
past	future
emotionally intense, slow	emotionally intense, mercurial
cyclic time	instantaneous time
proximate senses (touch, taste, smell, sound, body movement)	**long-distant sense** (sight)
women	**men**
private, parochial realms	**public realm**

2. Place is primary in the Stone and the Bronze Ages

All ancient societies divided their physical environment into a *proportion* of places versus spaces, just as we continue to do today. However, those proportions differed from those typical of contemporary societies, in that Stone Age and Bronze Age magical societies had many more places than spaces. When the great religions emerged, the proportion of the physical environment considered place decreased and the proportion of area considered space increased. Why was this?

One reason was that the actual rate of change in society increased, while the attitude toward change became more accepting. In Chapter 2 we established that magical societies of the Stone and Bronze ages valued continuity and did not welcome change. It stands to reason that a preference for stability would also foster a preference for places. In addition, the rate of change in these societies was slow: hunting and gathering societies lasted tens of thousands of years before the emergence of horticulture; and horticultural villages lasted another 5,000 years before the rise of states and cities. In contrast, starting in the Axial Iron Age, rates of communication and transportation speeded up, and empires rose and fell more quickly. People found they could cope with change and as their attitude toward change became more positive, this was reflected in a larger proportion of the land being organized as spaces.

Another reason had to do with the differences between magic and religion. In chapter 13 we saw that in magical societies the sacred presences are provincial, being grounded in the local rivers, water holes, and rocks. Earth spirits, gods, and goddesses are immanent in the world, and the psyche is diffused. Physical places contain the various qualities of the ancestors, or totems, who have domain over particular areas. Because these beings are immanent—that is, close to human beings—they are known and predictable, just like the places they inhabit.

Conversely, because universalistic religion understands the human presence on earth in the context of a "Fall" from an original paradisiacal condition, individuals were discouraged from becoming too attached to where they were. Value was placed on change and self-improvement. This supported the organization of the physical environment as spaces. In addition, because God was transcendental to what human beings experience, he was unknown and unpredictable; and if the sky gods were transcendent, inhabiting the stars, completely invisible, and present everywhere, then they were nowhere in particular. Villages and cities lost their sacred power and became more secularized and material in the experience of religious people. The value of places declined.

Finally, the increased commercial activity of Greece, India, and, to a lesser extent, China during the Axial Iron Age made these societies more cosmopolitan and prone to build empires. They were expanding. This implied the need to engage with strangers both within and between states, and also required learning to live with unpredictability. Cosmopolitan cities became sites for the construction of public spaces.

There were no empty, secular geographies in tribal societies. Everywhere was either a place or a space, with places predominating. For both hunter-gatherers and to a lesser extent for horticulturalists, the land was more like a womb than a wilderness. Before people in tribal societies traveled to another village they were expected to know which sacred presences ruled over the areas they were traveling through and they were taught techniques to protect themselves from being attacked or to avoid displeasing these powers.

Spaces in ancient societies were where bartering, gambling, or fighting might occur. The area one traveled to when going on a vision quest was also a space because it involved unpredictability, danger, and potential exhilaration. The boundaries where spaces began and ended were less clear and it was risky to become too attached to an area that was ill-defined. Emotional experiences in spaces probably became easily "scattered" rather than "planted." There was greater attachment to places because places were usually closed systems with clear boundaries.

What became of ancient places with the rise of states and cities? In order to answer this question I will compare modern industrial cities to pre-industrial cities. Modern cities are sites of spatial explosion. Compared to rural areas, modern cities are

more *concentrated*—i.e., crowded;
more *intense*—in pace of movement and
    exchange of information;
more *diverse*—in cultural and recreational
    activities and services;
more *exotic* in population—containing a
    greater cultural variety of
    immigrants, with people who are less
    rooted; In addition, cities have
more *choices* of job opportunities and
    diversity of goods and services;
more *unpredictability* and *novelty*;
more *individualism* and less interdependence;
more *anonymity*;
more *noise*;
more *danger*; and
more *homelessness*.

In short, modern urban existence entails a profusion of audio-visual stimulation, demands, and confrontation with others. Bronze Age and Iron Age cities had many of these characteristics of industrial cities in seed form.

The transition of cities from a pre-industrial condition to industrialism in some ways parallels the urban transition of the Bronze and Iron Ages:

(1) In pre-industrial cities there were *more places than spaces;* this situation was reversed in later industrial cities.

(2) Within pre-industrial cities a single space was used for many activities. In industrial cities there is a more specialized use of spaces, where one space goes with one activity.

(3) In ancient cities there were *unconcealed differences between castes in mannerisms, clothing, and dialect.* Lyn Lofland (1973) calls this "overt heterogeneity of the populace"; in industrial cities differences within classes a hidden or understated. Lofland calls this a "masked heterogeneity" in public space.

(4) In pre-industrial cities *space was less monopolized by commerce* than in later industrial cities.

At the center of the Bronze Age city was a ceremonial center that acted as a little cosmos; this ceremonial center was often constructed near a sacred plant or tree. From there the four directions radiated out through and beyond the city to realms which the gods and goddesses were thought to inhabit. Sacks (1980) showed that city planning was essentially a psycho-spiritual activity:

Often the most geographically permanent and regular features such as the sun, moon, stars mountains, rivers and sea become the most . . . arresting. . . . Associations with the sun such as light, warmth, life and birth are placed in the sun's path, especially in the east and above. Their opposites such as darkness, cold and death belong to the west and below. In the mythical-magical mode, this means that directions actually are thought of as the places or "homes" of these feelings and functions. (Sacks 1980, 152-153)

Sacks notes that

In India, cities were supposed to be designed according to a mandala replicating a cosmic image of the laws governing the universe. Manuals of architecture defined the shape of this mandala as a square. . . . Time enters the mandala by coordinating the signs of the zodiac and space does so by orienting the square towards the four . . . cardinal points. (Sacks 1980, 156)

Propitious sites for the location of settlements in China were determined by studying 'earth currents.'. . . The cosmic breath follows earthly channels in a way comparable to the flow of blood in the human body. . . . Geomancy was used to locate Chinese cities and Chinese cities were conceived of as cosmological symbols. According to Chinese ritual books, cities were to be square in shape, orientation to the cardinal directions and enclosed by walls with twelve gates, one for each month (Sacks, 1980, 157)

In agricultural states, at the beginning or end of the construction of any sacred or important building there was a ceremony that integrated the new area or building into the sacred universe of the inhabitants. The attributes of buildings and streets, and especially their relationships to the geographical directions (north, south, east, or west) were informed by psychological experience.

In other words, the functions of buildings were inseparable from sacred geometry and the human psyche. There was no pure geometrical space that could stretch out infinitely and which could be filled with arbitrary contents. Everything was already filled, and filled with a very structured psycho-sacred world. By comparison, in modern geography the four directions of the compass are drained of sacred principles and of any human experiential qualities.

The movement from village life to urban life created a special set of interpersonal problems for the inhabitants of Bronze Age cities. In the first place, in tribal societies face-to-face kin-groups were the basic unit. Even in chiefdoms with thousands of people, the duties and obligations a person fulfilled were based, to some extent, on personal knowledge of specific kin members.

In a village, the presence of strangers was not taken for granted. According to Lofland (1973), their presence in villages created an extreme reaction. In isolated tribal societies, strangers were not even seen as human. If they were powerful, they might be seen as gods or deceased ancestors. Tribal people either made strangers kin through a ritual, or strangers were expelled or killed. With the rise of cities, strangers had to be humanized in order for everyone to get along. It was no accident that universalistic religions advocated for tolerance and even love of strangers.

The streets of Bronze Age cities were scenes crowded with extreme examples of the human condition. People with diseases or serious psychological problems were an integrated part of public life, since there were no state agencies or hospitals to house the physically or mentally disabled. There were no prisons, and public punishment for crimes included beating, branding, the plucking out of eyes, and the cutting off of limbs. Sacred sacrifices were also a normal part of street life.

With no specialized places for learning or recreation, children played in the streets. There were no specialized places for public entertainment; public squares and plazas could be used if room could be found. Activities piled up on top of each other, with many going on simultaneously and close by. In contrast, industrialized cities typically have specialized spaces whose use is strictly scheduled.

In pre-industrial cities the rate of exchange of goods and information was far slower than in industrialized cities, so that the *experience* of the timing of events was inseparable from *where* they were experienced. Distances were experienced as *sequences of encounters* as one moved from place to place. Further, people were encouraged to savor events because a high proportion were part of a sacred ecological network uniting people with trees, stones, and buildings. Public *places* such as monuments and temples were more important than public *spaces.* Unlike in modern cities, public spaces were not dominated by commerce; they were the domain for entertainment, festivals, games, and socializing. There were many more holidays celebrated in public than there are in modern cities.

In industrial societies *as the rate of trade and information speeded up, time began to unravel from the physical environment in people's experience.* The *experiential* meaning of space and time became separated from scientific and commercial understandings of geography and "clock" time. *The physical environment lost its psychological connection with events and became a mere neutral container for them.*

Within public spaces in the ancient world there was little segregation of buildings. Warehouses and workshops were all mixed together. Neither were animals completely separated from public life. Streets were filled

Figure 14.1 Comparison of Bronze Age Cities to Industrial Cities

Pre-industrial city	Industrial City
city is primarily sacred spaces smaller	**city is primarily secular** spaces larger
public realm not commercial decline of private realm	**public realm commercialized** expansion of private and parochial realms
mixed public realm: many activities going on in the same place at the same time	**specialized public realm:** single activities going on in different places at different times in economically poor areas, places and spaces "pile up" hospitals
maimed, diseased, blind, scarred and diseased were in public children being tutored on the streets children play in streets no sewers or indoor plumbing body relief in public	children in public schools children play in playgrounds and parks sewers and indoor plumbing body relief in private or bathrooms
public beatings physical punishment: branded, loss of eye, limbs, scarlet letter sacrifices	prisons sacrifices outlawed
warehouses, workshops, houses all mixed	special segregation of work and home retail and wholesale: zoning
public thick with street-life: mixture of humans/animals: pigs, horses	**public thinner with street-life:** subordinated to transportation and shopping animals separated from city life but for pets less robust public life: intentional activities
robust public life: dancing, music story-telling, parades many holidays	less holidays
slow transportation--time slower walking for lower classes litters or horses for upper classes time inseparable from space-place experience	mass transport-- time faster mass transportation time separated from space-place experience: empty containers
commerce on the street: flea markets less specialized places for public entertainment use public squares, plazas	commerce in stores specialized buildings
Caste differences overt in language/appearance	**Class differences masked in language/ appearance**
people are what they wear rich and poor integrated in public differentiation in <u>design</u> of dress, materials costumes dictated by laws elite speech is different	people are where they stand rich and poor segregated in public subtle distinctions fashions speech differences between classes more subtle

with humans, horses, pigs, and barnyard animals. In some Bronze Age cities there were no sewers or indoor plumbing. Street life was thus an extreme mix of decay, feces, and urine underlying buying and selling, storytelling, and parades.

There is an interesting contradiction between social stratification and spatial integration. Unlike industrialized societies, ancient cities were small and different social castes were crowded together in integrated neighborhoods. This made it inherently problematic to distinguish one caste from another. *The upper castes preserved differences by accentuating rigid codes of appearances and speech.* Lower classes were legally bound to wear clothes made of different materials from those the upper classes wore. There was no such thing as fashion in ancient cities: one wore the clothing appropriate to one's social caste. In this detribalized atmosphere of strangers, rigid codes of appearance and language were attempts at building a sense of predictability into social relationships.

In short, ancient cities must have been very intense, with the extremes of activities more or less randomly juxtaposed to each other: beggars walking near aristocrats; storytelling on one street going on simultaneously with a parade on another, and torture on still another; sacrifices being offered while dancing and singing occurs close by; children playing games of chance as prostitutes and the insane egg them on.

As Lofland argues, the city created a new kind of human being—the cosmopolitan—who was able to relate to others in new ways that city living made not only possible but necessary. The individual gained the capacity for superficial, fleeting, and restricted relationships. He could be civil.

3. Decline of place in the cities of the Axial Iron Age

As we saw in chapter 13, as the great religions arose, the psyche became compressed within the individuals, society and nature became far more secularized, and a monotheistic deity became more transcendental on the one hand and global on the other.

With the rise of agriculture in the Bronze Age, people became more settled on the land and in the newly risen cities. As people became more civilized, and as social-economic and technological forces introduced more predictability over the natural environment, there grew a stronger distinction between what was cultivated and what was wild. "Cultivation" referred to the act of tilling the soil and tending crops, but it also meant having civilized culture or refinement. All of this affected how space and place were conceived, leading to the following changes:

(1) The land outside the cities and the cultivated fields became a space—wilderness.
　　This included biophysical nature.
(2) Space *within* cities expanded somewhat.
(3) Places became concentrated and crystallized into
　　(a) specific buildings, including in temples or monuments in the cities, and
　　(b) specific fields and gardens in the countryside.

The Axial Iron Age cities bridged the abyss between the Bronze Age sacred cities and the secularized industrial cities, but stand far closer to the ancient world. Most of the elements in Bronze Age cities remained in the Axial Iron Age, but cracks in their hierarchical unity are showing.

In the Axial Iron Age the adoption or creation of universalistic religions often went with empire-building, and both spreading the word of God and spreading political and economic power required that the areas being exploited be secular, profane, and spatial. If nature was to be brought under the domain of humanity and if other societies were to be converted to the new monotheism, they must be understood as spatial wildernesses.

The idea of humanity's chartered dominion over nature (and non-believers in magical societies) which calls for turning places into spaces has its origins in western sacred traditions. Places that were pregnant with false gods had to be transformed into spaces that could accommodate a placeless transcendental deity.

Figure 14.2 Spaces and Places under Magical and Religious Systems

Stone and Bronze Age Magic	Iron Age Religion
Sacred realm dominates secular realm	Secular realm expands
place has psychic energy independent of people	place is becoming a neutral, empty container for contents
place and space inseparable from body direction (up, down, right, left)	place and space separate from the body (compass directions--north, south, east, west)

Hunter-gatherers/Simple horticulturists	Agricultural states	Commercial empires
place dominant, diffused in land or focused in gardens	place dominant concentrated in buildings fields	place declines
little space	space becomes wilderness	space expands becomes wilderness
(society an extension of nature) integrated with wild animals	(society distinct from nature) integrated with domesticated animals	(society separated from nature) distance from animals
biophysical nature a womb no wilderness	biophysical nature a wilderness city and fields are a womb	biophysical nature a wilderness wilderness includes nature and other societies city and fields are a womb
	society is placial	society becomes more spatial
sacred presences diffused in places	sacred presences concentrated in places	sacred presence placeless

At the same time, as we have seen, within the cities of the Axial Iron Age more areas were opened up to commerce (and a secularized science and politics, in the case of Athens).

As we will see in the next chapter, the alphabet was instrumental in detaching people from places while encouraging the building of a spatial community of strangers. Aristotle provided a conceptual basis for secularizing the physical environment by claiming that *places were simply empty containers no longer filled with psyche.*

Universalistic religion supports a spatial orientation on earth because globalizing tendencies require travel to unknown areas and dealing with strangers; religion's abstract nature discourages attachment to particular places because these are provincial. Concurrently, secularized notions of society and the biophysical world are more conducive to a spatial orientation. The commercialization of society requires buying and selling among strangers, which requires risk. The spatialization of nature means that nature will be seen as infinitely open, an area to which objective questions (i.e., scientific inquiry) can be posed without concern for the will and intentions of gods and goddesses.

4. Sense hierarchies: proximate senses vs. long-distance sense

Does the type of society an individual lives in affect whether sight, touch, smell, taste, sound, or movement is valued or depreciated? Did hunter-gatherers use their senses in the same proportion as people living in agricultural states? Did Paleolithic hunter-gatherers use the same proportion of the senses as hunter-gatherers living in the Axial Iron Age? And—more directly to the point of this book—do men and women use the same senses in equal proportion? If not, how much of this difference is biological and how much results from social and historical factors?

In *From Earth Spirits to Sky Gods* I discussed briefly how even within a given society, people do not use their senses equally. Also, the use of the senses evolves throughout the lifespan: touch and smell emerge, first while sight is the last to develop. In addition as a person learns to manipulate tools effectively the use of the senses becomes mediated by the senses that are most required to manipulate the tool. We are all specialized in some senses more than others, depending on the work we do.

Further, there are differences in the senses' range of influence. When two people are pressed up against each other all the senses are available—touch, taste, smell, sight, and sound. Yet while we can *see* a part of the person, we cannot see the whole person unless we step 3 to 6 feet away. The senses that have the shortest range are taste, followed by touch and smell. You can hear a person speak at a much longer range, and you can still see a person even after you can't taste, touch, smell or hear them. For this reason taste, touch, smell, and sound have been called the "proximate senses" while sight has been labeled the "long-distance" sense.

It is not just the stage of individual development or the kind of tools one uses that determines which sense gets used. The type of society and point in history determine "path of least resistance" for which senses are likely to be used. This is deeply connected to whether people practice magic or religion and whether the physical location is understood primarily as a place or a space.

When we enter into places and spaces we engage these socio-ecological zones with our senses—we touch, smell, hear, and see things. In some cases we even taste parts of our environment. Some senses are more easily used with places and others with spaces. By implication, if pre-Axial Age societies used places more than spaces, then they were more likely to use some senses more than others. Conversely, if, during the Axial Iron Age spaces became more prevalent, then a different sense would have been used more prominently.

I have said that places tend to be known, predictable, and cozy. These characteristics go at least as much with the proximate senses of taste, touch, smell, and sound as they do with sight. The kitchen is a great *place* because of the smells and tastes available there. On the other hand, spaces tend to be unknown, unpredictable, and expanding. Space goes with sight. As we saw in an earlier section, in tribal and agricultural societies, place matters more than space. Therefore in pre-Axial Iron Age societies emphasizing place we are likely to find more of an appreciation of the proximate senses. If Axial Age civilizations emphasized space over place, then we can expect to find that in these societies the long-distance sense of sight mattered more. We will see examples confirming this in the next section.

What is the relationship between the use of the proximate and long-distant senses on one hand, and magic and religion on the other? In chapters 11 and 12, I briefly suggested that people practicing magic *saturate the senses* in order to achieve an altered state of consciousness. The monotheistic religions, however, consider it dangerous to use the senses to achieve an altered state of consciousness because they fear that doing so will pull people back to the animal world. They attempt to deprive the senses. To the extent that universal religions indulge the senses at all, sight is preferred. This follows because sight is the least involved, most distant of the senses.

Thus social evolution has been characterized by a movement from the use of the proximate senses to the long-distance sense of sight. Earlier I said that how we use our senses is inseparable from the tools we use. The alphabet—a linguistic tool—was instrumental in revolutionizing the sense ratios in favor of sight. It also supported the development of space over place and sky-god religion over magic. As we will see later, the ecological setting—altitude, climate, and geography—also affects sense rations.

To summarize so far:

Stone Age and Bronze Age societies	Iron Age societies
primitive and secondary magic	universalistic religions
sensory saturation	sensory deprivation
proximate senses = touch, taste, smell, sound	long-distance sense = sight
place	space

5. Proximate senses in Stone Age and Bronze Age magical societies

The subtitle of David Howes' and his colleagues' book, *Varieties of Sensory Experience*, is "Towards an Anthropology of the Senses." In this book, various cultures are compared with regard to their preferred use of the senses. I discussed some specifics of this in my previous book (Lerro 2000). In general what Howes, et al., show is that:

(a) People in pre-industrial societies have a *more developed sense of the proximate senses* such as smell, sound, and body movement. In the case of body movement, Howes et al. argue that, instead of dancing to a single beat, the Tiv of Nigeria move four different parts of their bodies to four different rhythms within a single piece of music.

(b) In pre-industrial societies *other senses than sight are used extensively as metaphors* for important social processes. For example, the Ommura of Papua New Guinea use the phrase "knowing his nose" to summarize the character of a man. The Dogon claim that "good words smell sweet and bad words smell rotten." In the mythology of the Hopi the word is thought to have come into being by sound, not light. When the Suya say they have learned something, they say "it is in my ear."

(c) Parts of the environment are classified using senses other than sight, such as by smell.

For example, many different kinds of incense (pleasing and unpleasing) are burned to call down the spirits. Each spirit is partly classified according to its smell, which the incense is supposed to evoke. Sacred presences are also classified according to their tastes.

Specific foods are set out for various sacred presences according to their palettes in order to influence them.

Perhaps the most depreciated sense in modern times is that of smell. But as Classen, Howes, and Synnott (1997) tell us, this wasn't always the case.

> The native inhabitants of New Guinea are . . . extremely alert to the olfactory cues of the rain forest. . . . Interestingly whereas in the West sight is considered *the* distance sense, smell often outdistances sight in the experience of forest dwellers like the Umeda. They know that smell can give them knowledge of things hidden to the eye. (Classen, et al., 1997, 98)

The sense of smell in some societies is the organizer of seasonal calendars:

> In the jungles of the Andaman Islands as one after another of the trees and climbing plants come into flower it is possible to recognize a distinct succession of odours.... [They] have constructed their calendar on the basis of this cycle, naming the different periods of their year after the fragrant flowers that are in bloom at different times. Their year is thus a cycle of odours. . . . (Classen, et al., 1997, 95)

Yearly calendars were directly connected to the planets, which were also believed to emit smells:

> Batek Negrito deities live in a cool fragrant land of fruit blossoms in the sky. The sun is believed to have a bad smell of raw meat, acquiring its stench by passing through the land of corpses after it sets in the west. The Batek avoid excessive heat themselves, and say that the moon runs away from the heat and foul smell of the sun. Humans are caught between their two celestial bodies, their own bodies being composed of both. With our hot blood, sickness and death resemble the hot, putrid sun. In their preference for coolness and their deligt in fragrance,

however, they imitate the moon. . . . (Classen, et al., 1997, 116-117)

The Batek Negrito myth concerning the origin of food shows how the deities are affected by smells.

> All foods originally came from one being, a giant bearcat. The deities create the different edible plants and animals by killing the bearcat, scattering its parts abroad and turning each piece into a different kind of plant or animal. . . . For the Batek Negrito, to cook different plants and animals together would be to try and reverse this original process of food creation and blend separate food categories back into a unitary whole. Such an act would . . . constitute a rejection of the creative work of the deities and naturally provoke their anger. (Classen, et al., 1997, 107)

In pre-Axial Age societies incense was used to climb to the gods. Among the Batek Negrito:

> In a tree burial, the corpse is dressed in a colourful sarong, wrapped in a sleeping mat and laid inside a lean-to built in the branches of a sturdy hardwood tree. Incense resin is then burnt under the tree by the head of the corpse. This is supposed to enable the soul already located about the earth . . . to waft to the afterworld on the incense smoke. (Classen, et al., 1997, 151)

Smell is used in various tribes to increase the chances of a successful hunt.

> Odour not only determines the edibility and aesthetics of food in various cultures but it also makes possible the very procurement of food. For the Wamira, the Trobrinders, the Batek Negrito the Desana and the Ongee, acquiring sufficient food depends on carefully and properly manipulating the olfactory environment . . . for the Ongee, hunting for food is a game of olfactory hide and seek. A

successful hunt involves restricting the release of the hunters odour and locating and releasing all the odour of the prey. . . . These practices are based on the belief that animals and plants are part of the same olfactory network which interrelated humans and spirits. (Classen, et al., 1997, 145)

In the royal households of the ancient Egyptians, perfumes used included as many as twenty ingredients. They were available as toilet waters, oils, and powders. What's more, different perfumes were used for different parts of the body and were used by both men and women.

In pre-Axial Age societies smells were a vital part of rites of passage. In fact, smells were used as elements of socialization:

[B]abies, for example come into the world in a gush of natural smells and need to be socialized into the odours of culture. . . . The inhabitants of the Tanimbar Islands of Indonesia traditionally 'smoked' a newborn child over the household fire for the first few weeks of life. . . . [I]t is only when a child receives a name . . . [and] becomes a socialized human being, at the age of about six months, that she or he ceases to be a serious olfactory liability. (Classen, et al., 1997, 135)

In ancient households, cushions and bedclothes were filled with dried herbs, and clothes and storage chests were incensed. Even domesticated animals did not escape the deluge of scenting.

In the ancient world perfume and food were not differentiated. Foods could be perfumed and perfumes could be and were, at times, eaten (unlike modern perfumes, ancient perfumes were not poisonous). Incense was burned after dinner as an offering to household gods and perfume was offered to guests the way we offer coffee.

In the ancient world, ruling groups used *superior* smell, rather than lack of it, to govern. In a very real sense, the lower classes did smell worse, given the kind of work they did as

butchers, tanners, fishmongers, and dyers of cloth (who used urine as a cleaning agent). Women were believed to have an inferior smell of celestial origin:

This underlying foulness of women was expressed in the ancient association of women with the moon, which in turn was associated with corruption. Men, on the other hand, were linked with the sun, considered productive of sweet scents. From this perspective, the tradition of perfuming brides in the ancient world could be understood in part as a kind of cultural processing whereby naturally foul, disruptive women were symbolically turned into sweet, obedient helpmates. (Classen, et al., 1997, 38)

Classen, Howes, and Synnott conclude that:

Olfactory symbolism thus was used very effectively to pass value judgments on different groups of people in antiquity. Given the strong emotional and physical reactions of pleasure or disgust which smells inspire, such an olfactory classificatory system would have been a potent aid to maintaining different classes in their proper place in the social order. (Classen, et al., 1997, 38)

6. Ecological and technological reasons for the rise of sight

Until now I have treated the use or non-use of the senses as more or less determined by type of social structure, and as coinciding with the social construction of places and spaces. I have treated the senses as if they were independent of the ecological setting. But can altitude, climate, and land topography influence which senses are used? When Constance Classen (in Howes 1991, 251-252) compared two tribal cultures of South America, she found that in the highland areas cold dulls the appreciation of touch and odors are not well diffused through the thin atmosphere. Hearing, however, is accentuated by the acoustics of the mountains and the sense of sight is strengthened by the open sky and the mountains. In contrast, when people live in the tropics, where the physical environment is close at hand, the proximate senses are strong while sight is weakened by the lack of penetration into the forests.

The tendency toward sensory deprivation in dry, cold climates is collaborated by James DeMeo (1998) in his study of the deserts of the Near East. DeMeo argues that the people who inhabit the area he calls "Saharasia" began to experience sensory deprivation beginning about 5000 to 4000 BCE, as deserts appeared and grew.

According to DeMeo, the childrearing swaddling practices of herders provide clear evidence for the depreciation of touch among desert-dwelling peoples. The head of the infant was tied against a cradleboard to keep it steady as the mother walked across the irregular land formations. This, according to De Meo, led to cranial deformation. In general, herders are not very physically affectionate with their children.

It seems likely that the wide-open spaces of the herder's domain would make the proximate senses less important and the distant sense of sight more important.

To what extent will the empirical characteristics of the land affect whether people will tend to make a space or a place out of it? Does the climate, topography, or the altitude influence whether something becomes a place or a space? A look back at the comparative chart of the psychological experience of place and space in an earlier section of this chapter makes it difficult to imagine people attributing the characteristics of place to the Sahara desert. This is one of the most barren, bleached out and sanitized areas on Earth, an area that has unpredictable weather, that seems to expand forever, and that provides little coziness or comfort. The life of nomadic pastoralists in the Archaic Iron Age must have expanded space and diminished places. Perhaps now we can have a better appreciation for the *ecological* reasons why sensory deprivation and depreciation of the proximate senses arose along with the universalistic religions.

Marshall McLuhan (1962) and Harold Innes (1951) argued that the tools a society uses become a kind of "extrasensory perception" to the people in that society. The predominant tools used in a society will skew the sense ratios of the participants. In the Axial Iron Age an important new tool was the alphabet. With the alphabet came an increasing amount of writing and reading. As Eric Havelock (1963) points out, when people first began to read, they read out loud, maintaining their sense of sound. But when reading became private, the ear was silenced and the eye was able to accelerate its traversal of the page. Then reading and writing both become silent activities excluding all senses but the eye. Howes et al. (1991) relates a story of a tribal people who thought that an anthropologist's ears were swollen because he was taking notes rather than listening. For this tribe, remembering was inseparable from listening. In the Axial Iron Age, the relative importance of the ear and the eye was reversed. This will be explored in greater depth in the next chapter on the development of hyper-abstract reasoning.

In summarizing our work on the senses, we are saying there were two movements:
(a) from sensory saturation to sensory deprivation, and
(b) from the proximate senses to the long distance sense of sight,
   Both were affected by
(a) the ecological setting in which the societies were nested, and
(b) the kinds of technology available to the society at the time.

What we want to know is, what are the conditions under which the ecological setting will be the primary determinant in sense ratios and under what circumstances will technology play that role? Figure 14.3 gives an overview of the situation.

On the whole, in *tribal societies* sense ratios are determined *by ecological conditions* while in *state societies* technology overrides the ecological setting. At one extreme on the left of the chart are hunting-gathering societies and simple horticulture societies that live in lush environments. They might be characterized as "high proximate," because they combine oral means of social transmission with a landscape (jungles and forests) that lends itself to touch, taste, and smell. Tribal societies living in austere

Figure 14.3 Impact of Ecology and Technology on Sense Ratios

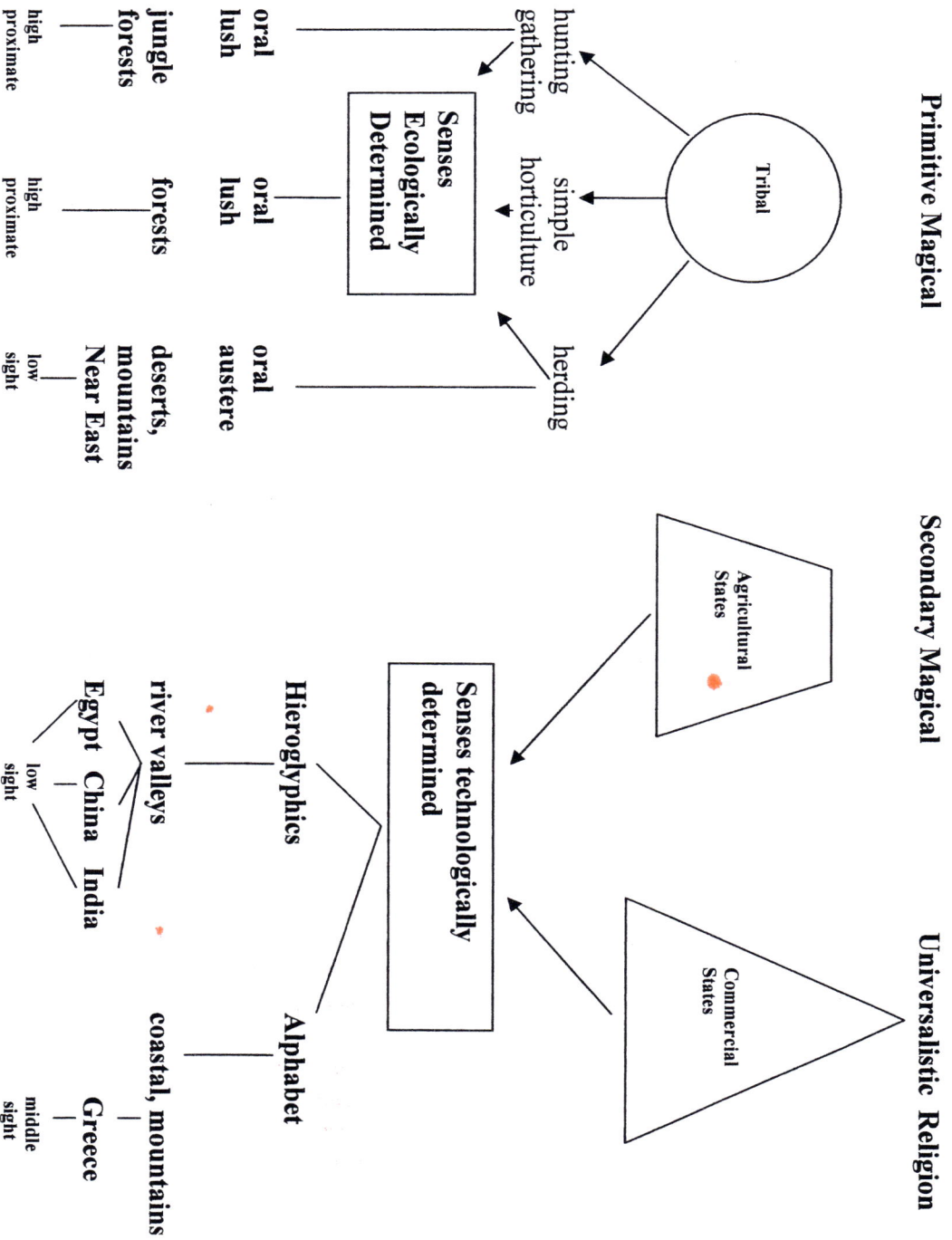

Primitive Magical   Secondary Magical   Universalistic Religion

Tribal

hunting
gathering

simple
horticulture

herding

**Senses
Ecologically
Determined**

oral
lush

oral
lush

oral
austere

jungle
forests

forests

deserts,
mountains
Near East

high
proximate

high
proximate

low
sight

Agricultural
States

Commercial
States

**Senses technologically
determined**

Hieroglyphics

Alphabet

river valleys

coastal, mountains

Egypt China India

Greece

low
sight

middle
sight

environments, whether in the deserts or in the arctic, whether they are herders or hunter-gatherers (Inuit), will be conflicted. Living in the snow where there are few landmarks and the line where the land ends and the sky begins is vague, Inuit hunters must develop an acute sense of sight. Yet as a tribal society the importance of hearing remains, because they must pass on their culture orally. I call them "low sight."

Agricultural states are in a similar position. River valleys support the cultivation of sight, but despite the presence of hieroglyphic writing, all but about 1% of the population remain oral. I call these societies "low sight" as well. It is in the commercial states of the Axial Iron Age that sight comes into its own. This is because the terrain of mountains and seacoasts (specifically in Greece) supports sight, while the invention of the alphabet and coined money also supports the cultivation of writing and reading. I call this period "middle sight." (It was only after the 15th century with the inventions of the printing press, the microscope, and the telescope that the term "high sight" is justified.)

Broadly speaking, in tribal societies the ecological setting primarily determines sense ratios because the feedback loop between these societies and the biophysical world is more immediate. At the other extreme, in the Axial Iron Age social human relations with biophysical nature are increasingly mediated by social relationships, technology, economics, and politics. These considerations will then determine which senses are at the top of the hierarchy.

There is a thread that unites chapters 12, 13, and 14. Place, sensory saturation, and the proximate senses support and sustain primitive and secondary magic. The proximate senses permeate places and create a coziness that is strengthened by a diffused psyche, which magical activities try to influence. Space, sensory deprivation, and sight go with the emergence of sky god religion. Space and sight distance the rest of the senses from the ecological setting as the psyche is compressed inside the bodies of individuals. As space is secularizing and expanding nature and depreciating places, it makes room for the worship of a placeless, transcendental deity.

8. Women, places, and the proximate senses

In chapter 7 I stated that while there are certain occupations that are not gender-specific (such as craft production, sacred communion, pottery-making, and horticulture) there are many others that are indeed gender specific. Here again is that sampling:

Men	Women
hunting large game	fuel gathering
metal-working	preparing drinks
smelting ores	gathering
lumbering	preparing wild plant foods
woodworking	dairy production
making musical instruments	laundering
trapping	water fetching
boat-building	cooking
stonework	child-rearing
working in bone, horn and shell	
mining	
quarrying	
bone-setting	

In addition, there are other areas that are, on the whole, dominated by men, including warfare, politics, economics, and big-game hunting. Further, most of the forms of work that men do appear to have the following five qualities:

(a) they involve greater strength and stamina,
(b) they are more dangerous or risky,
(c) they are not easily interruptible,
(d) they require high levels of skill and training, and
(e) they require long periods of time away from home base.

If we focus on properties (b) and (e), and compare them to the differences in characteristics between places, spaces, and sense ratios, we see an interesting correlation. *The areas in which men engage in activities are typically regarded as "spaces." Conversely, the areas in which most women in ancient societies engaged in their daily activities were regarded as "places."* Figure 14.4 summarizes this section. To be sure, there were exceptions to the rule. For example, when men were engaging in activities that were not easily interruptible—like stonework or woodworking—they occupied a place, not a space. At the same time, many of women's work activities were secular and material—that is, spatial rather than placial—like dairy production and water fetching. Yet the sense used by men performing these activities more often than not was sight. Women, on the other hand, used the proximate senses at least as much as sight.

Let us compare some of the dominant activities men and women performed in hunter-gatherer bands, horticultural villages, agricultural states, and commercial civilizations, and examine which senses were being used and whether the areas in which these activities were performed were spaces or a places.

As we have seen, in general hunting and gathering societies were dominated by a placial orientation in the organization of ecological zones. These places were diffused across the land and could be metaphorically understood as a "womb." The work of most men in band

societies was to engage in hunting, which requires a combination of sight, kinesthetics, listening for sounds, and making sounds. Because hunting is dangerous and the outcome of the hunt is unpredictable, these areas are best designated as "spaces." Making war occurs in a space, since it is adventurous, dangerous, and the outcome is unknown. Both hunting and warring are cold, and emotions are clearly mercurial.

Gathering also requires keen sight but also touch, smell, and taste in order to distinguish edible from poisonous tubers and roots. While gathering took women away from the immediate campsite, it had more predictable yields than hunting, and involved little risk. The areas where women gathered were best understood as places. Women performed two other activities that are exclusively female, and which skew them in the direction of the proximate senses: child rearing and food preparation. In raising children, touch, smell, and sounds are at least as important as sight. In the making of drinks and food, taste and smell are primary. Both child rearing and food preparation occur in places, since they are predictable, bounded, involve security, and involve cultivating "slow," "thick" interpersonal emotions.

Insofar as the general political relations of hunter-gatherers are egalitarian, men and women share these areas together. Since the politics of band societies was egalitarian and largely consensual, this meant that both men and women needed to listen carefully. Since politics involves deciding future policy, the area in which it occurs is a space.

Trade involves going to a buffer zone and haggling with people from other societies over goods. Men did this far more often than did women. If the content of trade was food, the proximate senses would be involved. But unless the intention was to build a confederacy in which the principles of generalized reciprocity would be in operation, the goods exchanged would be durable. The senses used by men would be sight—for examining the items carefully, and reading of body language. Men would also listen for voice inflections to detect deception. Touch, taste, and smell would not have been significantly required in trading. Since trading is risky, unpredictable, and potentially hostile, it occurred in a space.

As we saw in the chapters on sacred systems, sensory saturation was practiced in communal rituals. The magical circle was a place, since it involved much controlled preparation—i.e., the gathering of rocks, incense, and other correspondences. The preparation of music and costumes was also predictable and familiar. On the other hand, the techniques used by a shaman for curing and healing—fasting and meditation—relied more on sensory deprivation. Further, the areas designated for vision quests were more spaces than places, since what was discovered was unpredictable and dangerous. While communal rituals involved both men and women, shamans were men far more often than women.

Simple horticultural societies continued to be dominated by place, perhaps even more so than hunter-gatherers. This was because men ceased to do big game hunting and spent a great deal of time clearing the land for women to plant gardens. While women's work expanded in importance, it was cyclic and predictable. In complex horticultural societies, commodity production for an external market began. The workshops and market places that emerged in these societies are understood as essentially as spaces, because trade involves risk and low-grade hostility. As in hunting-and-gathering societies, men did the trading most of the time. Furthermore, in these societies both men and women began to understand the land outside of the area they were cultivating less as a womb and more as a wilderness—that is, a space.

In simple and complex horticultural societies, the sense ratios may have expanded a bit in the direction of the proximate senses. Both men and women engaged in craft production, whether pottery or woodworking. Pottery requires a strong sense of touch (in both molding and firing) and sight. Woodworking requires the same skills, with the addition of smell. The making of musical instruments requires all the senses but taste.

Stone working requires sight and touch, and boat building requires sight. Both these activities are male-dominated. The activity of gardening—which was dominated by women—requires a sense of touch, smell and sight. The domestication of animals requires the same skills as raising children—touch, sound and smell. While both men and women could spin and weave, women more often performed these activities—which required a strong sense of touch and sight. Village societies had more children, which meant that with more time spent on childrearing and cooking, women would have relied increasingly on their proximate senses.

On the whole, prior to the rise of stratified societies

(1) The non-domestic work of men required the sense of sight more than did the activities of women. The latter's work had a higher percentage of involvement of the proximate senses.

(2) Women worked in two spheres in which the proximate senses played essential roles—childrearing and cooking.

(3) There were few activities that women performed in which sight was the leading sense, or activities that men performed that were dominated by the proximate senses.

In Bronze Age agricultural states there were major changes in how men and women located themselves in places and spaces. Trade expanded considerably in agricultural states, and merchants were, in effect, "space" travelers. They traveled to other lands by ship, shaking off the provincialism of their local habitat. Merchants were almost always men. Within agricultural states the use of the wheel for chariot transport for the upper classes sped up the pace of social life (which tended to make the area spatial). There was now a greater division between what was cultivated—the city and the fields—and what was left over—wilderness. In tribal societies, all women's work was parochial and placial. In agricultural states, except for priestesses, respectable women withdrew from the parochial to the private realm of the domestic household where they engaged in the placial activities of cottage industry. Most men in agricultural states were peasants and engaged in farming, another placial activity.

As we saw earlier in this chapter, space expanded with the appearance of cities. Though the city was dominated by the ceremonial center (a place), the presence of strangers, and an expanding diversity of activities tended to open up spaces. Lower-class women did work in public, engaging in menial jobs and engaging in music, dance, and storytelling just as men did. But for middle- and upper-class women, being seen in public was not good for one's reputation. Though a priestess in an agricultural state performed sacred ceremonies in the temple (a place), the same temple became a space when she managed the divine household. She supervised many industries, including brewing and milling.

With the invention of hieroglyphics in the Bronze Age, differences in the use of sight between men and women became more lopsided. Priests were in charge of writing systems, and thus it was they whose sense ratios were most skewed toward sight. Priestesses in agricultural states also developed sight because they kept track of the temple expenditures. Both priests and priestesses used all the senses in their secondary magical ceremonies. Men replaced women in the fields as plow-based agriculture replaced horticulture. Farming grain does not require the same touch-and-taste skills as does garden planting; the former also involves more kinesthetic movement. Agriculture was men's province.

As we saw earlier in this chapter, herding societies are located in arid environments in wide-open spaces that discourage the use of the proximate senses for both genders. Even touch, in which women were normally immersed during childrearing, declined in the harsh child-rearing practice of swaddling.

In the Axial Iron Age, at least in Athens and in middle Ganges India, spaces grew larger as commerce expanded. The flea markets in agricultural states were essentially marginal and the vestiges of kin group obligations and duties between groups remained. The centralized redistribution center coordinated by divine king was not governed by commercial relationships. In the Axial Iron Age, kin groups weakened and it became easier to exchange goods and services. The use of coined money was like adrenaline to the economy of some Axial Age civilizations. The marketplace (a space) grew considerably. Meanwhile the emergence of a secular politics taking place at the polis and informally in the agora, tended to secularize public space. While the Axial Iron Age city was a far cry from an industrialized city, it was a more secular and spatial city than Bronze Age cities.

To what extent did women have spaces in Axial Age Athens? Women were excluded from all politics, and no middle- or upper-class women could be seen in public. Essentially Axial Age women engaged in the same domestic cottage industry as in the Bronze Age.

Axial Age men dominated public spaces, from the polis to the marketplace to the brothels.

The decline of places within Axial Age cities worked against both women and men, in that life was more exciting (for about 20% of the men) and less secure (for everyone else). The invention of the alphabet democratized the use of the sense of sight, but only for 20% of the population—all of them males. The use of coined money required only the use of sight, and since commodity production and the exchange of coined money took place in public squares, women were not part of these processes.

The purpose of this chapter is to show that the organization of the physical environment *legitimizes and sustains* gender hierarchies over time. The rise of sight at the expense of the other proximate senses was one psychological ingredient in encouraging women to internalize institutionalized male dominance.

As long as people lived in egalitarian hunter-gathering societies and simple horticultural societies, and in non-crisis situations, the fact that these societies were dominated by the conservative qualities of place was not a problem for women. But under conditions of social stress—including population pressure and resource depletion—learning how to live in spaces was important. Men had the edge here because their activities in these egalitarian societies were already more spacial. Once gender hierarchies emerged in agricultural states, having public spaces in which to organize was crucial to forming an opposition to institutionalized male dominance. As long as women had little or no experience operating in spaces—and in dealing with unpredictable, risky situations—it would be difficult for women to self-organize against men.

At the same time, the increased use of sight goes with the ability to distance oneself from the immediate task or environment to compare and contrast relationships between objects and to think more abstractly (as we will see in the next chapter). Since women did not have the opportunity to cultivate their sense of sight, this worked against their ability to challenge the gender hierarchy that had emerged.

Figure 14.4 Speculative Use of Sense Ratios, Space and Place in Ancient Societies

PALEOLITHIC AGE

Men	Both	Women
hunting: space sight, sound, kinesthetic		**gathering : place** sight, touch, smell, taste
making war : space (recursive throughout) sight, sound, kinesthetic		**child rearing: place** (recursive throughout) touch, smell, sound **cooking: place** (recursive throughout) taste, smell
	politics: space sound (listening)	
trading (recursive throughout): space sight, sound	**sacred activities—** **communal: place** sensory saturation: all the senses	
sacred activities: space individual- shamanistic sensory deprivation--fasting, meditation sight--vision quests kinesthetic--dancing		

NEOLITHIC AGE
craft production: place

Men	Both	Women
woodworking--touch, smell, sight	musical instruments sight, sound, touch	pottery--touch, sight
clearing the land: place kinesthetics boat-building--kinesthetics, sight		**planting: place** touch, smell, sight domestication of small animals-- touch, sound, smell spinning and weaving--sight and touch
stone-working: sight, touch	**BRONZE AGE**	
writing (hieroglyphics) economic data and myths sight--recording myths		writing hieroglyphics: recording economic data sight--tracking divine household expenditures
farming: place plow: kinesthetics	**temple activities: place**	**cottage industry: place**

ARCHAIC IRON AGE

Men	Both	Women
sight, sound (anti-proximate senses) **herding camels, sheep, goats: place** sight, sound		harsh child-rearing practices--non-touch **tending to animal milk products: place** dairying-- touch, smell, taste, sound tanning leather--touch, smell, sight
	AXIAL IRON AGE	
writing: alphabet sight **coined money: commerce/market: space** sight **politics--Greek polis: space** discussion--sound **brothels: space**		

Cognitive Evolution in the Bronze and Iron Ages: The Economic and Political Roots of Hyperabstract Thinking

In the last chapter I discussed how women were more limited to the proximate senses than men during the Bronze and Iron Ages, and how this contributed to the internalization of oppression. In this chapter we will study the second of three elements in women's internalization of institutionalized male dominance—reasoning.

The purpose of this chapter is threefold: first, to show how a new kind of reasoning—what I call "hyperabstraction"—was rooted in technological, economic, and political evolution in the ancient world. This is the subject of most of this chapter. Second, I will show how this process impacted some men differently from the way it affected most other men and virtually all women. Third, I will discuss how the lack of opportunity for women to develop their hyperabstract thinking skills contributed to their internalization of institutionalized male dominance.

In order to convey the meaning of what I'm calling "hyperabstraction" let me begin by defining *abstraction*. The ability to think abstractly is common to all human beings as a result of the cultivation of language, which allows us to think beyond the here-and-now. The process of abstraction can be broken down into three moments: extraction, deliberation, and generalization.

Let's suppose I am in the middle of an argument with my partner about how much we can afford to spend on a new car. The process of abstraction begins the moment I use my thinking about this particular problem to compare it to my past and future problems in this relationship and to problems outside my relationship. For example, after a bitter fight about the car, I begin to *extract* the essential elements of this problem from its inessential or accidental properties. For instance, we spent a lot of time in the argument "spinning our wheels" in fruitless mutual accusations. At the same time, I have noticed my partner eating an orange and watching a fly buzz around my sandwich. The orange and the fly are accidental events in this situation that are best left ignored. However, the mutual accusations do matter.

I *extract* this part of the experience out of its context and I *deliberate* about it. I compare our present problem with the car to how we have fought about other issues in the past as well as issues we may encounter in the future, such as whether or not we want children or whether or not we want to live the rest of our lives in the United States.

The last moment of abstraction comes when I *generalize* beyond the particular problems in my relationship and I think about how I fight at work, with neighbors, or with friends. Do we also spin our wheels in mutual accusations?

The heart of abstraction is the capacity to distance oneself from the here and now—present time and local space/place. I define "hyper-abstraction" as an *increase* in the ability to

(1) distance oneself from local time and space/place in the process of extracting the essential from the inessential,

(2) project further back and forward in time and more distantly in space/place in the process of deliberation,

(3) generalize to a greater range of situations, and

(4) self-reflect on the thinking process itself, independent of sensory experience in the process of deliberation.

This chapter is about how three inventions—hieroglyphics, the alphabet, and coined money—mediated the transition from abstraction to hyperabstraction. People began to think in a hyperabstract way because they began to work in occupations that required the cultivation of this skill in order to use inventions. As we will see in this chapter, neither the inventions nor the skills were available to women. This affected women's capacity to challenge the authority of men or to build an alternative movement. The following is an overview of where we are headed:

Social Structure	Paleolithic	Neolithic	Bronze	Iron
Internal Economic distribution	tallies	simple tokens	simple/complex tokens cuneiform	
External Economic distribution	bartering	commodity production	proto-money (grains, gold bars)	coined money
Cultural transmission	oral storytelling	oral storytelling	oral storytelling	written alphabet
Sacred tradition	animism	animism	polytheism	monotheism

1. The economic roots of hyperabstraction: internal redistribution systems in the Bronze Age

An increase in abstraction in the economic realm was driven by a growing number of raw materials together with an increased circulation of goods. A surplus of food production in the middle and late Neolithic Age required more complex methods of tracking the redistribution of goods within society. The upper classes in Bronze Age states had to learn to think more abstractly in order to manage this redistribution.

We might begin our discussion with Bronze Age civilization with the advent of picture writing as a means of accounting, and describe all that went before as having consisted simply of "oral" tribal culture and the developing rudiments of pictorial script. But Denise Schmandt-Besserat (1992) argues that the antecedent of writing was not a simpler two-dimensional script, but three-dimensional counting devices she calls "tokens." In addition, the relationship between oral sacred traditions and written sacred traditions was not a direct one; it was mediated by economic relations. This means that side-by-side with oral sacred traditions there arose economic accounting systems that progressed from tallying to tokens, to writing on clay tablets. It was only as a by-product of writing on clay tablets for economic purposes that writing came to be used for sacred purposes.

The movement from Paleolithic tallies through Neolithic plain tokens to Bronze Age complex tokens to pictorial writing reveals an evolving process of *social* abstraction which, according to Vygotsky's theory of learning, is a precursor to the *internalized* capacity of individuals to reason abstractly. We will return to this point in the last section of this chapter.

According to Schmandt-Besserat, there are two kinds of counting—reckoning and accounting. Reckoning is simply counting, or calculating how many of an item there are.

Accounting is the more complex process of tracking the inputs and outputs of a system.

The history of human notations goes all the way back to at least the Upper Paleolithic—29,000-15,000 BCE—when hunters used notched sticks, and etched bones and antlers to keep track of animal skins or lunar phases. Each unit of a group was tallied with one notch. The notches do little to reveal what was being counted, and so they could only have been useful in small communities where only a few items needed be recorded.

Yet even in this simple system there were elements of abstraction. As Logan (1995) points out, the marks isolated the object from its context. Also, recording the item on the bone separated the information from a particular knower, and made the item recorded public knowledge. It displayed information for all to use. Hence we see the first of three elements of abstraction—extraction.

During the Neolithic Age, notches and pebbles were either supplemented or replaced by clay tokens. Tokens were small three-dimensional geometrical shapes that stood for a certain quality and quantity of goods. Clay was more adaptable to human notion and allowed tokens to be designed freely for economic purposes. Clay tokens also lent themselves to being organized into a larger system:

> The greatest novelty of the new medium . . . was to be a system. There was not only one type of token carrying a discrete meaning, but an entire repertory of *interrelated* types of tokens each with a corresponding discrete meaning. For example, besides the cone, which stood for a small measure of grain, the sphere represented a large measure of grain, the ovoid stood for a jar of oil. The system made it feasible to simultaneously manipulate information concerning different categories of items. . . . It became

possible to store with precision unlimited quantities of information concerning an unlimited number of goods without the risks of failure of human memory. (Schmandt-Besserat, 1992, 161)

According to Robert Logan (1986) these tokens could stand for the following:

(1) A ban (6 liters) or bariga (36 liters) of grain, of which there were three varieties—barley, wheat, and emmet;
(2) Jars of oil;
(3) Containers of foodstuffs such as butter, berries, or dates;
(4) Livestock—primarily sheep and goats—differentiated by age, sex, and breed in units of one, ten, and one hundred head;
(5) Wool, cloth, and different types of garments;
(6) Measures of land expressed in terms of the amount of seed required to sow it;
(7) Service or labor expressed in the time units of days, weeks, and months.

Clay was a useful medium because it is easy to find, easy to work with, and flexible, so that no special tools or skills were needed to make tokens. Small tokens could be arranged and rearranged into groups of any composition and size, while notches engraved on bone, once made, were not erasable. The tallying of notations was irreversible: once notches on a bone were made, the bone was "used up" as a means of tracking. On the other hand, plain tokens could be used and reused to track new economic exchanges. Finally, while tallies were limited to tracking only quantitative information, tokens conveyed qualitative information as well: the type of item being counted could be indicated by the token's shape.

To summarize:

tallies	tokens
probably counted time or objects	counted economic items
made of bone or pebble	made of clay
not systematically related	systematically related

fixed and irreversible
quantitative only (non-specific)
(independent of products)

could be reorganized, hence reversible
quantitative and qualitative
(tied to products)

Tokens were less abstract than pictographic writing because the quantity recorded was never independent of the quality of the particular object being used as a symbol. This meant that arithmetic, algebra, and geometry could not develop until it was possible for numbers to be abstracted from physical objects and studied for their own sake. To study numbers independent of context is the essence of the fourth element of hyperabstract reasoning, in which the inventions of the human mind (in this case numbers) are reflected upon without the burden of application.

Schmandt-Besserat has unearthed 8000 specimens of tokens from 116 sites in Iran, Iraq, the Levant, and Turkey. The process of using representations began in simple horticultural societies around 8000 BCE with 24 tokens and grew to more than 200 by the time of the rise of states and cities in the Near East around 3300 BCE. The shapes of tokens included spheres, discs, cylinders, cones, ovoids, triangles, and tetrahedrons. These were further differentiated with markings, incisions, and punched holes.

First plain tokens were used for keeping track of the products of farming, such as animals or measures of cereals. These tokens were probably loose and exchanged hand-to-hand. While their three dimensionality made them more flexible than notched tallies, the volume of tokens required made the long-term storage of recorded information problematic: small artifacts can be easily separated from one another and it is difficult to keep them in particular order over long periods of time. As societies became more complex, these plain tokens began to be stored in hollow envelopes. According to Logan,

It is presumed that the envelopes were used to consolidate all of the tokens employed in a single transaction. The surfaces of the envelopes were marked with the seals of the individuals involved

in the transaction and hence the envelopes served as a receipt or a contract (Logan, 1995, 89)

However, there were problems with the new system, in that the envelopes when sealed obscured the counters. The contents could not be verified without breaking the envelopes open. The solution to this problem was a major though probably inadvertent step in the evolution of writing:

Accountants resolved the problem by imprinting the shapes of the tokens on the *surface* [my emphasis] of the envelopes prior to enclosing them. The number of units of goods was still expressed by a corresponding number of markings. An envelope containing seven ovoids bore . . . seven oval markings. . . . The seals signaled ownership [and] obligation authority. . . . (Schmandt-Besserat, 1992, 7)

As bureaucracy increased during the Bronze Age, complex tokens were developed to keep track of products manufactured in workshops—such as textiles, garments, luxury items, bread, and oil. Whereas plain tokens were simply smooth shapes, complex tokens had a greater variety of shapes and contained punctuated markings such as lines and circles. These complex tokens were more refined and more uniform in character. In addition, for the most part, complex tokens were not stored in envelopes but were strung together by their perforations and held by a solid bulla—an oblong clay tag bearing seals of the individuals involved in the transaction. Bullae were attached by strings to form a kind of necklace. They were not passed on hand to hand but were kept in archives.

Let me summarize the differences between plain and complex tokens:

Plain tokens
smooth shapes
not stored (simple horticulture)
stored in envelopes (complex horticulture)

represented animals, cereals
casually made
(fired at low temperatures)
passed on hand-to-hand

Complex tokens
perforated shapes with markings

stored in envelopes
stored on bullae (agricultural states)
represented manufactured products
more standardized

kept in archives

As people learned to use these tokens, their thinking would have become more complex. Complex token-using involved a transition—
(1) from reckoning to accounting;
(2) from irreversible markings on tallies to reversible use of tokens allowing repeated use;
(3) from quantitative data to quantitative and qualitative data;
(4) from tokens used at-large to tokens being contained in hollow envelopes or stringed bullae.

The following is both a summary of where we've been and a preview of where we are headed. The transition from tokens to writing involved the following stages:

(summary up to this point)
(1) types of tokens at large and passed hand to hand
(2) tokens enclosed in an unmarked envelope
(3) tokens enclosed in a marked envelope
(4) abandonment of envelopes for bulla
(preview of where we are headed)
(5a) abandonment of bullae for *tablets with impressed signs* that stood for abstract numbers
(5b) abandonment of bullae for *tablets with incised signs with a stylus* that stood for commodities
(6) development from incised signs of pictorial writing and alphabets used for purposes other than economic transactions

(7) use of pictorial writing for self-reflection on numbers-mathematics
(8) use of the alphabet for self-reflection on words—sacred literature, myths

Figure 15.1 summaries this entire section. Figure 15.2 adds to this section and anticipates other sections in this chapter.

Between the use of envelopes for storing complex tokens and pictorial writing are two intermediate stages (5a and 5b). We can see an abstract process at work in the movement *from a three-dimensional handling of tokens to a two-dimensional representation of tokens on a surface,* whether the two-dimensional representation is on an envelope or a bulla. The drawing of signs of the object on the surface is a midway stage between the handling of three-dimensional symbols and the use of a pictorial writing system—which differs from impressed or incised signs. Impressed or incised signs were *intended as a substitute for the tokens.* According to Logan (1995) it took another 50 years for people to realize that the actual tokens in the envelope were *redundant* if the impressions were already on the outside. It wasn't until this realization sank in that tablets began to replace the hollow envelopes.

Tablets began as solid clay balls with markings. The signs *were not pictures of the items they represented* (this would be picture writing) but rather *pictures of the tokens used.*

Out of incised signs came the development of what Logan calls the "logogram," which is a two-dimensional visual sign abstractly representing the written form of a single word (Egyptian hieroglyphics and Chinese characters are examples of logograms). Furthermore, two kinds of logograms can be distinguished:

pictograms, which represent the words they designate pictorially;

ideograms, which represent the *ideas* of the words they represent.

Logan goes on to point out that while the incised tablet led to the development of pictograms and ideograms, the impressed tablet did not. Why was this? Because semantically *impressed* markings were merely flattened, two-dimensional versions of the three-dimensional tokens, in that they shared the same outline and markings as the tokens themselves. All movements from tallies to simple and complex tokens to impressed markings represented either an increase in the variety and number of tokens or morphological changes within the tokens. They did not require qualitative changes in the mental process of abstraction.

Incising signs into logograms did represent a leap in abstraction, since a pictograph is a representation of a word in pictures.

With both incised and impressed tablets, the gradual loss of volume, concreteness, and tactility in representations indirectly led to a revolution in how people thought. The display of information with two-dimensions made it possible to see more data at a single glance, think more globally about the data, and classify and analyze the data more sharply.

Until now we have discussed the movement from the concrete to the abstract in terms of objects used (tallies or tokens) and containers (envelopes or bullae). Now we will turn our attention to numbering systems.

Each reckoning or accounting device implies a particular mode of counting. In simple hunting-and-gathering societies, where goods are not stored, the repeated addition of one unit to an imprecise idea of a total number was adequate to fulfill the needs of accounting. There were one, two, three, and "many." No one needed to determine a large number precisely—as in 41 coconuts. This approximate method of tracking was adequate as long as the

principal means of economic exchange was generalized reciprocity rather than hierarchical redistribution, where precision did matter.

Concrete counting emerged in the token economy of Neolithic and Bronze Age societies. In their redistribution systems, words for numbers were tied to the concrete object the numbers stood for. Tokens were differentiated depending on whether humans, canoes, or coconuts were the objects being counted. An example of concrete counting can be seen in an exchange between anthropologist Jack Goody and the Lo Daga of Northern Ghana. When Goody asked them to count for him, the answer was, "Count *what?*".

The Lo Daga didn't respond by counting "one, two, three, four, five." That would be abstract counting.

In planting societies the invention of tokens provided new ways of handling data, which resulted in cardinality in numbering—which implied grasping the notion of sets. Counting animals or jars of oil no longer meant "adding one more" and then pointing to a collection. Rather, one cylinder token stood for one animal, two cylinders stood for two animals, and so on.

The second major change that tokens brought about was object specificity. The token system required particular counters to deal with each type of commodity. By adding qualifiers to quantifiers of tallying, plain and complex tokens *fused* quantity to quality.

> Ovoids were used to count jars of oil and spheres to count measures of grain; vice-versa jars of oil could only be counted with ovoids and measures of grain with spheres. . . . The fact that tokens varied with each commodity suggests that they reflected a conceptual level at which *only units of the same kind could be counted together* [my emphasis]. In other words tokens seem to be conceived for manipulating data with a system of concrete counting. (Schmandt-Besserat, 1992, 190)

There were still no abstract numbers such as one, two, and three separated from any particular object or concrete commodities. This meant there was no sense of counting the total number of jars or oil together with bags of grain to arrive at the total number of commodities. To do this would imply that numbers could exist *across* categories of objects, and that numbers can be independent of objects.

Just as impressed markings and incised signs represented an intermediary stage between tokens and picture writing, so concrete counting (cardinality and object specificity) served as a transitional device between the use of tokens and abstract counting (yet to be discussed). In concrete counting, each number is fused with quality; in abstract counting, numbers are separable from the items being counted.

Abstract counting introduced signs that were universally applicable, and that permitted counting of dissimilar objects together. Later they also made it possible for people to begin to reflect on the relationships between and among numbers—which was the basis of mathematics (hyperabstract counting).

Now we are in a position to examine the relationship between numerals and letters. In abstract counting, numerals became the symbols encoding abstract numbers, while pictographs originated as representations of concrete objects. Once numbers became independent of particular items, it was possible for letters to develop an existence independent from that of commodities. When letters emerged, they were first used in Bronze Age texts in the transcription of stories of gods and goddesses; it was later, in the Axial Iron Age, that they became a true alphabet. Thus both numerals and letters emerged from abstract counting:

It was not by chance that the invention of pictography and phonetic writing coincided with that of numerals; instead, both were the result of abstract counting. *Once dissociated from any notion of number, the pictographs could evolve in their own separate way* [my emphasis]. The symbols formerly used for keeping accounts of goods could be expanded to

communicate *any* [my emphasis] subjects of human endeavor. As a result items such as "head of a man" or mouth, that never had a token, were expressed by a picture. . . . Finally symbols could function phonetically, representing not objects, but in particular cases, sounds. (Schmandt-Besserat, 1992, 194)

At first abstract numerals and abstract letters were both used for economic purposes. But as these numbers and letters were reflected on, this resulted in the discipline of mathematics on the one hand and the development of the alphabet on the other. Both were applied to expanding intellectual storage systems—a body of mathematical knowledge on the one hand, and literature on the other. When abstract numbers and letters are applied to the relationships within their disciplines as well as to the outside world, we can call them "hyperabstract."

Summarizing this information in terms of social evolution yields the following general timeline:

8000-3500 BCE: the use of concrete counting, in which quantity and quality are fused;
3150-3100 BCE: abstract counting is applied to the number of commodities; quantity and quality are separated *in economics;*
3100 and beyond: "hyperabstract" counting emerges, and self-reflection on abstract counting is applied to (a) mathematics (b) literature and sacred systems.

All forms of notation—whether tallies, tokens, pictographs, or numerals—extract information from its context, separate knowledge from a specific knower, and make knowledge socially available. All notations express movements in collective abstraction. However, the later in history we go, the more the process of abstraction accelerates.

At the beginning of this chapter I said there are three trends that can be traced in abstract thinking: extraction, deliberation, and generalization. Let us see how these trends developed in the economic evolution from tokens to pictographs and then from concrete

Figure 15.1 From Tallies to Tokens to Cuneiform

Time period	Type of counting	Material used	Containers	Contents Counted	System
Upper Paleolithic 29,000-15,000 BCE	tallying one-to-one enumeration	notched sticks, etched bones antlers	at large	time, animal skins quantity not qualities	unsystematic reckoning
Mesolithic 15,000-8,000 BCE	tallying	pebbles shells	at large	time	unsystematic reckoning
Neolithic 8,000-3,400 BCE	plain tokens concrete counting	clay balls tangible tactile-3D	at large quantity-quality merged	cereals, animals	systematic accounting
Bronze Age cities 3,400-3,250 BCE	complex tokens concrete counting	clay balls incised, perforated punctuated	plain envelopes	handicraft manufactured	systematic accounting taxes, tribute
3,250-3,150 BCE			tokens impressed on envelopes		
			tokens stored on stringed bullae		
3,150-3,100 BCE	no more tokens abstract counting	clay	tablets impressed-2D-visual		
3,100 BCE	abstract counting	clay	tablets incised 2D-visual	split between quantity-quality	accounting taxes, tribute
			concrete commodity incised signs	abstract numbers impressed signs	accounting
after 3,100 BCE	hyperabstract counting	clay	words picture writing/ideograph phonetic--alphabet	numbers	sacred texts mathematics

Figure 15. 2 Stages of Hyperabstraction Applied to Abstract Counting, Coined Money, Writing and Monotheism

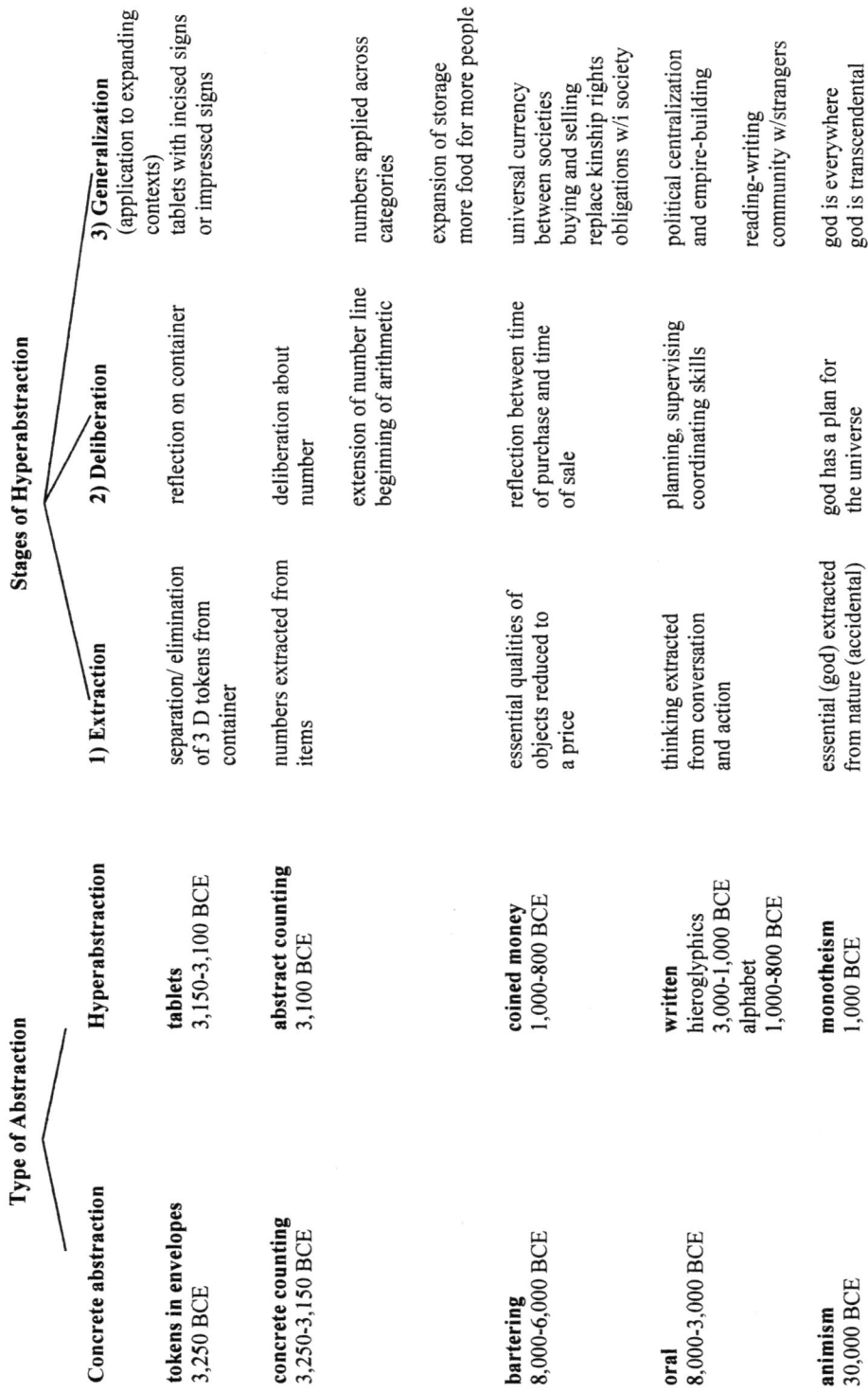

Type of Abstraction		Stages of Hyperabstraction		
Concrete abstraction	Hyperabstraction	1) Extraction	2) Deliberation	3) Generalization (application to expanding contexts)
tokens in envelopes 3,250 BCE	**tablets** 3,150-3,100 BCE	separation/ elimination of 3 D tokens from container	reflection on container	tablets with incised signs or impressed signs
concrete counting 3,250-3,150 BCE	**abstract counting** 3,100 BCE	numbers extracted from items	deliberation about number	numbers applied across categories
			extension of number line beginning of arithmetic	expansion of storage more food for more people
bartering 8,000-6,000 BCE	**coined money** 1,000-800 BCE	essential qualities of objects reduced to a price	reflection between time of purchase and time of sale	universal currency between societies buying and selling replace kinship rights obligations w/i society
oral 8,000-3,000 BCE	**written** hieroglyphics 3,000-1,000 BCE alphabet 1,000-800 BCE	thinking extracted from conversation and action	planning, supervising coordinating skills	political centralization and empire-building reading-writing community w/strangers
animism 30,000 BCE	**monotheism** 1,000 BCE	essential (god) extracted from nature (accidental)	god has a plan for the universe	god is everywhere god is transcendental

to abstract counting (see Figures 15.1 and 15.2 for more visual guidance). In the movement from concrete to abstract counting, quantities are extracted from qualities; the deliberation process includes self-reflection about number independent of the specific items counted, which results in the extension of the number line and the beginnings of mathematics. Generalization occurs (a) when numbers are applied across categories and are no longer tied to particular items, which results in (b) expansion of storage possibilities because of the extension of the number line, in turn because of the increased scope of the items counted; at the same time, there is an increase in (c) the degree of access to more people.

We can see the growth of hyperabstraction also in the movement from the use of tokens to the use of cuneiform. First tokens are used at-large and then collected in envelopes or strung on bullae. Abstraction begins when signs for the tokens and numbers of the tokens are extracted from the manipulation of the tokens (tokens at-large) or the images of the tokens on the envelopes or bullae. A deliberation process occurs when accountants realize that holding the tokens in envelopes is redundant if the tokens are represented on two-dimensional tablets. Generalization occurs when the tablets are used to track commodities by incising signs for commodities and for abstract numerals. A further generalization occurs when writing on tablets for economic purposes through abstract counting opens up the possibility for writing about non-economic aspects of human life (sacred traditions), as letters become freed from their original context—just as numbers were.

2. Economic roots of hyperabstraction: external trade

Schmandt-Bessarent makes it clear that plain and complex tokens, and the first writing systems, were all used to keep track of the *internal* redistribution practices of societies coordinated by an elite. Even in the trading that occurred in Bronze Age states in peripheral markets it is unlikely that complex tokens were used as a medium of record keeping. The use of tokens never trickled down to subsistence farmers for tracking the grain harvested or seeds set aside, probably because these could be estimated visually. But what about economic transactions *between* societies? Was there an evolution to that process as well?

In hunting and gathering societies and simple horticultural societies, commerce between members of the society was unacceptable; trade was limited to barter with other bands or tribes. The first bartered items were not commodities but "leftovers," as commodities are artifacts that are made with the intention of trading. In complex horticultural societies, work specialization made it possible for people to craft objects not only for sacred ceremonies but to sell to other societies; bargaining also began to occur among people within the same society. In chiefdoms, the dominant forms by which goods and services were transmitted were kinship rights and obligations; but as commercial exchanges grew, the process of exchange became more complex and cumbersome lacking some medium of accounting. It became more and more unwieldy to bargain and haggle to trade commodity for commodity, without a fluid medium of exchange—something that was durable and not reducible to another product.

Bartering product for product captures people in present space and immediate time. All trading is on-the-spot. If a good is unavailable, people must either choose something else or go home empty-handed

During the Bronze Ages, a more durable medium was used to mediate trading relationships between states. This consisted of various types of grain stored in small, tied sacks that could be weighed. Eventually the sacks of grain were replaced by gold and silver bars. These exchanges were still unwieldy and no single standard of currency applied to all states. Gold and silver bars did not resolve the problem of growing commodity exchanges taking place within peripheral markets in states. This problem persisted throughout the Bronze Age.

The invention of coined money in the Axial Iron Age allowed people to organize all products in terms of uniform prices, which held both within and between societies. A trader could come to a trading zone with no products to trade, and simply buy what he wanted with money. Axial Iron Age Greece and India produced national currencies that quantified a growing number of exchanges.

Sohn-Rethel (1978) described coined money as a social abstraction that teaches people to think across local space and present time. The use of money extracts the essential—the quantity or standard—from the following accidental characteristics that were part of pre-money economies: (a) the qualitative properties of commodities which make them different from each other; (b) the role and status of the person buying or selling; and (c) the uniqueness of the situation—how desperate the person is for the exchange.

Money also permits deliberation between the time of purchase and the time of sale. Money buys time. It allows people time to think about whether they want to buy something, because the physical burden of bringing objects to and from the market is eliminated. To trust in a coin that has no immediate use value (it cannot be immediately eaten or worked with) over a tangible product shows self-discipline and confidence in these social representations' capacity to stand up over time.

Money also results in generalization: because there is a universal system of equivalence—a price—it makes for an expansion of trade between societies. The invention of money allowed a greater number of people within a given society to be involved in social circulation. In Bronze Age states only an elite used both complex tokens for internal distribution and gold bars for trading purposes outside society. The emergence of coined money in the Axial Iron Age spread social circulation both within and between societies. While the use of money was still based on social class, for most people in agricultural states this invention offered some benefit, because it allowed them to participate more actively in an economy in which goods were being exchanged at an increasing rate.

Based on the work of Schmandt-Besserat it is possible to assert a possible relationship between internal and external economic exchange. Both are based on social abstractions. As far as I know there has been no explicit study of the relationships between tallies and barter, and plain tokens and commodity production. My guess is that there is a close relationship and that each form of internal economic exchange supported and sustained a corresponding form of external economic exchange. Perhaps the invention of plain tokens stimulated commodity production. Once commodity production emerged, it may have stimulated the production of complex tokens. And once hieroglyphics were used in the redistribution system, this may have stimulated the development of coined money.

Internal exchange		External exchange
tallies	Paleolithic	barter (use value)
plain tokens	Neolithic	commodity production (exchange value)
complex tokens	Bronze	barley, gold and silver bars
proto-mediated exchange hieroglyphics		
alphabet (internal and external)	Axial Iron	coined money (internal and external)

3. How hieroglyphics and the alphabet supported hyperabstract thinking

The evolution of counting, accounting, and writing systems is inseparable from the stratification issue of who gets to count and who gets to write. As a result of the wealth from crop production arising from the use of the plow, it became possible for the first time in history to divide the labor force into full-time mental workers and full-time physical workers. This division—and, inevitably, centralization—of the political process meant that mental workers "thought" much more than they "acted." Priests and to a lesser extent merchants were full-time mental workers who made their livings centralizing production and distribution within society and trading with other societies.

In order to do the job of politically centralizing a society, a mental worker must cultivate the abstract thinking skills of coordinating the input and output of the redistribution center, systematically supervising others, and projecting a plan for society in the future. Coordination, supervision, and planning require that an administrator not allow himself to be buried in sense data or detail. He must extract the essential from the nonessential qualities of the goods being handled. He must stay focused on coordinating the detail in one area with detail from other parts of the system. The priest or priestess must also deliberate and think about how to coordinate the actions of others. Lastly, in order to plan for society, the administrator has to generalize by imagining the future context and anticipating what will probably happen before it actually happens.

One of the fruits of the mental-physical division of labor in the Bronze Age was that upper-class mental workers had both the time and the occupational responsibility to think about thinking. This reflective process probably would not have gotten far without writing, because writing captures thoughts and allows them to be reorganized, improved, and self-consciously manipulated. Since the priests and priestesses in upper-caste Bronze Age states could give orders to others to carry out actions,

this freed them to be able to cultivate a life in which a cycle of reading-thinking-writing-and more reading could develop and take on a life of its own. This spiraling process led to thinking about thinking—"thinking squared." This in turn made it easier to organize thinking processes into categories, compare them to other categories, prioritize the categories, and work out the logical inconsistencies between thoughts.

In everyday life we are presented with problems, we use ours minds to solve them, and then new problems arise. Thinking is generally rooted in the need to take action to solve problems. In tribal societies, thinking and doing went together through a wide variety of semi-specialized activities. But when people cannot "see" their cognitive processes through some kind of external storage system, the thought processes vanish when conversations with others end or when projects get resolved, either in success or failure. The idea of extracting thinking from this process of problem-solving and scrutinizing it for separate examination can only come about through writing or some other external storage system. Further, it can only develop when people are paid to think—i.e., when they become full-time mental workers.

All societies have to determine how to transmit their most important social knowledge across generations. One of the byproducts of the evolution of writing is that it serves as an external storage system for social knowledge.

Of course, societies had transmitted culture previously, in the absence of writing systems. As Eric Havelock (1963, 1978) has pointed out, people in oral cultures developed very sophisticated devices for collective memory, using story, drama, poetry, music, and dance, all of which provided a unified experience that encouraged people to remember by saturating their senses and creating an altered state of consciousness. Sympathetic magical practices not only served sacred purposes by casting a spell over people, but fulfilled the pragmatic function of providing a memory theater.

The stories told were dynamic and easy to understand because they were based on the common experiences of all members of that society. Conflicts around universal polarities such as danger-security, love-betrayal, leaving-joining others, and aggression-justice were portrayed. The stories were rooted in rituals connected to particular times of the year and particular places, so they were reinforced in time and space. The people in the rituals became identical with the sacred beings the myths were retelling. Memories were locked in the bodies of participants through song and dance, and these memories returned as soon as music and movement opportunities presented themselves. These rituals resembled a mass hypnosis.

The emergence of hieroglyphics in secondary magical societies in the Bronze Age, and the alphabet during the Iron Age, weakened the necessity of using myths, dramatization, and the arts to support collective memory. This is one reason why, as I have argued in chapter 12, dramatization in secondary magical societies (ceremonies) and religion (pageants) became less participatory. With writing, these traditions were detached from the people enacting the story, the storyteller, the time and place of the ritual, and the sense data and emotions that went with it. The stories became isolated, privatized, and deliberated about. Those who could read and write could communicate with strangers, and this undermined loyalty to one's kin group or society. They could see their culture more objectively, independent of the need for storing memories.

David Abram (1996) makes the point that human language did not always separate us from biophysical nature. It was *written* language that did this. The language of hunter-gatherers partly evolved from making and listening to the sounds of other species. In order to survive in the jungle, foragers must become sensitive to the sounds and cries of other animals in order to catch them. Further, they must have been able to feint these sounds in order to lure these animals out of hiding. It likely required years of practice and social learning to refine these techniques. To make exclusively *human* sounds when living in the jungle would keep potential prey away. On the other hand, to be incapable of listening to the sounds of dangerous animals threatened their lives.

The rise of picture writing involved the transfer of attention from biophysical nature to the two-dimensional surface of parchment or tablets, to symbols of animals rather than call-and-response relationships. Even so, with picture-writing animals were visually depicted, even though in static images. With the alphabet, all visual images were left behind as sounds and letters became abstracted and inherently meaningless, their meaning arising solely from their arrangement and the relatively arbitrary assignment of definitions, spellings, and pronunciations to them. Learning to write and read transformed ear-biophysical relationships with places to a visually centered expansion of the human community into distant spaces.

It is no accident that the Sumerian, the Egyptian, the Chinese, and the Harappan civilizations, as land-based river-valley civilizations, contributed to the development of pictographs, but not the alphabet. The latter was the work of more mobile herding societies—the Hebrews and others on the Arabian peninsula, as well as Phoenician and Greek trading societies. This is probably because these latter societies needed a more portable, less image-based writing system with which to conduct external trade. In the Bronze Age civilizations, pictographs were used either to track internal economic redistribution or for sacred purposes.

The transition of writing from hieroglyphics in the Bronze Age to the alphabet in the Axial Iron Age corresponds to contemporaneous transitions from secondary magic to universalistic religion and the emergence of written law. In the case of the Babylonians, before the code of Hammurabi (1900 BCE), there was no theory of jurisprudence and writing was confined to economic administration. Hammurabi refined both writing and the legal systems.

> Hammurabi . . . had the task of coordinating and uniting a vast multicultural, multiracial and multilingual society consisting of previously semi-independent walled cities that had

constantly warred against each other. In order to rule such an empire, coordinate its economic and agricultural activities and command the loyalty of its diverse geo-political entities, he had to appease each element of the society and satisfy them that they were being treated fairly and equally with all the rest . . . ensuring uniformity of measures, commodity prices, professional fees and transport tariffs throughout the empire. (Logan, 1986, 76-77)

Before the Hebrews developed a writing system, their gods were sensuous and pluralistic

(Elohim); Yahweh at the time of Abraham, Isaac, and Jacob was just another tribal god of this herding society. But this soon changed:

The God of Moses takes on an even more abstract formulation reflecting the abstraction of alphabetic writing. . . . YHWH is invisible to his people. He cannot be looked upon or the people will perish. The people are forbidden to make any images of their God. (Logan, 1986, 91)

Here is a summary of the impact of writing on thinking in the transition from tribal to state societies.

Stone Age tribal	Bronze and/or Iron Age States
Writing	
weakens	**strengthens**
dramatization	description
(myth and art)	(history)
present time	past and future time
local place	global space
sensory saturation	sensory deprivation
proximate senses	sight
participant-storyteller mimesis	solitary study
intersubjectivity	objectivity
story-telling mystery	logical-cause-effect
	scriptures
animism	monotheism

4. Theoretical implications: the socio-historical nature of abstraction

Usually people characterize abstraction as a thinking process that goes on in people's heads. In this chapter I have challenged this notion by arguing that abstraction is embodied in the social relations between people and results from the invention of tokens, tablets, picture writing, the alphabet, and coined money. Further I am suggesting that who gets to cultivate their reasoning processes depends on the group's access to these inventions. The invention of complex tokens, tablets, and picture writing in part was possible because of a great split between mental and manual labor which

occurred in the first agricultural states in the Bronze Age. It was the upper classes of priests and, to a lesser extent, priestesses who used these tools. The inventions of the alphabet and coined money occurred in the Axial Iron Age and these inventions were more democratic, spreading to middle-class merchants.

But what does the social nature of abstraction mean? Russian psychologist Lev Vygotsky (1978) and his followers (Wertsch 1985a, 1985b; Lektorsky 1984; Bakhurst 1991; Leontiev 1981; Mikhailov 1980; Panov 1985) claimed that the human mind is foundationally social. They argued that all new psychological skills are first learned not privately by a mighty attempt to pull oneself up by one's own bootstraps, but by cooperating with other people. These activities must be structured, ongoing and meaningful. It is only after this cooperative activity that the new skills are imported into the psyches of individuals, so that these individuals can reproduce those collective processes in private without the help of others. The third stage (and this is implied but not stated by Vygotsky) is when privatized skills are applied by an individual to new social contexts beyond the original setting in which it was learned. Thus the basic movement of abstraction is social—psychological—social:

(1) "Local interpersonal" skills are learned in a specific, localized context;
(2) "internalization" skills occur when these skills can be performed alone;
(3) "global interpersonal" skills are learned when they are applied to contexts beyond the original setting in which they were taught (local interpersonal).

Vygotsky's model gives us a specific description of how society gets inside people's heads and hearts. Then it shows how society changes when thinking individuals act upon society.

What is the relationship between Vygotsky's three stages of learning and the three stages of abstraction? Extraction, deliberation, and generalization are the processes that go on in people's heads as part of the internalization phase.

Vygotsky devoted his life to demonstrating the social roots of psychological development in children. As a way of summarizing his ideas, let us explore a mundane scenario: suppose a father and daughter decide to bake cookies together. The father may give the little girl the job of mixing eggs, flour, and cookie mix, supervising her while at the same time as doing other parts of the process himself. First the child will learn how to manipulate the tools involved with cooking, with the help of her father. If the cookies turn out well, the process is repeated a number of times with the little girl performing a growing number of functions that used to be performed by her dad. This is the local-interpersonal stage. Once all of the skills have

been mastered, the dad can withdraw and encourage the girl to make cookies on her own. If she does this successfully, she has mastered the internalization stage.

Now let us suppose that the father finds out there is going to be a block yard sale in a couple of weeks. He encourages his daughter to bake cookies for the sale. This will require a new set of social skills, including learning to be more objective. As long as the decision of which kind of cookies to make was limited to her dad and herself, the basis of what to make was only local interpersonal, because the context is the domestic household. But to make cookies for both neighbors and strangers requires (a) making cookies on a much larger scale, requiring more planning and a greater division of labor and (b) learning to make new kinds of cookies, some of which she might not even like. This requires that she survey the people in the neighborhood as to what cookies they would like. This third stage involves finding out more about how the world works beyond her family. This last stage is global-interpersonal.

This type of learning is not limited to childhood socialization. In adult work settings, when we enter into a new job, the training program is equivalent to the local-interpersonal stage. One learns the job by following someone who has already done it—a mentor. The internalization stage occurs when the skills learned can be performed alone. The global-interpersonal stage occurs when the skills that have been internalized can be applied to volunteer work for a political cause, a church, or some other social context outside of work.

Now we are in a position to address the relationship between Vygotsky's three stages and the inventions discussed in this chapter. What happens when a new tool emerges—like complex tokens, tablets, coined money, or the alphabet—yet *no social group* has completely mastered its use? Answer: Everyone has to figure it out as they go. This is how history happens.

Vygotsky himself did not do research on the application of his theory of learning to world history, but he supported the work of his colleague Luria (1976) which was along these lines. In this section I will

(1) group the political and technological inventions discussed earlier into what I am calling Vygotsky's "local interpersonal stage";

(2) discuss how these skills get internalized (Figure 15.3 has done this in graphic form);

(3) show how the internalized skilled gets passed on across generations and then applied to sacred traditions.

Figure 15.4 shows how these stages might be applied to the invention of new tools in the movement from the Neolithic to the Bronze Age.

In this section I am claiming that Vygotsky's three stages of learning can be applied to how certain social castes and classes first learned to think in a hyperabstract way by using new tools. In other words, the movement from tokens to tablets, from concrete to abstract counting, from cuneiform to the alphabet, from bartering, the use of gold and silver to coined money are all examples of social hyperabstract thinking. They first appeared at work, in economic and political contexts. Why should this have been the case?

In our first chapter on history shaping we saw that there is one activity that stands behind the production of all social structures—human labor. In reaction to recurring population pressure and resource depletion crises in the late Neolithic Age, people reorganized their tools and changed their economic and political institutions, including the making of tokens and the production of commodities. In order to respond collectively and creativity to these crises, people labored in technological, economic, and political settings. *In the realm of world history these settings are the site for the local interpersonal stage of Vygotsky's theory.* Once these skills were internalized through extraction, deliberation and generalization, they were applied to wider social contexts—for example, to sacred systems.

Figure 15.4 divides the application of Vygotsky's three stages into three intergenerational cycles, reading across the top from left to right. The first cycle consists of adults going through the three phases *within a single generation.* I call this "macrolevel stage one": it represents socio-historical change in the

late Neolithic Age. The second cycle, in the middle of the page, is the three-step process by which these adults transmit what they've learned to their sons and daughters. This I call "microlevel one" because it deals with the developmental change of the individual in the next generation—the son or daughter of the priest or priestess. The third cycle, on the right of the page, includes the three stages these former adolescents face as adults when confronted with a *new* crisis. I call this macro-level stage two because it returns to the socio-historical dimension but in a new way. (New tools such as the alphabet and coined money would be applied if we stretched Figure 15.4 to include the Iron Age.)

As priestly redistributors learned to manipulate the social abstractions of plain and complex tokens and apply them to economic exchanges, they internalized these abstractions. This came after many years of working with the tokens and from repeated opportunities to supervise, coordinate, plan, delay gratification, and universalize. And all of this in turn came about as a result of centralizing political relations. Over time, redistributors learned to extract images and numbers from tokens and to apply these images and numbers to tablets with impressed or incised signs. The global interpersonal moment of Vygotsky's stages came when adults applied these skills beyond the original economic and political sphere, to sacred beliefs that became a more abstract form of secondary magic.

Now that we have completed one cycle of Vygotsky's theory, as applied to social evolution, let us see how the same process might have acted across generations. These are the microcycle stages 4–6. *The third macrophase of social evolution (parents applying their skills to non-laboring contexts) overlaps with the first stage of individual development in the scribe or merchants' son or daughter.* Adults used to working with plain and complex tokens and coined money will unconsciously apply these social abstract skills to how they raise their children, how they play with them, how they punish them, and what they teach them. Typically a person who makes a living manipulating social abstractions, whether they

Figure 15.3 Vygotsky's Theory of Cognitive Evolution In History

All higher psychological processes begin and end as social processes. They originate first in structured, meaningful, cooperative and recursive local interpersonal relations between people. Only later do these skills become internalized, private and independent skills which individuals carry out alone. Finally these skills are reapplied to the social world in larger contexts then those in which they were originally formed.

Three Stage Process:

Micro-level of individual Life-cycle	Category	Macro-level of World History
Socialization by parents for child's individual survival.	**Cause**	Population pressure and resource depletion necessitates new laboring contexts for social survival.
Engagement between parents and child in playing and learning new skills, roles in problem-solving.	**Stage 1** **Local Interpersonal**	Occupational cooperation of adults as they labor and learn new technologies, economics and political systems.
Private, independent problem-solving.	**Stage 2** **Internalization**	Private independent problem-solving.
Application of new learning to non-domestic contexts: school, play with peers or other adults.	**Stage 3** **Global Interpersonal**	Application of new learning to non-laboring contexts: child-rearing, recreation, sacred activities.

be coined money, checks, or credit cards, will carry that way of reasoning beyond economic contexts. Perhaps the games priests or merchants played with their sons and daughters involved the manipulation of plain and complex tokens, just as the game of "monopoly" prepares children for life in a capitalist economy.

Once these teenagers learned these micro-skills from adults through problem-solving and role-playing, they internalized these skills. They learned to extract, deliberate, and generalize without having to be around their parents in order to do it. Finally, these children began to practice their skills outside the home with other people, playing with peers or with other adults.

As adults, these former teenagers entered the macro-social world fully prepared to be redistributors or scribes. This is the Macrolevel 2, cycle three, stages 7–9. For illustrative purposes I will speed up social evolution and make these young adults deal with another social crisis later in the Bronze Age, which would force the collective invention of pictographic writing. Thus pictographic writing skills in stage seven would have been internalized by these young adults. Quantities were separated from qualities (extraction), quantities were deliberated about, and mathematics was invented. Mathematics was then applied to the expansion of storage and the more efficient use of food. In stage nine, these abstract thinking skills were again applied to sacred traditions, creating a more abstract form of polytheism or secondary magic.

6. Women and hyperabstraction

According to Vygotsky's theory, the extent to which women used hyperabstract reasoning was inseparable from how often they got a chance to use complex tokens and hieroglyphics in the internal redistribution system in the Bronze Age. How often were they able to use money and the alphabet when these emerged in the Axial Iron Age?

Since women more often than men worked in making clay pots, it is likely that women were also actively responsible for making plain and complex tokens. The handicraft production

of these tokens, however, was not the same as *using* them. It was the priests in agricultural states who were responsible for using tokens for redistribution/accounting purposes. This caste comprised only a fraction of the entire agricultural state population—according to Lenski (1987), about one percent. It is important to remember that only a tiny percentage of the men had access to this technology, and that the lack of this tool affected lower castes of men as well as all women.

As pointed out by Schmandt-Bessarat, when hieroglyphics began to be impressed or incised on two-dimensional tablets, those who first worked with them (whether for economic purposes or for sacred purposes) were men. Further, the invention of writing was important in justifying both gender and caste stratification. The new mythology was powerful not only because it became male-dominated, but because it was *written down*. But why would writing the myths down have provided political clout for the elite? How would this differ from *orally* passing myths on?

Oral myths are more easily changed, if for no other reason than that human memory is more malleable than a written scroll. In oral myths, each generation must have left out certain elements of the myth, and added new parts. In contrast to this, once the stories are written down, they are less subject to change unless change is deliberately intended. Written myths must have acquired an awesome quality and a formality that the oral myths probably lacked. Since *elite men* were in control by the time writing was invented, it was *their* myths that became awe-inspiring.

Writing must have been oppressive to women in another way. Whatever disenfranchisement women were already experiencing was now *codified in laws*. Activities that deviated from codes that were written on tablets and scrolls must have gained even more illegitimacy than they already had. Thus protest would have become even more difficult.

As noted earlier, the alphabet, once it emerged, proved to be a more democratic tool, because it was easier to learn and apply. Its use, at least in Greece, spread to the middle class and perhaps to lower-class farmers, but probably the people who learned to use it were all men. If participation in the polis was open to about 20% of the male population who were citizens, it is doubtful that women—who were altogether excluded from political participation—would have learned to use the alphabet. On the other hand, the women who were married to those male citizens probably indirectly benefited by their husbands' learning to read and write.

The emergence of coined money must have had a similar effect on the lives of women. As commodity production and markets within society expanded in the Axial Iron Age, the merchants who were at the center of the new wheeling and dealing were generally men. For women married to merchants, and to men in the social classes who actually exchanged goods at local markets, life might have improved somewhat. But women did not directly participate in the expansion of the economy.

In short, hieroglyphics, the alphabet, and coined money increased the distance between some men and most other men and women. What we must turn to now is the psychological impact of these tools on the lives of women. If writing and coined money helped to develop hyperabstract thinking, and women did not have access to these tools, then they would have been less encouraged to think in a hyperabstract way than were middle- and upper-class men. What exactly would this mean?

If women were discouraged from thinking in a hyperabstract way, this would have limited their thinking to present time and local place. Women in the Bronze and Iron Ages did not work in public as tribal women did. They spent their lives in the domestic economy; therefore they were not able to compare notes and identify commonalties. What is more, even if they could have done this, without a system of writing available to them it would have been very difficult to build a movement.

Among other things, a movement requires a reference point beyond the present. It must refer to past instances of injustice and it must project in writing a better future. Without this, a movement is not rooted in the stream of history. Writing encouraged just this

hyperabstract thinking skill of lifting oneself out of present situations and sense data and comparing the past to the future. Illiteracy would not make this impossible, but it would make it more difficult.

In addition, without the hyperabstract reasoning that came with writing there would have been less deliberation between one experience and other. If an individual's mind is lost in reacting to other people and to the demands for routine behavior, there is no time to analyze one's situation. One lives in a reactive mode as a way of life.

Without writing, women could not connect with other women who shared a common plight in other areas beyond the local kinship network. Movements usually cannot be successful against an existing order unless they get help or at least draw a sympathetic response from others who are not in the immediate vicinity.

Without the use of coined money, women would also have lost the possibility of cosmopolitan interactions, which could occur in trading centers. These areas—in Greece, the agora—not only provided a forum in which people could buy exotic goods, but invited a comparison between cultures. And this experience of cultural dissimilarity was in turn capable of undermining blind loyalties to family and one's social station. If women had limited access to trading centers, they would have been more isolated in their outlook.

In short, because women lacked opportunities to learn hyperabstract thinking, it was difficult for them to build a psychology of resistance. They were thus more likely to internalize their oppression.

Figure 15.4 Intergenerational Change in Hyperabstraction from the Neolithic to the Bronze Age

LATE NEOLITHIC AGE

Macrolevel 1

socio-historical change in parents

cause: population pressure/
resource depletion crisis

**1) local interpersonal change
in laboring practices**
Cooperatively learning and problem-solving
in new laboring practices in economics
and politics:

    plain tokens, complex tokens
    commodity production

2) internalization
Priests, priestesses and merchants
learn to extract, deliberate and generalize

Economic redistributors learned to extract
images from tokens and apply to tablets
with impressed or incised signs

3) global interpersonal
Application of new skills to non-economic
contexts. Child rearing, sacred tradition
outside the domestic setting

EARLY BRONZE AGE

Microlevel 1

socio-historical change in teenagers

cause: socialization by parents
for child's survival

4) local interpersonal
Priests, priestesses and merchants
teach hyperabstract skills to their teenagers in
problem-solving, role-playing,
playing games and handling artifacts

5) internalization
Teenagers extract, deliberate and generalize
privately in the absence of adult supervision

6) global interpersonal
Teenagers practice hyperabstract thinking
when playing with peers and while being adults

LATE BRONZE AGE

Macrolevel 2

socio-historical change as
teenagers become new adults

cause: population pressure
resource depletion crisis

7) local interpersonal
As teenagers become adults
they inherit the occupation of
priest, priestess or merchant.
Use of hyperabstract reasoning
to resolve new crisis:

    pictographic writing
    use of gold and silver bars

8) internalization
Priest, priestess learn to extract
deliberate and generalize--
abstract counting, arithmetic

9) global interpersonal
Application to non-economic contexts
and a more abstract form of secondary magic

Chapter 16

Collectivism and Individualism: Evolution of the Self

In this chapter we will complete our study of the forces of internalization that impacted women's psychology and supported institutionalized male dominance. In the first section we will explore exactly what it means to possess a "self" and the ingredients that go toward building one. In the next section I will discuss the forces of socialization that are the means for internalizing these ingredients.

In the first two sections I will treat the building of a social self as if it had no variation in social evolution. While all societies have to provide children with these ingredients, the types of selves that get built are not the same. Some skills are emphasized while others are downplayed, depending on whether the society is a tribe, an agricultural state, or a commercial farming society.

In the third section of this chapter I will highlight the difference between collectivist selves and individualist selves. We will see that,

just as Stone Age, Bronze Age, and Iron Age societies had different political, economic, sacred, ecological, sensory, and cognitive orders, so too the senses of self were also distinct. Individuals in tribal societies had "horizontal collectivist selves" and people in Bronze Age agricultural states had "vertical collectivist selves." It is only in the Axial Iron Age that we see the first signs of a "vertical individualist self."

In the fourth section I will explain why women had vertical collectivist selves and how this might have contributed to their internalization of oppression. In the last section I will explore how the forces of legtimation (discussed in chapters 12 and 13) and the forces of internalization (chapters 14 through 16) mutually support each other. Here is an overview of the place the self occupies in comparison to other differences we have addressed:

Stone Ages	Bronze Age	Axial Iron Age
egalitarian/rank	stratified caste	stratified class
primitive magic	secondary magic	religion
primacy of place	primacy of place	place declines, space expands
proximate senses	proximate senses	sight
concrete abstraction	incipient hyper-abstraction	hyperabstraction
horizontal collectivist self	vertical collectivist self	vertical individualist self

The horizontal collectivist self is conditioned by egalitarian political relations, primitive magic, proximate senses, a sense of place, and concrete abstraction; and it will in turn influence these forces. At the other extreme, the vertical individualist self is conditioned by class political relations, the presence of monotheism, the use of the long-

distance sense of sight, the organization of physical settings into spaces, and hyperabstract reasoning. At the same time, the individualist self helps reproduce the very relations that determine it.

1. Building a social self: learning objectivity and subjectivity

Human identity might be divided into three interacting layers. The first layer is temperament. This is the biological predisposition of the organism prior to being humanized by socialization. In psychology texts these characteristics include whether a person is introverted or extroverted, and whether an individual is "high-strung" or easygoing. The second layer of identity is personality. Personality results from the interaction between temperament and socialized environment over time. Personality consists of the characteristics of the individual that persist over time and across roles and situations. While personality is socialized, it refers to the biography of the individual. Society is relatively indifferent to the personality of individuals but it is quite concerned with the development of the third layer of identity, the self.

The self, like personality, is built from a combination of biological forces on the one hand and socializing forces on the other. However, the cultivation of a self primarily involves learning skills and cultivating attitudes that allow the individual to participate fully as a member of society. This involves being a recipient of social forces and being a co-constructor of those forces. In order for society to be transmitted across generations (history), those who developed selves must, as parents, help build the selves of their children so they are capable of working, raising children of their own, and transmitting their knowledge to the next generation. The self is the smallest unit of society.

The socialization of the self takes between six and ten years. According to Mead (1972), Hewitt (1991), and other symbolic interactionists, a cornerstone in the foundation of a self is learning to be objective and subjective.

What do we mean by objectivity and subjectivity? A brainstormed list of characteristics might look something like this:

Objectivity	**Subjectivity**
knowing what is going on outside	knowing what is going on inside
detached	involved, engaged
cold	having feelings
fair	biased
related to actions	related to inner states

Conventional wisdom would have us assume that the cultivation of objectivity is difficult, so difficult in fact that many adults never master it; while subjectivity is automatic or inborn and requires no development. This is not the case. A young child has neither objectivity nor subjectivity; both must be built.

The young child does possess a proto-social self that is pre-subjective and pre-objective. Young children are too lost in their own needs to see their caretakers as full beings living in situations and playing roles that are independent of themselves (this would require objectivity). Other people are seen by infants and young children as fragments and are used as means to satisfy their needs. At the same time, this proto-social self does not realize that its internal urges, emotions, fantasies are closed off to the scrutiny of others. In order to develop subjectivity there must be an awareness that one's inner life cannot be publicly scrutinized.

To build a social self one must—

(a) distinguish the inner world from the outer world
(b) learn language, both verbal and non-verbal
(c) manipulate tools effectively
(d) suppress or relativize biological urges
(e) cultivate a conscience
(f) learn to play in an improvised and a designed manner
(g) decipher the beliefs and customs of society

(h) master how to make and take roles
(i) learn the status and entitlements of people in roles
(j) learn to think abstractly about past experiences and future intentions
(k) navigate across routine, mildly problematic and crisis situations
(l) learn to cooperate in groups
(m) manage the tension between individual and social self-interest (I-me dialogues)

Some of the skills and concepts a child must learn as part of socialization cannot easily be categorized as either subjective or objective because they overlap both categories. These include learning to distinguish the inner world from the outer world, learning to use verbal and non-verbal language, and learning how to manipulate tools.

All beings must earn a living in the environment. We, in order to do this, must focus on what we need and find a way to engage nature in successfully appropriating it. Most other biological beings are limited to their physical anatomy—claws for raking, teeth for tearing, and beaks for pecking. Humans craft tools to enlarge their ability to harvest energy from the environment. Tools intensify our actions and allow us to reshape the world.

As we saw in the last chapter, language is vital in enabling the human species to live beyond the here and now. It allows us to share our experiences with others, speeding up the learning curve for everyone. It allows us to analyze and compare our common past experiences. Also language allows us to develop future plans together. Language is primarily social, but as a secondary gain the use of language invites reflection on a personal past and future. Without language thinking would be tied to the present.

Another requisite to cultivating objectivity is the development of a conscience. As all parents know, it is futile to expect a child to know what is right or wrong. It is also unrealistic to simply tell a child what is right and wrong and expect that information to govern the child's behavior from that point on. Tangible consequences—such as punishment for anti-social behavior—seem to produce better

results in this regard. There is a point however, at which the conversations between parents and children about beliefs and morals move from interpersonal to intrapersonal. In other words, the child internalizes these conversations with parents and makes them their own. When this occurs, the child has succeeded in building a conscience—or, in Freud's term, a superego.

Of course, having a conscience does not guarantee that the child will do what the parents want. But if the child does not enact the beliefs and morals of the parents she or he will be aware of the conflict and probably feel guilty about certain actions. Prior to this internalization of conversations, guilt and remorse do not exist. Avoiding wrongdoing is merely a matter of fearing punishment or following what the parents want because of an anticipated reward. To build a conscience the child must also eventually decode society's morals and beliefs; these become the contents of the conscience.

One of the most important skills a young person must learn is how to take and make roles. Roles are a predictable range of expected actions and attitudes that are embedded in specific situations. Roles arise from a conscious or unconscious division of labor between people because the goals of a situation can be achieved more efficiently and successfully that way.

For children, learning to play roles and play them in situations is not coextensive in time. Children first learn what roles are, and they do this through play. Mead identifies three stages in learning how to play in roles:

(1) *Preparation.* In this first stage, the child is still mastering language, tool manipulation, and her body, and is also developing an conscience. S(he) imitates the actions of others without understanding that they are roles, nor does she understand the meaning of the roles.

(2) *Play.* In this stage the child begins to understand roles, but can only play the roles of significant others *one at a time.* Secondly, the child cannot see himself from the perspective of others. I have called this (Lerro, 2000, 121–122) "improvised play," which involves "let's pretend" games in which the imagination is cultivated at the expense of structure. Roles,

rules, and purposes are invented, changed, and ended quickly at the whim of the child.

(3) *The game.* At this stage (what I call "designed play"), the child can assume the perspectives of several others at the same time. In addition, the individual can now see herself from the perspective of others. Here imagination is tempered by playing in games that have roles, rules, and expectations built into them before the game begins and are not subject to modification. Designed play teaches structure, self-discipline, and co-operation over extended periods of time.

Learning to play in roles is a precondition for taking on roles in earnest. Learning to play roles seriously involves not only learning what the codes are—the beliefs and values of the participants in general—but also that some roles involve order-giving and order-taking. Every role has a status and a range of entitlements as to what is expected, permitted, and prohibited. This is the origin of prestige, influence, privilege, and power as discussed in chapter 1.

At first the child does not understand that all roles are rooted in situations. Thus deciphering situations constitutes another important skill. Different situations require us to play different roles. In every situation there are at least eight dimensions:

(1) meaning (what is happening?)

(2) purpose and hopes (why is it happening?)

(3) power base (who is making it happen?)

(4) rules (what is permitted and forbidden?)

(5) roles (is there a place for me?)

(6) customs (what is expected?)

(7) physical setting—furniture, artifacts (where is it happening)

(8) timeline (when is it happening? how long will it last?)

A routine situation is one that is stable and repetitive, and in which most or all of these questions are answered in the same way by all of the people in the group. In routine situations these dimensions are usually taken for granted and not explicitly discussed. Lack of clarity or disagreement among people, especially in the first four dimensions, destabilizes routine situations and leads to either problematic or crisis situations.

For example, on most days when I teach a class I encounter a routine situation. I come into the classroom and most of the students are sitting away from the front of the room. They understand they are in a classroom, they are students trying to get a decent grade, and I am the teacher. They are expected to ask questions, to bring paper and pens to write with, and to take turns when speaking. I don't have to tell them that they cannot spontaneously come to the front of the room and sit on my desk, begin moving furniture around, or leave without offering a reason. The dimensions of the situation, as unconsciously agreed on, do not require discussion.

A mildly problematic situation is one in which unexpected, minor novel events stretch the boundaries of the eight dimensions without calling the situation itself into question. Some of the eight dimensions come to the level of group consciousness because they must be discussed and negotiated in order for the situation to re-stabilize. Sometimes mild problematic situations emerge not because of events, but because a significant number of people in the group misunderstand some of the dimensions of the situation or are in conflict about them.

In the example of a classroom, a mildly problematic situation might arise if a number of students question my absence policy or grading criteria in front of other students. My power base, the rules for the class, and the timeline are being tested. But the reasons for why we are here and the expectations about what we are doing remain in place. Whether this situation returns to routine or escalates into a crisis depends on how everyone in the room negotiates the controversy.

A crisis situation occurs when either most of the dimensions are called into question, or only the most important ones such as the meaning, purpose, or power base are called into question. A natural disaster that rocks a school can immediately change a routine situation into a crisis. It ends the educational situation and forces the same group of people to renegotiate how they are to be together in a collapsing building. Because the situation has changed, all of the dimensions of situation have to be reorganized.

When children first enter a social milieu they enter it not knowing anything about roles or situations. Their proto-social self imposes their personality on the situation, oblivious to the roles people are playing and the type of situation they are in. The first step for the child is to understand that people play roles and with these roles go certain expected behaviors. In addition, they must learn that the same person can play *many* roles in the course of a day, not just the one role of mom or dad. They must understand that roles are *detachable* from particular people. Roles can be played by anyone, not just the people they know. The next step is to learn how these multiple and detachable roles will change depending on whether a person is in a routine, mildly problematic, or crisis situation.

Designed play (Mead's "the game") socializes children to respect structure and perseverance in order to participate in routine situations. Improvised play (Mead's "play") teaches people how to be imaginative when a group is faced with a crisis situation. When an individual operates in a routine situation he or she is role *taking,* entering a role that is already in place. When an individual is operating in a crisis situation she or he is role-*making,* creating the role (with others) on the spot.

So far the ingredients that go with cultivating objectivity include understanding how to play roles and learning how to change roles as situations dictate. In addition to this the young child must learn mentally to move from present time (their lifetime) and local geography (the domestic household) to past and future time (world history) and global geography (beyond the domestic household). Cultivating a generalized "other" means understanding society as global on the one hand and historical on the other.

This is what Mead meant when he characterized cultivating objectivity as consisting of developing a "generalized other" inside one's mind. The generalized "other" is an internalized sense that other people, and the situations they find themselves in, are objective and independent of the internal expectations and wishes of the child and her parents. For example, this means coming to realize when at school that other children have parents who do not have the same beliefs about religion that her own parents do. It means understanding that not all people around the world have computers in their homes, that even many families within the same city do not have a computer.

The child comes to realize that the domestic household which she thinks is *the world* is, in fact, a tiny slice of a world, and that it is surrounded by many other domestic households which are in turn dominated by much larger social institutions which exist in places s(he) may never go. In other words, the things the child once saw as absolute become relative to a much larger world.

On the one hand a child must learn that the roles she masters are small aspects of historical structures that have come into being *before* her individual lifetime and are likely to remain *after* she dies. On the other hand the fully socialized individual does not assume that the roles that happen to exist in her lifetime are *eternal.* The role of computer programmer is unique to the 20th century. It hasn't always existed. In sum, just as the individual understands the relativity of the domestic household as the world, so too does he come to understand that the roles he plays in his lifetime are a tiny part of world-history in the making.

But what about an individual's *subjectivity,* or what symbolic interactionists call the individual's "biographical self"? According to Mead, developing a sense of subjectivity is impossible without first understanding what it means to be objective. Once objectivity is understood, one's personal identity can be seen in perspective—as relatively small, but also unique. The proto-social self of the child comes to comprehend that her inner life is not on display to others; that others are not simply an audience for the child's personal dramas. Other people have individual lives that are unique to them, theirs to make for better or worse. This awakening allows the child to think about, fantasize, and act towards himself not as the center of the universe but as a unique being among other unique beings.

Just as the individual must understand the social world as expanding in geography and time, so she must come to see her own life as having wider temporal and geographical reach. The budding self realizes that it has a past and a future as well as a present. The individual must be able to reflect on past experience not only in the service of his present situation, but also in where he wants to go. At the same time this individual self must come to see that its ability to shape and change things can extend beyond the domestic household to all of society. In other words, just as the individual comes to understand the world as expanding in time and space, so she comes to see the same process, at least a microcosmic version of it, going on in her life.

Once an individual develops a picture of an independent objective world on the one hand and a distinct subjective world on the other, a unique problem presents itself. The existence of the objective world means that there are constant *expectations that other people in social groups will have* of me. Yet at the same time, because I understand how to navigate these roles and situations, I have a greater chance of transforming these roles and situations in the service of *what I want*. The problem now is to reconcile social self-interest and individual self-interest.

Once the outer and inner worlds are clearly distinguished, negotiations must take place. Mead calls the part of the individual that has internalized the expectations of others the "me" part of the self. The part of the self that represents the interests of the individual in relation to society is the "I" part. Mead called the subsequent negotiation between the I and the me part the "I– me" dialogue. These two sides cooperate and compete with each other; they haggle, trade, and plead for their respective interests when in roles and situations.

Here is an example. Suppose an individual in a tribal society sees a member of his kin group headed toward his hut expecting to visit and be fed. The "I" part of this person thinks to himself, "here comes so-and- so, the loafer, expecting a free handout. I should leave quickly so I don't have to entertain him." The "me" part counters with, "no, he is my kinsman and I am responsible for treating him as one of my own." The "I" part rebuts this by saying, "but he is such a loafer, he wouldn't do the same for me." The "me" part counters with, "but the members of his family would be upset with me and they are not loafers. I don't want to start trouble with them." The "I" part tries a compromise: "maybe I could be with him for a few minutes and pretend to be sick in order to send him on his way."

Earlier in this chapter I said that the ability to develop a generalized "other" and a biographical self requires living in the present with an *expanded* sense of time and space. In order to do this an individual must learn to think abstractly. In the last chapter we defined abstraction as having three moments:

(1) to extract the important from the unimportant properties of objects and situations in the present;
(2) to deliberate how these essential properties connect to both a group and an individual past experience, together with individual and group future plans; and
(3) to generalize as to how to use these essential properties in other situations.

Conversely, thinking in a concrete way would imply:

(1) an inability to distinguish the essential from the inessential properties of things, and hence a tendency to become lost in the accidental properties of a situation—the passing of a butterfly, a burp, or the smell of food in the next room;
(2) having little sense of how what is going in the present might be connected to past experiences, and a consequent inability to think clearly about the future; and
(3) an inability to learn from situations and apply to new ones, leading the individual to repeat many of the same reactions regardless

of where they were or whom they were with.

The movement from concrete to increasingly abstract thinking is described in Piaget's stages of cognitive development.

Now that we have completed our survey of the building blocks of the self, we will examine how differences in the socializing forces of these building blocks contributed to the differences in the kinds of selves produced in tribal societies, agricultural states, and commercial farming states.

2. How forces of socialization form collectivist and individualist selves

The division of social identities into individualist and collectivist has been researched by a number of psychologists (Triandis 1995; Segal, Dasen, Berry, and Poortinga, 1990; Smith and Bond-Harris, 1994) and is a main staple of courses on cross-cultural psychology. For the purposes of this book we are interested in the *origins* of this difference and how this difference is connected to the building blocks of the self. But what exactly do we mean by "collectivism" and "individualism?" Let me begin with how each identity orients itself in relation to society and nature.

Individualism is a set of beliefs and practices that assumes that: (a) The individual is separate from kin-groups and nature; (b) the inner world is more a source of identity than objective actions; and (c) the individual is more important than the group. Collectivism is a set of beliefs or practices that assumes the reverse: (a) The individual is interdependent with society and nature; (b) the outer world of objective actions matters more than does inner experience; and (c) the group is more important than individual.

But where do these assumptions come from? Do individuals just decide for themselves which set they like better? Hardly. Technological, political, and economic social structures create institutions for socializing these individuals. People in these institutions will teach other individuals the building blocks in ways that will create and sustain dominant social relations.

People in Stone Age and Bronze Age societies were conditioned to negotiate the building blocks of self as collectivists. With the rise of individualism in the Axial Iron Age, individuals engaged the building blocks differently because there are new assumptions about the relationships between the individual, society, and nature. A tribeswoman living in a simple horticultural society would not have had the same "I-Me" dialogue as a merchant in the Axial Iron Age. She would not have faced the problems of role-making and role taking in the same way; nor would she have felt and thought the same as the merchant about dealing with crisis situations. But exactly how did this difference come to be?

In our society, in the course of growing up, the building blocks discussed in the first section of this chapter are constructed from the interaction of at least seven forces of socialization: the nuclear or extended family; the educational system, especially teachers; the mass media, including TV, movies and the internet; sacred influences such as churches; the government, which promotes patriotism and loyalty to the state; participatory and spectator sports; and lastly, friends. The question the socializing forces address is what the individual is supposed to be and do.

The first factor that impacts whether or not a person develops an individualist or a collectivist self is the *number* of socializing forces that support individualist or collectivist assumptions. If three institutions support individualism and four support collectivism, the result will be confusion. This is what happens to immigrants or refugees who come from a collectivist society to the United States. But in most cases a society is predominantly either individualist or collectivist, so there is less confusion.

The second factor is the degree of conflict and harmony between forces of socialization. In industrial capitalist societies even when all of the socializing forces are individualist, if they are vying for control over the individualist's choices of identity—soldier, rock musician, or family man—they may cause confusion. Further, they suggest that *any one of these identities is possible*. As Berger (1967) points out, it is because an individual sees conflicting choices that he comes to see the relativity of all social institutions. This reinforces the assumption that the individual is prior to the group, and the constraints on an individual are not as great as the possibilities.

In an industrial capitalist society it is likely that the messages of family and mass media will conflict; the messages of friends may conform to neither; while the government and the churches could be at odds with each other, given the separation of church and state. Identity-crisis questions like "Who am I" and "What is my place in society" are unique to societies that promote individualism. Not all individuals in all societies ask these questions, which wouldn't be raised unless a *variety* of answers were possible. For a variety of answers to be possible there would need to be socializing forces that give different answers to these questions.

Berger goes on to argue that in societies with the least division of labor, the sources of socialization tend to all reinforce the same assumptions and are not in competition with each other. They will produce the most conformity and obedience. If we examine the socializing influences of egalitarian societies, we see that the main ones are the family, kin groups, and local clans. Whatever tensions may exist between these groups, they nevertheless give the individual more or less the same message—that group expectations are primary. Methods of transmission in tribal society are oral. There is no mass media, and in Bronze Age states the centralized government and sacred institutions are often identical. There are rarely counter-institutions that actively compete with collectivism unless the society has been invaded by individualists. While there might be some loyalty conflicts between the peasant traditions in the villages and the expectations of the government, these are caste societies where people do not question their place in society. The only social group within the society that might have proto-individualist tendencies consists of the merchants, who travel to other societies and may recognize the relativity of their own society's way of doing things.

So far I have suggested that the formation of the self is inseparable from the development of the building blocks discussed in section one. Then I argued that the formation of the building blocks within the individual is mediated through (a) the *content* of what society needs—i.e., an individualist or collectivist self, and (b) the *forms* of the socializing influences. This includes the *number* of socializing institutions and whether these institutions are *competing or cooperating* with each other. Now let us look more closely at the process by which the building blocks are transmitted from the various social forces into the individual's psyche. As we saw in the last chapter on cognitive evolution, Vygotsky claims that all new psychological skills originate first as cooperative social relations between people, then become internalized, and are finally applied to larger social contents.

Let us take the building block of tool use. For example, how might a young child learn how to catch fish for her family? Her father or mother may show her how to pick a piece of wood that is neither too yielding nor too rigid; how to choose and attach a string; and how to select and catch the bait. This is the first of Vygosky's stages of learning, the local interpersonal stage. The internalization stage will come when the young girl can master all of these skills by practicing them herself. The global interpersonal stage occurs when the child is able to fish by coordinating her efforts with members outside her family so that the entire society can be fed.

In a state society there are still more socializing influences, so that Vygotsky's three stages of learning intersects more socializing forces. For example, the son of a merchant may learn mathematical calculations from his father, using bags of barley or millet as a form of money. But the son may also learn from the accounting practices of priests involved in managing the temple household. Therefore the young man has two socializing influences in the local interpersonal stage. At the global interpersonal stage he might apply what he has learned in trading with societies his father never traded with.

Let me summarize the processes of socialization. In order to participate in society, an individual must build a self. This is done by mastering skills that take many years to develop. How well or badly these skills are learned depends on a variety of socialization forces. The process of how the socialization forces interact with an individual over his or her life-span can be meaningfully broken into Vygotsky's three phases of learning.

In the next section we will study how the actual content of the building blocks differs, depending on whether the society is collectivist or individualist.

3. Individualist vs. collectivist selves

In this section I will propose the specific ways in which people in the Stone Ages and Bronze Ages might have differed in how they were socialized to use the building blocks and thus to construct *collectivist* selves. I will contrast this Stone-Age, Bronze-Age collectivist pattern with how the middle and upper classes during the Axial Iron Age were socialized to use the building blocks to create an *individualist* self.

I call societies "horizontal collectivist" because, with the exception of complex horticultural societies, they are politically and economically egalitarian. The people in these societies are collectivist not just because their socializing influences are unified, but because there is no class or caste conflict over access to resources or political decision-making processes.

However in rank and stratified societies, even though the socializing influences may be continue to be unified, the increased specialization of labor and the differentiating access to resources and political decision-making processes create real material differences between ranks and castes. The resulting rivalries represent conflicting group self-interests which act as a potential platform for the later formation of an individualist self. I call people living in Bronze Age agricultural states "vertical collectivists" because they still put the needs of society as a whole before their individual identity, despite the fact that there are real material differences between them. As we will see, individualism first emerged in Greece in the Axial Iron Age. These selves are called "vertical individualist" because these selves were supported by the class basis of their societies.

I will begin by contrasting how collectivists and individualists differ in how they understand their relationship to society and nature. While infants from all societies must distinguish themselves from their social environment (more specifically from the mother), in individualist societies the child comes to understand herself as separate not only from her mother, but eventually from all of society and the natural world. The collectivist child learns to distinguish himself from his mother as he grows up, but he never imagines himself as separate and autonomous from his society or the natural world. On the other hand, the nature of cooperative, organic relationships does not extend outside his group. Collectivists do not tolerate strangers. The latter are either brought into the kin group through a ritual or ceremony, or they are expelled or killed. Collectivists imagine their relationship with the social and natural world in an *organic* way, as if they themselves were an organ in the body of society or nature. The organ has a function to perform within the whole. If the organ gets separated from the body it dies.

The individualist imagines her relationship to society and nature in the form of a *contract.* First the individual separates herself from the kin group, but then must determine how to relate to the social and natural worlds after the separation. The nature of the relationship appears to the individualist as voluntary and instrumental. In the first place, the individualist reconnects with society on a non-kin basis— whether as a buyer and seller of commodities, or through an exchange of ideas with strangers. Nature is understood as a means to an end rather than an end in itself. Lastly, for the individualist the primary connection to the sacred is with a transcendental monotheistic source that is sustained through free will. The Buddha, Socrates, and Plato all had individualist selves.

The Archaic Iron Age herding or trading societies were the places where society and nature changed from being inseparable aspects of the sacred world to being means to an end. For the nomadic Hebrews, Yahweh mediated the relationship between Hebrew tribe members. There was an agreement (the covenant) between God and the Hebrews to meet at the end of history. Everything the tribe did in in history counted in God's judgment of them. Instead of society being a permanent part of a sacred cosmology embedded in nature, both society and nature became a means to achieve spiritual ends in a spiritual world that was transcendent of both nature and society.

In the case of India, while the Buddha was seriously involved in the political reform of society, his primary interest was not in society for its own sake but in how his philosophy and practice would help people to achieve a spiritual state in a transcendental world beyond society.

Now let us turn to the specific building blocks and examine how individualists and collectivists negotiate them differently. Let us begin with language. In tribal societies there is no full-time division of labor wherein people occupy themselves with a single job all day long. Furthermore, there is no separation between people who do mental work and people who only do physical work. It is only with the rise of social surplus in the Bronze Age that some people are enabled to be pulled off food production to specialize in arts and crafts, trading, administrating, or policing other people. As Ernest Gellner (1988) points out, there is a direct connection between the specialization of labor and the specialization of language.

Gellner points out that as people in tribal societies move from one work setting to another, the words they use to describe their work experiences are not specialized because they do not work long enough at any one job to develop a specialized language that only that group of people can understand. Secondly, people engage with many of the same people in many different contexts. This means that when a female gatherer talks with another female gatherer, she is also having a relationship with that woman in many other contexts besides gathering. They may meet each other in childcare, in tanning leather, in weaving, and as participants in a ritual. In order to maintain

group solidarity the language must expand far enough to cover a variety of social contexts. This means that language can be intentionally ambiguous.

With the rise of agricultural states, society becomes stratified and split into castes. As these castes specialize more in fewer work settings, the language that develops becomes more specialized because people are becoming more skilled at what they do. As members of the various castes typically do not have frequent conversations with others outside their caste, except for perfunctory exchanges of deference or superiority, each caste develops a specialized language that goes with the work its members do. In sum, horizontal collectivists in tribal societies diffuse language across many contexts and use language in a less specialized way. Vertical collectivists and vertical individualists focus language to very few specific contexts and have a more specialized vocabulary.

Further, collectivists (whether horizontal or vertical) are better at role-taking than are individualists. For one thing, the collectivist accepts his role in the way an organ "accepts" its role in the body—the role is necessary to the functioning of the whole. In tribal societies and in agricultural states, individuals play a number of roles, but collectivists do not make a major separation between their personality and the roles they play. A servant in an agricultural state does not complain to other servants that her "true self" is being held back in her job. She doesn't argue that her personality is more suited to being a priestess. Further, because the rate of change in their society is generally slow, collectivists are most at home in role-taking in routine situations.

At the same time this assumption of conservatism should not be carried too far. Nomadic egalitarian societies and even ranked herding societies are probably very good at role-making and dealing with crisis situations because they are smaller in numbers, there is less material wealth, they are constantly having to move, and, if they live in inhospitable ecologies, they have to work very hard.

On the other hand, in agricultural states there were fewer roles, these roles were hierarchically organized, and they were probably experienced more as straitjackets. Because people in agricultural states are more sedentary than people in either hunting and gathering or horticultural societies, the former were probably the least comfortable with change. The self was much more at home with role-taking and routine situations than was the case with horizontal collectivists. Having any experience in transforming situations would be very foreign, almost like a crack in the cosmic order.

In part because individualist selves have psyches that are focused inside the skin rather than diffused in nature, individualists often play roles but identify with them less. This is because for them social relations are imagined to be contractual and so roles are instrumental and temporary. For the individualist self, one's unique personality is what gives definition. For example, the Buddha had no difficulty in encouraging adults in his society to leave their families (role-taking in a routine situation) to become wandering spiritual seekers, an activity in which they would have to discover or create new roles and be challenged by novel situations which the Buddha intentionally created as part of a spiritual practice (role-making in problematic or crisis situations). The major connections with others are less with the kin group and more with strangers in other places or with a transcendental reality. Since the rate of change is quicker in the Axial Iron Age, individualists are generally more comfortable with change and are better at the role-making that is required in more recurrent crisis situations, as we will see.

Earlier we said that cultivating a generalized "other" involved an expanding sense of time and place/space. This leads to the realization that the world is objective and independent of an individual's intentions or will. This realization includes a comprehsion that roles are (a) multiple, (b) detachable, (c) global, and (d) historical.

What are the differences between individualists and collectivists in how objective they become? Collectivist selves generally have a more difficult time being objective. Horizontal collectivists will easily understand roles as multiple because of the lack of division of labor in their societies. However, horizontal collectivists will have a difficult time imagining roles as detachable, because their roles are an extension of their kin-group responsibilities, which are linked to their ecological settings and their sacred worlds. Further, because collectivist societies are more provincial, they tend to absolutize the roles that are played and are less aware that the roles they play in their society are similar to the roles played by people in other tribal societies in other areas of the globe. The collectivist self will have no trouble with the historicity of roles when it comes to understanding that they exist beyond their generation. In fact, they probably imagine these roles as eternal.

What will be difficult for the collectivist self is the fact that new roles emerge as part of the historical process, while other roles are marginalized or vanish. On the whole, collectivists are more inter-subjective rather than objective. This means they will be very loyal to their group's beliefs and customs and will have difficulty judging fairly a criticism of the group's ways if it comes from someone outside the group, even if it is valid. On the whole, collectivists are more inter-subjective rather than private and objective. The individualist self is more objective and inclusive of strangers on the one hand, and private on the other.

For the collectivist, selves care very little about their biographies. Certainly the major landmarks in life such as initiation rites, marriages, and separations are remembered, but what matters for the collectivist is the *group* past. The individual's unique experiences are not reflected on, or imagined to be anything special.

Because the individualist understands himself as separate from the group, his individual development is more important. As mentioned earlier, sages and prophets of the great religions separated from their group's past and traveled on a spiritual journey unique to themselves.

Related to the biographical self is the perceived locus of control. Cross-cultural psychologists make a distinction between external and internal locus of control. Collectivists have an external locus of control, meaning that what happens to the individual is imagined to be caused by forces beyond their control. This external control may be imagined as issuing from sorcery on the part of people in other societies, the unknown machinations of sacred presences, or just luck. Because the psyche is understood as diffused, the individual takes less responsibility for control over what happens in their individual development.

Because the individualist's psyche is focused within, individualists take more responsibility for what becomes of them in their past, present, or future. While most individualists believe in some monotheistic sacred source, that source gives them some autonomy to control their lives and they are accountable to their deity for their choices. Individualists have an internal locus of control.

For every individual self-identity reality is divided into two realms: the *internal* realm of thoughts and feelings, and the outer world of *actions*. As it turns out, individualists and collectivists locate their biographical self on different sides of this division. Luria (1976) studied the difference between the personalities of peasants still living in the rural areas of Russia approximately ten years after the revolution, as compared to other peasants who had moved to the cities and had been subjected to industrialization. He found there was a difference in how they evaluated their own personalities.

Luria found that peasants inhabiting rural areas answered questions about their personality by referring to *other people*—who, they believed, were a better judge of their own personality than they themeselves were. They did not refer to their own assessment of their inner states to determine who they were. For collectivists, the ultimate determinant in their personal identities is how their actions affect others. While the collectivist must self-reflect on the feedback received by others in order to become more sensitive to her social environment, the self-reflexive moment is in the service of others. It does not face inward and it is not imagined as detachable from actions.

While the individualist self must also reflect on how his actions affect others, this is not the main locus of his attention. He allows the self-reflective part to have a separate life of its own. He pays attention to it, independent of his external actions. In Luria's study, the former peasants who were going to school and living in cities were much more willing to reflect on their personalities, weigh their strengths and weaknesses, and analyze and evaluate themselves without referring to others.

The value of self-reflection is supported by the universalistic religions that emerged at around the same time as individualism itself. These religions argue that inner states are at least as important as actions. If evil thoughts are unaccompanied by actions, this does not necessarily let the individual off the hook. When the Buddha encourages his disciples to become more spiritual, he doesn't require that they solicit the opinions of those they may work with. He expects self-reflection. When Socrates encourages his followers to know themselves, he is expecting internal examination, not feedback from the world.

Let us turn to the next building block—the navigation of routine and crisis situations. When a routine situation becomes problematic or a crisis, there are a number of possible outcomes. The crisis situation can lead to degeneration, a return to a routine, or a transformation of the situation, which in society as a whole can mean either reform or revolution. How would collectivists and individualists differ in how they handle such situations?

As might be expected, because of the collectivist self's perceived interdependence with others, it is less at home challenging the existing order in attempting to transform situations. Artisans or peasants in agricultural states at best may question the abuses of the upper classes, but this is only in the service of having things "get back to normal." They lack the resources, free time, education, and ideological support to question the existing order.

In the ancient world it was the members of the upper classes—the sages and prophets such as Buddha, Confucius, Lao Tze, and Socrates—who had the resources, education and self-confidence to transform crisis situations in their society in the service of reforms. It was possible not only to break away from their caste origins, but to question the existing society as a whole, and to form an ideology opposing it. Universalistic religions were reform movements highlighting the abuses of secondary magic.

Sages and prophets demonstrated a capacity to transform situations. The ability to transform situations in the service of reform requires, first, that society be large enough to afford a more-or-less full time division of labor; second, that the division of labor be stratified so there are potential conflicts among the groups; third, that the competing classes must have enough resources, leisure time, and education to develop an ideology and a plan for reform. The first two are necessary but not sufficient conditions for reform.

The question of whether one prefers role-taking and routine situations or role-making and problematic situations is directly connected to our last building block, the "I-Me" dialogue. In all societies individuals have to face a potential conflict between their individual self-interest and the group self-interest. In egalitarian societies, in the overwhelming number of times individual self-interest is synonymous with the self-interest of society as a whole because these societies are egalitarian. Thus for horizontal collectivists the I-me dialogue was more or less fused.

Among members of rank and stratified societies a conflict between individual and social self-interest emerges because there are real political and economic inequalities. The I-Me dialogues among vertical collectivists are real; but, because of the expectations of society, the Me side will win out. As might be expected, the I-Me dialogue for the individualist often can result in the victory of the "I" over the "Me."

In all societies prior to the Axial Iron Age, "I–Me" dialogues are about individuals and their relationship with kin groups or social castes in which roles are clear. But as far as I know Mead never considered what the expansion of identifications beyond the local group might do to this internal dialogue. Partly the Axial Iron Age is about a movement from identification with a particular community to a more global community of strangers. This meant that in addition to an "I-me" dialogue there would have been a larger internal dialogue that existed between strangers in two new realms, commerce and religion.

A significant aspect of this increased rubbing-of-shoulders with strangers was the need for altruism. I define altruism as having the following ingredients:

- It is voluntary (rather than necessary) activity that is done out of generosity (not scarcity);
- it is costly to the altruist and at the same time highly valuable (but costless) to the community;
- its motive is to improve other people's conditions (personal gratification is secondary); and
- it is given to strangers, not to members of kin groups.

Altruism is most likely to be pursued in religious communities attached to universalistic religions.

The opposite of altruism is heteronomy, or selfishness. Heteronomy, in which the individual tries to gain the most from people with the least amount of expense, so that self-interest comes before the community, can be voluntary or involuntary. In short, heteronomy is the pursuit of self-interest at the expense of society. More times than not heteronomy was practiced by all social classes in everyday secular activities, but most especially by merchants.

Paradoxically, *both* altruism and heteronomy appear as alternatives only in the Axial Iron Age, and for individualist selves. Collectivists do not behave in a heteronomous way because they do not engage with strangers on a consistent basis. They are not heteronomous within their society because this would threaten their survival. In general it might seem that collectivists are altruistic, because they always put the group before themselves. But our specific definition of altruism does not really describe what collectivists do. In the first place, the collectivist does not voluntarily give, she necessarily gives for her survival. Personal motives are not secondary. Collectivists are giving in their self-interest. Moreover, there is a cost to the community, because the economy of reciprocity implies that the collectivist has a right to expect specific others to do things in return, although when and where these things are done is often left vague. Finally, collectivist giving goes to the clan or kin-group, not to strangers living in other societies or within the same society.

In short, *having an individualist self is a pre-condition for either altruism or heteronomy.*

Initiators of reform movements have to have strong individualist selves and confidence in their rising sacred or ethical beliefs in order to withstand the attacks of the existing order while they are building their alternative community. They generally have to renounce their kin group and cast their destiny with the alternative community they are building. With the rise of individualism, the relationship with society becomes dramatic. One can work to weaken society by acting heteronomously, or work for social transformation the way the prophets and sages of the universalistic religions did.

To summarize: Until the Axial Iron Age, collectivists had "I-Me" dialogues that were either diffused (horizontal collectivists) or weighted on the side of the "me" (vertical collectivists). They did not have internal dialogues about strangers because there were not a critical number of strangers in any given society. Individualists continued to have "I-Me" dialogues about family and relatives, but the "I" side of the dialogue tended to win more often.

So how do we understand the rise of either altruism (in the pursuit of universalistic religion) or heteronomy (in the pursuit of commerce) in new situations among strangers rather than kin groups? What does this do to Mead's "I-Me" dialogues? How can we translate the individualist's relationship to strangers into an internal dialogue involving both altruism and heteronomy?

I suggest that the term "I–We" might stand for the relationship between the individual and the growing community of strangers that the universalistic religions are attempting to cultivate. The "We" part of the internal dialogue goes beyond the "Me" which is associated with a kin group or clan. It is a higher, alternative community that is being built between societies of strangers based on altruism. Conversely, in secular commercial situations with strangers, when an individual is contemplating whether to take advantage of a stranger he will no longer be having an "I-Me" dialogue. To represent this situation I propose the term "I–They." Summarizing this in a visual form:

collectivist	context	individualist	
I-me dialogue favoring "me" provincial (little applicability)	families/kin strangers	I-Me dialogue favoring "I" cosmopolitan	
		commerce heteronomy "I-They"	religion altruism "I-We"

Presenting the possibility of social transformation in the ancient world in these terms suggests that it is completely an upper-middle class and upper class movement. Does this mean the lower classes had no social movements in the ancient world? Essentially it does. The reasons for this will be discussed in the next chapter.

In the chapter immediately preceding this one I argued that hyper-abstract reasoning begins in the Bronze Age with the division of society into mental and physical workers. The fruits of the work of mental laborers include hieroglyphic writing, abstract counting, and a more centralized currency. However, three additional inventions in the Axial Iron Age—the alphabet, coined money and the political forum of the polis in Athens—increased *hyperabstract* thinking. To what extent these three inventions contributed to the rise of the

Figure 16.1 Collectivist vs. Individualist Selves

Collectivists	Building Block	Individualist
Paleolithic, Neolithic, Bronze Age	time period	Axial Iron Age
1) organic connection w/society nature	inner world outer world	1) separation from kin-group and nature — Contractual relationship with strangers and with a transcendental source
2) less specialized language	learn language	2) more specialized language
3) self inseparable from role taking inter-subjective	generalized other	3) self detachable from roles: role-making objective--private
4) group past and future	biographical self	4) individual past and future
external locus of control	locus of control	internal locus of control
self determined by actions	location of self	self determined by self-reflection
5) good at mastering routine situations	situations/ transformation	5) good at dealing with crisis or social transformation
6) emphasizes "me"	I-Me dialogue	6) emphasizes the "I" — "I-They" dialogue or "I-We" dialogue — heteronomy altruism
7) concrete abstraction	forms of abstraction	7) hyper-abstract reasoning

individualist self is hard to say. My point is simply that there was a deep relationship between the rise of the individualist self and hyperabstract reasoning. For example, here is a list of the skills and characteristics that go with the individualist self:

- a more specialized form of language
- images social and natural relations as a contract
- internal locus of control
- separation of self from roles
- role-making as opposed to role-taking
- a more objective generalized "other"
- situational transformation
- preoccupation with subjective states of consciousness
- individual development conceived of as separate from the group
- "I–me" dialogue weighted on the side of the "I"
- "I–we" dialogues and "I–they" dialogues
- heteronomy or altruistic behavior

All of these skills and characteristics require one or all of the hyperabstract processes we defined in the last chapter. As it turns out, in order to think in a hyperabstract manner the individual must imagine his or her mind separate from the senses, the body and action, just as the self must be imagined as separated from society and nature. The individualist self splits her or his hyperabstract reasoning between a spiritual world of building altruistic relations with strangers and a secular world of potential manipulation of strangers in commercial transactions.

It is important to remember that only a few upper-middle-class and middle-class merchants, aristocrats, and prophets in Persia, India, China, and Greece had individualist selves and were developing a hyperabstract form of reasoning. The lower classes within these societies were still collectivists and still used concrete forms of abstraction. Wealth buys distance, leisure time, and resources to cultivate a private identity and to think in a more abstract manner. Figure 16.1 summarizes the differences between collectivist and individualist selves.

4. Women as Collectivist Selves

Until the Axial Iron Age, all selves were collectivist. As we have seen, when individualist selves emerged they were unique to upper-middle-class and upper-class sages, aristocrats, and merchants. Furthermore, these people were all men. What did it mean for women in the ancient world to have a horizontal or vertical collectivist identity? What would it have meant for women to have an individualist identity?

Women living in egalitarian societies had a horizontal collectivist self, just as men did. This meant that while they had a feeling of connection with the social and natural world, their place in the scheme of things was probably not perceived as limiting because the division of labor into roles (and the language that went with those divisions) was not so specialized as it was to become in the Bronze Age. Like the men, they were not concerned about their personal past and future, but focused their concerns on the history of the group. Women's external locus of control was only a sense that as an individual, sacred forces were beyond her control. As a group member practicing magic, the woman believed that her group could affect the natural order. Women in egalitarian foraging societies would have had to be somewhat familiar with dealing with problematic and crisis situations, since a nomadic lifestyle would keep any group from getting too comfortable. This was less the case in horticultural societies, because living in villages in a sedentary lifestyle tends to stabilize and deepen the habit of dealing with routine situations.

As with all horizontal collectivists in egalitarian societies, social self-interest and individual self-interest were essentially synonymous. However, women's primary responsibility for child rearing would probably have made her stress more the "Me" part of the "I–Me" dialogue than the men would. Lastly, women would tend to think, like the men, in a less abstract way because these societies lacked the technology to plan for long-term consequences.

The vertical collectivist self was somewhat of a liability for women in agricultural states. In these caste societies a woman's roles were probably experienced as straitjackets and the language, while specialized, was confined to the caste she belonged to. Loyalty to her civilization's past and future must have been experienced as a contradiction since it was not *her* group that reaped the material benefits of such loyalty. The experience of an external locus of control would have been more accentuated, since in secondary magical societies it is the priests and priestesses, not significant numbers of the population, who call down the deities.

Since agricultural states are even more sedentary than horticultural societies, people in the former would likely have even less experience in transforming situations. Most women in the Bronze Age would barely have had an "I" to participate in "I–Me" dialogues. This would be so not only because of their low social status but because of child-rearing responsibilities and the large number of children that women were expected to raise. Last, most women in the Bronze Age would have had little reason to think in a hyperabstract way since it was all they could do to maintain themselves and their extended family.

Priestesses in agricultural states had the most contradictory status attributes, and so it is probably among them that a proto-individualist self for women might have emerged. For a priestess, feeling an inseparable connection with the social and biophysical world would not have been experienced as limiting, since she had a high place within the hierarchy. The specialized language she learned, which went with managing the divine household, was probably liberating since she was at the pinnacle of the knowledge base of her society. While her identity was inseparable from the various roles she took on, the roles themselves must have been enjoyable and empowering. It was not as if there was another way she wanted to be, but could not be. Her biographical self was rooted in her civilization's past and its relationship to the goddesses and gods, and this was something to be proud of—since structurally she was close to the goddesses and gods. Her locus of control was external, but it

must have been closer to the way women in egalitarian societies might have felt, because through her magical ceremonies she could actually effect change. The movements of members of the divine household were watched closely by the population, and for royal or priestly women every routine situation was sacred. Every movement was thought to be sympathetically linked with the workings of the cosmos above and the earth below. While the "I-Me" dialogue was heavily weighted on the side of the "Me," it was less severely so in this case than in that of lower-class women, because priestesses had servants to take care of their children. Priestly women in the Bronze Age had to develop some skills at hyperabstract reasoning, because these were required for the management of the temple economy.

The type of self that Axial Iron Age women had was probably less restrictive than that of lower-class women in the Bronze Age, but not as expansive as that of priestesses in the Bronze Age. On the whole, the self available to women in the Bronze Age was of higher status than that in the Axial Iron Age, but the number of women who could become priestesses was severely limited. For men, the Axial Iron Age opened up an individualist identity to about 20% of the male population. A woman might have reaped indirect political benefits from her husband's individualism, but virtually all women remained vertical collectivists.

Because in Greece and India commerce had entered into social relationships, women's place in society and nature was no longer as secure as it had been. The transcendental nature of monotheism and the secularization of society and nature had an indirect effect on the typical woman. Her language was less specialized than that of her priestly sisters in the Bronze Age, because there was now more movement across classes than across social castes. However, since women did not occupy positions of power in the Axial Age, they were not in a position to learn a specialized language which could work for women's benefit. Women's roles in the Axial Iron Age were inseparable from their identity, and since women rarely left the house they were most at home in routine situations.

Woman's biographical self was probably less rooted in a group past, because city life in the Axial Iron Age had considerably weakened kinship relations. Her external locus of control would be about the same as that of lower caste women in the Bronze Age. She probably felt helpless to control her life through sacred interventions, because goddesses had either disappeared or been marginalized. She must also have felt helpless to control her material life: She was still excluded from the art, philosophy, and politics of the time. The "I-Me" dialogue would have been weighted on the side of the "Me," and there was little opportunity to develop hyperabstract thinking, since there were no public political positions open to her.

What did women lose in not having an opportunity to develop an individualist self? What could the development of an individualist self have done for their capacity to mount an opposition to the system that exploited and repressed them? On the one hand, women lost an opportunity to make a connection with strangers beyond the kin-group in the Axial Iron Age. In the Bronze Age, merchants who were most likely to develop an individualist self were all men. In the Axial Iron Age, there were few if any opportunities for women to be wandering scholars, merchants, or sages. This meant that women's selves would not have moved much beyond kin-group or caste connections.

Without a specialized language of power, which Priestesses in agricultural states possessed, women in the Iron Age were denied an opportunity to develop a vocabulary that took them away from the language of mundane conversation. With the exception of Bronze Age priestesses, specialized language among other Bronze Age castes would have been more confining than liberating. When an individual can imagine herself outside the roles she plays, roles become more relative and malleable. Switching roles or imagining new roles become real possibilities. Women in the ancient world did not imagine themselves as having a secret self hovering inside over all the roles being played, so there wasn't a sense of possible alternative identities.

When an individual can conceptualize a personal past and future, he or she can learn from the past and project plans for the future. Without attention to one's individual practice, one's life becomes enmeshed in the life of the group. Possessing an internal locus of control brings with it a sense that one has the power to control what becomes of oneself. Locating one's identity within oneself means that how one's actions affect others is less important. An individualist self is less concerned with how one's actions may affect the kin group or the family. By developing the "I" side of the "I-Me" dialogue, the individual is constantly refining what she or he wants and why.

An individualist self can imagine changing the world, because situations and roles are relative rather than absolute. An individualist self can choose to work in the interests of a better society (altruism) or against the interests of society (heteronomy). It was male individualist selves who made these choices, not women.

In general, the individualist self experiences a heightened sense of objectivity beyond the loyalty to kin group in the form of strangers in other times and places. On the other hand, the individualist self cultivates a sharper sense of subjectivity beyond the roles, rules, and expectations of family and kin. The individualist self has far greater potential to be a reformer or a revolutionary

Figure 16.2 integrates the relationships between the legitimizing forces (chapters 12 and 13) and the internalizing forces on the subordination of women. This section shows why women's subordination to men even within collectivism partly explains why there wasn't a women's movement in the ancient world.

I will briefly describe some of the connections between these phenomena, which will be followed by charts that summarize some of the relationships. For the moment, it is less important to grasp the movement from primitive magic to secondary magic to religion over time or the movement from place to space over the course of history. Rather, it is essential to understand how primitive magic is both the cause and the consequence of place, the proximate senses, concrete abstraction, and the collectivist self at a given moment in time. Conversely, religion is both the cause and consequence of space, sight, hyperabstraction, and the individualist self within a given moment in time—the Axial Iron Age.

Tribal primitive magic and tribal psychology are characterized by porous boundaries. Just as the collectivist self is understood as organically tied to society and the natural world, so in primitive magic the psyche is diffused into the biophysical world. Furthermore, just as the collectivist self does not separate its psyche from the places inhabited, so in the sacred world of magical creation myths consciousness is never separate from matter.

In addition, the places that these collectivist selves occupy are thought to have psychic properties that feed back into this collectivist self, and the senses used by the collectivist self—especially smell and sound—have especially permeable boundaries. All of these tendencies are governed by concrete abstraction, in which the mind is embedded in practical action on physical reality. This mind does not spend much time contemplating invisible deities or a cosmopolitan brotherhood with strangers in distant lands. Thinking in concrete abstractions does not invite extensive introspection, which would lead to reforming oneself or society.

For the vertical collectivist self of stratified Bronze Age states there is a sense of passivity relative to external forces. The external local of control which comes from caste position goes with the psychic properties that places possess. Vertical collectivist selves do not enter a new area as a space in which they feel they can impose their collective will as if the area were a neutral container. This passivity goes with the characteristics of the proximate senses used. As

Tuan says, unlike the eyes which can initiate opening and closing, ears and the nose are already open and people have to react to what comes through these senses.

When concrete abstraction is applied to magical practices in hunting and gathering societies, the result is instantaneous time. Just as in concrete abstraction there is less surveying of the deep past, in tribal societies there is an immediate present orientation in the relationship between magical practice and effect. No one thinks, "first we practice the ritual and then it has an effect on the animal." The magical practice is assumed to have an immediate impact. Just as the collectivist self cannot separate her individual psychology from social roles and role-taking, neither can she separate her psyche from the dynamics of nature. Nature is not experienced as having its own laws independent of human wishes and fears. In animistic causality everything in nature happens for a reason, everything is a sign of something mysterious and meaningful. There is no chance or necessity in nature.

Finally, in tribal societies the collectivist self has a group past, and this group past is bound to stories which are themselves embedded in the places wherein the people have settled. These settings in turn are rooted in the proximate senses of smell and sound, which may be the most powerful of all the senses in jogging specific memories of the past.

Conversely, the vertical individualist supports and reproduces sky-god religion in the Axial Iron Age. What each has in common is separation from the kin group, and an identification with a wider circle of strangers. In the case of the individualist self this makes for expanding commerce within and between societies. At the same time there is a separation and secularization of the biophysical environment, which allows the individualist self to develop a science independent of sacred influences. The separation of humanity from nature supports the transcendental nature of religion. Both the world of strangers and otherworldly religion embody the characteristics of space over place.

When the self is understood as independent of society and nature, this makes the now disenchanted biophysical environment a space that is infinite and expanding, in which an individual can wander using the sense of sight to promote objectivity and distance while supporting science. The hyperabstract reasoning of this individualist self also invites the rational calculation of merchants buying and selling. In the religious realm, hyperabstract reasoning makes it easier to imagine an invisible god that created matter, because in hyperabstract thinking it is possible to think about thinking, independent of having to use thinking to engage in conversations or perform actions.

For the religious individual a compressed psyche gives free will and allows for a sense of destiny (rather than fate). For the individualist self destiny includes dreams of self-improvement because of an internal locus of control, and dreams of social reform because he imagines society is based on an expanding contract which unfolds not in cyclic repetitions but in linear history.

Concrete abstraction, primitive magic, places, the proximate senses, and the collectivist self work well for both men and women as long as societies remain politically and economically egalitarian. But as societies become stratified, these sacred systems and their attendant psychology become liabilities for essentially all women and most men below the middle class. On the one hand the new stratified order is reinforced by religion, the individualist self, space, sight, and hyperabstraction. This new orientation is foreign to most men and all women. On the other hand, the sacred systems and psychology used become marginalized and dismissed as superstitious, backward, and inferior.

Figure 16.2 Composite Figure for Sacred Traditions and Psychology:
Legitimation (Chapters 12, 13) and Internalization (Chapters 14, 15, 16)

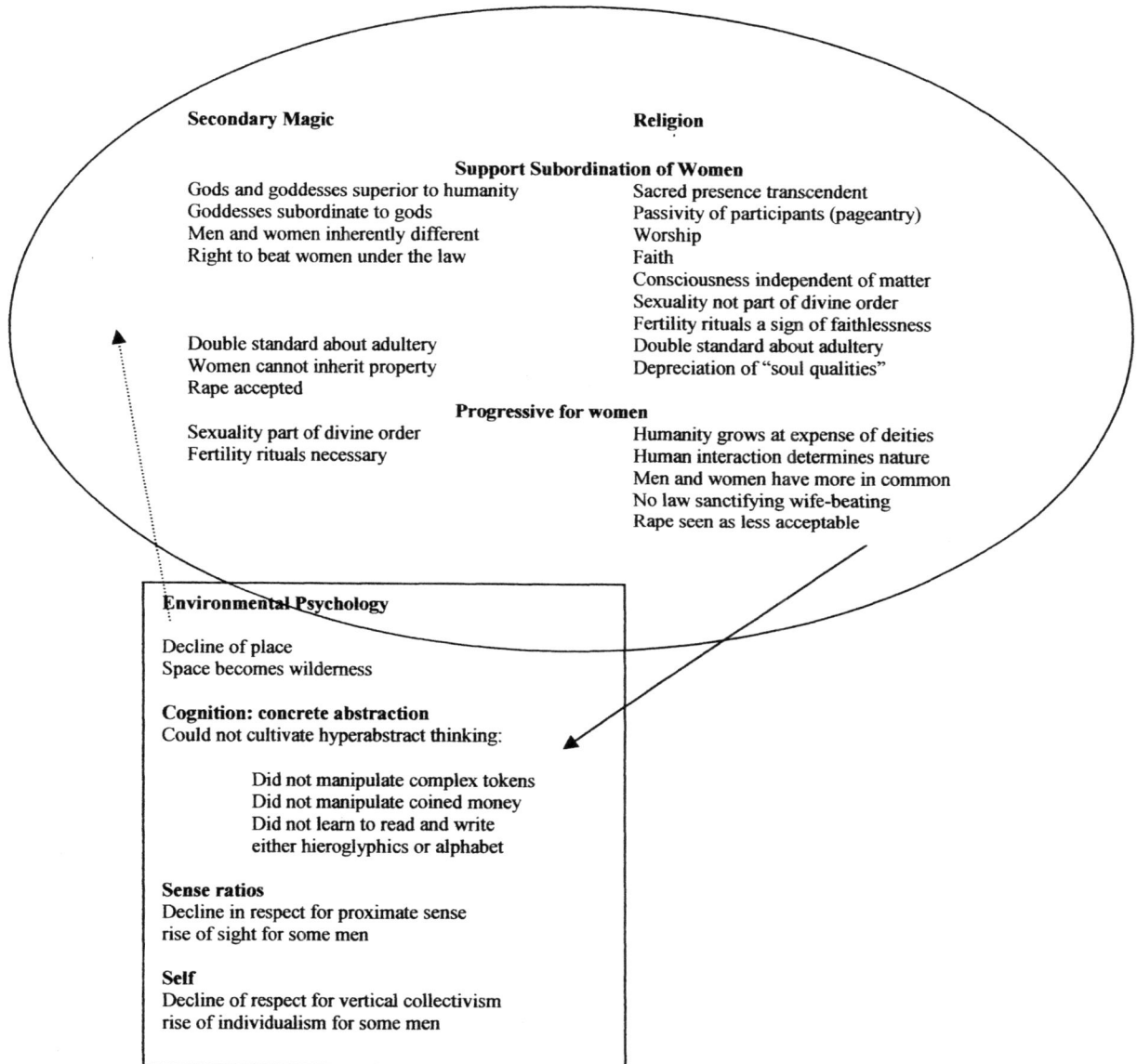

Secondary Magic   **Religion**

Support Subordination of Women

Gods and goddesses superior to humanity   Sacred presence transcendent
Goddesses subordinate to gods   Passivity of participants (pageantry)
Men and women inherently different   Worship
Right to beat women under the law   Faith
                                               Consciousness independent of matter
                                               Sexuality not part of divine order
                                               Fertility rituals a sign of faithlessness
Double standard about adultery   Double standard about adultery
Women cannot inherit property   Depreciation of "soul qualities"
Rape accepted

Progressive for women

Sexuality part of divine order   Humanity grows at expense of deities
Fertility rituals necessary   Human interaction determines nature
                                               Men and women have more in common
                                               No law sanctifying wife-beating
                                               Rape seen as less acceptable

Environmental Psychology

Decline of place
Space becomes wilderness

Cognition: concrete abstraction
Could not cultivate hyperabstract thinking:

> Did not manipulate complex tokens
> Did not manipulate coined money
> Did not learn to read and write
> either hieroglyphics or alphabet

Sense ratios
Decline in respect for proximate sense
rise of sight for some men

Self
Decline of respect for vertical collectivism
rise of individualism for some men

Part VI

Phase 4: Collusion—
Why Women Reproduced
Gender Hierarchies

Chapter 17

Dissent, Mobilization and Revolution: Why There Was No Women's Movement in the Ancient World

The purpose of this chapter is to examine why, in the light of events described in this book, there was no women's movement in the ancient world. In order to do this I will:

(a) provide an overview of the events grouped into four cycles of female subordination,

(b) examine Chafetz's implied conditions for maximizing male dominance,

(c) summarize Marvin Harris's model for why societies change,

(d) explore the necessary and specific conditions for the emergence of social movements, and

(e) compare the conditions of the ancient world to the conditions for social movements.

In chapters 5 and 6 I presented a socio-ecological description of the origins of what I call informal male dominance, which was followed historically by the development of institutionalized male dominance. I argued that informal male dominance occurs periodically in egalitarian societies depending primarily, according to Reeves-Sanday, on whether the subsistence resources are in scarce or abundant supply, and on which sex is thought to embody the forces of nature that people depend on. Institutionalized male dominance began in complex horticultural societies and was consolidated in Bronze and Iron Age states. Within institutional male dominance I have identified five phases:

(1) Enmeshment—men have power over women in the public economy, but this is tempered by cross-cutting cleavages such as skill at work, age, and status of the product in which it is possible for women to have more influence, prestige and privilege than men.

(2) State coercion—men's power over women is rooted in the infrastructure of society, including the political economy and the military. Overlapping cleavages emerge in which women are subordinate solely because of their gender.

(3) Legitimation—men's power over women is reinforced by superstructural systems, such as sacred beliefs and education, which justify this power.

(4) Internalization—men's power is imported into the psychology of women. This results in habits of deference, attitudes of low self-esteem, and lack of assertiveness.

(5) Collusion—men's power is reproduced by women's work as women reproduce over time the institutions that oppress them.

These five stages go through four cycles. While all five stages are present in rudimentary form in all four cycles, some stages are primary in some cycles and dormant in others. Here is an overview:

cycle 1—enmeshment-collusion—complex horticulture—late Neolithic Age

cycle 2—coercion-collusion—agricultural states—early Bronze Age

cycle 3—coercion-legitimation—agricultural states—middle and late Bronze Age

cycle 4—legitimation-internalization—
    collusion—commercial farming states—
    Axial Iron Age

In chapters 8 through 16 I added other
events and processes that influenced women's
condition in the ancient world. Figure 17.1
includes events that are related to the stages of
submission. Figure 17.2 is a causal model of
social evolution in the ancient world and
includes events that are not directly gender
related.

Let us begin by reviewing the events
themselves.

1. Integration of events into the four cycles of women's subordination

Whenever arguments are made for the
absence of male dominance in the past, they
usually begin with the earliest possible period—
usually with hunter-gatherers. While gender
hierarchies were less likely to occur in hunter-
gatherer societies than in any other social
formation, not all hunting-and-gathering
societies were the same. During the period of
big-game hunting under the harsh conditions of
the Ice Age (20,000 years ago), there would have
been, according to Reeves-Sanday's model,
extreme informal male dominance. There
would have been stressful social conditions and
segregated work patterns, together with the
hunting of large animals. Even in parts of the
world where game resources were ecologically
abundant, as long as subsistence was tied to big
game there would have been informal male
dominance, though in a milder form than in
areas of scarcity.

As big-game hunter-gatherer societies ran
out of large prey, they began to switch over to
small-game hunting, and this inadvertently
nudged gender relations in the direction of
minimum or no male dominance. Under
abundant ecological conditions these kinds of
societies had integrated work and child-rearing
practices. In addition, these societies practiced
magic, they were dominated by place, and they
used multi-sensual perception; individuals in
these societies possessed collectivist selves and
thought in terms of concrete abstractions. All

of these social and psychological characteristics
applied to both men and women. Historically,
this is the period between about 10,000 and
8,000 BCE. Politically and economically, these
societies remained egalitarian.

When small-game resources became
seriously depleted these hunting societies began
to supplement their diet by planting fruits and
vegetables and by domesticating small animals.
These simple horticulture societies were
conflicted in terms of Reeves-Sanday's criteria
for informal male dominance: There was a
return of segregated work patterns and of child-
rearing practices, but there was no reliance on
large animals. Small animals were domesticated
by the women and women controlled the
planting. There were two pervasive conditions
that lent themselves to the re-emergence of male
dominance—chronic warfare and men's
biological predisposition for aggression. The
dominance of place, multi-sensual perception, a
collectivist personal identity, and concrete
abstraction remained characteristics of simple
horticulture societies.

In chapter 5 we saw that the roots of gender
inequalities go deeper than the roots of caste or
class inequalities—which appear with the rise of
rank and stratification. As seen in figure 5.4,
there are some common conditions which both
forms of inequality share and there are
important differences. For example, biophysical
circumscription will work toward the
formation of rank and stratification, whereas
migration works toward the formation of
gender inequalities. Also, while an abundance
of resources concentrated in a small area is
likely to lead to rank hunting-gathering
societies, a scarcity of resources will tend to
provoke gender hierarchy.

The movement from informal male
dominance to institutionalized male dominance
goes with the rise of rank relations. It is rooted
in the strategy chosen by simple horticultural
societies to deal with the problems of
population pressure and resource depletion.
This movement occurred around 6000 BCE in
arid areas of the Near East with limited pristine
natural resources, areas that were geographically
circumscribed by mountains or deserts. As we
saw in chapter 5 in our discussion of

Sanderson's theory of the origins of inequality, simple horticultural societies fight over scarce land and the victorious group reorganizes society in the form of a hierarchy, partly to put itself in power and partly to resolve the ecological and demographic crisis.

In complex horticultural societies, women continue to plant but there is the beginning of the practice of breeding of large animals—which are controlled by men. In chiefdoms, commodity production arises and this is also controlled by men. In addition, as we saw in chapter 6, a sexual double standard appears among the chiefly lineage. Chiefly men are allowed many wives while chiefly women are expected to be monogamous. Commoner women are subject to rape.

It might seem odd to characterize these gender relations as "enmeshed" when it seems that men had considerably more power than women. However, as we saw in chapter 6, this power was somewhat tenuous. For one thing, women's labor was considered sacred while men's was not; for another, women were active in the public arenas and worked with other women. Women had access to skilled positions, and unmarried commoner women were sexually free. Marriage was not an economic necessity for any woman, as the woman's kin group entitled her to subsistence rights. Moreover, male dominance was somewhat situation-specific. For example, kin sisters had control over brothers, and young men had to defer to older women. Though politically and economically there was rank inequality between chiefs, district managers, and commoners, gender inequalities were cross-cut by female rights and privileges in some situations. The predominance of primitive magic, place, multi-sensual perception, a collectivist self, and concrete abstraction among all social members tempered this first form of institutionalized male dominance.

Whatever overlapping cleavages existed in gender relations in complex horticultural societies were made crystal clear with the rise of agricultural societies. When the land of complex horticultural societies became depleted another struggle between groups occurred. But this time the struggle wasn't between egalitarian groups; it was between groups that were already ranked. The emergence of the plow made it possible to stay in the same place, feed a growing population, and have a surplus available for trade. This surplus wealth made possible a full-time specialization of labor. In this second cycle of subordination, a military caste emerged that protected the ruling elite from the rest of the population.

All of this was terrible news for women. The invention of the plow meant that planting was taken over by men. Thus women lost control of the primary means of production. Women disappeared from public life and became limited to working in the domestic economy. Women were now kept from the solidarity with other women which comes from working in public. The upper classes continued to practice polygyny but all women were expected to be monogamous. Women's value as workers sank so low that female infanticide became a regular practice.

As we saw in chapter 10, the Bronze Age was peppered by natural disasters which some say were caused by the impacts of comet debris, including asteroids and meteorites. These impacts caused climatic downturns, leading to famines. In addition, as William McNeill (1976) and Jared Diamond (1997) have pointed out, agricultural states and cities were great breeding grounds for disease.

In cycle three, in the middle Bronze Age, the invention of the spoked wheel for chariot warfare along with the domestication of horses increased both the reality and threat of state coercion. Pastoralists made devastating use of these innovations; their raids on planting societies became more lethal, thus compounding existing social stress in those societies. As Reeves-Sanday says, where there is social stress male dominance is not far behind.

It was in cycle three that the forces of legitimation became formidable. In chapter 1, I defined legitimation as a set of institutionalized processes used by those with coercive power to induce those in submission to comprehend their submission as being necessary, socially beneficial to all, part of a cosmic order, inevitable, and eternal.

One of the fruits of the full-time division of labor was a split between mental and manual labor. Men monopolized mental work. As we saw in chapter 14, when writing systems first emerged they were used for economic purposes; but slowly these systems began to be used for recording myths. The gods and goddesses came to reflect the material interests of the men in power. The cosmic order was presented in an increasingly abstract and static way, and the abstract nature of the cosmos reflected the thinking process of the men in power. If the social order was embedded in the cosmos and the cosmos was presented as static, then the existing social order was understood also to be eternally the same, always serving the interests of the ruling priesthood. The changlessness of the new sky-god deities was underscored by the use of bronze to depict them, thus emphasizing durability and lack of wear-and-tear, as compared to stone or wood sculptures.

In addition, when natural disasters occurred and the sources of these natural disasters were identified in the sky (comets, asteroids or meteors), this also tended to make people identify the sacred presences as male. Previously, there were both male and female gods and goddesses in the sky, just as there were male and female goddesses on the earth. However, there was a higher proportion of male gods in the sky than female, and vice versa. When comets were seen in the sky and the debris impacted the earth and was seen as "causing" earthquakes, floods, etc., this reinforced the power of gods over goddesses. This is discussed by Clube and Napier in section five of chapter 14. Frymer-Kensky supports this by reporting that goddesses become more marginalized in the middle and late Bronze Ages.

Meanwhile, changes in magical practices also disadvantaged women. Secondary magic was somewhat less participatory than primitive magic, and included more reification of sacred presences. The dynamics between sacred presences and humanity changed in secondary magic from primitive magic as an expression of the movement from egalitarian to stratified political relations. An increasing passivity of humanity can be seen in the following ways: a movement from an emphasis on ritual (action) to storytelling (talking); a movement from human beings recreating the world through magic to co-creating with gods and goddesses; gods and goddesses being clearly more powerful than humanity, whereas earth spirits and humans were more or less equal; and a concentration of magical power in specialists—priests and priestesses—with the rest of the group being more passive. The effect of secondary magic was to justify stratified political relations. This worked against women.

Secondary magic was in place before natural disasters, but when the disasters occurred goddesses went from being subordinate to being marginalized. In chapter 11 we saw that the impact of the stress of natural disasters makes gender relations more hierarchical in favor of men, and this was expressed in less-democratic processes of decision making and social coordination.

The reification of sacred presences worked not only against women, but against all stratified groups. The process of reification can be seen in the movement away from the prominence of forces in primitive magic to the prominence of beings in secondary magic. When sacred life is depicted primarily as a movement of forces there is a sense in which people believe they can participate in changing the world. Sacred activity is in "liquid" form, easy to change. When sacred life is depicted through beings, it becomes more "solid" and harder to change. From there it is a short step to believing that sacred presences are eternal and unchangeable.

The addition of writing to the process of education created a split between the upper classes and the rest of the population, which continued to rely on storytelling. Because written myths were transmitted via a new mysterious technology, and because they were backed by the pomp and ceremony which surrounded upper-class activities, lower-class storytelling must have seemed archaic and ineffectual by comparison. The replacement or vilification of the sacred presences of the lower castes by the superior sky-gods must have become incorporated into people's sacred

Figure 17.1 Summary of Events that Supported Female Subordination:
Cycles One and Two

Pervasive constraints: Biological— male aggression, competition, status seeking, promiscuity

INFORMAL MALE DOMINANCE

Periodic crisis: Ecological/ demographic— population pressure-resource depletion

Paleolithic hunter-gatherers, Neolithic simple horticulturalists : 30,000-6000 BCE

lineage traced through the male line	segregated child rearing practices
patrilocal residency	segregated work patterns
high chronic warfare	

INSTITUTIONALIZED MALE DOMINANCE

Periodic crisis: Ecological/ demographic—population pressure-resource depletion

conflict between groups over scarce land
arid climate and scarce pristine resources, geographic circumscription

Stages of subordination	Cycles

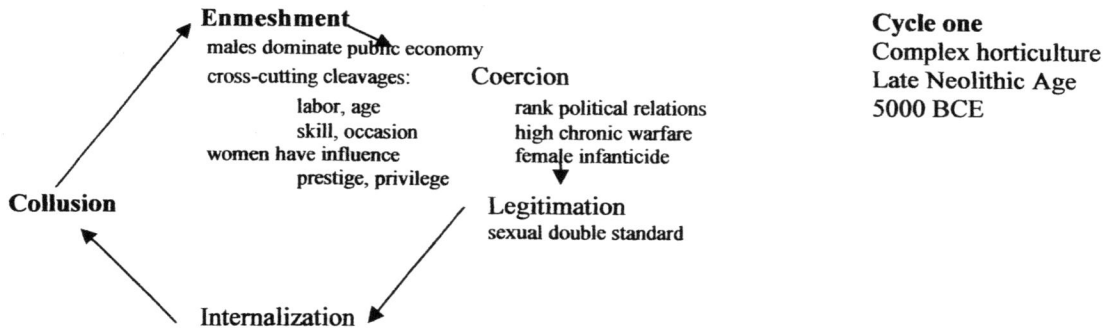

Enmeshment
males dominate public economy
cross-cutting cleavages:
    labor, age
    skill, occasion
women have influence
    prestige, privilege

Coercion
rank political relations
high chronic warfare
female infanticide

Legitimation
sexual double standard

Collusion

Internalization

Cycle one
Complex horticulture
Late Neolithic Age
5000 BCE

Periodic crisis: Ecological/ demographic— population pressure-resource depletion

Natural disasters, comet debris

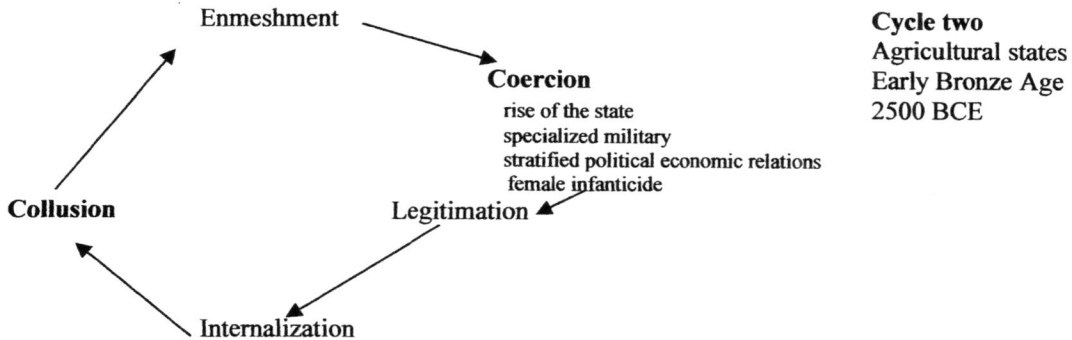

Enmeshment

Coercion
rise of the state
specialized military
stratified political economic relations
female infanticide

Legitimation

Collusion

Internalization

Cycle two
Agricultural states
Early Bronze Age
2500 BCE

Figure 17.1 Summary of Events that Supported Female Subordination
Cycles Three and Four
INSTITUTIONALIZED MALE DOMINANCE

Pervasive constraints: Biological— male aggression, competition, status seeking, promiscuity

Stages of Subordination	Cycles

Periodic crisis: Ecological/ demographic—population pressure-resource depletion

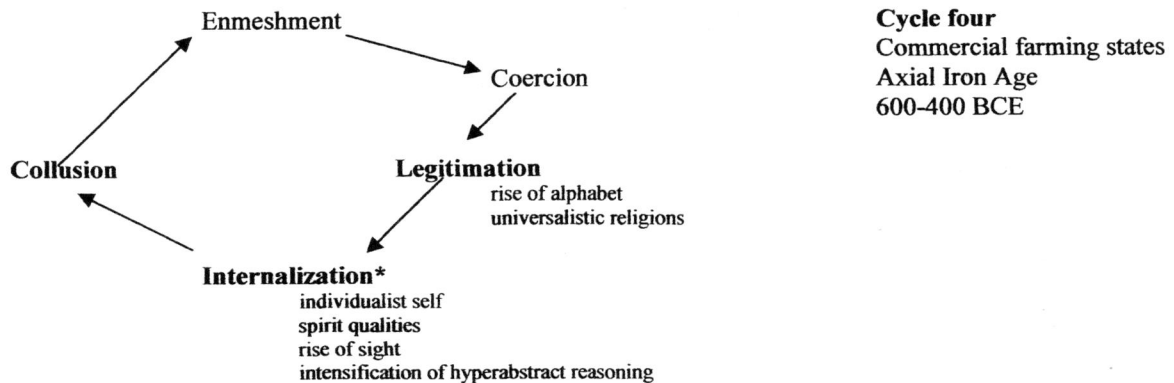

Natural disasters, comet debris

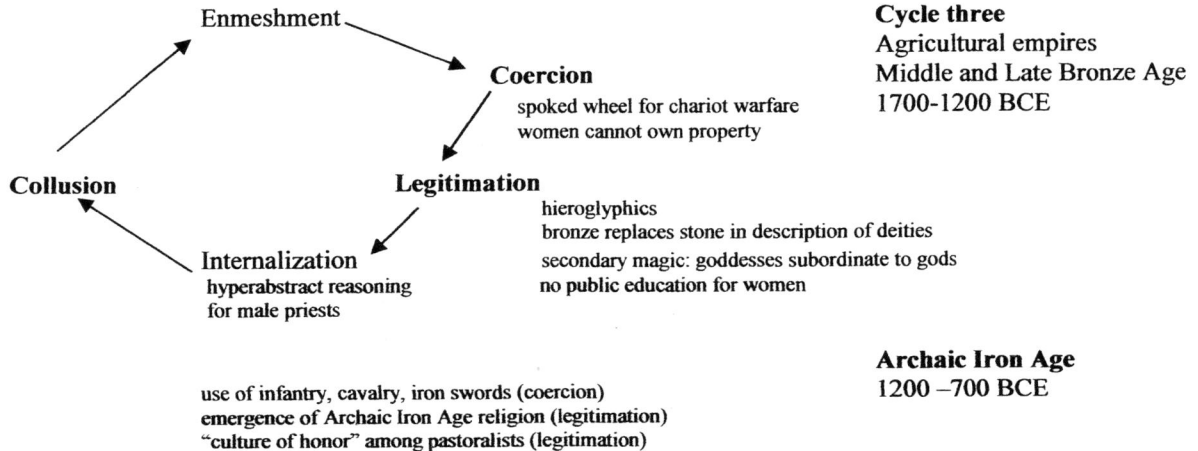

Enmeshment

Coercion
  spoked wheel for chariot warfare
  women cannot own property

Collusion

Legitimation
  hieroglyphics
  bronze replaces stone in description of deities
  secondary magic: goddesses subordinate to gods
  no public education for women

Internalization
hyperabstract reasoning
for male priests

Cycle three
Agricultural empires
Middle and Late Bronze Age
1700-1200 BCE

use of infantry, cavalry, iron swords (coercion)
emergence of Archaic Iron Age religion (legitimation)
"culture of honor" among pastoralists (legitimation)

Archaic Iron Age
1200 –700 BCE

Periodic crisis: Ecological/ demographic—population pressure-resource depletion

Enmeshment

Coercion

Collusion

Legitimation
  rise of alphabet
  universalistic religions

Internalization*
  individualist self
  spirit qualities
  rise of sight
  intensification of hyperabstract reasoning

Cycle four
Commercial farming states
Axial Iron Age
600-400 BCE

---

* Applies only to upper class and middle class men. These qualities create distance between these classes and the lower classes on the one hand, and all women on the other.

education, creating an educational system based on subordination. Women unconsciously passed on these traditions to their daughters, justifying the rule of the male elite. In addition there was no secular public education for women in either the Bronze or Iron Ages. Because women did not have any public identity, they had little space to speak of and their ecological zones were dominated by a conservative placial orientation. Meanwhile, hyperabstract reasoning emerged as a force which began to separate a few scribes from the rest of the population.

The Archaic Iron Age is not a stage through which most societies passed, but war-like pastoral invasions affected planting societies in the Old world, and pastoralists used iron weapons and cavalry to break down other societies. This in turn made target societies more violent, once they acquired these techniques themselves. The culture of honor was a legitimizing force within pastoral societies.

During the Axial Iron Age natural disasters temporarily subsided, alleviating social stress. This stress reduction was reflected in the depiction of monotheistic deities as being less harsh than the polytheistic deities in the Bronze or Archaic Iron Ages. The spread of the alphabet was a necessary condition for the spread of monotheism, which continued to legitimize women's inferior status. The polis as an institution further legitimized women's subordination by excluding them from political discussions. The use of coined money and iron tools improved women's status indirectly. All of these factors expanded space rather than place.

In tribal societies thinking and doing went together. When there was a full-time division of labor in the Bronze and Iron Ages, five to ten percent of the population became mental workers. As we saw in chapter 14, these mental workers engaged in what I call hyperabstract reasoning. Those who were excluded from such occupations continued to think in concrete abstractions. This limited their ability to challenge the existing order. Most people's minds degenerated because their work required less and less thinking. The rise of monotheism further encouraged not only abstract thinking, but the use of the rational side of the mind, the "spirit" side of the psyche, at the expense of the non-rational or "soul" side of the psyche.

As we saw in chapter 13, the rise of a spatial orientation toward socio-ecological zones went with the use of sight as the leading sense. Since women were excluded from mental work, they continued to use the proximate senses and to be placially oriented. While both these perceptual-orientational tendencies worked well for people in tribal societies, they became liabilities in state societies.

Finally, when the individualist self first emerged in the Axial Iron Age, it was in the exclusive possession of upper-class men.

2. Toward a materialist theory of the emergence of gender hierarchies

Now let us return to Janet Chafetz's macrostructural theory of gender stratification and examine how well her model captures the specific processes and events that transpired in the ancient world, and determine to what extent it needs to be modified.

In figure figure 4.1, the major components—what she calls the independent variables (i.e., high population density, the high ratio of men to women, the presence of high technology, and environmental harshness or threat)—seem to fit well with the events described in the previous section. However, environmental harshness should be expanded to include the impact of transient climatological, geological, and astronomical events. This would take into account natural disasters, climate changes, famines, and plagues that historians are just beginning to factor in.

Another major component missing from figure 4.1 is biological constraints. As we saw in chapter 7, the work of evolutionary psychologists needs to be included in a comprehensive materialist theory. While biological factors certainly do not determine the emergence of institutionalized male dominance, male aggressiveness, status, and competition have a great deal to do with the fact that if political hierarchies emerge, it will be men rather than women at the top.

Figure 17.2 Materialist Dynamic Catalyzing Institutionalized Male Dominance

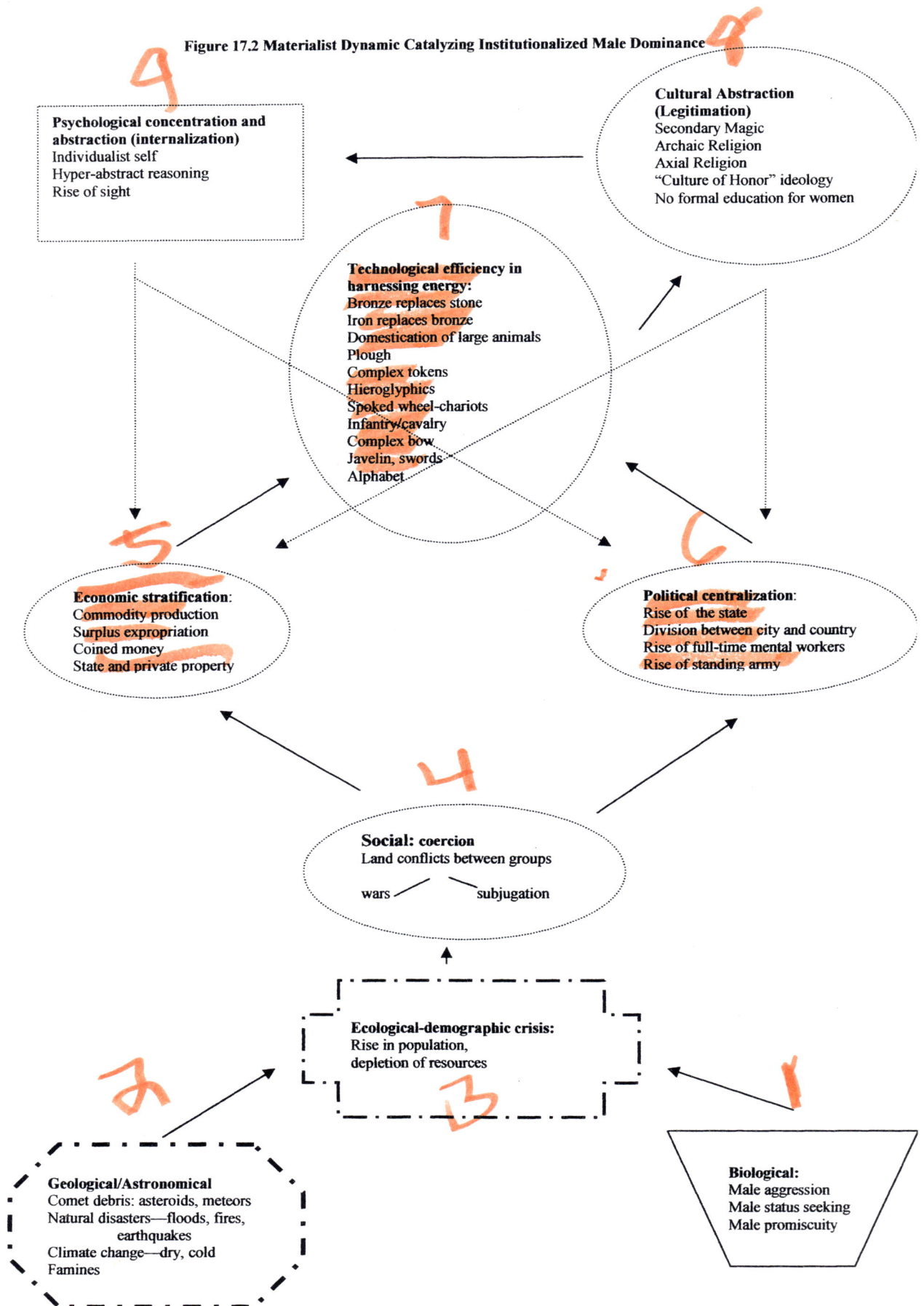

Psychological concentration and abstraction (internalization)
Individualist self
Hyper-abstract reasoning
Rise of sight

Cultural Abstraction (Legitimation)
Secondary Magic
Archaic Religion
Axial Religion
"Culture of Honor" ideology
No formal education for women

Technological efficiency in harnessing energy:
Bronze replaces stone
Iron replaces bronze
Domestication of large animals
Plough
Complex tokens
Hieroglyphics
Spoked wheel-chariots
Infantry/cavalry
Complex bow
Javelin, swords
Alphabet

Economic stratification:
Commodity production
Surplus expropriation
Coined money
State and private property

Political centralization:
Rise of the state
Division between city and country
Rise of full-time mental workers
Rise of standing army

Social: coercion
Land conflicts between groups

wars   subjugation

Ecological-demographic crisis:
Rise in population,
depletion of resources

Geological/Astronomical
Comet debris: asteroids, meteors
Natural disasters—floods, fires,
     earthquakes
Climate change—dry, cold
Famines

Biological:
Male aggression
Male status seeking
Male promiscuity

Within the primary variables, the political dimension is missing. I suspect this area has been collapsed into the category of "surplus economic production." It seems to me that the scheme would benefit from the addition of another component labeled "political decision making processes." There is no conflict I can see between the rest of her dependent variables and the material described in this book.

Chafetz's category of secondary variables includes ideology. This is supported by the events described in this book, since it appears from my research that sacred traditions are more the consequence than the cause of institutionalized male dominance. Both secondary magic and monotheism need to be specified in this section.

More importantly, her model is missing a psychological component to explain how social processes become internalized in individuals, and how people are thus programmed to reproduce the macro-structural institutions. Vygotsky's theory of learning fills in this void perfectly. Without it, we have biophysical and social forces acting on mindless individuals. We need to explain how people's minds become submissive.

In sum, while Chafetz's theory of gender stratification can be broadly applied to the ancient world, there are too many components missing in order for it to work well as a conceptual basis for accounting for the events in the ancient world.

Let us turn to Marvin Harris's model of social evolution, as described in figure 1.3. Though Harris's theory is not specific to the origin of gender relations, its general structure is closer to what we need in order to explain the events of the ancient world. Chafetz and Harris are both materialists in that they both explain social change by reference to ecology, demography, technology, economics, and politics. Neither is a reductionist because both allow for belief systems to influence material systems—though they agree that belief systems are not as important. Like Chafetz's theory, Harris's cultural materialism lacks a geological-astronomical component, a biological component, and a psychological dimension. However, Harris's approach is less abstract, and includes a richer delineation of activities that go with the categories he does give us.

In the light of these reservations I have included a chart I have developed which groups the events in the ancient world with Harris's dimensions of socio-culture, adding the biological, geological-astronomical, and psychological dimensions. I call this the Harris-Vygotsky model. Because Vygotsky's theory of psychological learning itself is strictly materialist, I am confident that Harris would have no major reservations with Vygotsky; and I am also confident that Vygotsky would appreciate the overwhelming majority of Harris's work. I do not know what either would think of the geological-astronomical dimension, and neither would likely want to have much if anything to do with the biological component I have introduced.

From Figure A at the end of the introduction we saw three types of influences on women: pervasive, periodic, and emergent. Pervasive factors are always operating. These are biological forces that are indicated by the hard line in the shape of an inverted trapezoid. Periodic factors are those that come into play on a regular basis but can be absent for long periods of time. These are ecological and demographic forces, along with geological and astronomical forces. They are indicated with dashed lines. Finally there are emergent forces, which come about only at certain points in the history of social evolution for the first time. These are economic, political, technological, and cultural in nature and are indicated with elliptical shapes that have dots around them. Psychological changes are also emergent, but since society and psychology are not the same thing, I have given psychology the shape of a rectangle.

The depth of the shading in the various shapes indicates what I think are the ultimate determining factors in the subordination of women. It would be easy to think that forces such as biology—which are pervasive—would have the strongest influence. But this is not the case. The most powerful influences are the most darkly shaded, which are the ecological, demographic, economic, political, and technological changes. The geological-astronomical and the biological are secondary, supporting causes. The cultural and the psychological dimensions essentially react to and legitimize these other variables but are not themselves responsible for causing institutionalized male dominance.

3. Necessary and sufficient conditions for the emergence of social movements

Given all the events in Figure 17.2 that contributed to women's subordination, why were there no women's movements in the ancient world to fight against these conditions?

Throughout this book I have argued that human beings are constitutionally social beings. This means that the most powerful constraints on human actions are social institutions and the events which occur within them. At the same time, optimal conditions for human transformation also lie in social groups and the social situations people find themselves in.

In two of the classical experiments in social psychology—the Asch experiment on conformity and the Milgram experiment on obedience—situational factors were predictive of whether people would obey, conform, or resist. In the case of the Milgram experiment, when people were placed in a very prestigious environment in the presence of a prestigious authority figure, and there was no visible conflict either among the authority figures or among the group being tested, the participants "shocked" individuals well beyond what any psychological expert would predict. This made the average person appear cruel. However, when some of the situational factors were altered, the participants did not go along with the authority. When the experiment was held in a less prestigious location, with a less prestigious authority figure, more people spoke out. When the authority figures conflicted with each other, or when someone in the group spoke out against what was being done in front of the participants, more people refused to cooperate.

Situational factors were crucial in the Asch experiment as well. In response to a question about the relative length of two lines, many participants changed their answer after they found out they were greatly outnumbered by people who had given different answers. The tendency to conform varied with the number of people who were represented as having given conflicting answers. If women have a greater or lesser inherent biological tendency than men to obey or conform, this was not shown in either experiment's outcome. Neither were personal psychological differences helpful in explaining the results.

Extrapolating the results of these two significant experiments to the question at hand, it would appear that women's subordination in the Bronze and Iron Ages cannot be explained by either the biology of women or by their personality. If biology were really the main factor, then women in egalitarian societies and women today would be far more subordinate than they are. It is the presence or absence of certain social conditions that results in subordination, or that makes resistance movements more or less likely to arise.

Though conditions in society may be unbearably bad for some castes or classes, people do not automatically rebel. Conversely, people's social conditions might actually be improving and people will join resistance movements anyway. The reasons people rebel or fail to rebel have little to do with psychological qualities such as lack of nerve, motivation, or altruistic intention. If social conditions work against a class of people, then psychological motivation or heroic personalities among some members of this group will not be sufficient to enable them build and sustain a movement. So too, if the social preconditions are present, average people with little personal courage may find themselves swooped up into a movement.

According to social evolutionary theory, all human action (even individual action) is either directly or indirectly social. Virtually all individual and group actions implicitly or explicitly contribute to maintaining and reproducing the existing order. By their labor, people collude with dominant institutions when they reproduce them. However, individual and group actions sometimes challenge or resist the dominant institutions, and people occasionally work to build microcosms of a new social order. Periodically there are events in society that briefly challenge a social system—events such as riots—which are called "collective action." When collective action endures a longer period of time as an organized resistance against a particular injustice, it is called a "protest." When protests are connected to a more systematic opposition to the status quo of society, it is called a "movement." Collective action, protests, or movements should be understood as points on a spectrum.

Marx and McAdam (1994) argue that collective action involves group action in settings in which institutional guidelines are non-specific, vague, inadequate, in dispute, or lacking altogether. Collective action can be intentional or unintentional; overt or covert (a conspiracy); heroic and altruistic or opportunistic and exploitative; violent or non-violent. In collective action it is not so much that behavior arises from an absence of rules, but that new rules are made on the spot. It involves role-making which takes place in crisis situations.

Conversely, institutional action or collusion consists of practices that reproduce the existing order by fulfilling routine situations and role-taking. Much institutional behavior has the potential to become collective action, turn into a protest, and then develop into a movement. Conversely, collective action, protests, and social movements usually have some institutional foundation.

For an individual to engage in a collective action, let alone to join a socio-political movement, is an exceptional act; it is not typical human behavior. Most people are socialized into believing in the inherent justness of the existing social order and so they maintain and reproduce the existing order through institutional action (such as working). People engage in collective actions only when driven to an extreme point where social crisis is linked to crises in their personal lives, and these crises are linked consciously to the way society's institutions work. Even when this is the case, people may engage in a collective action without joining a movement. This is because they may live in a historical period in which there is no social movement with which to link.

Social movements themselves are only likely to emerge under very specific material conditions, as we will see.

What are the necessary conditions for resistance movements? In studying racial and ethnic minority movements in the United States, Farley (1995) identifies six social evolutionary pre-conditions, and five conditions more specifically related to social movements. The six evolutionary conditions are

1. the rise of urbanization
2. the rise of industrialization
3. economic expansion
4. rising educational levels
5. mass communications
6. international examples of successful liberation

The conditions more specific to social movements are:

7. dissatisfaction (relative deprivation)
8. a network of communication
9. resources
10. a sense of efficacy
11. leadership

It could be argued that, because the experience of racial and ethnic minorities is not the same as the experience of women, these conditions do not apply. But in her later work, *Gender Equity*, Chafetz (1988) identifies almost exactly these conditions in explaining the rise of women's movements.

Let us examine why these conditions would need to be in place.

(1) *Urbanization*: Material wealth and social complexity are preconditions for both coercion and for resistance movements. One of the consequences of an increase in material wealth is that not everyone needs to be involved in food production; this leads to the formation of social classes, distinct occupations, and new institutions. In order for an elite to wield control over other social classes they must be supported by a full time military. Those specializing in other occupations build the foundations of educational systems, communication systems, and transportation

systems, which also support that coercion. However, once these institutions and systems are built, they have the potential to be used by resistance movements as well. Furthermore, in cities, as opposed to rural areas, the differences between rich are poor are easier to see because social castes or classes are more concentrated. The same observations could be made regarding wealth and power differentials between men and women.

(2) *Industrialization*: Industrialization allows people the time and space to recognize commonalties and to build a class or gender consciousness, because life in the factory forces people into one space for long periods of time. In addition, industrial production is super-socialized. If the performance on one's job demands working together cooperatively with others, then it becomes easier to imagine effectively cooperating with others to do something about difficulties or dangers on the job. Industrial societies with a capitalist base also tend to have more protection for oppositional movements—freedom of assembly, voting, and protection for unions.

(3) *Economic expansion*: People are more likely to fight for what they want when their basic needs are not under attack. In times of economic expansion, new job opportunities open up and class mobility becomes a more realistic possibility. At the same time, the expansion of the economy makes class divisions less of a threat because it appears that there is more for everybody. In the case of gender relations, economic expansion may ease tension in the relationship between women and men.

(4) *Mass communication*: No movement has a chance of success unless it can spread itself beyond its origin and coordinate its activities with other protest or movement centers. The presence of regional and national newspapers, radio, television, and the Internet allows movement groups to know what is going on everywhere within the society, and to know what similar or linked groups are doing elsewhere. The movement can also use mass media to broadcast its message to the general population.

(5) *Rising educational levels*: As people become more educated they see a bigger picture of the world than the one they have been raised with. Being more educated usually means becoming familiar with strangers in other times and places, which may challenge family, caste, and kin loyalties. This is especially important to women, who have to challenge their allegiance to husband, family of origin, and/or their sole role as child raiser.

(6) *International examples of successful liberation*: It is very helpful for any group seeking to challenge the existing order to know of other similar groups in other places that have been and are being successful. This is important not only for ideological inspiration but because successful movements in other places can put pressure on the home country for better conditions.

All of these conditions are *necessary* but *not sufficient* in order for a movement to appear. According to Farley, favorable conditions more specific to social movements include the following:

(7) *Relative deprivation*: This condition is deeply connected with urbanization and industrialization. Are people more likely to rebel the worse their conditions get? At first glance, it may seem so. After all, if people have enough they become content and develop a material stake in the existing order. Conversely, it would seem that once things get very bad people then would have no choice but to rebel. Actually neither of these generalizations is true. Absolute deprivation does not lead to activism. It leads to hopelessness and preoccupation with immediate and momentary survival problems. If people have no reason to expect or hope for more, they will be less discontented with what they have. The lack of resistance movements under absolute deprivation, however, doesn't mean people are automatons who are too stupid to be frustrated. A person may feel very angry, but the intensity of a person's rage or feeling of hopelessness is no indicator of his or her likelihood to join a protest or movement.

According to relative deprivation theory, people join socio-political movements only when they come to believe their conditions are oppressive or unfair *compared to other groups* close at hand. Sociopolitical movements are partly a product of people's changing interpretation of what is happening. The supporters of movements will be those who suffer relative deprivation. These are the people whose expectations are rising but who feel held back in their upward movement.

People who suffer relative deprivation feel entitled to more than they are getting. To have that expectation of entitlement, there must be contradictions between the dominant ideology of a society and what it delivers, and contradictions between the deprived group's legal, political, and economic formal status and its actual status compared to other groups in terms of everyday life. The group members must be able to compare their situation with that of others in society who are like them in other ways, for whom those contradictions are less severe. Thus if women have the right to vote, but make only 72 cents for every dollar a man makes for the same work, the comparison between women's legal status and their actual status becomes glaring.

(8) *Communication*: No matter how much members of a group have in common, if they do not have a system of communication available to enable them to discuss what is happening to them, to compare experiences, and to enable them collectively to decide what to do to further their interests, they cannot act collectively. Communication is also important for building alliances with other, sympathetic groups. While mass communications can help a movement, the presence of mass communications media does not guarantee that a group will build a network out of this opportunity.

The basis of resistance to subordination is the knowledge that one is not alone in one's experience. This involves more than bonding with the people in the immediate situation. If one knows that other people in other places and at other times have felt a similar situation to be unjust and have fought against it, this provides hope and inspiration to continue resistance. People need to be inspired by stories of other times and places, of beings not so different from them who were part of the same struggle as they are.

However, the process of resistance partly involves groups of people getting together and coining new words to describe their situation. If they do not have a language through which to understand and interpret their conditions and express their protest, they will define their experience more passively in the terms used by the dominant society. In developing a language of protest and in alternative model building, women have to be able to develop an ideology they can pass on from generation to generation. For this it is necessary that they can write and read. Without literacy, women are more closely constrained in their efforts to find answers to social problems to their individual lifetimes. It is very difficult to develop and sustain ideas, especially a systematic analysis of social problems and possibilities of solution, if one is limited to oral traditions. Under such circumstances, ideologies of resistance would be next to impossible to develop.

As was said at the beginning of this chapter, maximum resistance is likely when a group is socialized in its education at home and on the job to challenge authority, to be curious, and to test reality rather than merely to adapt to it.

(9) *Resources*: The theory of resource mobilization argues that the presence of discontent resulting from relative deprivation, and of available communication systems, is not enough to build a movement unless there is an organizational resource base to mobilize and support efforts at sociopolitical change. People have to be able to express their discontent within a collective political framework that can sustain itself over time. If the challengers are to win the struggle they must have access to and control of sufficient resources. *Resistance movements arise from increases in the level of resource availability*. This is one reason why it is important for movements built from the poorer classes to link up with sympathetic members of wealthier classes to help them with equipment, funds, access to buildings, and donations of time. Access to resources is closely connected to economic expansion.

(10) *A sense of efficacy*: Even if a group feels relatively deprived, has put internal communication systems in place, and has access to adequate resources, if they lack a sense of confidence, this can be enough to stop them. Complaining by itself is not enough. People

must also have a vision of alternative models of how society could be ordered, and of their place in the transformation. Without this vision the goals of the movement will be more easily defined by the existing order. Movements will be built on the basis of attempts to get rid of problems, rather than on that of setting goals to build a new society. It is also important that the group's alternative model must be practical. Participants must be able to see in concrete terms that potential gains really do outweigh the costs of what might happen to them as a result of their involvement in movement activities. If the costs are too high and the benefits too vague, potential candidates will not join.

(11) *Leadership*: Farley (1995) explains that some theorists claim that leadership is not an independent factor because if the other conditions are in place, leadership will naturally emerge. Whether or not this is the case, leadership is important for inspiring people, sustaining their enthusiasm, developing an ideology, and planning strategies.

But even if all of these conditions are present, this is no guarantee that most people will join. In looking at the case of minority movements, Farley cites four reasons why most people do not join social movements, which I paraphrase:

(a) acceptance
  (i) they have become convinced by the ideology of those in power that these elites truly are superior
  (ii) they don't accept the superiority of the dominant group but feel the movement is not really strong enough to do anything about it
  (iii) they accept their status and win small psychological battles against those with privileges;
(b) scapegoating—they take their frustration out on other members of their group;
(c) avoidance—they avoid contact with those in power as much as possible, which would remind them of their subordinate status; for them, substance abuse might be an outlet that enables avoidance;

(d) seeking assimilation (tokenism)—they accept the system and make serious efforts to rise out of their group of origin.

However, social movements, in order to be successful, do not need for most people to be directly involved. They do need most of the above 11 conditions to be in place in order to have a chance of success. The first five conditions might be called necessary conditions. This is because without them, a movement is not possible. However, the presence of the first five conditions is no guarantee a movement will appear. The first five conditions are a foundation for the rest. Without the first five conditions, the other conditions may emerge, but they will not enable a movement to emerge. I am not suggesting that the fulfillment of all of these conditions is enough to make a movement successful. It only means that a movement will emerge.

If we use these eleven conditions to gauge the likelihood of women rebelling against the institutionalization of male dominance in the ancient world, we will see that most of these circumstances were absent.

4. Why there was no women's movement in the ancient world

Let us compare what we have learned of the events and processes in the ancient world that led to the subordination of women with Farley's conditions under which social movements arise. One thing to be aware of in making this comparison is that Farley's work is based on racial and class movements, not women's movements. While there is great overlap, gender movements are not identical with other social movements. For this reason I will add two dimensions not mentioned by Farley.

(1) *Urbanization*: Tribal societies do not have protests, let alone social movements, partly because differences between groups are not so severe that people feel something must be done about them. In addition, such societies do not have the social systems in place to sustain a social movement. Bronze and Iron Age cities had caste, class, and gender disparities

to justify protests and movements, and they had the material wealth to afford full-time mental workers. However, the elite in these societies squandered their wealth on "conspicuous consumption." Unlike early capitalists, they didn't invest their wealth in science and technology, which might have resulted in the mass transportation, communication, and educational systems that a social movement needs. Ancient elites did not invest in developing the social infrastructure.

In Iron Age states, some class mobility might have given women raised expectations. In some Iron Age states with cosmopolitan populations that are not held to kinship or caste loyalties there could be more direct competition for jobs, but these were monopolized by men. What mobility was possible was possible for men, not women. Women had no public life to speak of in either Bronze or Iron Age cities.

(2) *Industrialization*: Pre-industrial cities—whether in the Bronze or Iron Ages—did not have nearly the concentrated collective production of a factory in the industrial age. In order for castes, classes, or women to identify common needs and build protest or reform movements, group members need to be at the same place at the same time over months and years. Women's work life has to be collective and public. Women must also have the experience of cooperative performance on a job in which the product is the interdependent result of all their efforts. Examples in industrial society are working in a textile mill or an auto assembly line. As miserable as these jobs can be, the product is co-created together by all of the workers, even if their individual work constitutes an alienated creativity.

The habit of making a product together on the job acts as a model for learning to cooperate together on and off the job to build a movement. Solitary work such as cottage industry or even handicrafts, such as women did in preindustrial societies, does not lend itself to this experience.

Even if women in Bronze and Iron Age societies had worked together in public, these societies lacked the democratic institutions that would have allowed women to organize themselves legally. In order to oppose the authorities, groups need democratic institutions in place so that group members can openly discuss events and challenge the status quo. There was no constitution in the ancient world to allow the formation of unions, or to confer freedom of the press or freedom of assembly. Agricultural states were theocracies. There were no political parties. All political positions were either inherited or appointed by the upper castes. Political power was exercised in one direction—from the top down. The individual right to dissent was unheard of. In the Axial Iron Age there was certainly more democracy in the Greek polis, but women were excluded. In Bronze Age agricultural states, democratic institutions did not exist for anyone.

Finally, a condition which comes about with industrialization not mentioned by Farley, but very pertinent to the conditions of women, is capital-intensive technology—in other words, tools that use an energy source such as coal or oil, and thus do not require considerable human strength for their operation. One of the most important conditions that help build the women's movement was the development of machines that required relatively little human muscle-power. While it is difficult for most women to work with a plow and oxen, anyone can drive a tractor. The industrialization process opened up the possibility for women to do a far greater range of jobs, because the tools used were far less labor intensive. Chafetz stresses the importance of this in both her works (1984, 1988). It was no accident that women lost control of planting when the plow was invented and large animals were required for pulling it. Both the plow and the handling of large traction animals were far more labor-intensive than using digging sticks to cultivate gardens.

(3) *Economic expansion*: While Bronze and Iron Age societies were wealthy, relatively speaking, the wealth was static and top-heavy. It was static because there was no "free market" with dramatic expansions and contractions (or depressions). Because the state controlled the economy, changes in material wealth came primarily from colonization or victorious warfare. Also, the elites in agricultural states owned a much higher proportion of the relative

wealth of society than did the elites in industrialized societies (excluding the elites of the electronic-information age). These were caste societies and so new opportunities for mobility were not easily forthcoming. This was true not just because mobility would violate social norms but because elites did not invest much in the social infrastructure. There were not many new jobs to be had.

(4) *Mass communication*: There were no mass communication systems in Bronze or Iron Age states. Without regional or national newspapers, telephones, telegraphs, or television (let alone the internet), whatever social movements that might have emerged would have been isolated and crushed. People need to travel, compare living conditions, and build solidarity with workers in other societies. Women need to talk to other women beyond their own society to identify common problems.

(5) *Rising educational levels*: A sign of a good education is that one (a) has mastered the existing body of information of one's society and (b) is able to compare it with the bodies of information of other societies. In order to accomplish these tasks, reading and writing are usually essential. In the case of women in the ancient world, neither (a) nor (b) was the case. Women in the Bronze Age mastered only the portion of the societal information that crossed caste lines. Women received no formal education except possibly in music. In Axial Iron Age Greece, a woman's basic functions were to provide male heirs for her husband, provide him with cheap labor, and watch over the house.

In the Bronze Age, priestesses may have learned to write hieroglyphics and to keep records in order to manage a temple economy. But priestesses were a minuscule percentage of women in these societies. With the possible exception of the hetaerai women in Axial Age Greece, women did not read or write even after the alphabet had been invented.

Finally, a broad education requires traveling beyond your society. The only social caste in the ancient world that did this was that of the merchants, and that caste was composed entirely of men.

(6) *International examples of successful liberation*: The women's movement in the 19th century was inherently internationalist. Many women active in the movement were socialists, and socialism explicitly committed itself to internationalism. In the 20th century, the women's movement was prominent in socialist countries and, though the relationship between socialist governments and the women's movement was far from idyllic, state socialism in the former USSR and the social democracy movement in the Scandinavian countries provided women with concrete social achievements. Women in other nations were thus able to point to such achievements as achievable goals in their own countries. In ancient times in the Old World, there was no women's movement elsewhere to provide inspiration.

Let us turn now to Farley's more specific conditions for social movements to arise.

(7) *Dissatisfaction (relative deprivation)*: The basis for relative deprivation is a set of conditions that leads one to see deficits in one's own group's condition as essentially a social problem. There is either a contradiction between the condition of one group and others usually thought to be on an equal level (one group typically having more power and wealth than another), or a contradiction between the ideology of the society and the actual carrying out of its policies. In either case, people in a certain group feel entitled to more than they are getting.

In Bronze Age and Iron Age agricultural states, women suffered more from absolute deprivation than from relative deprivation. For one thing, in none of these societies were there other movements—class or race movements— with which women could compare their own status and prospects. For another, there was no dominant ideology of gender egalitarianism that was contradicted by women's actual condition. With these two conditions absent women, would not have felt relatively deprived.

(8) *A network of communication*: Coercion depends not only on keeping subordinated groups isolated from each other, but on keeping the middle and upper castes from being sympathetic to them and aligning with them.

The social distance between castes in the great Bronze Age civilizations was far greater than between classes in industrial capitalist societies. All social castes understood their position as the natural order of things and as legitimate. There were no doubts about social location, nor was there an ideology of mobility to support the movement of individuals from one social caste or class to another. The same was true in Axial Iron Age Greece, though to a lesser extent. The religious prophets of the Axial Iron Age did exhibit some elementary spirit of resistance. For example, the Buddha challenged caste distinctions, and the Hebrew prophets fought sacred wars in the effort to overcome their captivity at the hands of other civilizations. But no Axial Age prophet, as far as I know, supported equal treatment for women.

In part, the absence of a network of communication was caused by women not having words for their experience of oppression; that is, they lacked a language of protest. Consider, as an analogy, the experience of a molested child. Before a young girl possesses the word "molestation" to define an experience, she might simply exhibit unusually intense emotions of fear and shyness. She does not possess the knowledge that (a) other children have had the same experience, (b) there are words for this experience, and (c) others have condemned this activity as immoral. Without these conditions, the child will probably not identify her experience as a social problem.

However, in our society she will eventually hear other little girls talking (perhaps in group therapy) about the same experience, and will learns words that label the problem and propose a solution to it. Now she will have a different set of emotions—humiliation, anger, and zeal in doing something about it. The situation now becomes a social problem. A similar process is associated with the process of coining and learning terms such as "sexual harassment" and "racism."

Women in agricultural and commercial states lacked this language of description and protest. The basis of the formation of such a language is a time and place to talk about common experience. Because in the Bronze and Iron Ages women disappeared from public life, they had little opportunity to talk with one another. They were not likely to have identified their problems as social problems.

(9) *Resources*: The extent to which women in Bronze and Iron Age civilizations had access to resources is deeply connected up with the question of whether these societies were economically expanding and whether the majority of women had access to middle- and upper-class men and women who could help them. Because these societies lacked a dynamic economy and because caste relations separated women from different social groups, the vast majority of women lacked resources to build and sustain a movement.

(10) *A sense of efficacy*: The absence of a movement does not mean that women were brainwashed and never complained, that they didn't wish ill on individual men or even perform acts of calculated violence against them. But all of these thoughts, words, and deeds represent interpersonal engagements, not structural critiques. A woman may be upset with the abusive way a priest, aristocrat, or merchant treats her, but is less likely to quarrel publicly with the institutions of the priesthood or aristocracy. Oppressed groups do not begin to question the structure of social relations unless there is an alternative—at least in ideological form—with which to replace it. There was no such ideology in the ancient world. Without this alternative and the visibility of many other women who seemed prepared to act, women in the ancient world would have lacked this sense of efficacy.

(11) *Leadership*: Finally, women have to be able to imagine themselves in leadership positions within these alternative structures. One of the psychological requirements for a good leader is the cultivation of an individualist self, a self whose identity in roles is not so comfortable that it inhibits him or her from transforming situations rather than accepting them as given. Developing an individualist self would have allowed a woman not to care so much what other people thought, because she saw herself as independent of kin groups and society as a whole. This individualist self has an internal locus of control and imagines itself to

be in control of its inner life; it is less subject to what authority figures or social conventions expect. Furthermore, it recognizes and acts on its own self interest even at the expense of the authorities.

Another psychological skill required of leadership is the capacity to distance oneself from the present in order to imagine future possibilities. Leadership also requires long-term planning. These skills require hyperabstract thinking. The power of hyperabstract cognition is more likely to encourage dissent than is concrete abstraction. First, a woman possessing hyperabstract cognition could have seen further into the past and the future. Therefore, she would be more likely to see through the relativity of the present social forms. She would be able to plot, strategize, and think critically. Second, a woman with hyperabstract reasoning would have been able to relativize existing social institutions in terms of space. A woman with hyperabstract reasoning, if she were a merchant or a priestess, would likely have known about other cultures through the activities of trade and wars. This would have meant that her own society would be understood as *a* world rather than *the* world.

Women in Greece could not separate themselves from their social context. They defined themselves in terms of filling men's needs. Neither would women have had a sense of identity beyond their social roles. How could they? Their whole existence was defined by men. It takes a tremendous amount of self-confidence for any person to define their identity as separate from the roles expected by the group. With the sole exception of priestesses in the Bronze Age, only upper-class men were in a position to do this. Neither would women have had an I-me dialogue that emphasized their own needs. Women would not have had any of these qualities because they were not taken seriously as personal beings. Women had vertical collectivist selves that had great reverence for authority.

Women in the Axial Iron Age never occupied social positions in which a separate psyche could be cultivated. Even in the Dionysian rituals, where women had some emotional and physical release from their frustrations, they explained their behavior as the result of being possessed by the god. While men like Socrates or Plato, who had individualist selves, could take personal responsibility for their actions, women in this period could not do so. Women could not have survived making individual choices that were at variance with social norms. The Greek polis was a place where this could be done, but women were not allowed there. Their collectivist self-identity was too attached to kin groups and the authorities to permit them to engage in dissent, protest, or help build a movement.

A woman would have to feel powerful enough in order to take over positions of responsibility from men in dominant positions of the existing order. As we saw in chapter 14, certain social foundations would have been necessary to enable women to develop this kind of thinking; such foundations would have included access to administrative positions in which the individual is engaged full-time in mental work. With the exception of priestesses in Bronze Age agricultural states, women were not trained in administrative positions, and so they would have had no opportunity to develop hyperabstract thinking. Woman's consciousness, consequently, must have been in the service of conversation or actions, not self-reflection.

Applying Farley's 11 conditions for social movements to women's situations in Bronze and Axial Iron Age civilization reveals that only one of the 11 conditions was in place. Figure 17.3 summarizes the lack of these conditions in the ancient world. When combining the absence of the conditions for a social movement with the presence of all of the events grouped under the stages of subordination, it is no wonder that women colluded in their labor in reproducing the male-dominated institutions in their own lifetimes and in the next generation. Nothing like Marx's notion of practical-critical activity would have existed. The conditions under which both class and gender movements emerge with the most vitality came into being in the second half of the 19th century and persisted throughout the 20th century.

Before leaving this subject, I would like to address an objection that may have arisen in the minds of some readers. *Weren't there oppositional movements in ancient history—for example, slave and peasant revolts—which occurred without industrialization or mass communication? Could these be considered social movements? If so, why weren't there "women's revolts" as well?*

Such revolts undeniably took place, but they are better characterized as "rebellions' or "protests" rather than social movements for a number of reasons. These groups were challenging the abuses of people in authority, not the structure of authority itself. Moreover, they did not form coalitions with other groups that questioned the existing order. Second, these rebellions or protests were typically organized around immediate concerns. They had little, if any, sense of being part of a history (both past and future) that must be carried on beyond a single generation. Neither did they have a sense of relationship to other areas around the world, the way the current women's movement, global justice movement, or the civil rights movements do.

There were indeed oppositional religious movements in the Middle Ages, typified by the Anabaptists, which did call into question the political order. These might be called "primitive social movements," because although their desire was to call everything into question, they did not have the means to carry out their alternative program. They did not form coalitions with other groups, they did not persist beyond a single generation, and they did not unite with others beyond their local areas. They would have had to have a critical mass of people to have a chance to become successful, and for this they would have needed mass communication and industrialization.

There were good reasons why there were no women's revolts to parallel the slave, conscript, and peasant revolts in the ancient world. In pre-industrial times slaves or peasants could revolt and *yet still keep their families in tact.* Women have too many cross-cutting loyalties to husbands, brothers, and sons to call their unequal relationship with all these people into question. The family as a basic unit of society would have been threatened. It is only now, with some day-care institutions in place, the beginning of experiments in artificial insemination, and some economic independence from men, that women can consider breaking away from their families to some extent and aligning themselves with other women. For this reason it makes sense that the women's movement would be a late-arrival movement.

*   *   *

In closing, I want to stress that neither informal nor institutionalized male dominance means that women have no rights, privileges, influence or power. Further, while all men benefited in various degrees from the privileges of being men, most men lost political and economic power in the Bronze and Iron Ages. Finally, men as a group did not consciously seek to dominate women. To reduce cultural evolution to an historic "battle of the sexes" grossly simplifies the situation and ignores the fact that, initially, the emergence of male dominance was one of many byproducts of a more primary struggle between groups within society (which were not based on gender) for power under ecological and demographic stresses which entire societies faced.

Figure 17.3 Necessary and Specific Conditions for the Emergence of Social Movements

A) Necessary conditions for building a social movement

*1) Urbanization—material wealth and social complexity—*Yes.

Yet surplus is not reinvested in the social infrastructure. In Axial Iron Age, social mobility limited to men.

*2) Industrialization—cooperative labor in a concentrated space—*No.

No opportunity to meet at the same place and time to compare experiences. No democratic institutions under which to organize: freedom of assembly, freedom of the press; unions. Technology is very labor intensive.

3) *Economic expansion*--No.

Ancient civilizations were relatively static economically and top-heavy in wealth distribution.

4) Mass communication--No.

There were no mass communication systems in the ancient world.

5) *Rising educational levels*--No.

Women were neither socialized to master a wide range of knowledge within their societies, nor were they familiar with knowledge bases of other societies. The overwhelming majority of women could not read, write or travel.

6) *International examples* of successful liberation--No

No women's movement to draw from in other parts of the world.

B) Specific conditions for building a social movement

7) *Dissatisfaction (relative deprivation)*--No

Absolute deprivation--no contradiction between women to contrast with class or class movements.
No contradiction between ideology of society and what it practices.

8) *Networks of communication*--No

Caste distinctions kept other social castes from building alliances.
Weak sympathy for caste oppression in the Axial Iron Age . No connection made with women.
Lack of a language of protest.

9) *Resources*--No

Economic stagnation and caste division prevented this.

10) *Sense of efficacy*--No

Lack of an alternative ideology.
Lack of visibility of other women willing to act.

11) *Leadership*--No

Lack of experience in administrative positions of leadership.
No individualist self.
No hyperabstract cognition.

Bibliography

Chapter 1. History-Shaping

Berger, P. (1967) *The Social Construction of Reality.* Anchor.

Harris, M. (1977) *Cannibals and Kings.* Vintage.

_____ . (1988) *Culture, People and Nature.* Harper Collins.

_____ . (1979) *Cultural Materialism.* Random House.

Marx, K. (1906) *German Ideology*

_____ . *The Communist Manifesto*

Ollman B. (1976) *Alienation.* Cambridge University Press.

Chapter 2. The Anatomy of Ancient Societies

Bernal, J. (1971) *Science in History: Volume I.* MIT Press.

Childe, V. (1951) *Man Makes Himself.* Mentor.

_____ . (1954) *What Happened in History.* Penguin.

Cohen, M. (1977) *The Food Crisis in Prehistory.* Yale University Press.

Crone, P. (1989) *Pre-Industrial Societies.* Blackwell.

Diamond, S. (1987) *In Search of the Primitive.* Transaction.

Fried, M. (1967). *The Evolution of Political Society.* Random House.

Hass, J. (1982) *Evolution of the Prehistoric State.* Columbia University Press.

Johnson, A., Earle, T. (1987) *The Evolution of Human Societies.* Stanford University Press.

Lenski, G. (1987) *Human Societies.* McGraw-Hill.

_____ . (1977) *Power and Privilege.* University of North Carolina Press.

Ober, J. (1989). *Mass and Elite in Democratic Athens.* Princeton University Press.

O'Kelly, C., Carney, L. (1986) *Women and Men in Society.* Wadsworth.

Polanyi, K. (1957) *Trade and Market in the Early Empires.* Free Press.

Sahlins, M. (1972) *Stone Age Economics.* Aldine.

_____ . 1966) *Tribesmen.* Prentice-Hall.

Sahlins, M., Service, E. (1970) *Evolution and Culture.* University of Michigan Press.

Sanderson, S. (1991) *Macrosociology.* HarperCollins.

_____ . (1990) *Social Evolutionism.* Blackwell.

_____ . (1995) *Social Transformations.* Blackwell.

Tainter, J. (1988) *The Collapse of Complex Societies.* Cambridge University Press.

Chapter 3. The Place and Misplace of Goddesses

Bachofen, J. (1987) *Myth, Religion and Mother-Right.* Bollingen.

Briffault, R. (1959) *The Mothers.* Atheneum.

Campbell, J. (1964) *Masks of God: Occidental Mythology.* Viking.

Ehrenberg, M. (1985) *Women in Prehistory.* University of Oklahoma Press.

_____ . (1982) *Masks of God: Primitive Mythology.* Penguin.

Eisler, R. (1988) *The Chalice and the Blade.* Harper and Row.

Eller, C. (2000) *The Myth of Matriarchical Prehisory* Beacon.

Davis, Philip (1998) *Goddess Unmasked.* Spense.

Fisher, E. (1979) *Women's Creation.* McGraw-Hill.

Frymer-Kensky, T. (1992) *In the Wake of the Goddesses.* Free Press.

Goodison, L. Morris, C. (1998) *Ancient Goddesses.* University of Wisconsin Press.

Harrison, J. (1959) *Prolegomena to the Study of Greek Religion.* Meridian.

Lerner, G. (1986) *The Creation of Patriarchy.* Oxford University Press.

Motz, L. (1997) *The Faces of the Goddess.* Oxford University Press.

Neumann, E. (1972) *The Great Mother.* Bollingen.

Neumann, E. (1954) *Origin and History of Consciousness.* Princeton University Press.

Shlain, L. (1998) *The Alphabet and the Goddess.* Viking.

Sjoo, M., Mar, B. (1987) *The Great Cosmic Mother.* Harper and Row.

Stone, M. (1976) *When God was a Woman.* Harvest.

Chapter 4. Socio-Ecological Theories of Gender Hierarchies

Chafetz, J. (1988) *Gender Equity.* Sage.

Chafetz, J. (1984) *Sex and Advantage.* Sage.

Engels, F. (1968) *Origin of the Family, Private Property and the State.* International Publishers.

Guttentag, M. Secord, P. (1983) *Too Many Women.* Sage.

Hurst, B. (2000) *Social Inequality.* Allyn and Bacon.

Chapter 5. Informal Male Dominance

Fried, M. (1967) *The Evolution of Political Society.* Random House.

Reeves-Sanday, P. (1981) *Female Power and Male Dominance.* Cambridge.

Sahlins, M. and Service, E. (1970) *Evolution and Culture.* University of Michigan.

Sanderson, S. (1991) *Macrosociology.* HarperCollins.

Chapter 6. Cycles of Female Subordination

Keuls, E. (1985) *The Reign of the Phallus.* University of California Press.

Lerner, G. (1986) *The Creation of Patriarchy.* Oxford University Press.

McElvaine, R. (2001) *Eve's Seed.* McGrawHill.

Pomeroy, S. (1975). *Whores, Wives, and Slaves.* Schocken.

Roontz, S., Henderson, P. (1986) *Women's Work, Men's Property.* Verso.

Van Der Veer, R. Valsinger, J. (1993) *Understanding Vygotsky.* Blackwell.

Ward-Gailey C. (1987) *Kinship to Kingship.* University of Texas Press.

Wertsch, H. (1985) *Vygotsky and the Social Formation of Mind.* Harvard University Press.

Chapter 7. Is Origin Destiny?

Berry, J. (1992) *Cross-Cultural Psychology.* Cambridge University Press.

Blum, D. (1997) *Sex on the Brain,* Penguin.

Brown, D. (1991) *Human Universals.* McGrawHill.

Buss, D. (1999) *Evolutionary Psychology.* Allyn and Bacon.

Gaulin, J., Mc Bruney, D. (2001) *Psychology.* PrenticeHall.

Goldberg, S. (1993) *Why Men Rule.* Open Court.

Low, Bobbi. (2000) *Why Sex Matters.* Princeton University Press.

Sanderson, S. (2001) *Evolution of Human Sociality.* Rowman and Littlefield.

Chapter 8. Noble Savage or Brutish Barbarian?

Keeley, L (1996) *War Before Civilization*. Oxford University Press.

Kelly, R. (2000) *Warless Societies and the Origin of War*. University of Michigan Press.

Tavris, C., (1992) *Mismeasurement of Woman*. Simon and Schuster.

Nisbett, R., Dov Cohen (1996) *Culture of Honor*. Westview.

Chapter 9. Chariots, Infantry and Nomadic Invasions

Drews, R. (1988) *Coming of the Greeks*. Princeton University Press.

_____. (1993) *End of the Bronze Age*. Princeton University Press.

Mallory, J. (1989) *In Search of the Indo-Europeans*. Thames and Hudson.

Nisbett, R., Dov Cohen (1996) *Culture of Honor*. Westview.

Chapter 10. Fire, Water and Comet Debris

Allan, D. and Delair, J. (1995) *When the Earth Nearly Died*. Gateway.

Baillie, M. (1999) *Exodus to Arthur*. Batsford.

Clube, V., Napier, B. (1982) *The Cosmic Serpent*. Faber and Faber.

_____. (1990) *The Cosmic Winter*. Blackwell.

Diamond, J. (1997) *Guns, Germs and Steel*. Norton.

Fagan, B. (1999) *Floods, Famines and Emperors*. Basic Books.

Goldsmith, D. (1977) *Scientists Confront Velikovsky*. Cornell, University Press.

Greene, M. (1992) *Natural Knowledge in Preclassical Antiquity*. Johns Hopkins Press.

Gribbin, J., Gribbin, M. (1996) *Fire on Earth*. St. Martin's.

Huggett, R. (1997) *Castastrophism*. Verso.

Keys, D. (1999) *Castrastrophe*. Ballentine Books.

Lewis, J. (1996) *Rain of Iron and Ice*. Helix.

Peiser, B., Palmer, T., Bailey, M. (1998) *Natural Castastrophes During Bronze Age Civilisations*. Archaeopress.

Mc Neill, W. (1976) *Plagues and Peoples*. Monricello.

Pellegrino, C. (1994) *Return to Sodom and Gomorrah*. Avon.

_____. (1991) *Unearthing Atlantis*. Vintage.

Schoch R. (1999) *Voices of the Rocks*. Harmony.

Steel, D. (1995) *Rogue Asteriods and Doomsday Comets*. Wiley.

Velikovsky, I (1950) *Worlds in Collision*. Doubleday.

Chapter 11. Natural Disasters and Gender Stress

Aptekar, L. (1994) *Environmental Disasters in Global Perspective*. G.K. Hall.

Barkun, M. (1986) *Disaster and the Millennium*. Syracuse University Press.

Barnett, R. Biener, L. (1987) *Gender and Stress*. Free Press.

Bawden, G. Reycraft, R. (2000) *Environmental Disaster and the Archeology of Human Response*. University of New Mexico.

Bell, P., Greene, T. (1996) *Environmental Psychology*. Harcourt Brace.

Bookchin, M. (1987) *The Rise of Urbanism and the Decline of Citizenship*. Sierra Club.

Enarson, E. Morrow Hern, B. (1998) *The Gendered Terrain of Disaster*. Praeger.

Gifford, R. (1997) *Environmental Psychology*. Allyn and Bacon.

Miller, D. (2000) *Introduction to Collective Behavior and Collective Action.* Waveland.

Moghaddam, F. (1998) *Social Psychology.* W.H. Freeman.

Oliver-Smith, A., Hoffman, S. (1999) *The Angry Earth.* Routledge.

Tavris, C., Wade, C. (1998) *Psychology.* PrenticeHall.

Chapter 12. Primitive and Secondary Magic

Cornford, F. (1957) *From Religion to Philosophy.* Harper Torchbooks.

Dodds, E.(1951). *The Greeks and the Irrational.* University of California Press.

Durkheim, E. (1957) *Elementary Forms of Religious Life.* Free Press.

Eliade, M. (1958) *Cosmos and History.* Harper Torchbooks.

_____. (1978) *A History of Religious Ideas: Volume I.* University of Chicago Press.

_____. (1982) *A History of Religious Ideas: Volume II.* University of Chicago Press.

_____. (1958) *Patterns of Comparative Religion.* Meridian.

Evans-Pritchard, E. (1965). *Theories of Primitive Religion.* Oxford University Press.

Feuerstein, G. (1987) *Structures of Consciousness.* Integral Publishing.

Frankfort, H. (1946) *The Intellectual Adventure of Ancient Man.* University of Chicago Press.

Frymer-Kensky, T. (1992) *In the Wake of the Goddesses.* Free Press.

Gebser, J. (1986) *The Ever-Present Origin.* Ohio University Press.

Hillman, J.(1977) *Revisioning Psychology.* Harper and Row.

Lerro, B. (2000) *From Earth Spirts to Sky Gods.* Lexington.

Lloyd, G. (1979) *Magic, Reason and Experience.* Cambridge University Press.

_____. (1990) *Demystifying Mentalities.* Cambridge University Press.

_____. (1992)*Polarity and Analogy.* Cambridge University Press.

Radin, P. (1959) *Primitive Religion.* Dover.

Roberts, K. (1995) *Religion in Sociological Perspective.* Wadsworth.

Chapter 13. Archaic and Universalistic Religion

Chakravarti, U. (1987) *The Social Dimensions of Early Buddhism* Oxford University Press

Clube, V., Napier, B. (1982) *The Cosmic Serpent.* Faber and Faber.

_____. (1990) *The Cosmic Winter.* Blackwell.

Frymer-Kensky, T. (1992) *In the Wake of the Goddesses.* Free Press.

Fung, Y. (1967) *A Short History of Chinese Philosophy.* Free Press.

Hatab, L. (1992) *Myth and Philosophy.* Open Court.

Lerro, B. (2000) *From Earth Spirts to Sky Gods.* Lexington.

Lewis, M. (1990) *Sanctiioned Violence in Early China.* State University of New York Press.

Ling, T. (1976) *The Buddha.* Penguin.

Mumford, L. (1956) *The Transformations of Man.* Harper Torchbooks.

Murray, G. (1955) *The Five Stages of Greek Religion.* Anchor.

Nielson, N. (1993) *Religions of the World.* St. Martin's.

Sharma, R. (1983) *Material Culture and Social Formations in Ancient India.* MacMillan.

Vivante, B. (1999) *Women's Roles in Ancient Civilizations.* Greenwood.

Whyte, L. (1959) *The Next Development in Man.* Mentor.

Chapter 14. Environmental Psychology and Sense Ratios

Altman, I., Low, S. (1992) *Place Attachment*. Plenum.

Casey, E. (1997) *Getting Back into Place*. University of Indiana Press.

Classen, C. (1993) *Worlds of Sense*. Routledge.

Classen, C. Howes, D. Synnott, A. (1994) *Aroma*. Routledge.

Havelock, E. (1963) *Preface to Plato*. Harvard University Press.

_____. (1978) *Greek Concept of Justice*. Harvard University Press.

Howes, David (1991) *The Varieties of Senosry Experience*. University of Toronto Press.

Innes, H. (1951) *The Bias of Communication*. University of Toronto Press.

DeMeo, James. (1998) *Saharasia*. OBRL.

Gallagher, W. (1993) *The Power of Place* HarperCollins.

Lofland, L. (1973) *World of Strangers*.

_____. (1998) *The Public Realm*. Aldine De Gruyter.

Mc Luhan, M. (1969) *Gutenberg Galaxy*. Signet.

Ong, W. (1988) *Orality and Literacy*. Routledge.

Sack, D. (1980) *Conceptions of Space in Social Thought*. University of Minnesota Press.

_____. (1992) *Place, Modernity and the Consumers' World*. Johns Hopkins University Press.

Schneidau, H. (1976) *Sacred Discontent*. University of California Press.

Sjoberg, G. (1965) *The Preindustrial City*. Free Press.

Tuan Y. (1974) *Topophilia*. PrenticeHall.

Wilson, P. (1988) *The Domestication of the Human Species*. Yale University Press.

Chapter 15. Cognitive Evolution in History

Abram, D. (1998) *The Spell of the Sensuous*. Pantheon.

Bakhurst, D. (1991) *Consciousness and Revolution in Soviet Philosophy*. Cambridge University Press.

Cazeneuve, J. (1972) *Lucien Levy-Bruhl*. Harper and Row.

Cole, M. (1996) *Cultural Psychology*.

Goody J. (1977) *The Domestication of the Savage Mind*. Cambridge University Press.

Havelock, E. (1963) *Preface to Plato*. Harvard University Press.

Lektorsky, V. (1984) *Subject Object Cognition*. Progress.

Leontiev, A. (1981) *Problems of the Development of the Mind*. Progress.

Levy-Bruhl L. (1975) *The Notebooks on Primitive Mentality*. Harper and Row.

Logan. R. (1986) *The Alphabet Effect*. William Morrow.

_____. (1995) *The Fifth Language*. Stoddart

Luria, A. (1976) *Cognitive Development*. Harvard University Press.

Mikhailov, T. (1980) *The Riddle of the Self*. Progress.

Sohn-Rethel, A. (1978) *Intellectual and Manual Labor*. Humanities Press.

Schmandt-Besserat, D (1992) *Before Writing*. University of Texas Press.

Van Der Veer, R., Valsinger, J. (1993) *Understanding Vygotsky*. Blackwell.

Wertsch, H. (1985) *Vygotsky and the Social Formation of Mind*. Harvard University Press.

Chapter 16. Collectivism and Individualism

Charon, J. (1998) *Symbolic Interactionism*. PrenticeHall.

Gellner, E. (1988) *Plough, Sword and Book.* University of Chicago Press.

Hewitt, J. (1991) *Self and Society.* Allyn and Bacon.

Mead, G. (1972) *Mind, Self, and Society.* University of Chicago Press.

Segal, Dasen, Berry, and Poortinga. (1999) *Human Behavior in Global Perspective.* Allyn and Bacon.

Smith, P., Bond-Harris, M. (1994) *Social Psychology Across Cultures.* Allyn and Bacon.

Triandis, H. (1995) *Individualism and Collectivism.* Westview.

Chapter 17. Dissent, Mobilization and Revolution

Chafetz, J. (1988) *Gender Equity.* Sage.

Farley, J. (1995) *Majority-Minority Relations.* PrenticeHall.

Marx,T., McAdam, D. (1994) *Collective Behavior and Social Movements.* Prentice Hall.

Miller, D. (2000) *Introduction to Collective Behavior and Collective Action.* Waveland.

Index

extreme informal male dominance 111,
112, 114, 115, 117, 376

F
Fabbro, David 180, 181, 184
facultative genes 146
Fagan, Brian 210
faith 57, 81, 155, 183, 231, 282, 283, 286,
371
fast sex 153, 167
fasting 327, 330
feminist spiritualists 1
feuding 169, 170, 185
Fisher, Elizabeth 131, 230
foraging 29, 31, 34, 35, 37, 39, 49, 81, 107,
111, 114, 116, 117, 160, 181, 184, 185,
186, 187, 234, 275, 366
forces of socialization 351, 357
formal coercion 120, 125, 128
formal democracy 280
Fothergill, Alice 242, 243, 245, 248
Frazer, Sir James 79, 80, 259
Fried, Morton 30, 38, 43, 87, 180
Frymer-Kensky, Tikva 6, 59, 75, 269, 270,
271, 272, 273, 274, 284, 285, 287, 378

G
Gailey, Christine Ward 124, 126
gardening 37, 107, 173, 327
Gaulin, Steven 146, 148, 149, 152
Gaulin and McBurney 146, 148, 149, 152
Gellner, Ernest 360
gender conspiracy 164
gender equality 5, 48, 88, 110, 114, 116,
118, 167
gender hierarchies 110, 136
gender hierarchy 1, 2, 3, 4, 5, 6, 8, 27, 83,
84, 88, 95, 98, 99, 100, 109, 122, 127,
137, 143, 259, 328, 329, 376, 381
gender inequality 83, 86, 88, 90, 98, 115,
116, 118, 162, 167, 245
generalization 331, 337, 339, 340, 341, 345,
346
generalize 331, 332, 342, 348, 350, 356
generalized other 355, 356, 361, 365, 366

generalized reciprocity 32, 138, 290, 326,
336
geographically circumscribed 41, 107, 376
Gilgamesh Epic 131
Gimbutas, Maria 54, 61, 62, 63, 68, 75, 76,
80, 191, 195, 196, 197
global interpersonal 345, 346, 347, 350,
358
global interpersonal stage 358
God 54, 55, 58, 62, 70, 78, 81, 131, 132,
147, 149, 209, 210, 262, 269, 279, 280,
283, 284, 285, 286, 287, 289, 302, 304,
305, 313, 317, 344, 360
god 3, 6, 11, 27, 54, 55, 65, 69, 73, 74, 75,
79, 82, 111, 132, 133, 139, 202, 216, 235,
259, 265, 267, 268, 270, 271, 272, 273,
274, 281, 283, 284, 298, 301, 302, 303,
304, 305, 306, 320, 325, 339, 344, 369,
370, 378, 392
goddess spirituality 74
goddess theorists 2, 60, 61, 64, 68, 77, 79,
80, 81, 83, 191, 195
goddesses 1, 3, 4, 6, 11, 42, 50, 54, 56, 57,
61, 62, 64, 65, 66, 68, 69, 70, 72, 73, 74,
75, 77, 78, 79, 80, 81, 82, 121, 128, 130,
134, 135, 139, 260, 267, 268, 269, 270,
271, 272, 273, 274, 275, 276, 277, 280,
284, 285, 286, 289, 291, 302, 304, 305,
306, 313, 314, 319, 337, 367, 368, 371,
378, 380
gods 11, 27, 42, 50, 54, 56, 57, 64, 65, 66,
69, 68, 70, 71, 72, 73, 74, 75, 76, 77, 81,
82, 83, 99, 121, 128, 130, 134, 135, 139,
198, 218, 224, 260, 264, 265, 267, 268,
269, 270, 271, 272, 273, 274, 275, 276,
277, 280, 283, 284, 285, 286, 289, 291,
301, 302, 303, 304, 305, 313, 314, 315,
317, 319, 321, 322, 337, 344, 367, 371,
378, 380
gods and goddesses 11, 50, 70, 77, 81, 82,
260, 267, 269, 270, 272, 273, 274, 275,
276, 277, 284, 285, 286, 289, 291, 302,
314, 319, 337, 371, 378
gold and silver bars 340, 341, 350

120, 121, 124, 128, 129, 132, 134, 135,
143, 147, 149, 150, 151, 154, 159, 164,
165, 166, 185, 193, 194, 197, 198, 203,
205, 209, 214, 218, 221, 224, 227, 234,
235, 242, 243, 245, 248, 251, 253, 260,
261, 265, 266, 269, 270, 271, 272, 273,
274, 276, 277, 281, 285, 288, 289, 296,
301, 305, 309, 310, 311, 312, 313, 314,
315, 316, 317, 318, 319, 320, 322, 323,
325, 326, 327, 328, 330, 331, 340, 343,
344, 349, 351, 354, 355, 356, 358, 359,
361, 363, 366, 367, 368, 369, 370, 371,
376, 377, 378, 381, 385, 386, 387, 388,
389, 391, 392, 393, 394

places 99, 309, 311

plain tokens 332, 333, 334, 335, 338, 341,
350

Plato 280, 289, 291, 359, 392

plow 1, 35, 41, 44, 73, 89, 108, 129, 131,
132, 139, 164, 165, 287, 328, 330, 342,
377, 389

polarities 235, 268, 269, 275, 276, 284, 342

polis 50, 51, 133, 139, 204, 289, 328, 330,
349, 364, 381, 389, 392

political-economic inequality 115

politics 2, 11, 16, 27, 29, 30, 48, 49, 53, 79,
81, 83, 108, 118, 139, 143, 144, 153, 156,
157, 164, 166, 175, 275, 284, 298, 299,
300, 319, 325, 326, 328, 330, 350, 368,
383

polyandry 37, 53

polygamy 33, 37, 306

polygyny 37, 44, 93, 119, 136, 185, 377

polytheism 1, 6, 11, 54, 55, 56, 57, 77, 81,
82, 99, 135, 259, 260, 267, 274, 279, 284,
286, 287, 291, 302, 305, 332, 348

polytheistic 6, 68, 70, 80, 82, 263, 266, 268,
269, 274, 284, 301, 302, 303, 304, 381

population 1, 3, 4, 9, 16, 17, 18, 24, 28, 31,
33, 34, 35, 38, 40, 41, 42, 50, 51, 53, 59,
74, 76, 81, 83, 87, 89, 90, 91, 92, 94, 97,
98, 99, 103, 104, 105, 106, 107, 108, 111,
112, 113, 126, 128, 129, 130, 131, 135,
144, 154, 159, 161, 170, 171, 172, 175,
177, 178, 180, 182, 184, 185, 186, 187,

189, 194, 195, 198, 200, 204, 205, 227,
230, 231, 232, 233, 234, 236, 242, 245,
246, 249, 250, 251, 252, 253, 255, 292,
294, 295, 299, 300, 301, 314, 325, 328,
346, 347, 348, 349, 350, 367, 376, 377,
378, 379, 380, 381, 382, 386, 389

population density 34, 40, 53, 89, 90, 91,
92, 94, 112, 185, 186, 230, 232, 234, 236,
255, 381

power 1, 2, 5, 8, 15, 16, 20, 23, 24, 26, 27,
30, 36, 38, 39, 40, 42, 43, 44, 48, 51, 52,
54, 59, 60, 67, 69, 70, 71, 72, 73, 74, 75,
76, 77, 82, 83, 84, 85, 86, 87, 88, 91, 93,
95, 96, 97, 98, 99, 103, 106, 109, 110,
111, 112, 113, 114, 117, 119, 120, 121,
122, 124, 125, 126, 127, 128, 130, 131,
132, 135, 137, 143, 145, 152, 155, 156,
157, 158, 159, 161, 162, 165, 166, 190,
191, 192, 198, 203, 204, 205, 228, 240,
241, 242, 245, 248, 251, 253, 261, 264,
266, 267, 270, 271, 272, 274, 276, 278,
282, 283, 285, 286, 287, 288, 292, 293,
294, 296, 297, 298, 299, 304, 305, 313,
317, 354, 367, 368, 375, 377, 378, 386,
388, 389, 390, 392, 393

practical-critical activity 121, 392

prayer 260, 282, 283, 305

pre-Socratics 280, 291

predisposition 145, 147, 156, 158, 159, 164,
165, 166, 204, 352, 376

presentational 261, 263, 266

presentational recreation 266

prestige 16, 30, 35, 36, 37, 43, 75, 83, 90,
91, 97, 109, 110, 111, 112, 114, 116, 117,
118, 119, 122, 124, 125, 126, 136, 144,
145, 166, 238, 251, 354, 375, 379

prestige/privilege 109

priestesses 42, 51, 74, 81, 130, 136, 139,
262, 272, 276, 289, 305, 327, 328, 342,
344, 350, 367, 368, 390, 392

primitive communism 32

primitive magic 5, 7, 11, 33, 70, 259, 262,
265, 266, 267, 268, 269, 275, 276, 277,
278, 279, 282, 324, 351, 369, 370, 377,
378

primitive social movements 393

private 15, 16, 25, 32, 33, 39, 66, 67, 78, 83, 84, 86, 87, 99, 160, 161, 169, 230, 244, 249, 263, 273, 274, 283, 293, 294, 300, 310, 312, 316, 323, 327, 345, 347, 361, 365, 366, 382

private realm 67, 310, 316, 327

privilege 22, 27, 30, 39, 43, 44, 52, 59, 74, 85, 86, 87, 103, 109, 110, 111, 117, 119, 120, 122, 124, 125, 128, 129, 130, 143, 145, 158, 161, 162, 166, 191, 193, 241, 251, 275, 278, 289, 292, 299, 306, 354, 375, 377, 379, 388, 393

privileges 44

problem-focused coping 241, 243, 253

problematic or crisis situations 354, 361

problematic situation 121, 354, 363

professional warriors 199

progress 28, 29, 39, 44, 55, 58, 65, 82, 105, 169, 170, 171, 174, 209, 251, 304

protest 36, 301, 348, 385, 386, 387, 388, 389, 391, 392, 393, 394

proximate senses 6, 11, 99, 136, 309, 312, 319, 320, 323, 325, 326, 327, 328, 330, 331, 344, 351, 369, 370, 381

psychological workload 238

public 15, 16, 24, 27, 29, 35, 36, 37, 38, 40, 42, 44, 48, 49, 51, 66, 82, 83, 84, 85, 86, 87, 88, 90, 93, 95, 98, 99, 110, 111, 114, 117, 119, 122, 125, 127, 129, 130, 133, 136, 138, 139, 153, 156, 157, 158, 159, 161, 164, 166, 228, 238, 239, 242, 244, 246, 247, 248, 249, 251, 253, 270, 273, 274, 277, 287, 294, 305, 310, 312, 313, 314, 315, 316, 328, 333, 349, 368, 375, 377, 379, 380, 381, 389, 391

public realm 84, 85, 164, 310, 312, 316

Pythagoras 280, 281, 289, 291

Q

Qi 297, 301

R

raid 47, 49, 76, 173, 174, 175, 176, 177, 178, 179, 182, 184, 190, 193, 194, 197, 198, 203, 204, 205, 206, 208, 217, 377

raids 76

rank 4, 7, 11, 16, 26, 27, 37, 38, 39, 40, 43, 44, 48, 49, 51, 52, 59, 67, 87, 88, 103, 105, 107, 108, 109, 110, 114, 115, 116, 118, 122, 124, 125, 126, 128, 136, 138, 139, 153, 164, 190, 267, 282, 292, 303, 351, 359, 360, 363, 376, 377, 379

rank and stratified societies 16, 26, 27, 59, 109, 110, 359, 363

rank social relations 16, 34, 109

rapier 199

rebellions 120, 206, 271, 295, 393

reckoning 332, 335, 336, 338

redistribution 34, 36, 39, 40, 114, 138, 139, 328, 332, 336, 340, 341, 342, 343, 348

Reeves-Sanday, Peggy 4, 48, 59, 75, 87, 88, 99, 110, 111, 114, 115, 116, 117, 119, 375, 376, 377

reform movements 264, 363, 364, 389

reification 23, 24, 25, 26, 27, 28, 70, 121, 378

reify 23, 24

relative deprivation 385, 386, 387, 390, 394

religion 2, 3, 5, 6, 7, 11, 54, 55, 57, 62, 63, 64, 68, 74, 77, 78, 79, 80, 81, 82, 83, 130, 135, 144, 145, 149, 216, 224, 259, 260, 261, 262, 263, 264, 266, 267, 268, 269, 272, 274, 277, 279, 280, 281, 282, 283, 284, 286, 287, 288, 289, 291, 299, 301, 302, 303, 304, 305, 306, 313, 315, 317, 318, 319, 320, 323, 324, 325, 343, 351, 355, 361, 362, 363, 364, 369, 370, 371, 380, 382

religious monotheism 99

representational 261, 263

resistance movements 120, 121, 384, 385, 386, 387

resource depletion 1, 3, 4, 17, 18, 28, 38, 83, 99, 104, 105, 107, 108, 111, 113, 126, 128, 171, 186, 328, 346, 347, 350, 376, 379, 380

About the Author

Bruce Lerro is an adjunct college teacher who has taught in a wide range of working adult populations in junior colleges, as well as in business, military, prison and alternative settings, for the past fifteen years. He has developed over twenty courses ranging across the disciplines of macro-sociology, socio-historical psychology, comparative mythology and religion, political economy, and world history. Bruce instructs regularly at many colleges and universities including Dominican University, Golden Gate University, and Columbia College. Besides being a writer and teacher, Bruce is also a representational artist with fine-art training in pen and ink drawing. He lives with his partner, Barbara MacLean, a career counselor, in Oakland, California, where Bruce aspires to be a Renaissance man and complains that he was born in the wrong century.

ISBN 141202141-3